Anonymus

The Manuscripts of the House of Lords, 1690-1691

Anonymus

The Manuscripts of the House of Lords, 1690-1691

ISBN/EAN: 9783742844842

Manufactured in Europe, USA, Canada, Australia, Japa

Cover: Foto ©Thomas Meinert / pixelio.de

Manufactured and distributed by brebook publishing software
(www.brebook.com)

Anonymus

The Manuscripts of the House of Lords, 1690-1691

HISTORICAL MANUSCRIPTS COMMISSION.

THIRTEENTH REPORT, APPENDIX, PART V.

THE

MANUSCRIPTS

OF THE

HOUSE OF LORDS,

1690–1691.

Presented to both Houses of Parliament by Command of Her Majesty.

LONDON:
PRINTED FOR HER MAJESTY'S STATIONERY OFFICE,
BY EYRE AND SPOTTISWOODE,
PRINTERS TO THE QUEEN'S MOST EXCELLENT MAJESTY.

And to be purchased, either directly or through any Bookseller, from
EYRE AND SPOTTISWOODE, EAST HARDING STREET, FLEET STREET, E.C., and
32, ABINGDON STREET, WESTMINSTER, S.W.; or
JOHN MENZIES & Co., 12, HANOVER STREET, EDINBURGH, and
90, WEST NILE STREET, GLASGOW; or
HODGES, FIGGIS, & Co., LIMITED, 104, GRAFTON STREET, DUBLIN.

1892.

[C.—6822.] *Price 2s. 4d.*

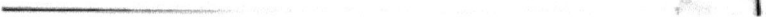

INTRODUCTION.

THE present volume begins with the Recognition Act, the first measure passed by the new Parliament, which met on 20 March 1689–90, with a Tory majority in the Commons, and with Caermarthen, the Lord President, as Prime Minister. The Bill, as introduced by the Whig Duke of Bolton, declared the Acts of the Convention-Parliament to be laws of the realm, and recognised William and Mary to be "rightful and lawful" * Sovereigns. The divisions, which, as usual, are recorded, show how even was the contest in the Lords. The declaratory clause, after being carried with amendments by a majority of three, and ordered to be reported separately by a majority of five, was rejected on report by a majority of six. A fresh Clause was then drawn, as a compromise, recognising the new Sovereigns as in the Bill of Rights, to which the Whigs added another, by a majority of seven, "enacting" † that the Acts of the last Parliament were laws and statutes of the Kingdom. The Bill, thus recast, passed the House without a division, and, to the general surprise, was returned from the Commons without amendment (No. 237).

The Whigs, defeated in the Commons on their Abjuration Bill, which was rejected on 26 April by 192 to 165, brought another Abjuration Bill on 1 May into the Lords. The history of this Bill, which has been confused by historians with the former one, can now be clearly traced. It consisted originally of four Clauses, the last containing a Declaration, or, as it was called, a "Recognition and Declaration," recognising, acknowledging, and declaring William and Mary to be sovereigns of

* These words, as Burnet rightly states (IV. 41), were in the original Bill, which Ralph, who pretends to correct him (II. 194), had evidently never seen.

† Substituted for "declared and enacted." Burnet here is wrong.

right,* and promising to stand by them and their Government against James and his adherents. This Declaration was to be subscribed by every male above 16, on pain of paying double taxes and forfeiting the elective franchise, and, if a member of either House of Parliament, or a person holding any office or employment, civil, military, or judicial, or being in the Royal Household, of incurring the penalties in the Act of 30 Car. II. The Bill was read a second time and ordered to be committed without a division, the King being present during the debate, but the order was challenged by the Tories two days later, when it came to be acted on, and was affirmed by 48 to 33, Nottingham being teller for the minority. Then began a series of long and heated debates, lasting till the Prorogation on 23 May, and marked by a quarrel between L. North and L. Lovelace, and another between L. Kingston and E. Monmouth, whom the House ordered to "demean themselves peaceably" to each other. The record of proceedings bears out Burnet's statement, that "the House was so near an "equality in every division, that what was gained in one day, "was lost in the next." The clause containing the Declaration, which was taken first, was lost by three votes in Committee, and rejected again, when re-offered, by the House on Report. In place of it, various alternative drafts were proposed, two of them by Warrington and Monmouth for the Whigs, and three by Caermarthen, Devonshire (the L. Steward), and the Bishop of London for the Tories, and another expedient was suggested in the Assertory Clause of the Bill of Rights, which was rejected by a majority of six. These drafts do not, unfortunately, exist, but Burnet, whose account of the Bill is in the main confirmed, gives a clue to their contents.† The House finally adopted Caermarthen's Declaration, which had been

* Macaulay, the only historian who has inspected this Bill, now published for the first time, strangely omits to mention the first part of this Declaration, which was the main point of contention. It was a renewed attempt, in fact, of the Whigs to obtain that explicit assertion of the *de jure* sovereignty of William and Mary, which they had failed to obtain in the Bill of Rights and in the Recognition Act just passed.

† "The Abjuration in the Bill," he says, "was properly an oath of a special fidelity to the king, in opposition to King James. The Tories offered, in bar of this, a negative engagement against assisting King James or any of his instruments, knowing them to be such, with severe penalties against such as should refuse it" (II. 46). Burnet himself was for the Abjuration in the Bill (*ib.* 44).

reported together with that of the Bishop of London. With regard to the question who should make the Declaration, thus amended, the Committee, acting on instructions from the House, who exempted "the universality," agreed that it should be subscribed by all officers ecclesiastical,* civil, and military (judicial officers were now excepted), mayors, bailiffs, Heads of Houses, Halls and Colleges and Schoolmasters, as well as by Members of both Houses of Parliament, who had been exempted however, by a Whig majority of eight, from the disability, in case of refusal, to sit and vote. At this point the Bill dropped in Committee, and was never finally reported (No. **265**).

The changes recently made by the Tories in the Lieutenancy and Militia of London, which occasioned the next party contest, will be seen by comparing James' Commission of 1 Oct. 1688 and William's first Commission of 19 March 1688–9 with the one of 15 March 1689–90, framed by Caermarthen and Nottingham, in concert with the Bishop of London, for which the Commons (24 April) voted, by a majority of 49, an Address of Thanks to the King. Undeterred by this vote, the Whig opposition in the Lords moved (1 May) for a Select Committee to inspect the Commissions and ascertain who were the advisers of the change. The motion was rejected by 45 to 43, but the enquiry sought for was conducted, within certain limits, by a Committee of the whole House, whose report was only prevented by the Prorogation. The papers and proceedings, including a scrutiny of panels in connection with the charges of jury-packing, show how nearly the Whigs succeeded in their object of obtaining a thorough examination of the abuses of the Court party in the previous reign (No. **267**). Their attempts, however, to prevent the passing of the Bill for reversing the *Quo Warranto* judgment proved a failure. Counsel were heard for the Corporation, who objected to "reversing" and thereby acknowledging the validity of, a judgment which as they insisted and wished to see declared, had been void and illegal from the first, but the counsels' request for further time to prepare their arguments, though allowed by a majority of 7 in Committee, was refused by the House, on Report, by a

* This is the first mention of the clergy, who, as Burnet rightly remarks, were not included in the Bill as introduced. Ralph's criticisms (II. 197) serve only to show his ignorance of the Bill.

Tory majority of 3, obtained by proxies. Nottingham himse took the chair in Committee. The Judges were heard as to the word "reversed," and also on the question whether a Corporation by prescription could forfeit its being, a point on which the two Chief Justices and Justice Ventris gave their opinions in the affirmative, and the Chief Baron and Justice Eyre in the negative. The Committee refused to wait to consult the remaining Judges, and passed the Bill without amendment, in which shape it received the Royal Assent on 20 May (No. 299).

Under date 16 May will be found the text of another, but abortive, Bill promoted by the Tories, for enforcing the penalty of 500*l.* imposed by the Act of 1672 on office-holders who failed to take the Oaths and Test,—a penalty which, as the preamble declared, had been evaded by "Papists* and other evil-disposed persons" in the reign of James II., by colour of dispensations. The Bill, which passed the Commons by 137 to 91 votes, was restricted to "offenders of greater degree," but extended from Privy Councillors to town clerks. Its provisions were to be executed by five commissioners appointed by the Crown, whose powers, including the conviction of offenders, subject to an appeal to a jury at Quarter Sessions, were to cease on 24 June 1691. The forfeitures were to be paid through Receivers General into the Exchequer, a clause being added that the money should be placed to a distinct account, and applied solely to the expenses of the French war and the reduction of Ireland. The Whigs failed in the Commons, by 93 to 176, to reject this clause, but they succeeded by 10 votes (160 to 150) in adding on the third reading a proviso exempting those who had accepted any office during the Interregnum. In the Lords the Bill was committed by a majority of only 3, but dropped in Committee after an amendment requiring the possession of a real and personal estate of 3,000*l.*, to make the offender liable to the forfeiture† (No. 274).

* Dalrymple states that the Bill was brought in specially to affront the Dissenters, and adds that, "to make the affront the stronger, when a motion was made in the Commons for levying the penalties from Papists, it was overruled." —Memoirs i. 418.

† Luttrell wrongly adds (21 May) that the Lords' amendments provided that the party should be first convicted by a jury. This provision, it appears, was in the Bill as it came from the Commons.

The Bill declaring the hereditary revenues of the Crown to be vested in their Majesties, which also dropped with the Session, purported to give effect to the first of three Resolutions* passed by the Commons on 28 March, in settling the revenue, before granting their Supply (1 April) of 1,200,000*l.* for the expenses until the following Michaelmas. After vesting all the revenues enjoyed by James II. on 10 December 1688 in William and Mary, it made those revenues, with the sanction of the new Sovereigns, a fund of credit for raising 250,000*l.* for the reduction of Ireland and the French War, and authorised loans to the Exchequer to that amount, on the security of the Excise duties and the profits of the Post Office (No. **275**).

On 23 May both Houses adjourned till 7 July, after which they were prorogued by successive Commissions. With regard to the Regency Act, passed in view of the King's intended departure for Ireland (4 June), and providing for the exercise of the government, during his absence, by the Queen in his name and her own, the opinions of the 10 Judges consulted will be found recorded at length. All of them agreed that the King could not delegate his power to the Queen without an Act of Parliament, but as to the Commons' proviso and the amendment added to it by the Lords, each of which was ultimately embodied in the Act, Pollexfen differed from Holt and Atkyns in condemning both as contradictory to the rest of the Bill (No. **260**).

After a recess rendered memorable by the naval disaster of Beachy Head (30 June), and the victory of the Boyne (1 July), Parliament reassembled on 2 October 1690, about a month after William's return from Ireland. The Earls of Salisbury and Peterborough at once petitioned to be released from their two years' imprisonment in the Tower. After consulting the Judges, when the two Chief Justices, being asked as to the general effect

---

* The second resolution, to which effect was given by an Act of this session (1 W. & M. c. 8), dealt with the non-hereditary portion of the Excise, which had been granted to Charles II. in lieu of the feudal services then abolished (12 Car. II. c. 23 and c. 24), and was now granted to William and Mary for life. The third resolution dealt with the Customs, which had been granted to Charles II. and James II. for life, and were now granted to William and Mary for four years. Each of these branches of revenue was made a security for raising a supply, fixed altogether at 1,000,000*l.* from these sources, the remaining 200,000*l.* of the grant being a [illegible] to be raised by a Poll Bill.

of the Act of Grace, declined to give an opinion on Parliamentary proceedings, the Lords refused, by a majority of eight in a House of only 50, to discharge them then, but admitted them to bail; and four weeks later, on report from a Committee appointed after a debate which, according to Burnet, was aimed in reality against Caermarthen, they decided that impeachments were discharged by a dissolution or a prorogation, and accordingly released them. The papers laid before the Committee are important, as showing the materials on which this constitutional question was decided (Nos. **283** and **286**). Four days later (6 October), L. Torrington, who had been committed to the Tower, by order of the Council, after the battle of Beachy Head, petitioned the Lords for his liberty or a trial by his peers. His privilege of peerage being disallowed, he was removed to the Marshalsea, by a warrant signed by the Commissioners appointed to act as Admiral in his place, and laid on the Table (13 October) by L. Pembroke, the first Lord of the Admiralty, who had been sent with L. Devonshire, after the disaster, on a special mission of inquiry to the Fleet. The Resolution affirming the legality of the warrant was carried by 32 to 17, in accordance with the unanimous opinion of the Judges, who added, in reply to a further question, that his commitment was equally in the power of the Privy Council (No. **285**). The Act, however, vesting in the Commissioners, in view of his trial, the powers of the Lord High Admiral, which passed a third reading by 25 to 17,* was held by nearly all the Judges to be a merely affirmative and therefore needless enactment (No. **307**). Under date of 23 December will be found the text of a more important, but abortive, measure of the Commons, the Irish Attainder Bill, which arose out of the necessities of Supply (No. **370**). No less than 18 provisos of exemption were added in Committee by the Lords, who, unlike the Commons, allowed each Petitioner a hearing by one Counsel. These amendments (No. **374**), whether intentionally or not, proved fatal to the Bill, which dropped with the adjournment on 5 January 1690–91, caused by the King's impatience to proceed to the Hague. Another Bill brought up from the Commons, purporting to prevent the hindrance of business by the numerous and often frivolous election petitions

* Ralph (ii. 248), who is followed by Macaulay, gives the numbers incorrectly.

and transferring their consideration from a Committee to the House, was negatived on the same day (No. **377**).

The next Session did not begin till 22 October 1691, three days after William's return from the Netherlands, and a month after the pacification of Ireland by the surrender of Limerick. While the Commons, after voting 3½ millions for the vigorous prosecution of the war with France, were considering the Ways and Means, the Lords (2 December) ordered the Commissioners of Accounts, appointed by the Act of the previous January, to present their Report, which five days later was accordingly done. This Report, which Macaulay regretfully supposed to have been lost,* is among the archives, and will be found set out in full, together with the Commissioners' Answers to various questions addressed to them in the course of the inquiry that followed (No. **468**). No words are needed to show the importance of this national balance-sheet, and the light it throws on the abuses of place and office and the scandals connected with the administration of the public funds. The exposure, however, led to no immediate reform, the Lords ultimately abandoning their investigation, and the Commons wasting their energies in debates full of barren recriminations. The Act for abrogating the Oath of Supremacy in Ireland, the effect of which was to exclude all Papists there from places of public trust and the practice of the law and medicine, had occasioned a contest between the two Houses earlier in the Session. The Lords' proviso exempting those whose rights had been guaranteed by the treaty of Limerick, which the Commons refused to accept until after three Conferences, was an addition, it appears, made at the instance of Lord Nottingham, after the Bill had been reported from Committee (No. **441**).

Among papers relating to trade and commerce, a Lords' Bill of November 1690 for the more effectual restraining the trade with France (No. **350**), which was rejected after a first reading, throws some light on the evasions of the Act of 1688, prohibiting the importation of any French commodities until August 1692. That Act, as is known, had condemned all such goods to be destroyed, but a value was set upon them, based, with some

* A copy appears to exist among the Harleian MSS. (No. 7101), according to an extract and reference in Ruding's *Annals of the Coinage*, III. 369.

exceptions, on the Book of Rates, one-third of which was to go to the person seizing them. The Bill proposed, by lowering these rates, to prevent the importation of French goods, by way of merchandise, under colour of sham prizes, and also to encourage privateering, which, as the preamble complains, had been forborne by British merchants, while French privateers infested the coasts. The question of privateering was reserved for the continuing Act of 1693, but the prohibition of French trade was enforced by two earlier enactments. One of these, containing some restrictions on the sale of wine by retail, which were opposed by the Vintners (No. **379**), imposed heavy penalties on the non-destruction of French imports. The other took its origin in a Bill introduced by Lord Newport, making it high treason to maintain any correspondence or commerce with the French. This Bill was recast, after consulting the Judges, before it left the Lords, the penalties of high treason being restricted to the exportation of arms and munitions of war, and the going into France without leave, while the exportation of any other commodities was made to entail a præmunire, and returning from France without leave, imprisonment, a proposal to treat the last offence as high treason being rejected by a majority of eight (No. **482**). A result of the prohibition of French brandies appears in an Act for encouraging the distilling of spirits from corn,* which was opposed by the Distillers' Company and by the Sugar merchants and refiners (No. **375**). A private Act for encouraging and better establishing the manufacture of white paper (No. **272**), which, as stated in the preamble, had been attempted in this country without success, while vast quantities had been imported from France, forbade the exportation of rags, and continued for 14 years the monopoly enjoyed by the Company established by letters patent of James II. Two appeals which came before the House (Nos. **470** and **508**) throw some light on the origin of this Bill, which was opposed by the paper makers of Chipping Wycombe, as depriving them, in the interests of patentees who were not inventors, of the the advantages to be expected from the exclusion of French

* "Sir Robert Howard," writes Luttrell (22 Nov. 1691), "has tried to distil spirits from wheat, and has brought it to great perfection, to make it as strong as brandy itself."

paper. A further instance of the growing jealousy of exclusive rights on the part of joint-stock companies appears in connexion with the Act for confirming the privileges of the Hudson's Bay Company, which was opposed by the London merchants trading to New York and New England, the Company urging, on the other hand, that they had spent 15,000*l.* in retaking the Colony from the French, and that the fur trade, unless managed by a Company, would be lost, as private traders would not trade in difficult times (No. **271**). The prohibition of French salt led to difficulties in victualling the Fleet, which are explained in some evidence in support of an Act for exempting from destruction, on that account, the lading of two prizes taken during the war (No. **480**). A consequence of the extraordinary dearness of coals during the continuance of the press-warrants,* was the appointment of a Select Committee of enquiry early in 1690, at whose instance a Bill was drafted by two of the Judges, (No. **247**), reviving for seven years the Act of 1664 for regulating their measures and prices. The Bill dropped in the Commons with the Session, but was re-introduced and passed in the following October (No. **284**). An unsuccessful attempt to suspend the Navigation Act, in regard to the restrictions imposed on the employment of foreign seamen (No. **376**), deserves notice in connexion with the question of manning the Navy. A clause imposing penalties on the rescue or concealment of impressed seamen was added by the Lords, and a special proviso was offered by Lord Nottingham for encouraging the importation of naval stores. With regard to the woollen trade, the grievances occasioned by the duty of alnage, which was finally abolished in 1698, are set forth in connection with a Bill (No. **369**) for transferring the collection of the duty from the farmers under the Duchess of Richmond to the Custom House, which appears to have suffered shipwreck on the question of compensation. A Bill promoted by the Pin-makers' Company, but laid aside in the Commons, supplies some details with regard to a minor branch of industry, once protected by Statute, which is stated to have much decayed of late in consequence of foreign competition (No. **289**).

* They were recalled in April 1691. Ralph II. 273. A complaint of impressment, in breach of privilege, appears in No. **262**.

A Bill of some importance deserves notice as advocating an economic heresy denounced by Locke.* It proposed to check the drain of bullion from the kingdom, caused by the higher price of silver abroad, by raising the standard of what was then virtually the currency of the nation, and reducing the intrinsic value of the new Crown piece from 5s. to 4s. 9d. This expedient of lowering the weight of the coins, while retaining the old names, which was advocated a few years later by Lowndes, but resisted by Montague, in his Act for reforming the scandalous condition of the coinage, was supported by the working goldsmiths but opposed by the leading London merchants, including Sir John Houblon, the first Governor of the Bank of England; and the Bill finally dropped in Committee (Nos. **330**, **353**).

To the legal historian these pages are rich in matter of interest. The alleged irregularities in the administration of the law had occasioned the appointment of a Committee of Enquiry in November, 1689, which was re-appointed two days after the meeting of the new Parliament in March 1690, but no further proceedings are recorded. A Bill, however, was introduced on 4 April, "for the benefit of the subject in relation to the practice and execution of the law" (No. **244**), purporting to remedy a variety of corruptions and abuses. The Bill, as amended, extended the penalties imposed by earlier Statutes on the buying and selling of offices to Ministers of State and judges, and a form of oath was prescribed for all persons holding any place of trust or profit. Counsel had to swear, before being admitted to practice, that they had not made any present to any judge, and if neglecting to appear for their client, or failing, in such cases, to return the fee in time to provide a substitute they incurred a fine of 100*l*. There are provisions also for regulating the fees payable to Counsel as well as officers, for shortening Orders of Court, for preventing the abuses of injunctions in Chancery, for securing the proper custody of documents, and for punishing undue practices on the part of attorneys. Bills of Exceptions were declared to lie not only in civil, but also in criminal causes, as to which a further change was made by rendering jurors liable to attaint for false verdicts. To prevent delays of judgment, "owing to the discontinuance of Parliament or default or neglect of the peers,"

* Essay on the Value of Money, published in 1691.

a Committee of Lords was to be chosen every Parliament to execute the powers given by the Act of 14 Edward III. The Bill dropped with the Session, but the subject of law reform was revived by the Lords early in the following one, when the Judges were ordered to prepare two Bills, one for regulating the Court of Chancery and the other the Courts of Common Law. The latter of these does not appear to have been presented, but that which is probably the former of them—namely, a Bill for reforming divers abuses in the Court of Chancery and in other Courts of Equity—was introduced on 22 Oct. 1690 (No. **304**). Its provisions revived the notable dispute set on foot in the time of Lord Ellesmere (1616) by the then Chief Justice Coke, as to the power of a Court of Equity to give relief after or against a judgment of the Common Law, and mark the jealousy entertained of the Chancery, partly as a Court of prerogative, but more especially since the recent development of the whole system of equity by Lord Chancellor Nottingham. All English Bills in courts of equity were abolished, as representing a jurisdiction usurped in defiance of previous statutes. No injunctions for the stay of suits were allowed, unless security was given in the Common Law Court for due prosecution, but a clause, retained in Committee by 11 votes to 2, confirmed the power of Common Law Courts to grant prohibitions to Courts of Equity. To protect mortgagees against suits for redemption often "twenty or thirty years after they had been in possession,"* it was enacted that such suits should be brought within two years at the latest. The Bill was opposed by the Commissioners Keck and Rawlinson, but supported by Chief Justices Holt and Pollexfen, Chief Baron Atkyns and seven of the Common Law Judges Counsel being heard also, by desire of the King, on the point of prerogative. It dropped after recommitment, and the matter ended in a reference to a Select Committee, who, after taking further evidence, ordered Keck and Rawlinson to prepare a new Bill (which does not appear, however, to have been drafted), to prevent delays and length of suits, to regulate fees, to join a majority of Judges with the Chancery in rehearing causes, and

---

* In an appeal brought in 1690 from a decree in Chancery of 1647, counsel for the appellant argued, in justification of the long interval that had been suffered to elapse, that "redemptions have been after a longer time than this" (No. **303**).

to provide for sufficient costs and damages. Another measure, originating in the Lords but lost in the Commons, proposed to deprive the Chancery of its jurisdiction in Bills of Review, which, as the preamble objected, were brought before the same Judges who tried the cause before, and had been confined of late to error appearing on the face of the decree, without looking into the proofs taken in the cause. This jurisdiction was now transferred to the Exchequer Chamber, as in the case of Writs of Error, and the cause was to be reheard and decided, subject to an appeal to Parliament, by five Common Law Judges, including a Chief Justice or Chief Baron. The Lord Chancellor, Lord Keeper, or Lords Commissioners might be present, if they pleased, to give their opinions, but were not allowed to vote (No. **438**).

With regard to the laws affecting debtors and creditors, an attempt appears in a Bill of 1690 already noticed (No. **244**), to anticipate the reforms achieved by the Act of 1697, in preventing escapes with the connivance of officers, and abolishing the scandals of Whitefriars. A variety of other abuses are recited in a Bill, introduced in the Lords, but abandoned after a first reading, which appears to have been framed chiefly in the interests of the creditors of imprisoned debtors, with the view of enabling them to satisfy their own debts out of those due from others to their prisoners (No. **322**). The vexatious process for the recovery of small debts under 40*s*. forms a subject of complaint in two attempted enactments. One of these is a Lords' Bill, rejected on the third reading, for abolishing in such cases the writ of *Capias*—a suggestion put forward some years before by Chief Justice Hale,*—with a view of putting an end to the practice of dragging small suits into the Courts at Westminster and subjecting small debtors to mesne process and arrest, in disuse of the ancient County Courts and contrary to the intention of the Statute of Gloucester (No. **266**). The other is for erecting a Court of Conscience for Southwark (Nos. **363**, **364**), similar to that which had existed in the City of London since the reign of Henry VIII., and those which it had been attempted in 1689 to erect at Greenwich and Norwich.† An important

* See Chapter vii. of his "Considerations touching the Amendment or Alteration of Laws" in Hargrave's Tracts, Vol. i., pp. 280-4. Hale reckoned that the 40*s*. of the time of the Statute of Edw. I. was worth about 6*l*. in his day.

† Calendar, 12th Report, App., Part vi., Nos. **198** and **195**.

amendment of the criminal law, making robbery, wherever committed, a capital offence, and extending the penalties of such felony to the buyers of stolen goods, owed its origin also to the Lords (No. **424**); the remainder of the Act was added by the Commons.

The prevention of clandestine marriages by minors forms the subject of a Bill of October 1691, reviving an earlier one of 1689, but lost, like its predecessor, after leaving the Lords, where it was largely amended in a Committee presided over by Bishop Burnet (No. **395**). A Bill for the same purpose had been brought into the Commons in November 1690, but had been let fall,* notwithstanding an incident at the time which, it was thought, would favour its passing. This was the abduction of a young heiress of sixteen, Mary Wharton, who was dragged from her coach in London and forcibly married to a Capt. Campbell, an act for which Sir John Johnston, one of the accomplices, was hanged at Tyburn, the King, it was said,† refusing to pardon him unless her friends desired it. A clause to annul the marriage was introduced in the Bill then pending in the Commons, but was rejected as irregular. Leave was given, however, to bring in a Private Bill for that purpose, which passed into law after the Lords had taken evidence on a petition of the Earl of Argyll, the brother of Capt. Campbell (who had fled from England), objecting that the marriage had been consented to (No. **361**).

In connexion with the long-vext question of the trial of peers and the procedure in cases of treason, two Bills, each of which was before the Lords in November 1691, explain a further stage in the dispute which was first adjusted by the Act of 1695. One of these was a Lords' Bill (No. **417**) for regulating the trials of peers and commoners, a revival of their Bill of 1689, as then sent to the Commons, where it dropped. It was introduced on 6 November 1691, but laid aside after commitment, in favour, apparently, of another one, brought up from the Commons on the 18th (No. **442**), for regulating trials for treason, which embodied several of its main provisions. This Bill the Lords

* "Upon consideration," says Ralph (ii. 253 *note*), "that the Bill was attended with many inconveniences, and might hinder many younger brothers from making their fortunes."

† Luttrell. 18 Dec. 1690.

amended by tacking to it regulations for the trial of peers, providing that during a recess, as well as during a Session, the whole body of the peerage should be summoned in cases of high treason—a stipulation inserted, but afterwards withdrawn in deference to the Commons, in the Bill of 1689, re-affirmed by a Resolution and Standing Order of the Lords in January, 1689–90, insisted on now, with the result, if not the purpose, of delaying the passing of the Bill, and finally agreed to by the Commons in the Act of 1695.

Conspicuous among a number of Private Bills, relating mostly to the tenure and settlement of landed estates, and possessing only a local or personal interest, there are two for the relief of the City Orphans, whose property, entrusted to the Corporation of London by a feudal right of high antiquity, had been lost by the disastrous closing of the Exchequer in 1666, and whose wrongs had grown by neglect into a public scandal. Each of these Bills, introduced into the Lords on 15 November 1690 (No. **329**) and 11 November 1691 (No. **434**), was rejected in the Commons, to whom the Orphans had previously applied in vain for redress. The papers and proceedings explain fully the main points of contention, namely, by whom—whether a Judicature, a Court of Inquiry, or Commissioners—the necessary investigation was to be conducted, and how far, and by what means, the Corporation should discharge its liabilities.

With regard to questions of personal privilege, some papers illustrate the abuses connected with the grant of protections to peers' servants, which were abolished by Standing Order in 1711. A scrutiny undertaken in March 1690, which occasioned an order vacating those granted in the last Parliament, and requiring all future ones to be registered, showed no less than 52 standing in the name of Lord Morley in London alone (No. **241**). A further order of 13 Oct. 1690 cancelled all protections entered in the previous Session, some of which, including one sold for 45s. to a surgeon to enable him to evade his creditors, were found to have been counterfeits (No. **251**). In the course of a debate shortly afterwards arising out of a petition against some high-handed proceedings of the Earl of Lincoln, it was proposed to prohibit protections altogether. The motion was lost by 43 votes to 25, and the House agreed to allow them, as before, to the menial servants of peers (No. **372**), but they were refused to attorneys and solicitors in a case brought forward by the Bishop of St. David's (No. **423**). Those applied for by the King's servants are few in number, as was urged in their defence when they were abolished in 1693.* Three cases occur in which they were allowed (Nos. **288, 362, 385**); but a Gentleman Pensioner, who had accused Lord Lovelace of having turned out half the band, whose offices were claimed as freeholds, to make room for friends of his own, was ordered to be arrested for libel (No. **352**). The claim of privilege in bar of ordinary law-suits, though less frequent since its disallowance in 1685 to peers acting only as trustees, still led to occasional complaints, as for instance, in connexion with a dispute between the Earl of Salisbury and his younger brothers respecting their father's estate, when the Earl was ordered to waive his claim (No. **336**), with a *cause célèbre* concerning the will of Christopher, late Duke of Albemarle, in which privilege was refused to the Earl of Bath beyond a certain date (No. **308**), and with a claim of the Earl of Monmouth, as to which some curious details are recorded, to the management of an idiot's estate (No. **490**). Privilege was allowed to the Bishop of St. Asaph in some proceedings relating to church lands (No. **341**); but Bishop Burnet failed, on a division, to avoid a writ obtained against him by the Dean and Chapter of Windsor, for refusing to institute a clergyman to a living of which they were the patrons (No. **320**). A proposal to take away all privilege from peers who neglected to attend the House for a whole Session was put forward but afterwards withdrawn during an inquiry in 1690 as to the ways of punishing absent Lords and compelling their attendance (No. **314**).

Two further cases of privilege show the variety of grievances entertained by the House. One of these appears in a petition of the Duke of Norfolk, claiming the right, as head of the Court of Chivalry, to marshal funerals, in opposition to the

---

* These relate only to claims preferred by petition to the House, not to "writs of protection" granted by the King. One of these—the latest instance, according to Blackstone (Com. III. 289)—was granted by William in 1692 to Lord Cutts, to protect him from being outlawed by his tailor (3 Lev. 332).

King-of-Arms, and complaining of a prohibition from the Court of Exchequer—a legal question left undecided by the Committee for Privileges, after taking the opinion of the Judges (No. 461). The other was a complaint by Lord Longueville of having been assaulted, in a *fracas* at the Playhouse, by a sentry of the guard, which ended in the King's giving orders, at the desire of the House, to whom he had referred the petition, that no soldiers should be on duty there in future, and suspending the players from acting till they had begged pardon for the affront (No. 493).

A claim of peerage, as to which full particulars are recorded, relates to the barony of Howard de Walden, which had fallen into abeyance, by the death of the Earl of Suffolk in 1689, between his two daughters and coheirs. The question was, in whose favour the abeyance should be terminated, a point fully argued in this Calendar, but not decided until 1784 (No. 502).

The Appeals are numerous, but comparatively few of them represent cases deemed important enough to be reported in the Courts below. Some noteworthy exceptions, however, are found, in each of which the Judges were consulted, as, for instance, those relating to the rights of children of the half-blood under the Statute of Distributions, a point on which the Civilians also were heard (No. 239), to the admissibility of a Scotch judgment as evidence in support of a decree in Ireland (No. 504), to the forfeiture of an estate tail—the manor of Dauntsey, in Wilts—by general words in an Act (No. 397), and to a Writ of Error brought *per saltum* from the Court of Exchequer, which the House, after a long argument, rejected as incompetent on the authority of a Statute of Edward III. (No. 252).* Three appeals relate to disputes between the lord of the manor and his customary tenants (Nos. 250, 368, and 497); and some details of local interest appear in a case concerning certain privileges connected with Weyhill fair

* Chief Baron Atkyns, who presided, as Lord Keeper, at the hearing of this case of E. Macclesfield *v.* Starkey, throws a sidelight on the proceedings, in a treatise published in 1699. "The Lords," he says, "were on the point of reversing the judgment in the Exchequer, but being by one of the Judges, then also sitting on the upper woolsack, put in mind of the statute of Edw. III., they forbore to proceed to do any more upon it, referring it to the order limited by that statute."—*The True and Ancient Jurisdiction of the House of Peers*, p. 31.

(No. 415), and in some litigation with regard to the office of Warden of the Fleet, together with "all the shops of Westminster-Hall," thereto belonging (Nos. 299, 373, and 429). There is an Appeal brought against the son of the notorious Scroggs, in respect of his father's purchase of Weald Hall, in Essex (No. 458). A Respondent in another Cause is ordered to beg Chief Justice Holt's pardon for having presented a petition reflecting on his conduct in the Court below (No. 477), and there is a case in which the Lord Commissioner Rawlinson attended, by order, to explain the non-execution by the Court of Chancery of a judgment of the House, in regard to which the Committee absolved him, but directed him to censure the Registrar (No. 431).

A few miscellaneous items may be mentioned in conclusion. Under date of 18 November 1691 will be found the contents of a packet of intercepted papers, which had been found on board a French vessel, captured on its way to join Chateaurenaud off the Irish coast, and which were alleged by Caermarthen's son, Lord Kiveton, to include a letter from Nottingham to Sir Ralph Delaval, the commander of the English squadron sent to Ireland. The matter, as will be seen, proved a mares-nest, but it led to two Conferences, after an inquiry in the House, in the course of which Bishop Burnet read the letters which were in French, and Lord Ashburnham acted as interpreter for the French captain, who was examined at the Bar (No. 443). Lord Kiveton figures further in a quarrel with Lord Granville, some details of which are given, and which occasioned an order for the arrest of both parties (No. 309). The Master of the Rolls petitions the House for the delivery of his writ of assistance, which had been granted to his predecessors, but was withheld by a messenger of the Court of Chancery (No. 354). A Protestant, who was engaged to be married to the daughter of a Papist, prays that her father may be prevented from removing her to a nunnery—a petition which led to a hearing of both parties (No. 351). Papists were still excluded from the precincts of the House; one of them, found walking in the Court of Requests, was handed over by Lord Lovelace to Black Rod, but discharged on its appearing that he had been summoned in reference to some business before the Commons (No. 360).

An anonymous warning of an alleged design to blow up the Houses led to a search of the vaults and cellars (No. 348), a precaution observed with due formalities to this day at the beginning of every Session.

E. Fairfax Taylor.
Felix Skene.

HISTORICAL MANUSCRIPTS COMMISSION.

THE MANUSCRIPTS OF THE HOUSE OF LORDS.

1690.

237. March 26. William and Mary Recognition Act.—Amended Draft* of an Act for declaring the Acts of the late Parliament begun and held at Westminster the 13th day of February 1688, to be of full force and effect by the laws of this realm, and for recognising their now Majesties King William and Queen Mary to be by the laws of this realm our rightful and lawful Sovereign Liege Lord and Lady King and Queen of these Realms.—Whereas it is necessary for the peace and settlement of these realms that the minds of all the subjects be united in and under the Government by the Divine Providence so happily established by many good and wholesome laws made and enacted in the late Parliament begun the 13th day of February 1688 and from thence by Prorogation continued till the sixth of February 1689,† Be it therefore declared *adjudged* ‡ and enacted by the King and Queen's Most Excellent Majesties, by and with the advice and consent of the Lords Spiritual and Temporal and Commons in this present Parliament assembled and by the authority of the same, That all and singular the Acts made and enacted in the said Parliament were, are, and of right ought to be deemed, [adjudged] ‡ taken and esteemed to be the laws of this Realm.

And the Lords Spiritual and Temporal and Commons in this Parliament assembled do humbly pray Your Majesties that by the Authority of this present Parliament it may be declared, enacted, and established, And be it declared, enacted and established That we do recognise and acknowledge that your Majesties King William and Queen Mary are and of right ought to be by the laws of this realm our most rightful and lawful Sovereign Liege Lord and Lady King and Queen of these realms of England, France and Ireland, in whom the Imperial and Royal State, Crown and Dignity of these realms, with all the rights and prerogatives thereunto belonging, are rightfully and entirely vested, And thereunto most humbly and faithfully we submit ourselves, our heirs and posterities. [Offered this day by the D. Bolton and, after debate, on question, read 1ª (L. J., XIV., 438). The subsequent proceedings were as follows:—

1 April. House in Committee. The Bill read through.

---

* As reported from C. W. H. on 5 April. The whole of this draft was ultimately superseded by Annex (*f.*) with amendments.

† For the addition proposed here to the Preamble see Annex (*d.*).

‡ These two amendments were reported on 5 April (L. J., XIV., 450). The first of them is supplied here from Annex (*e.*) below.

House of Lords MSS.

1690.

Title read and postponed.
Preamble read and postponed.
First enacting clause read.*

After debate on the Bill, Committee moved to adjourn the debate to Thursday [3 April].

Ordered to report accordingly.

House resumed. *E. Bridgewater* reported as in L. J., XIV., 445. House to be in Committee on 3 April, and the Judges to attend. (MS. Min.)

3 April. House in Committee. E. Bridgewater in the Chair.

First enacting clause read. *Proposed* instead of this clause ("Whereas all and singular the Acts made in the late Parliament, etc., except such as were temporary").† House moved that a Sub-Committee be appointed to draw up a Bill upon the debate. After debate, the clause was read.

A clause offered by the Lord Cornwallis read.

A clause offered by the Lord President read.‡

An Act in the Statute Book read: for amoving all questions and disputes concerning the assembling and sitting of this present Parliament. 12 Car. II., c. 1.

The clause in the Bill read, upon which the debate has been. *Question:* Whether this clause shall pass without any alteration or amendment? Resolved in the *Negative.*

House resumed. House adjourned during pleasure. *Ordered* to report for a further day. House resumed. *E. Bridgewater* reported accordingly. House moved to sit *de die in diem* until the Bill be expedited. *Question:* Whether this House shall resolve themselves (*sic*). *Ordered* to proceed in a Committee of the whole House on the Bill to-morrow. *Question:* Whether this House should be resolved into a Committee *de die in diem* until this Bill be expedited? *Question:* Whether this Question shall be put? Resolved in the *Negative.* (MS. Min., L. J., XIV., 448.)

4 April. House in Committee. E. Mulgrave in the Chair. The Order for the business of the day read.

First enacting clause read. *Moved* that leave may be given to bring in a clause to declare that the validity of this Parliament does not depend upon the last.

The clause read, brought in by the Lord President,‡ and the clause in the Act. After debate, *Question:* Whether the word ("confirm") shall be one part of the amendment to this clause? Resolved in the *Negative.* Contents 25; Not-Contents 34. Tellers, E. Nottingham and E. Monmouth. Then this *Question* was put: Whether the word ("declared") shall stand in this Bill? Resolved in the *Affirmative.* Contents 33; Not-Contents 27. Tellers, E. Nottingham and E. Monmouth.

House resumed. *E. Mulgrave* reported that the Committee have made some progress in the Bill, and have resolved that the word ("declared") shall stand in the first enacting clause. After debate upon the irregularity of reporting without Order from the Committee, House again adjourned during pleasure.

E. Mulgrave in the Chair. After debate, what should be reported to the House, it was proposed to go on with the clause. *Question:*

---

* The MS. Min. add here as follows: "House resumed. E. Scarsdale took the oaths. House adjourned during pleasure."

† *See* Annex (*a*.).

‡ *See* Annex (*b*.).

Whether the Committee shall now go on with the clause? Resolved in the *Negative*. Contents 24; Not-Contents 36. Tellers, E. Stamford and E. Feversham. After debate, *Question:* Whether it shall be reported to the House what votes have passed at this Committee? Resolved in the *Negative*. Not-Contents 30; Contents 28. Tellers, E. Stamford and E. Feversham. Leave asked to dissent. *Ordered* to report that the Committee desire the House may be put into a Committee again to-morrow at 10 o'clock to proceed in this Bill.

House resumed. *E. Mulgrave* reported as ordered. House agreed, and ordered accordingly. (MS. Min., L. J., XIV., 449.)

5 April. House adjourned during pleasure, and put into a Committee on the Bill. E. Bridgewater in the Chair.

The clause read. House moved that the word ("adjudged") may be added in this clause.

A clause read, offered by the Lord Steward. [Query, Annex (*c.*) or (*d.*).] The clause read again. After debate,

A clause read, offered for a preamble. [Query, Annex (*c.*) or (*d.*).]

Question: Whether the word ("adjudged") shall be put into the Bill after the word ("declared") and before the words ("and enacted")? Resolved in the *Affirmative*. Contents 33; Not-Contents 30. Tellers, E. Stamford and E. Nottingham. The clause was read with the word ("adjudged") in. Line 12. Leave out the word ("adjudged"). The clause read with the last word ("adjudged") left out. After debate, whether this clause shall pass as it is now amended. *Question:* Whether this clause shall pass so amended? Resolved in the *Affirmative*. Contents 35; Not-Contents 32. Tellers, E. Stamford and E. Kingston.

After debate, *Question:* Whether the House shall now go on with the other clause in the Bill? Resolved in the *Negative*. Contents 31; Not-Contents 36. Tellers, E. Stamford and E. Kingston. *Ordered* to report what the Committee has done.

House resumed. *E. Bridgewater* reported the two amendments to the first clause.* Leave given for dissenting. *Question:* Whether to agree with the Committee? Resolved in the *Negative*. Contents 30; Not-Contents 36. Tellers, E. Stamford and E. Feversham. A debate arose, whether to go on with the Bill now, or adjourn till the 7th. *Resolved*, That it is the opinion of this House, that all the Acts passed in the last Parliament begun the 13th day of February 1688, are good laws to all intents and purposes whatsoever. *Question:* Whether the House is of that opinion? *Previous Question:* Whether this Question shall be now put? Resolved in the *Affirmative*. *Ordered* to go into Committee on the 7th, and no other business to intervene. (MS. Min., L. J., XIV. 450, 451).

7 April. House adjourned during pleasure into a Committee on the Bill. E. Bridgewater in the Chair. *Proposed* that the House be resumed, and a Bill brought in for penalties upon any that deny the validity of the laws.

The recognizing clause in the Bill read.

A clause in the Bill of Rights read twice.

A clause read, offered by E. Monmouth.

Agreed, that the clause be drawn up for recognizing their Majesties just as in the Bill of Rights.

A clause read, drawn by E. Monmouth.

* *See* Annex (*e.*).

House of Lords MSS.
—
1690.

Proposed that a Sub-Committee withdraw. 1. That it is an asserting clause; 2. That it is measured by the Bill of Rights.

E. Mulgrave.	E. Nottingham.
E. Monmouth.	E. Pembroke.
E. Rochester.	L. Bishop of Sarum.
D. Bolton.	
E. Shrewsbury.	

They withdraw to draw the clause. [The proceedings of this Sub-Committee are not recorded in Com. Book.] *D. Bolton* reported that the Sub-Committee have drawn a clause and ordered him to report it. It was read ("We your Majesties'").* Asked if it was the opinion of the Committee that this clause be part of the Bill. *Agreed*, that this clause be part of the Bill.

A clause offered for to follow the last for declaring the Acts of the last Parliament good. The clause read again; then read with amendments proposed; then amended and read at the Table. The clause read again. After debate, *Question:* Whether this clause shall pass without any alteration or amendment? Resolved in the *Affirmative.* Contents 36; Not-Contents 29. Tellers, E. Kingston and E. Monmouth.

The Preamble of the Bill read that was postponed, and agreed to be left out.

The Title postponed read; another agreed:—("An Act for recognizing the King and Queen, and for avoiding all questions touching the Acts made in the Parliament assembled at Westminster in the first year of their Majesties' reign, 13 Feb. 1688"). *Ordered* to report that the Committee have gone through the Bill as it is.

House resumed. *E. Bridgewater* reported the Bill with amendments. The amendments read.

Title read again and agreed.

First enacting clause read, for recognizing, and agreed to.

Then the other clause read, and agreed to.

Ordered to be engrossed. (MS. Min., L. J., XIV., 453.)

8 April. Read 3ª, an Act for recognizing the King and Queen, and for avoiding all questions touching the Acts made in the Parliament assembled at Westminster the 13th day of February 1688.

Title agreed to be amended, and instead of ("King and Queen") put in ("King William and Queen Mary").

Proposed to put in ("And be it enacted"). Agreed to be put in, and then read thrice and agreed.

Leave given to dissent.† *Question* put: Whether this Bill shall pass? Resolved in the *Affirmative.* Bill sent to the Commons (MS. Min., L. J., XIV., 455).

---

* *See* Annex (*f.*).

† The expunged Reasons for the Protest on the third reading are printed in Thorold Rogers' "Protests of the House of Lords." Vol. I. p. 97. The proceedings which led to their being expunged are thus recorded in MS. Min.:—

10 April. House moved to consider whether any Lord may enter what Reasons he pleases upon a Protestation. The Protestation moved to be read. The Protestation of 8 April read out of the Journal. After long debate upon the first Reason, the first Reason read in the Protest. Leave for dissenting. *Question:* Whether the Reason now read shall be expunged out of the Journal? *Previous Question:* Whether this Question shall be now put? Resolved in the *Affirmative. Main Question* put and resolved in the *Affirmative.* Then the House went into debate upon the Second Reason in the Protest of 8 April. The Second Reason read out of the Journal Book. *Question:* Whether this clause that has been last read shall be expunged out of the Journal? Resolved in the *Affirmative.* Contents 38; Not-Contents 28. Tellers, E. Monmouth, E. Nottingham. House moved to consider

On 10 April the Bill was returned agreed to without amendment (L. J., XIV., 458), and on the 14th it received the Royal Assent (*ib.* 463). 2 W. & M. c. 1.]

Annexed :—

(*a.*) 3 April. Draft clause as follows: "Whereas all and singular the Acts made and enacted in the late Parliament begun the 13th day of February, 1688, and from thence continued by prorogations and adjournments until the sixth day of February, 1689, were, and except such Acts as were made temporary and are expired, are and of right ought to be deemed, adjudged, taken and esteemed to be the laws of this realm, and that no doubt or scruple ought to be made thereof by any person whatsoever; And whereas their Majesties, King William and Queen Mary, are, and of right ought to be by the laws of this realm, our rightful and lawful sovereign liege Lord and Lady King and Queen of these realms of England, France and Ireland, in whom the imperial and royal state, crown, and dignity of these realms, with all the rights and prerogatives thereunto belonging, are rightfully, lawfully and entirely vested; Be it enacted by the King and Queen's Majesties, by and with the advice and consent of the Lords Spiritual and Temporal and Commons in this present Parliament assembled, and by the authority of the same, that from henceforth all persons that shall by words, writing, or printing, maintain or assert that all or any the Acts made and enacted in the aforesaid late Parliament, except such Acts as were made temporary and are expired, are not of full force and virtue, or are not the laws of this realm, shall be committed to gaol, there to remain without bail or mainprize the space of , and forfeit to their Majesties pounds; And be it farther enacted by the authority aforesaid that from and after the day of , all persons that shall by words, writing or printing, maintain or assert that their Majesties King William and Queen Mary are not lawful and rightful King and Queen of these realms of England, France and Ireland and all other the dominions thereunto belonging, shall suffer the pains and penalties hereafter expressed, that is to say for the first offence and for the second offence." *Endorsed* as read this day, and again on 5 April.

(*b.*) 3 April. Amended clause, as follows: "Whereas during the late difficulties and exigencies of affairs (by reason of the abdication of the late King James the Second) the Lords and Commons, being assembled at Westminster the 13th day of February in the year of our Lord 1688, were from thence continued by Prorogation and Adjournment until the 6th day of

---

of the alteration in the Journal of the word ("no") in the Protestation of the 5th April. *Ordered* that it be referred to the Committee on the Journal Book.—11 April. The Questions that were made and put yesterday were read, in order to their being entered in the Journal Book, and whether the clauses read yesterday to be expunged out of the Journal, shall be inserted in the Questions. After debate, the questions were read again. *Question:* Whether the Votes made yesterday shall be entered as they are now read, without any alteration? Resolved in the *Affirmative.* Contents 35; Not-Contents 24. Tellers, L. Chandos and L. Cornwallis. *D. Somerset* desiring that, since the Reasons in the Protestation are expunged, he having protested for those very Reasons, he might have leave to take out his name; it was accordingly granted, as also that any Lord who has entered his name to the said Dissents, may do likewise so, if he please. (MS. Min., Comp., L. J., XIV. 459, 460.)

House of Lords MSS.

1690.

February 1689, and then dissolved by the King and Queen's Majesties, in which time several Acts were passed by and with the advice and consent of the said Lords and Commons assembled as aforesaid, which being of necessary use are fit to be continued [and confirmed]; Be it therefore enacted by the King and Queen's most Excellent Majesties, by and with the advice and consent of the Lords and Commons in this present Parliament assembled, and by the authority of the same, that all and singular the Acts made or mentioned to be made by their said Majesties by and with the advice or consent of the Lords and Commons upon or since the said 13th day of February, 1689, and all and every the clauses, sentences and Articles in them and every of them contained, shall be and hereby are ratified, [confirmed and] enacted and declared to have the full force and strength of Acts of Parliament, according to the tenure (*sic*) and purport thereof, and so shall be adjudged, deemed and taken to all intents and purposes whatsoever, as if the same had been made, declared and enacted by authority of this present Parliament." The remainder of this sheet of paper is cut off. *Endorsed* as read this day and again on 5 April. [Offered by the L. President in place of the first enacting clause, and amended on 4 April by omitting the words in square brackets.]

(*c*.) 5 April. Draft (in clerk's hand) of portion of preceding, amended by adding the words in italics, as follows; "Whereas during the late difficulties and exigencies of affairs by reason of the abdication of the late King James the Second *and of the throne thereby becoming vacant and the King and Queen's accepting the Crown upon this express condition among others, that the Oaths of fidelity and obedience should be taken by all persons in all cases where the Oaths of Allegiance and Supremacy were to be taken by virtue of any former laws*, the Lords and Commons assembled at Westminster were on the 13th of February, 1688 . . ." *Endorsed* as read this day.

(*d*.) 5 April. Draft of proposed addition to the preamble of the Bill, viz., "after the preamble as in the Bill" to add as follows:—"And whereas the Throne becoming vacant by the abdication of the late King James, the Lords Spiritual and Temporal and Commons of this Kingdom, convened by the Prince of Orange's circular letters, did agree upon and frame a new Instrument of Government, by which the Prince and Princess of Orange were declared King and Queen of this realm, and in which among other things it was agreed that the present Oaths of fidelity and obedience should be established and substituted in the room of the former Oaths of Allegiance and Supremacy, to be taken in all cases where the said Oaths of Allegiance and Supremacy were heretofore required, and that the said Convention, being afterwards turned into a Parliament by their Majesties' Consent, did take the said Oaths according as directed by the above said Instrument of Government; Be it therefore, etc., as in the Bill." *Endorsed* as read this day.

(*e*.) 5 April. Amendments in first enacting clause of Bill as originally introduced, viz.:—

After ("declared") add ("adjudged").

[After ("deemed")] leave out ("adjudged").

[Made in C. W. H. and reported this day. L. J., XIV., 450.]

(*f.*) 7 April. Draft of Bill (partially amended),* as reported first from the Select Committee, and then, with amendments, from Committee of the whole House this day. The original Draft consists of the words printed in Roman type below, and as finally amended, by omitting the words in square brackets and adding those in italics, forms the Act, which is given here in full, with the exception of the two amendments on third reading, which are separately noted.

An Act [made] *for recognizing the King and Queen*† *and* for avoiding *all* Questions touching the Acts made in the Parliament assembled at Westminster [in the first year of their Majesties' reign] *the thirteenth day of February, one thousand, six hundred, eighty-eight.*

We, your Majesties' most [dutiful] *humble* and loyal subjects, the Lords Spiritual and Temporal and Commons, in this present Parliament assembled, [recognising and declaring that] *do beseech your most Excellent Majesties, that it may be published and declared in this High Court of Parliament, and enacted by authority of the same, that we do recognise and acknowledge* your Majesties *were*, are and of right ought to be by the laws of this realm our [most rightful and lawful] Sovereign Liege Lord and Lady King and Queen of England, France and Ireland, and the dominions thereunto belonging, in [whom] *and to whose princely persons* the Royal State, crown and dignity of the said realms, with all [the rights and] *honours, styles, titles, regalities*, prerogatives, *powers, jurisdictions, and authorities*, [thereunto] *to the same* belonging *and appertaining*, are *most fully*, rightfully and entirely [vested] *invested and incorporated, united and annexed*, [and thereunto most humbly and faithfully submitting ourselves; For] *And for* the avoiding of all disputes and questions *concerning the being and authority of the late Parliament assembled at Westminster the thirteenth day of February, one thousand, six hundred, eighty-eight*, we do most humbly beseech your Majesties that it may be [declared, and be it declared and] enacted,‡ by the King and Queen's most Excellent Majesties, by and with the advice and consent of the Lords Spiritual and Temporal and Commons, in this present Parliament assembled, and by authority of the same, That [the Lords Spiritual and Temporal and Commons assembled at Westminster the 13th day of February 1688 and continuing to sit and act as a Parliament, with their Majesties' Royal concurrence and by their consent, were a good and lawful Parliament, and that] all and singular the Acts made and enacted in the said Parliament *were and* are laws and statutes of this Kingdom, and as such ought to be reputed, taken and obeyed by all the people of this Kingdom.

238. March 26. Worthenbury Chapel Act.—Amended draft of an Act for separating and making the chapel of Worthenbury a distinct church from the parish church of Bangor. The amendments in both Houses were purely verbal. [Read 1ª this day. Royal Assent, 14 April. L. J., XIV., 438, 463. 2 W. & M. c. 2, in Long Calendar.]

---

* The only amendments marked on the Draft are to omit the words ("declared and be it declared and"), and the portion beginning with ("the Lords Spiritual") and ending with ("and that").

† Amended on third reading, as in the Act, by leaving out ("the") and adding ("*William*") and ("*Mary*"). The amendment is imperfectly entered in L. J., XIV., 455.

‡ Amended on third reading as in the Act by adding ("*and be it enacted*").

House of Lords MSS.

1690.

Annexed:—

(*a*.) 28 March. Instrument releasing to Sir Roger Puleston of Emrall, in the county of Flint, all right, &c., to the tithes and presentation of the parish church, rectory, or parsonage, of Worthenbury, and empowering him to use the most speedy way to separate the said Church from that of Bangor. *Signed* Thos. Lloyd. *Attested* Thos. Pemberton, John Shore. *Dated* 27 Nov. 1689. [Read in Committee this day. Com. Book.]

(*b*.) 28 March. Similar Instrument, dated and attested as preceding. *Signed* Wm. Lloyd. [Read in Committee this day. Com. Book.]

(*c*.) 5 April. Letter from E. Derby to E. Stamford declaring his consent to the Bill. [Read this day in Committee, being a reply to a letter ordered to be sent by E. Stamford on 28 March. Com. Book of dates.]

(*d*.) 5 April. Lords' Amendments. [Made in Committee and ordered to be reported this day. (Com. Book.*)]

239. March 28. Watt *v.* Crook.—Petition and Appeal of John Watt and Francis Camfield and Elizabeth, his wife. George Watt died intestate in 1688, possessed of a personal estate of nearly £10,000, and administration was granted to the Petitioners, John Watt and Elizabeth, being his only brother and sister of the whole blood. His sister by the half-blood and her husband, Peter Crook, then brought a Bill in Chancery, claiming, under the Act for the distribution of Intestates' Estates, an equal share of the personal estate, and the Court of Chancery on 11 February 1689 decreed accordingly. Petitioners are advised that it is not within the meaning of the Act, that persons of the half-blood, who are so little regarded in the law, as that they can never come to inherit any of the real estate of a person of the whole blood, but rather that it will escheat, should come in for any or at most for more than a half share of the personal estate. *Signed* by John Watt; *Countersigned* Ambrose Phillipps and Tho. Filmer. [Reported this day from the Committee for Petitions. (L. J., XIV., 445. Pet. Book, 28 March.) The Cause was first heard on 8 May.† *Attorney-General* (for Appellant): Speaks to the Act and the usual practice of the Court. Stat. Hen. VIII. Marriage is greatly to the disadvantage of the first. I consider the words. There are no express words in this case in the Statute. Cites several cases. *Mr. Levinz* (for Appellant): These words in the Statute, "according to law," are according to the Ecclesiastical law. Three out of four cases have gone otherwise in Chancery. *Serjeant Hutchins* (for Respondent): Take it to the Common law we are right. We are in equal degree and are entitled to an equal share with the brothers and sisters of the whole blood. In the case of *Furner* v. *Laws* the half-blood [was held] equal. Cites case of Mr. Milborne. There is no degree but equal; they are before nephews or uncles. Reads part of the Statute of Frauds and Perjuries. Every brother and sister shall have an equal share. In 1677 and all along it has been done. Cites Stapleton's case and L. Winchelsea's case. *Mr. Finch* (for Respondent): Cites the words of the Act, [to show] what the meaning of the words "in equal degree" is. The question [was] before your Lordships [in] the case of the Duke of Suffolk. The question is: Who is in equal degree upon the personal estate? The case of *Smith* v. *Tracy* is against them. Counsel withdraw. *Ordered* to hear the

* The Journal omits to mention these amendments.

† The MS. Min. of April 17 (Comp., L. J., XIV., 467) and May 3 contain entries that the cause is to be heard "the next free day."

Civilians on Monday next in the Cause.—On the 12th the Civilians were called in. *Mr. Walter:* The case was left by Mr. Attorney on this point of the half blood. I speak to the whole blood; the designs of the persons deceased, the Common Law cannot go on it. It is the consideration of the blood that makes this case. He reads Justinian in Latin in this case. *Mr. Oldish* (for Crooke): The law of Justinian is a revolt [? novelty], and has been otherwise many hundreds of years. The Canon Law mentions not one word of it. The power of the Ordinary to distribute by the Statute. The Statute of Westminster, 2nd Chap., 19th, 21 Hen. VIII., that ascertains who is the prochien amie. They withdraw. *Ordered* to be reported on the 15th, and the two Chief Justices then to be present and give their opinions. —On the 15th, the House being moved to hear the judges, the *L. C. Justice Holt* said: The question is whether, if a man be possessed of a personal estate and has a brother of the whole and one of the half blood, the half-blood should have an equal share. I am of opinion that the half-blood ought to have the same share. I confess it is hard, but we are bound by the Statute. It has been determined in the case of *Smith* v. *Tracy*. The law has been constantly held so, and though it is hard, yet the words of the Act bind us up. *L. C. Justice Pollexfen:* I am of the same opinion on the same grounds. Though they cite divers authorities, all this signifies nothing, unless it had been received here. It never did receive in this kingdom. There being no law, it could not be but as directed by the Act, which binds us up. The half and whole are in equal degree. Here they are both brothers and cannot be otherwise. If there was reason for making it otherwise, that is before your Lordships. *Ordered* That the decree be affirmed. (M.S. Min., May 8, 12, 15.) See *Shower's* Cases in Parliament, p. 108, 2 *Vernon* 124, and 2 *Ventris*, 317.]

Annexed:—

(*a.*) 2 April. Answer of Peter Crook and Elizabeth, his wife. The Lords Commissioners of the Great Seal decreed in favour of Respondents upon mature deliberation and long debate. The decree is just, the half-blood being as near a kin to the intestate as the whole blood, as has been adjudged both before and since the Statute of Distributions. Pray that the Appeal may be dismissed with costs. *Signed* by Respondents; *Countersigned* H. Finch and G. Hutchins. *Endorsed* as brought in this day.

(*b.*) 26 April. Petition of Respondents that the Appeal may be dismissed for want of Recognizance. L. J., XIV., 476.

(*c.*) 29 April. Petition of Appellants that either side may have a Doctor of the Civil Law to be heard in the cause, the sole point in difference being what share those of the half-blood are entitled to by virtue of the Statute of Distributions, and Petitioners being advised that the construction of that Act will much depend on the practice in the Courts of the Civil Law both before and since the said Statute. L. J., XIV., 478.

240. March 28. Patents (Vacating) Bill (Needwood Forest). —Amended draft of an Act for making void certain Letters Patents therein mentioned. The preamble as amended, is identical with that in the Act of 1695–6 (7 and 8 W. & M. c. 40), the amendments being as follows: "And whereas since the said decree the said [several sums] *sum* of seven thousand pounds [and likewise the sum of four hundred pounds, being the value of the said premises at Sheerness, have] *hath* been repaid, notwithstanding which the said Letters Patents and Grant have not been surrendered, yielded up, cancelled or vacated." Then follows

House of Lords MSS.

1690.

a clause being the same as § i. of the Act, except in not containing the words ("from the time of making and granting thereof as if the same "had never been made and granted") and in reading after ("heredita- "ments whatsoever therein mentioned") the words ("shall at all times "hereafter remain, continue and be and so be adjudged to remain, continue "and be in their present Majesties, their heirs and successors for ever, of "such and the like estate and in such manner, form and condition to all "intents, constructions and purposes as if the said Letters Patents had "never been had or made.") [Read 1ª this day. L. J., XIV., 441. On 8 April, *Mr. Ward* and *Mr. Dodd* were heard for Mr. Rupert Browne. Mr. Dodd stated that Mr. Browne had sent Mr. Vernon the £7,000, "and, says he, you shall have a third part of the Forest." (M.S. Min., 8 April.)—On 22 April *Mr. Ward* (for Mr. Browne): £7,000 and £400 for Sheerness was paid. The Grant expresses £7,000 as the consideration. Many rents are reserved. Mr. Browne desires interest for the £7,000. *Mr. Dodd* (for same): There are three distinct sums. The £7,000 is the consideration money, for which we hope to have interest. Neither the mortgage nor the interest has been paid. We only desire to be reimbursed our money. *Serjt. Tremaine* (for Bill): They paid £7,000 and £400 for the whole, and next day sold half for £7,000; so they had a good bargain. The soil they had was proved to be worth £3,200. The Patent was obtained by surprise. It passed as none ought, I am sure, and as none ever passed before. There is no reason for the interest, for the King never received the money. *Serjt. Thompson* (for Bill): They are persons guilty of as great a fraud as can be in cheating the King. *Mr. Ward*: Mr. Browne did not get the Grant. *Mr. Dodd* denies there is a surrender. This is the first time they pretended Mr. Browne had the Grant. Several witnesses were examined and stated that Col. Vernon acknowledged he was £3,300 in Browne's debt. *Samuel Boheme* stated that the Patent was in the joint interest of Browne and Vernon. Rest as in L. J., XIV., 470. (MS. Min., 22 April.)—The proceedings in Committee, of which E. Bridgewater was chairman, are thus recorded. 26 April. *Resolved*, That Mr. Browne shall have £4 10*s*. 0*d*. per cent. per annum for the £3,300 principal, viz. £930.* *Mr. Browne* is called in and proposes that his money may be paid out of the timber and cord wood. *Agreed* That it shall be raised out of timber and cord wood already felled and to be felled, and that the King shall have the refusal of the wood so to be sold for the use of the Navy. *Agreed* That some one of the Judges be desired to draw a clause to that purpose. —1 May: *Mr. Browne* is called in and asked what profits he has had out of the forest since the grant to Col. Vernon? He says he had no profits at all. *Mr. Vernon* says the same. A clause for the repayment of Mr. Browne's debt out of the wood in the forest is read.—7 May. *Mr. Browne* is called in, and being asked whether he claims the office of chief Ranger of the Forest, he says he does not, but he believes Col. Vernon's executors do. *Ordered* That the Lord Steward be spoken with herein.—10 May. *Mr. Browne* is called in, and being asked what wood he has already cut down, he says neither he nor Col. Vernon have cut down any wood since the Patent. *Ordered* That there shall be a clause to make Mr. Browne accountable for any wood he may have felled. A resignation of the office of Ranger of Needwood Forest, dated 5 Dec. 1689, is read. The Bill was then ordered to be reported with amendments. (Com. Book, April 26, May 1, 7, 10.) It was laid aside in the Commons after a first reading. C. J., X., 417. *See also* No. 270.]

---

* It appears from the amendments to (*c*.) and (*d*.) that this 4*l*. 10*s*. 0*d*. was afterwards changed to 6*l*.

Annexed :—

(*a.*) 26 April. Proviso against alienation of the premises by Letters Patent. Comp. § vi. of the Act. [Added in Committee this day at the end of the Bill. Com. Book.]

(*b.*) 26 April. Proviso for restoring all rights, etc., as they existed before the Letters Patent. Comp. § vii. of the Act. [Added in Committee this day after preceding paper. Com. Book.]

(*c.*) 7 May. Amended clause corresponding, with variations, to § iii. of the Act. The amendments are to substitute five for three Commissioners and to make the axe-bearer for the time being one of them, and to make interest payable at 6 p.c. instead of 4½ p.c. [Read on 1 May and added this day, after amendment, to follow the two preceding provisoes. Com. Book.]

(*d.*) 7 May. Amended clause naming Charles Egerton, Esq.; Sir Walter Bagott, Bart.; George Vernon, Esq.; Henry Cavendish, Esq., Axe-bearer; Joseph Saunders, of Barton, Gent.; Villers; of Hanbury, Senr., Gent.; John Haynes, of Uttoxeter, Collector, Richard Cope, of Sherrald Lodge, Poysinge; William Salt; William Turton, Esq.; and John Every, of Burton, Esq. as Commissioners for setting out the wood to be felled, for payment to Rupert Browne of £4,521. The amendments are to except ship timber from being cut, and to change the sum of £4,213 5*s.* 0*d.* to £4,521, consequentially on altering the rate of interest. [Substituted for part of preceding clause, which, as amended, was added this day in Committee, Com. Book.]

(*e.*) 10 May. Proviso, corresponding with § ii. of the Act, except in reading, instead of ("Offices of Steward....chase of Needwood") the words ("office of chief Ranger of the forest of Needwood"), and in omitting the words ("by lawful conveyances") and ("have "not forfeited their offices or done or suffered any causes of forfei- "ture thereof by Nonuser, Disuser, Abuser or otherwise"). [Added in Committee this day, after Annex (*c.*) Com. Book.]

241. March 28. Protections.—Lists of Protections endorsed as brought in this day (L. J., XIV., 441). [On 24 March the House, on motion, ordered Lists of Protections* to be brought in by the Sheriffs of London and Middlesex, the Bailiff of Southwark, the Marshal of the Marshalsea, and the Steward of Westminster (MS. Min., L. J., XIV., 436). On 28 March the Sheriffs, &c. were called in and delivered the Lists below on oath, Philip Perry, Thos. Hooper, Edw. Brewster, Jonathan Horwood, and William Eyre being sworn at the Bar. The House considered the Lists the same day.† *Ordered*, that all the absent Lords have notice that have Protections on their names and they not here. In regard to the first List (*a*) the following notes appear :—

Duchess of Buckingham :—Declared that she has no privilege of Parliament.

L. Cholmondeley :—Not allowed, the L. Cholmondeley disowning it.

E. Carlisle :—To be acquainted with (*sic*).

Danby :—To have notice (*struck through*). He comes up and disowns them.

E. Bath :—Says he knows nothing of Chapman ; he will withdraw Hebblethwaite.

Bp. of St. Davids :—Notice.

---

* *See also* 12th Report, App., Part VI., No. **223**.

† An Order, in MS. Min., for considering them the next day is cancelled.

House of Lords MSS.

1690.

E. Devon :—The Sheriff called in and told there is one Wharton protected by E. Devon. He says some of these names were turned over by his predecessor. Mr. Rouse to attend.

Denbigh :—John West is his menial servant.

D. Grafton :—Declares his protections void.

E. Huntingdon :—Notice.

House declares that all Protections of the last Parliament are void.

Howard :—Notice.

Lovelace :—Knightley Purefoy.

Lincoln :—Barbara Roche, a servant, James Crosby, Sam. Lunn, Thos. Ford.

Lichfield :—Absent; to have notice.

Morley and Mounteagle :—Notice to be given to him.

Mulgrave :—Protection disowned.

E. Montague :—Notice.

D. Northumberland :—To have notice.

Norfolk :—Denies them.

Oxford :—Thos. Exton withdrawn.

E. Pembroke :—Withdrawn; out of doors.

E. Radnor :—John Ferrers, menial servant.

Suffolk :—Sir Thos. Williams, menial servant, John Dixon, Henry Hatcher withdrawn.

D. Southampton :—Withdrawn, all but Harder.

D. Schonberg :—Vacated.

Somerset :—Richard Lotteridge (*sic*). His Grace says he never did nor never will grant Protections.

Protection Sheriff this Parliament (*sic*): Notice. [*See* (*b.*) below.]

Poultry and Wood Street Compter since last Parliament. [*See* (*c.* below] :—

Byron :—Notice.

L. Denbigh :—Josiah Webster disowned.

Borough of Southwark. [*See* (*d.*) below.]

All Protections to be vacated and none allowed but what are entered in the office of the Clerk of the Parliaments; and that the order be printed and published. House acquainted that the Doorkeepers of this House are afraid to be pressed. *Hancock* called in. He says he is afraid, but nobody threatened him. He withdraws. *Ordered* that the persons who have counterfeited any Lord's Protections be sent for to attend this House. (MS. Min., L. J., XIV., 441.)

The Lists are as follows :—

(*a.*) List of Protections (126) entered in the office of the Sheriff of Middlesex, viz. :

Aylesbury :—
*Dr. Nathaniel Johnson.
Bath :—
Henry Heblethwaite,
Thos. Chapman.
Byron :—
John Selby.
*†Anthony Dugna,
Anthony Dugna.
Mary, Duchess of Buckingham :—
Thos. Paulden.

Clarendon :—
†John Watts,
John Logge.
Cholmondeley :—
†Thos. Beczley [Beasley in (*c.*)].
Carlisle :—
Thos. Durffey,
†James Chevalier,
†Wm. Jennison,
†Wm. Pickard.

* These names occur also in Annex (*b.*).
† These names occur also in Annex (*c.*).

Dorset, L. Chamberlain :—
†Peter Dugna,
Sir John Clayton,
†Jane Sandys,
Hugh Montgomery,
Thos. Neale,
Leonard Simondson,
Marquis de Monpouillon.
Note.—All these are certified by his Lordship to be their Majesties' menial servants.
Danby :—
†Abraham Barrington,
Christopher House.
Dartmouth :—
†Henry Griffith.
St. Davids :—
†Dr. Nathaniel Johnson.
Devonshire :—
Wm. Wharton.
Denbigh :—
John West.
Grafton :—
Philip Elwes,
†Thos. Throgmorton.
John Wood.
Huntingdon :—
John Johnson,
†Rainald Grahme [Randolph Graham in (*c*.)].
†Knevett Hastings,
†Edward Williams.
Hungerford :—
John House.
Howard :—
Dorothy Walker.
Lovelace :—
Knightley Purefoy.
Lincoln :—
James Crosby,
Barbara Roche,
Samuel Lunn,
Thos. Ford.
Lichfield :—
John Cuthbert
Lindsey :—
Noell Ansell.
Morley and Mounteagle :—
†Thos. Knott,
†Richard Hewett,
Thos. Lamplugh,
Luke Cropley,
Thos. Gray,
Nathaniel Mooring,
John Bulbeck,
†Wm. Maddocks,
Ralph Wrenn,
†John Preist,
†Richard Worth,
Francis Peacock,
Robert Mynn,
Richard Rogers,
Wm. Boundey,
John Fendell,
Thos. Lamplugh,
†Sir Robert Nightingale,
Thos. Woodward,
John Grove,
Scipio Acland,
John Wright,
Robert Bradshaw,
John Cooper,
†John Osmond,
Francis Percival,
†Ambrose Venn,
†John Sykes,
†Richard Charnock,
Jeremiah Keene,
†Margaret Pinckney,
Joseph Beson,
John Pennington,
†William Jay,
John Harrod,
Richard Taylor,
Philip Carter,
†George Rogers,
†John Glover,
†John Jeanes,
†Richard Raynes,
†John Newman,
†Henry Wilson,
Joseph Tubbe,
†Henry Bryan,
Thos. Sharpe,
Bernard Gould,
Thos. Farrington,
John Starth,
Thos. Griffin,
Christopher Escott,
†Richard Rogers.
Note.—All withdrawn but about nine.
Mulgrave :—
John Naylor.
Montague :—
*†James Mellett.

* These names occur also in Annex (*b*.).
† These names occur also in Annex (*c*.).

HOUSE OF LORDS MSS.

1690.

Marlborough :—
†Anthony Freeman.
Noted: Withdrawn.
Northumberland :—
Charles Pryor,
John Swift,
Frederick Harder,
Thos. Potter,
John Pollexfen,
†James Versprite [Versprett in (*c*.)].
*†Wm. Jones,
*Mary Knowles,
*†Simon Spatchurst.
Norfolk :—
Arthur Squibb,
Edmund Howard, Esq.
Oxford :—
†Thos. Exton.
Pembroke :—
John Bathurst, Esq.
†Cornelius Vermuyden, Esq.
Radnor :—
John Ferrers.
Suffolk :—
†Sir Thos. Williams,
John Dixon,
Henry Hatcher.
Southampton :—
Francis Lund,
†Frederick Harder,
Wm. Denny.
Schonberg :—
†Thos. Handerook [Hambrooke in (*c*.)],
†Joseph Drinkwater,
Thos. Beare,
Nathaniel Day.
Somerset :—
†Richard Liverseidge [Liverside in (*c*.) and Letteridge in MS. Min., 28 March].
Wilts :—
Edward Strode,
Edmund Eyre.

Signed: Thos. Hooper, Undersheriff of Middlesex.

(*b*.) List of Protections (6) entered in the office of the Sheriff of Middlesex since the last Session of Parliament. *Signed:* Thos. Hooper, Undersheriff.

(*c*.) List of Protections allowed in the Poultry and Wood Street Compters since the last session of Parliament, viz. :—

L. Morley and Mounteagle -	Matthew Tite.
	John House.
E. Suffolk - - -	Sir Thos. Williams, Bart.
L. Howard - - -	G. Hockenhull, Senr.
L. Byron - - -	Anthony Dugan.
L. Denbigh - - -	Josiah Webster.
E. Marlborough - -	Anthony Freeman.

Noted, since disallowed.

Signed: Phil. Perry and Edw. Brewster.

(*d*.) 28 March. List of Protections entered in the office of the Bailiff of the Borough of Southwark, viz. :—

	Allowed.	Dated.	Signed.
John Wadlow -	5 June 1685 -	28 May 1685 -	Bucks.
John Palmer -	21 Sept. 1685 -	16 July 1685 -	Lucas.
George Rose -	25 Sept. 1685 -	15 Aug. 1685 -	Lincoln.
John Smalley -	2 Feb. 1685 -	28 Jan. 1686 -	Hunsdon.
Humfrey Roberts	4 June 1689 -	29 April 1689	Southampton.
John Garland -	20 Feb. 1689 -	18 Feb. 1689 -	Lincoln.
William Jennings	20 Mar. 1689 -	20 Mar. 1689 -	Morley and Mounteagle.

Unsigned.

* These names occur also in Annex (*b*.).
† These names occur also in Annex (*c*.).

(*e.*) List of persons (60) protected in the Court of their Majesties' Palace of Westminster since their Majesties' accession.

The List contains the following names, besides those noted in (*a.*) above :—

E. Clarendon -	- Levi de la Haye.
L. Morley and Mounteagle -	Morgan Jenkins.
	Hugh Lente.
	Wm. Parkehurst.
	Sam. Parkehurst.
	George Penney,
E. Lincoln - -	- John Garland.
Don Pedro Ronquillo	- John Gasper Keeling.
L. Brandon - -	- Bandolph Burges.
L. Dunblane - -	- Jervas Scroope.
	Jervas Scroope.
E. Winchelsea -	- Wm. Mansfield.
L. Howard - -	- G. Hockinghull.

Signed : Fra. Whitestone. *Dated* 27 March 1690.

(*f.*) Return (written under the Order of the House of the 24th) stating that the Steward of Westminster has no protection entered in his office nor in the Head Bailiff's office. *Signed :* Jonathan Horwood, Dep. Ball.

242. March 29. Loleworth Manor Act.—Amended draft of an Act respecting Loleworth Manor, entitled as in L. J., XIV., 442. Lords' amendments purely verbal. None in H. C. [Read 1ª this day; Royal Assent 2 May. *Ib.* 442, 483. 2 W. & M. c. 10 in Long Calendar.]

Annexed :—

(*a.*) Consent of John and Susanna Edwards to the passing of the Bill. *Dated* 29 March, 1690. *Attested* by R. Walker and Ben. Mills.*

(*b.*) Similar consent of A. Smith, Jas. Altham, Hen. Hedworth, R. Ingram, and W. Gore. *Dated* 29 March, 1690. *Attested* as preceding.

(*c.*) 4 April. Rough notes of proceedings in Committee, including amendments made this day. [No entry of proceedings in Com. Book.]

243. April 1. Harleford House Act.—Amended Draft of an Act for the sale of the capital Messuage or Mansion house of Harleford and Manor of Great Marlow and other lands in the County of Bucks. *Endorsed :* Lord and Lady Falkland's Act. Lords' amendments are to insert the names of Trustees, and a verbal amendment. None in H. C. [Read 1ª this day; Royal Assent 2 May. L. J., XIV., 444, 483. 2 W. & M. c. 12 in Long Calendar. *See also* Com. Book, 12 April.]

243*. April 3. E. Ranelagh *v.* Sir J. Champante.—Petition and Appeal of Richard, Earl of Ranelagh, Sir James Hayes, Knt., and John Bence, Esq., Executor of John Bence, deceased. Complains of a Decree and Orders of the Court of Exchequer in respect of a balance of 24,159*l.* 8*s.* 8½*d.*, claimed on two accounts by Respondent. The circumstances of the case are set out in the Appeal of "Dashwood *v.* Sir J. Champante" (12th Report, Appendix Part VI., No. **214**). Appellants are unable to prove their objections to the accounts, which have

* They were sworn at the Bar on 3 April. (MS. Min. No entry in L. J.)

House of Lords MSS.

1690.

been tampered with and falsified, until Respondent produces the necessary vouchers, books, and papers. *Signed* by Appellants; *Countersigned* by H. Finch and James Sloane, who certify that there is good cause of Appeal. [Read this day, L. J., XIV., 447. The Cause was heard, on the revived Appeal (Annex (*c.*) below) on 6 March 1692–3. *Mr. Finch* (for Appellants): If this be a stated account, it will ruin the Undertakers. *Sir Thomas Powys* (for Appellants): The difference arises upon two accounts. The first thing will be whether Roberts had any authority to make up such an account. Roberts says he did not take it to be an account concluding. Sir John admits to us he had mistaken as to 12,000*l.*, and thereupon there were 12 leaves cut out in the charge and discharge. Reads several orders and the Commission to the Undertakers, and depositions of Roberts and others. *The Solicitor-General* (for Respondent): The great objection is the balance of it is very high. As to Mr. Roberts not having a sufficient authority, it stands as I will show you. Sir James Hayes was fully intrusted by them. They have accepted the vouchers, and then it is plain that they did deliver up the vouchers. They had them in their custody, and the delivery up we will plainly show. As to the tearing out the leaves by their witness it is plain that so much is taken off for their advantage. He that tore out the leaves swears the very same sums were put in other leaves. *Mr. Ward* (for Respondent): The Account was confirmed by the Barons of the Exchequer in Ireland. Roberts' authority was a very good authority. Reads many depositions to prove the delivery of the vouchers, &c. They accepted the vouchers and then refused to give a receipt. Deposition of Robert Curtis read; he believes the vouchers were delivered. The Plaintiff charged himself with all receipts and disbursements. The vouchers were in the custody of John Hayes. Reads decree in Ireland. *Mr. Finch* heard in reply. *The Solicitor-General* and *Mr. Ward* heard. Counsel withdraw. Question put: Whether the Report shall be now made? Resolved in the Negative. Contents 27; Not-Contents 34. *Ordered* to be reported to-morrow. —On 7 March, the Speaker reported, and after debate, the Decree was reversed by 32 to 25. Tellers, E. Manchester and E. Radnor. (MS. Min., L. J., XV., 277, 279.) *See also* 2 *Vernon*, 395.]

Annexed:—

(*a.*) 10 April 1690. Answer of Sir John Champante, Knt. Prays that the Appeal may be dismissed with Costs. Similar to Answer in Appeal of "Dashwood *v.* Champante." *Signed* by Respondent. *Endorsed* as brought in this day.

(*b.*) 27 Feb. 1692–3. Petition of Richard, Earl of Ranelagh, Rachael, Lady Viscountess Dowager of Falkland on the behalf of herself and others, Executors of Sir James Hayes, Knt., deceased, and of John Bence, Esq., Executor of John Bence, deceased. Pray that the Appeal, which has abated by the death of Sir James Hayes, may be revived. *Signed* by Petitioners; *Countersigned* James Sloane. L. J., XV., 251.

(*c.*) 28 Feb. 1692–3. Petition and Appeal of Richard, Earl of Ranelagh, Rachael, Lady Viscountess Dowager of Falkland on the behalf of herself and others, Executors of Sir James Hayes, Knight, deceased, and of John Bence, Esq., Executor of John Bence, deceased. Similar to above Appeal of 3 April 1690. *Signed* by Appellants; *Countersigned* by Thos. Powys and James Sloane, who certify that there is good cause of Appeal. [Read this day. L. J., XV., 253.]

(*d.*) 1 March 1692–3. Answer of Sir John Champante, Knt., to preceding. Similar to previous Answer (Annex (*a.*) above). *Signed* by Respondent; *Endorsed* as brought in this day.

244. April 4. Law (Reform) Bill.—Amended* draft of an Act for the benefit of the subject [in relation to] *regulating* the practice and execution of the Law.—§ i. Whereas their Majesties, in giving their Royal Assent to the Bill of Rights, and in other actions of their reign, have shown their desires and endeavours that their subjects may enjoy the full benefit of the laws of the land, For the better preventing for the future certain corruptions and abuses in relation to the administration and practice of the said laws, which, having prevailed by long custom, stand in need of particular remedy, and encouraging and promoting industry in practisers, students and clerks employed in any cause, business, office or profession concerning any of their Majesties' Courts of Law or Equity, Be it therefore enacted by the King and Queen's most Excellent Majesties, and by and with the advice and consent of the Lords Spiritual and Temporal and Commons, in this present Parliament assembled, and by authority of the same,† That the several laws made in the 18th and 20th years of King Edward III. to prevent Ministers of Justice to take presents and gifts of private persons, and the laws made in the 12th year of King Richard II. and in the 5th and 6th years of King Edward VI. against buying and selling of offices, and the pains and penalties therein ordained and appointed, shall extend to all ministers of state, judges, and justices of all Courts at Westminster and all other Courts of their Majesties, their heirs and successors, whatsoever, without saving or exception of any, and that all person or persons who [do now or] shall hereafter enjoy‡ any office or offices or places of trust or profit whatsoever within this realm of England shall at the entering upon their respective offices take the usual oaths for the due execution thereof and swear as follow:—

I, A.B., do swear that I have not directly or indirectly given, taken or received, and will not hereafter directly or indirectly take, give or receive any sum or sums of money, or any bond or assurance for the payment of anything, for the office unto which I am now admitted, or for making, naming or ordaining any officer, minister or clerk within this realm of England, dominion of Wales, or town of Berwick-upon-Tweed. So help me God.

And all and every person or persons now in office, some time before the ending of *Trinity* term next ensuing in one of their Majesties' Courts at Westminster or in the Quarter Sessions where he or they reside or inhabit, and every other person or persons at any time hereafter entering upon the execution of any office, shall within the space of three months next after his admission or entrance thereunto take the said oaths in like manner together with the usual oath belonging to their office.

§ ii. And whereas to prevent the danger of partiality in judges, it has been provided by two several laws, the one made in the 8th year of the reign of King Richard II., the other in the 3rd year of King Henry VIII.,

---

* The additions are shown by italics, the omissions by square brackets. These amendments are inserted here from the list of amendments (Annex (*c.*) below), being identified by the marginal references in the draft.

† This first clause, here following, was eventually superseded by Annex (*e.*) below.

‡ The MS. Min., 30 April, add two amendments which are not given in Annex (*c.*) below, viz., to substitute ("be admitted into") for ("enjoy") and to read in the same line ("any or every office") instead of ("any office").

that no man shall be justice of assize or Gaol Delivery within the County where he was born or doth inhabit, some questions having been made whether the said statute extend to the justices in the Great Sessions or Circuits in Wales; It is hereby enacted and declared that the said justices in Wales [are and] shall *from henceforth* be deemed and taken to be within the remedy and provision of the said statute to all intents and purposes, as much as if they were particularly named therein; And all grants and commissions *granted or to be granted from henceforth* contrary to the said statutes are hereby declared void and of none effect in the law.

§ iii. And whereas presents and gifts made to the judges by counsel at law is (*sic*) equally pernicious to influence the Court to favour causes, as if their clients gave the same, for prevention whereof, Be it enacted that all and every *Serjeant*, Barrister *or other practitioner* at law shall within the space of *four* months from the *first* day of *Trinity term* next ensuing, and every other *Serjeant*, Barrister, *or other Practitioner* before he or they be admitted to practise [as Counsel shall together with the usual oaths upon their admission swear as follow] *shall take the oath following*:—

I., A.B. do swear that I will not by myself or other *directly or indirectly* give or make any present to any judge *or judges* whatsoever of any Court or to any other person to *his or* their use. So help me God.

§ iv. And whereas many Counsel at law take fees of their clients for attending and pleading their causes, yet neglect to do the same, Be it enacted that every counsel at law who shall receive a fee to attend and plead in any cause at a certain time and place and shall neglect to do the same accordingly, or shall not return the fee or fees received so timely that his client may if he think fit with the said fee provide him another counsel, shall incur the penalty of *one hundred pounds*, whereof one moiety shall be to the King and Queen their heirs and successors, and the other moiety to the person or persons will sue for and recover the same by action, bill, plaint or information in any of their Majesties' Courts of Justice, and upon conviction shall pay to the party grieved three times the value of the loss and damage sustained by the neglect or offence aforesaid, and for the second offence shall be disabled after conviction thereof to practise in any Court whatsoever.

§ v. And whereas by the neglect of the law made in the 3rd year of King James I., *chapter seven*, attorneys and solicitors do charge their clients with excessive fees and unnecessary demands, and wrong the counsel at law of their fees by setting their names to pleas and other proceedings without their knowledge or consent; Be it therefore enacted that every attorney or solicitor offending against that Statute shall be duly punished according to his offence as that Statute directs, limits and appoints.

§ vi. And to avoid vexation and extortion, one or more table of fees to every office shall on or before the ending of *Trinity* term next be hung up therein and kept open and visible to all comers in every Court, office or place where any such fees are payable, and in default of hanging up or keeping such table or tables the person or persons who shall receive the said fees either for themselves or others, shall incur the penalty of *twenty pounds each term the tables shall not be so hung up*, to the uses aforesaid, to be recovered as in like cases of penalties incurred is provided.

§ vii. Be it likewise enacted that all Bills in Chancery or the Exchequer, filled with impertinent matter to increase the charge of defendants who are to pay for the copies of them, shall be proceeded upon no otherwise than is usual with Bills which contain matter of scandal; and in every case where the plaintiff in either Court dismisses his own Bill, or if either plaintiff or defendant appears upon hearing the cause to have prosecuted or defended vexatiously, full costs shall be decreed; nor shall any injunction be granted in Chancery to stop proceedings at law, until such time as the defendant has had convenient time to put in his answer according to the distance of his habitation from London, and if any injunction be obtained upon a false suggestion, the party injured shall be adjudged to be in the same condition and forwardness as to his proceedings at law as he might have been in common course if no such suggestion had been made. And all orders in Chancery and the Exchequer shall have only the ordering part without lengthening them out with any recitals of the allegations of counsel on either side.

§ viii. And to the intent that all Commissioners to take answers and depositions in Chancery may duly execute the said Commissions, Be it enacted that every such Commissioner shall, before he sit upon any such Commission, take an oath in Chancery, or before the next Justice of Peace for the county where he executes the said Commission, for the due execution thereof, which oath, keeping to the substance without any particular form, every Justice of Peace is hereby empowered to administer.

§ ix. And to the end that poor men as well as rich may receive equal justice, Be it enacted that if any officer, lawyer, attorney or solicitor ask or take any fee or other profit or reward from any person or persons admitted to sue in formâ pauperis or to admit him, the person or persons so offending shall for the first offence forfeit the sum of *fifty pounds* to the uses aforesaid, to be recovered as in like cases of penalties incurred is provided, and for the second offence, being lawfully convicted thereof, shall be disabled to practise or enjoy any office or employment whatsoever.

§ x. And whereas many persons be arrested upon mesne process and to answer the action be forced to give special bail to the Sheriff in the county and afterwards before some judge of that Court whereout the process issued, which is very grievous to persons living remote from London, and at the end of the cause, if the defendant renders himself, the bail is discharged; Be it therefore enacted that where the person arrested shall execute a warrant of attorney to confess or acknowledge a judgment of the value demanded and to appear to the writ and stand the event of trial, he shall be excused from giving bail or any further security.

§ xi. And whereas many families have been ruined by the negligent keeping of bills, answers, depositions and other pleadings and proceedings in Chancery, by reason none but practising attorneys or their clerks are entrusted by turns with the care and custody thereof, who in favour to their clients may embezzle, rase and deface their adversary's evidences without being discovered in whose turn the fact was committed, which renders the party grieved remediless; and whereas King James I. in the like case, by advice of his Council, not only committed the care and custody of filing and keeping affidavits to proper and fit persons, but settled and granted the fee which, for the great benefit thereby accruing to the public, hath continued a patent office with a fee distinct and apart from the Six Clerks ever since; and whereas not any fee is of right due or payable to any attorney or clerk for filing the proceedings, or any settled fee for searches, yet they make suitors pay for filing every proceeding 3*s*. 4*d*. and 4*s*. 4*d*. at least, and for every search

HOUSE OF LORDS MSS.

1690.

one term 1s. and take what they please for further searches; For prevention whereof, be it enacted that the care and custody of all bills, answers, depositions and other proceedings in Chancery shall for the future be committed to a proper and fit person or persons, to (*sic*) whom the King and Queen, their heirs and successors, shall by sign manual think fit to constitute and appoint during good behaviour; And that the person or persons so constituted shall receive and take only one shilling for filing every proceeding and for the search of every term only four pence and no more, and shall by himself or sufficient deputies attend the said office at proper times and seasons or usual office hours for doing of business. And be it further enacted that the person or persons so entrusted with the filing and keeping proceedings shall not suffer any practising attorney or clerk to carry any proceedings out of the office without taking notes or memorandums under their hands to return the same back to the office in some convenient time; And the person or persons appointed to be the officer or officers shall take an oath as other record-keepers usually do before the Master of the Rolls for the time being to be faithful in the execution thereof, and shall further swear not to defraud the Six Clerks or their under clerks of any copies which of right belong to them. And if any attorney, clerk, solicitor or other neglect or refuse to record and file any bill, answer, deposition or other proceeding or to return proceedings duly back to the office, he or they so neglecting or refusing shall for every offence incur the penalty of forty shillings to be levied by distress and sale of the offender's goods; And for that end the Master of the Rolls for the time being is hereby empowered in a summary way without legal forms to hear and determine all complaints in relation to this matter, and shall have four pence for every summons, one shilling for the order or decree and eight pence for his warrant or execution; And the person or persons by him empowered to distrain and make sale of the offender's goods shall deduct the same out of the forfeiture and give the remainder thereof to the informer and return the overplus, if any be, of the money raised upon distress and sale of the goods to the offender.

§ xii. And be it further enacted, that in case the officer or his deputy do or shall defraud the Six Clerks or their under clerks of any fees due for copies, he or his deputy so offending shall not only pay treble the value received and taken for any such copies to the party grieved, but shall forfeit the sum of forty shillings, to be levied by the Master of the Rolls' warrant and distributed as aforesaid, and shall be further subject and liable to suffer as in the case of perjury, being duly convicted in any of the Courts of Justice.

§ xiii. And whereas many persons charged in execution for debt and damages or both are by the connivance of the Marshal of the King's Bench and Warden of the Fleet permitted to go abroad at their pleasure and thereby become remiss or negligent in the payment of their debts, Be it enacted that, if any person so in execution in either of the said prisons be found out of the prisons other than by Habeas Corpus or rule of Court, it shall and may be lawful for any person or persons whatsoever to arrest such without any writ or warrant and carry him or her to the county gaol of the place where he or she shall be so taken, there to be kept until the said debt or damages for which he or she is so in execution be fully satisfied.*

* Compare 8 & 9 Will. III. c. 27., s. 1.

§ xiv. And whereas there are many privileged places in and about London and Westminster and Southwark where unreasonable opposition is given to the lawful execution of legal process, and where many desolate persons do shelter themselves and their effects; For remedy thereof, Be it enacted, that if any person or persons shall oppose, hinder or disturb the lawful execution of process or execution against the person, goods or estate of any person whatsoever, the offender or offenders herein shall be adjudged guilty of felony and shall suffer as felons with the benefit of clergy.*

§ xv. Provided that this Act shall not take from the privilege of the Royal Palace.

§ xvi. And whereas divers tradesmen and others withdraw themselves and their effects into remote and unknown places, and though they have debts owing to them, the creditors can receive no benefit thereof elsewhere than in the City of London, Be it enacted that any creditors for any certain sum of money shall and may in all places within the Kingdom of England attach so much of the debts due to their debtors in the hands of any person or persons indebted to their said debtors as is or shall be due to the said person or persons hereby authorized to attach, and after judgment or outlawry and proof of the debt, such creditors shall have execution for so much of the same as shall be due to such creditors against the person so indebted to such debtors. And be it further enacted that, in all cases where persons are mutually indebted to each other, each party may make stoppage and deduction of so much as is owing to him or her by the other; and upon motion bringing what he or she shall allege to be all the remainder into the Court where the action is commenced, the plaintiff shall proceed at the peril of paying all the costs of suit.

§ xvii. And whereas many Acts of Parliament for attainting of jurors for false verdicts have become ineffectual by reason the punishment in an attaint is so grievous that one jury will very rarely attaint another, and whereas the freedom from attaints in criminal causes has encouraged many extravagant and murderous verdicts; Be it enacted that an attaint shall lie in criminal as well as civil causes, and that the judgment upon an attaint in civil causes shall have no other effect than the payment of treble damages to the party grieved by the false verdict, rendering every such juryman incapable of being a juryman or giving any evidence in any cause; And in criminal causes every such juryman shall incur the like disability, and, where the verdict has wrongfully occasioned the death of any person, shall pay the [sum of] *third part of what he was worth at the giving such verdict* to the husband or wife of the party injured by such verdict, and if there be no husband, to the next of kindred.

§ xviii. It being some question whether a Bill of Exception allowed by the Statute made in the 13th year of King Edward I. is intended otherwise than in civil causes, Be it enacted and declared that such Bills of Exception in like manner as is provided by the said Act shall lie in criminal as well as civil causes.

§ xix. And whereas it is provided by a law made in the 14th year of King Edward III. that delays of judgment in other Courts shall be redressed in Parliament, which has been rarely put in practice, by reason of the discontinuance of Parliament or default or neglect of the Peers of this realm in Parliament assembled, Be it enacted that from henceforth a Committee of Lords shall be chosen at every Parliament in like manner as is appointed by the said Act, in order to execute the said powers thereby given.

* Compare 8 & 9 Will. III. c. 27., s. 15.

House of Lords MSS.

1690.

§ xx. And whereas many good laws made in former reigns,* viz. 51 Henry III. st. 5; 3 Edward I. capp. 18, 19; 6 Edw. I. c. 14, 10 Edw. I. stat. Rutl.; 27 Edw. I. c. 2; 6 Hen. IV. c. 3; 7 Hen. IV. c. 3; 33 Hen. VIII. c. 39; 27 Hen. VIII. c. 24; 27 Hen. VIII. c. 10; 7 Edw. VI. c. 1; 18 Eliz. c. 5; 22 and 23 Car. II. c. 22, avail not to suppress the corruptions or undue practices thereby intended to be remedied, because officers and attorneys, enriching themselves by non-execution or mis-execution of the laws, and [winking] *conniving* at others' disobedience, have of late years escaped unpunished, to the great scandal of the Government; For prevention whereof, and that fines, pains or penalties wilfully incurred may not for the future be withdrawn and concealed, and that the pains and penalties incurred by inadvertency and not out of any ill design may be compounded and discharged with mercy and moderation, Be it enacted That the Lord Chancellor, Keeper or Commissioners of Great Seal, High Treasurer or Lords Commissioners of the Treasury for the time being, Under Treasurer, Judges and Barons shall make necessary rules and orders or other provisions in their respective courts and places, as much as in them lies, to prevent all undue practices in officers and attorneys; And that the person or persons refusing to make such rules, orders and provisions, and the officer or attorney or other disobeying them shall for every offence incur not only the penalties of the laws already in force against all such their undue practices, but shall further incur the penalty of *five hundred pounds*, whereof one moiety shall be to the use of the King and Queen, and the other to the informer, to be recovered as other penalties are herein before mentioned and expressed to be by trial and conviction in some of their Majesties' Courts of Justice.† [Read 1a this day, and committed to a Select Committee on the 5th. (L. J., XIV., 448, 450.) The Bill appears to have originated in the proceedings of the Committee appointed to enquire into Irregularities in the Courts of Westminster Hall.‡ The Committee, of which E. Stamford was Chairman, met on April 7, 8, 9 (only to adjourn), 10, 11,§ 12 (L. J., XIV. 460), 12 and 14, when the Bill was ordered to be reported with the amendments given above (Com. Book). On the 10th *Sir William Wogan* was heard as to the clause relating to Wales. On the 12th the two *Chief Justices* were heard against the first clause, which had been postponed in order to hear them. They said they have now a right vested in them of disposing of offices. They have a right, a freehold, and hope it shall not be taken away. They hope they have done nothing to forfeit it. Then, after reading the saving in 5 and 6 Edw. VI. c. 14, the Committee added a Proviso in their favour (Annex *a.* below) and further desired them to draw up a clause as to Counsels' fees (Annex *b.* below).—On report on the 21st, the Bill was recommitted in order that the officers of the Courts might be heard by Counsel. (L. J., XIV., 469.)—On the 24th, in C.W.H., L. North in the Chair, Counsel were called in on the Petition and asked what they had to say against the Bill. *Sir Charles Porter:* If the Bill passes, it will be very prejudicial to the persons. Speaks to the Oath and reads it. *Mr. Ward* is heard also. They withdraw. *Lord North* said he desired the Counsel to withdraw, because he was not fit to collect evidence. Counsel being called in again, *Mr. Ward* objected that the words "of trust or profit" might extend to all, and were a snare upon

* The Acts here mentioned, which are given in the margin of the Bill, were added as an amendment.

† Here are marked for addition the Provisos A. and B. *See* Annexes (*a.*) and (*b.*) below.

‡ *See* Calendar, 12th Report, Appendix, Part VI., No. 160.

§ The MS. Min. of 11 April have the following "Law Bill ordered to be revived. Committed."

all the people. The law was very full already; and as for the clause about the Judges in Wales, it might as well be said that a man born in Middlesex might not be a Justice in Westminster Hall. *Sir Charles Porter:* There is a clause that takes away the giving of any special bail. This we offer as a thing of great moment. Counsel withdraw. House resumed. *Lord North* reported that Sir Charles had spoken as to the sale of Offices; that it would discourage young gentlemen, and that the Oath was very extensive.—On the 26th, in C. W. H., E. Bridgewater in the Chair, the Title and Preamble were read and postponed. First Enacting Clause read. The Oath read. Statutes 18 and 20 Edw. III., 12 Ric. II., and 5 and 6 Edw. VI. read. House moved to hear the Judges upon the Clause, and that a day may be appointed for hearing them. *Question:* Whether the Judges shall be heard to this point now? Resolved in the Negative.—On the 30th, in C. W. H., L. Cornwallis in the Chair, the first Enacting Clause was read. Leave out ("do now or") and for ("enjoy") read ("be admitted into"), and read ("any or every office") instead of ("any office"). *Moved,* to hear the Judges upon the Clause. *Pollexfen, C. J.:* Your Lordships will take into consideration to what these Statutes extend. If the small fees are taken away, then all the inferior officers must be maintained. A Clause read. Agreed that the Clause be made two Clauses. The Clause read. The first Clause left out and this inserted. *Ordered* to report this and to ask leave to sit on Friday. (MS. Min.; L. J., XIV., 480.)—On 14 May a motion was made that the Bill be revived and that Tables be hung up in the offices of their Fees. A Paper was offered.* The Committee of the whole House was revived, and an order made concerning Tables of Fees as in L. J., XIV., 498. (MS. Min.) Nothing further recorded. The Bill finally dropped with the Session.]

Annexed:—

(*a.*) 12 April. Amended Proviso, marked A., as follows:—"Provided "always that this Act or anything therein contained shall not in "any wise extend to any office or offices whereof any person or "persons is or shall be seized of any estate of inheritance, nor "that it shall in any wise extend or be prejudicial or hurtful to "any the Chief Justices of the King's Courts commonly called "the King's Bench and Common Pleas or to any of the Justices "of the Assize that now be or hereafter shall be, but that they "and every of them may do in every behalf touching or con-"cerning any office or offices to be given or granted by them or "any of them as they or any of them might have done before the "passing of this Act, *and that they or any of them shall not be "obliged to take the before-mentioned oaths,* anything [above-"mentioned] *herein contained* to the contrary in any wise "notwithstanding." [Added in Committee this day, after hearing the Chief Justices. Com. Book.]

(*b.*) 14 April. Amended Clause, marked B., as follows:—"That for "the restraining extraordinary charges and fees to counsel,† Be it "enacted that in any case to be moved, debated, tried or heard in "any Court of law or Equity within this Kingdom, the Counsel "to be retained and employed in such motion, debate, trial or

* Perhaps Annex (*f.*) below.

† A proposal to restrict Counsels' fees was made before the Committee on Irregularities in Courts of Law. (Calendar 12th Report, Appendix Part VI., No. 160.) A Bill was offered to that Committee by E. Macclesfield "for regulating the law," and another Bill was read "for regulation of the Courts of Justice." A memorandum adds that E. Bridgewater, the Chairman, took the two Bills till the next meeting of the Committee, to consider of them. (Com. Book, 17 Jan., 1689–90.)

HOUSE OF LORDS MSS.

1690.

"hearing shall not exceed the number of three for any one party, "plaintiff or defendant, demandant or tenant, to be heard in any "such motion, debate, trial, or hearing. And the fees to be given "to counsel in any such motion, debate, trial, or hearing shall not "exceed the sums following, That is to say:—To any one "counsel upon or in any motion, not exceeding *ten shillings.**— "Upon or in any Writ of Error other than upon or in special "verdicts and upon or in every demurrer, where no special "argument is necessary, not exceeding *twenty shillings.—Upon "any demurrer where special argument is necessary, Not ex-"ceeding five pounds.*—Upon or in any special verdict, Not "exceeding *five pounds.—Upon every trial except trials at "Bar, Not exceeding twenty shillings.—Upon every trial at "Bar, Not exceeding three pounds.*—Upon or in every hearing "*of a cause* in any Court of Equity, *Not exceeding three pounds.* "—Upon *arguing of any demurrer in a Court of Equity, Not "exceeding twenty shillings.—Upon hearing any exceptions to "a Master's Report, Not exceeding twenty shillings.*" [Prepared by the Chief Justices, by direction of the Select Committee, and added this day. Com. Book, April 12, 14.]

(*c.*) 14 April. Lords' Amendments in Select Committee, made on April 7, 8, 10, 11, 12 and 14 and reported this day. Com. Book of dates. [*See* text of Bill and (*a.*) and (*b.*)]

(*d.*) 21 April. Petition of Shem Bridges, Wm. Tempest, Richard Aston, Tobias Eden, officers in the Courts of Law and Equity, and of many more officers in the said Courts. Their estates and freeholds, for which they have paid great taxes, being concerned in the Bill, they pray to be heard by Counsel. [Read in the House this day, and Bill recommitted that Petitioners might be heard. (L. J., XIV., 469 and MS. Min.) *See* notes to Bill above.]

(*e.*) 30 April. Clause enacting as follows:—"That the Statutes "made in the eighteenth and twentieth years of King Edward "III. the twelfth year of King Richard II. and the fifth and "sixth year of King Edward VI. and all and every other statute "against buying or selling of offices heretofore made and now "remaining in force, shall be from henceforth put in due execution "according to the true intent and meaning thereof." [Substituted this day, in C. W. H., for the first clause, after C. J. Pollexfen had been heard. MS. Min.]

(*f.*) *Undated.* Petition addressed to the Right Hon. Lord Ossulston, as follows:—"The Exchequer consists of three sorts of Officers, Common Pleas, Revenue and English or Duchy side. Duchy Court. Two provincial Courts, Bishop's Court in every diocese, King's Bench, Common Pleas, Exchequer and Chancery in Counties Palatine, Sheriff's Courts and Courts of Record in divers towns, whereof the Sheriffs can give best accounts. Marshalsea for the Verge of the King's Palace. Stepney Court at Ratcliffe, in Com. Middlesex. Flint Court in Southwark. Mayor and Sheriff's Court in London. Sheriffs, Gaolers (2), Counters in London. Clerk of Assizes and of the Peace in every County. Welsh Courts, whereof the Judges can give your Lordships the best account. Stannary Court in Cornwall. Barmote Court in Derbyshire and Wirkesworth. Several Courts in Nottingham and Derbyshire." Prays that their Lordships will not postpone

* The word ("twenty"), inserted also as an amendment, is struck out.

the Bill for want of an account of these Court fees. A clause is inserted in the Bill,* that every officer shall at or before the ending of Term next cause an exact Table of the just fees due and belonging to every office to be hung up and kept therein for public view, and shall not take any other or greater fees unless the Parliament think fit to make any alteration therein.

(g.) *Undated.* Paper notes as follows:—"Wellington Court. Exchequer. English side and Revenue side. Cinque Ports. Marshalsea. Peverell Court. Nantwich Court. Lord Mayor of London's Court. The Sheriff's Court. The Court of Record of Stepney."

245. Apr. 5. Sir Hugh Middleton's Estate Act.—Amended Draft of an Act for confirming a Settlement made by Sir Hugh Middleton, Bart., for a separate maintenance for Dame Dorothea, his wife, and for other trusts, and for the better enabling Trustees to sell part of his estate for payment of his debts. The Lords' amendments are interlined on the Draft. No amendments in H. C. [Read 1ª this day. Royal Assent 2 May following. L. J., XIV., 450, 483. 2 Will. and Mary, c. 14, in Long Calendar. *See also* Com. Book, 9 April.]

Annexed:—

(a.) 9 April. Consent of Sir Hugh, dated 3rd April, and read before the Lords' Committee this day. Com. Book.

246. Ap. 5. Berenger's Estate Act.—Amended Draft of an Act to enable Thomas Berenger, Esq., to sell lands for payment of his debts. The Lords' amendment is interlined on the Draft; the Commons' amendment on the Roll. [Read 1ª this day. Royal Assent 2 May following. L. J., XIV., 450, 483. 2 Will. and Mary, c. 16, in Long Calendar. *See also* Com. Book, 10 April.]

Annexed:—

(a.) 10 April. Amendment in Lords' Committee this day. Com. Book.

247. April 7. Coals Bill.—Amended draft of an Act for reviving a former Act for regulating the measures and prices of Coals. As amended, it differs only from the Act of 2 W. & M., Sess. 2, c. 7, in the date of its coming into force, viz., May instead of December. The Lords' two amendments to this draft are to substitute this date for the word ("henceforth") and to fix "seven" years as the period (originally left blank) for the continuance of the Act. [The House on 31 March appointed a Select Committee to inspect the reasons of the extraordinary prices of Sea Coal in London and Westminster, and what is fit to be done to prevent them for the future (L. J., XIV., 443). The proceedings of this Committee were as follows:

1 April. L. Ossulston in the Chair. *Ordered* that Mr. Freeman, Mr. Arnold, and Mr. Bridgeman, three of the Justices of Peace for the City of Westminster [and Sir Patience Ward] † attend on the 4th, and that the Lord Mayor send at the same time two or three Aldermen of the City of London, who are not concerned in trading in coal.—4 April. L. Ossulston in the chair. *Sir John Laurence, Sir Thomas Kinsey, Sir Thomas Lane,* and *Mr. Bridgeman* are called in, and propose that the Act of 16 and 17 Car. II., for setting prices of coals, which is now

* *See* § v. of the Bill.

† This name is struck through.

expired, may be revived. That they are desired to inspect the wharves and see what store of coals is there. They say that in 1665, when the like was done, they had like to have been sued for it. The way, they say, to make coals cheap, is to grant a convoy of two or three ships and seamen to bring coals, without being pressed. They propose that there may be an order of the House; that they may have a power to swear them as to their stock; that there may be a voluntary stock and ground for store places; there will then be a year's provision always, and the price to be submitted to the Barons of the Exchequer. They deliver in a Proposition, which was made to the King by the City in 1672, which is read. They pray the revival of the Act 16 and 17 Car. II., concerning coals. *Mr. Middleton*, an officer at Paul's, desiring to be heard, and being permitted so to do, says that from Michaelmas 1687 to 1689 there have as many coals come to London as have at any time since 1660 in two years. 650,000 chaldrons have come in in that time. The Act 16 and 17 Car. II. c. 2 is read. Adjourned to 7 April. (Com. Book.)

4 April. The House on report from the Committee, ordered Mr. Baron Nevill and Mr. Baron Turton to draw the above Bill (L. J., XIV., 449), which was read 1ª this day (*ib.* 452), amended in Committee (Com. Book), reported, read 3ª and sent to the Commons on 9 April (L. J., XIV., 457), where it dropped with the Session. *See also* No. 284.

248. Ap. 7. E. Essox's Estate Act.—Draft of an Act to enable Algernon Earl of Essex, to make a wife a jointure, and for raising of moneys for payment of £6,000 borrowed to make up the Lady Morpeth's portion. The Commons substituted, in the preamble, ("with other remainders over") for ("the remainder in fee in himself and his heirs"), and added the Clause on a separate schedule before the Saving Clause. The rest of their amendments are interlined on the Roll. [Read 1ª this day. Royal Assent 2 May following. L. J., XIV., 452, 482. 2 W. & M., c. 10, in Long Calendar. *See also* Com. Book, 10 April.]

249. April 7. Mun *v.* Bickerstaffe.—Petition and Appeal of Thomas Mun, Esq. Petitioner, commanding the "Victory" under letters of marque, had, during the Dutch war in 1672, captured two prizes, the "Justice" and the "Smith," belonging to the States General, and assigned them by bill of sale to Sir Charles Bickerstaffe, to have them condemned for him. Sir Charles had got them condemned in the Admiralty Court in Scotland, and had sold them for nearly £6,000, but had never paid Petitioner his share of the proceeds. Appeals from a dismission of his Bill in Exchequer for an account, and prays that Sir Charles may be ordered to answer. *Signed* by Appellant; *Countersigned* William Wogan and William Ettricke. [Reported this day from the Committee for Petitions. L. J., XIV., 453. Pet. Book, 1 April. Counsel were called in on 6 May, pursuant to order of 28 April (L. J., XIV., 477). *Mr. Serjeant Levinz* (for Appellant): The Appellant had a Commission under the Duke of Richmond. He seized two ships, the "Smith" and the "Justice." The Duke was to have a tenth. He attends the Duke to Denmark and he makes a Bill of Sale to Sir Charles Bickerstaffe. This, he says, was upon trust that he should be accountant. House informed that Sir Joseph Williamson is concerned and others as members of the House of Commons. *Mr. Hutchins* heard to this, says this was accounted for. Sir J. Williamson is concerned. *Sir Charles Porter* heard to this, and states the case, and says Sir J. Williamson is concerned. Counsel withdraw. Nothing ordered. (MS. Min. No entry in L. J.)]

Annexed :—

(*a*.) 16 April. Answer of Sir Charles Bickerstaffe, Knt. The prizes had been taken by the Duke of Richmond, the Lord High Admiral of Scotland, when on his way as Ambassador to Denmark, by means of the pinnace and some of the crew of the Frigate "Portland," Captain Guy, which the Duke borrowed, and Petitioner, a servant of the Duke's, was sent home with them, to have them condemned on the Duke's account. Respondent had been the Duke's Executor and Deputy Admiral, but had made over his interest in the Duke's estate to Sir Joseph Williamson, Knt., and his Trustees, Sir John Lowther of Whitehaven, Bart., and Matthew Johnson, and Sir Joseph ought to have been made a party to the Appeal. Respondent further disclaims all liability for the "Justice," which had been sold by Archibald Clinkard, his fellow Prize Commissioner. Petitioner ought further to be barred by the Statute of Limitations. *Signed* by Respondent; *Countersigned* Geo. Hutchins. *Endorsed* as brought in this day.

(*b*.) 28 April. Petition of Appellant for a short day for hearing. L. J., XIV., 477.

250. April 8. Hudlestone *v.* Mounsey. — Petition of Andrew Hudlestone, Esqre. Wm. Mounsey, and 53 others, customary tenants in the vill of Matterdale and Barony of Graystock in Cumberland, claiming common of pasture upon the lands of Hutton Moor, Westermellfell and Redmire in Petitioner's Manor of Hutton John, brought an action against him in the Exchequer to restrain him from impounding their cattle. A trial at law in the Common Pleas was directed, and a verdict obtained in favour of Mounsey's claim with regard to Westermellfell, and thereupon the Court decreed that the other 53 tenants were equally entitled with Mounsey, although ten of the Jury certified that their verdict referred only to Mounsey. Appeals against Decree. L. J., XIV., 447. *Signed* by Appellant; Sam. Buck and B. Tonstall, whose signatures are copied, are the Counsel certifying that there is just cause of Appeal. [The cause was heard on 4 Dec. *Sir William Williams* (for Appellant): Common or no common is properly triable at law. We say we were ready to try this at law. *Sir Francis Winnington* (for Appellant): We pray that [even] if it were regularly proceeded in, yet it is hard that a man's right should be precluded. The Jury never intended to find but for one and not for all. *Sir Robert Sawyer* and *Mr. Ward* spoke for the Respondents. The Speaker having reported, the House dismissed the Appeal. (MS. Min., L. J., XIV., 578.).]

Annexed :—

(*a*.) 30 April. Answer of William Mounsey and 53 others. The Certificate of the Jury was improperly obtained, and ought not to weigh against the account of the trial given by the judge who tried it. *Endorsed* as brought in this day.

(*b*.) 8 Nov. Petition of Appellant for day for hearing and for an Order for Sir Wilfrid Lawson, Bart., John Pattinson, Thomas Ben, and John Huddleston to attend as Witnesses. L. J., XIV., 545. [Witnesses ordered (on motion) to attend. MS. Min., 1 Dec.]

251. April 9. Protections.—Counterfeit Protection to Richard Kirby, Chirurgeon, as follows:—" To all Serjeants, Bailiffs, Press-Masters and other Officers and persons concerned, to whom these presents shall come, Greeting. Whereas I have thought fit to accept the Bearer hereof,

House of Lords MSS.

1690.

Richard Kirby, Chirurgeon, to serve me in some particular affairs; Now these are strictly to require and charge you, and each and every of you, not to arrest, attach, impress, stop, hinder, or molest the said Richard Kirby, Chirurgeon, in any wise howsoever during such his service or within the space of forty days next after the date hereof, as you and every of you will answer the contrary at your perils. Given under my hand and seal the fourth day of April, 1690." Here follows what purports to be the signature of "Lord Kingston," in the same handwriting as the attestation, viz., "April 4, 1690. This protection allowed by me, Clerk of the Parliament House. Witness my hand, Jo. Browne." [This and the next paper were read in the House this day (L. J., XIV., 457) and the following evidence was given: A woman said Kirby bought the Protection of two men, Thomas Talcott and Thomas Garston, and that there were other Protections. Thomas Garston confessed he sold one for 40*s.* to Bignell, and that Talcot and James Reeks forged it. It was written according to Reeks' directions by Cranwell the Scrivener at St. Mary Hill against the church at Billingsgate, who received 1*s.* for it. Garston alleged he was Head Ranger of Greenwich Park. He was sentenced to be pilloried, the Chief Justice, on being asked what he would do if he were before him, answering, Pillory, for ears he cannot. MS. Min., April 9 and 11. L. J., XIV., 461.]

Annexed:—

(*a.*) 9 April. Similar counterfeit Protection to Richard Bignell, Mason.

(*b.*) 11 April. Deposition of Richard Bignell and John Richards. On the 2nd inst. Deponents with the wives of Rich. Kirby and Thos. Talcot met Thos. Gaston at the King's Head on Tower Hill, where Gaston showed them a Protection pretended to be signed and sealed by E. Kingston, and filled up for Richard Kirby, Chirurgeon, but would not part with it unless the money were ready, and thereupon Bignell producing him a guinea down, he promised him also a Protection, which Bignell received from him that night, and paid him the rest, amounting to 18*s.* 6*d.* Kirby being discontented and doubting the legality, Deponents went to Mr. Walker, at the Office of the Clerk of the Parliaments, who said the Protection was a counterfeit, and ordered Deponents to take up Gaston or his confederates, which they did, and brought him before Justice Crofts at Greenwich, who, after Gaston had given them bond and security for a sixth part of what they received, by a watch valued at 40*s.*, bound Deponents over to prosecute him. [Richards was examined this day at the Bar. MS. Min.]

(*c.*) 11 April. Deposition of Richard Kirby. Deponent was introduced by Talcot to Gaston, as being a friend of Lord Kingston and one who could help him to a Protection against his creditors. He agreed with Gaston accordingly for 45*s.*, and was to have the protection the Wednesday following, but slacked in going when the day came. Talcot's wife then came and told him that, if he did not come at once, he could not have it at all, as Gaston was going to the Clerk of the Parliaments to have the Protections signed. Thereupon Deponent's wife and Bignell went to Tower Hill for two Protections to Gaston, who, as they were informed at his lodging, had gone to the Parliament House. Deponent's wife went on to Talcot and paid him 40*s.*, and Talcot and one Watts brought Deponent the counterfeit Protection. Deponent, on seeing it, saw at once it was forged. Talcot said that if it were not good, he should have a fresh one or his money back, and next Monday it was to be remedied; but Deponent being dissatisfied went with Bignell and Richards to Mr. Walker, who refused to own the handwriting, and Deponent then sent to have them taken up. Gaston pretended he was to have but 5*s*., the other 40*s*. being for the Steward. [Sworn this day, when also Kirby was examined at the Bar. MS. Min.]

252. April 10. E. Macclesfield *v.* Starkey.—Petition of the Defendant's son, Thomas Starkey. His father has just had notice of the hearing being fixed. He is in Cheshire, and his Counsel, Mr. Finch and Mr. Serjeant Tremayne, are both out of town. Prays the hearing may be put off to some other day next week. *Endorsed:* Nothing done on it. MS. Min. [The Writ of Error was brought in on 7 Dec. 1689 (L. J., XIV., 365). On 15 April, Counsel being called in to argue the Errors, *Serjeant Thompson* (for Plaintiff) said the question was whether or no the action would lie, or whether it were not sufficiently barred. *Mr. Conyers* (for Defendant) states the case and his reasons for this presentment having been made by the proper persons. The Grand Jury are the representatives of the whole County. *Mr. Finch* also appeared for Defendant. *Serjt. Thompson* having replied, the Speaker reported the case, and, after debate, it was *proposed* that a Committee should be appointed to examine this business in relation to the Statute 31 Edw. III. c. 12. The Statute read. Stat. 20 Car. II. c. 4. *Proposed* to call in the Counsel to be heard whether the cause is regularly before the House. *Proposed* to ask the Counsel whether this is within that Statute. *Question*, Whether Counsel on both sides shall be heard at the Bar presently? Resolved in the *Affirmative*. Contents 32, Not-Contents 24. Tellers, E. Scarsdale and E. Rivers. Counsel called in. Speaker asked if they had anything more to offer. *Serjt. Thompson* says they came to know what their Lordships had to command of them. They withdraw. *Agreed* to ask them whether the cause had gone though the regular steps in the Court below, as it ought. Counsel called in again. *Serjt. Thompson* is of opinion it did. *Mr. Conyers* thinks it did not; nor are they ready to speak to it at present. *Serjt. Thompson* speaks to it and says he is prepared for it. *Mr. Finch* desires further time to prepare to answer Serjeant Thompson's argument. A Committee was then appointed to examine precedents of Writs of Error returned into the House of Lords, without having been argued in the Exchequer Chamber. (MS. Min., 15 April, L. J., XIV., 465-6.)—On 17 April, in Select Committee, the Writ of Error between Santen and the King is read, of 29 Car. II., which was brought into Parliament according to the Statute.* *Mr. Atwood* said he had searched precedents and found none from the Exchequer but the above. Stat. 31 Edw. III. c. 12 read. *Ordered* to report that the Order is defective, and to desire the power of the Committee may be enlarged, so that they might hear Counsel. *The Chief Justices* are asked whether the Statute is full enough to take away a Writ of Error on a Judgment given in the Exchequer till Judgment is given in the Exchequer Chamber before the Chancellor and Treasurer? Also, If a Writ of Error be brought immediately before the Lords, whether the subject is barred of an Appeal which the Statute allows? No Writ of Error from the Common Pleas lies before the Lords, but must first come to the King's Bench. There is as much reason for the bringing a Writ of Error directly from the Common Pleas to the Lords as from the Exchequer. They desire they may hear Counsel. (Com. Book.)

* L. J., XIII., 129, 167.

House of Lords MSS.

1690.

21 April, *L. Cornwallis* reported that the Committee have made some progress, and desire that the Order of Reference may be amended, as they are restrained to the Statute of Edw. III., and that they may hear Counsel, to inquire whether the Lords may proceed to correct errors before they have been brought before the Treasurer and Chancellor in the Exchequer Chamber. *Ordered* accordingly. (MS. Min., L.J., XIV., 469.)—*Eod. die.* In Select Committee, the Order made this day in the House is read. *Serjt. Thompson* (for Plaintiff) speaks to a Writ of Error lying from the Exchequer before the Lords in Parliament. As they have jurisdiction of all causes determined in the King's Bench and Chancery, he knows not that the Court of Exchequer can pretend to any privilege of exemption from appeal. Coke 4, Inst. 25. Before the Statute of 31 Edw. III. there was an appeal to the Lords. 18 Edw. III., No. 40, in the Parliament Rolls. 1 Ric. II. William Delapole's Case.* Writs of Error were redressed by Parliament or by special Commission. Baron Savile's Reports; Writs of Error were to be directed as they were at Common Law, and Writs of Error did lie at Common Law. The question is whether a Writ of Error must of necessity be brought first in the Exchequer Chamber? This Act was an affirmative Act. It took not away the jurisdiction. 1 [Coke's] Reports, fol. 11, Pelham's Case. This Act has no negative words to take away the subject's appeal to the Lords as it was at Common Law. Stat. 27 Eliz. c. 8 is read. Many statutes have been made for explanation of this Statute of Edw. III., such as 31 Eliz. c. 1, 16 Car. II. c. 2, 20 Car. II. c. 4. An Appeal comes from Chancery to the Lords without a Bill of Review. *Mr. Atwood* (for Plaintiff) quotes Bracton 1, fol. 2. Riley's Placita, Appendix, fol. 428, 22 Edw. I., fol. 1, 30 in Memoranda Scaccarii. The Lord Saye's Case. The Cause is respited and referred to Parliament. Riley, 35 Edw. I., fol. 429, 430. Fleta, Lib. 2 c. 2: the Exchequer more immediately depends on the Lords than other Courts. *Boughey* v. *Ramsden*, 22 Car. II.: a Writ of Error was brought before the Lords, and the Record retained, and execution awarded.† *Mr. Trevor* (for Defendant): They have produced no precedents since the Act 31 Edw. III, and if there be no precedent, I am sure the Committee will expect good reason for such a construction as they put on the Act. As to the Act of 27 Eliz., it makes strongly against them. The jurisdiction of the House of Lords is that it is the last resort. There is usage on our side from the time of making the Act. *Mr. Finch* (for Defendant), speaks to Mr. Thompson's Bill of Review and to the Record in Pelham's Case. This comes not regularly before the Lords. No cause comes hither originally before the Lords. You cannot take it up in the middle of it. The Party has no option to go before the Chancellor &c. or before the Lords. Quotes Stat. 31 Eliz. c. 1. The Lords are the ultimate jurisdiction, the highest Court of Judicature. This cause comes *per saltum*, without going to the regular Court where it should have gone. *Serjt. Thompson:* This Cause is properly before the Lords. Parliament Roll, No. 135. *Holt, C.J.:*‡ The question is whether a writ of Error lies in Parliament before being brought into the Exchequer Chamber? It does not lie in Parliament till a Judgment be given in the Exchequer Chamber. The Counsel have produced no precedent to the contrary. No precedent appearing, constant practice is a great evidence to us in Westminster Hall. The bringing

* These two cases are cited in Coke 4, Inst., fol. 105, in margin.

† L. J., XII., 385.

‡ Holt was Counsel for Starkey below, Sir W. Williams appearing for E. Macclesfield. *See* Howell's State Trials, X., 1360.

it into Parliament is contrary to the very words of the Statute. This deprives the other party of the advantage the Act gave him. At Common Law no person can come to Parliament if right can be had elsewhere, and there is no precedent to the contrary. Plowden's Commentaries, fol. 206, in the Case of *Stradling* v. *Morgan*. The reasons of the Law disallow of this way of procedure, and the Writ of Error is not properly before the Lords. *Pollexfen, C. J.:* Quotes Stat. 14 Edw. III. c. 5, 21 Edw. III. Cotton's Abridgement, 56, 71. 1 Ric. II. Cotton's Abridgement, 124. What has been said of Writs of Error from King's Bench is nothing to this business. This not having been in so long time practised, I hope your Lordships will not now alter it. *Atkyns, C. B.:** Quotes 11 Edw. III.; the case of Agar and Candish †; 14 Edw. III., case of *the Abbot of Ramsey* v. *Countess of Kent*. Coke 4, Inst., fol. 106.‡ In 18 Jac. I., fol. 175-6, a Committee was chosen by the Lords to inquire into their privileges and judicature, and they employed Mr. Selden, fol. 11, 25, fol. 88, 95.§ 22 Hen. [Edw.] III., Haddeloe's Case.‖ In cases of Writs of Error there ought to be first a Petition to the King, and the King writes on it "Fiat Justitia." *Ordered* to Report what has been said by the Counsel and the Judges. (Com. Book, 21 April.)—On 25 April *L. Cornwallis* reported the arguments of Counsel on both sides, as follows: Mr. Thompson cited from Coke's Institutes two instances on the Parliament Rolls before 31 Edw. III., one being William de la Pole's Case. There was only one since that Statute, a Writ of Error in the King *v.* Santen. He cited Savile's Reports and Pelham's Case in Coke's Reports. The question was whether the Statute abridged their Lordships' power which they had before the Statute, which he said it did not. The question was whether the Statute had made it necessary to follow it only. If the subject had no election, it might prove mischievous. The Writs were brought into Parliament; yet he insisted there was another way to proceed before they brought them. He insisted much on that. 31 Eliz. c. 1, 16 Car. II. c. 2, and 20 Car. II. c. 4, were all explanatory of the Statute of Ed. III. He cited 27 Eliz. c. 8. Mr. Atwood said their Lordships' jurisdiction was never questioned in Common Law. There was no Court to go to but Parliament before the Statute of Edw. III. If they were excluded before the Appeal to the Chancellor, they were excluded

---

* *See* Atkyn's *Treatise of the true and ancient jurisdiction of the House of Peers*, 1699. "The Lords" he says "were upon the very point of reversing the Judgment in the Exchequer, but, being by one of the Judges, then also sitting on the upper woolsack, put in mind of the Statute 31 Edw. III. c. 12, they did forbear to proceed to do any more upon it, referring it to the order limited by the Statute," p. 31.

† *See* Moore's Reports, p. 564.

‡ Coke, who in the passage quoted, refers to the precedent of 11 Edw. III. as follows: "Hil. 11 Edw. III., in *Libro Rubeo* in Scaccario, fol. 322, the case of John de Lecestre, Chamberlain of the Exchequer, a notable precedent."

§ This reference is explained by a passage in Atkyns *ut supra*, p. 30. "In 18 Jac. I., folio 175 of the Lords Journal, "I find" he says "an entry of 30 Nov. in that year, that a Committee had been named by the Lords to take into consideration the customs and privileges of the Lords' House, and the privileges of the Peers, and that a sub-committee had been named, who had express power to reward such persons as by their warrant should search among the records for privileges and customs, and that Mr. Selden had been appointed for that purpose, and had taken much pains on it. On fol. 208 of the Journal of James, on 14 Dec. the Committee reported. On fol. 91 I find the title of the Committee to be a Committee for searching for precedents for judicature, accusations, and judgments anciently used in this High Court of Parliament." What copy of the Journals is here referred to, is not clear. It is not the MS. Journal. Comp. L.J., III., 65, 67.

‖ *See* Hadelow's Case in Year Book 22 Edw. III.

after. Mr. Trevor said he doubted not but that a Writ of Error lay to their Lordships after having been before the Chancellor and Treasurer. Precedents before the Act could not be made use of since the passing of the Act. By the words of the Act he could find no election in the party. In 27 Eliz. there were express words, that the party should have election. Mr. Finch said that he conceived the case came not regularly before their Lordships. He insisted there was no election for the party in this Statute; in the Statute of the Queen there was. He denied that the Lords could award execution in Boyley's [Boughey's] case. Mr. Thompson replied. L. C. Justice Holt gave his opinion in it. The question, he said, is whether this Writ of Error is well brought. He is of opinion that it is not, and he expected precedents but found none. The Statute is positive by the words. At the Common Law nobody can come to Parliament for relief, if it is to be had anywhere else. L. C. Justice Pollexfen said that if there be no precedent in this case, it will be hard to make one in this case. If a Writ of Error should come immediately before the House, it might be mischievous. Since there are no precedents, he would be loth to leap over the Statute. The L. C. Baron said there is a precedent in 11 Edw. III., the Case of Agar and Candish, Coke 4, Inst. 176, Hadlow's case, and case of the Countess of Kent. None ever was brought but by King's fiat. The Committee did not order any Report of the Committee but what was said by the Counsel. *Ordered* that the Writ of Error be referred to the ordinary course of law, etc. as in L. J., XIV., 474. (MS. Min., 25 April.).]

253. April 11. Lewknor's Act.—Petition of Jane the wife of John Lewknor Esqre. praying to be heard by Counsel against the Bill, as it passed the Commons so quickly that she had no time to make her application there. [Read this day and referred to the Committee, but withdrawn subsequently on Petitioner being told that the Bill would not prejudice her Jointure. L. J., XIV., 460, and Com. Book, 15 April.]

254. April 11. E. Shaftesbury's Estate Act.—Amended draft of an Act for the making some provision for the daughters and younger sons of Anthony Earl of Shaftesbury. The amendments, both in the Lords and in the Commons, are purely verbal. [Read 1ª this day. Royal Assent 2 May following. L. J., XIV., 460, 483. 2 W. & M. c. 11, in Long Calendar. *See also* Com. Book, 12 April.]

Annexed:—

(*a*.) 12 April. Lords' Amendment in Committee this day. Com. Book.

255. April 21. Writ of Summons (L. Willoughby de Eresby).—Writ of Summons, dated 19 April, to Robert Willoughby de Eresby, Chr., who took the Oaths this day. L. J., XIV., 469.

256. April 21. Foden *v.* Farrington.—Petition of Edward Foden Esqre. Petitioner's brother Thomas married one Bridget Leigh, and made two jointures upon her, the second restricting the first, and Petitioner was made Trustee under the second settlement, to pay off debt. After Thomas died, his widow married one John Farrington, and the first jointure was set up and upheld by the Court of Chancery in 1679 and an Account with Petitioner ordered. The Master, contrary to the Decree, charged Petitioner with his receipts, but would not allow his disbursements; and Petitioner put in exceptions to his Report, which were overruled by Lord Chancellor Jeffreys without a full hearing. Appeals against the Decree confirming the Master's Report.

Signed by Appellant; *Countersigned* Charles Porter and H. Finch. [Referred to Committee for Petitions this day (L. J., XIV., 469), and presented, on their report, on the 25th (L. J., XIV., 474; Pet. Book, 25 April). The Cause was heard on 5 Dec., *Sir Charles Porter* and *Mr. Finch* appearing for Appellant, and *Mr. Trevor* and *Mr. Bowles* for Respondent. (MS. Min.).]

Annexed:—

(*a*.) 3 May. Answer of John Farrington. The Decree was after a full hearing. Prays that the Appeal may be dismissed. *Endorsed* as brought in this day.

(*b*.) 8 Nov. Petition of Appellant for a day for hearing. L. J., XIV., 545.

(*c*.) 3 Jan. 1690–1. Petition of Respondent. The costs he has received are not a third of what he has expended. Prays the repayment thereof to the Appellant may be suspended, until the account can be settled in Chancery. L. J., XIV., 615.

(*d*.) Copy of the Judgment of the House, of 5 Dec. 1690, appended to preceding. L. J., XIV., 580. *In extenso*.

(*e*.) Appellant's Exceptions to the Master's Report, showing £95 not excepted to. Appended to (*c*.) above.

(*f*.) Affidavit of Respondent, sworn before S. Keck on 2 Jan. 1690–1, that he has spent near £500 in prosecuting the cause for fourteen years in Chancery, and that the Costs of the Appeal have ruined him so that he is not worth £5. Appended to Annex (*c*.) above.

257. April 22. Forester's Estate Act.—Amended Draft of an Act to enable Sir Humphry Forester to settle and dispose lands [by the consent of Sir Humphry Winch, his father-in-law]. The Lords left out the above words in square brackets, and the rest of their amendments are interlined on the Draft. No amendments in H. C. [Read 1ª this day. Royal Assent 2 May following. L. J., XIV., 470, 483. 2 W. & M. c. 13, in Long Calendar.]

Annexed:—

(*a*.) 23 April. Lords' Amendments in Committee this day. Com. Book.

258. April 23. Fenwick's Estate Act.—Consent to an Act to enable Sir Robert Fenwick to sell lands for payment of debts. Whereas a Settlement was made between Wm. Fenwick, of Bywell, Northumberland, and his eldest son Sir Robert Fenwick, Knt., of the one part, and Richard Lord Preston, by the name of Sir Rich. Graham, of Netherby, Bart., Reynold Graham, of Nunnington, Co. York, John Clavering, of Chappel, Durham, Esq., and Mathew Heron, of Kirkheaton, Northumberland, Esq., and Roger, Christopher, Edward, Lodowicke, Thomasine, Mary, and Dorothy Fenwick, Wm. Fenwick's remaining children, and Margaret Fenwick, wife of Sir Robert, and sister of Lord Preston, on the other part, which settlement omitted provision for Sir Robert's second wife and for payment of debts, the persons signing consent to the Bill, provided no lands are sold for the payment of debts, but Shortflat and Mill, which are £125 per annum. *Signed* by Roger and Edward Fenwick, brothers of Sir Robert, and Matt. Heron and John Clavering. *Dated* 29 Oct. 1689. [Read in Committee this day, when also Sir George Fletcher was desired by Lord Preston to give his consent. (Com. Book.) The Bill was brought from the Commons on 12 April. Royal Assent 2 May following. 2 Will. & Mary c. 15 in Long Calendar.]

259. April 25. Clarke *v.* Baden.—Petition and Appeal of Edward Clarke, Esq. Petitioner was a younger son of the late Henry Clarke, of Wilts, Entering Clerk in the Alienation Office, and, with a view to his marriage with a person of considerable fortune, his father settled £100 a year out of the said office, but exacted a bond for £1,800 from Petitioner with condition to pay £800, which Petitioner had paid, and an agreement not to disturb his father in his office nor to receive the £100 a year during his father's life, which Petitioner had carried out. After his father's death, Robert Baden, his administrator and principal creditor, sued Petitioner on the Bond, and Petitioner having brought a Bill in Exchequer for relief, the Court made a decree against him in November 1689, from which Petitioner appeals, praying for a stay of proceedings in the meantime. He cannot bring a Bill of Review without performing the Decree. *Signed* by Appellant; *Countersigned* R. Sawyer. [Reported this day from the Committee for Petitions. (L. J., XIV., 474. Pet. Book, 25 April.) The cause was heard on 11 Dec. *Sir Ambrose Phillipps* (for Appellant): The question is on a bond. 7 April 1677 an annuity was granted. Mr. Baden is a creditor. A bond to Sir John Bladwell to be delivered up. *Mr. Masters* (for Appellant): We say the bond was given upon this agreement. *Sir Francis Winnington* (for Respondent): This is only a matter of ill words in a family. As to the Cause there is nothing in it. Mr. Clarke dies and we could not recover the money. The Court of Equity will never relieve against the penalty of the bond. *Mr. Craford* (for Respondent) heard. The Speaker then reported and the Appeal was dismissed. (MS. Min. L. J., XIV., 586.).]

Annexed:—

(*a*.) 3 May. Answer of Robert Baden. He had purchased the Bond of one John Steele for £50. The alleged Agreement was only by parole, and fraudulent and clandestine between father and son, to deceive Appellant's wife, and should not avail against the law. *Endorsed* as brought in this day.

260. April 26. Regency Act.—Amended* draft of an Act for the exercise of the Government by Her Majesty during His Majesty's absence. After a preamble as in the Act, the Bill proceeds thus: "Be it enacted by the King and Queen's Most Excellent Majesties, by and with the advice and consent of the Lords Spiritual and Temporal, and the Commons in this present Parliament assembled, *and by the authority of the same*, That whensoever and as often as it shall happen that his said Majesty shall be out of this realm of England, the regal power and government of the Kingdom of England, Dominion of Wales, and Town of Berwick-upon-Tweed, and the plantations and territories thereunto belonging, be administered and executed by the Queen's most Excellent Majesty in the names of both their Majesties, during only such his said Majesty's absence out of this realm of England." [Read 1ª this day; Royal Assent 20 May. L. J., XIV., 475, 504. 2 W. & M. Sess. 1, c. 6. On consideration of the Commons' Amendments on 8 May, the Judges were heard as to the first new Proviso, to which some words were proposed to be added. *Holt, C. J.*: This is the first time that I ever heard of it. I desire time. *Pollexfen, C. J.*: I desire time and desire the question to be stated in writing. *L. Cornwallis* proposed a question to be asked the Judges. The first question read. *E. Monmouth's*

* The only Amendment made by the Lords to the Bill as first sent to the Commons is the one marked by italics. MS. Min., 28 April. L. J., XIV., 477.

question proposed and read. *L. Godolphin's* question proposed and read. The first question read again. The four questions read and agreed to. The House then ordered the Judges to give their answers tomorrow. (MS. Min., 8 May. L. J., XIV., 488.) On the 9th the Judges were heard. *Holt, C. J.:* We have met, ten of us, on this business. [He reads the first question.] Upon consideration of the whole Bill, I conceive the King's power is altered so far as in his absence, and it appears that after his return he has the same power. This is an alteration. As to the second question and two concurrent administrations, the amendments do constitute two concurrent regal powers. Until these amendments, there was no power; now there are two and not a superior one. With regard to the third question, as for commands, I think, it being concurrent, the last command is to be obeyed. So it is *vice versâ*; if the King and Queen contradict one another, the last is to be obeyed. As to the fourth question, about the King's pleasure under his sign manual, that is answered before. On the fifth question, as to the Patent, it may. I speak for myself, Mr. Justice Powell and Gregory. *Pollexfen, C. J.:* As to the first question, I agree with what C. J. Holt has said and delivered. As to the second question, I should agree if we agreed upon the Proviso. I am unsatisfied whether it be not a void, repugnant Proviso.* I take it so to be. He speaks to the words of the clause or amendment, if the Queen, in his absence, passes any Act of Parliament. If this be good, it debars the King from his acts of regal power. It is a question whether this be not contradictory one to the other. I am confounded at the bigness of the thing and shortness of the time. All the others will fall on this: if the proviso is void, all falls upon the Queen. He speaks to the other questions. The L. C. Baron could not be there. *Rokeby, J.:* I am amazed in the question. The act made in the last Parliament directs the sole power in the King. As to the first question, I apprehend it is a great diminution of his power. While he is absent, he is not King. As to the second question, concerning powers, if it be a good proviso, it does constitute two powers. While I disobey one, I disobey the other. *Eyre, J.:* I take all the questions to be one. I agree with my Lord Chief Justice, that it constitutes the power in the Queen, but it is but temporary. I take the latter command is to be obeyed. I take the law to be the same in the two last questions as to the signet and seal. This might be inconvenient, were it not sweetened in the person in whom it is settled. I cannot see that the Proviso is contradictory to the Bill. It is only dispensing for a time, and this Proviso is but a further explanation of it; though there cannot be two sovereign powers, but there may be one sovereign power in two persons. *Ventris, J.:* This puts a power in the Queen. As to the second question, that will consist upon the proviso. The Proviso is consistent with the Bill. If they interfere, the latter is to be obeyed. The Proviso is not void. If the least interval of time, the last is to be obeyed. — *Moved* that the Judges may have more time. Some words offered to cure all objections: "but that "every such Act and Acts shall be as good and effectual as if his Majesty "were within this realm, and shall not be contradicted or controlled but "by his Majesty only during his absence." *Moved*, to ask the Judges whether these words would do? *Holt, C. J.:* Eight of us agreed that those words would do. He reads the clause with these words. *Pollexfen, C. J.:* (After reading the words); This declares if the Queen passes an Act it does ex-rule and bar the King. *Moved* that the Judges have time until Monday to consider of the Bill. *Moved*, that the Judges give their opinion whether, if the King shall have occasion to go out of the Kingdom, he may not delegate his power to others?

HOUSE OF LORDS MSS.

1690.

The question was then put as in L. J., XIV., 491, and resolved in the Affirmative, after a division, by 41 to 21. (MS. Min., 9 May.)—On 12 May the Judges were heard. *Holt, C. J.:* As to the last question, ten of us met and are all of opinion that without such an Act of Parliament the King cannot delegate to the Queen. Some of us gave our opinion to the amendment to the Proviso. I see no difficulty if these words be added. The other Judges said they concurred in that opinion. The Proviso read with the amendment. *Moved*, to hear all the Judges. *Pollexfen, C. J.:* I do apprehend I think it repugnant, contradictory and void in law. We all agree that if in any Act of Parliament a Proviso is contradictory to the premises, the Proviso is void. If there cannot be two Kings or two Queens in regal power at the same time by the laws of England, if there was need of a settlement in Philip and Mary's time, if there cannot be two Kings or two regal powers by the laws of England, then the question is how can this clause stand with it? The penning of this clause is the reason in this case. The words are contradictory to the former. [He reads the clause as amended with these words.] The words are too much or too little. If this Proviso be contradictory, then this will be subject too. *L. C. Baron:* I take it that the sole question is on the Proviso, and whether it be contradictory. I conceive it is not contradictory, but explanatory only. It is not now that the sole power is in the Queen. I take it the Proviso comes in very properly. The Proviso and the amendment make it very plain. *Dolben J.:* Speaks to the first question, on which the Judges gave their opinions the other day. They do in no manner clash with the Bill. They explain and make it appear well. The Proviso is not contradictory, but explanatory. The Proviso with the amendments fully answers all the objections. *Nevill, B.:* First question; how far the amendments, &c. I take it, it does not settle two concurrent jurisdictions. As to the amendment, it is not repugnant but only explains it and directs how far it shall be exercised. It is explanatory and consistent. *Lechmere, B.:* The questions are too big for me. I looked upon the Act of Settlement, and though these clauses and Act are consistent, yet I cannot see how they are consistent with the Act of Settlement. [Reads several parts of the Act of Settlement.] Under this Government we act. How far they are consistent, I submit, I doubt it is not safe. *Eyre, J.:* It is not repugnant; it is only explanatory. The enacting part had put the sole power in the Queen during the King's absence. Now the proviso leaves it to the Queen still, where the King pleases. *Turton, B.:* The question is whether the Proviso is contradictory or in keeping. I conceive they are explanatory only. *Holt, C. J.:* Replies to what Pollexfen, C. J. said. The purview of the Act is to sole power, and then I should be of that opinion. I do not take it to be so. It only says she "shall and may" do so, if the King does not contradict it. It is a necessary proviso and very consistent. The Proviso was then read, with the words to be added. A question proposed to be asked the Judges, and read, viz., Whether the King may not by commission in his absence empower persons to raise forces in case of invasion or insurrection, and for applying the Great Seal for the necessary carrying on the Government, with a proviso that they do not act but by the consent and approbation of the Queen from time to time, signified by her setting her hand. The Proviso was then agreed to with the amendment, and the House named Managers for a Conference. (MS. Min., 12 May. L. J., XIV., 493.) The Lords' amendment to the proviso was agreed to by the Commons on the 13th (L. J., XIV., 495).]

261. April 26. Vyner's Estate Bill.—Draft of an Act for confirming certain Articles of Agreement made between the Creditors and Executors of Sir Robert Viner. Confirms Articles of Agreement made between Thomas Viner, surviving Executor of Sir Robert (the other Executor, Francis Millington, having renounced) and Sir Thomas Meres, Knt., Sir John Moore, Knt., Daniel Sheldon, John Creed, and Thomas Langham, Creditors of Sir Robert, and representing three-fourths of his debts, and constitutes the said Creditors and Richard Morley and Joseph Hornby, Trustees for sale of Sir Robert's Estate and payment of his debts. It further annuls all accounts between Sir Robert and Bridget, Countess of Danby, touching the management of her estate by Sir Robert during her minority. [Read 1ª this day. L. J., XIV., 475. A Petition against the Bill was presented (see *a.* below), and the Bill appears to have dropped in Committee. Com. Book 29 April, and 6 May.]

Annexed:—

(*a.*) 29 April. Petition of Sir John Marsham, Bart., Sir Robert Marsham, Knt., Wm. Edwards, John Russell, and divers other Creditors of Sir Robert Viner. Pray to be heard by Counsel against the Bill, which will be prejudicial to their securities. [Read before the Committee this day. Com. Book of date and 6 May.]

262. April 26. E. Carnarvon's Privilege (Hempson).—Affidavit of William Clayton. States that, in pursuance of their Lordships' order of the 25th, Deponent, being deputed by Black Rod, arrested Henry Washington, for impressing one of E. Carnarvon's watermen, but that Washington, after promising to go with Deponent, got on board his ketch with some pressed men, after the latter had illtreated Deponent, and said he did not care a farthing for the House or its Order. L. J., XIV., 475. [On the 25th E. Carnarvon moved the House that, as he was going yesterday to Greenwich, they took his waterman out of the boat from him, and he said he would acquaint the King and Council and House of Lords with it. His Lordship's two servants were called in and the waterman's boy and sworn. Asked what was done to his Lordship's waterman. The pressmaster called him aboard, and he went and took hold of the waterman and swore, God d—— him, they would have him. My Lord said it was his man. He drew his sword and swore he would have him or my Lord. I was fain to row him with the boy home. *William Mires* says the same. They pulled my Lord twice on his knees. My Lord said he would complain to the King. The Pressmaster said that the papers on the wall showed there were no Protections. *The Waterman's boy* says the same, and that they pulled my Lord twice on his knees. They withdraw. The servants called in again. Asked who it was that did this? It was the gunner of the "Defiance," and he took hold of my Lord and drew his sword three times. *Ordered* as in L. J., XIV., 474. (MS. Min., 25 April.)—On the 29th, *Washington*, the gunner, being brought to the Bar, was told of the complaint against him. He said "I did press this man, I did not know him to be my Lord's man. I "had orders from the Captain to let none go." *Q.* "You offered "violence to my Lord's person and said you would have one of them?" *A.* I desired to have one of the watermen. Bid answer if any people in the boat did it? He gives no answer to this. He withdraws. *Washington* and Clayton called in again. *Asked*, Why did not you obey the warrant when served on you? You broke his sword and escaped. *A.* I offered no violence to his Lordship's person. I offered him a boat to carry him home. *Clayton* says, I went to him and demanded the waterman. He said I might take him. He asked me what he should do with his prest men. I went with them to the ship, and then he broke the sword and I told him it was an Order of the House of Lords. He said he did not care for that; he was in the King's ship. They withdraw. House moved to punish this fellow. *Ordered* as in L. J., XIV., 478. (MS. Min., 29 April.)—On 3 May, Washington's petition (Annex below) being read, he was called in and kneeled down and was reprimanded, and having asked pardon of the House was ordered to be discharged. (MS. Min., 3 May. L. J., XIV., 484.)]

Annexed:—

(*a*.) 3 May.—Petition of Henry Washington, Gunner of H.M. Ship "Defiance." Prays to be released, that he may repair to his Majesty's Service. L. J., XIV., 484. [His Petition was first read on 1 May, MS. Min. No entry in L. J.]

263. April 30. Hoby's Estate Act.—Amended Draft of an Act for the granting unto Elizabeth, relict of John Hoby, Esq., and now the wife of the Lord Henry Alexander, son and heir apparent of Henry Earl of Stirling in the kingdom of Scotland, one Annuity or yearly Rent Charge of £450 for her life in satisfaction of £500 a year in lands which she was to have for her jointure. The Lords' amendments are purely verbal. Those in the Commons are to substitute for "Elizabeth Hoby," the widow, words describing her as married again. [Read 1ª this day; Royal Assent 20 May. L. J., XIV., 480, 504. 2 W. & M. c. 26, in Long Calendar. *See also* Com. Book, 4 May.]

264. May 1. Writ of Summons. (L. Ferrers.)—Writ of Summons, dated 6 Feb., to Robert Shirley de Ferrers, Chr., who took the Oaths this day. L. J., XIV., 480.

265. May 1. Abjuration Bill.—Amended Draft of an Act for the better securing their now Majesties King William and Queen Mary and the peace of the Kingdom against the attempts of the late King James and his adherents to disturb the same.

§ i. Whereas it hath been found necessary unto all Civil Government and bodies politic that the members thereof should in some kind declare their union and oblige themselves to support, assist and defend their respective bodies politic and the Government of the same against all the enemies and disturbers of their peace, and divers laws and statutes have heretofore been made in this Kingdom for the same purpose and intent, when there have been occasion to direct and establish the manner of succession to the Crown and Government; And whereas the Lords Spiritual and Temporal and Commons in Parliament assembled have declared and established the Crown and Royal dignity of these kingdoms to be lawfully vested in their now Majesties King William and Queen Mary, and have in the names of all the people of these realms humbly and faithfully submitted themselves and their heirs and posterities unto their said Majesties and faithfully promised to maintain and defend them to the utmost of their powers with their lives and estates against all persons whatsoever that shall attempt anything to the contrary; To the end therefore that the union of all the subjects of these realms in a firm and steadfast resolution to maintain and defend the Crown and Government as the same is now established may be made known and declared, that all of them may personally bind themselves thereunto for discouraging all the enemies of the public peace,* [Be

* The rest of the clause, included within this square bracket, was rejected in C. W. H. on 12 May. (MS. Min.)

it enacted by the King and Queen's most Excellent Majesties, by and with the advice and consent of the Lords Spiritual and Temporal and Commons in this present Parliament assembled and by the authority of the same, that from and after the day of no peer of this realm or a member of the House of Peers shall vote or make his proxy in the House of Peers, or sit there during any debate, nor shall any Member of the House of Commons vote or sit there during any debate after their Speaker is chosen, until such Peer or Member shall from time to time respectively audibly repeat and subscribe the Recognition and Declaration hereafter mentioned and set down at such time and place as the Oaths now required to be taken, where mentioned in an Act made the thirtieth year of the reign of King Charles the Second entituled An Act for the more effectual preserving the King's person and Government by disabling Papists from sitting in either House of Parliament, on pain to incur all and every the respective penalties, forfeitures, incapacities and disabilities appointed by the said Act for persons offending against the same.]

§ ii. And be it further enacted that every person, as well Peer as Commoner, who on the day of shall have, bear, or execute any office or employment, civil or military, or shall hold or enjoy any place of judicature in any of their Majesties Courts, or shall have the profits or the trust of any such office or place whatsoever within the Kingdom of England, Dominion of Wales, or town of Berwick-upon-Tweed or in their Majesties' navy or in the islands of Jersey or Guernsey, or shall be of the household or in the service or employment of their Majesties or of their Royal Highness, who shall reside or be within the City of London or within the distance of thirty miles from the same at any time before the day of next ensuing, shall before the end of Easter term 1690 make or subscribe the [Recognition and]* Declaration hereafter mentioned and set down in their Majesties' High Court of Chancery or Court of King's Bench at such time as is required by an Act made in the five and twentieth year of the reign of King Charles the Second, entituled an Act for preventing dangers which may happen from Popish Recusants, concerning taking the oaths therein mentioned, and every such person not being or residing within the said city or within thirty miles of the same within the time aforesaid shall on or before the day of in the year 1690 at the quarter sessions for the county or place where he shall reside or be on the day of make and subscribe the [Recognition and]* Declaration hereafter set down in open Court between the hours of nine and twelve in the forenoon, and that every person who at any time after the day of shall be admitted into, enter upon or take any such office, place or employment as aforesaid, profits or trust of the same, or be of the household or in the service or employment of their Majesties or their Royal Highness as aforesaid, shall at such term or sessions next after the same make and subscribe the [Recognition and]* Declaration hereafter set down in such Court and at such time as is required respectively by the said last mentioned Act concerning the oaths therein mentioned, all which shall be required of and put upon record in the respective Courts on pain to incur all and every the respective penalties, forfeitures, incapacities and disabilities appointed by the said last-mentioned Act for persons offending against the same.

§ iii. And it is further enacted by the authority aforesaid, that all and every the Sheriffs of the several counties of England and dominion of Wales and the Mayor or Chief Officer of the town of Berwick-upon-Tweed

* Left out in C. W. H. on 12 May (MS. Min.)

HOUSE OF LORDS MSS.

1690.

shall cause this Act to be published in all and every the parish churches of this Kingdom of England, Dominion of Wales and town of Berwick-upon-Tweed, and shall cause a printed copy of this Act to be delivered unto and left with the chief officer of every of the said parishes and the Mayor, Bailiff or head officer of every city, town, and Corporation, and the constable or tithingmen of all and every the said parishes shall and are hereby required to provide a well bound paper book which shall be kept and preserved in all times hereafter for a Register book in all and every the said parishes, and shall cause the Recognition and Declaration in this Act set down to be fairly written therein, and shall before the day of in the year 1690 summon and require at convenient times and days all and every the males above sixteen years of age within the precincts of all and every the said parishes to appear in their respective parish churches after Divine service to hear this Act read, and all and every of them the said males shall and are hereby required to make, repeat audibly and subscribe in the presence of three at the least the Recognition and Declaration in the words hereinafter in this Act set down, and all and every of the said persons refusing or neglecting to make, repeat and subscribe the said Recognition and Declaration within the time herein limited shall from and after such refusal or neglect be taxed, assessed and shall be obliged to pay a double share or proportion, in respect of his real and personal estate, of all parish charges and duties to church or poor or otherwise and of all and every other taxes, subsidies and impositions whatsoever that now are or hereafter shall be imposed by Act of Parliament for the service of their Majesties and Kingdom, and shall also be and is hereby declared to be incapable to give any vote in the elections of members for Parliament; and all and every the Sheriffs and other officers neglecting their respective duties by this Act enjoined, shall forfeit and incur the penalty of one hundred pounds of English money, to be recovered by action of debt, bill, plaint or information by him or them that will sue for the same, wherein there shall be allowed no essoyn or wager of law or any more than one imparlance.

[§ iv. And be it enacted that the Recognition and Declaration hereby intended and appointed to be made and subscribed shall be in the words following. I, A.B. do truly, firmly, assuredly and in the sincerity of my heart think and do hereby recognize, acknowledge and declare that the late King James the Second having abdicated the Government, and their Majesties King William and Queen Mary having accepted the Crown and Royal dignity of the Kingdom of England, France and Ireland and the dominions thereunto belonging, according to the resolution and desire of the Lords Spiritual and Temporal and Commons assembled in a full and free representative of this nation, their said Majesties did become, were, are and of right ought to be by the laws of this realm our Sovereign Liege Lord and Lady King and Queen of England, France and Ireland and the Dominions thereunto belonging, And I do sincerely and faithfully promise that I will stand to, maintain and defend their said Majesties and the Government under them, to the utmost of my power with my life and estate, against the late King James and his pretence of right of title to the Crown and Royal Dignity and all his adherents therein, and against all the open and secret attempts of him and them to disturb or disquiet their said Majesties in their enjoyment and exercise of their Royal power and authority.*] †[Read 1^a this day. L. J., XIV., 481. On 3 May, on reading the Order of the day for going into a Committee of the whole House, it was proposed that the absent

* The Declaration is given, but not quite correctly, by Luttrell, 2 May 1690.

† Immediately after the order for the second reading on 2 May, the following entry, not in L. J., appears in MS. Min. "The injunction of the House be laid on the L. North and the Lovelace, between whose Lordships some words have passed."

Lords be summoned. After debate, House *moved* that directions be given to the Committee that a Peer's not signing the Declaration shall not incapacitate him from sitting in this House. After debate, order for the business of the day read again. *Question*, Whether the House shall now proceed upon the business of the day according to the Order now read? Resolved in the Affirmative. Contents 48, Not-Contents 33.* Tellers, E. Nottingham and E. Warrington. House adjourned during pleasure. E. Bridgewater in the Chair. The Bill read through. House resumed. *The Lord Bishop of Bristol took the Oaths, etc.*† House adjourned during pleasure. The title read and postponed. The preamble read. Committee *moved* to postpone all the paragraphs to the Declaration, and settle that first. *Question*, whether all the paragraphs shall be postponed to the Declaration? Resolved in the Affirmative. Contents 40, Not-Contents 32. Tellers, E. Stamford and E. Kingston. Then the Declaration in the Bill was read. Another Declaration proposed and read by the Clerk. Read again. The latter part of the Declaration read in the Bill. A Declaration, offered by Lord Warrington, read; read again; read again. A paper drawn by the Lord Steward read. Assert the right of King William to deny the right of King James. The L. Warrington's paper read. The promising part of the Declaration in the Bill read. *Proposed* that the Declaration brought by the Bishop of London be for those that are not in office universal, and another for officers and places of trust and only to relate to them. *Moved*, That this test may extend to officers only. *Moved*, That the Declaration be put to military and civil officers only. The Declaration read by the Lord in the Chair. I, A.B., do sincerely etc., as in L. J., XIV., 484. After debate, *Question*, Whether the question for putting the Clause‡ to be part of the Bill was the first stated question? Resolved in the Negative. Contents 33, Not-Contents 39. Tellers, E. Stamford and E. Feversham. Then the Question was proposed, whether the Clause‡ shall be put to all officers, civil and military? Then this question was put: *Question*, Whether the word ("only") shall be added to that question? Resolved in the Affirmative. Contents 38, Not-Contents 35. Tellers, E. Stamford and E. Feversham. Then the *main Question* was put, Whether this Clause shall be part of the Bill and be put to all officers, civil and military only? Resolved in the Negative. Contents 35, Not-Contents 38. Tellers, E. Feversham and L. Lovelace. Ordered to report matter of fact. House resumed. E. Bridgewater reported that they had postponed the clauses in the Bill to the Declaration and then came to the Declaration following, that they sat a great while and then they put the several questions as above, which were carried as above, and had rejected the said Clause.§ . . . *Proposed* to agree with the Committee in this Report. *Ordered*, That the debate be adjourned to Monday morning next, the first Clerk and all the Lords to attend. (MS. Min., 3 May. L. J., XIV., 484–5.)

On 5 May, the Speaker having stated the Report, it was *moved* that the Reporter report again. The Report read as reported by E. Bridgewater. After debate, Question proposed, Whether the Declaration stated shall be offered to all officers, civil and military? *Question* put, Whether to agree with the Committee that the word ("only") shall be added to the said question? After debate, on *Question* whether the

---

* Luttrell (2 May 1690) gives the figures wrongly as 51 and 40.

† These words in italics are struck through. Comp. L. J., XIV., 485.

‡ The word "Clause" here clearly refers to the Declaration in the Bill.

§ Here follow these words: "E. Kingston and E. Monmouth. Injunction of the "House to demean themselves peaceably to each other."

House of Lords MSS.

1690.

word ("only") shall be part of the question? Resolved in the Negative. Contents 39, Not-Contents 45. Tellers, E. Warrington and V. Weymouth. *Main Question* put, Whether to agree with the Committee that the Clause shall not be part of the Bill, nor put to all officers, Civil and Military only? Resolved in the Affirmative. The House agreed with the Committee. *Moved* to receive a paper offered by L. Warrington. *Moved* to adjourn and be put into a Committee upon the Bill. *Moved* that direction be given to the Committee to draw a Clause out of the Bill of Recognising, (No. 237) and Bill of Rights. *Moved* to consider of the question in the Committee for postponing all the paragraphs in the Bill to the Declaration. *Moved* that directions be given to the Committee that nothing may take away the right of voting in Parliament. After debate, *Proposed*, That the not taking of the Declaration should be no longer a punishment on any Lord than until Ireland shall be reduced. *Proposed* being bound to the peace in great sums of money for refusing the Declaration, and to be disarmed. After debate, *Question* put, Whether there shall be no penalty in this Bill to disable any person from sitting or voting in either House of Parliament? Resolved in the Affirmative. Contents 46; Not-Contents 38. Tellers, E. Feversham and E. Warrington. *Ordered*, That the House be put into a Committee to-morrow at ten of the clock in the forenoon. (MS. Min., 5 May. L. J., XIV. 485–6.)

On 6 May, after reading the order of the day, a Clause was offered to be referred to the Committee. *Agreed* that it may be offered at the Committee. After debate, House in Committee. E. Mulgrave in the Chair. *E. Monmouth* offers a declaratory clause. Proposed to have the Lord Bishop of London's clause read which was offered the other day. After debate, the Lord Bishop of London's clause read. The E. Monmouth's clause read. *Proposed* to take both the clauses* together and take them as the subject matter to debate on. *Agreed*, that both be taken into consideration. The Lord Bishop of London's clause read. House moved that these words be added ("nor will I correspond . . . . adherents, knowing or believing them to be such"). House moved to leave out ("Church and State"). It was read so. *Agreed* to stand in, and *agreed* that this Clause be part of the Bill. House resumed. E. Mulgrave reported that the Committee desire they may sit again on Thursday next. (MS. Min., 6 May. L. J., XIV., 487.)

On 8 May, upon debate whether the House shall be adjourned or go upon the business of the day, *Question*, Whether the House shall be now adjourned. Resolved in the Negative. House in Committee. E. Bridgewater in the Chair. The Declaration offered by E. Monmouth read. A debate arose for leaving out the declaring words in the Clause. The Declaration read again. The declaratory part read. A new Clause offered by the Lord President to be read. After debate, the clause read twice. A debate arose whether there shall be a declaratory clause. After long debate, *Question* proposed, Whether there shall be a declaratory clause or not? The declaratory part read out of the Bill of Rights. *Question* proposed, Whether this assertory clause now read shall be passed as part of the Declaration? *Question*, Whether this question shall be now put? Resolved in the Negative. Contents 33; Contents 39. Tellers, E. Stamford and E. Kingston. The clause read that was brought in by the Lord President. *Agreed* and ordered to be part of the Bill. *Moved* to put in these words ("I do own no Allegi-

* Neither of these "Clauses" or Declarations, nor in fact any of the five alternative Declarations proposed are unfortunately preserved; but the substance of the Tory proposals is given by Burnet (Hist. ii. 46).

"ance to the late King James"). *Ordered* to report both the Clauses, that of Tuesday and this to-day. House resumed. E. Bridgewater reported the Clause agreed to on Tuesday last and the Clause now agreed on. The first Clause was read. The other read. *Question*, Whether the first clause shall stand and be part of the Bill? *Previous question*, Whether this question shall be now put? Resolved in the Negative. The second clause *agreed to*, and Ordered to sit again to-morrow in a Committee on the Bill. (MS. Min., 8 May. L. J., XIV., 489.)

On 9 May, the House was *moved* that the clause may be read which was reported from the Committee last night and which was agreed on by the Committee on the 6th inst. *Ordered* that the debate of this be adjourned to Monday next at ten o'clock in the forenoon. (MS. Min., 9 May L. J., XIV., 491.)

On 12 May, the order of the day for the House to be put into Committee read. The Lord Bishop of London's clause read. *Moved* to put the House into a Committee on the Bill to consider who shall take the clause agreed on last. The other clause read, agreed on by the Committee and the House. The other clause read. *Moved* to go into a Committee to consider what persons shall take the Declaration agreed on and what the penalties shall be. *Proposed* to know what persons shall take this Declaration. *Agreed*, That there shall be no Declaration to the universality. To all officers, ecclesiastical, civil and military, and both Houses of Parliament and to such as the Government shall suspect. *Ordered*, That the debate to the Lord Bishop of London's clause shall be adjourned to to-morrow. Committee to consider who shall take the Declaration agreed on by the House on the 8th inst. House in Committee. E. Bridgewater in the Chair. Title read and postponed. Preamble read and postponed. First enacting clause read and rejected, beginning Sheet 4, l. 10. and ending Sheet 7, l. 5., and [agreed] that the consideration of what shall be in its stead shall be postponed. Second enacting clause in relation to officers read. In Sheet 9, line 4, Sheet 10, line 10, and Sheet 11, line 11 leave out ("recognition and"). *Agreed* ("the Officers ecclesiastical, civil and military, "mayors, bailiffs, Heads of Houses, Halls and Colleges and School-"masters"). *Question*, Whether the Members of both Houses of Parliament shall take and subscribe this Declaration in the Act. Resolved in the Affirmative. *Ordered* to report matter of fact. House resumed. The Earl of Bridgewater reported as in L. J., XIV., 494. (MS. Min., 12 May.)

The Sub-Committee appointed to draw a clause containing this Declaration was revived on the 17th of May and ordered to report on the 20th (L. J., XIV., 501); but no further proceedings are recorded. The Bill was never reported from the Committee of the whole House.]

Annexed:—

(*a*.) Draft of portion of a clause* as follows:—"Be it Enacted etc. That all and every the members of either House of Parliament for the time being, and all and every person and persons that shall bear any office or offices Ecclesiastical, Civil or Military, or shall receive any pay, salary, fee or wages by reason of any Patent or Grant from their Majesties, or shall have command or place of trust from or under their Majesties or from any of their Majesties' predecessors or by their authority or by authority derived from them, and all heads of Colleges and Halls in both the Universi-

* Apparently in E. Monmouth's hand. *See* Notes above.

HOUSE OF LORDS MSS.

1690.

ties and elsewhere within this realm and all Ecclesiastical persons, Schoolmasters and Masters of Hospitals and all Mayors, Aldermen, Bailiffs and Constables."

(*b.*) Draft of portion of a clause as follows:—"And be it further Enacted by the Authority aforesaid, That all and every person or persons that shall be admitted, entered, placed or taken into any office or offices Civil or Military, and all Ecclesiastical persons and all heads of Colleges and Halls and Schoolmasters and Masters of Hospitals and all Mayors and Bailiffs and the Members of both Houses of Parliament . . . ."

266. May 1. *Capias* for Small Debts Abolition Bill.—Commons' Engrossment of an Act to take away all Process of *Capias* for debts or damages under Forty shillings. Whereas by a Statute made in the sixth year of the reign of King Edward the First, called the Statute of Gloucester, it was provided that no proceeding shall be in any of the Courts of Record of Westminster, for any debt or damages, unless the same amounted to forty shillings and above, but that such small demands should be tryed or heard and determined in County Courts, Hundred Courts, and Courts Baron of lords of manors, being no Courts of Record, wherein the proceedings were only by distress in mean process and sale of goods of the defendant for the debt and damages in which he should be condemned, And whereas the laws and statutes that subjected the bodies of the defendants to arrests and to be in execution for debts and damages were never intended to be extended to such debts and damages as did not exceed the sum of forty shillings, notwithstanding which, by indirect ways and means, such processes and proceedings have been of late, as well in the Courts at Westminster as in the Court of the Marshalsea, the Courts held in several Corporations and divers other Courts of Record, against many persons for such small demands, and they have been arrested on mean processes and charged in execution for the same, to the utter undoing of many families and subverting the ancient course of the common law, and thereby the said ancient courts have been rendered in a manner totally useless; For remedying whereof, be it enacted by the King and Queen's most Excellent Majesties, by and with the advice and consent of the Lords Spiritual and Temporal and Commons in Parliament assembled and by the authority of the same, that the mean process in every action or suit to be commenced for the recovery of any debt or damages not exceeding the sum of forty shillings in any and every Court or Courts whatsoever shall be by summons of the defendant or reasonable distress of his goods only. And that for the more speedy and effectual proceeding thereon, if any person or persons, defendant or defendants, after due execution of any summons at the suit of any person or persons, plaintiff or plaintiffs, to be issued out of any Court by delivering a true copy of the same to the defendant or defendants, or by leaving such true copy for such defendant or defendants at the dwelling house of such defendant or defendants, or place of his, her, or their usual residence or abode, or after such defendant or defendants have been, by virtue of any process at the suit of the plaintiff or plaintiffs, issuing out of any Court, distrained by his, her, or their goods, shall not appear according to the purport of such process, that then it shall and may be lawful for the plaintiff or plaintiffs to file his, her or their declaration against the defendant or defendants in the Court or Courts where such cause shall be depending, and to proceed in his, her, or their suit as if the defendant had appeared. And be it further enacted by the authority aforesaid that the body of the defendant shall not be taken or charged in execution in any case whatsoever where the debt or damages that shall be recovered, besides costs of suits, shall not exceed the sum of forty shillings, but the plaintiff shall and may have and use all other remedies for obtaining of the debt or damages so recovered as he might have done if this Act had not been made. *Parchment Collection.* [Brought from the Commons this day. L. J., XIV., 481. On 2 May, read 2ª * and 3ª, and a debate arose whether the Judges shall be heard before the Bill pass. *Moved* that the debate be adjourned until to-morrow. *Ordered* accordingly. After the Royal Assent had been given to some Bills, a debate arose whether anything can intervene before the going on upon the debate of the Engrossed Bill. *Proposed* to adjourn. On question, adjournment negatived by 52 votes to 41, E. Warrington and E. Rochester Tellers. (MS. Min., 2 May. Compare L. J., XIV., 482.) On 3 May, the debate was resumed, and it was proposed to add a Rider that the Bill should continue in force but for three years. After debate, the question that the Bill do pass was negatived. MS. Min. L. J., XIV., 484.]

267. May 2. Lieutenancy of London.—Paper entitled "Names of the Lieutenancy of the City of London." *Noted* at foot: Or any seven or more of them, whereof one of the quorum to be always there. Dat. apud Westm. 19º die Martii, anno primo Gul. et Mar. *Endorsed* as brought in this day. Begins "Sir John Chapman Knt. Lord Mayor." Ends "Jeremiah Whichcott, Esq." The names are identical with those in Annex (b^2). The subjoined analysis includes the contents of this, as well as of two other Commissions, annexed hereto, viz.:—

No. 1. Commission of 1 Oct. 1688 (Annex (*r*) below), containing - - - - - -	77 names.
No. 2. Commission of 19 March 1688–9 (the above), containing - - - - - -	96 ,,
No. 3. Commission of 15 March 1689–90 (Annexes (*a*), (b^1), and (*c*) below, containing - -	129 ,,

Names in Nos. 1, 2, 3.

§Ashurst, Sir Wm.
§*Dashwood, Sir Sam.*
§Edwin, Sir Humphry.
§Fowle, Sir Thos.
Hedges, Sir Wm.
Jeffrey, Sir Robert.
Jolliffe, John.
Kiffen, Wm.
Laugham, Thos.
§Mathews, Sir John.
Newland, Sir Benjamin.
§*Pritchard, Sir Wm.*
§*Raymond, Sir Jonathan.*
Russell, Sir Wm.
§*Turner, Sir Wm.*
Thorowgood, Sir Benjamin.
Underhill, Edward.
§*Vandeputt, Sir Peter.*
Warren, Wm.

Names in No. 1 only.

§The Lord Chancellor.
§Butler, Sir Nicholas.
§Bawden, Sir John.
Berry, John.
Bathurst, Sir Benja.
Bludsworth, Sir Thos.
Bull, John.
Crispe, Henry.
§Daniell, Sir Peter.
Dodson, Sir Wm.
Davall, Sir Thos.
Duncomb, Chas.

* MS. Min. No entry in L. J.

§ Marked with a Q, as of the Quorum, the presence of one of these so marked being necessary to constitute a Court. See Annex (*r*) below.

House of Lords MSS.

1690.

Edwards, Sir Jas.
§Firebrass, Sir Basil.
Griffith, Sir Thos.
Graham, Richard.
§Hooker, Sir Wm.
§Jenner, Mr. Justice.
Knightly, Sir Robert.
Lewis, Sir Simon.
Lucy, Jacob.
Loades, Henry.
Mawson, John.
Moore, Sir John.
Mundey, Jas.
North, Sir Dudley.
§Parsons, Sir John.
Paravicini, Sir Peter.
Pepys, Wm.
Rodbard, Thos.
Rawlinson, Sir Thos.
§Shower, Sir Barth., Recorder.
Short, John.
§Thompson, Sir Sam.
Werden, Sir John.
Wiseman, Sir Edward.
Wythers, Wm.
Winberry, Wm.

Names in No. 2 only.

*Bristow, Rich.
*Chamberlain, Chas.
*Crispe, John.
*Cox, John.
*Dyer, Lawrence.
Godfrey, Michael.
*Hammond, John.
Hudson, John.
*Harrison, Edmund.
§*Lane, Sir Thos.
§Love, Will.
*Morice, John.
*Onslow, Richard.
§*Pollexfen, Sir Hen., Atty. Gen.
*Smith, John.
*Sedgwick, Obadiah.
*Walker, Wm.

Names in No. 3 only.

Adams, Sir Robert.
§Beauchamp, Richard.
Bedingfeild, Robert.
Barron, Arthur.
Boulter, Edmund.
Cutler, Sir John.
Chamberlain, Jas.
Carpenter, Wm.
Clarke, Henry, Deputy.
Coggs, John.
§Desbovery, Sir Edward.
East, John.
Floyer, Peter.
Gilburne, Percival.
Gore, Wm.
Genew, John.
§Hudson, Jas.
§Hussey, Wm.
§Hoare, Richd.
Hornby, Joseph.
§Hooker, Wm.
Joy, Peter.
§Jeffreys, Jeffery.
§Kent, John.
Midgely, John.
Nightingale, Jeffrey.
Normansell, Richd.
Norton, Roger.
Peirce, Richd.
Smith, Jas., Draper.
Smart, Joseph.
Sawyer, John.
Strong, Wm.
Tempest, Wm.
Withers, Will., Sen.
Wood, Thos.

Names in Nos. 1 and 2 only.

§Chapman, Sir John.
*Gardner, John.
Tulse, Sir Henry.

* These names compose the second list in Annex (b^3) below.

§ Marked with a Q, as of the Quorum, the presence of one of these so marked being necessary to constitute a Court. *See* Annex (*r*) below.

Names in Nos. 1 and 3 only.

§Alie, Richard.
§*Box, Ralph.*
§*Beaker, Edward.*
Colson, Thos.
§*Charleton, Nicholas.*
§*Goslin, Sir Wm.*
Hawes, Nathaniel.
§*Jefferys, John.*
§*Kinsey, Sir Thos.*
Nicholls, John.
Quiney, Adrian.
§*Rich, Sir Peter.*
Smith, Sir Jas.
Steventon, John.
§*Vernon, Sir Thos.*
Ward, Sir James.
Wallis, John.

Names in Nos. 2 and 3 only.

§Alleyn, Sir Thos.
§Ashurst, Sir Henry.
Allen, Daniel.
Adams, John.
§Birch, John.
Bowles, Joseph.
Bodington, Jas.
§Clayton, Sir Rob.
Chamberlain, Francis.
§*Child, Francis.
Coventry, Walter.
Cooke, Thos.
§Cooke, John.
*Clarke, Edward.
Denew, Jas.
§Fleet, Sir John.
§Frederick, Thos.
Flavell, John.
Foach, John.
Faulkner, Wm.
Gosfright, Francis.
Grange, Ralph.
§Herne, Joseph.
Houblon, Peter.
Houblon, Jas.
*Houblon, John.
Hatley, Henry.
Jarrett, Will.
Johnson, John.
Kenrick, Andrew.
§Lawrence, Sir John.
§*Lethieullier, Christopher.
Lethieullier, Sir John.
§Mordant, Sir John.
Mercer, Daniel.
Moore, Francis.
§*Pilkington, Thos.
§Papillon, Thos.
Powell, Samuel.
Roberts, Sir Gabriel.
Robinson, Leonard.
Rayley, John.
Raworth, Robert.
§Stampe, Sir Thos.
§Sambrooke, Sir Jeremiah.
Sitwell, George.
Scawen, Wm.
Scriven, Joseph.
Shaw, Thos.
Thorold, Chas.
Tench, Nathaniel.
§Treby, Sir George, Recorder.
§Ward, Sir Patience.
Westerne, Thos.
Whittingham, Robert.
Wessell, Abraham.
Whichcott, Jeremiah.

[On 1 May, the Order made on motion on 29 April for considering the State of the Nation (L. J., XIV., 479. MS. Min.), being read, it was proposed that a Committee be chosen to enquire of the cause of the decay of credit, and to inspect the men of the Lieutenancy of the City of London, and ascertain who were the advisers of the change of the Lieutenancy. A Committee was ordered to enquire into the present state of the City Militia and the late alteration. *Question:* Whether it shall be referred to a Select Committee? Contents, 43; Not-Contents, 45. Tellers, L. Chandos and L. Lovelace. Resolved in the Negative. *Or-*

* Entitled "Sir" in No. 3 Commission.

§ Marked with a Q. as of the Quorum, the presence of one of these so marked being necessary to constitute a Court. *See* Annex (*r*) below.

HOUSE OF LORDS MSS.

1690.

dered to be referred to a Committee of the whole House to-morrow. *Moved* to be referred to the Committee to examine whether credit be not lost, and which way it may be regained. *Ordered*, That the Clerk of the Crown send in to-morrow a List of the Lieutenancy of London that are now in, and of those that are put out. (L. J., XIV., 481. MS. Min.)—On 2 May these lists were brought in. (*See* paper above and Annex (*a*.) below.)—On 5 May, further lists, attested by the Lord Mayor, together with Lists of the Officers of the City Militia, were delivered in by the Clerk of the Lieutenancy (*see* Annexes (*b*.) to (b^5) below), pursuant to orders of the 2nd and 3rd inst. (L. J., XIV., 483, 484, 486.)—On 7 May these lists being read, it was *moved* that it be referred to the Lord Mayor and Court of Aldermen to examine the character of the persons named in the lists and give the House an account of them. *Moved*, to enquire into particulars and instances in those that were of L. Russell's jury. *Proposed*, That the King be made sensible of the advice he has had. *E. Monmouth* names Sir James Smith. He is chosen a Colonel. He was some way accessory to all the misfortunes of the late reign. He let go Brent, and lay in prison three months. Who was in his place? One who took the Sacrament according to the Church [of England]. This man, Sir Robert Clayton, went and prevented the body of the Court of Aldermen in waiting on the King; and his Lieutenant-Colonel was Sir Francis Child, and in his room is a traitor. *Proposed*, that all accusations against any of the Lieutenancy be in writing upon oath. *Proposed*, that a Committee be appointed to examine and inspect these things and to examine upon the heads in his declaration. *Proposed*, that a day be appointed for any persons who shall come to the Bar upon oath and make an affidavit; and that the Committee be ready to receive proofs upon oath. *Moved*, to name a day for anyone to bring in anything in this matter, or otherwise it may fall. House *moved*, that a Committee be appointed to receive complaints upon oath or record against any now in the Lieutenancy or Militia of the City of London. On question, resolved in the *Negative*. *Ordered*, that Saturday next be appointed to receive complaints, upon oath or record, against any persons now in the Lieutenancy or Militia of the City of London. (L. J., XIV., 488. MS. Min.)—On Saturday, 10 May, it was *moved* to call in Broome, and that he may show the panels of L. Russell's and Cornish's juries. Broome not attending, Henry Cornish was called in, and asked in the words of the Order. He withdrew. The Order read. Whether they can say anything against any man in the Lieutenancy? Can you inform my Lords anything of any person in the Militia or Lieutenancy, that makes him obnoxious to this Government? Objection being taken by *Cornish* and *Key*, when called as witnesses, to the want of a proper summons, House *moved* for a summons to persons to give information, and that a general summons be sent to the Common Council. *Agreed* to send summons to any particular persons named by a Lord. Three questions were finally agreed upon (L. J., XIV., 491. MS. Min.), and evidence was taken upon each as follows:—

Question 1. What have you to object against any person now in the Lieutenancy or Militia of the City of London in relation to the Government?—On 10 May, *Mr. Cornish:* If your Lordships had expected a general account, I should have received a summons. Several are of the City Lieutenancy that were concerned in my father's murder and are in this record. (He reads their names.) Thomas Langham was of the jury, and is of the Lieutenancy. I have nothing further but Percival Gilburn, of the Grand Jury. (He was called in again and delivered the Record that was taken off the file.) *Mr. Key:* All I have to say is that Lieut.-Col. Quiney, when they swore North and Rich, brought the soldiers in upon the hustings. He turned out several. I would have gone in. He refused me and offered to strike me. I was upon the hustings, and going off, I was taken up and carried in again by four or five captains. They squeezed me. They cried "Down with the rogue into the pit." Sir William Pritchard took me by the arm and squeezed me and told me I was a rioter. My Lord Mayor said "Go home, Mr. Key." They would not let me. At last they did. I ran the gauntlet. They kicked me a great way. I was one of the takers of the Poll. I was of the Livery of Merchant Taylors' Company. I was appointed a supervisor of the Poll. . . . I can say nothing more than I have said. *Mr. Baker:* I have no acquaintance with any of them. I know nothing of my own knowledge. *Sir H. Hubert:* Nothing.* *Mr. Jekyll:* Adrian Quincy came with armed soldiers into Guildhall. Quincy took the Aldermen by the shoulders and put them out. Sir James Smith bailed Brent. He seized a cheesemonger's widow for keeping a conventicle in her house, and he kept the money in his hands, and the Churchwarden came and demanded a third part. He sent for the woman. This I have from them that had it from the woman's own mouth. (MS. Min., 10 May.)—On 16 May, *the Lord Mayor:* "It has been my unhappiness to suffer under all governments in King Charles' time, and now I am afraid we are coming to the Egyptian bondage again."—Witness is told to answer only to the question.—"When we were upon the duty of electing the Mayor and Sheriffs in 1682, when we came to take the poll, I presume we had the majority of two or three to one. The poll was adjourned to Tuesday in Whitsun Week. We were sent to the Tower. We were brought to the King's Bench. It was ordered that those men who had the fewer hands might be Sheriffs. Sir Dudley North and Sir Peter Rich—they must be the men; they were imposed on us. All that would not concur with them were clapt up. Sir James Smith and Sir James Edwards commanded one Quincy to keep us off the hustings, and so Mr. North and Rich were sworn. Quincy commanded the guns and pikes. He took Sir John Lawrence and others and thrust them into a corner, and said if they would not be quiet, they should feel military discipline. Sir James Smith by name commanded to strike them and keep them off. *Sir John Houblon:* I have nothing to object against any particular person. I was not concerned in the government until this Revolution. *Sir Christopher Lethieullier:* I never was in any part of the government till of late. I have nothing to say against any. *Samuel Hoare:* I know nothing. *Mr. Knightley:* I have no objection against any person His Majesty shall put in to the Lieutenancy. When the Sheriffs were to be chosen, I was to attend at the choice. One Quincy had the command of the soldiers, and he would not let us in. When the Lord Mayor came, we went again. The soldiers in the Hall would not let us go up. Sir John Lawrence went to go up. I got up at last upon the Hustings. "My Lord," said I, "here are others to come up." Sir James Smith said, "What have you to do here?" I said: "If your Lordship does not swear these, P[apillon] and D[ubois], I come to protest against your actions." *Obadiah Sedgwick:* I have nothing to say in respect of any of those gentlemen. I lived quietly at home before this Revolution. Some of the now Lieutenancy did send me to prison. I have always been an attender at Church. They fetched me out of my house at 12 o'clock at night. I take the warrant

* Here it was moved to explain the question by adding the words ("in the late times").

House of Lords MSS.

1690.

to be an illegal commitment. (Reads several names of those that signed it, and also the King's warrant of 20 June and their order of 21 June 1685.) *Mr. Hogg:* I can inform something of the choice of Sheriffs. I think Mr. Beaker is of the Militia. I happened to be in Guildhall, I saw a customer and asked him if he heard his, Sir P[eter] R[ich's] name? He said, "No, but we had a sign given us, when we were to call out 'A Rich'." *Leonard Robinson:* I happened to be of the Common Council when the Charter of London was resolved to be surrendered. These were for the surrender, Sir R. Box, John Midgeley, Deputy Hawes. I was chosen for one to defend the Charter. There were several questions proposed. The Instrument that was brought down, was brought by Lieut.-Col. Fr[ancis] Griffith. After we had polled, it was carried that we would not surrender. Sir William Pritchard said he would see who durst oppose the King. I was concerned in the whole matter of the choice of Sheriffs, I was chosen to take the poll. Sir William Pritchard was Lord Mayor. We were kept off the hustings by train-bands; Lieut.-Col. Quiney kept us off. Quiney showed me a copy of an order of several of the Lieutenancy, with several names to it, that ordered him so to do. Mr. Borrett is Clerk. Mr. Gilbert Nelson, Mr. Watson and Mr. Wade can affirm what I say. *Gilbert Nelson:* I have nothing to say to whom the King puts in. Sir Peter Rich and Sir Dudley North stood; Mr. Papillon and Mr. Dubois were chosen. They took upon them the Shrievalty. Sir William Pritchard was put up, I was sent to gaol by Sir William Pritchard for being at the Coroner's. *Ra[lph] Watson:* I can speak to the Surrender of the Charter of the City. The Instrument came down. I was one of the Common Council. It was debated. The Lord Mayor, Sir William [Pritchard], gave his judgment upon the question. It was upon the affirmative for the surrender. "You shall have a poll," said he, "and come in at the little door, that I may see you." Mr. John Midgeley polled for it. I think there were one Major, a scrivener Griffith, Lieut.-Col. Steventon for surrender. Obadiah Cowcutt can inform of words said of the King. (*See* Annex (*o*.) below.) *Mr. Wade:* I can only speak to the Charter. I was of the Common Council when Sir W. Pritchard was Lord Mayor. The question was proposed: Who would be for the King in the surrender of the Charter? He said he would see the faces of them that were against the King in the surrender of the Charter. *Peter Essington:* I know many of them were in the Lieutenancy in King James' time. I know several that made an Address to King James: Sir W. Pritchard, Sir James Smith, Sir R. Box, Sir Thomas Vernon, Nicholas Charlton. The following were of the Lieutenancy and made great heats in the Hall in 1682 and 1683: Sir W. Pritchard, Sir John Raymond, Sir R. Jeffreys, Sir Benjamin Newland, Sir R. Box, Sir W. Goslin, Sir Thos. Vernon, Nicholas Charlton, Mr. Thomas Langham, Lieut.-Col. J. Hudson, Mr. Percival Gilburn, Mr. J. Midgeley, William Withers, Sir Robert Reding, Lieut.-Col. Steventon, Mr. Carpenter. These I have named were for surrendering. Sir W. Pritchard passed an Act in Common Council. At the second reading the question was denied. 8th Oct. 1688 in the Gazette shows it, and they are now in the Lieutenancy. (MS. Min., 16 May.)—Recalled on 22 May, and asked whether he knows any busy in surrendering the City Charter and instant in bringing City Sheriffs and seizing persons without legal warrants? Lieut-Col. Quiney and Capt. Edwards were in Guildhall on Michaelmas day, and kept them from the hustings. He commanded to load, and if the citizens would come on, to fire on them. Quiney took up several citizens in Monmouth's rebellion. They imprisoned about 300 for a month; these were against their election. Some of us in the Compter—that endangered our lives. Col. Quiney was one [of those who arrested us.] They carried us as criminals, and brought us back so. Asked whether they were Charter men? I believe they were of both sorts. I was always a Charter man. Twenty-five of this Lieutenancy were of those that imprisoned us. I have the Paper, and all that are marked with a cross* are of this new Lieutenancy. (He reads the Address out of the Gazette.) The gentlemen that used us so were very kind to the Mass house. I said to Sir William Pritchard "Will not this be accounted for?" "Pooh, Pooh," said he, "if others disturb the peace, we will keep it." (MS. Min., 22 May.) On 16 May, *Mr. J. Jekyll:* I went to take my leave of Col. Sidney before he died. He told me the Sheriffs had just been with them, and he told me he had locked them in and told them he laid his blood at their doors. Mr. Langham, that is of the Lieutenancy now, was of Cornish's jury and Lord Russell's grand jury. He was of Oates' jury. Mrs. Gaunt was executed, and he was on her jury. Sir Benjamin Newland was foreman of the jury when the City were rioters, when there was none at all. Twelve of us were indicted as rioters. Sir J. Matthews was of that jury—the Rioting Jury—and also Percival Gilburn. *Ferdinando Burleigh:* (Delivers copies of the records, giving lists of the juries.) Langham was on Cornish's jury. I am a stranger to the City. When the Lord Mayor was arrested, I went with the Coroner, and Sir William Pritchard said we should be ruined. They said they would give no appearance. I find several on the juries. Delivers a copy of the Lieutenancy's order for Quiney to keep the Citizens out. (*See* Annex (*p.*) below.) *Mr. Bateman:* I have nothing to say to the question. I asked Sir William Turner about my father upon an information that lay before him. I went to Sir William and asked for it. He asked if it was against the King? I said it was to save his subject's life. He said I should not have it. I saw it in a book in Sir William Turner's hand. I know nothing as to any other things. *Mr Kitchen:* As to Sir William Turner I can speak. Some time before Bateman's trial, I went to Sir William Turner. I found this examination in his book. I went to Mr. Burton and Graham, that I might have it. I went to Sir William and he said he should not do it. (MS. Min., 16 May.) —On 17 May, *John Borrett:* I am now Clerk. I was not in the last reigns. I have brought the books. I can say nothing more. *Sir John Lawrence:* I can say little; it is so long ago. While I was upon my duty in the election, I was very severely used by Lieut.-Col. Quiney. He would have put me out of the Hall. A company of the Green regiment was brought into the hall, and we were driven into a square bit of ground. I stood my ground. He laid violent hands on me, and I was dismissed the government. There were others. I took notice of none but him. I know nothing more. *Samuel Tucker:* In 1682 we were at the election of Sheriffs. One Captain Ed[wards] was with a Company in the Ward. Col. Quiney was within. He denied admission to me. I had a right of voting. His files did as he commanded. I saw within the Hall Sir John Lawrence. They denied coming until the Lord Mayor came. I got into the Hall after some hours staying. I saw Mr. Papillon offer to swear. Mr. Genew was there, and Mr. J. Genew and Mr. J. Blackmore thrust me off the hustings. They said not one word to me, but thrust me off from the hustings. *Jervas Byfield:* I do not very well understand the question. I know a great many of them. Sir Peter Rich took upon him to be Sheriff of London without any

* *See* Annex (*r.*) below.

House of Lords MSS.

1690.

choice. Sir Dudley North was polled three to one against him. Sir William Pritchard—we never chose him. Several were indicted for rioters. They indicted seven in twenty-one that were not there. Sir Benjamin Newland was foreman of the jury. Jeffreys gave the names to the jury of those whom they should find Not Guilty. *Deputy John Bickley:* In the year 1683 I was in the Common Council. Sir R. Box and Capt. Griffith were for delivering up the Charter. *Mr. William Walker:* I can speak upon the Quo Warranto. [I am of the] Ironmongers' Company. I went and attended His Majesty to Windsor. We attended Sir Robert Sawyer. It was His Majesty's pleasure. We signed such an Instrument as he had sent. I desired him to sign it, that we might call a Committee. I attended him [with] the Instrument. They sent to Mr. Burton. He sent me a letter. They had me before the Lord Mayor. I told the Lord Mayor I was Master. They procured a new Charter. They sent to me for the key of the seal of the Company. Sir Robert Jeffreys sent to me. They opened the box of the seal and put the Company in [*illegible*]. Sir Robert Jeffreys was Master. Thomas Heatly was Clerk of the Company. (Witness speaks to Burton's letter, and reads it.) This was after we had signed the Instrument. *Henry Chandler:* I live out of the liberty of the City and know nothing of it. Our Charter was surrendered; Sir Peter Rich moved in Court for its surrender. Quiney kept us from going up to the hustings. *Mr. J. Broome:* I do not come to make complaints. The Aldermen are my masters. I was unkindly used by them. A writ of Mandamus came for swearing Papillon and Dubois. I was in a public employment. I pressed an appearance. They said they would give no direction, and yet they said they would not indemnify me, nor let their counsel appear for me. There was a return of the Writ. I applied myself to Sir William Pritchard for an appearance. He refused it. The *latitats* were directed to me. After this, in Common Council I was removed and put out of my office. *Slingsby Bethell:* I was undone upon prosecution upon the pretended riot at Guildhall, when I was not there, and three of the jury are of the Lieutenancy—Percival Gilburn, Sir Benjamin Newland and Sir John Matthews. No evidence at all was given, nor were my witnesses called in, who could have proved I was elsewhere. *Henry Stroud:* I can say nothing particularly. There was something of an Instrument read by Capt. Griffith. I was committed prisoner by the Lieutenancy in King James' time. *Thomas Hunt:* In respect to this Government I know nothing, I am of the Ironmongers' Company. I am an officer. I appeared at the summons in the Hall. We agreed on a Petition to His Majesty. The first person that moved was for it. I thought it not consistent with the oaths I had taken to the Ch[arter]. I was put into custody by one Spencer, who is now in the Militia. He showed me no warrant. Quiney laid his hands on me. This was in the Duke of Monmouth's time. *Hedges:* Twenty-four hours I was at the Compter. About a month at Draper's Hall. (MS. Min., 17 May.)—On 22 May, *Mr. Thomas Cuthbert:* I lived in the country at that time, I know nothing. *Mr. Robert Cuthbert:* I know nothing. I know when the Charter of our Company [was surrendered], I was turned out, and can say nothing. *Mr. Peter White:* I know nothing. I sat in the Common Council when the Charter business was on. I must confess I cannot forget the last Council, I remember Sir William Pritchard and several were for the surrender. We got nothing but by polling, and we were threatened. I opposed the surrender. The names were to be kept after we had voted. It was one in the Common Council who threatened me; who it was, I cannot tell. *Dr. Thomas Gardiner:* The former Lieutenancy were very positive to have the Charter delivered. Griffith, Langham,

Withers and others. They sent files of Musketeers to break open my door. One Pearce came to my door and searched my house, as they pretended, for arms. I saw no warrant. Many of my neighbourhood came to the Lord Mayor and said they would send for me, for I was one of Lord Shaftesbury's jury. I was in the panel, but did not appear *Christopher Forster:* The late Lieutenancy committed me to prison. I know not who were then or now in the Militia. *Sir Thomas Hawton:* I think there are some in now that were very obnoxious, as Col. Quiney. I was turned out of the Company because I was not for the surrender. They are very ill men. I believe several were for the delivery of the Charter. Sir William Turner and Sir William Pritchard were for it; about eighteen, and we were turned out. *Thomas Rawlinson:* Not of my own knowledge. *Sir Peter Daniell:* I have nothing to object against them. I believe them to be good men. *Richard Normansell:* I know all of them. They are of different judgments, but they acted equally, I think and are fair men. *Mr. Eldred:* In the year 1682 or 1683 we had a ward. The candidates were Hawkins and Dubois. Sir William Pritchard shut up the poll. We desired a scrutiny. Sir Dudley North was [returned],* and they removed to a place in favour of some men upon the choosing of an Aldermen. I know nothing of surrendering charters. I know of no undue practices in the choice of Sheriffs. *Thomas Wilson:* I know not whether I may speak of Sir William Pritchard, being a mayor. The Ward was adjourned to St. Sepulchre's. I was to take the poll between Hawkins and Dubois. Sir William Pritchard came. Asked if they had done. He said "No, shut up the books," which was done. Soldiers were set against the Mass house, to guard it. Thos. Salter was Lieutenant; he commanded those soldiers. *Thomas Adams:* I know none. *Robert Blackborne:* Of the city I know nothing, I can speak to our Company, the Fishmongers'. A writ was brought to Sir Symon Lewis, and he called a Court. Sir Symon Lewis, Mr. Withers and Capt. Griffith were for it. The major part were for it. The L. C. Justice North; we had a difference in the Company. I was there when Sir Peter Rich was chosen. It was the worst election I ever saw. There were handkerchiefs held out, and then they cried "A Rich! A Rich!" and then he was chosen, as they said. *Mr. Peter Houblon:* I cannot charge my memory long. At the time of the Charter they turned us out of the Company. I was taken out of my bed by the Lieutenancy and imprisoned. Lieut.-Col. Pearce of the now Militia and Major Spencer carried me away, and I was 13 or 14 days in prison, because I would not vote for the delivery of the Charter. Major Spencer told me I should repent it as long as I lived. *Mr. F. Moore:* I am no freeman of the City. I know nothing of the matter. (MS. Min., 22 May.)

Question 2: Whether you know any of those that are guilty of any illegal practices since the year 1680?

Mr. Jekyll: I have a list at home, if your Lordships give me time. (MS. Min., 10 May.) *The Lord Mayor:* I gave your Lordships an account of Sir James Smith and Quiney. *Sir John Houblon:* I know nothing of my own knowledge. *Sir Christopher Lethieullier:* I know nothing of my own knowledge. *Samuel Hoare:* I know nothing. Col. Quiney stood at the door and kept us from going into the Hall. I was concerned as an elector; I had a voice. I wonder I was summoned up. I know nothing of Sir James Smith. *Mr. Knightley:* I know not who are in or out; but that some are in very obnoxious to the City. *Obadiah Sedgwick:* I know nothing of that . . . . As for the Charter of the Grocers' Company, 12 April 1684, I attended to do my duty as an

* Luttrell, 16 Dec. 1682.

House of Lords MSS.

1690.

Assistant in the Company. Sir James Edwards moved for the surrender of the Charter. Mr. Pearce, Sir R. Box, and Percival Gilburn were to go with the Charter. I opposed the surrender of the Charter. Mr. Pearce is now Lieut.-Col. *Mr. Hogg:* I know nothing. *Gilbert Nelson:* I do not know what is called "illegal." They carried me to gaol for several days, almost one month. Lieut.-Col. Pearce and C[aptain] Le Neve said they had an order from the Lieutenancy for it. The Warrant was signed Evans. *Mr. Wade:* I know nothing. *John Borrett:* I do not know. *Jervas Byfield:* Mr. Langham was one of Mr. Cornish's jury. Sir William Russell carried away the Charter of the Skinners' Company. He brought Sir George Jeffreys and Jenner's letter and Mr. Graham's letters to hire off Mr. Browne. . . . Then we were turned out. His fault was for arresting Sir William Pritchard. *Deputy John Bickley:* Not of my own knowledge. (MS. Min., 17 May.) —*Mr. Peter White:* I have nothing to accuse anybody of. *Christopher Forster:* I know nothing of my own knowledge. *Thomas Rawlinson:* Not of my own knowledge. *Sir Peter Daniell:* I know nothing. *Thomas Adams:* I know not who are in the present Lieutenancy. Capt. Griffith was for resigning the Charter. *Freeman:* What I have to say is to Sir William Pritchard. There was an Alderman made in the Ward of Farringdon Without. Sir William gave no precepts. He adjourned to St. Dunstan's. It tended, I believe, rather to make Sir Dudley North an Alderman than let the people have the right to chose. He came and commanded the books to be shut up. A scrutiny was denied. I verily believe Sir Dudley North was not chosen. I was in the hall when the soldiers were there, when the two persons that were legally chosen were not sworn. I saw a great rudeness; I know not the persons. I was taken up in Monmouth's Rebellion. It was said to be from the Lieutenancy. They took our words that night, and then we were confined for a month. The officer sent for me. Capt. Phillips, now a Captain, was then an Ensign. *Mr. Peter Houblon:* I know nothing. (MS. Min., 22 May.)

Question 3: Whether you know any of them were of the Lord Russell's, Mr. Cornish's or Colonel Sidney's Juries?

Mr. Jekyll I do know several were. *Mr. Broome:* I went by order of my Lord Mayor and took lists, and by comparing them I find they were of some juries. Sir Thomas Fowles was of the panel of the jury. Can give a better information on Wednesday next. (MS. Min., 10 May.) *The Lord Mayor:* I cannot answer to it. I was in the King's Bench. *Sir John Houblon:* I know nothing of my own knowledge. *Sir Christopher Lethieullier:* I answer as to the others. I never was concerned in any other thing till the [one] now thrust on me. *Samuel Hoare:* I know nothing. *Mr. Knightley:* I know nothing of it. *Obadiah Sedgwick:* I know nothing of my own knowledge. *Mr. Hogg* I know nothing. *Leonard Robinson:* I have no further knowledge than the public trials. *Gilbert Nelson:* I did not concern myself. *Ralph Watson:* I know no one but by hearsay. *Mr. Wade:* Nothing. (MS. Min., 16 May.)—*John Borrett:* I did not attend the trials. *Samuel Tucker:* Deputy Langham was of Alderman Cornish's jury. Sir Thomas Rawlinson was foreman of the grand jury. (MS. Min., 17 May.)—*Mr. Peter White:* I know nothing. *Dr. Thomas Gardiner* It is said credibly that Mr. Langham was of Cornish's jury. *Christopher Forster:* I know nothing of my own knowledge. *Thomas Rawlinson* I was with several citizens in prison, but they knew not for what. *Mr. Robert Blaney:* I can say as to the jury about the Riot. Thomas Langham was on Cornish's jury. Sir John Matthews, Sir Benjamin Newland and Mr. Percival Gilburn were on the Rioter's Jury. *Mr. Peter Houblon*: I know nothing. (MS. Min., 22 May.)

On 22 May the above evidence was ordered to be reported by the Speaker the next day, and the Lords to be summoned. (MS. Min. L. J., XIV., 505.) The report, however, was never made, the adjournment on the 23rd putting a stop to further proceedings.]

Annexed:

(*a*.) 2 May.—Paper entitled "Names of the Commissioners of Lieutenancy for the City of London." *Noted* at end of list: "Or any seven or more of them, whereof one of the quorum to be always there. Dat. apud Westm. xv. die Martii, anno secundo Gul. et Mar." [1689–90]. *Endorsed* as brought in this day. Begins "Sir Thos. Pilkington;" ends "Edmund Bolter, Esq." The List is identical with that in Annex (b^1) below.

(*b*.) 5 May.—Letter of 3 May from Sir Thomas Pilkington, Lord Mayor, to the House of Lords, certifying that the five lists, appended, are true lists of the present Lieutenancy and Officers in the Militia of the City of London, as of the former Lieutenancy and Officers in the Militia before their Majesties' present Commission of Lieutenancy, and of those that were displaced and put out. [This and the five following papers appended hereto, are endorsed "List of the Lieutenancy, delivered by the Clerk of the Lieutenancy pursuant to order of 2 and 3 May, 1690, and received this 5 May."]

(b^1.) List of their Majesties' present Commissioners of Lieutenancy of the City of London, per Commission dated 15 March, 2 W. & M. [1689–90]. Identical with Annex (*a*.) above. The names are given in the analysis of the three Commissions above, Commission No. 3.

(b^2.) List of the Field Officers, Captains, Lieutenants and Ensigns in the Militia of the City of London, as they are now commissioned by their Majesties' present Commissioners of Lieutenancy for the said City, 3 May, 1690. The names are given in the second column below, those in the first column being the late officers, taken from Annex (b^5) below:—

Annex (b^5).	Annex (b^2).
White Regiment.	
Colonel.	
Sir Thos. Pilkington, Knt., Lord Mayor.	Sir William Pritchard, Knt., Alderman.
Lieut.-Col.	
William Pilkington.	John Steventon.
Major.	
Peter Essington.	—
Captains.	
John Ward,	Thos. Aungier,
Benjamin Davis,	Benjamin Page,
Peter Carpenter,	John Condley,
Thos. Hammond,	Richard Amery,
Thos. Sealy.	John Ward.

House of Lords MSS.

1690.

Annex (b^5).	Annex (b^3).

Lieutenants.

John Pilkington (Capt.-Lieut.),	Giles Baker (Capt.-Lieut.),
Philip Whiteman,	Thos. Forshaw,
George Heath,	Chas. Chandlis,
Thos. Bent,	John Tayler,
John Shorey,	Henry Turner,
James Bett,	Richard Fletcher,
William Meekins,	Thos. Bent.
Richard Fletcher.	

Ensigns.

Henry Hewett,	Richard Tottey,
Thos. Sheffeild,	Richard Timms,
Sam. Gibbs,	William Cocke,
George Prince,	William Thompson,
Obadiah Mesmacutt,	Thomas Elwes,
Robert Nardan,	George Prince.
Francis Thorneborrow,	
Thos. Scriblehill.	

Orange Regiment.

Colonel.

Sir Robert Clayton, Knt., Alderman.	Sir James Smith, Knt.

Lieut.-Col.

Sir Francis Child, Knt., Alderman.	Edward Becker.

Major.

Thos. Cuthbert.	Richard Kinsey.

Captains.

Nathaniel Long,	John Leighton,
John Somer,	James Shuter,
Edward Jenkins,	John Phillipps,
John Symon,	Josiah Wiseman,
Joseph Stratton,	John Butler.

Lieutenants.

Joseph Hyde (Capt.-Lieut.),	Daniel Barton (Capt.-Lieut.),
Humphrey Pickfott,	Thos. Salter,
Richard Barnes,	John Reynolds,
John Rose,	Henry Relfe,
Henry Coxhed,	James Pooley,
Richard Wise,	Sentley Whitehead,
Daniel Neald,	Thomas Cox,
James Gillam.	Valentine Avery.

Annex (b^3).

Ensigns.

Russell Alsopp,
John Allen,
Thos. Hartley,
Benjamin Rumsey,
Michael Gammon,
Richard Brookes,
Isaac Hadley,
John Mead.

Annex (b^5).

Richard Marshall,
William Wickes,
John Gough,
Francis Goodman,
——— Peascod,
Stephen Farmer,
Henry Kite.

Blue Regiment.

Colonel.

Sir Patience Ward, Knt., Alderman.

Sir Peter Rich, Knt., Alderman.

Lieut.-Col.

Samuel Wickins.

Richard Pearce.

Major.

Charles Milson.

William Woodroffe.

Captains.

Gilbert Nelson,
William Webster,
Robert Silke,
Samuel Westall,
Thos. Edlyn.

Robert Silke,
Thos. Seely,
John Fryth,
Henry Daniell.

Lieutenants.

William Nicholls (Capt.-Lieut.),
John Alexander,
George Jarrard,
William Holday,
William Stevens,
Charles Harbin,
Thos. Rowse,
John Richards.

Nicholas Ward (Capt.-Lieut.),
John Palmer,
John Ticknor,
Charles Harbin.

Ensigns.

Giles Fermin,
Thos. Woodman,
Edward Wood,
Joseph Buckingham,
Andrew Phillips, Junr.,
Henry Balchin,
Francis Taylor,
John Edlin.

Hopewell Hoare,
Martin Vadenanker,
Henry Balchin.

Annex (b^3).	Annex (b^2).
Green Regiment.	
Colonel.	
Sir Thos. Stampe, Knt., Alderman.	Sir Jonathan Raymond, Knt., Alderman.
Lieut.-Col.	
Humphry Willett.	Adrian Quiney.
Major.	
John Hillman.	Thos. Spencer.
Captains.	
Robert Lancashire,	Thos. Hodges,
Richard Wightwicke,	Daniel Fowle,
Ezekiel Hutchinson,	Joseph Drake,
Thos. Emes,	Thos. Crane,
John Jellings.	Nicholas Donning.
Lieutenants.	
William Phillipps, (Capt.-Lieut.),	William Haywood, (Capt.-Lieut.),
John Bullon,	Thos. Bracey,
John Wood,	John Hinde,
John Cave,	Isaac Urry,
John Andrews,	George Heath.
Thos. Todd,	
John Tickner,	
—— Sharpe.	
Ensigns.	
John Foden,	William Paxton,
Thos. Willett,	Richard Howes,
Richard Cooke,	Thos. Brayne,
John Lancashire,	Ferdinando Gunter.
Richard Jobber,	
James Barrington,	
Cornelius Jesson,	
George Haille.	
Yellow Regiment.	
Colonel.	
Sir William Ashurst, Knt., Alderman.	Sir Thomas Stampe, Knt., Alderman.
Lieut.-Col.	
Robert Hatton.	Francis Griffith.
Major.	
Henry Hatley.	John Hilman.

Annex (b^3).	Annex (b^2).

Captains.

Mark Stretton,	Robert Lancashire,
John Adams,	Richard Wightwicke,
John Ayres,	John Loveday.
Samuel Mabbs, Senr.,	
William Churchill.	

Lieutenants.

Thomas Jenkins, (Capt.-Lieut.),	William Phillipps, (Capt.-Lieut.).
Samuel Smith,	
Thos. Manwairing,	
Jeremiah Francis,	
Samuel Ball,	
Moses Burton,	
Samuel Mabbs, Junr.,	
John Fowkes.	

Ensigns.

Edward Fauconbridge,	
John Rivett,	
—— Rose,	
Jonathan Forward,	
Jonathan Sandford,	
Robert White,	
Samuel Clarke,	
Edward Powell.	

Red Regiment.

Colonel.

Sir Thomas Lane, Knt., Alderman.	Sir Thomas Kinsey, Knt., Alderman.

Lieut.-Col.

Francis Kenton.	James Hudson.

Major.

Richard Tilden.	John Genew.

Captains.

Richard Joyce,	Edward Chevall,
Benjamin Dry,	John Mould,
Anthony Cornewell,	Edward Shrawley,
Daniel Wray,	Nathaniel Lang,
John Lane.	Henry Minchard.

Annex (b^5).	Annex (b^5).

Lieutenants.

William Whitehead, (Capt.-Lieut.),	Nicasius Russell, (Capt.-Lieut.),
William Winepresse,	John Stockesbury,
John Staples,	Christopher Atkinson,
William Kempe,	Thos. Farrington,
John Feild,	Henry Drult,
Thomas Lane,	William Stevens.
John Burchill,	
Christopher Gold.	

Ensigns.

William Smith,	Edward Catchmead,
Jeremiah Mitchell,	Roger Weekes,
Anthony Stretton,	John Whitehurst,
Jeremiah Hurt,	James Carpenter,
—— Cocke,	Josuah Hill,
Thos. Shaw,	Hugh Mayo.
George Cresser,	
Nicholas Ogden.	

(b^3.) Paper containing (1) List of their Majesties' late Commission of Lieutenancy for the City of London, as their names stand in the Commission dated 19 March, 1 W. & M. [1688-9], and (2) Names of their Majesties' former Commissioners of Lieutenancy for the City of London, lately displaced or put out.—The first of these Lists, containing 96 names, is identical with the first paper above. The second contains the names marked with asterisks in the analysis above.

(b^4.) List of the New Commissioners added to the Lieutenancy by their Majesties' present Commission.—The names are those appearing in the analysis of the Commissions above as being in No. 3 only and in Nos. 1 and 3 only, with the omission here of James Hudson.

(b^5.) List of the names of the late Field-Officers, Captains, Lieutenants and Ensigns in the Militia of the City of London, as they were commissioned by their Majesties' late Commissioners of Lieutenancy for the said city in the first year of their Majesties' reign. [For contents see Annex (b^5.) above.]

(c.) List entitled "The names of their Majesty's new Commissioners of Lieutenancy for London. Dated xv. die Martii 1689. *Subscribed* xiii. die Maii 1690. Fer. Burleigh. Identical with list in Annex (b^1.), beginning "Sir Thomas Pilkington" and ending "Edmund Boulter."

(d.) 16 May.—List of jurymen empanelled and sworn on the indictment of Sir William Russell, Thomas Walcot, William Hone and John Rouse at Justice Hall, in the Old Bailey, in July, 1683. The names in italics are marked as sworn.

Sir Richard Alie,	*Benjamin Thorowgood,*
Peter Paravicini,	*William Longmore,*
Benjamin Skutt,	*John Price,*
Peter Harman,	*Francis Brerewood,*

William Withers, Senr.
William Lovell,
John Debnam,
Percival Gilborne,
Henry Wood,
John Cooper,
Samuel Newton,
Henry Wagstaffe,
Thomas Blackmore,
Thomas Larner,
John Potts,
Leonard Bates,
John Fencill,
Bartholomew Ferriman,
Spencer Johnson,
James Kolke.

Noted. ꝑ. Petr. Rich, Ar. et Dudley North, Mil. Vic. *Signed;* Examined 13 May 1690. Fer. Burleigh. [Delivered in this day by F. Burleigh. MS. Min.]

(*e*.) 16 May, 1690.—List of jurymen empanelled and sworn at the trial of The King *v.* Sir William Russell and others at Justice Hall on 12 July, 1683. The names in italics are marked here, and are those of the jury at Sir W. Russell's trial, as given in Annex (*f*.) below, and in *Howell's State Trials*, ix. 591.

Coleman St. Ward :—
Sir James Ward,
Sir Thos. Davall,
Arthur Baron, Esq.,
Thos. Moffitt,
John Martin,
Thos. Hodges,
§Will. Fitzacherly,
‡*Will. Rouse.*

Tower Ward :—
‡Peter Joy,
*†‡John Pelling,
Thos. Percy,
*†Will. Winberry,
Thos. Normansell,
Rich. Meynell,
Will. Pellatt,
**Jervas Seaton,*
Rich. Burden.

Aldgate Ward :—
James Lucy,
Peter Jones,
‡Will. Crouch.

Billingsgate Ward :—
‡Hen. Loades,
Hugh Strode,
Rob. Mellish,
Abr. Wright.

Broad St. Ward :—
Pet. Ayleworth,
Will. Danes,
John Steventon,
*Will. Rutland,
‡*Will. Fashions,*
*‡*Thos. Shorte,*
‡Sam. Skinner,
*†Theophilus Man,
Geo. Baker,
Rich. Kent, Esq.,
‡Gorlington Chapman [Jermingham Chaplin in Annex (*h*.)].

Dowgate Ward :—
Rich. Hamond,
‡Francis Chamberlain,
*‡John Genew,
John Ridges.

Bishopsgate Within Ward :—
John Ruston,
Joel Andrewes,
Rich. Izard.

Bridge Ward :—
*†‡John Short, Sen.,
*†Thos. Nicholls [Nicholas],
Roger Mingay.

Candlewick Ward :—
‡*Geo. Toriano,*
‡*Will. Butler,*
Will. Parker,
‡*Jas. Pickering.*

Lime St. Ward :—
John Hall,

---

* These names form the jury at the trial of Walcot and Hone, as given in Annex (*f*.) and *Howell's State Trials*, ix. 521.

† These names form the jury at the trial of Rouse, as given in Annex (*f*.) and *Howell's State Trials*, ix. 639.

‡ These names appear also on the jury panel at the trial of Cornish and Gaunt in 1685. *See* Annex (*h*.).

§ Appears also on jury panel at the trial of the King *v.* Barnardiston. *See* Annex (*k*.).

House of Lords MSS.

1690.

Matt. Gibbon,
Thos. Ainger,
Rob. Masters,
Luke Pead,
Christopher Johnson,
Phil. Perry,
Step. Gittings,
Will. Warren.

Walbrook Ward :—
John Westbrooke,
John Tempest,
John West,
Edward Le Neve.

Langbourne Ward :—
Will. Gerrard,
Anth. Mingay,
Nath. Hornby,
Hen. Collyer,
‡Jas. Smith,
Thos. Lowfeild,
Thos. Jenny,
Sam. Hanckee.

Cripplegate Ward :—
Rob. Aske, Esq.,
Thos. Jeve,
Hugh Noden,
Rob. Brough,
John Mallory,
Thos. Yate,
§Will. Crispe,
‡§John Walkley,
‡*Thos. Oneby.*

Farringdon Within Ward :—
Francis Griffith [*Noted:* now Lieut.-Col.],
Peter Pickering,
Edward Rigby,
†‡Rich. Hoare,
†Thos. Barnes,
†Hen. Robins,
†Hen. Kempe,
John Owen,
Will. Symonds,
Thos. Grice [? Price. *See* Annex (*i.*)].

Farringdon Without Ward :—
Paul Weekes, Esq.,
‡Roger Reeve,
†§Edward Reddish,
†Edward Kempe,
Will. Browne,
‡Ambrose Istead,
‡Thos. Fowles,
Thos. Hammond,
Thos. Fitzer,
§Thos. Dring,
§Hen. Baldwin,
Robert Fowles,
‡Thos. Rawlinson,
‡Will. Warne,
Val. Castillion,
‡Jervas Wilcox,
‡Jas. Smith.

Aldersgate Within Ward :—
§Peter Floyer.

Aldersgate Without Ward :—
‡Robert Scott,
John Andrewes,
Jer. Wright,
‡Jas. Sheldrake.

Cordwainer Ward :—
Thos. Coulson.

Vintry Ward :—
John Pecke,
John Hoyle.

Castle Baynard Ward :—
‡Sir Will. Dodson,
‡Sir Edw. Wiseman,
Will. Gosling,
Nich. Alexander,
*Nich. Charleton,
*Christ. Pitt,
*†‡Rob. Beddingfeild,
Thos. Warren.

p̄. Petr. Rich, Ar. et Dudley North, Mil. Vic. Ex[d]. xii[o]. die Maii, 1690. Fer. Burleigh. [Delivered in this day by F. Burleigh. MS. Min.]

---

* These names form the jury at the trial of Walcot and Hone, as given in Annex (*f.*) and *Howell's State Trials*, ix. 521.

† These names form the jury at the trial of Rouse, as given in Annex (*f.*) and *Howell's State Trials*, ix. 639.

‡ These names appear also on the jury panel at the trial of Cornish and Gaunt in 1685. *See* Annex (*h.*).

§ These names appear also on the jury panel at the trial of Bateman. *See* Annex (*i.*).

(*f*.) 16 May.—Paper containing names of the jurymen at the trials at Justice Hall in July 1683 of (1) The King *v.* Sir William Russell. *Noted:* Examined by Tanners' Book 13 May, 1690; Fer. Burleigh; (2) The King *v.* Thos. Walcot and William Hone. *Noted:* Examined 13 May, 1690. Fer. Burleigh; and (3) The King *v.* John Rouse. *Noted* as No. 2. [Delivered in this day by F. Burleigh. (MS. Min.) For names see Annex (*c.*) and notes.]

(*g*.) 16 May.—Names of the jurymen empanelled and sworn on the indictment of Henry Cornish and Charles Bateman at Justice Hall on 14 October, 1685. The names in italics are marked as sworn.

Percival Gilborne,	*Will. Withers, Jun.*
Barth. Ferriman,	*Thos. Deacon,*
Thos. Blackmore,	*Rich. Browne,*
Thos. Symonds,	*John Barnard,*
Will. Watton,	*Thos. Mills,*
Thos. Barnesly,	*Will. Fownes,*
John Greene,	*John Luker,*
Thos. Amy,	John Allen,
Joseph Baggs,	Hugh Strode,
John Reynolds,	Will. Clarke,
Rob. Blackmore,	Job Voere,
Joseph Caine,	Will. Currer.

þ. Thoma Kinsey, Mil. et Benjamin Thorowgood, Mil. Vic. Examined 13 May, 1690. Fer. Burleigh. [Delivered in by F. Burleigh this day. MS. Min.]

(*h*.) 16 May.—Names of jurymen empanelled and sworn* at the trial of The King *v.* Henry Cornish and Elizabeth Gaut [Gaunt], Prisoners at the Bar, at Justice Hall in October 1685. The list contains, besides the names noted in Annex (*e.*) above, the following:—

Sir William Russell,	John Midgley,
Sir Michael Hicks,	John Carpenter,
Sir John Mathews,	*Thos. Langham,*
Sir Thos. Griffith,	†*Ambrose Isted,*
Sir John Clarke,	Kenelm Smith,
Sir Thos. Vernon,	Ralph Lee,
Sir Edward Boveree,	Will. Moyer,
Sir Rich. Alie,	Thos. Lefeild,
Sir Ralph Box,	Jas. Woods,
Sir Thos. Hartopp,	*Thos. Pendleton,*
Arthur Baron, Esq.	Sam. Hinton,
Benjamin Scutt,	Nich. Smith,
†*Thos. Rawlinson,*	Thos. Peircehouse,
Thos. Goddard,	*John Grice,*
Will. Gore,	†*Thos. Oneby,*
John Kent,	Rich. Cotton,
Edward Griffith, Esq.	John Foster,
Will. Withers, Sen.	Thos. Sergeant,

* The names marked here as sworn, which are printed in italics, form the jury at the trial, as given in *Howell's State Trials*, xi. 413. Cornish is there stated to have challenged 35 of the panel.

† These names occur also in Annex (*e.*) above.

HOUSE OF LORDS MSS.

1690.

Jas. Richardson,
Will. Cloudsley,
Rich. Holford,
Thos. Crane,
Lewis Wilson,
Hen. Wood,
Will. Tigh,
George Pecke,
Francis Brerewood,
Will. Longmore,
John Price,
Walter Acton,
Stephen Coleman,
Rob. Clavell,
Will. Long,
John Wells,
Maurice Mosely,
John Pott,
Thos. Lardner,
Jas. Kelke,
John Perrott,
Thos. Ashby,
Noel Bassano,
Paul Sherman,
Will. Humfreys.

Return. p̃. Thom. Kinsey, Mil. et Benjamin Thorowgood, Mil. Vic. *Noted:* Examined xii. die Maii, 1690. Fer. Burleigh. [Delivered in by F. Burleigh this day. MS. Min.]

(*i.*) 16 May.—Names of jurymen empanelled and sworn at the trial of The King *v.* Charles Bateman, &c. at Justice Hall in the Old Bailey on 9 Dec. 1685. The names in italics, noted here as sworn, form the jury as given in *Howell's State Trials*, xi. 470.

Sir Thos. Griffith,
Rich. Ailay, Esq.,
Will. Lovell,
Rich. Williams,
John Canham,
Patrick Barrett,
John Palmer,
Dalby Thomas,
Bernard Salconstall,
Rob. Cade,
James Rayner,
**Edward Reddish,*
*Hen. Baldwin,
Sam. Newington,
Anth. Merry,
Geo. Lilborne,
Dan. Fowle,
**Peter Floyer,*
Laurence Cole,
John Cooper,
John Loveday,
Thos. Hammersly,
*John Walkely,
Jas. Carte,
Francis Smyth,
Gilbert East,
Ralph Hatly,
Rich. Mytton,
*Thos. Dringe,
Geo. Grove,
John Carpenter,
John Jackson,
Geo. Purefoy,
Thos. Bassett,
Rich. Furnis,
Thos. Ashby,
John Rogers,
John Bellinger,
Jas. Saunders,
Rob. Stevens,
*Will. Crispe,
Rob. Fowle,
Arthur Middleton,
John Ricketts,
Peter Andrews,
John Bland,
Thos. Cooper,
Geo. Bowers,
John Willey,
Thos. Price,
Martin Simpson,
Paul Kerry,
Edw. Decane,
Thos. Oliver,
Rich. Greenewood.
Nath. Camfeild,
Will. Mace,
Will. Bould,
Rich. Knewstubb,
Thos. Walton,
Job Harris,
John Perrott,
Benj. Dyes,
Nich. Beard,
John Fletcher,
Ben. Skynner,
Christ. Kemble,
Will. Wade,

* These names occur also in Annex (*e.*) above.

Geo. Copping,	John Dryden,
John Baker,	Jas. Evitts,
John Freeman,	Edw. Cooke,
Sam. Beavis,	Fenix Johnson,
Phil. Hunlocke,	Thos. Bryan,
Geo. Reeve,	Joshua Sabine,
Rich. Jackman,	Thos. Savage,
Will. Taylor,	Sam. Stringer,
Will. Pride,	Thos. Croxon,
Rich. Austin,	Thos. Dawson,
Rob. Roberts,	Will. Ayliffe,
Rich. Norman,	John Hilliard,
John Johnson,	John Marriott,
Rich. Fletcher,	Thos. Holmes,
Nath. Hewitt,	Joseph Hudson.
Jas. Hall,	

ß. Thoma Kinsey, Mil. et Benjamin Thorowgood, Mil. Vic. Examined 13 May, 1690. Fer. Burleigh.

(*k.*) Names of jurymen empanelled and sworn at the trial of The King *v.* Samuel Barnardiston, late of London, Bart. The names in italics, noted here as sworn, form the jury as given in *Howell's State Trials*, ix. 1334.

Thos. Vernon,	Rich. Alie,
Percival Gilborne,	Will. Fitzacherly,
Edward Boveree,	Rob. Raworth,
Will. Withers, Sen.,	Barth. Ferryman,
Jas. Woods,	Will. Jarratt,
Rob. Master,	John Debnam,
Sam. Newton,	Francis Brerewood,
Geo. Toriano,	Spencer Johnson,
Kenelm Smith,	Will. Bridges,
Thos. Goddard,	Will. Gore,
Thos. Amy,	Will. Harman,
Rich. Blackborne,	Jas. Smith.

Respons. Sam. Dashwood, Ar., Peter Daniell, Ar. Exam. per Record. 13 May, 1690.

(*l.*) Names of juryman empanelled and sworn at the Trial of The King *v.* Samuel Johnson. The names marked as sworn are in italics. The jury is not given in *Howell's State Trials.*

Thos. Honylove,	Matt. Walker,
Jas. Woods,	Jos. Smart,
Jas. Smyth,	Humphrey Stokes,
Rich. Goodlad,	Thos. Metcalfe,
Thos. Lefeild,	John Lee,
Thos. Death,	Peter Wade,
Claude Hayes,	Anthony Mingay,
Bernard Mynn,	*John Storey,*
Will. Baxter,	*John Reynolds,*
Edw. Alder,	*John Harman,*
Thos. Jenney,	*John Price,*
Sam. Hankee,	Will. Withers,
Nath. Dodson,	*Francis Brerewood,*
Thos. Mason,	*Hen. Wood,*
Kenelm Smith,	*Hen. Gold.*
Will. Jerratt,	

Respons. Petrus Daniell, Ar., Sam. Dashwood, Ar. Exam. per Record. 13 May, 1690. Fer. Burleigh.

House of Lords MSS.

1690.

(*m.*) 16 May.—Names of jurymen empanelled and sworn at the trial for riot of Thomas Pilkington, Samuel Shute, Henry Cornish, Lord Grey de Werke, Sir Thomas Gould, Sir Thomas Player, Slingsby Betholl, Francis Jinkes, John Deagle, Richard Freeman, Richard Goodenough, Robert Kaye, John Wickham, Samuel Swynocke, Joshua Brooks, William Miller, John Jekyll, Senior, Thomas Charleton, Dorman Newan, John Jekyll, Junior, Benjamin Allsopp, Mathew Meriton, John Trenchard and Jervas Byfeild. The names in italics are marked as sworn and are given in *Howell's State Trials*, ix. 235.

Sir Ben. Newland,	Thos. Symonds,
Sir John Mathewes,	*Sam. Newton,*
Sir John Buckworth,	Spenser Johnson,
Sir William Russell,	*Will. Whatton,*
Sir Thos. Griffith,	John Fencill,
Sir Edward Wiseman,	Thos. Barnesly,
Sir James Ward,	*Geo. Billers,*
Sir Thos. Davall,	Thos. Amy,
Percival Gilborne,	Nath. Budd,
Henry Wagstaffe,	Will. Skinner, Jun.,
Barth. Ferriman,	Will. Withers, Jun.,
Thos. Blackmore,	Thos. Deacon,

Respons. Dudley North, Mil. et Peter Rich, Mil. Vic. Exam. per Record. 13 May, 1690. Fer. Burleigh.

(*n.*) List of names entitled "Die Jovis 28° die Septembris 1682. By the Lieutenancy. Forenoon, at the Lord Mayor's and at Guildhall. Present." The list is as follows:—

The Right Hon. the Lord Mayor,	John Stevenson,
Sir George Waterman,	Thomas Cowden,
Sir James Edwards,	Edward Beaker,
Sir William Pritchard,	John Wallis,
Sir Henry Tulse,	John Nicholls,
Sir James Smith,	William Parker,
Sir John Peake,	Henry Loades,
Sir John Chapman,	Peter Ayleworth,
Sir Symon Lewis,	John Shorte,
Sir John Mathewes,	Richard Alie,
Sir Benjamin Newland,	Benjamin Scutt,
Sir William Dodson, and	Hugh Strode, and
Sir John Buckworth, Kn^{ts}.	William Carpenter, Esq^{rs}.

Marked. Examined 14 May 1690 out of the Lieutenancy Book. Fer. Burleigh. [*See* Luttrell, 28 Sept. 1682.]

(*o.*) 16 May.—Paper stating as follows:—"About Christmas after the then Prince of Orange landed, Mr. Benjamin Page did say that the Prince was a very ill man for invading his father's right, and that it would not be long before he would be served as Monmouth was. This was spoken off the sign of the St. John Baptist's Head in Whitecross Street near Cripplegate; present Mr. Fearne, Mr. Camnon, Mr. Gilles, and General Osberne." *Signed* Obadiah Cowcutt. *Endorsed* as delivered in by him this day. [A witness, Mr. Watson, having stated to the Committee that Cowcutt could inform of words spoken of the King, *Cowcutt* was called in, and, being sworn, made a statement, as above, which he was ordered to put in writing. MS. Min., 16 May.]

(p.) 18 May.—Three papers, *endorsed* "Orders out of the Lieutenancy Books. Copied 18 May 1690," vizt. :—

(1.) Jovis, 28 Septembris 1682, past 12 o'clock. At the Right Honourable the Lord Mayor's house.

Present.

The Right Honourable the Lord Mayor.

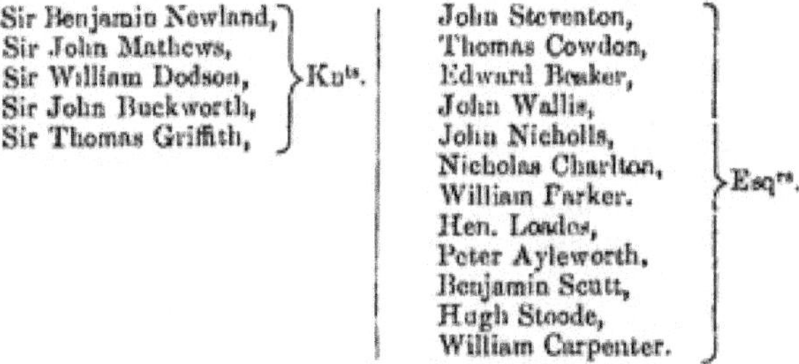

Sir Benjamin Newland,	Knts.	John Steventon,	Esqrs.
Sir John Mathews,		Thomas Cowdon,	
Sir William Dodson,		Edward Beaker,	
Sir John Buckworth,		John Wallis,	
Sir Thomas Griffith,		John Nicholls,	
		Nicholas Charlton,	
		William Parker.	
		Hen. Loades,	
		Peter Ayleworth,	
		Benjamin Scutt,	
		Hugh Stoode,	
		William Carpenter.	

Ordered, That Lieutenant-Col. Quiney shall not only stay on his guard till 8 at night, as ordered by the Commissioners in the morning, but shall with his company keep off all persons from going upon the hustings (as in the morning order is required) on any pretence whatsoever (unless he receives the order in writing of the Lord Mayor for so doing) for the preventing of any such disorders as were committed by the number of persons who kept so great a noise in the forenoon And *Ordered*, That the Lieut.-Col. shall send for one company from the Exchange to guard in the Guildhall-yard till 8 at night and to obey the orders of the Lieut.-Col., and at 8 the three companies to draw off and be dismissed, and that the Captain that comes from the Exchange shall have a short order sent to him to be commanded by Lieut.-Col. Quiney with the like order in case of any tumults as formerly.

To Lieut.-Col. Quiney
these

(2.) 8 Octobris 1683.

Present.

Sir John Peake,	Lieut.-Col. Cowdon,
Sir Henry Tulse,	Mr. Stroude,
Sir Robert Adams,	Mr. Lucy,
Lieut.-Col. Steventon,	Mr. Wythers.
Lieut.-Col. Beeker,	Mr. Parker,
Lieut.-Col. Quiney,	Mr. Langham.

This Report was now presented and read as follows :—

To the Right Honble. the Lord Mayor and the rest of his Majesty's Commissioners of Lieutenancy for the City of London.

We, whose names are subscribed, being lately appointed a Committee to draw an Order for the Commanders to observe on the guards, and we have drawn it as followeth :

That the Commanders shall, without fail, at the time of their going on till the time of their going off the guards, not only keep strictly all their soldiers on the guards but also keep there themselves and not go anywhere to refresh themselves upon pain of being punished for the same as a neglect of duty in the Commander and a great default in the soldier. And for the better performance thereof, every Commander shall call over his Roll at 9 of the clock at night and 5 of the clock in the morning, or at any other hours may be most convenient, and take an exact account of all such as are absent and make return thereof to the next Lieutenancy. And in case any Commander shall be remiss herein, the Commissioners will take care to supply those defects by commissionating such as will carefully observe their orders, that the King and the City may be served with that safety as the law intends. And that neither the Lieutenant, Ensign, Serjeant, Corporal or Sentinel shall presume or offer to suffer any soldiers nor to go off themselves of the guards without the leave of the Captain, upon pain of being punished according to law. And that no Captain shall presume to go out of town or be off the guard unless by leave from the Commissioners or real sickness; And that no inferior officer shall be absent without leave from the Captain, and that this order be read at all times publicly, that all the Company may plainly understand the same. And that after candle-lighting each Commander shall without fail cause six links at least to march with the Company and march with their files six deep. All which we submit to the Commissioners. Dated the 8th October, 1683.

Edward Booker, William Dodson,
Thomas Langham, William Withers,
Adrian Quiney.

Which report was well approved of and ordered to be forthwith printed and sent to each Commander.

(3.) 21 Junii 1685. By his Majesty's Commissioners of the Lieutenancy for the City of London.—By virtue of a warrant under his Majesty's Seal Manual, dated the 20th inst., whereby his Majesty doth command the Lieutenancy of London to apprehend all disaffected and suspicious persons within the City, particularly Nonconformist Ministers and such as had served against his Royal father or late Royal brother of blessed memory, and for detaining them in safe custody till further order, and the horses of such to be secured, his Majesty's said Commissioners do hereby order you to whom this is directed immediately this night, with such officers as you shall judge necessary, civil or military, to enter the houses of the persons undernamed and them to apprehend and secure in safe custody, to be kept till further order; And thereof fail not and make return thereof to the Lord Mayor to-morrow, and what horses you secure and who stand engaged for being delivered when called for. [Delivered in to the Committee this day by Ferd. Burleigh. MS. Min.]

(*q*.) 22 May.—Paper endorsed "Address of the Lieutenancy of London," as follows:—4 Octobris 1688. By his Majesty's Commissioners of Lieutenancy for the City of London. Agreed, That Mr. Justice Jenner, Sir Henry Tulse, Sir Bartholomew Showers, Sir Robert Jeffreys, Sir James Smyth, Sir Peter Daniell, Sir Benjamin Bathurst, Sir Dudley North, Sir John Parsons, the two Sheriffs, Esqre Colson, Sir Thomas Griffith, Sir William Dodson, Esqre Lucey, Lieut.-Col. Steventon, Lieut.-

Col. Becker, Esqre Graham, Esqre Crispe, Esqre Mundey, and Esqre Langham (and any other of the Commissioners that will go), do attend his Majesty with the following Address, vizt. :—

To the King's Most Excellent Majesty.

The humble Address of your Majesty's Commissioners of Lieutenancy for the City of London.

We cannot but with enlarged hearts return your Majesty our most sincere and humble acknowledgment of your peculiar care and acts of bounty and mercy towards this your ancient and famous City of London, who amidst the many and more important affairs that might at this juncture employ and take up your Royal thoughts, have not yet left us without a security, but by this your Majesty's Commission has put our preservation into our own hands, by suffering us to constitute of our own body such officers as we hope and doubt not will prove most zealous for the safety and honour of your Majesty and the defence of our selves and families. We must confess our lives and fortunes are but a mean sacrifice to such transcendent goodness, but we do assure your Majesty of our cheerful offering of both against all your Majesty's enemies who shall disturb your peace upon any pretence whatsoever. *Examined* by J. Borrett. *Endorsed* as brought in this day. [On 17 May Mr. Borrett, the Clerk of the Lieutenancy, was ordered to give a list of those who made the Address. MS. Min. *See also* Luttrell, 4 Oct. 1688.]

(*r*.) 22 May.—Paper entitled "Sir John Eyles, Lord Mayor pro tempore. Commission of Lieutenancy dated October 1, 1688." *Noted:* "Seven makes a Court, whereof one of those marked with Q."* On the second page is written as follows:—

July 17, 1685. Present.

The Lord Mayor,	Adrian Quiney,
Sir James Smith,	Edward Becker,
Sir James Edwards,	John Wallis,
Sir John Moore,	Thomas Cowden,
Sir William Prichard,	Henry Loades,
Sir Simon Lewis,	George Toriano,
Sir John Mathews,	John Jeffreys,
Sir William Russell,	John Short,
Sir William Dodson,	Hugh Strode,
Sir Robert Adams,	William Wynbury,
Sir Edmund Wiseman,	William Carpenter and
John Steventon,	William Warren, Esq^rs.

Sir,—These were present when those disaffected persons (as they pretended) were discharged. You desired a list of those that were present when they were committed. Their names are not in this Book, but they are in one of those books that the House of Lords has at present.—*Endorsed:* Delivered by Mr. Essington 22 May 1690.

* The names in this Commission are embodied in the analysis given in the note to principal paper above. The 25 names there in italics were stated by Essington to have been those in the new Commission who imprisoned witness and others. (MS. Min., 22 May.)

House of Lords MSS.

1690.

268. May 9.* L. Howard of Escrick's Privilege (T. Peacock).—Petition of Thomas Woodhouse, now in custody of a messenger by order of the House, on behalf of himself and one Wanton Dunning. Petitioner and Dunning, being two bailiffs of the Sheriff of the county of York, arrested in April last Thomas Peacock, of Nunington, at the suit of one Mr. Bullock, for a debt of thirty pounds, and have been committed on the complaint of Lord Howard of Escrick, who informed the House that Peacock was his menial servant. Petitioner is heartily sorry for the offence, and being a very poor man, with a wife and a great charge of children, prays that he and Dunning may be discharged. L. J., XIV., 490.

269. May 10. London (*Quo Warranto*) Act.—Petition of the Lord Mayor, Aldermen and Commons of the City of London in Common Council assembled. Pray to be heard by Counsel on the Bill for reversing the Judgment in a *Quo Warranto* against the City of London. L. J., XIV., 491. [On 13 May Counsel were called in in the case of the City of London against the Bill. *Mr. Trevor* (for the City upon their Petition): It appears by the Bill that it is for the good of the City. We would have the word ("reversed") left out of the Bill. Now if it be reversed it was a good judgment.—The Lords took notice that it was to be in a Committee of the whole House. Counsel withdrew. House *moved* to hear Counsel at the Bar in a Committee, pursuant to the Order. House in Committee. E. Nottingham in the Chair. Counsel called in again. *Mr. Trevor* (for the City): I offer that the word ("reversed") be struck out of the Bill, for reversing acknowledges it to be good until reversed. This is of that consequence, that I cannot undertake of those things, for want of time. We pray that we may have some time to consider of that point, and desire that that word be struck out of the Bill and the Judgment declared void. *Mr. Ward* (for the City). Desires time. The, Judgment is that the liberties of the City should be seized into the King's hands as forfeited. It reverses, annulls and makes void an illegal judgment. Now this is a Corporation by prescription. We hope to find by looking into our books that this is the first judgment of the kind. In most humble duty we pray some short and convenient time for this. Counsel withdrew. Reported that they desire further time. After debate, House *moved* to give time until Thursday. *Question*, whether any longer time shall be allowed to the City of London to be heard by their Counsel to this Bill? Resolved in the Affirmative. Contents 43; Not-Contents 36. Tellers, E. Feversham and E. Warrington. *Moved*, that House be moved to be put into a Committee again to hear this business on Thursday. House resumed. *E. Nottingham* reported that the Committee had sat according to order, and that they have thought fit to allow further time for the City of London to be heard by their Counsel to this Bill. After debate, *Question*, whether to agree with the Committee?—Resolved in the Negative. Contents 42; Proxies 2 = 44. Not-contents 40; Proxies 7 = 47. Tellers, E. Feversham and E. Warrington. Leave to protest. House in Committee. E. Nottingham in the Chair. Counsel called in and told the Lords expect that what you have to say you now offer. [*Mr. Trevor*]: I shall give some reasons for the word ("reversed") to be left out, and that it may be declared to be void for those reasons. 1. The preamble says it is an illegal judgment. If illegal it stood good till reversed. 2. That the Bill directs new choices. They have chosen officers pursuant to their ancient constitutions. It will reflect upon them. Why should not they

* The MS. Min. of this day have the following entry: "House moved that the footmen may not lie on the table. The Gentleman Usher ordered to forewarn them."

continue in for the year? 3. It is desired that the privilege of bringing money for orphans may be lost. We desire reasons may be inserted in the preamble of the Bill why the judgment was illegal. All offices in the City are bought and sold. We desire that may not be and a clause inserted to prevent the sale of offices. *Mr. Ward:* [We desire] that it may be declared to be a void judgment. This Judgment is given by an information in a *Quo Warranto*. The City plead they are a Corporation by prescription. They admitted them, by bringing an information, to be a Corporation, and yet judgment was given that they were no Corporation, because they took excessive toll and petitioned for a Parliament. If they misdemeaned themselves, yet they may be punished; but how they should be no Corporation (*sic*). If this be admitted, it follows as a consequence that a Corporation that sends men to Parliament may be ousted by the judgment in the *Quo Warranto*. This will be the case of all Corporations, where they are Corporations by prescription. 1. Choosing officers 26 May; that they may continue to the usual times. All the officers have been chosen according to the ancient constitution of the City. 2. They desire to abridge themselves of orphans' money. 3. Offices are one of the greatest inconveniences that may be to be sold. That they may come in by proper election. Counsel withdrew. House resumed [to receive a Message]. House adjourned during pleasure. E. Nottingham reported what was urged by Counsel on both sides. The Bill was read through. *Proposed*, that the House may be adjourned for a time to consider and to hear the Judges' opinion on the word ("reverse"). *Ordered* to report that the Committee have made some progress, and that the House be moved to appoint to-morrow morning the first business, and that some Judges attend and all the Lords be summoned. House resumed and so reported, to which the House agreed and ordered it accordingly. *Moved*, That several persons may be summoned; their names read. *Ordered* that the said persons be summoned.* (MS. Min., 13 May. L. J., XIV., 495-6.)

On 14 May, the House being put into Committee, E. Nottingham in the Chair, the title of the Bill was read and postponed. Preamble read and postponed. First enacting Clause read. House *moved* that the Judges give their opinions on the word ("reverse"). *E. Nottingham* gave the Judges an account of what the Counsel said on that point. *Holt, C. J.:* The reversal of a judgment is upon a Writ of Error, as a judgment against law. A judgment may be good until reversed, if given by a legal Court. If a judgment be given in a Court where there is no power of cognizance, then it is void. It is used till set aside, if given by a legal Court. *Pollexfen, C. J.:* A Writ doth lie to reverse this. But in this [case] we cannot deny that the Court had a jurisdiction. It is but voidable, and stands good until reversed. The word implies the judgment was in force until reversed. *L. Chief Baron [Atkyns]:* This Bill has with it a judicial part. This Bill is in the nature of a Writ of Error. Your Lordships will consider that there is Error in the judgment. Question, what the effect of these words is. If you declare it was void, then it was so from the beginning; but, as my Lord C. Justice Pollexfen says, the acts are good until this Bill is passed. The Counsel observed this

* There is here an expunged entry that the "House was moved That the business appointed for tomorrow may be adjourned to another day; That the persons summoned may have notice not to attend tomorrow"; and an expunged Order to adjourn to Friday (the 16th).

House of Lords MSS.

1690.

judgment was grounded upon a *Quo Warranto;* and the grounds of it. There is an absurdity or contradiction in the Record, and therefore [it is] void from the beginning. The Record is not before you in the Bill. I think the Counsel were in the right, that if there be a contradiction in the Record, it is void. *Eyre, J.:* I differ from the L. Chief Baron. This coming by Bill, you can consider only in the legislative and judicial (*sic*). The word ("reverse") is an equivocal term. If voidable, yet if reversed, it is void from the beginning. The Court that gave the judgment had jurisdiction. It is a judgment till reversed. If you declare it null and void, then it was void from the beginning. *Proposed* to ask the Judges whether a Corporation by prescription and sending burgesses to Parliament can forfeit their Charter of Corporation? The enacting Clause read in the Act for declaring the Ship-money void. After debate, *Question* asked, whether the franchise that a Corporation enjoys by prescription may be forfeited? *Holt, C. J.:* I conceive it may. Then this question was put to the Judges, whether a Corporation by prescription may forfeit its being? *Holt, C. J.:* I take it what is surrenderable is forfeitable. If they may surrender they may forfeit. *Pollexfen, C. J.:* In all times I considered of this thing, I thought it was never possible or legal for a Corporation to forfeit its being. I leave it to those reasons and authorities that are now in print. *L. C. Baron* [*Atkyns*]: They cannot forfeit their being. I am fully of opinion it cannot be forfeited. *Eyre, J.:* I have given my opinion on this. If surrenderable, it may be forfeited. As it may be surrendered, so it may be forfeited. *Ventris, J.:* I was of opinion there could be no surrender, that it could dissolve its capacity, and I am now of opinion that as they cannot surrender, so they cannot forfeit. I can find no precedent of a proceeding against the being of a Corporation. There never was one precedent found in this case. *Moved* to send for the rest of the Judges. *Proposed, that the Judges be summoned to attend presently, and that in the meantime the House will go on with the other parts of the Bill and with the clause postponed if the Judges come not by five o'clock.** After debate, the question was proposed, whether the Judges that are now absent shall be sent for? *Question*, whether the word ("now") shall be added to that question. Resolved in the Negative. *Main Question* put, whether the Judges that are now absent shall be sent for? Resolved in the Negative. *Question*, whether the House shall be now resumed? Resolved in the Negative. Contents 29, Not-Contents 41. Then the first enacting Clause was read again. After debate, *Question*, whether to pass this clause without any amendment? Resolved in the Affirmative. The next enacting Clause read, in re, facto et nomine agreed. The next Clause read and agreed to. Proviso read concerning Sheriff's Courts and agreed to. Next Clause agreed to. Next agreed to. Proviso agreed to. Next Clause agreed to. Clause concerning trustees for tolls, &c. read and agreed to. Proviso read for continuance of officers and the time for choosing again. House moved to resume the House and to sit again to-morrow the first business. The Clause read again for the time of elections. *Question*, whether to agree to this Clause? Resolved in the Affirmative. Next Proviso read and agreed to. Next enacting Clause read and agreed to. Swearing sheriffs, read and agreed to. The next Clause agreed to. Proviso for leases and all the rest to the end of the Bill. The title

* These words in italics are struck through.

postponed read again and agreed to. The postponed preamble read and agreed to. *Ordered* to report the Bill without any amendments. House resumed, and E. Nottingham reported it so. *Question*, whether the House shall be now adjourned? Resolved in the Negative. The Bill was then read 3ª and passed and a Message sent to inform the House of Commons. Royal Assent 20 May. L. J., XIV., 504. 1 W. & M. Sess. 2. c. 8.]

270. May 12. Patents (Vacating) (Needwood Forest) Bill.—Lords' Engrossment of the Bill of 28 March (No. **240**) including the amendments made in Lords' Committee. *Parchment Collection.* [It was ordered this day to be sent down to the Commons and bears the words "Soit baillée aux Comons;" but another Engrossment must have been sent down. L. J., XIV., 492.]

271. May 14. Hudson's Bay Company Act.—Petition of the Merchants of London, trading to New York and New England. Sets forth that New York and New England are English Colonies and take off vast quantities of the manufactures of this kingdom (as by the Custom House books will appear), the chief returns for which are beaver and other furs. The trade of these colonies employs a great quantity of shipping and, next to the Newcastle trade (now the French have in effect beat us out of our Newfoundland fishery), is the greatest nursery for seamen this kingdom has left. Nova Scotia or Acadia, now part of Canada, adjoining to the territories of Hudson's Bay, was formerly an English Colony, until by a treaty between England and France it was delivered into the hands of the French at terms agreed on, which terms were never complied with. Petitioners are well assured of the settlement and strength of these colonies, and that there is at this time nothing wanting to make his Majesty master of all the French interest in those parts, and thereby of the sole trade of beaver and all furs, but his Commission for government and commands to that end. But Petitioners are very much surprised at a Bill passed by the Commons and sent up to their Lordships to establish a boundless charter with sovereign power granted by Charles II. to the Hudson's Bay Company (a small number of men with an inconsiderable stock and no ways serviceable to the nation), upon a mistaken suggestion that they would discover a new passage into the South Seas, when in truth there is no such passage yet discovered, but under this cover a useless monopoly set up, which, if established by Act of Parliament, will not only deprive the colonies of the whole trade of furs and so destroy the trade of this nation, but also settle the French interest in those parts to that degree that it will not be in the power of the English nation ever to remove them. Pray to be heard against the Bill. *Signed* H. Slaughter, Humphry Edwin, Joseph Dudley, Jonathan Davis, James Fyton, John Jackson, Gerard Van Heythuysen, Francis Tierens, Thomas Crome, Jer. Johnson, R. Hackshaw, Samuel Ball, Gilbert Bant, Valentine Crüger, Thos. Lane, Thos. Phipps, and William Artelby. L. J., XIV., 497. [In Committee, on 15 May, *Mr. Phipps* offered exceptions in writing to the Hudson's Bay Charter, which were read and delivered in. *Mr. Serjeant Thompson* (for the Bill): The trade is of great advantage to England and it cannot be managed but by a Company, for if the trade be laid open, it will certainly be lost, for private persons will not trade in difficult times. It stands the Company in considerable sums of money to maintain our fortresses, by which we carry on our trade. *Mr. Squib* (for the Bill): It has cost the Company £15,000 to retake the

Colony from the French. They have been at £200,000. charge. There are 105 shares in the Company. Any of the Company that has £100 in stock has a vote. They can take any man into the Company that they please.—Reasons, from some other persons, in writing against the Bill are offered and read. They pray that a clause may be added relating to beaver. They withdraw. The Bill is read by paragraphs. Sk. 5, line 2 for ("fourteen") read ("seven") (Com. Book, 15 May). The Bill was then reported with this amendment. L. J., XIV., 498. Royal Assent 20 May. *ib.* 504. 2 W. & M. Sess. 1. c. 15.]

272. May 15. Paper Act.—Petition of the Mayor, Aldermen and other inhabitants of Chipping Wycombe, in the county of Bucks. In the parish of Chipping Wycombe there are eight paper mills, employing fifty families in making white paper. Most of the paper makers have been bred apprentices to the trade, and can and do make good white printing paper. If they should be prohibited from making any such white paper above four shillings a ream, as by a restraining clause in the Bill now before their Lordships is proposed, they and their families or the greatest part of them, will in a short time inevitably become chargeable to the said parish, where they are legally settled inhabitants, having been brought up to no other trade. Petitioners are exceedingly burdened with poor, and if the said paper makers likewise become chargeable, Petitioners and the rest of the inhabitants will not be able to pay taxes and provide for them, but will be intolerably oppressed and utterly impoverished. Pray their Lordships to prevent the passing of the Bill with the said clause of restraint. L. J., XIV., 499. [The House going into Committee on the Bill on 17 May, E. Rochester in the Chair, the Bill was read through. Counsel called in. *Serjeant Thompson* (for several Paper makers): It cannot be denied but we made very good paper before their pretence, and they got their patent on that account. There are many mills, the inheritance of several persons. Now the French paper is prohibited, there is much expectation of advantage in this trade. This will slacken our industry. They desire only to make as good as they can. They have engrossed the rags about the town. It is but a notion to say 4*s*. I offer to the Dean of Windsor. At the House of Commons there is seeming kindness, and we hoped those mills should be accepted. They have got a proviso that they will take our mills of us. *Sir William Williams* (for the Dean etc. of Windsor): If it be a design to set up the lucre of private persons, That they in France make it cheaper. The trade upon the general prohibition will devolve a great trade upon the mills. Why should not every mill make as good paper as they can and sell it at the highest price that may be? That which concerns the Dean of Windsor is the case of every particular mill. We will not, says the Chapter, wrong our tenants to set up others, and if this project takes, our mills must be let to whom they please; the patents, (*sic*) they renew their leases. These tenants must lose their fines, and all must truckle to this Company. *Mr. Trevor* (for Petitioners): If these mills cannot work as usual, the several families in the town must starve. They can now make no paper at all. They will engross all the materials of white paper. The Corporation, they say, will employ you; but they are settled here, and cannot follow to other places. *Mr. Ward* (for the Bill and Patentees): I desire to premise to your Lordships there is no check at all upon others. No paper above 4*s*. has been made but by this Company. They cannot of themselves make any higher writing and printing papers This has been an invention brought into England by this Company.

They have attempted to destroy the Company and to destroy this manufacture. We hope to make it appear that this is as useful and necessary as may be. As it is useful and necessary, so we hope your Lordships will establish us. We do no wrong to the Church of Windsor. We will give the rents. None of the dependencies of Wycombe are taken off. *Mr. Darnell* (for the Bill): Whoever opposes this Bill, the French trade is at the bottom. We will give unquestionable security for their rent. They can make no writing paper. They may come into the Company. This has been the interest of France, we can show. We pray that this new invention may receive encouragement, as we think every new invention ought to do. *Serjeant Thompson:* We desire only to have leave to make as good as we can. We desire but the same equal liberty with them. We can never have any further industry in this case. *Sir William Williams* (in reply): We made as fine as these men can make before the French paper came into England. That Proviso is not for the Chapter. We complain of this Proviso. The Patent asked for is not confirmed in every part. Counsel withdraw. House resumed* . . . . . . House adjourned during pleasure upon the Paper Bill. E. Rochester reported what was said by the Counsel against and for the Bill. House resumed† . . . . . . House adjourned during pleasure on the Paper Bill. E. Rochester in the Chair. The Patent produced. Title and preamble read and postponed. First enacting Clause read. Part of the Patent read. House resumed. E. Rochester reported that the Committee desire a Select Committee may be appointed to consider the Patent and the Bill and report. (MS. Min., 17 May. L. J., XIV., 501.)—The proceedings of this Select Committee on 19 May are thus recorded. E. Rochester in the Chair. The Charter is read. The Bill is read by paragraphs. The title agreed. The preamble agreed. The first Clause in 4 sk. postponed. The last Clause in 4 sk. postponed. The first part of the next Clause, that relates to the time of closing the books, postponed. In sk. 6 the first Clause that there may be liberty of transferring interest by letter of attorney, if it be found necessary; this to be considered again, if there be any other amendment in the Bill. *Question:* Whether to agree to the price as in the clause in sk. 7. Contents 12; Not-Contents 10. Resolved in the Affirmative. A Proviso relating to the Dean and Chapter of Windsor's Mills is read and rejected. A Proviso on behalf of the ancient Paper-makers is offered. *Question:* Whether the Clause in the Bill relating to the Church of Windsor shall stand in the Bill? Contents 23; Not-Contents 10. Resolved in the Affirmative. *Question:* Whether the Company shall be obliged to take off all Mills as by the last Clause relating to Windsor? Contents 2; Not-Contents 18 (*sic*).‡ Resolved in the Affirmative. The postponed clauses are read and agreed to. Ordered to be reported without amendment. (Com. Book, 19 May. L. J., XIV., 502.) Royal Assent 20 May. 2 W. & M. Sess. 1. c. 16.]

Annexed:—

(*a*.) 15 May. Petition of the ancient Paper-makers of this Kingdom against the Bill. Sets forth that one Brisco, Bladen and others obtained Letters Patent from James II. to be a Corporation and have the sole making of white writing and

* Here follow the proceedings in "Dod *v.* Burrowes." L. J., XIV., 501.

† Here follows the Message from H. C., agreeing to the Hudson's Bay Company Bill. L. J., XIV., 501.

‡ Evidently a mistake for "Contents 18; Not-Contents 2."

printing paper, they being not the inventors of the said art. Those Letters Patent, being the grant of a plain monopoly, were void in the law, as all grants of that kind are, being contrary to the common law and statute laws of this realm, and against the benefit and liberty of the subject. The Bill is to confirm and establish those Letters Patent and to disable Petitioners from making any paper above 4s. the ream, which will ruin above a thousand families of Paper-makers, who have served their apprenticeships and are more skilled in the art than the Patentees, and have time out of mind made paper from 3s. to 20s. the ream. Several of Petitioners have taken long leases of paper-mills at great rents, some at £70, others at £80 per annum, and contracted for the making of great quantities of paper, which mills will become useless, if the Bill passes. The granting to particular persons the sole power of making paper will enable them to advance the price of paper as high as they please, which will be grievous to the subject; whereas the manufacture of paper being free and without restraint to Petitioners, there will consequently follow a far greater supply of all sorts of white writing and printing paper for the necessary use of this Kingdom, and will prevent the ingrossing the same by the Patentees, who hitherto have employed but five mills, or not the twentieth part of those employed by Petitioners. Petitioners conceive that an Act of this kind is without precedent, and by its example may prove mischievous to all trades. Pray to be heard against the Bill. *Signed* Edward Spycer, Jer. Francis, Edward Queich, William Harris (their marks), and George Gill, Robert Slade, William Blackwell, John Slocombe, John West, Richard West, Thomas Morris, William Russell, Alexander Russell and James West. L. J., XIV., 499.

(*b*.) 15 May. Petition of the Dean and Canons of Windsor. The Bill, notwithstanding the Proviso touching Petitioners, inserted by the Commons, will damnify the Church of Windsor in its inheritance to the value of near £100 per annum. Pray to be heard by Counsel. *Signed* Greg. Hassard, Dean. L. J., XIV., 499.

273. May 16. Writ of Summons, dated 15 May, to John [Hough] Bp. Oxford, who took the Oaths this day. L. J., XIV., 500.

274. May 16. Test Act (Enforcement of 500*l*. Forfeitures) Bill.—Commons' Engrossment * of an Act for vesting certain Forfeitures of Five hundred pounds in their Majesties, and for the speedy levying thereof. § i. Whereas a good and necessary Law for preserving the Religion and Government established in this kingdom was made in the five and twentieth year of the reign of King Charles the Second entituled An Act for preventing dangers which may happen from Popish Recusants, whereby, among other things, it was enacted that all and every person and persons that should be admitted, entered, placed, or taken into any office civil or military, or should have command or place of trust from or under the said King his heirs or successors, or by his or their authority or by authority derived from him or them within this realm of England, dominion of Wales or Town

* The amendments made in C. W. H. by the Lords, are inserted in the text from Annex (*a*.) below, being identified by the marginal numbers on the Engrossment.

of Berwick-upon-Tweed, or in the King's Navy (other than such as are therein excepted), who should neglect or refuse to take the Oaths of Supremacy and Allegiance therein mentioned, or the Sacrament of the Lords' Supper, or to make and subscribe a certain Declaration therein set down, at the times and in the places and manner thereby appointed and required, and yet after such neglect should execute any such Office or Employment, being thereupon convicted in manner as in the same Act is appointed, should (besides other great and grievous penalties) forfeit the sum of five hundred pounds, to be recovered by him or them that should sue for the same; And whereas, in the reign of the late King James the Second divers evil disposed persons, Papists and others, in notorious violation and contempt of the said law, having refused or neglected to take the said Oaths and Sacrament and to make the said Declaration, did nevertheless, after the times expired in which they ought to have done the same, presume to execute divers of the said Offices and Employments, by colour of dispensations and other undue pretences, by means of which, and other like courses, the religion, laws and liberties of this kingdom were in imminent danger of being subverted, and great troubles and charges brought upon this kingdom; and for that it is just and also merciful (the rest being discharged), that part of the forfeitures of the offenders of greater degree, who have been the cause or instruments of the public calamities, should be taken, and the same applied toward the support of the great charges of the kingdom, and for the easing of their Majesties' good subjects; Be it therefore enacted by the King and Queen's most Excellent Majesties, by and with the advice and consent of the Lords Spiritual and Temporal and Commons in this present Parliament assembled, and by the authority of the same, That every person who, at any time during the reign of the said late King James, was or took upon him to act as a Privy Councillor or officer of their said Majesties' Household, Judge, Lieutenant of a County, Deputy Lieutenant, officer in the Militia, Army, or Navy, above the degree of a Lieutenant, or as Commissioner for any part of the said late King's Revenue, Customs, Treasury, Ordnance, or Stores, Sheriff, Justice of Peace of any County at large, Mayor [or Chief Magistrate] of any City or Town Corporate, or Recorder, Steward or Town Clerk thereof, *having a real and personal Estate of the value of £3,000 or upwards above their debts** (other than such as now are, or on the first day of August last were, officers of or in their Majesties' Army or Navy), *and* having refused or neglected to take the said Oaths or Sacrament, or to make and subscribe the said Declaration, did, after the time expired in which he ought, according to the said Act, to have done the same, execute any such Office or Employment as aforesaid, shall, notwithstanding any Dispensation or other pretence whatsoever, forfeit and pay to their Majesties the sum of five hundred pounds for and in respect of every such Office or Employment so by him executed; and the said sum and sums is and are hereby vested in their Majesties, *by the ways and means hereafter directed by this Act*; and every such person shall be debtor and accountant to their Majesties for the same, and shall be discharged of and from all other actions and suits depending or to be brought for the same.

§. ii. And for the more speedy and effectual convicting of the said offenders and levying the said sums, Be it enacted by the authority aforesaid, That Commissions shall before the four and twentieth day of June,

* "The Lords" says Luttrell (21 May 1690), "have added a Proviso or two, that none should pay who are not worth 3,000*l*., and that the party should first be convicted by a jury." This last statement, as will be seen from § x. of the Bill as sent from the Commons, is incorrect.

1690, be issued forth under the Great Seal to such persons and in such manner as their Majesties shall appoint for the putting this Act in execution, and the persons therein named or appointed Commissioners respectively, or any five of them for the matters and according to the powers herein mentioned, shall be and be taken to be a Court of Record, and they or any five of them at such times and places as they shall think fit from time to time, with or without adjournment summarily and without the formalities of proceedings in Courts of Law or Equity, may and shall, upon the testimony of witnesses upon oath, confession of the Party or by any other lawful ways and means, and with all the expedition that the nature of the proceeding and justice will admit, examine, hear and determine the matters aforesaid and make a Record of every such offence under their hands respectively, which Record so made shall to all intents and purposes be taken and adjudged to be a full and perfect conviction of every such offender for every such offence to entitle their Majesties to the said sum of five hundred pounds, from which conviction there shall be no Appeal or Review otherwise than is hereafter provided, nor shall any Writ of Error or Certiorari lie for removal of the same.

§ iii. And for the better proceeding in the premises, Be it also enacted, That the said Commissioners or any three of them shall issue out Notes or Warrants under their hands, thereby warning all persons accused or suspected to be offenders in this behalf to appear before them at such time and place as shall therein be specified, and upon appearance of the said parties summoned or upon default of appearance and oath made of due notice given for that purpose (which oath and all other oaths necessary for the execution of the powers given by this Act the said Commissioners are hereby empowered to administer), the said Commissioners may and shall proceed to make such determination and conviction as aforesaid, and such service as is usually allowed to be good in any cases of Subpœna shall be accounted to be a good service of the Notes or Warrants aforesaid.

§ iv. And be it forther enacted, That all the determinations and convictions which shall be made by authority of this Act, shall be recorded in a book or books, to be provided for that purpose, and signed by five or more of the said Commissioners.

§ v. And be it further enacted, That there shall be Receivers General appointed by their Majesties, unto whom or their lawful deputies the several sums of five hundred pounds payable by any person or persons upon such conviction shall be paid, and the same shall by the said Receivers be paid into the Receipt of their Majesties' Exchequer, the said Receivers retaining to their own use two pence in the pound and deducting also thereout such sums of money as by allowance of the Lord High Treasurers or Commissioners of the Treasury shall be paid or laid out for necessary charges of and about the premises.

§ vi. And be it further enacted, That a duplicate or true copy of every conviction, signed by five or more of the Commissioners and also by the Receiver or Receivers respectively, shall be certified into their Majesties' Court of Exchequer within thirty days after the conviction; and the same so certified shall be a charge upon the respective offenders for the money by them payable upon such convictions, if the same have not before been paid to the respective Receiver as hereby is appointed, Upon which charge such process as may in any case of debt by the law or statutes of this realm be issued shall be forthwith awarded and issued out of the said Court for the speedy and effectual levying the said sums of five hundred pounds or so much thereof as shall not have been paid to the Receiver or Receivers as aforesaid; for which purpose every

Receiver shall upon every duplicate by him signed, to be transmitted into the Exchequer, express what part of the said several sums is paid, or that the same are wholly paid or unpaid, as the truth of the case shall be, and the said Commissioners shall also certify into the said Court of Exchequer all recognizances taken by virtue of this Act and not discharged.

§ vii. And be it further enacted, That every person convicted by virtue of this Act and not acquitted of the same upon appeal, shall, within three months after such conviction, pay the sum or sums of five hundred pounds payable by him thereupon to the respective Receiver or Receivers, who shall thereupon give to the said person an acquittance for the same, which Acquittance shall be a full discharge to the said party for the said money, and also by and upon the said payment and acquittance the said person shall be and is hereby pardoned and discharged of and from all penalties, forfeitures and incapacities whatsoever for or in respect of the respective offence or offences, upon the conviction whereof the said money is so paid; But if the said person shall not within the time aforesaid pay the said sum or sums as aforesaid, he shall be liable not only to the said process of the Exchequer, but likewise to all other the penalties, forfeitures, disabilities and incapacities mentioned and appointed in the said Act made in the five and twentieth year of the reign of King Charles the Second.

§ viii. And for the enabling the Commissioners to proceed with effect, Be it enacted by the authority aforesaid, that the Clerks of their Majesties' Courts of Chancery, King's Bench and Sessions of the Peace, and all witnesses and other persons in this behalf concerned, being thereunto reasonably required by the said Commissioners or any five of them, shall attend the said Commissioners and produce their Books, Rolls and Records and give their testimony, and in case any of them shall refuse or neglect so to do or to do such other thing or things as the said Commissioners shall require by virtue of this Act, that then they may commit such persons into any of their Majesties' prisons, there to remain and be kept in safe custody without bail or mainprize until he or she shall yield obedience to that which is so required.

§ ix. And be it further enacted, That every of the said Commissioners, before he enter upon the execution of this Act, shall take an Oath before three other of the said Commissioners, which they are hereby authorized and required to administer, the tenor whereof shall be as followeth, vizt.:—

"I, A.B., do swear that, according to the best of my skill and " knowledge, I will truly, faithfully, and impartially demean myself in " the execution of an Act of Parliament, intituled An Act for vesting in " their Majesties certain forfeitures of five hundred pounds, and for the " speedy levying of the same, and that I will not, for fear, favour, " reward, or affection, share or discharge any person against the tenor " of the said Act. So help me God."

§ x. Provided and be it enacted by the authority aforesaid, That where any person shall be aggrieved by any conviction, it shall be lawful for him to appeal from the same within twenty days after conviction, presenting his exceptions thereto in writing to any of the Commissioners convicting, who shall present and deliver the same in to the Justices at the next General Quarter Sessions of the Peace to be held for the county or place where such person so convicted shall reside at the time of such his conviction, which said Justices shall by a trial by a Jury, to be returned after the usual manner, finally hear and determine the said Appeal. Provided that none of the Commissioners convicting shall

House of Lords MSS.

1690.

sit at the determination of the said Appeal; and if the Appellant shall not prosecute with effect or shall not be thereupon acquitted, the said Justices shall award treble costs against such offender for his unjust Appeal. Provided that upon the delivery of such Appeal, the Appellant shall enter before one or more of the Commissioners convicting into a recognizance to prosecute the said Appeal with effect, and pay treble costs in case he shall not be acquitted upon the same; and if such recognizance be not entered into, the Appeal shall be null and void.

§ xi. And be it further enacted by the authority aforesaid, That if any action, suit, plaint or information shall be commenced or prosecuted against any person or persons for whatsoever he or they shall do in pursuance or in execution of this Act, such person or persons so sued shall and may plead the General Issue and may give this Act and the special matter in evidence; And if the Plaintiff or prosecutor shall become nonsuit or forbear further prosecution or suffer discontinuance, or if a verdict pass against him, the Defendants shall recover their double costs, for which they shall have the like remedy as in case where costs by law are given to the Defendants.

§ xii. Provided always that the powers granted to the Commissioners by virtue of this Act shall continue and be in force until the four and twentieth day of June in the year 1691 and no longer.

§ xiii. Provided that nothing in this Act contained shall extend to any Sheriff who did receive the Sacrament of the Lord's Supper in order to enable himself to exercise his office, but could not be admitted to take the Oaths and Test by reason that no Sessions of the Peace was held in the county whereof he was Sheriff.

§ xiv. And be it further enacted, That all and every sum or sums of money recovered and paid by virtue of this Act shall be paid into the Receipt of their Majesties' Exchequer, and a distinct account shall be there kept of all such money, to the intent the same be applied for the prosecuting of the war against France and the reducing of Ireland and to no other use whatsoever.

§ xv.* Provided always that this Act shall not extend to charge any person or persons whatsoever who after the eighth day of October and before the thirteenth day of February 1688 accepted of any office or commission and executed the same without qualifying himself according to the said Statute made in the said five and twentieth year of the said King Charles the Second (in respect of such acceptance of such office or Commission only) if such person or persons do and shall before the first day of August next receive the Sacrament of the Lord's Supper according to the usage of the Church of England and at the next Sessions of the Peace for the county or place where he shall reside take the Oaths mentioned in Act (*sic*) of the last Parliament, intituled An Act for abrogating the Oaths of Supremacy and Allegiance and appointing other Oaths, and repeat and subscribe a declaration mentioned in the said Statute made in the said five and twentieth year of King Charles the Second.

Parchment Collection. [Brought from the Commons this day. L. J., XIV., 500. On 21 May, the motion for going into C. W. H. was carried by 24 votes to 21, E. Kingston and L. Ferrers, Tellers. In C. W. H., L. Cornwallis in the Chair, the Title and Preamble postponed. The 1st enacting Clause read. The Act of 25 Car. II. read, to see whether others were not made liable by this Act, who were not by the 25 Car. II. Then the amendments embodied in the text above were made in Clause i. (L. J., XIV., 504–5 *in extenso*), and

* This Proviso was added in the Commons on third reading by 160 votes to 70, (C. J., X., 416). Ralph (II. 200) gives the numbers wrongly as 160 and 150.

the Clause thus amended was agreed to (MS. Min., 21 May). Then progress was reported, and the Bill dropped with the Session.]

Annexed :—

(a.) 21 May. Lords' Amendments in C. W. H. this day. L. J., XIV., 501–5, *in extenso*. [Embodied in text above.]

275. May 19. Hereditary Crown Revenues Bill.—Commons' Engrossment of an Act declaring the Hereditary Revenues of the Crown to be vested in their Majesties. § i. Whereas the several rates, impositions, duties and charges upon Beer, Ale, Cider and other liquors mentioned in an Act of Parliament made in the twelfth year of the reign of his late Majesty King Charles the Second (intituled An Act for taking away the Court of Wards and Liveries and Tenures in Capite and by Knight Service and Purveyance, and for settling a Revenue upon his Majesty in lieu thereof), and thereby granted to the said King, his heirs and successors, and the rents, revenues, issues and profits of the General Letter Office, or Post Office, or Office of Postmaster General, and the revenue arising by granting Licenses for the selling and uttering wine by retail, and also all and singular other the Revenue and Revenues, Manors, Lands, Rents and Hereditaments, Estate and Estates whatsoever, whereof or wherein King James the Second, or any in trust for him was or were seized or possessed on the tenth day of December in the year of our Lord 1688, or whereunto he was then lawfully entitled of or for any Estate or Interest, did become and were lawfully vested and settled in our Sovereign Liege Lord and Lady, William and Mary, King and Queen of England, Scotland, France and Ireland, in right of the Crown of England for such Estate, Interest and Term respectively as the said late King James had in the same respectively upon the said tenth day of December, 1688, and the same and all and every the profits thereof respectively (except the revenue arising by Fire Hearths and Stoves, and such other of the premises concerning which it is otherwise ordained by any Act made in the Parliament held in the first year of their Majesties' reign, or in or by this present Act, and except such of the premises as have been granted, demised or let by their Majesties for and during the respective Estates or Interests granted of or in the same) may and ought to be raised, levied, collected, answered and paid to and enjoyed by their Majesties in the same manner and form, according to such rates and orders, and by such rules, means and ways, and under such penalties and forfeitures as by law the same might or ought to have been raised, levied, collected, answered, paid or enjoyed at the time aforesaid; Be it therefore declared and enacted by the King and Queen's most Excellent Majesties, by and with the advice and consent of the Lords Spiritual and Temporal and Commons in this present Parliament assembled, and by authority of the same, That all Acts of Parliament made for the granting, settling, levying, collecting, answering and paying the premises or any of them, or for the preventing frauds or regulating abuses therein or for the better ordering or recovering the same, and all powers, provisions, penalties, articles, clauses and things contained in the said Acts or any of them now are and stand in full force and shall be applied, practised, executed and put in ure for and concerning the respective premises according to the tenor and intent of this present Act.

§ ii. Provided nevertheless and be it enacted, That an Act of Parliament made in the first year of the reign of the late King James the Second (entituled An Act for settling the Revenue on his Majesty for life which was settled on his late Majesty for his life) shall be and is hereby repealed and made void, and that no article, clause or thing therein contained from henceforth shall be or be construed to be of any force or effect whatsoever.

§ iii. And whereas their Majesties have been graciously pleased to signify their Royal pleasure that they are contented (having regard to the present exigency of affairs) that the Revenues and Premises or any part thereof should be made a Fond of Credit for raising a present sum not exceeding the sum of £250,000 towards the reducing of Ireland and carrying on the war against France (not doubting but that their good subjects will in time provide for the taking off such anticipations); to the end therefore that their Majesties may be enabled to raise any sum or sums not exceeding in the whole the said sum of £250,000 upon the security of the said rates, impositions, duties and charges upon Beer, Ale, Cider and other Liquors, and also upon the said revenues, issues and profits of the said General Letter Office, or Post Office, or office of Postmaster General by this Act declared to be vested in their Majesties, Be it enacted by the authority aforesaid, That it shall and may be lawful to and for any person or persons, natives or foreigners, bodies politic or corporate, to advance and lend to their Majesties into the receipt of the Exchequer, upon the security of the said Rates, Impositions, charges and duties of Excise, and also upon the said profits of the said General Letter Office or Post Office, any sum or sums of money not exceeding the sum of £250,000 in the whole, and to have and receive for the forbearance of all such monies as shall be lent before the tenth day of June 1690 interest not exceeding the rate of 8*l.* per centum per annum, and for what shall be lent after the said tenth day of June interest not exceeding the rate of 7*l.* per centum per annum.

§ iv And to the end that all moneys which shall be lent unto their Majesties, not exceeding in the whole the sum of £250,000, may be well and sufficiently secured out of the said Revenues arising by the rates and duties of Excise and by the profits of the said General Letter Office or Post Office or Office of Postmaster General, with interest for the same not exceeding the respective rates aforesaid, Be it further enacted by the authority aforesaid, That from and after the first day of November 1690, the Commissioners and Governors for the management of the Receipt of the Excise at the head office in London or the major part of them shall separate and keep apart three parts (the whole in four equal parts to be divided) of the money arising by the rates and duties of Excise hereby declared to be vested in their Majesties, as the same shall from time to time arise or be paid into the said Office of Excise by the Receivers or Collectors of the same or by any other person whatsoever, and the Auditor and Comptroller of the Excise for the time being, or their respective deputies, shall keep a perfect and distinct account in books fairly written of the said three parts as the same shall come in, to which books all persons concerned shall have free access at all seasonable times without fee or charge; And the said Commissioners and Governors of Excise are hereby required and strictly enjoined from time to time to pay weekly, to wit, on Wednesday in every week, if it be not a holy day, and if it be, then the next day after that is not a holy day, the said three parts into the Receipt of their Majesties' Exchequer distinct and apart from the other moneys which he or they shall receive for their Majesties' use.

§ v. And also be it further enacted by the authority aforesaid, That from and after the first day of November 1690 until the first day of November 1693 there shall be continued and be within the City of London an Office for the General Receipt of the said issues, profits, rents and revenues of the said General Letter Office or Post Office, into which office all the moneys arising by the same, either within this Kingdom or without, shall be well and truly answered and paid into the hands of the Receiver or Receivers General for that purpose appointed or to be appointed for the receipt of the said issues, profits, rents and revenues, which said Receiver or Receivers General is and are hereby directed and required from time to time at the said Office to separate and keep apart three parts (the whole in four equal parts to be divided) of the whole receipt of the said moneys (as the same shall from time to time become due and be paid into the said Office by the several Receivers, Collectors or any others who are or shall be employed to pay the same); And the said Receiver General of the profits of the said General Letter Office for the time being is hereby required and commanded to keep a perfect and distinct account in books fairly written of the said three parts as the same shall come in, to which books all persons concerned shall have free access at all seasonable times without fee or charge; And the said Receiver or Receivers General for the time being of the said issues and profits of the said General Letter Office or Post Office is and are hereby required and strictly enjoined from time to time to pay weekly every Wednesday, unless it be a holy day and, if it be, then the next day after that is not a holy day, the said three parts of all such moneys as aforesaid into the Receipt of their Majesties' Exchequer distinct and apart from the other moneys which he or they shall receive for their Majesties' use.

§ vi. And be it further enacted by the authority aforesaid, That there shall be provided and kept in their Majesties' Exchequer, that is to say, in the office of the Auditor of the Receipts, one book in which all moneys which shall be paid into the Exchequer of or for the said three parts of the said rates and duties of Excise as aforesaid shall be entered apart and distinct from all other moneys paid or payable to their Majesties upon any account whatsoever, and one other book in which all moneys that shall be paid into the Exchequer of or for the said three parts of the said issues and profits of the said General Letter Office or Post Office as aforesaid shall be entered apart and distinct from all other moneys paid or payable to their Majesties upon any account whatsoever; And that all and every person and persons, natives or foreigners, bodies politic or corporate, who shall lend any moneys to their Majesties upon the credit of the said rates and duties of Excise or upon the said issues and profits of the said General Letter Office or Post Office respectively and pay the same into the Receipt of the Exchequer, shall immediately have a Tally of Loan struck for the same and an Order for his or their repayment, bearing the same date with his or their Tally, in which Order shall be also contained a Warrant for payment of interest for forbearance, not exceeding the respective rates aforesaid, for his or their consideration, to be paid every three months until repayment of the principal; And that all Orders for repayment of money shall be registered in course according to the date of the Tally respectively, without preference of one before another; And that all and every person and persons shall be paid in course according as his or their Orders shall stand entered in the said Register book respectively, so as that the person, native or foreigner, his or her executors, administrators or assigns, who shall have his or her Order or Orders first entered in the said respective books of Register, shall be taken and accounted as the first person to be paid upon and out of the said rates and duties of Excise, or upon and out of the said issues

House of Lords MSS.

1690.

and profits of the said General Letter Office or Post Office as the same shall respectively come in; And he or they who shall have his or their Order or Orders next entered, shall be taken and accounted to be the second person to be paid, and so successively and in course; And that the said rates and duties of Excise, as the same shall come in, and also the said issues and profits of the said General Letter Office or Post Office, as the same shall come in respectively, shall be in the same order liable to the satisfaction of the said respective parties, their executors, administrators or assigns successively, without preference of one before another and not otherwise, and not to be divertible to any other use, intent or purpose whatsoever. And if the said Commissioners or Governors of Excise, or the said Receiver or Receivers General of the profits of the said Post Office for the time being, shall refuse or neglect to pay into the Exchequer the said three parts of the moneys arising by and out of the said rates and duties of Excise or out of the said profits of the Post Office in such manner as they are before respectively required or enjoined to do, or shall divert or misapply any part of the same, then they for any such offence shall respectively forfeit their offices of Commissioners or Governors or Receivers General, and be uncapable of any office, employment or place of trust whatsoever, and shall be liable to pay the full value of any sum or sums so diverted or misapplied to any person or persons who will sue for the same by any action of debt, bill, plaint or information in any of their Majesties' Courts of Record at Westminster, wherein no essoign, protection, privilege, wager of law, injunction, order of restraint or more than one imparlance shall be granted or allowed.

§ vii. And be it further enacted, That no fee, reward or gratuity, directly or indirectly, shall be demanded or taken for providing or making of any such books, registers, entries, view or search as aforesaid, or in or for the payment of money lent or the interest as aforesaid by any of their Majesties' officer or officers, their clerks or deputies, on pain of payment of treble damages to the party grieved by the party offending with costs of suit; or if the officer himself take or demand any such fee or reward, then to lose his place also; And if any undue preference of one before another shall be made, either in point of registry or payment, contrary to the true meaning of this Act by any such officer or officers, then the party offending shall be liable, by action of debt or on the case, to pay the value of the debt, damages and costs to the party grieved, and shall be forejudged from his place or office; And if such preference be unduly made by any his deputy or clerk, without direction or privity of his Master, then such deputy or clerk only shall be liable to such action, debt, damages and costs, and shall be for ever after uncapable of his place or office. And in case the Auditor shall not direct the Order or the Clerk of the Pells record, or the Teller make payment according to each person's due place and order as afore directed, then he or they shall be judged to forfeit and their respective deputies and clerks herein offending to be liable to such action, debt, damages and costs in such manner as aforesaid; All which said penalties, forfeitures, damages and costs to be incurred by any of the said officers or any their deputies or clerks, shall and may be recovered by action of debt, bill, plaint or information in any of their Majesties' Courts of Record at Westminster, wherein no essoign, protection, privilege, wager of law, injunction or order of restraint shall be in any wise granted or allowed.

§ viii. Provided always and be it hereby declared, That if it happened that several Tallies of Loan or Orders for payment as aforesaid bear date or be brought the same day to the Auditor of the Receipt to be registered, then it shall be interpreted no undue preference which of those be entered first, so he enters them all the same day.

§ ix. Provided also that it shall not be interpreted any undue preference, to incur any penalty in point of payment, if the Auditor direct and the Clerk of the Pells record and the Teller do pay subsequent Orders of persons that come and demand their money and bring their Order before other persons that did not come to demand their money and bring their Order in their course, so as there be so much money reserved as will satisfy precedent Orders which shall not be otherwise disposed, but kept for them (interest upon loan being to cease from the time the money is so reserved and kept in bank for them).

§ x. And be it further enacted by the authority aforesaid, That every person to whom any money shall be due by virtue of this Act after Order entered in the books of Register aforesaid, for payment thereof, his executors, administrators or assigns, by endorsement of his Order may assign and transfer his right, title, interest and benefit of such order or any part thereof to any other, which being notified in the office of the Auditor of Receipt aforesaid, and an entry or memorial thereof also made in the respective books of Register aforesaid for Orders (which the officers shall upon request without fee or charge accordingly make), shall entitle such assignee, his executors, administrators and assigns to the benefit thereof and payment thereon, and such assignee may in like manner assign again and so toties quoties, and afterwards it shall not be in the power of such person or persons who have or hath made such assignments, to make void, release or discharge the same or any the moneys thereby due or any part thereof.

§ xi. Provided that nothing in this Act contained shall extend or be construed to repeal or alter an Act made in the last Session of the Parliament held in the first year of their Majesties' reign, intituled An Act for preventing all doubts and questions concerning the collecting the public Revenue or anything therein contained.

§ xii. Provided always and be it enacted, That nothing in this Act contained shall extend or be construed to extend to invalidate or confirm any Letters Patents or Grants under the Great Seal of England heretofore made of any gift, charge, annuity, sum of money or pension issuing, payable or to be issued or paid out of any of the Revenues by this Act declared to be settled or vested in their Majesties, but that all such Letters Patents or grants shall be of the same force and in the same condition, and the said Revenues liable thereto in the same and no other manner than if this Act had never been made, anything herein to the contrary in anywise notwithstanding.

§ xiii. Provided always and be it enacted, That nothing in this Act contained shall extend, or be construed any way to extend to the invalidating certain Letters Patents bearing date the twentieth day of February in the second year of the reign of the late King James the Second, and granted by the said late King James the Second to the Right Honourable Henry, Earl of Clarendon, Laurence, Earl Rochester and others in trust for their Royal Highnesses the Prince and Princess Ann of Denmark, containing a grant of the yearly sum of 30,000*l.*, issuing out of certain Revenues therein mentioned, but that the same shall be good and effectual in law; and the said Letters Patents are hereby certified and confirmed, anything herein contained to the contrary notwithstanding.

House of Lords MSS.

1690.

§ xiv. Provided that nothing in this Act contained shall be construed or taken to hinder any the growing and annual payment or payments due or payable, and to be due and to be due and payable to her Majesty Catherine the Queen Dowager out of the said Revenues by virtue of several Letters Patents already made to her under the Great Seal of England, but that the same shall and may be paid and received by virtue of the said Letters Patents as fully and amply as if this Act had not been made, anything before contained to the contrary thereof nothwithstanding.

§ xv. And forasmuch as the Hereditary Revenue belonging to the Crown hath been very much encumbered by pensions granted by Letters Patents in the reign of King Charles the Second, and King James the Second, to the great damage of the Crown and prejudice of the people; therefore, to prevent the like mischief for the future, and that the Monarchy may be supported, and the Hereditary Excise, Post Office and Wine Licences may always descend free from debts and Incumbrances to any succeeding King or Queen, Be it enacted and it is hereby enacted by the authority aforesaid, That all pensions or any sum of money which shall hereafter be granted by Letters Patents to any person or persons out of any part of the Hereditary Excise, Post Office or Wine Licenses shall cease and be determined at or upon the natural death of the King or Queen who shall make any such Grant, anything in this Act or any other to the contrary notwithstanding.

§ xvi. Provided always that this Act or anything therein contained shall not be construed or taken in any sort to avoid, impeach or prejudice a Grant by certain Letters Patents, bearing date the fourteenth day of May in the year of our Lord 1690, made during this present Session of Parliament by their Majesties to Arthur, Earl of Torrington and his heirs in consideration of his faithful services and for support of his Honour, of several pieces and parcels of ground and lands in the Great Level of the Fens called Peterborough Level or Bedford Level, containing by estimation 10,000 acres, be the same more or less, of the present yearly value of 1,409*l*. reserved rents thereout and after the determination of the leases thereof in being, of the yearly value of 3,000*l*. or thereabouts more or less; but the said Letters Patents and the grants of the premises therein made or mentioned to be made are hereby confirmed to be good and effectual in the law to him the said Earl and his heirs as well against their Majesties, their heirs and successors, as also against all and every trustee or trustees of the late Queen Maria, Consort of the late King James the Second, on whom the same were settled in trust for or to the use of the said late Queen, and her, his and their estates and interests in the premises are hereby vested in the said Earl and his heirs.

§ xvii. Provided always that nothing in this Act contained shall extend to vest any estate, right, title or interest in their present Majesties or either of them of, in or to any manors, lands, rents or hereditaments whatsoever that were the manors, lands, rents or hereditaments of Theodore Bathurst, of Lincoln's Inn, Esquire, and were seized into the hands of the late King James the Second by reason or means of any Office or Inquisition found by virtue or colour of one or more Commission or Commissions under the Great Seal of England, further or in any other manner than the same were vested in the said late King James the Second, anything in this Act contained to the contrary in any wise notwithstanding.

§ xviii. And be it enacted by the authority aforesaid, That the Chancellor of the Exchequer and other the Commissioners of their Majesties' Treasury now being shall and are hereby required at or before the second day of

June next ensuing to take the like Oath as by the laws of this realm is taken by every Lord Treasurer of England, as it is hereafter described and in the manner thereby directed, that is to say, the Chancellor of the Exchequer shall take the same before the Lord Chancellor or Lord Keeper or Lords Commissioners of the Great Seal of England or any two of the said Lords Commissioners of the Great Seal, and the said Commissioners of the Treasury shall take the said Oath before the said Chancellor of the Exchequer after he shall have taken the same as aforesaid; And all and every person or persons who shall from and after the end of this Session of Parliament be in those respective offices, shall in like manner take the same Oath before the said respective persons before they or any of them take upon him or them the execution of the said offices or any of them, any law or usage to the contrary notwithstanding; And the Lord Chancellor and Lord Keeper and Lords Commissioners of the Great Seal of England and Chancellor of the Exchequer for the time being respectively are hereby authorised to administer the said Oath accordingly, the tenor of which hereafter followeth.

"I, A.B., do truly and sincerely swear, in the presence of God, "that I will well and truly serve the King and Queen and their people "in the Office of Commissioner of the Treasury; that I will do right to "all manner of people, poor and rich, of such things as concern my "Office, and truly keep and dispend their Majesties' Treasure; that "I will truly counsel the King and Queen, and conceal and keep their "Counsel; that I will neither know nor suffer the King and Queen's "hurt, nor their disheriting, nor that the right of the Crown be decreased "by any means, as far forth as I may let it; and if I may not let it, "I shall make knowledge thereof clearly and expressly to the King "and Queen with my true devise and counsel; and I shall do and pur-"chase the King and Queen's profit in all that I may reasonably do. "So help me God." *Parchment Collection.* [Brought from the Commons this day, but dropped with the Session, after being reported without amendment from C. W. H. on 23 May. L. J., XIV., 502, 506.]

276. May 19. Pardon (General) Act. — Lists of Precedents relating to Acts of Pardon, ordered this day upon reading the Bill entituled An Act for the King and Queen's Majesties most Gracious, General and Free Pardon, and reported on 20 May. L. J., XIV., 503. [The Bill was brought in by the Lord President this day, by their Majesties' Command, and the Committee for Privileges were ordered to inspect Precedents. On 20 May the Precedents were reported and read, and it was proposed to read the Bill. House moved that the thing may be cleared, whether any persons concerned may be heard after the Bill read. Two questions proposed, (1) How often it is to be read? (2) When it is read, whether, upon hearing any person, you can strike out any names. *Agreed* that the Bill may be spoken to after being read. After debate, the Question as to reading the Bill was carried &c. as in L. J., XIV., 503. *Moved*, That all the Lords sit uncovered during the reading of this Act. After the Royal Assent had been given to some other Bills, the Speaker, on the King's withdrawal, reported the Bill of Pardon. *E. Huntingdon* moved that he may be heard by his Counsel before the Bill pass. *Bp. St. David's* desired to be heard, and spoke, and said, if the House thought what he said needed any explanation, he might be heard by his Counsel before the Bill pass. After debate, the question as to the Bill passing was carried as in L. J. MS. Min., 19, 20 May. *See also* L. J., XIV., 502–3, 506.] The Lists of Precedents are as follows:—

HOUSE OF LORDS MSS.

1690.

(*a*.) 19 May. List of Precedents, as follows:—

5 July, 32° Hen. VIII., allata a Domo Communium Bill Pardonacionis. (L. J., I., 151.)

9 July, lecta est Billa Pardonacionis. (*Ib.* 154.)

13 July, lecta est Provisio quædam, cum exceptionibus et correctionibus, generali Pardonacioni anneẍ. (*Ib.* 155.)

3° Edw. VI., 20 Jan. 1ª vice lecta et conclusa An Act of Pardon. (*Ib.* 382.)

1 Feb. 1ª 2ª et 3ª vice lecta est Provisio quædam anneẍ to the King's free Pardon. The said Proviso was signed by the King and Privy Council, as well as the Bill. (*Ib.* 398.)

10 April, 35 Eliz. 1ª vice lecta An Act for the Queen's General Pardon. (L. J., II., 190.)

43 Eliz. 1ª vice lecta An Act for the Queen's Majesty's most Gracious General Pardon, and sent to the Commons. (*Ib.* 257.)

26 May, 3° Jac. An Act for a General Pardon read and sent to the Commons. (*Ib.* 443.)

21 July, 7° Jac. 1ª vice lecta An Act for a General Pardon. (*Ib.* 654.)

23 July. The Commons at a Conference desire Sir Stephen Proctor may be excepted out of the same, or that the Bill which was depending concerning him may pass; whereupon the Lords appointed Mr. Attorney to attend His Majesty therewith and he in His Majesty's presence added a Clause for excepting him. The said Clause was read in both Houses. (*Ib.* 656–8.)

25 Car. II., 28 March 1673. Hodie unica vice lecta An Act for a General Pardon. There is entered the manner of passing the said Bill. (L. J., XII., 576–7.)

[Produced before the Committee for Privileges on 19 May, when Mr. Petyt was ordered to attend the next day with the Records of such precedents as he could find. Priv. Book.]

(*b*.) 20 May. Further List of Precedents, viz.:—

21 Dec. 6° et 7° Hen. VIII. Item introductæ sunt duæ Billæ, viz., Billa concernens Generalem Pardonacionem Domini Regis et Billa concernens les Avoures, quarum secunda per Communes assentita est, et prima habet octo provisiones annexas. (L. J., I., 56.)

22 Dec. Item Billa concernens Generalem Pardonacionem Domini Regis, cum novem provisionibus annexis. The provisoes are all signed by the King. (*Ib.* 57.)

10 April, 5° Eliz. Hodie 1ª vice lecta est Billa of the Queen's Majesty's most free and general pardon, quæ communi omnium Procerum assensu conclusa est. (*Ib.* 618.)

23 Dec, 8° Eliz. Item lecta est Billa of the Queen's Majesty's free and general pardon, quæ communi omnium Procerum consensu conclusa est. (*Ib.* 664.)

29 May, 13° Eliz. 1ª vice lecta est Billa touching the Queen's Majesty's most Gracious generaland free pardon, quæ conclusa est. (*Ib.* 700.)

14° Martii, 18° Eliz. Hodie introducta est a Domo Communium Billa for the Queen's Majesty's most Gracious and free Pardon. Conclusa. (*Ib.* 750.)

29° Martii, 27° Eliz. Hodie lecta est Billa An Act for the Queen's Majesty's free Pardon quæ communi omnium Procerum assensu conclusa est, et data servienti Gawdie &c. deferenda in Domum Communium. (L. J., II., 108.)

26 Maii, 21 Jac. Hodie unica vice lecta est Billa An Act for the King's Majesty's most [Gracious] general and free Pardon. Put to the Question, and generally assented unto. And the said Bill was sent to the Commons. (L. J., III., 410.)

[Produced this day by the Clerk at the Committee for Privileges. Priv. Book.]

(c.) 20 May. Mr. Petyt's Abstract of Precedents, viz. :—

42 E. III., cap. 2. It is assented that the pardon which the King made to his Commons the 30th year of his reign be holden in all points.

43 E. III., cap. 4. The King, at the request of the Commons, having regard to the great aids they had given him, of his special grace released and pardoned to his said Commons and every of them all manner of trespass of vert and venison done before that time in his forest.

Parl. 51 E. III., No. 22. After the 22nd of Feb. certain Bishops and Lords, the Chancellor, Treasurer, and Keeper of the Privy Seal and all the Justices by the King's appointment went to Sheen, where the King lay sick, and there, in their presence, the articles of the King's general pardon, as ensueth, were read, with other answers made to the Petitions of the Commons, as hereafter follow, whereunto the King agreeth and willed that they should the next day be read in the House, and to make the same the last day of the Parliament, which was done the next day accordingly.

Parl[t]. 5 R. II., No. 30. The Commons required of the King three manner of pardons to be confirmed by Parliament, viz[t]. the first touching Nobles and Gentlemen, who in resisting of traitors and rebellious villains, slew certain persons without due process of law. The second for such as were of those rebellious companies. The third for such as lived in peace without any rising, which was granted.

The Pardon for Nobles and Gentlemen.

The Pardons of the rebels being out of the towns of Canterbury, Bury St. Edmunds, Beverley, Scarborough, Bridgewater and Cambridge, except such persons whose names appear hereafter, being the principal and ringleaders of the Rebels, except Provers and Appealers of treason and felonies, and except such as slew Simon, Archbishop of Canterbury, late Chancellor, the Prior of St. John's, then Treasurer, and John De Cavendish, Chief Justice of the King's Bench, so as all men endamaged by such insurrection be not foreclosed of their due remedy.

The Pardon for such as lived in due obedience, as free from that insurrection.

No. 39. The Commons require a sight of the Pardons granted. Thereto was answered, that such was not the guise, but that the Commons should make petition for such Pardon in writing and that the King the last day of the Parliament should answer the same. And further, it was said that the King used not to grant anything to the Commons unless they also granted to him. The Commons answered that of the grant of the subsidies of wool and other staple wares, they would be advised. And it was answered for the King, that he would so be of any Pardon.

No. 40. The Commons being better advised granted a Subsidy, whereupon the Pardons granted were openly read before the House.

HOUSE OF LORDS MSS.

1690.

No. 105. The King, at the request of the Commons, enlargeth his Pardon for certain felonies and treasons, as may appear in the Record.

Parlt. 6 Ric. II., No. 43. The King, at the request of the Commons, granteth Pardon of all treasons and felonies done in the then late insurrection (except certain before excepted), and except John. Horne, Adam Carlile and Walter Sibell of London, then accused of horrible acts.

Ibid. No. 48. The King, at the request of the Commons, pardoneth all trespasses touching lands or tenements, trespasses done by the King's officers or other great Lords, and of Jurors and maintainers of quarrels.

Parl. 8 Ric. II., 30. Commons pray that a General Pardon of all felonies and other trespasses and offences may be granted. The King answers he will advise.

Parl. 21 Ric. II., No. 48. Sir John Bussey, the Speaker, declared before the King, how ready the Commons were to ease the King by some subsidy, and prayeth for the Commons a General Pardon. Whereunto the Chancellor, by the King's commandment, answered that the King would be advised until he knew of the Common's grant.

Parlt. 5 Hen. IV., No. 87. A General Pardon. Stat. Book, 5 H. IV., cap. 15. The King of his special grace, by assent of all the Lords Spiritual and Temporal, and at the request of the Commons in this present Parliament assembled, pardoned, etc.

Parlt. 2 H. V., No. 23. The King of his own meer mercy pardoneth all his subjects all forfeitures incurred by the Statute of Liveries of cloth and hats. Stat. cap. 8.

Parl. 4 H. V., No. 12. The King's General Pardon.

Parl. 18 H. VI., No. 31. The King's general Pardon of all treasons, felonies, forfeitures, and other offences.

27 H. VI. cap. 6. The King, by the advice, assent, and authority of Parliament, pardoned, &c. [Offered this day to the Committee, by Mr. Petyt, in pursuance of an order of the 19th. *Mr. Petyt*, in offering them, informed the Committee that he had not had time to look into the Records themselves. He believed there were several precedents in the Chapel of the Rolls which he had not in the Tower. The House to be moved that the Officer of the Rolls attend with such precedents of this kind as he shall find, and that Mr. Petyt be ordered to bring the Records mentioned in the Abstract delivered in by him. (Priv. Book, May 20).]

277. July 7. Prorogation.—Commission, signed by the Queen, and dated this day, for proroguing Parliament to 28 July. *Parchment Collection.* L. J., XIV., 508. *In extenso.*

278. July 7. Writ of Summons. (Bp. Exeter.)—Writ of Summons, dated 15 April 1689, to Jonathan (Trelawny), Bp. Exon, who took the Oaths this day. L. J., XIV., 508.

279. July 28. Prorogation.—Commission, signed by the Queen, and dated this day, for proroguing Parliament to 18 August. *Parchment Collection.* L. J., XIV., 509. *In extenso.*

280. Sept. 12. Prorogation.—Commission, signed by the King, and dated this day, for proroguing Parliament to the 2nd of October next. *Parchment Collection.* L. J., XIV., 512. *In extenso.*

281. Oct. 2. Salmon v. Jones.—Copy transcript of Record. [The Writ of Error was brought in this day. L. J., XIV. 515. The case related to an action in Exchequer in respect of some lands in the parish of Lanvar, co. Anglesey. The Cause was heard on 3 Dec. *Mr. Ward* (for Plaintiff): States the case and reads several cases in several Reports. *Sir Francis Winnington* (for Defendants): The question is whether the deed made by William Lewis amounts to a Covenant. Cites a case in Siderfin's Reports. Judges heard. *Holt, C. J.* and *Pollexfen, C. J.:* We gave the Judgment. *Nevill, J.:* I apprehend the estate does pass. *Eyre, J.:* It was the intent of the donor. It being contrary to the rules of law, this Conveyance is a false Conveyance. *Ventris, J.:* Is of the same opinion, and gives his reasons for it. The last judgment is good. The House then affirmed the judgment. (MS. Min. L. J., XIV. 577.)]

282. Oct. 2. Garter's Roll.—A List of the Nobility of England according to their respective Precedencies, the 2d of October 1690. *Signed* Thos. St. George Garter, 2d Oct. 1690. *Parchment Collection.*

283. Oct. 2. E. Peterborough and E. Salisbury.—Petition of E. Peterborough as follows:—

To the Right Honble. the Lords Spiritual and Temporal in Parliament assembled.

The humble Petition of Henry, Earl of Peterborow,

Sheweth,

That your Petitioner hath been kept Prisoner in the Tower of London for almost two years last past, not being charged with any crime upon oath that your Petitioner could hear of, to the great impairing of his health and estate. That notwithstanding a Dissolution and several Prorogations of Parliament have intervened, as also an Act of free and general Pardon, yet the Governor of the Tower refused to set your Petitioner at liberty, and the Court of King's Bench, although legally addressed unto, refused to order his enlargement, as your Petitioner is advised they ought to have done by law. Therefore your Petitioner humbly prays your Lordships' order for his discharge. PETERBOROW. L. J., XIV. 515. [The Petition being read, the House was moved to hear the Judges. *Holt, C. J.:* The Lord Lucas returned he was committed by this House. I minded his Counsel of L. Stafford's case. Then it was insisted that he was pardoned by the Act of general Pardon. Ordered, *That he shall be heard by his Counsel and their Majesties' Counsel on Monday next at ten of the clock in the forenoon, and that the Judges and the Earl of Peterborough be heard whether the Earl of Peterborough's Impeachment be pardoned by the Act of Grace.** (MS. Min. 2 Oct.).—On the 6th the Judges attended. *Holt, C. J.:* On 26 Oct. [1689] there was a message from the House of Commons to impeach the Earl of Peterborough. The question is whether this offence be pardoned? The time when he did it is not mentioned. If this offence was committed since 13 Feb. 1688, if since the matter of fact is pardoned (*sic*). *Pollexfen, C. J.:* I am of the same opinion and for the same reasons. If it was before Feb. 13 it is pardoned. The other Judges (*Dolben, Powell, Turton, Rokeby,* and *Nevill*) of the same opinion. House moved that a Committee be

* The words in italics are struck through and the Order altered to read as in L. J., XIV. 515.

appointed to consider and search for precedents whether Impeachments continue from Parliament to Parliament. *Proposed*, To ask the Judges, whether crimes whatsoever by prosecution whatsoever are not pardoned by the Act of Grace, if they be not excepted in the Act? Question asked the Judges, Whether all crimes whatsoever, however prosecuted, are not excepted in the Act? *Holt, C. J.:* Desires to be excused from answering, it being a thing that relates to both Houses of Parliament. *Pollexfen, C. J:* We find in our law books that we are not to give opinions in Parliamentary proceedings. After debate, Question, Whether the Lords shall be now discharged of their Imprisonment? Resolved in the *Negative*. Contents, 21; Not-Contents, 29. Tellers, E. Stamford and V. Newport. *Question*, Whether the Earl of Salisbury and the Earl of Peterborough shall be admitted to bail? Resolved in the *Affirmative*. Lords Committees appointed to inspect and consider precedents whether Impeachments continue *in statu quo* from Parliament to Parliament. The House then ordered that E. Peterborough and E. Salisbury be brought to the Bar to-morrow to be bailed. (MS. Min. 6 Oct. L. J., XIV. 516).—On the 7th, *E. Salisbury* brought as sureties Sir John Fenwick and Thomas Cholmondley. The two Lords having withdrawn, *Proposed* that Sir John Fenwick being under bail himself, should not be bail for another. The House did not allow of the bail. E. Salisbury called in again, and the Recognizance read, and E. Huntingdon and E. Thanet entered into Recognizance. The House then ordered the Lords to be discharged on bail. (MS. Min. 7 Oct. L. J., XIV. 518.)—On 30 Oct. upon consideration of the precedents of Impeachments reported from the Select Committee (See No. 286), the House, on motion, and after a long debate, ordered the two Earls to be discharged from their bail, the previous question being first put and carried. (MS. Min. 30 Oct. L. J., XIV. 538.)—On 13 Nov. the House appointed the 18th for explaining their vote of liberation (L. J., XIV. 550), but nothing, it appears, was done on the 18th beyond reading the order of the 13th. (MS. Min. 18 Nov.)]

Annexed:—

(*a*.) 2 Oct. Petition of James, Earl of Salisbury, as follows:—

To the Right Honble. the Lords Spiritual and Temporal in Parliament assembled.

The humble Petition of James, Earl of Salisbury,

Sheweth,

That your Petitioner by several warrants of commitment hath been kept Prisoner in the Tower of London for the space of a year and nine months last past, to the great impairing of his health and estate. That notwithstanding the late Act of free and general Pardon, the Lord Lucas (Chief Governor of the Tower) refuseth to set your Petitioner at liberty, without your Lordships' order in that behalf. Your Petitioner therefore humbly prayeth your Lordships to order his discharge. And your Petitioner shall ever pray.

Salisbury.

284. Oct. 2. Coals Act.—Amended draft of an Act for reviving a former Act for regulating the measures and prices of Coals. Identical with the Act (2 W. & M. Sess. 2, c. 7). [Read 1a this day: Royal Assent 20 Dec. L. J., XIV. 514, 600. Section ii. of the Act, relating to the employment of foreign seamen, was added by the Commons.* On

* The Commons' Amendments were considered and agreed to on 13 Dec. (MS. Min. No entry in L. J. of date).

1 Jan. 1690–1 the House made an Order for the Lord Mayor, &c. of London to put the Act into execution. L. J., XIV. 612. See also No. 247.]

Annexed:—

(a.) 23 Oct. Lords' Amendment to the Bill. It fills the space left blank for the date of the commencement of the Act with 1 Dec. 1690, as in the Act. [Made in Committee 21 Oct. and reported this day. Com. Book, 21 Oct. L. J., XIV. 529.]

285. Oct. 6. E. Torrington.—Petition of Arthur, Earl of Torrington, praying for his release. L. J., XIV. 517–8. *In extenso.* [Read this day and to be considered to-morrow (*ib.*).—7 Oct. Order of the business of the day and Petition of E. Torrington read. *Moved* that a Committee be appointed to consider what has been done with Peers when they have been committed in time of Privilege of Parliament. *Ordered* that it be referred to the Committee of Privileges to consider precedents of what has been done with Peers committed in time of Privilege for misdemeanours only (M.S. Min. L. J., XIV. 519).—8 Oct. In Committee of Privileges, *L. Cornwallis* in the Chair, Order of Reference read. E. Torrington's Petition read. L. Arundell's case read; 5 and 18 April 1626. E. Devon's case, 15 May, 1689; the Report of the Committee of Privileges read, and the House's judgment thereon, that no Peer ought to be committed for nonpayment of a fine. *Ordered* to report these two cases specially to the House, and to desire the House will hear them read. (Priv. Book.)—9 Oct. Committee ordered to report to-morrow. (MS. Min. L.J., XIV. 520.)—10 Oct. *L. Cornwallis* reports the two precedents. *Moved* that a Committee be appointed to examine the Lord in the Tower. That the King's Counsel bring a charge against him. That an application be made to his Majesty that the charge against E. Torrington be brought hither. *Ordered* that the debate be adjourned to the 13th (MS. Min. L. J., XIV. 520).—13 Oct. Order for the business of the day read. *E. Pembroke* brought a copy of E. Torrington's Commission,* and a copy of the Warrant for his commitment,† as drawn by the King's Counsel. The Commission read, dated 28 April 1690. The Commitment read, 25 (*sic*) July 1690. [*Proposed* to have the opinion of the Judges, whether by virtue of his Commission he has departed from his privilege, and ought to be tried by the Admiralty.]‡ After debate, Judges' opinion asked, whether E. Torrington was triable by the Act 13 Car. II. *Holt, C.J.*, said that, when it was put to them formerly, the Judges were of opinion he was triable by this Act, and they are now of the same opinion, he being not High Admiral, but an Admiral subordinate to the Admiralty. *Pollexfen, C.J.*, of the same opinion. *C. Baron* [*Atkyns*], of the same opinion. After debate, upon consideration of the Petition of E. Torrington, *Resolved* as in L. J., *i.e.*, that the Earl, having accepted a Commission from the Admiralty, has no privilege as a Peer to be exempted from trial by the Articles of War. Debate adjourned till to-morrow. (MS. Min. L.J., XIV. 521–2.)—14 Oct. Order for business of the day read. *Ordered* that the debate be adjourned to the 18th, and Judges to attend. (MS. Min. L.J., XIV. 522.)—18 Oct. Order for business of the day read. *L. Vaughan* acquainted the House

* Annex (*a.*).

† Annex (*b.*).

‡ The words included in square brackets are struck through. The Question originally proposed was, "Whether he has privilege of a Peer so as not to be tried by" (*sic*).

House of Lords MSS.

1690.

that he is committed by a Warrant from the Admiralty Board two days since. *Moved* to have the copy of the Warrant of Commitment to the Tower. *L. Lucas*, according to the opinion of the House, delivered the Order of Commitment. The first Order of Commitment to the Tower for high crimes and misdemeanours read. The Order for delivering E. Torrington to the Marshal read. Copy Order of Commitment of the Admiralty by which he is now committed read. The receipt of E. Torrington from L. Lucas to the Marshal read. *Proposed* to ask the Judges' opinion upon the last Warrant, by which he stands now committed. Judges asked whether the Warrant by which E. Torrington now stands committed is a legal Warrant? Whether the Warrant last read is a legal Warrant of Commitment? *Holt, C. J.:* The Commissioners may commit. The Lord Admiral may. [As to the] Question whether the Commissioners may, I conceive they may commit in all cases where the Lord High Admiral may. 19 & 20 Car. II. a case of Bernard, in the E. Marshal's Court. This was held to be a good commitment. For the matter, being acted in the Fleet, he has misdemeaned himself, contrary to his instructions. Where an offence is made triable, by necessary consequence of law he must be committed. As for his being a peer, I give no answer to it. *Pollexfen, C. J.:* The matter is a matter of war. It is a miscarriage there. This is triable by martial law, and the law of England, in times of war, allows of it. If martial law be allowed by common law, that which then is done by the superior to the inferior must be according to their law, and the common law cannot judge of this. As for the peerage, I meddle not with it. There was a law undoubtedly for the sea and the land. If the fact arises within the jurisdiction of the Admiral, the Commissioners may act as the Admiral. I conceive this warrant to be a lawful commitment. *L. C. Baron* [*Atkyns*]: I shall consider it as abstracted from the privilege of Peerage. I will consider it as abstracted from that Act. The Commissioners may act as a Lord High Admiral. They were crimes before the Statute of Car. II. Our law takes notice that there is a martial law in this Kingdom, and we presume they go according to their law. I think the Commissioners of the Admiralty had the power of a Lord High Admiral before this Statute. *Dolben, J.*: I make no question but this a legal warrant, the Commissioners of the Admiralty may do as before this Act was made. I think the Commissioners may proceed as a Lord High Admiral. *Nevill, B.:* I am of opinion it is a good warrant. These crimes mentioned in the warrant were crimes before the Statute, and the warrant is good. I conceive it is well made and good. *Powell, J.:* I conceive they have a good power to commit by the martial law, and that the warrant is good. *Rokeby, J.:* As to the person committing, I think it is not to be doubted but before the Statute the Lord High Admiral might commit and the King may delegate, and then they have the power. As to the matter, we give faith and credit to the martial law. I conceive it a legal commitment. *Turton, B.:* I conceive this is a good warrant of commitment. The Commissioners have the same power as the Lord High Admiral. *Question:* Whether this warrant last read of the Commissioners of the Admiralty, dated 15 October, is a legal warrant? *Resolved*, that the commitment is legal. (L. J., XIV. 521. MS. Min. 18 Oct.)—There are no notes of the debate on the 20th.—On 21 Oct., after debate on the Resolution, drawn on the previous day by the Committee, *Question* proposed to be put to the Judges: Whether the Earl of Torrington, for the offence mentioned in the commitment of the Lords Commissioners of the Admiralty, might not have been committed by the Privy Council.* *Question*, Whether the Judges shall be asked this question? Resolved in the Affirmative. Contents, 30; Proxies, 5—Total, 35. Not-Contents, 27; Proxies, 4—Total, 31. Tellers, E. Monmouth and L. Cornwallis. Then the Question was put to the Judges. *Holt, C. J.:* I am of opinion that the Privy Council have a power of committing. I never heard any objection against their committing. As [to why] the Privy Council may [not] commit in this case as well as others, I cannot see any reason. *Pollexfen, C. J.:* I am of the same opinion. The authority was always allowed good in our books. For offences committed beyond seas and in the islands they have committed, and I think they may. *L. C. Baron* [*Atkyns*]*:* I am of the same opinion that the Privy Council have a power of committing. 6 Edw. III. Sir John Graham and De la Zouche, both were committed. 2 Rich. II. Lady Nevill complained that John Bruce had taken away her grandchild, and committed. 2 Rich. II., No. 49, Commons' Petition . . . . be put to answer upon his freehold. Committed. 4 Rich. II. The Commons complained of a riot. The answer was that two serjeants should go and take them. The Petition of Rights, par. 3; there the Council had a right of commitment. I am satisfied that the Council might commit the Earl of Torrington. *Dolben, J.:* I am of the same opinion, they may commit in matters of State, and if anything be matter of State, this is. *Nevill, B.:* I take it to be clear the Council may commit. *Gregory, J.:* I am of opinion that the Privy Council in matters of State may commit. If they had not power to try, yet they had power in this case to commit. *Rokeby, J.:* The Lords of the Council have a power of committing, and it is of so absolute a necessity that the Government cannot consist without it, and have power for those crimes mentioned in the warrant. *Proposed* to agree with the Committee. *Proposed*, That an addition be made to the Resolution of the Committee. The Resolution and additional words read, viz. ("but that the committing him in that conjuncture is to be excused by reason of his having taken a Commission to serve at sea.")† *Question*, Whether to agree to this addition? Resolved in the *Negative*. Then the two next questions in L. J., XIV. 527 were also resolved in the *Negative*. *Question*, Whether to add the words ("to prevent its being drawn into example," &c. as in L. J.)? Resolved in the *Affirmative* (*sic*)‡ Contents 30; Not-Contents, 30. Tellers, E. Sta[mford] and L. North. *Question*, Whether the word ("only") shall be inserted in the Resolution. Resolved in the *Negative*. Leave to protest.§ *Question*, Whether to agree with the Committee in their Resolution. Resolved in the *Affirmative*. Contents, 32; Not-Contents, 17. Tellers, E. Mon[mouth] and L. North. (MS. Min. 21 Oct.) See also No. 307.]

Annexed:—

(*a.*) 13 Oct. Copy of E. Torrington's Commission to be Admiral of their Majesties Fleet. By the Commissioners for executing the office of Lord High Admiral of England, &c. To the Right

---

* L. J., XIV. 527. The question as first proposed, was, whether the Earl of Torrington, having been accused of an offence for which he was liable to a commitment by the Lords Commissioners of the Admiralty, might not have been at first committed for the same crime by the Privy Council.

† The words "L. Steward" are written in the margin against this proposed addition.

‡ This is a mistake of the clerk, the numbers being equal. *See* L. J., XIV. 527.

§ No such protest is recorded in the Journals. The protest in L. J., XIV. 535, was on the third reading of the Admiralty Commissioners Bill (No. 307).

Honourable Arthur, Earl of Torrington, hereby appointed Admiral of their Majesties' ships employed and to be employed in the present expedition. By virtue of the power and authority to us given, we do hereby constitute and appoint you Admiral and Chief Commander of their Majesties' fleet employed or to be employed for the present expedition, willing and requiring you forthwith to take upon you the charge and command of their Majesties' said fleet, as Admiral and Chief Commander accordingly, and authorising and empowering you to wear the Union Flag at the main topmast-head on board such ships of their Majesties' fleet, where you shall happen at any time to be; hereby willing and requiring all commanders, captains, masters, and other officers and companies of the said fleet to obey you as their Admiral and Chief Commander during this expedition, and you likewise to observe and execute all such orders and instructions as you shall from time to time receive from us, the Lord High Admiral of England or Commissioners for executing the office of Lord High Admiral for the time being. And we do hereby further authorise you, in case of neglect, disability or other default or neglect of any of the said officers or seamen, to displace them, and to appoint and constitute others in their stead. And for so doing, this shall be your warrant. Given under our hands and the seal of the office of Admiralty this 28th day of April 1690. *Signed:* Pembroke, Thos. Lee, J. Lowther, John Chicheley. By order of the Commissioners, J. Sotherne. A copy according to the entry thereof in the Books of the Admiralty Office. J. Sotherne. [Delivered to the House this day by E. Pembroke.] L. J., XIV. 521.

(*b.*) 13 Oct. Copy of Warrant by the Commissioners of the Admiralty for the commitment of E. Torrington to the Marshal of the High Court of Admiralty. Given under their hands and seals 15 July 1690. L. J., XIV. 523. *In extenso. Dated* in margin 15 October 1690. *Endorsed* as delivered in to the House by E. Pembroke this day. L. J., XIV. 521.

286. Oct. 6. Impeachments.—Papers delivered in to the Committee appointed to inspect and consider precedents whether Impeachments continue *in statu quo* from Parliament to Parliament. [The Committee was appointed this day, after hearing the Judges on the matter of the Earls of Salisbury and Peterborough (No. **283**). (L. J., XIV. 517.) They met, with E. Mulgrave as chairman, on Oct. 8, 11, 15, 18, 22, and 23, on which last day they ordered to report. On 8 Oct., the order of 19 March 1678–9, concerning Impeachments is read. The Order of 29 March 1673, concerning Judicature is perused, and part thereof read, viz., the precedent of 15 Edw. III., Nos. 8, 43, 49, the Archbishop of Canterbury's case; also that of 51 Edw. III., No. 96, Hugh Stafford's case. *Ordered*, That the clerks at the next meeting bring all the Journals in the Parliament Office, wherein any Impeachments are contained. *Ordered*, That Mr. Petyt attend their Lordships on Friday next at 9 a.m., in the Prince's lodgings, and give an account of all Impeachments which have been in Parliament and of the time which they have respectively depended.—11 Oct. *Mr. Petyt* is called in and gives account of what he has found concerning Impeachments continued from Parliament to Parliament:—1st Precedent: 4 Edw. III., No. 16, the L. Berkley's case* (of which he produces a true copy, which is

* *See* Paper (*a.*) below.

read), continued to the next Parliament, 5 Edw. III., No. 18. His bail is discharged. The Rolls of 9 Edw. III. are lost. Continued to the Parliament 11 Edw. III., Rot. Patent. Membrana 28. The copy produced is read. He is then discharged. 2nd Precedent: 15 Edw., Nos. 8 and 43. The Archbishop of Canterbury's case;* a criminal case continued to 17 Edw. III., No. 22, being another Parliament, wherein it is called an arraignment. *Mr. Petyt* believes it will appear more fully in the pardon, which pardon he is directed to look into and give an account the next meeting. 3rd Precedent: 50 Edw. III., No. 47. The case of Adam de Bury,† impeached. 51 Edw. III., No. 91, the Commons desire he may be included in the General Pardon. His pardon is in the Patent Rolls 51 Edw. III. Memb. 19. *Ordered*, That Mr. Petyt enquire whether there was a General Pardon that Parliament. John Lester's case,‡ the same Parliament. The Commons pray his pardon, but he finds none for him. *Mr. Petyt* says that on Monday he is to go out of town to keep the L. Coleraine's Court, and cannot return till Wednesday, so prays he may not attend till after that time. He is appointed to make further search for Precedents, and also for the Pardons he mentioned in the Archbishop of Canterbury's and Adam de Bury's cases, and attend on Saturday. The Precedent of the Bishop of London's case, 7 Feb., 25 Hen. VIII., is read. The Clerk attending the Committee gives account of what other precedents he has found,§ but none of them having been continued from Parliament to Parliament, save Visct. Stafford's. The proceedings thereon were read. *Ordered*, That the Clerk search what Conferences or Free Conferences were with the Commons upon Impeachments. *Ordered*, That the Keeper of the Records of the King's Bench attend on Wednesday with the Records of the proceedings relating to the Lords lately in the Tower upon Impeachments, upon their motions for their *Habeas Corpus* (Comp. L. J., XIV. 520).—15 Oct. The Journal wherein is the Free Conference in the case of E. Danby is perused, and the Free Conference of 10 April 1679 is read. *Mr. Harcourt*, Secondary in the Crown Office, attending with the Records of the King's Bench relating to Impeachments, is called in. He delivers in an Abstract of them,‖ which the Clerk is ordered to keep for the Committee, and Mr. Harcourt is directed to bring the names of the Judges who sat at the several times when the said writs of *Habeas Corpus* were demanded.¶—18 Oct. *Mr. Petyt* is called in and says that in a Parliament held 50 Edw. III., there was a General Pardon, but none were to have the benefit but those who took out particular pardons by such a time. In 51 Edw. III., Adam de Bury took a particular pardon, this at the instance of the Commons, and in that pardon is expressed his Impeachment at length. Says he knows not whether the Archbishop of Canterbury was impeached in 15 Edw. III., but there were proceedings against him at the suit of the King. Rot. Claus. 15 Edw. III., p. 3. *Prohibitio pro Rege.*** The Minutes then set out the other precedents delivered in by Mr. Petyt.†† After considering these precedents, the Committee ordered Mr. Petyt to bring at the next meeting a further account of all that appears to him in the Records in the case of Richard Lyons, and to search whether the Lords were not sometimes summoned by new writs upon the second sitting of the same Parliament. The Committee also ordered the Keeper of the Records

* *See* Paper (*b.*) below.
† *See* Paper (*c.*) below.
‡ *See* Paper (*d.*) below.
§ *See* Paper (*e.*) below.
‖ *See* Paper (*f.*) below.
¶ *See* Paper (*f*[1].) below.
** *See* Paper (*g.*) below.
†† *See* Papers (*h.*) and (*i.*) below.

House of Lords MSS.

1690.

in the Chapel of Rolls to attend at their next meeting and bring an account of all precedents.—22 Oct. *Mr. Grimes*, Keeper of the Records in the Rolls Chapel, is called in and asked what he has done as to the search concerning Impeachments. He says that there is nothing in the Rolls except Acts of Parliament. He withdraws. *Mr. Petyt* is called in. Says that in Rot. Parl. 50 Edw. III., No. 19, [in the case of] Richard de Lyons,* judgment is given against him in that Parliament, and he is put to fine and ransom at the will of the King. Rot. Parl. 51 Edw. III., Mem. 27.† Pardon "per ipsum regem et magnum concilium" granted after the Parliament, and the same day he had a pardon "per ipsum Regem." 1 Ric. II., No. 41, proceedings against Alice Perrers.‡ 1 Edw. IV., membr. 35 dorso "Concerning Writs of Summons to Parliament." Prorogued before met and writs sent to appear at a day after. Till Edw. IV., no Parliament was ever continued, and then a Parliament met twice or thrice. 21 Hen. VIII. no difference between adjournments and prorogations. 51 Edw. III., Nos. 95, 96, Hugh Falstolf's§ case, impeached the year preceding. Does not find that there were any proceedings against him after the Parliament. He withdraws.—23 Oct. *Ordered* to report all the precedents that have been produced either by Mr. Petyt, Mr. Harcourt, or the Clerk attending the Committee, and that the House be desired to appoint a day for considering the same. The Report was made on 30 Oct. (L. J., XIV. 536. *In extenso.*) The E. Mulgrave in making the report, acquaints the House that copies of most of the precedents are ready to be read, if the House so think fit, and that some of them being in Old French, Mr. Petyt's clerk, who transcribed them, waits, by order, at the door to read such of them as the House should direct. The Clerk was called in and read the case of Thomas de Berkeley. *Proposed* to consider three precedents, viz., Berkeley, the Archbishop of Canterbury, and Adam de Bury. 22 May 1685, read. 19 March 1678–9, read. House moved to discharge E. Sarum and E. Peterborough. 7 Jacob. Stephen Procter. After debate, rest as in L. J., XIV. 538. (MS. Min. 30 Oct.)] The papers delivered in to the Committee are as follow:—

(*a.*) 11 Oct. Extracts from Rot. Parl. 4 Edw. III., No. 16. "Thomas de Berkley, Miles . . . . . . Radulpho de Nevill, "seneschallo Hospitii Domini Regis etc.;" Rot. Parl. 5 "Edw. III., No. 18 "Item, en mesme le Parlement . . . . . à "prochein Parlement;" and Rot. Pat. 11 Edw. III., p. 1, mem. 28, "Rex omnibus . . . . . apud Westm. xvi die Martii. Per ipsum Regem." Certified as true copies by W. Petyt. The whole is *Endorsed:* The case of Thomas de Berkley. [Delivered in to the Committee this day by Mr. Petyt, Com. Book.]

(*b.*) 11 Oct. Extracts from Rot. Parl. 15 Edw. III., No. 8, "Et meisme cesti jour . . . . . en ceste fourme," No. 43, "Et "fait à Remember . . . . . c'est assaver," No. 44. "Primerent " . . . . . juggement rendu," No. 49. "Et fait a Remember " . . . . . nostre seigneur le Roi;" and Rot. Parl. 17 Edw. III., No. 22, "Fait a remembrer . . . . . pur ancenter illodges." *Endorsed:* The Case of the Archbishop of Canterbury. [Delivered in to the Committee this day by Mr. Petyt., Com. Book.]

(*c.*) 11 Oct. Extracts from Rot. Parl. 50 Edw. III., No. 47. "Item Adam de Bury . . . . . especiales petitions de Parlement;" Rot. Fin. 50 Edw. III., Mem. 25, "Rex Vicecomitibus

* *See* Papers (*k.*) and (*k*¹.) below.

† *See* Papers (*l.*), (*l*¹.), and (*m.*) below.

‡ *See* Papers (*n.*) and (*n*¹.) below.

§ *See* Papers (*o.*) and (*o*¹.) below.

"London . . . . . Per concilium in Parliamento;" Rot. Parl. 51 Edw. III., No. 91, "Item prie la Commune . . . . . quites et descharges;" and Rot. Pat. 51 Edw. III., Mem. 19, "Rex "omnibus Ballivis . . . . . Roberto de Assheton, Camerario "ipsius Regis." Certified as true copies by W. Petyt. *Endorsed:* The Case of Adam de Bury. [Delivered in to the Committee this day by Mr. Petyt, Com. Book.]

(*d.*) 11 Oct. Extract from Rot. Parl. 51 Edw. III., No. 90. "Item prie la Comune . . . . . quites et dischargez." *Endorsed:* The Case of John de Leycestre. Certified as a true copy by Mr. Petyt. [Delivered in to the Committee this day by Mr. Petyt, Com. Book.]

(*e.*) 11 Oct. List of Precedents. *Endorsed* "Impeachments in "the Parliament Office. 1690. Used and reported," as follow:—

Henry VIII.

25 Hen. VIII. Bishop of London impeached by the House of Commons.

James I.

3 March 1620. Sir Giles Mumpesson 23. Judgment against him.
30 May 1621. Sir John Bennett charged by Serjt Crew.
16 April 1624. L. Treasurer, E. Middlesex. Complaint against him.
19 May 1624. Commons' Complaint against Bishop of Norwich.

Charles I.

6 May 1626. Articles against E. Bristol.
13 & 15 May 1626. D. Bucks impeached by the Commons.
18 Dec. 1640. Archbishop Laud impeached of High Treason.
22 Dec. 1640. L. Keeper Finch impeached of High Treason.
29 Dec. 1640. Sir George Ratcliffe impeached of High Treason.
12 Feb. 1640. Sir Rob. Berkeley impeached of High Treason.
6 July 1641. Six Judges; charge against them.
20 July 1641. Bishop of Ely impeached, but no proceedings on it.
4 Aug. 1641. Charge against the thirteen Bishops.
30 Aug. 1641. E. Bridgewater impeached; no proceedings.
18 Dec. 1641. Daniel O'Neale accused of High Treason.
30 Dec. 1641. The Bishops' Petition and Protest, and they committed.

Charles II.

6 Dec. 1660. William Drake impeached by Message.
3 Jan. 1666. L. Mordaunt impeached at a Conference.
12 Nov. 1667. E. Clarendon impeached, but no Articles then.
24 April 1668. Sir W[m] Penn impeached by Message for Conference.
5 Dec. 1678. E. Powis, V. Stafford, L. Petre, L. Bellasis, and L. Arundell of Wardour impeached, but no Articles.
23 Dec. 1678. E. Danby impeached; the Articles then brought up and read.
21 Dec. 1680. Mr. Seymour impeached; Articles then brought up.

House of Lords MSS.

1690.

7 Jan. 1680. Sir W. Scroggs impeached; Articles then brought up.
26 March 1681. Fitzharris impeached; no Articles.

Then follows, in another hand, the statement of the proceedings against V. Stafford, which appears in the Report, L. J., XIV. 536. *In Extenso.* [Delivered in to the Committee by the Clerk this day. Com-Book.]

(*f.*) 15 Oct. Paper endorsed, "Mr. Harcourt's account of *Habeas Corpora* upon Impeachments," as follows:—

Die.	Turr. London.	——
Lunæ prox. post Quinq. Septiman. Paschæ 32 Car. II. Regis.	—	Hab. Corp. pro Domino Vicecomite Stafford. *Sir William Scroggs. Sir William Dolben. Sir Francis Pemberton. Sir Thomas Raymonds.*
Veneris in crastino Ascencionis, Domini anno supradicto. *Parliament dissolved.* 28 March 1681.	*Remittitur* -	Idem Vicecomes Stafford, ductus in Curiam et remittitur. *Sir William Scroggs (Chief Justice).*
Veneris prox. post tres Septiman. Paschæ 33° Caroli supradicti.	*Remittitur* -	Hab. Corp. pro Thoma, Comite Danby, Retorn. affilatur et remittitur. Die Sabbati prox. post Christi Ascencionem Domini sequent. *Sir Francis Pemberton (Chief Justice) and the same judges.*
Veneris in crastino Ascencion. Domini anno 34° Car. 2^{di}.	—	Hab. Corp. pro Thoma Comite Denby. *Sir F. Pemberton, or Sir Saunders. Sir Thomas Jones. Sir R. Holloway. Sir T. Walcot.*
Sabbati prox. - -	*Remittitur* -	Thomas, Comes Danby ductus fuit in Curiam super Bre. prædict. et ordinat. quod Bre. et retorn. affilentur, et remittitur.
Veneris prox. post crastinum Trin. anno supradicto.	—	Hab. Corp. pro. Thoma, Comite Danby.
Jovis prox. post xv^m Trin. anno supradicto.	*Remittitur* -	Thomas, Comes Danby ductus fuit in Curiam et remittitur.
Martis prox. post crastinum Pur. anno 34 and 35 Car. 2^{di} prædict.	—	Habeas Corpus pro eodem Comite. *Sir G. J. Hayes. Sir Richard Holloway. Sir Thos. Walcot. Sir Robert Wright.*
Mercurii prox. post Mens. Paschæ anno 35°.	—	Habeas Corpus pro eodem Comite.

Die.	Turr. London.	—
Martis prox. post Mensem Paschæ anno 35°. Hillar. 35 et 36.	—	Habeas Corpus pro eodem Comite.
Lunæ prox. post crastinum Pur anno supradicto.	*Remittitur* -	Thomas, Comes Danby ductus fuit in Curiam super breve de Hab. Corp. et remittitur, et ordinatum fuit quod ducetur item in crastino sed non.
Sabbati in Octav. Pur. anno supradicto.	—	Als hab. corp. pro eodem.
Eodem die - - -	—	Sic pro Willielmo, Comite Powys.
Eodem die - - -	—	Sic pro Henrico, Domino Arundell. Sic pro Johanne, Domino Bellasis.
Martis prox. - - Trad. in balliam.	—	Idem Comes Danby, ductus fuit in Curiam, committitur Marr. et postea traditur in Ballium pro comparent. ad prox. Parliamentum. Johannes, Dominus Bellasis ut supra, traditur in Ballium. Henricus, Dominus Arundell de Wardour et Willielmus Comes Powys, traduntur in Ballium ut supra.
Mercurii prox. post tres Septiman. Sanctæ Trin. Anno 1 W. et Mariæ.	—	Hab. Corp. pro Henrico, Comite Peterborough.
Lunæ prox. post Octav. Pur. Anno supradicto.	—	Hab. Corp. pro eodem Comite.
		Sic pro Jacobo, Comite Salisbury.
Lunæ prox. post Quinq. Septiman. Paschæ anno secundo W. et M.	—	Hab. Corp. pro eisdem Comitibus.
Martis prox - - -	—	Iidem Comites ducti in Curiam, retorn. affil. et ordinatum fuit quod ducantur iterum die Veneris prox.
Veneris prox. - -	—	Comes Salisbury ductus in Curiam. Remittitur.
Lunæ prox. post tres Trin. anno 2°.	—	Hab. Corp. pro eodem Comite Peterborough.

Vera Copia. S. HARCOURT.

[Delivered in to the Committee this day by Mr. Harcourt. Com. Book.]

(f^1.) Paper endorsed "Names of Judges in King's Bench since 1671."

House of Lords MSS.

1690.

(*g*.) 18 Oct. Extract from Close Rolls 15 Edw. III., p. 3, membr. dorso 'Prohibitio pro Rege,' as follows:—"Rex venerabili in Christo Patri et eadem gratia Archiepiscopo Cantuar. totius Angliæ Primati, Salutem. Cum pridem in Parliamento nostro apud Westm. in Quindena Paschæ proximo præterita convocato, quædam legibus et consuetudinibus Regni nostri Angliæ expressè contraria et regiæ dignitati nostræ nedum valde præjudicialia et probosa fuissent nimis importune petita quæ nisi per modum Statuti tunc promisissemus consignari dictum Parliamentum fuisset sine omni expeditione in discordia dissolutum et sic guerræ nostræ Franciæ et Scotiæ quas de consilio vestro ut scitis principaliter assumpsimus fuissent quod absit verisimiliter in ruina;

"Et nos ad evitandum tanta pericula præmissis protestationibus de revocando eum possemus commode quæ sit a nobis quasi invitis extorta fuerant illa sigillo nostro sigillari permiserimus illa vice.

"Et postmodum ea de consilio et assensu Comitum et Baronum ac aliorum peritorum ex causis legitimis quia defecit consensus noster declaravimus esse nulla nec nomen vel vim habere debere Statuti.

"Ac jam acceperimus quod vos unum consilium provinciale in crastino Sancti Lucæ proximo futuro apud London convocari mandastis, in quo co-episcopos vestræ provinciæ contra nos concitare et aliqua nobis prejudicialia circa revocationem dicti pretensi Statuti et in enervationem, depressionem et diminutionem jurisdictionis, jurium et prerogativorum nostrorum regalium, ad quorum conservationem astringimur vinculo juramenti, Necnon circa Processum inter nos et vos super quibusdam ex parte nostra vobis appositis pendentem statuere declarare super his censuras graves intenditis promulgare, Nos volentes tanto præjudicio convenit obviare vobis districte prohibemus ne quicquam quod in derogationem seu diminutionem regiæ dignitatis, potestatis et jurium Coronæ nostrorum seu legum et consuetudinum dicti Regni nostri aut in præjudicium processus memorati vel etiam in roborationem dicti pretensi Statuti vel alias in contumeliam nostri nominis et honoris, aut in gravamen vel dispendium consiliariorum vel obsequialium nostrorum cedere poterunt in dicto consilio vel alibi proponatis, statuatis aut aliqualiter attemptetis aut attemptari faciatis. Scituri quod si secus feceritis ad vos ut inimicum nostrum et nostrorum violatorem jurium gravius quo licite poterimus capiemus. Teste Rege apud Westm. primo die Octobris. Per ipsum Regem et Concilium." *Noted*. Convenit cum Recordo. W. Petyt. [Delivered to the Committee this day by Mr. Petyt. Com. Book. 18 Oct. L. J., XIV. 537.]

(*h*.) 18 Oct.—Statement endorsed "Mr. Pettit's Account of Impeachments," as follows: "May it please your Lordships, in "obedience to your Lordships' order of the 8th of this instant "October 1690, sent to me, to inspect and consider Precedents, "whether Impeachments continue in *statu quo* from Parliament "to Parliament, and to give your Lordships an account of all "Impeachments which have been in Parliament, and of the time "which they have respectively depended; I have made all the "diligent search I possibly could in this small time of your "Lordships' allowance, and here humbly submit this my col-"lection to your Lordships' great wisdom."

Rot. Par. 4 Ed. III., No. 1. Anno 4 Ed. III. Roger de Mortymer was upon the King's charge given to the Lords, adjudged to be drawn and hanged as a Traitor.

No. 2. In the same Parliament Simon de Bereford, as being of Council with the said Roger, had the like judgment.

No. 3. And so had John Mautravers, as being guilty of the death of Edmund, Earl of Kent.

No. 4. The like judgment was given upon Bogo de Bayons and John Deverell.

No. 5. And it was also assented and agreed, That Thomas Gournay and William Ogle should have such judgment for the death of King Edward II. as they who traiterously murdered him.

No. 16. And lastly, in the same Parliament, Thomas de Berkeley was accused ex parte Domini Regis for the same murder, tried and acquitted thereof, and afterwards bailed, etc.

Rot. Parl. 13 Edw. III. No. 8. Anno 15 Edw. III. The Archbishop of Canterbury prayed the King that, whereas he had been defamed through the realm, he might be arraigned in full Parliament, etc.

Rot. Parl. 21 Edw. III. No. 38. Anno 21 Edw. III. The Commons complain of the extortion used by certain merchants, who were farmers of the King's Customs of Wools, not naming the parties, for which they prayed remedy, and that the said merchants might be put to their answer in that Parliament for such outrage and distress done to the people.

Which Petition is thus answered: Let the Marchantz be called into Parliam^t. et eicut leur Repons.

No. 68. Whereupon John de Wesenham and Walter de Cheriton, Merchants, who were concerned in those complaints, prayed the King that he would command them to come before the Council, to answer whatsoever should be objected against them.

Rot. Parl. 42 Edw. III., No. 20.—Anno 42 Edw. III. Sir John de la Lee, Steward of the King's Household, was brought before the Lords and some of his Commons, in that Parliament, to answer several Articles against him, of which being not able to purge himself, he was sent to the Tower (No. 26), there to remain prisoner, till he had made fine and ransom, at the King's will.

Rot. Parl. 50 Edw. III., No. 17.—Anno 50 Edw III. Richard Lyons, Merchant, of London, was "empechez et accusez" by the Commons, whereupon he was in that Parliament adjudged to prison, etc.

No. 21. In that Parliament William, Lord Latimer, was likewise impeached and accused by the Commons, and had judgment then given upon him.

Nos. 31, 33, 34. And so had William Elys, John Pechee, and John, Lord Nevill, who were all impeached in the same Parliament by the Commons.

Rot. Parl. 51 Edw. III., Nos. 87, 89, 90, 92. Besides, Alice Perrers, and John de Leicester and Walter Sporyer, who, as they were all impeached, so were they all convict in this very Parliament, as appears by the Speaker's motion to the King for their pardons in the next Parliament, Anno 51 Edw. III.

House of Lords MSS.

1690.

Rot. Parl. 1 Ric. II., No. 38.—Anno 1 Ric. II. John, Sire Gomenys and William de Weston were severally arraigned "en plein Parlement," and in that Parliament had judgment given against them.

No. 41. In the same Parliament, Alice Perrers was brought before the Lords to answer to certain matters which should be objected against her "depar le Roi," which matters being denied by her and proved against her, she was in the same Parliament adjudged to be banished, etc.

Rot. Parl. 4. Ric. II., No. 17.—Anno 4 Ric. II. Sir Ralph Ferrers, Knt., was brought into Parliament under the guard of the Marshall of England, and there arraigned "depar le Roi" for suspicion of Treason, etc., and upon trial it seemed to the Lords he was innocent of that which he was charged with, and, therefore, he was bailed by pledges, body for body, to have him before the King and his Council, where, and when, and so often as it should please the King between that and the next Parliament.

Rot. Parl. 7 Ric. II., p. 1, No. 15.—Anno 7 Ric. II. The Bishop of Norwich was charged and impeached by the Commons of several misdemeanours, and had judgment (No. 23) given to make fine and ransom, according to the quantity and quality of his misdeeds.

No. 24. In the same Parliament, Sir William Elmham, Sir Thomas Tryvet, Sir Henry de Ferrers, and Sir William de Farndon, and Robert Fitz Ralph, Esq., were arraigned in Parliament at the request of the Commons, for receiving several sums, for giving up holds and fortresses, without the assent of the King or his Lieutenant, and in that Parliament judgment was given against them.

Rot. Parl. 7 Ric. II., p. 2., No. 11.—In the same year John Cavendish, fishmonger of London, complained, first, before the Commons of England, and after before all the prelates and Lords, being in Parliament, demanding surety of peace against Michael de la Pole, then Chancellor of England, the which was granted.

No. 13. Whereupon Cavendish accused him of bribery, of which the Chancellor cleared, first before Prelates and* Lords, and then before the Lords and Commons, in that Parliament.

Rot. Parl. 10 Ric. II., No. 6.—The Commons "compleignantz griefment" before the Prelates and Lords, of Michael de la Pole, Earl of Suffolk, late Chancellor of England, by several Articles, unto which the Chancellor made answer, and upon the many replications of the Commons, at last he had judgment to be fined, and imprisoned at the will of the King, etc. All which was done in one and the same Parliament.

Rot. Parl. 11 Ric. II., p. 1.—On the second day of that Parliament the Lords "Appellantz" exhibited their Petition to the King, concerning several Articles against diverse Lords and Commoners, whom they appealed of treason. Several of whom not appearing, and their default being recorded, judgment was given against them. After which, Sir Nicholas Brembre, a commoner, was brought prisoner before the King and the Lords, at the request of the said "Appellantz"; and the said Articles being read "en plein Parlement," he pleaded not guilty, which he was ready to defend with his body. Whereupon the Commons of the Parliament said, that they had seen and considered all the said

* The words "Prelates and" are interlined *in pencil*.

Articles, which they found to be true, and that they likewise, as much as in them lay, did also accuse the said Appellees, which they would have done, and it appertained to them to have done, had not the aforesaid Appellants pursued the said Appeals. Whereupon was answered by the Lords of the Parliament that the battle doth not lie in this case, but that they, upon examination of the Articles, would proceed to judgment.

Afterwards the Commons themselves "accusez et impechez" divers Commoners, Sir Robert Bealknap, Lord Chief Justice of the Common Pleas, Sir John Carey, late Chief Baron, and other Justices, etc. The Records were brought into the Parliament at the demand of the Commons, and the Commons accused the Justices for their untrue answer made unto sundry questions before the King at Nottingham, to the emboldening of the aforesaid offenders in their traiterous designs and attempts, etc. Unto which they answered, etc., were adjudged, etc., and all done in that Parliament.

After all which Appeals and Impeachments there followed another Impeachment of the Commons, entitled thus:—

Idem. M. 10. "Les Accusements et Empeschementz faits par les Communes du Roialme envers Simon de Beurley, Chivaler, John Beauchamp, Chivaler, John Salesbury, Chivaler, et James Barners, Chivaler, ensuent soug escripts dount les dits Communes prient Juggement en cest present Parlement," which was likewise given by the Lords in that Parliament.

Placita Coronæ in Rot. Parl. 21 Rich. II.—Anno 21 Ric. II. Edward, Earl of Rutland, etc. and six other Lords, and Scroop, Chancellor, appealed the Duke of Gloucester and the Earls of Arundell and Warr, and having delivered their Bill of Appeal to the King, sitting in his Throne of State, in the Great Hall within the Castle of Nottingham, with the Crown on his head, they offered to prove their accusation, "come vous tres redoute Seigneur et ceste haute et honurable Court, vostre Parlement, veilletz ordeigner."

Shortly after this, a Parliament being called at Westminster, the proceedings of those Appeals appear in a Roll, intituled, "Placita Coronæ coram domino Rege proximo post festum Exaltationis Sanctæ Crucis, anno regni Regis Ricardi 2[di] post Conquestum," etc.

Rot. Parl. 21 Ric. II., No. 15. And in the same Parliament, the Commons came before the King "en plein Parlement," and accused and impeached Thomas Arundel, Archbishop of Canterbury, of high treason. And upon their prayer for judgment against him, he was adjudged a traitor, etc.—Idem. No. 19. And in the same Parliament, the Commons "empechez et accusez" Sir Thomas de Mortimer of many high treasons. And because he was fled, it was ordained and established by the King and all the States of Parliament that a Proclamation should be made in England and Ireland to yield himself within three months after to the law, or else to stand convict and attainted, and to be adjudged a traitor to the King and realm.

Rot. Parl. 28 Hen. VI., No. 14.—Anno 28 Hen. VI. The Duke of Suffolk besought the King that he might be at his declaration of the great infamy and defamation that was said upon him by many people of the land, that he should be other than a true man to the King and to his realm, and that if any

HOUSE OF LORDS MSS.

1690.

man should say it in general or in special, he might make his answer in declaring of himself, as he was before the King and all the Lords and Commons in that Parliament. And then the Duke makes a Protestation of his great service and innocency, and requested that that Protestation might be enacted in that Parliament. After which the Commons required his commitment, but the Lords and Justices saw no cause for it, by reason their accusation was general. And then the Commons exhibit two Bills of Articles of Accusation and Impeachment against the Duke, "de quibusdam altis proditionibus, necnon offensis et imprisionibus, per ipsum ducem contra Regiam Majestatem factis et perpetratis." All which Articles they require to be enrolled, and that the said Duke might answer to them. Whereupon the Duke was committed to the Tower, and after [being] brought by writ before the King and Lords, the Articles were read to him, and he desired he might have copies, which was granted him, and he committed to the ward of minors, Stanley and Staunton, Esqrs., to be kept in a tower within the King's Palace of Westminster. Not long after, the Duke appeared before the King and Lords, and, kneeling, answered to the said Articles. And, afterwards, appearing again before the Lords, and being remembered by the Chancellor that he had not put himself upon his parage, was asked by him what he would say furthermore to that matter. And the said Duke answered, that some of those Articles were too horrible to speak more of them, and as to those Articles comprehended in the said Bill, touching the King's high person and the estate of the Realm, he trusted to God he had answered them sufficiently, and so he, not departing from his said answer, wholly submitted to the King's rule and governance. Wherefore the King commandeth the Lord Chancellor to say to him that, as touching the great and horrible things in the said first Bill comprised, the King held him neither declared or charged, and as touching the second Bill put against him, touching misprisions, which were not criminal, the King, by force of his submission, by his own advice, and not reporting him to the advice of the Lords, nor by way of judgment, for he was not in place of judgment, puts him to his rule and governance, that is to say (*inter alia*) that he should absent himself out of the kingdom for five years. And forthwith the Viscount Beaumont, on the behalf of the said Lords, both Spiritual and Temporal, and by their advice and assent and desire, recited, said and declared to the King's highness that what had been so decreed and done by his Excellence, concerning the person of the said Duke, proceeded not by their advice and counsel, but was done by the King's own demeanance and rule; wherefore they besought the King that this their saying might be enacted, in the Parliament Roll, for their more declaration hereafter, with this Protestation, that it should not be, nor turn in prejudice nor derogation of them, their heirs, nor of their successors in time coming, but that they may have and enjoy their liberty and freedom in case of parage hereafter, as freely and as largely as ever they, or any of their ancestors or predecessors had and enjoyed before this time.

Rot. Parl. 38 Hen. VI., No. 38.—And lastly, Anno 38 Hen. VI., the Commons accused and impeached the Lord Stanley of several matters done and committed by him, with relation to a rebellion, which had been lately raised by the Earl of Salisbury, on the behalf of the Duke of York; and prayed the King, that the said

Lord might be committed to prison, there to abide after the form of law. To this was answered "Le Roy s'advisera." *Signed* Guil. Petyt, Custos Recordorum apud Turrim, London. [Delivered to the Committee this day. Com. Book.]

(*i.*) 18 Oct. Statement endorsed "Mr. Pettit's Account of Impeachments," as follows:—"De Pardonationibus et Graciis factis per Regem Communitati Regni sui Angliæ, anno quinquagesimo Regis Edwardi Tertii.

Rot. Statutor, Mem. 1, No. 50; Rastall's Statutes, fol. 128. In a Parliament held anno L. Edw. III. by assent of the Prelates, Dukes, Earls, Barons, and others assembled at that Parliament, the King, forasmuch as that year was rightfully the year of Jubilee, or the year of Grace of his reign aforesaid accomplished, granted certain graces and pardons to his Commons of England. He pardoned (*inter alia*)—

1. All gifts, alienations, and purchases of lands, holden of him, without license.

2. All entries into lands, after the death of their ancestors, without suing them out of the King's hands.

3. He pardoned and released all fines, amerciaments, issues, forfeits, reliefs, and escuage, and all debts and accompts till the 40th year of his reign.

4. And also all manner of actions and demands which he had or might have by him, sole or else jointly with other persons against any of his said Commons.

5. The King also generally pardoned the suit of his Peace, for all manners of felonies done or committed before the said 50th year, with the outlawries, if any were thereupon pronounced. Except always treasons, murders, common thefts, and also rapes upon women.

But it was the King's mind that none should enjoy anything of the said graces and pardons of felonies, unless they pursued their charters in especial, betwixt that and the Nativity of St. John Baptist then next coming.

De Exemplificatione Gratiarum in Parliaments factarum, Mem. 13.—Pursuant to this Act of Pardon, and reciting it in a Roll, intituled 'Rotulus Pardonationum de anno 51 Edw. III.' amongst many hundreds more, who then sued out their particular pardons, we meet with—

1. Ricardus de Lions, Cives et mercator London, and

2. Adam de Bury,

who also took out their pardons, and that too in common form with the rest.

Rot. Parl. 51 Edw. III. But in a Parliament, anno 51 Edw. III., upon the Commons' request by their Speaker (amongst other things made)—

1. That Richard Lions might be restored to the law, and his goods and chattels.

2. That Adam de Bury might be contained 'En la Pardon en cest present Parliament grante,' and that he and his pledges might be quit and discharged.

The King granted to each of them special pardons, wherein their Impeachments, and the judgment given against Lions in 51 Edw. III., are fully recited.

So that upon the whole matter I humbly conceive that these Charters of Pardons were different and distinct pardons, from those which Lyons and Bury pursued upon the King's General Pardon granted to all the Commons in the Parliament of 50 Edw. III. *Noted in margin:* Lion's pardon is enrolled in the Patent Rolls 51 Edw. III., Membr. 21. Bury's pardon is enrolled in the Patent Roll 15 Edw. III., Membr. 19." [Delivered to the Committee this day.]

(*k.*) 22 Oct. Extract from Rot. Parl. 50 Edw. III., No. 19. "Par quoy le dit Richard . . . . . les portz D'Engleterre." *Endorsed:* Judgment against Richard Lyons. [Delivered in to the Committee by Mr. Petyt this day. Com. Book.]

(*k*[1].) 22 Oct. Translation into English of preceding extract. Appended to preceding.

(*l.*) 22 Oct. Extract from Rot. Parl. 51 Edw. III., m. 27. "Rex omnibus Ballivis . . . . xvi. die Martii. Per ipsum Regem et magnum Concilium." *Endorsed:* Richard Lyons' Second Pardon. Certified as a true copy by Mr. Petyt. [Delivered in to the Committee by Mr. Petyt this day. Com. Book.]

(*l*[1].) 22 Oct. Note showing that the pardons of Richard Lyons bear date 14 days after the Parliament ended. Appended to preceding.

(*m.*) 22 Oct. Extract from Rot. Pat. 51 Edw. III., m. 24. "Rex omnibus Ballivis . . . . xvi. die Martii. Per ipsum Regem." *Endorsed:* Richard Lyons' third Pardon. Certified as a true copy by Mr. Petyt. [Delivered in to the Committee by Mr. Petyt this day. Com. Book.]

(*n.*) 22 Oct. Extract from Rot. Pat. 1 Ric. II., mem. 7, No. 41. "Item le xxii. jour de Decembr. . . . . contre l'ordinance avant dite." *Endorsed:* Proceedings against Alice Perrers. [Delivered in to the Committee by Mr. Petyt this day.]

(*n*[1].) 22 Oct. Note on the case of Alice Perrers. Appended to preceding.

(*o.*) 22 Oct. Extracts from Rot. Parl. 51 Edw. III., 95. "Et fait a remembrer . . . . fait a ycelles"; *ib.* 96, "Item les Communes prieront . . . devant eux trouvez coupable." *Endorsed:* The case of Hugh Fastolf. Certified as true copies by Mr. Petyt. [Delivered in to the Committee by Mr. Petyt this day. Com. Book.]

(*o*[1].) 22 Oct. Note on case of Hugh Falstolf. Appended to preceding.

287. Oct. 6. D. Southampton *v.* Bishop of Lichfield.—Petition of Charles, Duke of Southampton. The late Sir Henry Wood, in 1671, in consideration of a marriage to be had between his daughter Mary and Petitioner, conveyed his estate to Trustees, of whom Respondent was one, in trust to allow her 450*l.* a year for maintenance till the age of twelve, and 550*l.* a year until seventeen or marriage. He confirmed this settlement by will, and made Respondent and Lady Chester (another of the Trustees) his executors in trust for Mary, to whom he gave his personal estate. The marriage took place on 29th June 1676, before Dr. Fell, late Bishop of Oxford. Petitioner's wife died on 15 Nov. 1680, and since her death Petitioner obtained a Decree against Respondent, Sir Cæsar Cranmer and others for Sir H. Wood's personal estate, which Decree was affirmed on 14 April last by their Lordships, who ordered Respondent to waive his privilege in the cause. Petitioner in Michaelmas term last brought his bill in Chancery against Respondent and Cranmer, the only surviving trustees, to have an execution of their trust of the real estate, but Respondent insists on his privilege, and thus keeps Petitioner out of his estate, which belongs to him for life. Prays for leave to proceed in Chancery to compel Respondent to answer. L. J., XIV. 517. [This Petition and the Respondent's answer were referred to the Committee for Privileges. L. J., XIV. 528. The proceedings in the Committee on 7 Nov. are thus recorded. Counsel called in. *Mr. Trevor* (for D. Southampton): There was an agreement between King Charles and Sir Henry Wood on the Duke's marriage with Sir Henry's daughter. Respondent and Craumer are trustees by the settlement. Respondent is called trustee in the deed, and is plainly a trustee. The marriage took effect after sixteen, for though the lady was married before, yet she lived till after that age. The Deed says they are to have the estate for their lives, and depends not on the contingency of having issue male. *Mr. Dormer* (for D. Southampton): The intent of the Deed was to make a present maintenance for the Duke and his Lady, and a provision for their issue, if they had any. The Duke, in his Lady's life, received the mesne profits without any obstruction. *Attorney-General* (for Respondent): If you judge this matter to be a trust, you go upon the merits of the cause, and then we can have no relief in Chancery. The Bishop is heir to Sir Henry Wood, is heir to his daughter, and has been in possession these ten years. Sir Henry has appointed by his Deed that if his daughter have no issue male, the Bishop shall have the estate. Sir Henry gave them a personal estate of 20,000*l.* There is no more ground to infer a trust in point of issue than if there had been no marriage. *Sir William Williams* (for Respondent): If you say he is only a trustee, and has no interest, there is an end of the Chancery suit. The will and settlement make but one conveyance. If the marriage take effect and the Lady have issue male, then the estate shall be in trust for the Duke and Duchess. We have been in possession ten years since the death of the Duchess, and have received the profits all this while and were never till now disturbed. The will directs the estate to the Duchess for her life, and the Deed gives it her as his heir. Whether the Lady have issue or no, she is to have an estate for life. *Mr. Trevor:* The decision of your Lordships is no judicial determination of the suit below. Counsel withdrew. Order of reference of 22 Oct. read. Standing Order of 12 Nov. 1685 read, concerning Peers having no Privilege as Trustees only. Ordered to report as in L. J., XIV. 546. (Priv. Book, 7 Nov.)]

Annexed:—

(*a.*) 14 Oct. Answer of Thomas, Lord Bishop of Coventry and Litchfield. There is no trust or interest in any of Sir Henry Wood's estate declared or made to Petitioner unless he have issue by his wife Mary. Sir Henry by his will, confirming the settlement, devised his estate in failure of such issue to Respondent (his only brother) for life, with remainder to his sons in tail, with remainder to Lady Chester (his sister) for life, etc. The Duke's marriage with Mary was not according to Sir Henry Wood's intentions expressly declared in the settlement and will, for that, by the procurement of the Duchess of Cleveland (the Duke's mother), Mary within two months after Sir Henry's death, being then but about seven years old, was taken from Lady Chester, her guardian and married to Petitioner, and afterwards re-married to him when about twelve years old, but both times without the consent of any of the trustees or of her guardian. By agreement with Sir Henry 2,000*l.* a year was to have been settled on Petitioner's behalf for a jointure of Mary in case of marriage, but as the marriage was surreptitiously

House of Lords MSS.

1690.

obtained, nothing on the Duke's part was thought fit to be performed. The Duke, during his wife's lifetime, had upwards of 20,000*l.* by her, without settling anything on her in return. Mary having died without issue, the real estate belonged to Respondent for life, and he has enjoyed it accordingly for ten years undisturbed. Prays that the Petition may be dismissed with costs, as vexatious. L. J., XIV. 528.

288. Oct. 6. Reddish *v.* Ewers (Privilege).—Petition of Edward Reddish. Petitioner was, on the settlement of their Majesties' family, sworn groom of their Majesties Ewry in Ordinary, and has duly pursued his duties. Many years ago, he was security for his father and brother in some debts, which he is unable to pay, the fear of which caused him to enter his certificate of his being their Majesties' servant in the Sheriff's Office. Being in waiting on their Majesties, and having a great charge of their Majesties' table linen in his hands, Petitioner was arrested on 22 September last at the suit of Thomas Ewers, of Richmond, Gent., and carried to Newgate, without leave first obtained from the Lord Steward of the Household or the Board of Greencloth, contrary to the privilege of their Majesties' servants. Prays to be discharged and that Ewers and others may be punished. L. J., XIV. 516. [On 9 Oct. Mr. Ewers and Mr. Tissard the Under-Sheriff were called in. *Mr. Ewers:* I employed Mr. Barnard, but I know nothing of the method. I gave him no particular directions. *Mr. Tissard:* There was a general writ of *utlegatum* against his body and goods, and I desired him to keep out of the way. I know nothing of this execution upon the mesne process. At the suit of Samuel Phaire 200*l.* laid on him. *Mr. Ward* (Counsel for Petitioner): Opens Mr. Reddish's case and says he was in May 1689 sworn a King's servant. On 22 Sept. last he was taken in execution by Ewers and Tissard. *Tissard*, asked if he was not Under-Sheriff then, says he was. *Mr. Barnard:* Knows not that he was King's servant. 1 Jac. I., c. 13. *Mr. Fordish* says he acquainted Mr. Barnard that he was the King's servant. The Statute read 1 Jac. I., c. 13. *Ordered* as in L. J., XIV. 519. Reddish was again arrested in Oct. 1691. *See* L. J., XIV. 630, 632.]

Annexed:—

(*a.*) 9 Oct. Petition of Thomas Ewer, Esq. Reddish, an apothecary, became bound about ten years since with others to Petitioner in a bond for payment of 100*l.* and interest. Reddish left his trade about two years since and absconded, and Petitioner, not knowing how to recover his debt, employed Mr. Barnard, an Attorney, to endeavour to get it paid, and now finds that Reddish is a menial servant to their Majesties. Petitioner was in no way privy to Barnard's proceedings, beyond giving him a general authority, as an Attorney, to manage the concern. He is sorry for having fallen under their Lordships' displeasure, and prays forgiveness. [Read this day, and Ewer ordered to be discharged. L. J., XIV. 519.]

(*b.*) 13 Oct. Petition of John Barnard. Petitioner having in Trinity Term last sued out a writ against Reddish at the suit of Ewer, the writ was inadvertently lately executed on Reddish, in breach of privilege, while Petitioner was absent on the Western Circuit. Petitioner is sorry for his offence and prays to be discharged. [Read this day, and Barnard reprimanded and discharged. L. J., XIV. 521.]

(*c.*) 21 Oct. Petition of Jacob Broad. Petitioner, when arresting Reddish, did not apprehend that he was their Majesties' servant, having found, on search that he was lately a prisoner for a debt of 400*l.* in the King's Bench, whence he had escaped and had been outlawed. Is sorry for having offended in ignorance and prays to be discharged, to prevent his family from being ruined and becoming chargeable on the parish. [Read this day, and Broad reprimanded and discharged. L. J., XIV. 527.]

289. Oct. 10. Pinmaking Bill.*—Amended draft of an Act for the better encouraging the Art of Pinmaking, and keeping and setting the poor Pinmakers to work. †[Whereas the Company of Pinmakers of England and Wales were first incorporated by a Charter of King James I., bearing date the 28th day of April, in the third year of his reign, which Charter was since confirmed by King Charles I. by Letters Patents under the Great Seal of England, bearing date the 4th day of August in the 18th year of his reign, and afterwards confirmed by Letters Patents of King Charles II., bearing date the 28th day of November in the 13th year of his reign;] And whereas the art of Pinmaking is much decayed of late years by the clandestine importation of foreign pins, to the damage of the King and Queen's Customs, as also by the abuses of covetous-minded men, and by the great increase of pinmakers, pins are not so well and sufficiently made; ‡[The Pinmakers have humbly addressed themselves to the King and Queen's Most Excellent Majesties, the Lords Spiritual and Temporal, and the Commons assembled in Parliament, as the only means to preserve and restore the Art of Pinmaking, and save them from the misery they live in, to pass this Act; therefore] Be it *therefore* Enacted, by the King and Queen's Most Excellent Majesties, by and with the advice and consent of the Lords Spiritual and Temporal and Commons in this present Parliament assembled, and by the authority of the same, That §[the said Charters or Letters Patents made and granted to the said Company of Pinmakers by their said Majesties' Royal predecessors King James I., King Charles I., and King Charles II. be and are hereby ratified and confirmed to the Master, Wardens, Assistants, and Commonalty of the Art or Mistery of Pinmakers, their successors and assigns for ever; And that they the said Master, Wardens, and Assistants and Commonalty, shall peaceably and quietly have and enjoy all and singular grants, liberties, privileges, franchises, and free customs and all other things at any time given or granted to the said Company of Pinmakers by whatsoever name or names they were called, or which they now have, or any of their predecessors have had, by virtue of any Charters or Letters Patents of any of their Majesties' most noble progenitors, or by any other lawful ways or means at any time heretofore have had, possessed, or enjoyed, in as large and ample manner and form as they or any of them ever had, might, should, or ought to enjoy the same, and as largely to have and enjoy the premises as if the same were and had been particularly and specially declared and expressed with the best and most clearest words and terms in the law to all intents and purposes, And also all such by-laws, ordinances, and constitutions as the said Company and their successors have made or shall hereafter make, not being repugnant to the laws and statutes of this Kingdom; And also all and every such contract and agreement as hath been made between William Killigrew, Esq., under his hand and seal, and the said Company

* The additions are shown by italics, and the omissions by square brackets.
† Here is noted in the margin to insert Clause A. *See* Annex (*a.*) below, No. 1.
‡ Here is noted in the margin to insert Clause B. *See* Annex (*a.*) below, No. 2.
§ Here is noted in the margin to insert Clause C. *See* Annex (*a.*) below, No. 3.

of Pinmakers under the seal of their Hall, and every clause, covenant and article therein contained for the terms therein mentioned, whereby the said William Killigrew is obliged to furnish the Pinmakers with wire at a price certain to rich and poor alike, and to take off the pins made of the same wire from the rich and poor at the same price: And that the said William Killigrew shall sell the said pins to all shop-keepers and retailers for the same price as he, the said William Killigrew shall pay to the Pinmakers, which sizes and prices are hereafter mentioned, viz.: Of the best sort: 2 lb. 4 oz., 10/; 2 lb. 8 oz., 10/5; 2 lb. 12 oz., 10/10; 3 lb., 11/2; 3 lb. 4 oz., 11/8; 3 lb. 8 oz., 12/; 3 lb. 12 oz., 12/6; of the second sort: 2 lb. 4 oz., 9/; 2 lb. 8 oz., 9/11; 2 lb. 12 oz., 10/4; 3 lb., 10/8; 3 lb. 4 oz., 11/2; 3 lb. 8 oz., 11/6; 3 lb. 12 oz., 12/. Of the third sort: 2 lb. 4 oz., 8/6; 2 lb. 8 oz., 9/9; 2 lb. 12 oz., 9/10; 3 lb., 10/2; 3 lb. 4 oz., 10/8; 3 lb. 8 oz., 11/; 3 lb. 12 oz., 11/6. Short whites, of the best: 1 lb., 8/2; 1 lb. 6 oz., 8/8; 1 lb. 10 oz., 9/; of the second sort: 1 lb., 7/8; 1 lb. 6 oz., 8/2; 1 lb. 10 oz., 9/6; of the third sort: 1 lb., 7/2; 1 lb. 6 oz., 7/8; 1 lb. 10 oz., 8/. Lilikins:—The best sort: 9/; the second sort: 8/6; the third sort: 8/. Middle Whites:—The best sort: 2 lb. 4 oz., 10/2; the second sort: 9/8; the third sort: 9/2. Double long whites, *alias* Cawkins:—Of the best sort: 3 lb. 8 oz., 12/4; of the second sort: 11/10; of the third sort: 11/4; 4 lb. of the best sort: 13/1; of the second sort: 12/7; of the third sort: 12/1. Packets:—Of the best sort: 9 oz., 16/8; 11 oz., 20/; 13 oz., £1 3*s.* 6*d.*; 16 oz., £1 8*s.* 10*d.*; 20 oz., £1 17*s.* 6*d.*; 24 oz., £2 7*s.* 2*d.*; of the second sort: 9 oz., 16/2; 11 oz., 19/6; 13 oz. £1 3*s.* 0*d.*; 16 oz., £1 8*s.* 2*d.*; 20 oz., £1 17*s.* 0*d.*; 24 oz., £2 6*s.* 6*d.*; of the third sort: 9 oz., 15/8; 11 oz., 19/; 13 oz., £1 2*s.* 6*d.*; 16 oz., £1 7*s.* 10*d*; 20 oz., £1 16*s.* 6*d.*; 24 oz., £2 6*s.* 0*d.* Spanish pins: 6 lb. of the best sort, 16/8; of the second sort, 16/2; of the third sort, 15/8; 7 lb. of the first sort, 19/; of the second sort, 18/6; of the third sort, 18/; 8 lb. of the first sort, £1 1*s.* 0*d.*; of the second sort, £1 0*s.* 6*d.*; of the third sort, £1 0*s.* 0*d.*].

And be it further enacted by the authority aforesaid, that from henceforth no foreign pins made out of the obeisance of their Majesties' dominions, be imported into this Kingdom of England, dominion of Wales, town of Berwick-upon-Tweed, Kingdom of Ireland, or any of their Majesties' foreign plantations, or any parts thereof, nor used within the same, or put to sale or exchanged for other wares, upon the pains, penalties, and forfeitures hereafter following (that is to say), Every such person or persons who shall import or bring any such foreign pins into this Kingdom of England, dominion of Wales, town of Berwick-upon-Tweed, Kingdom of Ireland, or any of their Majesties' foreign plantations, or any part thereof, or put the same to sale or exchange [them] *such pins* for any other wares, shall forfeit double the value of them in money, and the buyer or exchanger of the same, or *the person* in whose custody they shall be found, shall forfeit the said pins and the value *thereof* in money, the one-third part *of all such money to go* to the King and Queen's Majesties *and their heirs and successors'* one other third part to the informer, and the other third part to the poor of the parish where such offence shall be committed, the same to be sued for by action of debt, bill, plaint, or information, in any of their Majesties, Courts of Record at Westminster, or within the county, city, borough, or town corporate where such offence shall be committed, wherein no essoyn, protection, wager of law, or injunction shall be allowed; and that all licenses heretofore or hereafter granted, had or made to any person or persons, contrary to the form, effect, and true meaning of this present Act, shall from henceforth, by the authority aforesaid, be clearly void and of none effect.

And be it further enacted, by the authority aforesaid, that for the preventing of the importations of foreign pins, and the sale or exchange of them as aforesaid, upon complaint and information given to [the justice] *any justices of the* peace [or any or either of them], within the respective counties, cities, and towns corporate [at times reasonable] *where such offences shall be committed*, he or they are hereby authorized and required to issue forth his or their warrants to the constables of [their] *the said* respective counties, cities, and towns corporate, to enter *in the day-time, together with any one member of the said Company* and search for such foreign pins in the shops, warehouses, dwelling-houses, or other places of such person or persons as shall be suspected to have any foreign pins [within their respective counties, cities, and towns corporate], to seize the same, that they may be cut and destroyed, any Statute, Act, or ordinance to the contrary, in any wise notwithstanding; *and that all pins stuck in papers not having the mark of the said Corporation shall be taken to be foreign pins.*

And be it further enacted by the authority aforesaid, That no person or persons from and after forty days next ensuing the end of this present session of Parliament, shall make or cause to be made any sorts of pins whatsoever, unless he or they shall have first served as an apprentice in the aforesaid art of pinmaking during the space of seven years at the least, neither shall they retain, or set to work in the said art, any person or persons other than journeymen that have lawfully served in that art, and apprentices lawfully bound in the said trade or art, nor above the number of three apprentices at one time, nor those for any lesser time than seven years, upon pain to forfeit ten pounds for every month, as he or they shall continue offending contrary to the true meaning of this Act, to be [received] *recovered* to the uses and in manner and form aforesaid.

[And be it further enacted by the authority aforesaid that no person or persons from and after the said forty days shall retain or set on work in the said Art of Pinmaking any person or persons from out of their Majesties' realms and dominions of England, Scotland, and Ireland, upon pain to forfeit ten pounds for every month wherein such person or persons shall so offend contrary to the meaning of this Act, to be recovered to the uses and in manner aforesaid.]

Provided always that nothing in this Act shall extend to charge any person or persons lawfully exercising the said Art with any pain or forfeiture for setting or using his or their own natural son or sons to the making or working of pins in his or their own house and houses, so as every such son or sons be bound indenture of apprenticeship for the term of seven years at the least, which term shall not be to expire before he or they shall be of the full age of twenty-two years, anything [abovesaid] *herein contained* to the contrary notwithstanding. *Endorsed:* "The Pinmakers' Bill." [Read 1ª this day; Committed to a Select Committee on the 14th. L. J., XIV. 520, 522. Com. Book, Oct. 16, 21. Laid aside, after a first reading, in the Commons. C. J. X., 451, 453.

(*a*) 23 Oct. Paper, entitled "Additions and Alterations to the Act for better encouraging the art of Pinmaking and keeping and setting the poor pinmakers to work." *Four pages.* It contains the following proposed amendments:—

(1.) First portion of Preamble (marked A in margin), as follows:—"Whereas by Letters Patents under the Great Seal of England, bearing date the 28th day of April, in the third year of the reign of King James I. over England, etc., all and

House of Lords MSS.

1690.

every the pinners and pinmakers of the City of London, and all and every person and persons using and exercising the mystery, trade or art of Pinners, or making of pins within the said City of London, and their successors were incorporated by the name of Master, Wardens, Assistants and Commonalty of the art or mystery of Pinmakers of the City of London; and diverse powers, privileges, benefits and advantages were thereby granted to them and their successors; And whereas the said Letters Patents and the said matters therein or thereby mentioned or granted were afterwards allowed, approved and confirmed by other Letters Patents under the Great Seal of England, bearing date the 4th day of August in the sixteenth year of the reign of the said King James I.; and whereas by other Letters Patents under the Great Seal of England, bearing date the 20th day of August in the eleventh year of the reign of King Charles I., all and every the Pinners and pinmakers of the City of London, and all and every other person and persons using and exercising or which should use or exercise the mystery, trade or art of pinners or making of pins within the realm of England and dominion of Wales are incorporated by the name of Master, Wardens, Assistants and Commonalty of the Art or mystery of pinmakers of the City of London; And whereas by other Letters Patents under the Great Seal of England, bearing date the 28th day of November in the thirteenth year of the reign of King Charles II., the said Letters Patents granted by King James I. and King Charles I., and all the matters and things therein contained, were ratified and confirmed, and diverse other liberties, powers, authorities, jurisdictions, privileges, benefits, advantages and other things are granted unto the said Master, Wardens, Assistants and Commonalty of the art or mystery of pinmakers of the City of London."

(2.) Concluding portion of Preamble (marked B in margin) amended, as follows:—" And whereas certain Articles of agreement, bearing date the 18th day of July in the second year of the reign of their Majesties King William and Queen Mary, are made between William Killigrew, of the parish of St. Martin's-in-the-Fields in the County of Middlesex, Esq., of the one part, and the said Master, Wardens, Assistants and Commonalty of the art or mystery of Pinmakers of the City of London of the other part, whereby amongst other things the said William Killigrew is obliged to provide for and sell to the said Master, Wardens, Assistants and Commonalty and all others of the said Company sufficient wire for their trade at the rates and prices therein mentioned, and to buy and take of all pins which they shall make at the rates and prices therein mentioned, and to sell the same to shopkeepers, retailers or any other persons for the same rates and prices and no more, as by the said articles enrolled in the High Court of Chancery more at large may appear; And whereas the said Master, Wardens, Assistants and Commonalty of the art or mystery of Pinmakers of the City of London have made their humble application to this present Parliament that the said respective Letters Patents and the said Articles may be established, ratified and confirmed by the authority of Parliament." *

* Proposed to be inserted in lieu of the words (" The Pinmakers have humbly, etc.) with which the preamble in the original bill concludes.

(3.) Enacting clauses (marked C in margin) as follows:—"All and every the said Letters Patents, and all and every the grants, liberties, powers, authorities, jurisdictions, privileges, benefits, advantages, causes, matters and things in the said Letters Patents or every or any of them contained, be and are hereby ratified and confirmed, and are by the authority of the present Parliament established and made good and effectual in the law to all intents and purposes, subject nevertheless to the said Articles of Agreement and all the matters and things therein contained; And further also that the said Master, Wardens, Assistants and Commonalty of the art or mystery of Pinmakers of the City of London and their successors from henceforth for ever, shall have, hold, exercise and enjoy all and every the grants, liberties, powers, authorities, jurisdictions, privileges, benefits, advantages, causes, matters and things in the said Letters Patents and every or any of them contained, subject nevertheless to the said Articles of Agreement and all the matters and things therein contained. And be it further enacted by the authority aforesaid, That the said Articles of Agreement and all and every covenants, clauses, agreements, matters and things therein contained shall from henceforth during the term and space of one hundred years therein mentioned be good, valid and effectual in the law, and shall be performed and observed according to the tenor, purport and true intent and meaning of the same Articles." [The above three clauses are among the amendments made on 21 Oct. and reported this day. Com. Book 21 Oct.; L. J., XIV. 529.]

(*b.*) 23 Oct. List of Lord's Amendments in Committee. [Made 21 Oct. and reported this day. Com. Book 21 Oct., L. J., XIV. 529.]

290. Oct. 18. Sir J. Caldwell.—Petition of Sir James Caldwell, Bart., praying to be released from the King's Bench, and that his wife Susanna, and James Stone, the Attorney employed in the case, and Cornelius Johnson, Serjeant, may be brought to condign punishment. Adds to what is set out in the Journal, that Petitioner's wife had been persuaded to leave him and deny her marriage, and had tried to force Petitioner to take a sum of money to quit his right to her estate. L. J., XIV. 521.

Annexed:—

(*a.*) 25 Sept. 1690. Certificate, of date, of the Earl of Dorset, Lord Chamberlain of His Majesty's Household, referred to in preceding.

291. Oct. 18. Burchet *v.* Durdant.—Copy Writ of Error and Transcript of Record, brought in this day, with Tenor of Judgment, pronounced 15 Nov. 1690 (L. J., XIV. 554) affixed thereto. Complains of a Judgment of the Court of King's Bench, affirmed by the Court of Exchequer Chamber, establishing the Defendant, Maria Durdant, in the possession of certain lands in Cobham, Surrey, from which she had been ejected in 1682 by the Plaintiff, John Burchet. Defendant claimed possession as lessee of William, the grandson of Robert Durdant, deceased, who had held the property until his death in 1668, under the will of his kinsman Henry Wicks, Esq., of Shere, Surrey, Paymaster of His late Majesty's Works and Buildings, who died in 1662. Plaintiff claimed as heir of his father John, of Kingston-on-Thames, under a settlement made after the death of Robert Durdant. The proceedings set forth the Will of Henry Wicks, and also two settlements of 1 Jan. 1662 and 20 August 1668. [The Cause was first heard on 14 Nov. 1690. The *Attorney-General* (for Plaintiff): Recites the Will. Cites case of Chaloner *v.* Bower. *Sir W. Williams* (for Plaintiff) desires to be heard after. *Mr. Trevor* (for Defendant): The question is whether this fine has barred the Defendant. George Durdant had an estate tail by the words of the Will. *Mr. Ward* (for Defendant): The true question is, whether George Durdant took any estate by Robert. The word "heir" is a good description of it. He has given an estate to the heirs male of the body of Robert. Cites King *v.* Rumball, 2 Croke, Sunday's case, foll. 244. Counsel withdrew. A debate arose whether Sir W. Williams should be heard in reply. He was called in and heard in reply. (MS. Min. 14 Nov.)—On 15 Nov., the Speaker having reported, the House gave judgment affirming the judgment appealed from. The Judges, who had been ordered the previous day to attend, do not appear to have been heard. (MS. Min. 15 Nov.)

Annexed:—

(*a.*) 27 Oct. Petition of Mary Durdant, Widow. Prays that the writ may be discontinued and judgment affirmed, the writ, which was returnable on the first day of the Session, not having been brought in within the time limited by the Standing Order. *Endorsed:* "Judgment affirmed, pursuant to the Standing Orders of the House."

(*b.*) 28 Oct. Petition of John Burchett, Gent., Plaintiff. Prays that Petitioner's Errors may be received, and the affirmation of the Judgment set aside, and issue joined and the cause heard. L. J., XIV. 533.

(*c.*) 6 Nov. Petition of same, that a day may be appointed for hearing. L. J., XIV. 542.

292. Oct. 18. Barbot's Naturalisation Bill.—Draft of an Act for the naturalization of John Barbot and others. Identical with the Bill introduced on 21 Jan. 1689–90. (*See* 12th Report, Appendix, Part VI., No. **218**), except in omitting the following, vizt.:—

Paul Boyer, son of Matthew and Claire Boyer; born at Montpellier,
John Baudoin, son of John and Margaret Boudoin; born at Tours,
Joachim Goudet, son of John and Jane Goudet; born at Montagnac,
Peter Guénon, son of Stephen and Mary Guénon; born at Xaintes,
Elias Nezereau, Senr, son of Elias and Judith Nezereau; born at Rochell,
John de Cleves, son of [blank] and [blank] De Cleves; born at St. Quentin,
Elias Nezereau, Junr, son of David and Mary Nezereau; born at Rochell,
Anthony Beraud, son of Anthony and Margaret Beraud; born at Tours,
Peter l'Ernoult, son of Philipp and Antoinette l'Ernoult; born at Amiens,

and substituting, in place of the two last named, the following:—

Margaretta Beraud, daughter of [blank] and [blank] Du Four; born at Tours.
Jane l'Ernoult, daughter of John and Antoinette Lason; born at Valenciennes.

[Read 1^{a} this day. L. J., XIV. 523. Dropped, after a first reading, with the Session.]

293. Oct. 18. De La Chambre's Naturalization Act.—Amended draft of an Act for naturalizing of Francis De La Chambre and others. The persons named in the Bill are the following: Francis De la Chambre, son of Daniel and Mary De La Chambre, born at Rouen, in France; John Moller, son of Henry Moller and Christianna Kretzer, born at Amsterdam, in Holland; John Vandermersch, son of John Vandermersch and Angujeta Kops, his mother, an infant of about twelve years of age, born at Haarlem, in Holland, and *Charles Issac, son of Peter Issac and Catharina Issac, born at Maestricht.* [Read 1^a this day: Royal Assent 20 Dec. L. J., XIV. 523, 600. 2 and 3 W. & M., c. 22 in Long Calendar. The only Amendment by the Lords is to add the name of Issac. Com. Book. 13 Nov. The Commons added the name of Symon Beranger. C. J., X. 504.]

Annexed:—

(a.) 13 Nov. Certificate that Francis De la Chambre and John Moller received the Sacrament this day at the parish Church of St. Mary Aldermary, London. *Dated* 21 Oct. 1690. *Signed* by the Minister, Curate, and Parish Clerk. [Produced in Committee this day. Com. Book.]

(b.) 13 Nov. Certificate that Carl Isaac is a Protestant, and received the Lord's Supper in the Protestant Lutheran late Parish Church of Trinity the Less, London, on 5 Oct. last. *Dated* 7 Oct. 1690. *Signed* by J. E. Edzard, Minister. [Read in Committee this day, and Isaac's name added to the Bill (Com. Book). He had been sworn at the Bar, in order to his being naturalized, on 23 Oct. (MS. Min.)]

(c.) Certificate that Godfrey Roosen, in the Parish of St. Bartholomew, Exchange, Merchant, received the Sacrament on 16 Nov. 1690 in the parish Church of St. Peter's, Cornhill. *Dated* 16 Nov. *Signed* by Will. Beveridge, Minister, and Richard Williams, Churchwarden. *Attested* by George Merttins and John Soutter.

(d.) Certificate that Francis Folchier, Minor Canon of the Cathedral Church of Norwich, received the Sacrament on 26 Oct. last. *Dated* 1 Nov. 1690. *Signed* Hen. Fairfax, Humfrey Prideaux, Prebendary, and Francis Stafford. [The name of Folchier does not appear in the Bill, but the certificate is appended thereto. He took the Oath at the Bar on 8 Nov. (MS. Min.)]

(e.) Certificate that Symond Beranger took the Sacrament this day in the parish Church of St. Mary Le Bow, London. *Dated* 1 Dec. 1689. *Signed* Tim. Puller, Minister, and John Lubbock, Churchwarden. *Attested* by Arthur Astley and Thomas Pennatt. *See* C. J., X. 504.

294. Oct. 20. Allen *v.* Fox.—Petition and appeal of John Allen, of London, Glass-Seller, and Mary, his wife. Thomas Fox left by will his leasehold houses near the Custom House, after the death of his wife Anne, to be divided equally between his children Stephen, the Petitioner Mary, and Anne, wife of Jonah Clarke, and also a legacy of 500*l.* to his grandson Thomas Fox when 24, and 25*l.* a year maintenance meanwhile, and 52*l.* a year annuity to one Sarah Nottingham, a poor widow. His wife and his son Stephen having died, Stephen's two sons, Thomas and Stephen, by Hester their mother and guardian, brought a Bill in Chancery against Petitioners and Jonah Clarke and wife for their father's third part of the rents and the 500*l.* and 25*l.* a year maintenance, and also for his customary part of the estate of Stephen Fox, the grandfather, he having been a freeman of London. Clarke and his wife also brought a Bill against Petitioners for their third part of the rents and an account of the residue of Anne Fox's estate, and Petitioners brought a Cross Bill against them, and the Court on 12 May, 34 Car. II., decreed an account for the estates of the grandfather and his wife according to both their wills. Hester's Bill being heard on 26 June of the next year, and the infants waiving the account of their customary part, it was decreed that they should have their third part, and that the 500*l.* should be secured and the 25*l.* maintenance paid to the infant Thomas by Petitioner Allen, as the executor of Anne Fox, the executrix of Thomas, deceased. Some time after, when Petitioners had paid Hester the third part of the rents and also 237*l.* for the infant's maintenance, Clarke and his wife began again to proceed on their decree, and obtained on 22 July last an Order for payment of 191*l.*, besides 400*l.* of the legacy out of Anne Fox's estate, which ought to be paid out of the estate of the grandfather. Prays that the decrees and orders may be reversed, and all proceedings stayed. *Signed* by John Allen; *Countersigned* by Charles Porter and Wm Whitelocke. [Reported specially this day from the Committee for Petitions for the House's direction. (L. J., XIV. 524. Pet. Book, 14 Oct.) The Appeal was heard and the decrees reversed on 18 Dec. (L. J., XIV. 596);* *Sir W. Whitelocke* and *Mr. Finch* appearing for Appellants, and *Sir Ambrose Phillipps* and *Mr. Trevor* for Respondents. The L. C. Baron was heard as to the custom of London, and stated that a man cannot waive it to his wife in London. MS. Min.]

Annexed:—

(*a.*) 5 Nov. Answer of Jonah Clarke and Ann, his wife. The Court of Chancery, on 7 May 1689, on hearing Appellants' exceptions to the Master's report, declared that the 500*l.* legacy could not affect the specific legacies of the leases of the houses, and on a rehearing on 4 Dec. 1689, Appellants were ordered to account for both estates, and, after deducting the said specific leases, to pay the 500*l.* to Thomas, the grandson, out of the securities taken by Anne for the same, and, if necessary, out of the overplus of Thomas' estate, the specific legacies being first deducted. Appellants' exceptions were again overruled on 22 July last. They are not prejudiced by the decrees and orders, being allowed the legacies and maintenance out of the estate of Anne, the executrix of Thomas, which they seek to have out of the estate of Thomas. The specific legacy ought to be first paid, and the sum should not be charged on the houses, which are not charged by Thomas' will. Pray that the Appeal may be dismissed with costs. *Signed* by Respondent Jonah; *Countersigned* Ambrose Phillipps. *Endorsed* as brought in this day.

(*b.*) 13 Dec. Petition of Appellants that the Respondent Hester may be ordered speedily to answer, and a short day appointed for hearing. L. J., XIV. 588.

(*c.*) 16 Dec. Answer of Stephen Fox, an infant of the age of 17 and under the age of 18, by Hester Fox, widow, his natural mother and guardian, and of the said Hester Fox and of Thomas Fox. The houses in question were worth 170*l.* a year, and the annual ground rent 50*l.* Set forth the wills of Thomas Fox and

* The MS. Min. of 19 Dec. have the following: "Words added to the Judgment in Allen v. Clarke, viz., ('and the 25*l.* per annum maintenance and the legacy unto Sarah Nottingham, widow')." These words appear in the Judgment of 18 Dec. L. J., XIV. 596.

his wife Anne, and the proceedings below. Respondents are not concerned in the allowances insisted on by Appellants. Pray that the Appeal may be dismissed with costs. *Signed* by Thomas and Hester Fox; *Countersigned* Sam. Buck. *Endorsed* as brought in this day.

295. Oct. 20. Phelips' Act.—Draft of an Act for the enabling the sale of the manor of Kempton and Kempton Park and other lands, late of Francis Phelips, Esq., deceased. [Read 1ª this day; Royal Assent 10 Nov. L. J., XIV. 524, 547. 2 & 3 W. and M., c. 2 in Long Calendar. For proceedings in Committee, *see* Com. Book, 23 Oct.]

Annexed:—

(*a.*) 23 Oct. Consent of Ann Phelips, widow of Francis Phelips, deceased, and of John Phelips, his brother, to the passing of the Bill. *Signed* Ann Phelips and J. Phelips. *Dated* 22 Oct. 1690. Attested by John Saer. [Produced before Committee this day. Com. Book.]

(*b.*) 23 Oct. Same of William Lightfoot, Gent., named in the Will of the late Francis Phelips. *Signed* Wm. Lightfoot. *Dated* 22 Oct. 1690. Attested by Richard Young. [Produced before Committee this day. Com. Book.]

(*c.*) 23 Oct. Same of Sir Thomas Fanshaw, of Jinkins, in the Parish of Barking, Essex, Knight. *Signed* T. Fanshaw. *Dated* 22 Oct. 1690. Attested by Matthew Skipp. [Produced before Committee this day. Com. Book.]

(*d.*) Statement of incumbrances and of the amount of the fee simple and trust estate. *Undated.*

296. Oct. 20. Hewley *v.* Wyvill.—Petition and Appeal of Dorothy Hewley. Petitioner's father, Christopher, a draper and citizen of York, on his marriage with Anne, youngest daughter of Sir William Caley, Bart., agreed to settle on her, in return for a portion of 700*l.*, a jointure of 130*l.* a year. In part performance of this agreement, Sir William paid 500*l.* towards the portion, and Christopher settled on his wife certain lands in Wistow of the yearly value of 20*l.* In 1670 Christopher purchased an inheritance of lands in Wigginton of the yearly value of 60*l.*, and nine days afterwards died, leaving a real estate of 130*l.* a year, and a personal estate of above 3,000*l.*, and two daughters, the Petitioner and her sister Anne. The Respondent, Francis Wyvill, having married his widow, suppressed the marriage articles of Christopher and set up a pretended will as made by him a few hours before his death, devising to his widow all his personal estate and also all his real estate for life, to the exclusion of Petitioner and her sister. Petitioner, on coming of age, brought an ejectment at law for a moiety of the lands descended to her, and obtained a judgment against her mother's pretended title. Respondents thereupon exhibited a bill in Chancery, and the Lord Commissioners decreed to them the lands during the lifetime of the Respondent, Anne, which Petitioners had recovered at law on a presumption that there were marriage articles settling a jointure of 130*l.* a year upon her. Appeals from this decree, the effect of which is totally to disinherit Petitioner and her sister. Prays that Respondents may be ordered to answer. *Signed* by Appellant; *Countersigned* Ambrose Phillipps. [Reported from the Committee for Petitions this day. (Pet. Book. L. J., XIV. 525.) An Order for witnesses was granted on 2 Dec. (MS. Min. No entry in L. J.) The Appeal was heard on 12 Dec. *Sir W. Williams* (for Appellant): The Appellant makes choice of Sir John Hewley for her guardian, and be delivers a declaration in ejectment. The special verdict finds there was no settlement upon them. We thought we were very well at law. Then a Bill was exhibited, and in Equity they decree him, notwithstanding the verdict at law. They say they believe there was a settlement, and decree the whole land in jointure, and leave the children without bread. The will was made in the afternoon, and the man died at night, and he was in a delirium two or three days. *Mr. Ward* (for Appellant): The Court of Chancery must presume that there were articles of 130*l.* a year. Sir John, who was concerned in the match (*sic*) Sir William stood upon 60*l.* a year. The verdict is plain, that the will passes no estate. It is a presumption of the Chancery to decree against the verdict. *Mr. Trevor* (for Respondent): We admit the verdict for Appellant. The decree, we think, was right. We say it was agreed that the land should be settled. We do not insist on a will to pass it in law. We say there were articles, and that Sir John Hewley had them. In equity she is to have this performed. He denies he had the articles. *Mr. Serjeant Belwood* (for Respondent): Reads Sir John's letter of 4 June 1672. Speaks as to the bigness of the estate. *Sir W. Williams*, in reply, speaks to the said letter. These are other articles. Reads indentures, &c. The Speaker then reported, and the decree was ordered to be reversed. (MS. Min. L. J., XIV. 587.)]

Annexed :—

(*a.*) 21 Nov. Answer and case of Francis Wyvill and Anne, his wife. Christopher in his will dated 7 Aug. 1670, recited that he had settled in his marriage articles, the jointure lands, to the value of 130*l.* a year, on the Respondent, Anne, his wife, and left her the whole of his personal estate, after payment of several legacies and debts, all of which have been duly discharged. The jointure lands were quietly enjoyed until Appellant was instigated to dispute the will, being the more encouraged to do so for that either she or some for her had the marriage articles and jointure deeds, or well knew that they were lost or that Respondents could not produce them. The Respondent, Anne, though not in any way bound to do so, gave up and secured to the Appellant and her sister 250*l.* apiece, to be paid them on reaching the age of 21, or marrying, and also maintained and educated them (until they were persuaded to leave her) for the cost of which only a very insufficient allowance has been decreed. The validity of Christopher's will has been proved in the Ecclesiastical Court, as also in a trial at Common Law. Pray that the Appeal may be dismissed. *Signed* by Respondents ; *Countersigned* by R. Belwood. *Endorsed* as brought in this day.

(*b.*) 24 Nov. Petition of Respondents for a day for hearing. L. J., XIV. 563.

297. Oct. 20. Rowe *v.* Gwynn.—William Cock, being seized of a moiety to himself and his heirs male of the manor of Maidencroft, leased it for 200 years to Luke Norton, Thomas Goodyear, and Henry Ward, after the death of himself and Elizabeth his wife, without issue male, and then suffered a common recovery to the use of himself and wife and heirs male, remainder to the right heirs of his father, John. Cock and his wife dying without male issue, the inheritance in fee descended to Edward Lucy, of whom Heath purchased the said moiety, taking the lease in his own name, and the inheritance in the names of trustees, one half in the names of Blanchard and Borough, and the rest in the names of others. Heath devised the lease to his sister, Jane Savage, and by his will directed his trustees to convey to such persons as his sister should name, in trust for her and her heirs. Blanchard and Borough conveyed their moiety accordingly to trustees named by her in trust for her for life, remainder to Charles Wharton and heirs, remainder in fee to Petitioner, and the trustees of the other moiety conveyed in trust for her and her heirs, and Jane Savage by will devised her estate to Wharton and heirs, remainder in fee to Petitioner. Wharton died without issue, and Petitioner brought his bill in Chancery against Dorcas Gwynn, executrix of Wharton, and Bees Gwynn, executrix of Jane Savage, for possession of the estate and an account of the profits. The Court decreed that if the other estate of Wharton were not sufficient to pay his debts, the lease should be assets for that purpose, and that Dorcas should enjoy the lands in the lease till an annuity given by Jane Savage's will to Henry Heath, and all Wharton's debts and costs of suit &c. were fully satisfied, and that afterwards one moiety of the lease should attend the inheritance for Petitioner's benefit, and the other be held by Dorcas Gwynn, who should receive the profits of the whole to her own use till the debts and annuity were satisfied. Petitioner brought a Bill of Review, but failed to have relief. Prays that the decree may be reversed, Petitioner being entitled not only to a moiety but the whole of Jane Savage's estate. *Signed* by Appellant; *Countersigned* Thos. Dyost and Robert Price. [Reported this day from the Committee for Petitions. L. J., XIV. 524; Pet. Book 14 Oct. The Cause was heard on 13 Nov. *Mr. Dyost* (for Appellant): The decree has given us only one fourth part. We claim under Mrs. Wharton and we conceive ourselves entitled to her full interest. The lease for years confounds this business. Charles Wharton, if he had been alive, would have had the full half. We desire what James Savage had, which Mr. Wharton should have had, if he had lived. *Mr. Finch* (for Appellant): We claim all that James Savage had. The decree has given us but a moiety. The land in question is the manor of Maidencroft. Case Goodyear and Clarke instanced; a lease to be a bar. *Solicitor-General* (for Respondent): The lease is taken for granted to be in being. The whole equity of the lease came to Francis Cleaver and Heath. Francis Heath has the term of the whole in him. *Mr. Trevor* (for Respondent): They have endeavoured to perplex the case by misinforming their Counsel and your Lordships. They made the Deed, 20 Nov. 1654. *Mr. Finch* replied. Counsel withdrew, and the Speaker having reported, the House dismissed the Appeal. (MS. Min. L. J., XIV. 551.)]

Annexed :—

(*a*.) 30 Oct. Answer of Dorcas Gwynn and Bees Gwynn. The Appeal mistakes the proceedings in Chancery. Heath was not entitled by the will of Jane Savage, as alleged, to both moieties of the inheritance and the whole term (which ought to attend it) after the death of Charles Wharton without issue. Neither Heath nor Savage ever had any interest in the inheritance, as was falsely suggested, further than as to one moiety. The E. Nottingham, on a rehearing, declared that the lease could not attend the inheritance further than Wharton had an inheritance, and his decree was affirmed by the late L. Chancellor on a Bill of Review. The other moiety of the inheritance is in Sir John Munson. Appellant has no right to relief. Prays that the Appeal, which is unfair and disingenuous, may be dismissed with exemplary costs. Signed by Respondents; *Countersigned* Richard Holford. *Endorsed* as brought in this day.

HOUSE OF LORDS MSS. — 1690.

298. Oct. 20. Beakbane *v.* Harford.—Petition of Thomas Beakbane. Thomas Nower, having had a lease in 1676 from Edward Hunsdon, and wife of certain tenements in Shoreditch for 51 years at a peppercorn rent for the first year, and 5*l.* a year afterwards, made improvements worth 32*l.* a year, and in 1678 assigned the lease to Petitioner. Hunsdon's widow afterwards married John Harford, to whom Petitioner duly paid the ground rent, but could get no receipts, Harford having an eye to the improvements and designing to get possession. In 1679 Harford, under pretence of arrears, delivered declarations in ejectment to the tenants, and obtained judgment by default. Petitioner then brought a Bill in Chancery, and Harford and his wife a Cross Bill; and a trial at law being had, by direction of the Master of the Rolls in 1683, as to whether the rent for Michaelmas 1679 had been paid or not, Petitioner obtained a verdict, which was confirmed on a new trial; and the Court in 1684 decreed to him possession. This decree was set aside on a re-hearing in 1685 by L. Chancellor Jeffreys, and Petitioner's Bill of review was subsequently dismissed on the ground that he had not paid costs or performed the decree complained of. Prays that this decree may be reversed. *Signed* by Appellant; *Countersigned* by W. Whitelocke and Nic. Archbolde. [Reported this day from the Committee for Petitions. (L. J., XIV. 524; Pet. Book 14 Oct.) The Appeal was heard on 17 Dec. *Mr. Munday* (for Respondent): We desire costs and that till the costs are paid, they may not go on. We have insisted in this case. *Sir William Thompson* (for Appellant): Opens the case. There are two verdicts, and this was a sufficient cause for the Chancery to proceed. *Sir Bartholomew Shower* (for Appellant): We had but 50*l.* in arrear. The Master of the Rolls directs two issues, and then they find this was paid. We exhibited our Bill and they a Cross-Bill, and then for us to be decreed to lose our whole estate. They never proceeded in a year or two after the verdict. We have proof for payment of this 50*l.* *Mr. Munday* (for Respondent): It received so public a detestation in Chancery, that none would appear for it. These verdicts were only to inform the conscience of the Chancery The Respondent by following this cause is undone. He married one Anne Hunsdon and she had an interest in some houses. We came to demand the rent; he would not pay it. The tenants were so poor and so distress could not eject. The Appellant comes and confesses judgment. We in our answer positively deny the payment. *Sir Thomas Powys* (for Respondent): This is a cause of such great iniquity that I wonder it is brought here. The lease is to re-enter if not paid in 14 days. There was a confederacy of swearers. Watts was convicted of perjury, and the decree made on their evidence was set aside. *Sir W. Thompson* replied. Counsel then withdrew and, the Speaker having reported, the decree was affirmed. (MS. Min. L. J., XIV. 595.)]

Annexed—

(*a*.) 1 Nov. Answer of John Harford and Ann his wife. The premises consisted of four small timber houses, worth 12*l.* a year. Nower covenanted to build five new houses at the cost of 150*l.*, instead of which he built six small houses of brick, fit only for very poor people, and often empty. Nower assigned his interest to one Hammond, who assigned to Appellant, formerly a turnkey in the King's Bench, who, finding the tenants unable to pay his rack-rents, designed to cause Respondents to re-enter for non-payment of his ground rent, and some years afterwards, with the help of false witnesses, to prove the ground rent paid and make Respondents account for the full rack-rents at which he had let the houses. With that design he forced Respondents to bring the ejectment, and suffered judgment against him by consent; and on execution being taken out, brought his Bill pretending he had paid the rent, and got one Watts, a person of ill-fame, and one Cornby, a common knight of the post, who had stood in the pillory at Rumford, to swear they had seen it paid. L. Jeffreys sent them to the Fleet for perjury, together with Appellant for suborning them. Pray that the Appeal may be dismissed with costs. *Signed* by Respondents, with their marks; *Countersigned* by James Mundy. *Endorsed* as brought in this day.

299. Oct. 20. Bromhall *v.* Johnson.—Petition and Appeal of Thomas Bromhall, infant, preferred by William Bromhall, his father and guardian. Petitioner's uncle, the late Thomas Bromhall, being seized in fee of the office of the Fleet, with 13 houses belonging thereto, and all the shops in Westminster Hall, worth 1,300*l.* a year, mortgaged the same to the value of 5,000*l.* On his death in 1678, the equity of redemption descended to Petitioner, his heir-at-law. Respondent, claiming under a pretended deed, brought a Bill in Chancery against the mortgagees and Petitioner, and on 4 July 1690 obtained a Decree. The deed was obtained by fraud and without valuable consideration, and was only intended as a security to Respondent for some small debts for which he was bound to the late Thomas, from which he has been indemnified, and for some small loans to him, which Petitioner is ready to repay. Prays that the Decree may be reversed. [Reported this day from the Committee for Petitions. (L. J., XIV. 524; Pet. Book 20 Oct.) The Appeal was heard on 8 Dec. The *Solicitor-General* (for Appellant): This is the particular care and charge of a Court of Equity, Appellant being an infant. If this should be an inheritance, it would be void. Cites case of *Swift v. Eyre*. *Sir Francis Winnington* (for Appellant): If the law be for my client, then we are in a safe case. Some words they may apply to run to the inheritance. Sir George Renell, 16 Car. II., I put it that the lease in law was void, so the estate in law remains in Thomas Bromhall. By the manner of granting it, that is void in law. If my ancestor will make a conveyance, the deed defective, yet a Court of Conscience cannot alter it. 6 Oct. 1677 is the [date of] the deed we petition against. He mortgages it for 2,000*l.*, and in May 1678 he mortgages it again for 1,500*l.* We agree to pay the 250*l.* *Sir Charles Porter* (for Respondent): I hope we shall maintain the decree. They confess Mr. Bromhall under his own hand declared the estate should go to my client after his death. The deed is very sufficiently attested and fully expressed, and it is so conveyed as in Equity it could be. *Mr. Finch* (for Respondent): It appears plainly that Johnson should have this Estate, and pursuant to this, he does grant it over to Johnson. They say they have cheated Col. Norwood in law. Mr. Mallow's mortgage cannot be much in this case. As to his going into the country, there is no proof of that. *Sir Francis Winnington* replies. Eliza Bromhall's deposition read. *John Clements* sworn to prove the deed was read at the hearing. This deed, says he, was produced at the hearing. This is (*illegible*) mortgage to creditors. *John Moore* sworn. Asked if he saw the deed in Court; by whom was it sealed, whether by Bromhall, and whether Johnson had notice of the deed. Reads depositions. *Mr. Finch* replies. Counsel having withdrawn, the Speaker reported and the House reversed the decree. (MS. Min. L. J., XIV. 582.)]

HOUSE OF LORDS MSS.

1690.

Annexed :—

(*a.*) 30 Oct. Answer of Henry Johnson. Appellant's uncle purchased in 1676 the inheritance of the office of Warden of the Fleet and the premises in question for 3,000*l.* and 800*l.* a year for 14 years from Henry Norwood, who thereupon granted the same by deed to John Cumerford for 500 years in trust to secure payment. Cumerford, by direction of Norwood and at the nomination of Bromhall, leased them to Respondent, and Norwood conveyed the inheritance to Bromhall. Bromhall having mortgaged them for 13,000*l.*, and intending them after his death for Respondent (having no children of his own), gave to Respondent by deed of 6 Oct. 1677 all the lease and term of years to come that Cumerford had leased to Respondent and all his own interest in the premises. The Court of Chancery decreed the redemption to Respondent. The deed was made fairly, without any fraud or surprise. Prays that the Appeal may be dismissed with costs. Signed by Respondent; *Countersigned* Charles Porter and H. Finch. *Endorsed* as brought in this day.

(*b.*) 30 Oct. Petition of Respondent. The Appeal is only brought to delay Respondent from the account decreed from Richard Manlove, the present possessor. Prays for an early day for hearing. L. J., XIV. 535.

(*c.*) 8 Nov. Petition of Respondent, that the Appeal may be dismissed for want of recognizance. L. J., XIV. 545.

(*d.*) 10 Nov. Petition of Appellant to be excused from putting in bail, being an infant, or that the same may be put in by some responsible friend, his guardian being in Shropshire. *Signed* Robert Price. L. J., XIV. 546.

(*e.*) 9 Dec. Petition of Respondent. Appellant's Counsel at the hearing yesterday alleged that Petitioner's deed in question was void in law, and prayed for a trial at law thereupon, and on the L. Chief Baron's reporting the matter to the House, their Lordships supposed that Respondent's Counsel had admitted that the deed was void, whereas they averred the contrary. Prays to be heard touching this matter and to by admitted to try the same at law. *Signed* by Respondent; *Countersigned* Thomas Brotherton. *Endorsed* as read this day and rejected. L. J., XIV. 583

(*f.*) 9 Dec. Copy of Deed referred to in preceding. Thos. Bromwall grants to his cousin the Respondent, in consideration of his furnishing William Howard with clothes to the value of 100*l.*, and of 296*l.* received from Respondent, and of Respondent's being bound in a bond for payment of 500*l.* and interest to Norwood, the lease and term of years to come, that Cumerford leased to Respondent, of the office of Warden of the Fleet and premises thereto belonging, and all Bromhall's estate and interest therein. *Certified* by Fr. Pemberton as a good deed, to carry the equitable estate and trust of of Bromhall to Respondent in the term. [Appended to preceding.]

(*g.*) 10 Feb. 1691–2. Petition of Appellant.—Since their Lordships' judgment, Appellant has tendered Respondent 396*l.*, but the latter has refused to accept it, and the Court below has ordered him interest and costs. Prays that the Court of Chancery may be directed to certify how much of this sum was really due, and that on payment thereof, without interest and costs, and Respondent's being indemnified from the bond, Respondent may be ordered to deliver up or assign the deed. L. J., XV. 69.

(*h.*) Affidavit of Thos. Bush, certifying to the debts mentioned in the deed of 6 Oct. 1677. *Sworn* 28 Jan. 3 W. & M.

300. Oct. 20. Mynn *v.* Thomas.—Amended* Petition and Appeal of [the Hononrable Robert Cecil, Esq., and Elizabeth his wife, relict and administratrix of Richard Hale, Esq., deceased, Rowland Mynn, Gent., and others] *Rowland Mynn, Administrator to the goods of Rose Hale (with her Will annexed), unadministered by Rowland Hale, son and executor of Rose Hale, Bernard Mynn and Dionis Davenant, widow.* In 1636, Rose Hale, widow, lent 1,300*l.* to Sir Samuel Thomas on a bond of 2,000*l.*, on which judgment was obtained in 1642. Sir Samuel died seized of a good estate in fee, which descended to the Respondent Anthony Thomas, who was liable to satisfy the said judgment. The debt being devised by will to the Petitioner Rowland Mynn and others, they endeavoured to extend the estate, but Anthony, to avoid payment, insisted for many years on a deed of settlement, whereby he claimed the estate as heir in tail and not as heir at law, and at length, when Petitioners had recovered a verdict against him and avoided the deed as fraudulent, he set up a title under a Statute acknowledged to one Dagnell, on which the estate had been extended in 1643 and which he for a small matter had bought in. The Court of Chancery set aside this Statute, and confirmed a Report finding that Thomas was overpaid in 1683 the sum of 4,020*l.*, but left Petitioners to proceed on the verdict instead of decreeing payment of what had been received over and above the Statute. The Conrt of Common Pleas, on Thomas bringing to it the money recovered on the judgment, would not allow Petitioners to proceed upon the extent, and the Court of Chancery subsequently refused to relieve them, so that Petitioners have barely 2,000*l.* for satisfying a debt of 1,300*l.* lent in 1636, which, with the interest, comes to above 10,000*l.* Appeal from the last decree of the Court of Chancery. *Signed* by Appellants; *Countersigned* Charles Porter and William Killingworth. [Reported this day from the Committee of Petitions. (L. J., XIV. 524; Pet. Book 14 Oct. 1690.) The Appeal was heard and dismissed on 12 Dec. (L. J., XIV. 588.) *Mr. Finch* (for Appellant): If the prior mortgage be satisfied, then the other shall come to the other mortgagee. We have not acknowledged satisfaction. He defends himself in Chancery against conscience, by keeping this Statute on foot. *Mr. Ward* (for Appellant): So long as this entail ought to be, we are kept out of it. Two very unjust things are set up against us; they are both discharged. If they come and say what is just, we will pay the debt and interest. *Sir Ambrose Phillipps* (for Respondent): There is a Statute to Dagnall. Because my client Thomas is in possession, they would have us account for interest or profit. The Court of Chancery never did it. *Sir Thomas Powys* (for Respondent): The decree is just; they receive their whole money and acknowledge satisfaction for it. We thought we should have been at quiet. The Chancery never gives more than the penalty (MS. Min.)]

---

* The amendment was to substitute the words in italics for those in square brackets.

Annexed:—

(*a*.) 29 Oct. Petition of Anthony Thomas, Respondent, for further time to answer. L. J., XIV. 534.

(*b*.) 6 Nov. Answer of Respondent.—Appellants, in the name of William Hale, having taken out execution on a verdict obtained against Respondent, the latter offered to pay 2,012*l*. into Court, being the whole sum received on the penalty of the bonds and costs on the judgment, but Hale refused to receive it. Respondent then obtained judgment in the Common Pleas for discharge of his lands from execution, and paid the sum into Court. The Appellant Mynn brought a Bill in Chancery for interest on the original debt of 1,300*l*. beyond the penalty of the security, and L. Chancellor Jeffreys on 18 Dec. 1685 dismissed the Bill, and the cause being reheard on 19 Nov. 1686, on the question of interest, the Court refused further relief. Appellants in 1686 received the 2,012*l*. out of the Court of Common Pleas, and are therefore satisfied their debt, as Hale has acknowledged. Mr. Cecil and his wife have no right to appeal, being only administrators of Richard and William Hale. It is against all law and equity that a plaintiff in a judgment should receive more than the penalty of his judgment. Prays that the Appeal may be dismissed with costs. *Signed* by Respondent; *Countersigned* by Ambrose Phillipps. *Endorsed* as brought in this day.

(*c*.) 25 Nov. Petition of Rowland Mynn, on behalf of himself and of Bernard Mynn, his brother, and of Dionis Davenant, widow, his sister. Prays that the Appeal may be amended by striking out the names of Cecil and his wife and adding those of his brother and sister, and that Respondent may have leave to amend his answer accordingly. L. J., XIV. 564.

(*d*.) 28 Nov. Petition of Rowland Mynn, Bernard Mynn, and Dionis Davenant for an early day for hearing. L. J., XIV. 569.

301. Oct. 21. Writ of Summons (L. Ward).—Writ of Summons, dated 6 Feb. to Edward Ward Chr. who took the Oaths this day. L. J., XIV. 526.

302. Oct. 21. Jones *v*. The King.—Petition and Appeal of Gaynor Jones, widow, and William Cross, Gent. Complain of a decree of the Court of Exchequer in 1688, as set forth in Appellant's former Petition of Appeal (*See* No. **78**) and also of a decree of 21 June 1690 upon a Bill of Review. Pray that the same may be reversed. *Signed* by Appellants; *Countersigned* William Williams and R. Britlum [Reported this day from the Committee for Petitions. (L. J., XIV. 526; Pet. Book 20 Oct.) The cause was heard on 20 Nov. (L. J., XIV. 560.) *Sir William Williams* (for Appellants): The case was tried in 1687 in Lancashire. The estate was found for the use of Popish priests in Lancashire. A Bill of Review was brought and the Court neither affirmed nor reversed the decree in Exchequer, but explained it and said the estate should be for some Protestant Ministers. The jury were mostly Papists. There is error in the Bill of Review; the Court ought to have affirmed or reversed the decree. *Mr. Finch* (for Appellants): The estate belonged to one Robert Charnock, and he conveyed to some for lives and then to Grace Bold, who levied a fine and settled it in Gaynor Jones for her children and to John Cross. In 1686 the Attorney-General exhibited an information against Gaynor Jones, that it was to go to Romish priests. There were 11 Papists on the jury and they found for the priests in Lancashire. *Attorney-*

General (for Respondent): The information was duly laid. They quarrel at the jury; I think they were fit to try this case. There is, they say, no law to bring these things to the King. We had a good decree and that was affirmed. *Solicitor-General* (for Respondent): The issue was quite properly directed. There is a difference between a void use and an unlawful use. The Speaker having reported, after debate it was agreed to call in Counsel again and ask them whether they could prove the jury and witnesses were Papists and whether the remainder men were parties to the suit. The decree was then affirmed. MS. Min. 20 Nov.]

Annexed:—

(*a*.) 30 Oct. Answer of Sir George Treby, Knt., their Majesties' Attorney-General. Charnock, a Romish priest, conveyed the lands to Grace Bold not for any good or valuable consideration, but for unlawful and superstitious uses. Grace Bold's pretended devise (if such there be) was made after the estate was forfeited and by the trustee for such unlawful uses. The jury were lawfully impanelled and returned, and Appellants should not be admitted to make allegations of their unfitness, not having challenged any of them at the time. The information was not prosecuted by Goden, nor had he any promise or grant, as alleged. Their Majesties have granted the lands by warrant to Sir Richard Standish, Sir Edward Chisenhall and other gentlemen of quality in the county, in trust for the augmentation of the vicarage of Leyland, which was very small and of low value. Prays that the Appeal may be dismissed. *Signed* George Treby. *Endorsed* as brought in this day.

(*b*.) 10 Nov. Petition of Appellants, praying their Lordships to accept the recognizance of James Evans, Gent., and postpone the hearing for a week, till Petitioners, who live at a great distance from London, can come to town. L. J., XIV. 546.

303. Oct. 21. Spiller *v*. Herbert.—Petition and Appeal of Henry Spiller, Esq. Sir Henry Spiller, Knt. Petitioner's late kinsman, being seized in fee of the manors of Kingsey and Tythropp and Haddenham and several other lands in the counties of Bucks and Oxon, of the yearly value of about 2,200*l*., settled the same in 1642 after his death to the use of Petitioner for his life, then to his first son in tail male and so to the tenth son of Petitioner's body, with divers remainders over, with a power of revocation in the case of the manor of Haddenham. In 1645 Sir Henry being taken prisoner by the then rebels and carried to Gloucester, Philip, then Earl of Pembroke, sent one Mr. Stephens to him to propose a marriage between James Herbert, the Earl's second son, and Jane, Sir Henry's granddaughter, upon which Sir Henry informed Stephens of the settlement, but told him that, if he might have his liberty to come to London, he would discourse with the Earl on the subject. Sir Henry finding, however, on discussing the matter, that the Earl would not come to any reasonable terms, refused to consent to the marriage and was sent prisoner to the Tower, and during his imprisonment, Jane was prevailed with to marry the said James—against Sir Henry's consent. In 1647 the Earl and James brought a Bill in Chancery against Sir Henry to compel performance of a pretended agreement for the marriage, binding Sir Henry to settle the three manors on James and his wife and heirs after his death and 600*l*. a year for their maintenance during his life, and though Sir Henry denied any such agreement and set forth the settlement, the Court decreed against him. In 1649 Sir Henry died without performing the decree, and the said James and his wife entered into the manors, and in 1652 sued Petitioner in Chancery setting forth the former decree. The Court ordered Petitioner to convey to James and his wife the manor of Haddenham, the same having been settled with a power of revocation, but declared as to the other two manors that they would be satisfied by a trial at law on the point of the marriage agreement and the alleged fraud in the conveyance thereof, but in 1662 the trial of this issue was ordered to be stayed till Petitioner had executed a conveyance of the manor of Haddenham, which he refusing to do, James and his wife have ever since received the profits of all the manors. Petitioner's Bill of Review was dismissed in 1662. Appeals against the decrees against Sir Henry and himself and the Order staying the said trial. Petitioner has lately returned from beyond seas, having been in much trouble. Prays that the original causes may be reheard on their merits, that Jane may be ordered to answer and that the decrees may be stayed and ultimately reversed. *Signed* by Appellant; *Countersigned* Charles Porter and Mainwaring Davies. [Referred this day to the Committee for Petitions. L. J., XIV. 527. On 29 Oct. Counsel were heard on the Petition before the Committee. *Sir Charles Porter* (for Appellant): No time occurs to any one to appeal to the House for relief, and we think we have a right to be heard. *Sir William Whitelocke* (for Lady Herbert): This Petition ought to be rejected. It is an Appeal from Decrees in 1647, 1652, and 1662, and he has never appealed since till now, and we cannot have the witnesses we might have had then. Your Lordships cannot do right if you receive this Petition, for here have been several settlements made since the decree and marriage, and Mr. Herbert is real purchaser of the estate, and if you inquire into the decree, you may do him wrong. *Sir Charles Porter:* Redemptions have been after a longer time than this. We have a good title at law. We have made our entries every five years, but the decree hinders us from trying at law. All my client's writings were burned in the Temple, so he could not well appeal sooner. The Committee then agreed to report the Petition as not fit to be received. (Pet. Book 29 Oct.) On report, the 30 Oct. the House ordered the Petition to be dismissed. (L. J., XIV. 538.)]

304. Oct. 22. Court of Chancery, &c. (Reform of Abuses) Bill.—Amended* draft of an Act for reforming divers abuses in the Court of Chancery and other Courts of Equity. Whereas by the Statute of Magna Charta it is provided that no freeman shall be taken and imprisoned or disseized of his freehold, liberties or free customs, or any otherways passed upon or condemned but by lawful judgment of his peers or by the law of the land; and whereas by the statute made in the fifteenth year of King Henry the Sixth, reciting that divers persons were vexed by writs of Subpœna purchased for matters determinable at Common Law, in subversion and impediment of the Common Law, it was enacted that no writ of Subpœna be granted from thenceforth till surety be found to satisfy the party grieved his damages and expenses if the matter of his bill were not made good; and whereas also by the Statute made in the fourth year of King Henry the Fourth it is recited that as well in pleas real as personal after judgment in the King's Court the parties were made to come sometimes before the King and sometimes before the King's Counsel to answer thereto anew, to the great impoverishment of the parties and in subversion of the Common Laws of the land; and it was thereby ordained and established that after

* The additions are shown by italics and the omissions by square brackets.

judgment given the parties and their heirs should be thereof in peace till the judgment undone by attaint or error, as had been used by the laws in the times of the said King's progenitors; it is, notwithstanding by long experience, manifest that the High Court of Chancery, proceeding by English Bill as a Court of Equity, not regarding the common laws of the Kingdom nor the fore-mentioned statutes, have, under pretences of equity, drawn into Chancery by English Bill almost all manner of causes tryable and determinable at Common Law and there for the greatest part (especially in causes of value) have proceeded upon English Bill and depositions of witnesses according to the course of the Civil Law, and by sentence and decree determined the same, whereby the subjects of this Kingdom have been and still are not only unreasonably vexed and impoverished with long, chargeable and ruinous suits, but deprived of their birth-right, their trials by jury, their witnesses being examined vivâ voce and proceeding and judgments concerning their estate and properties in the Common Law Courts, where they may have their remedies in case of wrong judgments by the laws provided, the common laws subverted and in danger of being totally destroyed and all men's estates and property brought to arbitrary determination. For remedy in the premises and for preserving the common laws of this Kingdom from being totally confounded and destroyed, Be it enacted by the King and Queen's most Excellent Majesties, by and with the advice and consent of the Lords Spiritual and Temporal and Commons in Parliament assembled, That the fore-mentioned Statutes and every of them shall be and are hereby confirmed and required to be duly observed and that for the future *no man shall sue in any Court of Equity by English Bill nor shall* the said Court of Chancery or the Court of Exchequer or any other Court of Equity or any of them, proceeding as a Court of English Bill, [shall not] proceed to decree or determine or give relief in any cause or matter properly suable or determinable or for which any action, suit or remedy properly lies at Common Law, but shall dismiss such suit or Bill and leave the parties to their remedy at Common Law.

And for avoiding such suits in Equity as are too often brought, upon untrue suggestions, only for delay and to keep men from recovery of their estates, debts or rights at common law, it having been found by experience that the Statute made in the third year of King James the First, intituled An Act to avoid unnecessary delays of execution, enacting that execution should not be stayed by Writ of Error unless the party that brought the Writ of Error became bound in the Court where the judgment is given to pay all damages, costs and charges if he did not prosecute his Writ with effect, hath been found to be a good and effectual law in that behalf; Be it therefore enacted by the authority aforesaid, That for the future no action or suit that is now depending or that shall be hereafter brought in any Common Law Court, shall be stayed or any person imprisoned or molested for or by reason of any injunction or order of any the said Courts of Equity, nor shall such injunction or order for staying of any such suit or action be of any force before good and sufficient security, by the recognizance of two or more good and sufficient sureties in the Court where such suit or action shall be so depending, shall be entered into and given to the person or persons whose suit is so to be stayed and in such sums of money as such Court shall judge sufficient for the satisfying all damages, costs, charges and expenses that the person or persons so stayed by the said injunction or order shall sustain or be at by reason of such suit in Equity, if so be the complainant have no just cause for such suit in Equity or shall not prosecute his suit there with effect or that the same be dismissed and

House of Lords MSS.

1690.

that no relief or suit shall be admitted in Equity to stay or avoid the proceeding upon such recognizance (except out of this Act and always provided that suits and injunctions or orders upon such Bills or suits in Equity as shall be brought only to have discovery by the defendant's answer, or by books or writing in his custody and to stay any suit at Common Law till such answer put in and if therein such book or writings, confessed in his custody, then till such books brought in, shall not be comprehended within this Act but be of the same force, though no security given, as they were before the making of this Act). [And that since the fore-mentioned Court of Equity have shown such little regard to the Common or Statute laws of this realm, some other way than what hath been must be provided.]

And whereas the Common Law Courts in Westminster Hall have in them established a power and jurisdiction to keep other Courts within their limits and jurisdictions, and to that intent are authorized to grant Prohibitions to such Courts as well of law as equity when they exceed their authority and encroach upon the laws; Be it enacted that it shall and may be lawful for every of the Common Law Courts in Westminster Hall to grant Prohibitions to the said Court of Chancery and Court of Exchequer and every of them, proceeding as a Court of Equity by English Bill, where they ought not, in like manner as hath been used or by the law they may do to other Courts of Equity.*

[And for the amendment of the law that gives no costs of suits upon Prohibitions], Be it further enacted that in all suits upon Prohibitions costs of suit shall be awarded to the *prosecutor*, plaintiff or defendant for whom the judgment shall be given, which shall be taxed as *is now practised in the several Courts respectively* in other cases.

And whereas mortgagees, plaintiffs in judgments, conusees of Statutes and Recognizances are (by the practice introduced in the said Courts of Equity) very often at great prejudice and inconvenience, being neither able to get principal or interest but forced to become bailiffs to the mortgagors to manage their estates and raise if they can their debts in length of time and by petty sums as the estate yieldeth it and subject to an equity of redemption and a suit and account in Chancery twenty or thirty years after they have been in possession, to their great vexation, charge and loss; for remedy whereof be it enacted, That where any man at the time of making this Act is in the real and actual seison or possession of any lands, tenements or hereditaments, by virtue of or under any mortgage thereof made or forfeited for non-payment or by virtue of any extent upon any judgment, Statute or recognizance, that the person or persons entitled to the equity or suit for redemption, his or their heirs, executors or assigns shall, if he or they will redeem, bring his or their suit for redemption within *two years* commencing from the *first* day of *March* next ensuing or else to be for ever foreclosed and barred; And that where any man hereafter by ejectment or otherwise recovers and thereupon or otherwise enters and be in the real and actual seison or possession of the estate or of the rents and profits thereof, the mortgagor defendant in such judgment or conusor, or any claiming by, from or under him or them having the equity or suit for redemption, if he or they will redeem, shall bring his or their suit for redemption within *two years* after such entry, seison or possession recovered or taken or be thereof debarred and precluded for ever, and that in such case where the mortgage or lands extended are redeemable after the mortgagee or extendor

* This clause was retained by the Committee by 11 votes to 2. *See* notes below.

or any under him have been in possession before any suit for redemption brought, the mortgagee or any extendor claiming under him shall not be compelled to account for the mean profits, but may detain the same in satisfaction for interest incurred since his being in possession or account for the same at his election; Provided always and except where the person having such equity of redemption is or shall be at the time of such entry possessed or seisin taken an infant, feme covert, of non sane memory, in prison or beyond the seas, and if in such case to have *one year* and no more after such his disability removed;

And be it further enacted that no trust or agreement concerning any lands, tenements or hereditaments made, declared or risen after the said *first day of May* shall be relieved in equity unless it be contained in writing and so alledged in the Bill exhibited for relief, unless possession hath been in the party for whom such trust shall be so alledged, and that no averment shall be hereafter admitted in any Court of Equity of any intention of the parties contrary to or to alter or change the sense or legal construction of any deed made after the said day.

Provided always that nothing in this Act shall extend to enable the Courts of Westminster Hall to grant Prohibitions to the Courts of Equity in the County Palatine of Durham; And be it further enacted that the Courts of Pleas there shall have power to grant Prohibitions to the Court of Equity there in cases tryable and determinable at Common Law.

[On 7 Oct., the House being moved that it be referred to all the Judges of England to draw a Bill to prevent the charges of of law in Chancery or regulating the Chancery, and that a Committee be appointed to draw a Bill upon three or four heads, made an order accordingly for the Judges to draw a Bill with all convenient speed to limit the power of the Court of Chancery and also to retrench the expenses and delays of such as sue in that Court, and to consider of the Statute 4 Hen. IV. c. 23. (MS. Min. L. J., XIV. 519.) On 14 Oct. the House appointed a Select Committee* to receive and peruse the Bills to be drawn by the Judges, viz., (1) for regulating the Court of Chancery, and (2) for regulating the other Courts in Westminster Hall of Common Law, the first of which was to be brought in to the Committee by the Judges on the 17th inst., and the second on the 28th inst. (MS. Min. L. J., XIV. 522.)—On 22 Oct. the above Bill was read 1[a], and on the 24th it was read 2[a] and committed to a Select Committee. (L. J., XIV. 529, 530, 539.) The Committee met first on 24 Oct., E. Bridgewater in the Chair, when they ordered that notice of their next meeting should be given to the Lords Commissioners for the Great Seal, the Barons of the Court of Exchequer, and the Chancellor of the Duchy, to enable them to be heard, if they pleased, on the Bill.—On 31 Oct., no one attending but the L. C. Baron and two Barons, the doorkeeper informed the Committee that he had served the notice on the Lords Commissioners and L. Willoughby. *L. C. Baron* [*Atkyns*] says that he and his brethren are willing to have the equity side in the Exchequer regulated. The Statutes mentioned in the preamble read. After making the first three amendments in the text above, the Committee heard *Sir Miles Cooke*, one of the Masters

* The proceedings, if any, of this Committee are not recorded; it differs in composition from the Select Committee appointed on the 24th, which was the one that considered the Bill. Comp. L. J., XIV. 522 and *ib.* 530, 539.

in Chancery, as to what he had to say against the Bill and particularly against the Prohibition mentioned in it. *Question:* Whether the Clause of Prohibition shall stand in the Bill? Contents, 11. Not-Contents, 2. Resolved in the *Affirmative*. The remaining amendments were then made and the Bill ordered to be reported as above amended.* (Com. Book Oct. 24, 31.)

3 Nov. The amendments being read, on report, the House disagreed to the first one, because the Lords Commissioners had not been heard, and then Ordered that notice should be given them as in L. J., XIV. 541. (MS. Min.)

6 Nov. The House being acquainted that the King, feeling himself much interested in the Bill, desired that his Counsel might be heard, ordered accordingly. (L. J., XIV. 542.)

7 Nov. Counsel called in for the Lords Commissioners, a chair being allowed for Sir W. Rawlinson, as infirm. *Sir W. Rawlinson* is heard to the several particulars in the Bill. The first enacting clause is to enact three Acts in force. I go to the matter of the Bill, and there are six new clauses in it. The first clause may be very mischievous to the subject. In an action of account that is triable at law; now if the Chancery should not proceed to this, it may be destructive to the trade of the Kingdom, and so all accounts touching Merchants will be ended. So for payment of portions, that is triable at law. If Equity did not meddle in this, the trustees might go away with the money. As for the second clause, [reads clause] this refers to the grant of injunctions by the Court of Equity until they have given security in the Courts of Law. This, in point of reason, is a *non sequitur*. The Chancery orders the money into Court, and I think it is good security, and so far the Chancery provides. That that is required is a greater importance. This, I take to be a bar of all proceedings in Chancery. He is to give security before the Court of Common Law with two sureties, and so the party is to come to town, 100 miles or more, for this. The Chancery has provided so far as to secure the surety. The next clause is the greatest moment in the Bill. [Reads clause.] The Judges have power to prohibit inferior Courts, and in the Courts of the Marches of Wales. That ever they had any jurisdiction of the Court of Chancery, that I never read of. Taking it for granted they have no such power, it will be fit for your Lordships well to consider how far it is fit to be done. There is an Appeal from Chancery to this House, but for this, whether you can control what they shall do, here is no provision. How far His Majesty will think fit that the Judges shall control his Majesty's Court of Conscience and Justices I cannot determine. He recites Mr. Howard's case. The L. Nottingham's decree was confirmed contrary to the Justices' opinions.† Now if this clause had been then, there must have been a Prohibition. And then if the Prohibition be not obeyed, the Commissioners, or so many of them as can be got, must be sent to the prison of King's Bench or some other prison with the Great Seal. Suppose this clause were passed, in what manner are the Judges to exercise this jurisdiction? Will they grant a prohibition before they hear his Equity? As to the last clause, in reference to trusts, all this we observe and take

---

* *See* text above and Annex (*a.*) below.

† *See Howard* v. *D. Norfolk*, in Freeman, pp. 71–7 and p. 80; 3 Cha. Ca. 1 to 54, and 2 Swanston, 454. C. Baron Atkyns contrasts L. Nottingham's conduct in this respect unfavourably with that of L. Keeper Bridgeman in the case of *Fry* v. *Porter*. *See* his *Inquiry into the jurisdiction of Chancery in Cases of Equity*, 1695, p. 29.

care in. If I purchase an estate in reversion, but [by] this clause you are shut out, if I had not the possession. *Sir Ambrose Phillipps:* We were ordered to attend. I move we may have a copy of the Act and time to be heard, the King's prerogative being concerned and so others of the King's Counsel. *Mr. Ward* (for the Attorney-General): Desires time and to have a day appointed. The House then ordered King's Counsel to be heard on the 10th. (MS. Min.; L. J., XIV. 544.)

10 Nov. King's Counsel being called in, *Sir Ambrose Phillipps* recites the preamble of the Act. Three Acts are recited, and three Acts to be confirmed. No injunction granted until security at Common Law. Recites as to a mortgagor and mortgagee. If your Lordships think to set the time, it may do well. Counsel withdrew. A debate arose on the Order, whether it should be limited that the Counsel speak to the prerogative only? On Question, resolved in the affirmative. Counsel are called in and told they are constrained to speak only to the King's prerogative concerned. *Sir Ambrose Phillipps* goes on to speak. The Court of Equity is as ancient as the Common Law. *Mr. Trevor:* This is the first time that this Court was so charged. It was resolved in the reign of James I. that the Court of Chancery might proceed to grant Injunctions.* The complaints are so general that I can give no answer. They are reflections more than anything else. I suppose there is a title properly tryable at law. Ejectments may be so often that there is no end. This Bill may direct a particular issue, and then there will be an end. If this passes, a man cannot sue in that Court which is most for the benefit of the subject. Consider this in relation to the person that is complained against. There must be liberty of answering, and the equity must be tried. Matter of fraud is relievable in Equity, as in shifted Bargains. The defendant moves for a Prohibition and then the Court judges there is no equity. How shall this be tried, whether fraud or not? by a jury it must be done; this must be by a jury, and if they find no fraud, then it is determined. No Error in fact can be assigned upon a Writ of Error, but what is upon the Record. If Equity find there is a fraud, then they cannot relieve him, and then they must examine all over again in paper, with witnesses, and there it must be tried over again and he must run through three Courts. Judgments are as much security as mortgages are and then there can be no relief from the Common Law. Will it be a benefit to the subject that a cestui qui trust shall carry away the Estate? In the Bill there shall be no averment against a deed in writing. Here is a latitude let in for shifts, and though he be dead, yet there will arise others. It is required that none shall have an Injunction in Equity before security in the Court from which it comes. A man's Equity is his defence, and if deprived of this, a man will be at the mercy of any to be cheated. This will be a very great hardship. *Sir William Williams:* I do not find this Bill totally against the Chancery. It is for reforming some encroachments of Chancery upon other Courts. I take the main matter to reform are the encroachments. If it should be convenient to be done, then the consideration is, how his prerogatives are concerned? The King entrusts them either to the Lord Chancellor or Lords Commissioners. There is little conveniency and no necessity in this Bill. The Bill tells you there are encroachments. The law then takes care of them. The Chancery, you well saw, will spread itself. What remedy does this Bill take for care of encroachments? Trust or no trust is most commonly examined in Chancery, and account or no account, fraud or not

---

* *See* Annex (*b.*) below.

House of Lords MSS.

1690.

fraud. The face of the deed is very clear. I cannot examine this in a Court of Law. Where then? It must be in Equity, and surely then this Bill is not fit to pass. Can the Common Law give relief on Bonds? Who is fitter to be trusted than this Court. There are many petty things that the law ought to be strengthened [in]. Who shall be judge between the Chancery and the Common Law? The Chancery undoubtedly have it. *Mr. Ward:* The King's prerogative is twofold. That which is best for the King's people is best for the prerogative. Counsel withdraw. *Ordered* that all the Judges and also the King's Serjeants be heard on the 12th. (MS. Min. L. J., XIV. 547, 549.)

12 Nov. The Serjeants being called in, *Serjeant Thompson* said he hoped to show that the Bill might be necessary. Before Hen. VI. he believed there were few instances of that Court taking notice of several causes. He takes notice of the several Acts recited in the Bill, and speaks to them particularly. Cites several cases, as a policy for a man's life. The Act recites that "Whereas the Chancery Courts have taken upon them." This matter of Prohibitions is ancient —1616, the dispute between Coke and Ellesmere.* It is not so extraordinary a thing as it is taken to be. There is an opinion that the Statute of Præmunire is in force. They withdraw. The Judges heard. *Holt, C. J.:* The Bill recites three Statutes. There has been an objection made against these Statutes as if the Chancery (*sic*); it is plain, say they, the Chancery never went against these Statutes. If they do imprison and take men's estates when they ought to relieve, it is contrary to Magna Charta. There are one or two cases wherein they do encroach. Suppose a man is near of kin to an intestate; he shall sue in the Ecclesiastical Court. It is every day's experience; they go into Chancery. What have they to do with this? If a decree be made in this case, they commit him and sequester his estate, and there is not one word in the Act for this. If this be not against Magna Charta, I know not what is. Secondly, for legacies out of a personal estate. He cannot be attached at Common Law, and yet they take it and sequester. Statute 4 Hen. IV. There shall be, &c. (*sic*). Does not the Chancery every day ravel into verdicts and direct new trials? Some surmise: Is not this contrary to the Statute? But, say they, the Chancery is not mentioned in the Statute. It has been the opinion of many that the Stat. Hen. IV. did bind the Chancery. 23 Hen. VIII. (*sic*); this was written in Crompton's Jurisdiction of Courts.† Glanvil's case in King James' time.‡ They cite an opinion in King James' time. 15 Hen. VI., fol. 4. As to Prohibitions, they have endeavoured to give some objections to this. It will hinder appeals to your Lordships. This is strange. Why should it be thought unreasonable for us to grant a Prohibition? We desire only a Prohibition where there is no Equity. Why may not the Judges of the law be trusted with the law. As to redemption of mortgages, why should a man that has a just debt complain? *Pollexfen, C. J.:* I will speak a few words because of what has been spoken to the King's prerogative. What has been objected to, the Judges of the Common Law by their oaths are bound to do this. We shall be careful to secure the King's prerogative. We are for it and not equity. There is nothing in this Bill against any Court of Equity. The law is the rule of right and wrong. As to the Bill, I wonder to hear any Counsel say that this is the first time that he has

* *See* 2 Swanston 24 *note* and authorities there cited.

† *See* Crompton, fol. 67, quoted by Atkyns *ut supra*, p. 46.

‡ *See Courtney* v. *Glanvil*, 12 Jac. Croke 343, 1 Rolles' Rep. 111 and Moore's Rep. 838.

heard this Bill is contrary to Magna Charta. As to 4 Hen. IV. they say that does not concern the Chancery. [Speaks to] Glanvil's case in Moore and Cary's Reports. It is not in the King's power to set up a Court of Equity. This is plain in all the books. Notwithstanding these Statutes, they have proceeded in Chancery. The Provisos are just and reasonable in this Bill. Deeds are the great and only security a man has. *Atkyns, C. B.:* In *Fry* v. *Porter* the L. Keeper Bridgeman said, "If I were of another opinion, yet I would be bound by the opinion of the judges."* As to the station I am in, the King is concerned one way or other in almost every case, and whether you will grant [it or not], Prohibitions lie to the Court in the King's concernment as in other Courts. *Dolben, J.:* This is not our concern but the public's. We cannot get one farthing by it. *Ordered* that the rest of the Judges be heard on the 14th (MS. Min. 12 Nov.; L. J., XIV. 550).

14 Nov. The Judges were further heard. *Dolben, J.:* I agree to what the Judges have said before me. I am of the same opinion with them. This Bill will give great ease to the people of England. They say, the Chancery is not within Magna Charta. There was no such Court at the time of Magna Charta. 22 Hen. IV. Case put whether the Chancery could grant [Prohibitions]. The Stat. Hen. IV. is in force; the enacting part is only what they ought to do. *Nevill, B.:* There is so much said by my brethren that there is very little more to be said. It is a law in being. This is a very good Bill, and will establish us in our estates and rights. *Gregory, J.:* This Bill is a good Bill. [Hob]art's Reports, 342, cites several cases. *Lechmere, B.:* I have not anything more to offer. I look upon it as a temperate, moderate thing. *Rokeby, J.:* I think it a very good Bill. *Eyre, J.:* The matter has been so fully spoken to, that I meant to answer what the Lord Commissioner Rawlinson said. I approve of the Bill as a very good Bill. I say the three Acts do all extend to the Court of Chancery, and have been violated by many in that Court. Rolle's Abridgment, Title "Chancery," Coke 3rd Inst. What answers does the Lord Commissioner give as to the first Statute? Says he, the Chancery does nothing against this Act. Speaks to all the heads mentioned by Lord Commissioner Rawlinson. My opinion is, there is nothing in this Bill that tends to lessen the King's prerogative in a Court of Equity. Frauds have always been the subject of equity. *Ventris, J.:* The Bill [contains] three charges. First, there is the charge of the breach of three Statutes, one of which is Magna Charta. Lamb[ard's]† Jurisdiction of Courts. No jurisdiction upon English Bill till after Edward VI. As to [the Statute of] Hen. IV. I refer to what has been said before. Coke, 20 Art. His hand is subscribed to this Article.‡ *Ordered* to be reported to the Speaker. *Question*, Whether this report shall be made to-morrow next after the Earl of Bath's business? Resolved in the *Negative*. Contents, 12; Not-Contents, 13. Tellers, E. Br[idgewater], L. North. *Ordered*, to report on Monday and Lords to be summoned and Judges to attend. (MS. Min. 14 Nov.; L. J., XIV. 553.)

---

* *See* 1 Mod. Rep. 313 (quoted by Atkyns *ut supra*, p. 29) and 1 Vernon, 77.

† Apparently a reference to Lambard's Archeion.

‡ Evidently a reference to Art. 20 of the Articles against Cardinal Wolsey, subscribed by the then L. Chancellor, Sir Thomas More, and given in 4 Coke Inst., fol. 92, viz.: "Also the said Lord Cardinal hath examined divers and many matters in the Chancery, after judgment thereof given at the Common law, in subversion of your laws, and made some persons restore again to the other party condemned that, that they had in execution by virtue of the judgment at the Common law." *See also The Jurisdiction of the Court of Chancery vindicated* (1 Reports in Chancery, App., p. 77), where the argument drawn from More's signature is attempted to be explained away.

17 Nov. The Speaker reported what was said by Sir W. Rawlinson and the other Counsel upon the Bill. House moved in debate that the Reasons given, 14 Jac. I., be read.* The Reasons were read from the Rolls Chapel. *Moved* to recommit the Bill and to have some of Chancery and some of Common Law to attend the Committee. *Moved*, that the Bill be recommitted to a Committee of the whole House. *Ordered* accordingly. House adjourned during pleasure. House resumed. House adjourned during pleasure. E. Fauconberg in the Chair. The Bill was read through. The title read and postponed. The preamble read and postponed. *Ordered* to report progress. (MS. Min. 17 Nov.; L. J., XIV. 556.)

19 Nov. Order read for putting the House into Committee on the Bill. *Question*, Whether the House shall be put into a Committee on the Bill tomorrow? Resolved in the *Negative*. *Ordered* that the House be put into Committee on the 21st inst., and the Judges to attend. (MS. Min. 19 Nov.; L. J., XIV. 558.)

21 Nov. House adjourned during pleasure. E. Fauconberg in the Chair. The first enacting clause read. A Lord desired the Judges may be asked whether this clause has any retrospect upon what the Commissioners have done? *Pollexfen, C. J.:* If they are suable for anything before this Act, they are liable. *Atkyns, C. B.:* This does not expose them more than before. We do not oppose a clause of indemnity. A clause, drawn by the Judges, is read. *Proposed* to ask the Judges whether, if there be matter of equity as well as law, the Court of Equity can relieve after judgment given? Whether the Judges at Common Law can consider the Equity? And, if so, whether there be any relief in Equity. *Atkyns, C.B.:* I take it they cannot. *Pollexfen, C.B.:* We must go according to the form of law, and there ought to be sure relief. Cites Glanville's case. After long debate, the clause was read as amended by the Judges, and with the amendments by the Committee formerly. An account [required of] how this Statute 4 Hen. IV. can take notice of the Chancery. *Holt, C. J.* heard to it. A clause offered by L. Cornwallis read. Proposed to ask the Judges why these exceptions should not be in the Bill? *Holt, C. J.:* Reads the exceptions. We can relieve and do every day in the case. As for the latter part, I think it reasonable. Proposed to leave the L. Cornwallis' clause to be considered by the Judges. The Judges asked what they say to this clause? *Holt, C. J.:* I do not see this clause is absolutely necessary. *Atkyns, C.B.:* I do not see any one of these things needful. A clause drawn by the Judges, is read.† *Question*, Whether the word ("demurrer") shall be added to this clause? Resolved in the *Affirmative*. The clause was read with the word ("demurrer") in it. *Question*, Whether this clause shall be part of the Bill? Resolved in the *Affirmative*. House resumed. E. Fauconberg then reported progress, and the House ordered to go into Committee again the next day. (MS. Min. 21 Nov.; L. J., XIV. 561.)

22 Nov. House adjourned during pleasure on the Bill. E. Fauconberg in the Chair. The first enacting postponed clause read as amended, and the clause with the words ("or obtained by demurrer") in it, read. The declaratory clause postponed. The words ("or by default") agreed to be inserted in the clause last night agreed on. *Proposed* to ask the Judges whether fraud is not the thing properly cognizable in Chancery? That a clause be drawn that the King's Bench may give remedy upon a fraud by vacating the deed, or otherwise. Clause drawn by the Judges, brought in and read. *Proposed* to put the Question, Whether this clause shall be part of the Bill? The clause read again. *Question*,

* *See* Annex (*b.*) below. † *See* Annex (*c.*) below.

Whether this clause shall be part of the Bill? Resolved in the *Affirmative.** *Agreed*, to go next on a clause for frauds in equity the next day of meeting. House resumed. E. Fauconberg then reported progress, and the House ordered to go again into Committee on the 24th. (M.S. Min. 22 Nov.; L. J., XIV. 562.)

24 Nov. House adjourned during pleasure on the Bill. E. Fauconberg in the Chair. The first enacting clause read, with the amendments, and two clauses agreed to. *Proposed*, that if one is deceived, and a verdict pass for one, and then a written pardon or a *Noli Prosequi* pass, it may be of disadvantage to the party. *Holt, C. J.:* The objection is strong and may be amended by some words in the Bill. Some words were added by the Judges to the Committee. *Moved*, that the Lords Commissioners, Sir W. Rawlinson and Sir Anthony Keck do attend this House tomorrow. Notice to be given to them to that effect House resumed. *Ordered* that the House go again into Committee. tomorrow. (MS. Min. 24 Nov.; L. J., XIV. 564.)

25 Nov. The House postponed going into Committee till the next day. (MS. Min. 25 Nov.; L. J., XIV. 565.)

26 Nov. House in Committee on the Bill. E. Fauconberg in the Chair. *Moved*, That the Lords Commissioners may have chairs. Two chairs were brought in, one at one end of the table, and the other at the other end. The second clause agreed to is read. The Lords Commissioners Sir W. Rawlinson and Sir A. Keck are brought in, and told the Lords had sent for them for their evidence. The clause is read again. The first enacting clause is read with the amendments agreed on, and the two clauses are ordered to be part of the Bill. The debate left off was whether this was not leaving the judgment of equity in the jury or in the Judges of the Courts of Common Law? *Proposed* to ask the Lord Commissioner Rawlinson how this is consistent, to distinguish between a criminal fraud and an equitable fraud? *Sir W. Rawlinson:* Recites the paragraphs of the Bill. I take it to be a qualification of the first clauses in the Bill. This takes it for granted as if the Statute of Hen. IV. did extend to Chancery. If the matter be duly weighed, the Chancery was not directly meant in that Statute. The Chancery is a very ancient Court of Equity. I find in Hobart's Reports, *Martin* v. *Marshal and Key*,† that Lord Hobart was of opinion that the Court of Chancery is a fundamental court. Equity is justice, and it is as necessary a Court of Justice as any Court in Westminster Hall. There are a hundred instances where equity arises after judgment given. The proceeding formerly was by several actions, but they have now found out a way by *ejectione firmæ*. They are tried now upon a feigned lessee and a casual ejector, and if the tenant acquaints the landlord, then the landlord is ousted. Now by the Statute Hen. IV. the party ought to be at peace, until attaint or Writ of Error, and so, *pro* and *con*, they have done it eleven times over. In Lady Ivery's case there were thirteen or fourteen trials. This has entitled us to a new equity in Chancery. There are Bills of peace in Chancery: that does not arise till after verdict. There are several sorts of frauds. *Sir A. Keck:* I am unprepared for this. I look upon that Bill to be a perfect shutting up of Chancery, and so as unnecessary a Court as that of the Common Law (*sic*). Two matters have occurred to me. The first is that of giving life to the Statute of Henry IV. The practice has been contrary to it ever since, and the law having run thus long, I thought it would have drowned the whole. The second is that of the

* *See* Annex (*d*.) below. † Hobart's Rep., p. 63.

House of Lords MSS.

1690.

Prohibition. I took this to be unreasonable. There may have been an appetite of Courts to gain one on the other. This is too well known. The Chancery is a Court by prescription. 14 K. J. it is decreed to avoid the ruin of the people. The question is whether that course can be inverted when all mankind have framed their concerns according to the practice of the Court of Chancery. If you have a bailee, and he received 1,000*l.* and the bailiff dies, it is lost unless the Chancery relieve you; the Judges cannot, unless they forfeit their oaths. A man has bonds; his house is burnt and his bonds are lost. He sues in Chancery. No; say the Judges, this the King's Bench has prohibited to other inferior Courts. They have granted a Prohibition in this case. A purchaser buys land with a rent reserved and loses his deed. He resorts to a Court of Equity and sets this forth. A Court will say, God forbid you should lose the estate. No, but Common Law can do this. There are frauds of several sorts. Barney of Norfolk; 70,000*l.* bargains drawn into in one year. These frauds cannot be examined at Common Law. Lord Ardglasse's case; Deny Muschamp and H. Muschamp* *Holt, C. J.* heard to the point instanced by Sir W. Rawlinson. Upon the point last mentioned, of trustees setting up the right for want of deeds of issue to the father, I would anybody should make such an instance. *Sir W. Rawlinson* heard to answer this. *Pollexfen, C. J.:* This comes to the last clause of the Bill. The law takes no notice of the trust. *Atkyns, C. B.:* I think he has no remedy in this case, if this Bill pass. *Eyre, J.:* He has relief, though this Bill pass. *Ventris, J.* heard. Words proposed to be added to the clause ("or upon a verdict in a case wherein there is matter of equity").† *Sir W. Rawlinson* and *Sir A. Keck* withdraw. House resumed. E. Fauconberg reports progress. *Ordered*, that the House be put again in Committee on the 29th, and Sir W. Rawlinson and Sir A. Keck to attend. (MS. Min. 26 Nov.; L. J., XIV. 567.)

29 Nov. House moved to appoint a Committee to draw a Bill for regulating Chancery, and that the three Chief Justices and Sir W. Rawlinson and Sir A. Keck attend the Committee. (MS. Min. 29 Nov.; L. J., XIV. 572.)

This Select Committee, E. Rochester Chairman, sat on Dec. 2, 6, and 16 (having been revived on Dec. 6 and again on Dec. 13, L. J., XIV. 581, 588). Their proceedings are thus recorded. On 2 Dec., *Sir W. Rawlinson* acquainted the Committee that Sir A. Keck was unable to attend at that sitting, having had a bad night. 1st Proposition (marked in margin 'Agreed.'): To prevent the unnecessary delays and lengths of suits depending in Chancery in reference to the whole proceedings in the cause. 2nd Proposition (marked in margin "Agreed"): To regulate the extravagant fees to the officers and the expenses in the suit. *Proposed* that no Commission be granted for examination of witnesses but which both parties shall join in. That no Commission shall be proceeded in but within a limited time. How to make the Register's Minutes taken in Court more plain. To restrain the Chancery from giving relief after judgment in cases not properly equitable after judgment. That no cases shall be relieved in Chancery after judgment in the Courts of Law, but where two of the Judges, if there have been two in the case, being summoned into Chancery, shall

* *See E. Ardglasse* v. *Muschamp*, 22 April 1684, reported in 1 Vernon, 237, 238. The Defendant Henry Muschamp and his cousin Deny Muschamp obtained the grant of a rentcharge from the Plaintiff, which was set aside by the Lord Keeper for fraud.

† *See* Annex (*f.*) below.

agree that they are fit to be relieved. Whether this may not be a proper expedient for the determining this matter; if not that they propose some other way. That the Lord Commissioner Rawlinson and the Judges meet and consider of some method to judge and determine what cases are fit to be relieved in Chancery and what not. That [marked in margin 'Agreed'] the Lord Commissioner Rawlinson and Sir Anthony Keck be desired to consider of the proposition following, viz.: "That no cases shall be relieved in Chancery after judgment in the Courts of Law but where two of the Judges, if there have been two in the cause, being summoned into Chancery, shall agree that they are fit to be relieved;" And to return their opinion to the Committee on Saturday next, the 6th inst.—On 6 Dec. the L. Commissioners Rawlinson and Keck and the two Chief Justices and Mr. Justice Eyre are present. *Sir W. Rawlinson* acquaints the Committee that he and Sir A. Keck have considered the Proposition committed to them at the last meeting and find it utterly impracticable and that it will increase the charge of the subject. Half the judgments that come to Chancery for relief have never been by any Judge and many of them by Judges that may be dead or are removed. Many are by confession. *Sir A. Keck:* This gives the Judges a negative voice in Chancery, where they have no affirmative voice in the absence of the Chancery. The L. Nottingham gave judgment in the Duke of Norfolk's case contrary to the opinion of the three Chiefs, and your Lordships confirmed that judgment. He proposes that on rehearing on Bills of Review, Judges may be joined and have a voice with the Chancellor. *Holt, C. J.:* It is seldom effectual to have a rehearing before the same persons. I believe that what Sir Anthony Keck proposes in that particular may do very well. *Pollexfen, C. J.:* I do not see but that good may come out of this. I believe it may have some good effect. It is against all judicature to have the same Judges try the same cause again. If the Chancellor name the Judges, he will (as has ever been done) send for the Judges that he knows to be of his own opinion in the case in dispute. *Eyre, J.:* Sir Anthony Keck's expedient will answer what is desired in a great measure, if there be a number of Judges, such as five or six of the senior Judges, and they may hear the cause on all the proofs that have been in it. The Judges own the proposition referred to be impracticable. *Sir W. Rawlinson:* We always thought it improper for the same persons to rehear. *Sir A. Keck:* It is absolutely necessary that the Chancellor be joined with the Judges and that the Judges alone may not rehear. The Chief Justices propose that the Commissioners or Chancellor may be excluded at the rehearing, and that they may be present to give their reasons for the judgment they have given. Sir A. Keck proposes there may be a majority of judges at a rehearing, and that judgment may be by plurality of voices. *Agreed*, That in Bills of Review some of the Judges be joined with the Chancery, who are to rehear the cause upon all the proofs, and that there be such a number of Judges as may be superior in number to the Chancery. *Agreed*, That sufficient costs and damages be provided for in this Bill. *Ordered*, That the Lords Commissioners for the Great Seal of England and Sir Anthony Keck be desired to draw a Bill upon these heads following, and to present it to the Committee with all convenient speed. 1. To prevent the unnecessary delays and the length of suits depending in Chancery in reference to the whole proceedings in the cause. 2. To consider the fees to the officers and the expenses in the suit, and regulate them where they find them extravagant. 3. That in Bills of Review some of the Judges be joined with the Chancery, who are to rehear the Cause upon all the proofs, and that there be such a number of Judges as may be superior

House of Lords MSS.

1690.

in number to the Chancery. 4. That sufficient costs and damages be provided for in this Bill.—On 16 December* *Sir A. Keck* informed the Committee that the Lords Commissioners and himself had not yet met, but that he had drawn some clauses. The clauses are read. He proposes they may be seen by the Lords Commissioners. He is desired to show the clauses to the Lord Commissioners. *Sir W. Rawlinson* being present, two of his papers are now given him, and *Sir A. Keck* promises to send the rest to him to peruse, which when they have agreed and put in form they will present to the Committee. (Com. Book Dec. 2, 6, 16.) No further proceedings are recorded.]

Annexed :—

(*a*.) 3 Nov. 1690. Lords' Amendments to the Bill. [Made in Committee 31 Oct., and reported this day. Com. Book L. J., XIV. 541. They are embodied in the text above.]

(*b*.) 17 Nov. Order of King James I. and decree in Chancery for a Rule to be observed by the Chancellor in that Court, exemplified and enrolled for a perpetual Record there. 1616. *Subscribed:* Concordat cum Recordo et examinat. per me W. Grymes. *Endorsed* as read this day. Com. Book. [Printed *in extenso*, under the above title, as an appendix to Cary's Reports in Chancery, p. 115 *ad fin*. Ed. 1650.]

(*c*.) 22 Nov. Amended clause as follows :—" And for the better explaining the said Statute made in the 4th year of Henry the Fourth, It is hereby declared and enacted that the said Statute shall not be construed to extend to any Judgment confessed *or obtained upon Demurrer or by default*,† or to any Judgment otherwise obtained where there is or shall be any deed of defeazance or agreement in writing signed by the party who shall obtain such judgment for avoiding the same." [Amended by adding the words in italics and then added to the Bill this day. MS. Min. Nov. 21, 22.]

(*d*.) 22 Nov. Amended clause as follows :—" And be it further enacted by the authority aforesaid, That where any person shall be convicted by verdict [if any] *or otherwise in any action which that party* [illegible] *his heirs, executors or administrators are hereby enabled to bring in any* of their Majesties' Courts of Record at Westminster for obtaining any Judgment, Statute, Recognizance, Conveyance, Obligation or other specialty *or contract in writing* whatsoever by fraud, that in such case the said judgment, statute, recognizance, conveyance, obligation, or other specialty *or contract in writing* shall be absolutely void to all intents and purposes whatsoever." *Noted:* Agreed 22 Nov. [See notes of date to principal paper above. The handwriting is that of C. B. Atkyns.]

(*e*.) Paper containing the following :—(1.) Provided nevertheless that the Judges in the Equitable Courts shall be liable to no censure or be drawn into any question for anything by them heretofore done [as Judges of Equity against these Statutes] *contrary to the aforesaid Statutes ;* (2.) Be it hereby declared that the fore-mentioned Statute [of 4 Hen. IV. did and doth] *and every of them did and do* extend to the [High] Court of

---

* On 15 Dec. the House, on motion, ordered Sir W. Rawlinson and Sir A. Keck to attend the Committee the next day to report what progress they had made in drawing the Bill. MS. Min. 15 Dec.; L. J., XIV. 590.)

† *See also* Annex (*f*.)

Chancery and to all other Courts of Equity; and be it enacted. *Noted* under this Clause: "This is postponed, to be considered with the preamble of the Bill."

(*f.*) 29 Nov. Amendment to clause in (*c*) above, viz., to insert after ("*default*") the words ("*or upon a verdict in a case wherein there is matter of equity*"). [This amendment is mentioned in MS. Min. of date, as having been proposed this day, but it is not stated whether it was agreed to. See notes to principal paper above.]

305. Oct. 22. E. Salisbury's Estate Act.—Amended* draft of an Act [to prevent the cutting off of the entail of the Earl of Salisbury's estate] *for limiting the power of James, now Earl of Salisbury, to cut off the entail of his estate.* After the recital of the marriage settlement, the preamble, with its amendments, reads as follows:—"That James, now Earl of Salisbury, in the reign of the late King James the Second (notwithstanding his being descended of a Protestant family and his being born and educated a Protestant) [became a Papist and was notoriously known to be reconciled to the Church of Rome] *hath deserted the communion of the Church of England*, and [being] *is become* zealously [engaged in] *affected to* the Popish interest and not [then or] yet having any issue of his body, [but designing all possible prejudice to your Suppliant, being a Protestant and the next inheritable issue to the said honour and estate in case the said now Earl should have no issue male,] did *in Easter term in the fourth year of the reign of the late King James the Second,* suffer [a] common [recovery] *recoveries* of [about 1,500*l.* per annum of the said estate] *several of the said manors, lands, messuages, tenements, and hereditaments* in the said counties of Essex [or] *and* Middlesex,† settled as aforesaid by the said recited Deed of Settlement, and thereby barred and destroyed (as to so much thereof) the remainder limited to your Suppliant; And he, the said now Earl [still] continuing [a Papist and persisting in his zeal for that party, and having conceived a very great prejudice against and hatred unto your Suppliant for no other reason in the world but your Suppliant being a Protestant and zealous for their Majesties' service and the present Government,] *to be zealously affected to the Popish interest as aforesaid,* Doth intend (as your Suppliant is credibly informed and hath just reason to believe) to suffer several other common recoveries [of all the residue] of the said estate, *not comprised in the said former common recoveries* [on purpose to bar your Suppliant of the said remainder and with a design to settle the said estate upon some persons of his own religion or convey the same to the use and service of the Romish party, he, the said now Earl, having seriously and publicly declared that he would leave your Suppliant a poor Earl and disinherit your Suppliant of all he could]." The remainder of the original draft consists of (1) the first enacting clause, amended, as in the Act, by twice inserting the words ("*not comprised in the said former common recoveries*"); (2) the Proviso restraining the Earl from committing waste, amended, as in the Act, of which it forms the first Proviso, by adding the words from ("*in the counties of Middlesex and Surrey*") to ("*time being or two of them*")‡; and (3) the Proviso,

* The additions are shown by italics and the omissions by square brackets.

† The Com. Book (4 Nov.) has an amendment to insert after ("Middlesex") the words ("of the yearly value of 1,500*l.* or thereabouts"). This amendment, however, is not written on the draft, and does not appear in the Act.

‡ Here are marked for insertion the Provisoes forming Annexes (*a.*) to (*e.*) below.

HOUSE OF LORDS MSS.

1690.

as in the Act, saving the rights of the younger children or creditors or legatees of the late Earl. *Endorsed:* Bill of Robert Cecil, Esq., Second son of James, the late E. of Salisbury. [Read 1ª this day, and Counsel ordered to be heard on behalf of E. Salisbury against the Bill on the 27th (L. J., XIV. 528). On the 27th Counsel being called in, *Sir W. Williams* (for E. Salisbury) said there were facts recited in the Bill which he desired might be proved. That was his hatred. *Mr. Ward:* We thought they should be heard against the Bill. He reads the part of the Bill that recites the point of hatred and shows they are the second son. We are the next in remainder. It is in my Lord's power and, if in his power, we question but it is his will. *Sir W. Williams* reads that part of the Bill which is to the hatred. *Mr. Dobins* (for E. Salisbury) reads another clause in the Bill. There ought to be something proved of this, or it ought not to be in the Bill. We deny any unkindness between my Lord and his brother. *Mr. Trevor* (for Mr. Cecil) says they have witnesses to prove the unkindness. Counsel withdraw. Counsel called in again and told if they have anything to offer by way of proof, they are to offer it. *Lady Mary Forester* (sworn): Asked what she knows of the Lord's intention? I heard him say to his priest he would cut off the entail of all his estate if he lived to the next term—about two years since—of every grant he had. *Mr. Trevor:* We have no other proof but this as to my Lord's declaration of his intention. Counsel withdraw. Speaker reported and after consideration thereof, Bill read 2ª and committed to a Select Committee. (MS. Min. 27 Oct.; L. J., XIV. 532.) The proceedings in Committee, of whom E. Rochester was chairman, are as follows:—On 29 Oct. the Bill read entire. The parties being called in, *Mr. Dobins* (for E. Salisbury) says he believes the parcels are truly recited in the preamble. The Deed of Settlement is produced and compared with the preamble of the Bill, and the several uses read. *Sir W. Williams* (for E. Salisbury) proposes that the Earl may have power to let leases and raise portions for younger children and annuities for sons. *Counsel* for Mr. Cecil says this Bill bars but part of the Estate. The Earl has already turned 1,500*l.* per annum into fee simple, and has also cut off the entail of 1,500*l.* more. *Mr. Dolbin* (for Mr. Cecil) says the Earl will have 12,000*l.* a year beside. It is therefore unreasonable to charge the entailed estate. The House being set, they withdraw. *Ordered,* That they attend tomorrow in order to prove the matter of fact that is in difference between them. (Com. Book 29 Oct.)—On 30 Oct. *Mr. Trevor* says the Earl has 1,500*l.* a year and that is not charged; and that he has suffered a common recovery on 1,370*l.* a year more. The values are agreed but the estate is encumbered with 16,000*l.* mortgages and 10,000*l.* bonds. There is but 120*l.* a year of the fee simple estate mortgaged. If the trust estate be sufficient to pay all the debts, then the fee simple estate is not to pay the mortgages. All the lands that are mortgaged are within the trust except 120*l.* per annum. The Earl's fee simple estate is worth more than 80,000*l.* *Mr. Dobins* gives in a note of debts owing by the late Earl and charged upon the estate, which is read. Part of the late Earl's will is read. *Mr. Fisher* says half the leases of the Exchange come out at one time and half at another time. The leases were made at first for 30 years. There are, he thinks, 12 years expired. The counterpart of the mortgage on the new Exchange for 10,000*l.* is produced, dated 17 July '88. The House being set, *Ordered* that both sides attend tomorrow. (Com. Book 30 Oct.)—On 31 Oct. Counsel being called in, *Mr. Trevor* says the Earl has a reversion in fee after Mrs. Dorothy Cecil's death, of 3,500*l.* per annum, and has also a reversion in fee after a term of 99 years worth 8,000*l*. He has 2,000*l*. a year in right of his Lady and 1,000*l*. a year more after the death of her mother. *Sir W. Williams:* The Earl has no estate that will give him credit to take up sixpence. *Mr. Eleazer Sadler* (sworn at the Bar) says he has looked over the counterparts of the leases of the new Exchange and some of them have 20 years and some 16½ years yet to come. He computes that there is a deficiency of 13,000*l*. besides annuities, which in all will make 21,000*l*. The annuities to the overseers are to be paid till the debts and portions are paid. *Mr. John Fisher* (sworn at the Bar) says he with others made a computation and, according to their judgment, there appeared above 13,000*l*. deficiency besides annuities. *Mr. Sadler* says he believes the Earl to be now 7,000*l*. in debt. Witness received the 10,000*l*. borrowed by the Earl. He received 7,000*l*. of it in Lombard Street and the rest of it in Fleet Street. He paid with part of it his father's debts and with the other part his own debts contracted before he travelled. The Earl's paternal estate for the last seven years has not been yearly 3,000*l*. a year. *Mr. Trevor:* The estate we desire will to Mr. Cecil be above 2,000*l*. a year clear. *Mr. Sadler* says he has heard the last Earl say that he had not 2,000*l*. a year when he came to the estate. *Mr. Dobins:* The Earl has now 5,000*l*. a year, and in less than three years he will have 3,000*l*. a year more. His Lady's present revenue is 2,000*l*. a year. The reversion after her mother is 1,000*l*. The remaining part of my Lady's jointure is 1,000*l*. a year more. Mr. Cecil will have but 5,500*l*., out of which he must pay 600*l*. a year annuities to 6 others, 1,500*l*. a year dower to my Lady and annuities to servants. (Com. Book 31 Oct.) —On 3 Nov., *Mr. Cecil* is called in and asked what estate he has out of his father's estate? He says he has 300*l*. per annum and that is charged out of the estate he would preserve. He has also 6,000*l*. odd money payable at 21 years or on the day of his marriage. *Agreed*, That this estate be charged with 5,000*l*. apiece to younger children, to be paid at 18 years of age and upon the death of any of them not to go to their executors, but to merge in the estate, and that some part of the estate be set out for that purpose. The Counsel are called in and acquainted therewith, and ordered to meet and word the Bill accordingly. (*See* Annex (*a*.) below.) *Counsel* for Mr. Cecil propose that the estate now in trust for 10 years, which is 3,500*l*. per annum, may be the fund to charge the portions with. *Ordered*, That they bring in a clause to that purpose tomorrow. (Com. Book 3 Nov.)—On 4 Nov. *Counsel* for Mr. Cecil offer a clause, according to the direction of the Committee, which the Counsel on the other side do not oppose. The Bill is read by paragraphs. The title is postponed. Some amendments having been made, *Mr. Eleazer Sadler* is sworn at the Bar, and being asked, says he never heard him say anything concerning the disinheriting his brother, but he has heard him say that he would cut off the entail. He never heard my Lord say that he would leave his brother a poor Earl. Then the clause beginning ("but designing") was postponed, on question, by 9 votes to 4, and the rest of the preamble was considered and amended, and agreed to, except the clause postponed. The Counsel agreed to meet and draw a clause concerning leases. The clauses already drawn by Counsel are read and postponed. *Ordered*, That Mr. Cecil may swear his witnesses on the 6th,* to be examined on the 7th. (Com. Book 4 Nov.)—On 6 Nov. *Mr. Dolbin* delivers in copies of the two recoveries suffered by E. Salisbury. The Bill is to be

* On the 6th the House ordered the following witnesses to be summoned: Lady Frances Holford, Lady Mary Forrester, Lady Margaret Cecil, Mrs. Elizabeth Adams, Mrs. Mary Boyer, and Mr. John Dalben. (MS. Min. No entry in L. J.)

worded in its proper place according to the recoveries now produced. The proviso concerning the Earl's making leases is offered and read, and agreed to with some amendments. (Annex (*d.*) below.) Another proviso touching a jointure is offered and read and agreed to after amendment. (Annex (*c.*) below.) Adjourned till the next day. (Com. Book 6 Nov.)—On 7 Nov. *Mr. Dolbin* (for Mr. Cecil) says that they have summoned Lady Frances Halford, but, she refusing to come, they have Lady Mary Forrester and Lady Margaret Cecil to prove what they have heard her say. *Mr. Dobins* (for E. Salisbury) desires that Lady Mary Forrester, having been examined at the bar, may not be again examined here. *Mrs. Elizabeth Adams* (sworn) says that she acquainted Lady Frances Holford that she was to attend this morning. She said she wondered her brother would put her upon a thing that would ruin her and her children. She was then in E. Salisbury's house, in her chamber. *Mrs. Mary Bower* (sworn) says she served Lady Frances Holford with the order for attending this morning, and she said she was not well. *Lady Margaret Cecil* (sworn) says that she has heard E. Salisbury say that he designed to cut off the entail of his estate; but she did not hear him say how he would dispose of his estate. Mr. Cecil was then beyond sea, and my Lord was then angry with him because, being sent to, he did not come to him. They withdraw. The Committee then resolved by 9 votes to 4 to move the House that Lady Frances Holford be sent for to be sworn this morning to be examined to morrow. (Com. Book 7 Nov.)*—On 8 Nov. *Mr. Dobins* offers a proviso for leasing Salisbury House, &c. which is read and agreed to with an amendment. (Annex (*e.*) below.) He offers another proviso to empower the Earl to make leases of any other part of the estate, which is read and rejected. (Com. Book 8 Nov.)—On 10 Nov. the amendments formerly made are read in the presence of the Counsel. *Ordered*, That the Bill be reported with the amendments, and that the House be acquainted that the clause in the Bill, to which the Lady Frances Holford was to have been heard, is left to be considered by the House. (Com. Book 10 Nov.; L. J., XIV. 546.) The House, on receiving this report, and learning from Black Rod that Lady Frances was too ill to attend, agreed that the clause in question, which related to the Earl's having expressed great unkindness or hatred to his brother, Mr. Cecil, should be left out. The Committee's amendments were then read and agreed to, and the Bill was recommitted, in order to draw a clause that Mr. Cecil should be tied up as to the 5,500*l.* a year, as E. Salisbury is by the Bill, and that C. J. Pollexfen and Counsel on both sides attend the Committee. (M.S. Min. 10 Nov.; L. J., XIV. 546.)—On 11 Nov. in Committee (on recommitment), the clause drawn by C. J. Pollexfen, as ordered by the House, is read. They withdraw. Counsel called in and told they must not speak against a clause drawn in pursuance of the order of the House, but they may speak against this clause. *Mr. Dolbin:* The two younger sons provided for by this clause are now in rebellion. We have great reason to believe them Papists, and your Lordships have ordered a Bill to be brought in that a Popish heir shall not inherit; and this clause is quite contrary thereto. There is a third brother, that is

* On the 7th, in the House, Mr. Dolbin being called in and sworn, said that he was with Lady Holford, and he could not be admitted into her presence. He sent up the order. It was then proposed at first to order that Sir Miles Cooke, a Master in Chancery, should attend her and take her affidavit of what she knew relating to the Bill. (M.S. Min.) The House then ordered Black Rod to attend her with the order. (L. J., XIV. 543.) On 8 Nov. the House ordered her to be attached. (*Ib.* 544.)

a Protestant, that is not taken care of by this clause. *Mr. Dobins* (for E. Salisbury) says he has not had time to consider the clause. They withdraw. *Ordered*, to report that the clause which has been drawn by C. J. Pollexfen in pursuance of the order of the House, being objected to by the Counsel, shall be left to the consideration of the House. (Com. Book 11 Nov.) The House, on receiving this report *eod. die*, agreed, after debate, to read the clause (Annex (*f*.) below), and afterwards rejected it by 31 votes to 24. Tellers, L. Lovelace and L. North. The Bill was then ordered to be engrossed with the amendments. (M.S. Min. 11 Nov.; L. J., XIV. 548.) An unimportant amendment was added on third reading on the 12th (*ib.* 550.) On 17 Dec. the Bill was returned from the Commons with amendments* (*ib.* 594) which were agreed to with an amendment, to which the Commons, after a conference, agreed (*ib.* 596, 597). The Bill received the Royal Assent on the 20th (*ib.* 600) 2 and 3 W. and M., c. 16, in Long Calendar.]

Annexed:—

(*a*.) 10 Nov. 1690. Amended proviso, marked A., enabling the Earl to make leases of any part of the estate *not comprised in the said former common recoveries*, except Hatfield, in trust to raise portions, not exceeding 5,000*l.* each, for his daughters and younger sons. As amended by adding the words in italics, it forms the second proviso in the Act. [Agreed to in Committee, 6 Nov., and reported this day. L. J., XIV. 546. *See* Notes above, Nov. 3, 4.]

(*b*.) 10 Nov. 1690. Clause and two Provisos, marked †. The Clause, which is cancelled, is as follows: "And be it enacted that if the said James, Earl of Salisbury, shall hereafter happen to have any younger son or sons, daughter or daughters, that shall live to attain to the age of 18 years or be married, and shall have made any lease or term for years out of any part of the residue of the lands and tenements above mentioned, not exceeding the yearly value of 2,000*l.* per annum, and other than the capital messuage, park, and demeans of the Manor of Hatfield, in the County of Hertford, to any person or persons in trust only for the raising of 5,000*l.* apiece for every such child or children that shall attain to the age of 18 years or be married, for a portion or provision of such child or children, to be paid at such respective ages or days of marriage, which shall first happen; that such lease and term shall be good and effectual in the law, and the trustees thereof possessed in trust only for the raising of such sums of money."—The two provisos that follow from the third and fourth provisos in the Act. [The two provisos were reported this day. L. J., XIV. 546. *See* Notes above, Nov. 3, 4, 6.]

(*c*.) 10 Nov. 1690. Amended Proviso, marked B., relating to a jointure. The portion amended is as follows: "any part or proportion [of the said residue] of the said estate, *not comprised in the said former common recoveries* then due and payable to the said James, now Earl of Salisbury, shall not exceed in the whole the yearly sum of *fifteen hundred* pounds per annum

---

* The Commons' amendments are given in C. J. X. 505. As finally amended by the Lords, they are annexed in two separate Schedules to the Act. A clause was offered, but rejected on third reading in the Commons on 17 Dec., for raising interest at 5 p. c. out of the lands chargeable with portions for the Earl's daughters and younger sons, for their maintenance till their portions should become payable. C. J. X. 510.

House of Lords MSS.

1690.

in bar of her claim of dower of any part of the same estate not comprised in the said former common recoveries." As thus amended, it forms the fifth proviso in the Act. [Agreed to in Committee, 6 Nov., and reported this day. L. J., XIV. 546. *See* Notes above, Nov. 6.]

(*d.*) 10 Nov. 1689. Amended Proviso, marked C., being, as amended, the sixth proviso in the Act. It enables the Earl, being in possession of all or any part of the [said residue of the] said estate *not comprised in the said former common recoveries* to make leases . . . so as there be reserved as much yearly rent for the premises as was reserved due to the late Earl at the time of his decease [if the same were then in lease], and that so much can be got or else as much yearly rent as can *without any fine* be got for the same; with power nevertheless [at the discretion of the said Earl] *for the said Earl by the consent of the two Chief Justices and Chief Baron for the time being, or any two of them in writing under their hands and seals,* to reduce the rents to be reserved in such *of the said* cases wherein shall be contained any covenants . . . and of all other parts of the said [residue of the said] estate (except the said Hatfield House) for any term of years [absolute] not exceeding the number of 21 years, [as for any other number of years determinable upon the death of one (*illegible*)] so as during every such term there be reserved due and payable for the hereditaments and premises, in such leases respectively to be comprised, [as much yearly rent as was reserved due and payable for the same to James, late Earl of Salisbury, at the time of his decease, if ever the same be got, or else as much yearly rent as really can be got for the same] *the best improved rent as can be got for the same;* and be it enacted . . . leases to be comprised. [Reported this day. L. J., XIV. 546. *See* Notes above under date 6 Nov.]

(*e.*) 10 Nov. 1690. Amended Proviso, marked D., for leasing Salisbury House, &c., being, as amended, the seventh proviso in the Act. The only amendment is to substitute the consent of the two Chief Justices, &c. for the Earl's discretion, as in Annex (*d.*) [Offered by Mr. Dobins and agreed to 8 Nov., and reported this day. L. J., XIV. 546. *See* Notes above under date 8 Nov.]

(*f.*) 11 Nov. 1690. Engrossed Clause as follows: Provided that nothing in this Act shall to (*sic*) prejudice any pardon or pardons to life or estate, that his Majesty shall grant to William Cecil or Charles Cecil, sons of James, late Earl of Salisbury, being now infants and conveyed privately to parts beyond the seas without the consent or knowledge of their guardians, if that the said William Cecil or Charles Cecil shall, at any time before they attain the age of 18 years, bring a certificate to his Majesty's Courts of Chancery or King's Bench or (*sic*) their having received the Sacrament in any Parish Church within the Bills of Mortality according to the Church of England, and do then and there take the oaths and subscribe the declaration required and enjoined by an Act made in the first year of their Majesties' reign, intituled an Act for abrogating the Oaths of Allegiance and Supremacy and appointing other oaths. [Rejected by Committee (on recommitment) this day. *See* Note to first paper above, Nov. 10, 11.]

306. Oct. 24. Letters Patent Vacating (Needwood Forest) Bill.—Amended draft of an Act for making void certain Letters Patent therein mentioned. The original draft is identical with the amended Bill of 28 March 1690 (No. **240**), except in omitting from the list of Commissioners, Joseph Saunders, Villers, Richard Cope, and William Salt. The amendments to this Bill are to substitute the sum of 4,669*l*. 10*s*. for 4,521*l*., and to add, as Commissioners, Sir Henry Every, Bart., Henry Every, Esq., his son, Thomas Ilsley, Deputy Axe-bearer, Charles Blunt, Esq., William Cotton, of Yoxhall, Esq., John Adderley, Esq., Bernard Whaley of Great Yoxhall, Esq., Gilbert Thacker, Esq., Poole, of Radbourne, Esq., and Walter Bagnold, of Burton, Gent. [Read 1ª this day. L. J., XIV. 531. In Committee the following were inserted as Commissioners, viz., Humfry Worley, Esq., Nicholas Hurt, Esq., John Newton, Esq., William Whitby, Gent., Joseph Haynes, Gent., John Hurd, Gent., John Noble, Gent., and Richard Blackburne, Gent. (Com. Book 19 Nov.) The names on the draft were substituted for these on Report (L. J., XIV. 567), the alteration having been agreed to by L. Steward and Mr. Browne. (MS. Min. 26 Nov.) The Bill was not read in the Commons. C. J., X. 488.]

Annexed:—

(*a*.) 26 Nov. Lords' Amendments to the Bill. [Made in Committee 19 Nov., and reported this day. Com. Book, L. J., XIV. 567.]

(*b*.) 26 Nov. List of Commissioners substituted on Report this day. L. J., XIV. 567.

(*c*.) Paper giving the Christian names of Mr. Whaley, Mr. Ilsley, and Mr. Poole.

307. Oct. 24. Admiralty Commissioners Act.—Draft of an Act concerning the Commissioners of the Admiralty. Identical with s. i. of the Act 2 W. & M., Sess. 2., cap. 2. [Read 1ª this day. L. J., XIV. 531. On 28 Oct., the Judges being heard in answer to the question propounded to them (*ib.* 533), replied as follows: *Holt, C. J.:* I am of opinion that the Lords of the Admiralty have both these powers. This is upon the Statute 13 Car. II. I think it is clear that before this Statute was made, the offence was triable by a Court Martial. We take notice there was such a law, and the Petition of Right takes notice that there was such a law. The law being so before, it is to be considered what alteration this Statute has made. This is an affirmative power, and no other than what was before. If they can grant a Commission, they may give leave for execution. I conceive this is not a penal law, but a merciful law. The Statutes 7 Hen. VII. and 3 Hen. VIII. are in express terms. If a soldier leaves his captain, it shall be felony. They were judged guilty of felony for leaving their conductor though he were not captain. This was the [opinion] of 9 Judges versus 3. *Pollexfen, C. J.:* Before this Act was made there was martial law. In times of peace there was some regulation for the Fleet. If they might then proceed, I see nothing in this Statute that takes away the former power, and they may proceed as if this Statute had not been made. The Statute is made for a general Statute for settling the Navy. I take this to be a particular Act, to be a law of itself. If you intend to proceed according to this Act, then I doubt whether any but the Lord High Admiral can do this. If you will proceed according to this Act, there must be then a Commission granted by the Lord High Admiral. *Atkyns, C. B.:* I am of the same opinion

HOUSE OF LORDS MSS.

1690.

with the L. Chief Justice Holt. Time out of mind there was a law martial and marine. About what matters they exercise their jurisdiction is known. L. Coke speaks of this law, and tells you by what rule they go. 5 Q. Eliz. is in express words, so I hold that the Commissioners of the Admiralty have the same power as the Lord High Admiral. *Dolben, J.:* I did make some doubt whether upon this Act they might do it. I see by the Articles that there is not one new Act in this Statute that was not before. I think it is clear the Commissioners may grant Commissions, and may do all that the Lord High Admiral may do. *Nevill, B.:* I doubt this Act does not reach the Commissioners of the Admiralty. What was the law before, is the law still. I think this is a penal law. I cannot be convinced that the Lords Commissioners of the Admiralty have the same power as the Lord High Admiral. *Gregory, J.:* I conceive that the Lords of the Admiralty have the same power as the Lord High Admiral. *Eyre, J.:* I am of the same opinion; that the Commissioners of the Admiralty may execute the same power as a Lord High Admiral by this Act. This Act modifies but does not alter the law. *Ventris, J.:* Admitting there had been no such law as 17 Car., I think it is plain they could. This was part of the Lord High Admiral's power by the common law. I am of opinion that the Commissioners of the Admiralty may grant a Commission within this law. Where there is a new power given to the Lord Chancellor or Lord Keeper, there it is held that the Commissioners cannot grant. There is a great deal of difference in the new matter. This is not new in the subject matter of it. I am of opinion that the Commissioners may act as Lord High Admiral. After debate, ordered as in L. J., XIV. 533. The third reading was carried on 30 Oct. by 25 votes to 17,* the tellers being E. Feversham for the Contents, and V. Weymouth for the Not-Contents. (MS. Min. Oct. 28, 30.)]

308. Oct. 27. D. Albemarle *v.* E. Bath.—Petition of Elizabeth, Duchess of Albemarle, Charles, Lord Cheyne, William Cheyne, Esq., and Doctor Peter Barwick. Christopher, late Duke of Albemarle, by his will dated 4 July 1687, and drawn, by his directions, by the L. C. Justice Pollexfen, left considerable legacies to the Duchess and named the other Petitioners as his executors. A suit was commenced in the Prerogative Court of Canterbury for proof of the said will, in which the Earl of Bath pretended to be concerned on pretence of a former will dated in 1675. The Earl, having failed in his appeal from an interlocutory order of the Court, stood upon his privilege, just as the cause was ripe for judgment, although he had not only brought himself into the cause, but had agreed that the cause should come to a speedy end, and had agreed further, as appeared by his own letter, to waive his privilege in Chancery, if the Duchess and others would do the like. Pray that they may be at liberty to proceed in the cause. [Read, with the annexed Petition, this day. L. J., XIV. 531. The E. Bath being heard, said he waived his privilege in Chancery, but he insisted on it in Doctors Commons. The letter mentioned in the Petition, and directed to the Duchess of Newcastle, read. The House then ordered as in L. J. *ut supra*. On Nov. 6 Counsel were first heard. *Sir Charles Porter* (for the Duchess): The Earl appeared personally there, and was going on till one sentence was given and another was ready to be given, when he insisted on his privilege. There were two Wills, the

* Ralph, whom Macaulay follows, without being able to find his authority, asserts that the majority was only two.

last exhibited by Dr. Barwick. The Earl would have adm[inistration] *pendente lite.* There were Commiss[ions of] delegates about February, 1689. On 2 June last the Earl insisted on his privilege. *Mr. Ward* (for the Duchess): Dr. Barwick comes in with a new Will wherein he is executor. The Pro[ctor] entered it in the book to proceed in the Cause. The Earl of Bath was present. On 28 Feb. 1689 he insisted. On 24 May the Cause was set down to be heard on 2 June, and then the Pro[ctor] comes and says my Lord insists on his privilege. We submit whether my Lord's actions are as his words would have done. If it were not a waiver, we have gone on in the wrong. *Sir Charles Porter* mentions the letter written by the Earl of Bath to the Duchess. The letter read by the Clerk at the Table. They offer the Act of Court and read it, wherein my Lord's Proctor, by special order of the Earl, prosecuted the Appeal . . . . *Mr. Trevor* (for E. Bath): This consists of matter of fact and the Letter. We do not deny but that there have been proceedings such as Counsel mention. They do not pretend there to be an express waiver but in the Letter, and that is against such a declaration. Whether they have shown anything that amounts to a waiver we must leave to your Lordship's judgment. As to the mischiefs they mention by the demurrer which was overruled, (*sic*). *Sir William Williams* (for E. Bath): They do not insist upon an actual waiving. There was a Will exhibited in the Prerogative Court by the Earl. There is a Will exhibited by Dr. Barwick on their part. The last Will must prevail, if allowed by receiving the Will. The Earl does not waive, but finds he could not examine his witness. I have no way to prove this but by insisting on my privilege [he says], and would not anyone do this? *Sir Charles Porter* (in reply): Instances the Bishop of Coventry's case, 12 April 1690 and offers to prove that the Earl of Bath in general [terms] said he did waive his privilege. *Arthur Moore* (sworn), says he waited on the Earl and acquainted him with the Duchess's [message], and the Earl said he would never insist upon his privilege against the Duchess. This was said in January three or four days after the letter read.—On 11 Nov. Counsel were called in. The allegation read as to the Duchess's instigation to the Duke to alter the Will. May and June 1687. Several allegations read. *Sir W. Williams:* Upon these allegations the question arose whether these allegations shall be allowed to be examined into. It was impossible for the Earl to do this. The Delegates were of opinion for giving further time. Now, we are here to know whether you will allow further time, and when he found the Court would not, then he reasonably insisted on his privilege. In 1681, after six years time, the Duke ratified that Will. *Mr. Trevor:* The Earl stands on his privilege that he may prove his allegation. Let it be admitted or allow him to examine to it. It is at the worst but a loss of time. Here are the opinions of the civil lawyers that witnesses may be examined if they come before sentence, and this is a good reason to stand upon privilege. *Mr. Finch* (for the Duchess): The question is whether, when the Earl had once waived, he should insist again. They never examine to the same allegation again. If there is new matter, then they examine after. The Earl once alleged he would put in no other allegation. The Judge received this, but not to delay the Cause. The Courts in Westminster Hall will not grant a Commission but upon very good grounds. As to the matter of the last Will, it appears to be a Will made by the D. of Albemarle upon the most solemn considerations imaginable. It was gained, they say, by importunity. The deed is under controversy. Suppose the Duchess did importune this, what then? Is [it] not made? *Mr. Ward* (for the Duchess): The time the Earl has had already is from 1689 and so down. The 3 Oct. was allowed to plead, and then the Earl's Counsel says, "I will go no further." Above half a year this Will was framing, it is on 19 sheets of paper. Three were delivered in three parts to three several persons. What is this Will impeached by? After all these things, the Earl has all this time and no allegation is put in, and therefore we humbly submit it to your Lordships. *Mr. Trevor* (in reply): We can examine before the Delegates, and therefore my Lord insists upon his privilege. *Sir W. Williams* replies. *Mr. Finch:* On 3 Oct. the Earl declared he would make no further allegation. The new allegation that came afterwards, was to the L. C. Justice Pollexfen here.—Civilians to be heard as to the hearing of witnesses. *Dr. Oldish:* Says he conceives the Earl ought not to have further time. There should be no further delays, therefore the cause is set down. In the tenth Article they were examined. They produced witnesses, they say, but have examined no witnesses. The question is whether witnesses can be heard vivâ voce after the closure of the Cause. It lays all open and is not admissible. This is never known to have been admitted. It will open a gate to perjury and subornation. It is directly contrary to all practice. *Dr. Pinfold:* This Cause is in the Court of Delegates and is past the Prerogative Court. This is nothing but an assignation of the Court. You shall be bound by that time. If new matter arises, they shall plead that likewise, or else the whole truth cannot be found out. They say we have not made use of the time. I confess we have not, because it is not material.—On 13 Nov. *The Speaker* reported what had been said by Counsel on either side. *Sir W. Williams* reads the depositions at the Bar concerning the Duchess making undue solicitations to the Duke for making his Will. *Question proposed:* Whether the Earl of Bath shall insist upon his Privilege? *Proposed*, that the Earl of Bath should have a further time for examining of witnesses. It is agreed that the Earl has waived his privilege. After debate, *Ordered* as in L. J., XIV. 551.—On 15 Nov. Counsel called in. Order read. *Mr. Finch:* We cannot admit that allegation to be true. Gives his reasons. The allegation reflects upon the Duchess. The Duchess never heard of the Deed. *Mr. Ward:* If we admit these allegations, it will be very hard, for we have denied all these things. This Lord has not asked any Commission to examine these things in Chancery. There are some things we cannot sever one from the other. *Dr. Oldish* (for the Duchess): We cannot admit these allegations. He did not desire any Commission on all these Articles. If we should admit, it would be beyond all practice. *Mr. Trevor* (for E. Bath): We answer the question that, if they will not admit the allegations, it is great reason we should insist on our privilege. *Sir W. Williams* (for E. Bath): They ought to allow us one allegation or we insist on our privilege. *Dr. Pinfold:* This Cause comes not within the rule I gave the last day. There is no fear of subornation in this case. *Proposed*, that time be given to the Earl of Bath until the first day of Easter next. *Ordered* as in L. J., XIV. 554, that the Earl should not claim privilege beyond that date. (MS. Min.)]

Annexed:—

(*a*.) 27 Oct. Petition of the Creditors of Christopher, late Duke of Albemarle, deceased, to same effect as preceding. 26 signatures: among them is that of Hans Sloane. L. J., XIV. 531.

309. Oct. 27. L. Granville.—Petition of Charles, Lord Granville, praying to be discharged from his confinement. *Endorsed* as read this day.* L. J., XIV. 532. [On 21 Oct. the House was moved to take notice of a quarrel between L. Granville and L. Keveton. The House was informed that some time the last week L. Not[tingham] had an account that there was a quarrel. He sent two letters to the L. President and another to the E. Bath. The guards found L. Granville. I acquainted the King with it, and he gave orders for securing the Lords with the Guards, but I cannot tell whether they have done it or not. E. Bath undertook and engaged to secure and bring his son to the House. *Ordered* as in L. J., XIV. 527. (M.S. Min. 21 Oct.) On 22 Oct. Sir Thos. Duppa gave the House an account that he had taken into custody L. Granville and Mr. Granville, but that he could not find L. Keveton or Mr. Stringer. L. Granville was sent for to his place and told by the Speaker: "The House has been informed of a quarrel or words between you and the Lord Keveton, and they have ordered me to lay the injunction of this House that you meddle no more in this." [L. Granville replied as follows:] "About a year since, I promised the King that I would never entertain any such quarrel, and I have religiously kept my promise, and have received no message from him, nor sent any to him." *Moved* to call in Isaac and Cranmer, Francis Thorpe, and Charles Wood, who were called in and sworn. Asked if they knew anything of any quarrel between the Lords. [*Mr. Isaac*]: On Wednesday morning I went to Mr. Granville, and he was under guard. I inquired, and was told the Lord Danby and Granville had a quarrel, and that Mr. Stringer was second to L. Danby and Granville to L. Keveton. I met Mr. Granville at the Coffee-house. I asked the Master of the Coffee-house: who went out with Mr. Granville? He said it was Mr. Stringer. I heard of them in Bow Street, and so I got suspicion. There was a stop, which made me overtake them. I followed them. They lighted at the Swan tavern. I stood under Somerset House Gate. I saw them in the balcony. Mr. Granville came out and went to his lodgings. I saw him send away his man. I went to [the] L. Pr[esident] and we went to a Captain of the Guards. *Mr. Cranmer* said: Mr. Isaac gave me the same account that he has given your Lordships. The House then made the orders as in L. J., XIV. 528. (MS. Min. 22 Oct.)]

Annexed:—

(*a.*) 27 Oct. Petition of same, to same effect as preceding. *Endorsed:* "Read 27 Oct., and be discharged." L. J., XIV. 532.

310. Oct. 28. Wentworth's Estate Bill.—Commons' Engrossment of an Act to vest some lands of John Wentworth, Esq., in Trustees to be sold, and for purchasing other lands with the money raised thereby, more to the convenience of the said John Wentworth's estate. Whereas John Wentworth, of Brodsworth, Yorkshire, Esq., cousin and heir of John Wentworth, late of Empsall, Yorkshire, Esq., deceased, or his trustees are seized of property called Coat Bank, Trantran, and Trantran Mires, in the parish of Morland, Westmorland, and Casterton and Casterton Fell, and Hutton Roof in the same County, and whereas the first named lands adjoin the Park of Right Honble. Sir John Lowther, of Lowther in said county, and are very subject to be trespassed upon by his deer and cattle, John Wentworth, now 18 years old, and his

* The MS. Min. of 24 Oct. have this entry: "A Petition of Charles, Lord Granville read, praying to be discharged." The date on the endorsement is, therefore, probably wrong.

mother Susannah are willing to sell them to Sir John; and also to part with the other lands, which are over 60 miles distant from the rest of Wentworth's property. The Bill therefore vests the said lands in Susannah Wentworth, Sir Henry Marwood of Busby, Yorkshire, Bart., and Joseph Washington, of the Middle Temple, London, Esq., as trustees to sell the first named to Sir John Lowther, and the rest to him or anyone else, and buy a more convenient estate in Yorkshire or elsewhere with the purchase money. *Parchment Collection.* [Brought from the Commons this day. Rejected after 3rd reading. L. J., XIV. 533, 540. *See also* Com. Book 1 Nov.]

311. Oct. 28. Scroope's Estate Act.—Amended draft of an Act for vesting divers lands in trustees, to be sold for the payment of certain debts of St. Leger Scroop, Esq., deceased. *Endorsed:* Mr. Aspin's Bill. [Read 1ª this day. Royal Assent, 20 Dec. L. J., XIV. 533, 600. 2 & 3 W. & M., c. 23, in Long Calendar.]

Annexed:—

(*a*.) 11 Nov. Lords' Amendment to the Bill, reported by Committee this day. L. J., XIV. 548. Com. Book Nov. 1.

312. Oct. 28. Cooke's Estate Act.—Amended draft of an Act for the enabling of trustees to sell certain Lands of Richard Cooke, deceased, to pay debts and to raise a portion for his daughter. [Read 1ª this day. Royal Assent, 20 Dec. L. J., XIV. 533, 600. 2 & 3 W. & M., c. 19, in Long Calendar.]

Annexed:—

(*a*.) 17 Nov. Lords' Amendment to the Bill. [Made in Committee and reported this day. L. J., XIV. 555. Com. Book 17 Nov.]

(*b*.) Affidavits and Certificates that Elizabeth Cook and Robert Maltyward are unable from sickness and infirmity to go to London.

(*c*.) Petition of Robert Maltyward that the Bill may pass.

313. Oct. 28. Daniel *v.* Leigh.—Petition and Appeal of John Daniell, Esq. Complains of three decrees of the Court of Exchequer ordering Petitioner to pay to Respondent, the husband of his sister Mary, the sum of 500*l.*, as her portion under a deed of settlement executed by Petitioner's grandfather in 1655, conveying certain lands in Daresbury, Newton, and Hatton, in Cheshire, to trustees for that purpose, after discharging the debts of himself and his son, Petitioner's father. The decrees are erroneous, as neither the trustees nor the executor or administrator of Petitioner's father (who received during the lifetime of Petitioner's father rents enough to discharge the said debts) are parties to the suit, and Petitioner's estate tail is barred by them, which was never charged by the deed of settlement with his father's debts. Prays that Respondent may be ordered to answer and that the decrees may be reversed. L. J., XIV. 535. Pet. Book 29 Oct. [The cause was heard on 4 Dec. *Mr. Ward* (for Appellant): The decree is to pay 609*l.* 19*s.* 4*d.*, or else to be foreclosed. We conceive this decree is strict upon us. *Sir W. Williams* (for Appellant): This decree charges our land, whereas our estate ought not to be charged by law or equity. *Solicitor-General* (for Respondent): It was put into his head that he was not to pay interest for the money. The trustees have dismissed themselves of all power. *Sir Robert Sawyer* (for Respondent): The father gave the interest and the son for the same time. Counsel for Appellant reply. Counsel withdrew, and the Speaker having reported, the Appeal was dismissed. M.S. Min. 4 Dec. L. J., XIV. 579.]

Annexed:—

(a.) 19 Nov. Answer of William Leigh, Gent. — Appellant's father gave Respondent a bond for 100*l.* part of his wife's portion, and the remaining 400*l.* was declared to form part of the sum of 1,200*l.* to be raised by the trustees, and was secured by deeds of lease and release. The appeal is vexatious and ought to be dismissed. *Endorsed* as brought in this day.

314. Oct. 31. Absent Lords.—Extract from Rot. Parl. 31 Hen. VI. (6 Martii), M. 15, No. 46. Contra illos Dominos qui non veniunt ad Parliamentum. "Memorandum quod ultimo die Februarii . . . . respondebatur sub hiis verbis: Le Roy le voet." Certified as agreeing with the record by W. Prynne, Custos Rotulorum in the Tower of London, 8 April 1668. *Endorsed:* Used 1690. [The House was put into a Committee this day to consider of ways and means to make Lords attend the House. Statute Rich. II. read, where Lords, according to custom, have been fined. 9 Nov. 1669 where Lords were fined. The fines in Hen. VIII. read out of "Modus Tenendi Parliamentum." A paper read in Latin, where the Lords had been fined for absence by Act Hen. VII. 31. *Proposed:* That any Lords that shall omit their attendance here one Session of Parliament shall lose the privilege of Parliament. A fine to be on all the Lords alike. *Proposed:* 100*l.* for each peer. Agreed on, and to be estreated into the Exchequer, and no privilege to be allowed against the execution of that sentence. Standing Order read. That an Address be made to the King that the money may be put into a Treasurer's hands, that it may be disposed of as the House shall think fit to direct and that the Bishops' fine shall be but 50*l.*; that the House shall be called that day sennight that any Session or meeting of Parliament shall begin; and that if any Lord absents himself after he hath been present without leave of the King or the House . . . . House resumed. E. Bridgewater reported as in L. J., XIV. 539. (M S. 31 Oct.). No further proceedings are recorded.]

Annexed:—

(a.) 31 Oct. Paper entitled "Abridgment of Records," as follows:—"31 Hen. IV., p. 653. A certain fine is specially taxed upon every Lord, for not coming to the Parliament, according to his degree; Method of Parliament, fol. 73. Let the names of the Lords be viewed who are summoned to Parliament, read and examined before the King, and of them that are not come, let their names be delivered to the King in writing, to ordain such punishment as he shall please; 3 Edw. III. Term. Pasc., fol. 175. The Bishop of Winchester was indicted in the King's Bench for departing from the Parliament at Salisbury; Coke Juris. of Courts, c. 44, 6 Rich. II. c. 4., Rot. Parl. 31 Hen. VI., No. 46, fines were set, &c. Every Lord, Spiritual and Temporal, except he can reasonably and honestly excuse himself, shall be amerced, &c. 3 Edw. III. 18. If a Lord depart from Parliament without license, it is an offence done out of the Parliament, and is fineable by the Lords. *Vide* Mod. Parliamenti in the Journal of Hen. VIII. anno 1."

315. Nov. 3. Barret's Estate Act.—Consent of the Countess of Donegall and Lord Ranelagh to the passing of the Bill to enable Dacres Barret alias Leonard, Esq., to raise 1,500*l.* on the reversion of his estate in Essex. [Produced before Committee this day. Com. Book. The Bill received the Royal Assent on 10 Nov. L. J., XIV. 547. 2 & 3 W. & M., c. 3, in Long Calendar.]

House of Lords MSS.

1690.

316. Nov. 6. Jeneway *v.* Bedford.—Petition of Robert Dickens and William Jeneway and Elizabeth his wife, for a rehearing. [Ordered to be rejected this day on report from the Committee for Petitions. L. J., XIV. 542. Pet. Book 29 Oct. *See also* Eleventh Report, App. Part II., No. **308.**]

Annexed:—

(*a.*) 15 Dec. 1689. Certificate of date that several of the legatees mentioned in the will of Edmond Arnold, and alleged at the hearing of the Appeal to be dead are still living.

(*b.*) 3 March 1690. Affidavit of date of Robert Dickens to same effect as preceding.

317. Nov. 8. Hildyard's Estate Act.—Amended draft of an Act to enable Phillip Hildyard, Esq. to sell lands in Surrey, and to settle lands in Lincolnshire in lieu thereof. [Read 1[a] this day; Royal Assent, 20 Dec. L. J., XIV. 545, 601. Com. Book 15 Nov. 2 & 3 W. & M., c. 29., in Long Calendar.]

Annexed:—

(*a.*) 15 Nov. Consent of Mrs. Katherine Vane, Elizabeth Hildyard and George Juyce to the passing of the Bill. [Produced before the Committee this day. Com. Book.]

318. Nov. 8. Hartstonge *v.* Lloyd.—Petition and Appeal of Sir Standish Hartstonge, Bart. Respondent brought a bill in the Chancery Court of Exchequer against Petitioner and John Weaver, Clerk, and others, claiming 75*l.* with interest in respect of a loan to Griffith Jones, who had mortgaged his lands for about 3.500*l.* to Sir Herbert Crofts, Bart., and assigned the redemption of the mortgage to Weaver, in trust to pay his debts amounting to 333*l.*, including the sum due to Lloyd. Jones, and Weaver sold the lands for about 4,500*l.* to Petitioner, who pleaded, in answer to the claim, that he was a stranger to any previous transactions between the two, but, in order that the trust, if any, might be performed, paid the 333*l.* to Weaver. The latter acknowledged the receipt of the sum, but stated that 100*l.* of it was a payment due to him by Petitioner in respect of some houses. The Court decreed against Petitioner, contrary to all justice, Weaver having received the money as the responsible trustee, and not proving a farthing paid by him in execution of the trust. Prays that the decree may be reversed with costs. *Signed* by Appellant. *Countersigned* by James Sloane and Rich. Turner. [Reported specially this day from the Committee for Petitions. (L. J., XIV. 545.) Petitioner stated to the Committee that he could proceed no further in the Exchequer, unless he brought a Bill of Review before the same Judges. (Pet. Book 29 Oct.) The Cause was heard on 3 Dec. *Sir Charles Porter* (for Appellant): For this there was a judgment of 100*l.* to secure 50*l.* There was a mortgage in 1678 for 800*l.* to Sir Herbert Crofts, the sum is about 2,700*l.* Weaver was a trustee, and the equity of redemption was in him. The Defendant says, this 70*l.* is my deed. In the Exchequer the decree was that Sir Standish Hartstonge should pay the 70*l.* and interest. Their trustee owns that Weaver has received the money. Admitting we had notice, yet shall not Weaver pay? *Mr. Sloane* (for Appellant): Sir Standish is a purchaser for valuable consideration. I conceive Mr. Weaver ought to pay it. This was Jones' own doing. The *Solicitor-General* and *Mr. Ward* were heard for Respondent. *Sir Charles Porter* replied, and Counsel having withdrawn, the Appeal was dismissed with 30*l.* costs. (MS. Min. 3 Dec.; L. J., XIV. 577.)]

Annexed:—

(a.) 18 Nov. Answer of Lewis Lloyd, Gent. Appellant was a purchaser with full notice of Respondent's debt, to which the estate he purchased was subject, and having taken a conveyance from Weaver, he stands in his place as a trustee. The Court left him to take his remedy against Weaver, as he should be advised. *Endorsed* as brought in this day.

(b.) 21 Nov. Petition of Appellant for a day for hearing. L. J., XIV. 560.

(c.) 2 Dec. Petition of Appellant.—Prays their Lordships to take off the costs imposed for his non-attendance, Petitioner not having received notice of the hearing till too late to get Counsel to attend. *Endorsed* as read this day; nothing done on it. MS. Min. *See* L. J., XIV. 573.

319. Nov. 8. Clarke *v.* Baden.—Petition of Respondent for an early day for hearing. L. J., XIV. 545.

320. Nov. 10. Dean and Chapter of Windsor *v.* Bishop of Salisbury.—Petition of the Dean and Chapter of Windsor. Petitioners, on the refusal of the Bishop of Salisbury to admit the Clerk whom they presented to him to be instituted to the living of West Ildeley, in the county of Berks, of which Petitioners are the Patrons, were driven, in order to prevent a lapse, to seek a remedy at law and sued forth a *Quare impedit*, returnable at the beginning of this term, but his Lordship insists on his privilege and threatens to punish Petitioners' agents as infringers of it. The Writ does not touch his Lordship, either in his ecclesiastical or temporal rights, but only requires the performance of a ministerial Act, to which he is bound *virtute officii*, and the not doing whereof will prejudice Petitioners and all other lay patrons in the like case. Pray for leave to proceed in their legal course for the recovery of their right. *Signed* George Hassard, Dean of Windsor. L. J., XIV. 547. [The Committee of Privileges to whom the Petition was referred, resolved by 10 votes to three that the Bishop had no privilege in this case. Priv. Book 10 Nov.; L. J., XIV. 549.]

321. Nov. 10. Universities of Oxford and Cambridge (Confirmation of Charters) Bill. Draft of an additional Act for the confirmation of the Charters, Liberties, and privileges of the Universities of Oxford and Cambridge. Whereas by one Act of Parliament made in the thirteenth year of the reign of the late Queen Elizabeth, intituled An Act concerning the several corporations of the Universities of Oxford and Cambridge and the Confirmation of the Charters, Liberties and privileges granted to either of them, it was amongst other things enacted that the Letters patents of the said Queen's Highness' noble father King Henry the Eighth, made and granted to the Chancellor and Scholars of the University of Oxford, bearing date the first day of April in the fourteenth year of his reign, and the Letters Patents of the said Queen made and granted unto the Chancellor, Masters and Scholars of the University of Cambridge, bearing date the six and twentieth day of April, in the third year of her Highness' most gracious reign, and also all other Letters Patent by any of the progenitors or predecessors of the said Queen made to either of the said Corporate bodies severally, or to any of their predecessors by whatsoever name or names the said Chancellor, Masters and Scholars of either of the said Universities in any of the said Letters Patents had theretofore been named, should from henceforth be good, effectual and available in the law to all intents, constructions and purposes to the then Chancellor, Masters and Scholars of

HOUSE OF LORDS MSS.

1690.

either of the said Universities, and to their successors for evermore, and according to the form, words, sentences and true meaning of every of the same Letters Patents, as amply, fully and largely as if the same Letters Patents were recited verbatim in the said Act of Parliament, any thing to the contrary in any wise notwithstanding; And that the then Chancellor, Masters and Scholars of either of the said Universities severally and their successors for ever, by the name of Chancellor, Masters and Scholars of either of the said Universities, should and might severally have, hold, possess and use to them and to their successors for evermore, all manner of manors, lordships, rectories, parsonages, lands, tenements, rents, services, annuities, advowsons of churches, possessions, pensions, portions and hereditaments, and all manner of liberties, franchises, immunities, quietances and privileges, view of frank pledge, law days and other things, whatsoever they be, the which either of the said corporate bodies of either of the said Universities had held, occupied or enjoyed, or of right ought to have had, used, occupied, or enjoyed at any time or times before the making of the said Act of Parliament, according to the true intent and meaning as well of the said Letters Patents by the said noble Prince King Henry the Eighth, made and granted to the Chancellor and Scholars of the University of Oxford, bearing date as is aforesaid, as of the Letters Patents of the said Queen's Majesty made and granted unto the Chancellor, Masters and Scholars of the University of Cambridge, bearing date as aforesaid, and, as according to the true intent and meaning of all other the aforesaid Letters Patents whatsoever, any statute or other thing or things whatsoever theretofore made or done to the contrary in any wise notwithstanding; And that as well the said Letters Patents of the Queen's Highness' said father King Henry the Eighth, bearing date as is before expressed, made and granted to the said corporate body of the said University of Oxford, as the Letters Patents of the said Queen's Majesty aforesaid made and granted to the Chancellor, Masters and Scholars of the University of Cambridge bearing date as aforesaid, and all other Letters Patents by any of the progenitors or predecessors of her said Highness, and all manner of liberties, franchises, immunities, quietances and privileges, leets, law days, and other things whatsoever therein expressed, given or granted to the said Chancellor, Masters and Scholars of either of the said Universities, or to any of the predecessors of either of the said Universities by whatsoever name the said Chancellor, Master and Scholars of either of the said Universities, or any of the said Letters Patents be named, were and by virtue of the said Act, should be from thenceforth ratified, established, and confirmed unto the said Chancellor, Masters and Scholars of either of the said Universities and to their successors for ever, any statute, law, usage, custom, construction, or other thing to the contrary in anywise notwithstanding. And whereas since the making of the said recited Act, the said Queen was pleased to grant to the Chancellor, Masters and Scholars of the said University of Cambridge other Letters Patents under her Great Seal for the benefit of the said University, bearing date the thirtieth day of August in the one and thirtieth year of her reign, and the late King Charles the First did also grant many additional privileges to the Chancellor, Masters and Scholars of the said University of Oxford, by his Letters Patents bearing date the third day of March, in the eleventh year of his reign. Be it enacted by the King and Queen's most Excellent Majesties, by and with the advice and consent of the Lords Spiritual and Temporal and the Commons in this present Parliament assembled, and by the authority of the same, that as well the said Letters Patents

House of Lords MSS.

1690.

made and granted by the said Queen to the Chancellor, Masters and Scholars of the said University of Cambridge dated on the said thirtieth day of August as the Letters Patents of the said King Charles the First made and granted to the Chancellor, Masters and Scholars of the said University of Oxford, dated on the said third day of March, as also all other Letters Patents and Charters by any of the predecessors of their Majesties kings or queens of this realm, whether before or since the said thirteenth year of the said late Queen Elizabeth made or granted to either of the said Corporate bodies of the said Universities severally, or to any of the predecessors of either of the said Universities by whatsoever name or names the said Chancellor, Masters, and Scholars in any of the said Letters Patents or Charters have been heretofore named shall be from henceforth good, effectual and available in law, to all intents, constructions and purposes to the now Chancellor, Masters, and Scholars of either of the said Universities respectively and to their successors for evermore, after and according to the form, words, sentences and true meaning of every of the same Letters Patents and Charters, as amply, fully and largely as if the same Letters Patents and Charters were recited verbatim in this present Act, anything herein to the contrary in anywise notwithstanding. And that all the said Letters Patents and Charters, and all manner of liberties and franchises, immunities, quietances, privileges, powers and authorities, leets, law days, and other things whatsoever in the said Act or in any of the said Letters Patents or Charters, expressed, given or granted to the said Chancellor, Masters and Scholars of either of the said Universities, or to any of their predecessors of the said Universities, or to any public professor, officer, or minister of either of the said Universities for the time being, or to the said respective Chancellors, Masters and Scholars, or any other person or persons in trust, for the benefit and support of such office or place, by whatsoever name or title the said Chancellors, Masters and Scholars, or the said professors, officers or ministers of either of the said Universities or other persons in any of the said Letters Patents or Charters be named or described, be and by virtue of this present Act shall be from henceforth ratified, established and confirmed unto the said Chancellors, Masters and Scholars of either of the said Universities, and their successors, professors, officers, ministers and their successors, according to the true intent and meaning of the said Act and all and every the said Letters Patents and Charters, notwithstanding any failure or want of form in law in the said Letters Patents or Charters or in any of them, any statute, law, usage, custom, construction or other thing to the contrary in anywise notwithstanding.

And be it further enacted, that all and singular Letters Patents or Charters, at any time heretofore made by any of the Kings or Queens of this Realm for the erection, foundation, incorporation or endowment of any College or Hall in either of the said Universities, or for the confirmation of any such Charters, Letters Patents or Grants to them, or any of them, made to or for the endowment, benefit, or advantage of any of the Governors, Masters, Provosts, Presidents, Rectors, Wardens, Principals, Students, Fellows and Scholars of the said Colleges, or Halls, or any of them respectively, by whatsoever name or names the said Governors, Masters, Provosts, Presidents, Rectors, Wardens, Principals, Students, Fellows and Scholars, or their predecessors, or any or either of them respectively in any of the said Letters Patents, Charters, Instruments, Grants, Indentures or Writings be or are incorporated or named, were and shall be reputed, taken and adjudged to have been good, perfect and effectual in the law for all things therein contained, according to the true intent and meaning of the same, any thing, matter or cause to the contrary notwithstanding.

And be it enacted that all and every the several respective and Corporate bodies of all and every of the said Colleges and Halls of either of the said Universities shall, and may severally have, hold, possess, enjoy and use to them and their successors for ever, all manner of manors, lordships, rectories, parsonages, lands, tenements, rents, services, annuities, advowsons of churches, possessions, pensions, portions and hereditaments, and all manner of liberties, franchises, immunities, quietances and privileges, view of frank pledge, law days and other things whatsoever they be, the which any of the respective Corporate bodies of the said College or Halls in either of the said Universities had held, occupied, or enjoyed, or of right ought to have had, held, used, occupied and enjoyed at any time or times before the making of this Act, according to the true intent and meaning of any such Letters Patents, Charters, instruments, grants, indentures or writings whatsoever, any law, statute, letters mandatory or other thing or things whatsoever heretofore made or done to the contrary notwithstanding.

And whereas in several of the local statutes, ordinances and rules of the Colleges and Halls in the said Universities established and made in former times, many rites and offices of superstitious devotion had been appointed to be said and observed in the said Colleges and Halls, by the Governors, Fellows or Scholars or other Officers and Ministers of such foundations, by saying or singing of masses, dirges, obits and the like Popish offices and services, contrary to the true profession of the Protestant true Reformed Religion by law established in this realm; Wherefore, to remove all occasion of doubts or scruples which may happen in the minds of weak men concerning such rites and superstitious offices, be it further enacted, that all such rites and offices of masses, dirges, obits, complines and other Popish offices and services of superstitious devotion contrary to the true profession of the said Protestant Reformed Religion which are mentioned, prescribed, established or expressed in any such local statutes, rules or ordinances, shall and are hereby for ever abolished to all intents and purposes whatsoever, and no oaths heretofore taken, or hereafter to be taken, by any manner of person or persons of any such college or hall for the observance of any of the said respective local statutes, rules or ordinances, shall be taken or deemed to be, or have been meant or intended to relate to any of the said rites and services, or any other such superstitious and Popish offices in any such statutes, rules or ordinances established or expressed, any of the said statutes or ordinances, or any other matter or thing to the contrary in anywise notwithstanding.

Provided also, and be it enacted, that upon all and every visitation of the said respective Universities, or either of them, and all and every the respective Colleges and Halls and the governors, masters, scholars, fellows, members and officers of the same, by what name or names soever they be known, called or distinguished, all proceedings, sentences and judgments against any offender therein shall be had and given according to the laws and statutes of this realm, or the customs and statutes of the said respective Universities or the several local statutes and ordinances of the said Colleges or Halls, or any of them respectively and not otherwise, any law, statute or usage to the contrary in anywise notwithstanding.

And whereas it was often threatened in the reign of the late King James that a Quo Warranto should be brought against the Chancellor, Master and Scholars of the University of Oxford, under the pretence that the number of printing presses by them used, and the lease of the right and interest of printing and comprinting all and all manner of books by them made, was not warranted by the foresaid Letters Patents of King Charles the first, granted to the said University; Therefore, for the better encouragement of printing in the said University, and for the promotion of learning therein, and to the intent that all scruples and controversies concerning the same may henceforth be removed, Be it enacted by the authority aforesaid, that it shall and may be lawful for the Chancellor, Masters and Scholars of the said University of Oxford, to have and use any number of presses, not exceeding sixteen, in the said University, and to make any lease or leases of all or of any part of their right or interest of printing and comprinting all and all manner of books granted to them by the aforesaid Letters Patents of King Charles the first, for any time of years not exceeding twenty-one. Provided nevertheless, that nothing in this Act shall extend, or be construed to extend, to the prejudice of the rights and privileges of the Master and keepers or Wardens and commonalty of the mystery or art of Stationers of the City of London; but that they shall have and enjoy the same rights and privileges as they might have done if this Act had never been made, anything herein to the contrary notwithstanding.

And whereas the advowson and perpetual right of patronage of the rectory of Newelme, otherwise called Ewelme, in the county of Oxford and diocese of Oxford, was granted to the Chancellor, Masters and Scholars of the University of Oxford, by Letters Patents of King James the First, bearing date the six and twentieth day of August in the third year of his reign, to the intent that the profits thereof should be received and appropriated for the better support and maintenance of the Regius Professor in Divinity for that University, and the advowson and right of patronage of the rectory of Somersham, with Colne and Pidley and others the chapels thereof in the county of Huntingdon and diocese of Lincoln, and the rectory of Terrington in the county of Norfolk and diocese of Norwich, were likewise granted by the like Letters Patents of the said King, bearing date on the said six and twentieth day of August in the said third year of his reign, to the Chancellor, Masters and Scholars of the University of Cambridge, for the better support and maintenance of the Regius Professor and Margaret Professor in Divinity of that University; And whereas the right and title to one of the prebends of the cathedral church of Worcester, was by the Letters Patents of King Charles the first, bearing date the fifth day of July in the third year of his reign, given and granted to the Margaret Professor of the University of Oxford for the time being, for the better support and maintenance of the Margaret professors of the said University for ever; Be it enacted by the authority aforesaid, that the said respective rectories of Newelme, otherwise called Ewelme, and Somersham with Colne and Pidley and the chapels thereof, and the said rectory of Terrington, with the rights, members and appurtenances of every of them and the profits thereof, shall be respectively appropriated and applied for the better support and maintenance of the said respective professors in divinity of the said respective Universities for the time being and their successors, in as full and ample manner as if they were instituted and inducted in the same in due form of law, and according to the true intent and meaning of the said respective Letters Patent and the respective grants thereof by the said King James, granted or mentioned to be granted, as aforesaid; And the said respective professors for the time being, their executors and administrators, are hereby enabled and empowered in the name of the respective Chancellor, Masters and Scholars to sue for and recover all tithes, oblations and obventions now due and in arrear, or which shall hereafter become due and payable within the said respective rectories, or either of them, or any the titheable places thereunto belonging, any law or usage to the contrary notwithstanding.

Provided always and be it enacted, that the said respective professors for the time being shall take care of serving the respective cures there, or shall allow out of the profits of the said respective rectories sufficient for the support and maintenance of a Curate in each of the said rectories, and that no Regius Professor or Margaret Professor in Divinity, as aforesaid, shall hold any of the said respective rectories, or receive the profits thereof, for longer time than he shall hold such his professor's place in the respective University wherein he shall be possessed of the same.

And be it likewise enacted, that the said Margaret Professor of the University of Oxford, being obliged to constant residence and duty in the said University, shall have and receive all profits and emoluments arising from the said prebend of Worcester, in as full and large a manner as if he actually resided in the said Cathedral of Worcester and performed his duty therein, any law, statute, or any usage of the said Church to the contrary in any wise notwithstanding.

Provided always and be it enacted, that nothing in this Act shall be construed to extend to certain Letters Patents of King Charles the First bearing date the one and twentieth day of December in the eleventh year of his reign, for the granting a canonry of Christ Church in Oxford to the Orator of the said University, but that the same shall be and remain of the like force and effect and no other, as if this Act had never been had or made, anything therein to the contrary notwithstanding.

Saving to all and every person and persons politic and corporate, their heirs and successors, and the heirs and successors of every of them other than the King and Queen's Majesties, their heirs and successors, all such rights, titles, interests, leases, entries, conditions, charges and demands which they and every of them had, might, or should have had in or to any of the said manors, lordships, rectories, parsonages, lands, tenements, rents, services, annuities, advowsons of Churches, pensions, portions, hereditaments and all other things in the said Letters Patents, charters, instruments, grants, indentures or writings or any of them mentioned or comprised by reason of any right, title, charge, interest or condition to them or any of them, or to the ancestors or predecessors of them, or any of them devolute or grown before the several dates of the same Letters Patents, charters, instruments, grants, indentures or writings, or by reason of any gift, grant, demise or other act or acts at any time made or done between the said Chancellor, Masters and Scholars of either of the said Universities of Oxford and Cambridge or any of them and others, and between any governor or master, students, fellows and scholars of any of the Colleges or Halls in either of the said Universities respectively, or the Corporate bodies of them, or any of them and others by what name or names soever the same were made or done, in like manner and form as they and every of them had or might have had the same before the making of this Act, anything therein contained to the contrary notwithstanding.

Provided always and be it enacted by the authority aforesaid, that this Act, or anything therein contained, shall not extend to the prejudice or hurt of the liberties and privileges of right belonging to the mayor, bailiffs and burgesses of the town of Cambridge and city of Oxford, but that they, the said mayor, bailiffs and burgesses, and every of them, and their successors, shall be and continue free in such sort and degree, and enjoy such liberties, freedoms and immunities as they or any of them lawfully may or might have done before the making of this present Act, anything in this present Act to the contrary notwithstanding. [Read 1ª this day. L. J., XIV. 547. No further proceedings.]

322. Nov. 11. Creditors and poor Prisoners Relief Bill.—Draft of an Act for the relief of Creditors and poor Prisoners.

§ i. Forasmuch as the undue execution of the Acts of the 22nd, 23rd and 30th years of the reign of King Charles the Second for the Relief and Discharge of poor distressed Prisoners for debt has been very grievous unto divers of their Majesties' most loving subjects, who have been much troubled by unnecessary summons and the irregular practice thereof, and although there was a colourable pretence of the prisoners giving in a schedule of their debts to their creditors, yet such prisoners kept their books, bills, and papers which proved the same, and it was likewise left in the power of the prisoners to discharge their debtors to the damage of their creditors, whose interest and desire it is to have their debts rather than the persons of the prisoners, since it is become the common practice of jailors and keepers of prisons, so soon as the creditor has put the law in execution against his debtor, that then the jailor and his accomplices do get what the prisoner has left and so defeat the just creditor of his debt. For remedy whereof and to supply other defects which have obstructed the good ends and purposes of the said Acts, Be it therefore enacted by the King and Queen's Most Excellent Majesties, by and with the advice and consent of the Lords Spiritual and Temporal and Commons in this present Parliament assembled, and by the authority of the same, That it shall and may be lawful to and for any Justice of the Peace of any county, city, town or liberty within the Kingdom of England, Dominion of Wales and town of Berwick-upon-Tweed, or any three or more of them, to hear the charge of the creditor against the jailors and prisoners and to determine as this Act directs, by letting the creditor not have only the benefit of this law against the jailor and prisoner, but also against the debtors of such prisoners for the benefit of the creditors as to all persons being in prison or upon bail or security or who are prisoners in the King's Bench prison, or to the Warden of the Fleet or in Ludgate or the Counters in London or the Gate-house at Westminster, or in any other prison elsewhere whatsoever within the Kingdom of England, Dominion of Wales or town of Berwick-upon-Tweed, and that it shall be lawful to and for the said Justices or any one of them within their respective limits or jurisdictions, at the desire or request of any creditor, to grant his warrant or summons gratis to bring before him or them the prisoner his debtor and there to examine him or her upon oath or any other witnesses what real or other estate he or she hath, which oath the said Justice or Justices are hereby empowered to administer, to know what effects are belonging to him or her or what debt or debts are then owing to him or her within any of their Majesties' dominions or elsewhere, and by whom and for what cause and upon what security, and also what right or title such prisoner hath to any estate real or personal either in possession, reversion or remainder, of all which a schedule shall be made and subscribed by the prisoner in the presence of such Justice or Justices and shall afterwards be fairly entered with the book-keeper hereafter nominated and appointed for that purpose by this Act, by way of debtor and creditor, and kept by him for the better information of the creditors of such prisoners, who or such of them as will join, may thereupon sue for such debts and estate, or so much thereof as will reasonably satisfy them, either in their own names or in the name of the prisoner; And that

House of Lords MSS. — 1690.

no action or actions to be brought for the recovery of the same shall abate or be discontinued or otherwise determined by the death of any such prisoner or prisoners, or for any other cause whatsoever, but that every such action or actions be proceeded upon, notwithstanding any the causes aforesaid, as if the said prisoner or prisoners were alive, and after such effects or estate so recovered and received, or enjoyed, their own debts and charges first deducted, to render the overplus to the prisoner, his executors or administrators, and after such effects, debts or credits, or any right or title to any estate, are entered with the said book-keeper and subscribed by the prisoner, that then and after that time it shall not be in the power of any prisoner to discharge, by release or otherwise, any debt in the schedule mentioned, or to release any right, title, or interest which such prisoner shall discover to have to any lands, tenements or hereditaments whatsoever, without the consent of his creditors.

§ ii. And whereas, upon strict enquiry into the condition of the prisoners, it doth appear, that there are many persons now in prison that have much more owing to them than they owe to their creditors, yet their debtors do take the advantage of their confinement and poverty, pretending they owe them nothing, or at least will not pay them, or that they cannot do it with safety, so that the prisoners, for want of money and liberty to prosecute the law with effect against their debtors, have been often non-suited, and verdicts passed against them, to the damage of their creditors, which if they had received, as in justice they ought, those debts would have paid their creditors. Therefore, be it enacted by the authority aforesaid, if any person now in prison, who, either in the King's name or his own, hath formerly sued his debtor for a debt due to the King or himself, in order to pay his just creditors, and hath by the debtor's contrivance or perjuries, or taking of evidence to the damage of the creditors, or that the prisoner's proofs were not fully heard, so that the King or plaintiff for the creditors had a verdict or non-suit passed against them, or that any decree be made in any court of equity against the King or such plaintiff for the causes aforesaid, or any of them, that then in every such case, upon the petition of any creditor or creditors of such prisoner as aforesaid, it shall be and may be lawful for the Chancellor, Lord Keeper, or the Lords Commissioners for the custody of the Great Seal of England for the time being, the Lords Chief Justice of either Bench, or any other of the King's justices, the Lord Chief Baron of the Exchequer or any other of the barons of the said Court, to grant the said party or parties a re-hearing, or a new trial, either in the name of the King, creditor or prisoner, either in the same or any other of their Majesties' Courts at Westminster, which may appear most for the benefit of the prisoner's creditors, without naming or finding a relator or paying any costs.

§ iii. And whereas merchants, drapers, mercers, goldsmiths and other persons who disburse money for their customer besides goods, in their way of trade, and are oftentimes long before they are paid or reimbursed, Be it therefore enacted by the authority aforesaid, that if any person now in prison, hath lent, paid, or laid out, for or by order of any customer now his debtor, any money on bonds, bills, payments of debts or otherwise than for goods in his way of trade for such prisoners, after discounting interest for what he hath thereof received, shall be allowed interest for all such money so lent, paid or lent out for the relief of such prisoner's creditors.

§ iv. And whereas for twelve years last past, there hath not been any charitable Act made for the relief of poor prisoners for debt, and then many persons not being able to take the benefit thereof, but remain still in prison and thereby are debarred of their just debts by the Statute of Limitation, which otherwise might be applied to satisfy their creditors; Therefore be it enacted, that no debtor to any prisoner, he or she, his or her executors or administrators, shall have any benefit or liberty to plead the Statute of Limitation to any debt or demand due to any prisoner that is in prison, whose debt is entered with the said book-keeper as aforesaid, if the prisoner can upon trial, prove his debt to be due; and if there appears any intricacy in the account or debt to the Court, the prisoner may be heard to explain it, though not as an evidence. And be it also enacted, that no debtor to any prisoner whose debt shall be entered with the said book-keeper, as this Act directs, shall be protected by any place at court or otherwise, only such as are allowed by privileges of Parliament. And be it also further enacted, that all creditors do enter their debt or charge against such prisoner their debtor, within months after the date of this Act, with the said book-keeper or his deputy, on penalty of being excluded the benefit of his debt and dividend, infants and persons beyond seas only excepted; but the said book-keeper is not to accept of any debt to be entered, except such as appears to be due by book, bill, bond, indentures, mortgages, statutes and specialities, or on an original entered, and that such debt is not barred by the Statute of Limitation.

§ v. And whereas, it is usual for jailers, at the taking of a prisoner into custody, immediately to extort money or goods from him, as well for favour, as under colour of giving advice to defraud his creditors, and to take bonds and judgments for chamber rent or liberty, and by the last Act use to certify who were true prisoners, and by that means did put in practice many frauds and cheats to the damage of the creditors; for prevention of such mischiefs, Be it enacted, that no prisoner be admitted or allowed to be so that doth not produce a record for the same, or some other sufficient testimony upon oath besides their own, and that if the jailer or keeper of prison hath taken, received, exacted or extorted any money or goods from any prisoner, upon any pretences whatsoever, more than his just fees and reasonable chamber rent, which being proved by the creditor, prisoner, or any other credible witness, then the Chief Justice or judge of the Court from whence the prisoner was committed, are hereby empowered and authorized, upon full proof of the fact before him or them, to find the jailer or keeper of prison in double the sum of money or damage which the prisoner has sustained, which if he refuse to pay to the prisoner's creditors, then the judge or judges by his or their warrants may commit him close prisoner to any jail or prison but his own, there to remain without bail or mainprise until he hath paid and satisfied the same, any law to the contrary in any wise notwithstanding.

§ vi. And whereas, in former Acts the prisoners in the several prisons gave in their effects to the clerk of the peace in the several counties, and are there kept without any benefit or relief to the creditors, Therefore be it likewise further enacted, that no person now in prison in the Fleet or King's Bench, or any other prison within the cities of London and Westminster, or the liberties thereof, or within five miles of the said cities, shall be admitted to have any benefit of this Act, until he or she hath not only given a schedule of his or her effects, as aforesaid, but also a copy of their commitment and causes with the deeds, evidences, bills, bonds, writings, books and papers relating to such estate or debts to (who is hereby nominated and appointed for that purpose) book-keeper at his office in some convenient place within or near the City of London, to be fairly and alphabetically entered in large strong paper book or books, for the perusal of such creditor or creditors who may take or have copies of the same; and also that the major part of any one of the prisoner's creditors in value shall have full power and authority to compound and agree with such prisoner or prisoners who shall take the benefit of this Act, as also to agree upon methods and rules to sue for the same, and of what creditor or other person or persons name or names to make use of for that purpose, and for settling a treasurer, attorney or agent for the recovery of the said prisoner or prisoners' debts (or any other of their debtors' debts) that any such prisoner shall give in an account of, as aforesaid, which said compositions and agreements so made by such creditors are to be entered for the satisfaction of the rest of the creditors, and what orders, compositions or agreements shall be so made and agreed unto and entered with the said book-keeper, and signed by such major part of the creditors in value shall be good and binding to all the other creditors of the said prisoner. And be it likewise enacted that the Justices of the Peace within their several counties, limits and precincts, or any three or more of them, are hereby empowered and authorised to nominate and appoint one fit person to be book-keeper within their respective jurisdictions, for the execution of this Act, in the same form and method as in the preceding clause and elsewhere by this Act is prescribed.

§ vii. And forasmuch as very many persons now detained in prison are so extremely impoverished by their confinement and otherwise, that they are totally disable to give any satisfaction to their creditors, so as their continuance in prison cannot possibly prove to be any advantage to their creditors, nevertheless it is to be presumed that any creditor will put himself to the trouble of putting this Act in execution against such a disabled prisoner that is like to remain and perish in jail, to the ruin of their families and the manifest prejudice of the kingdom in general, since many of them, if they were at liberty, are qualified to be very serviceable to the public; Therefore be it also further enacted, that all persons in prison or upon bail or security to the jailer for debt or damages, or for or upon any action or actions, or upon any mean process for debt, account, or trespass upon the case, which actions by prosecution of law may be judgments for debts or damages, or who have judgments entered upon record against them, or are charged in execution, or imprisoned upon attachments for debt, or upon outlawries before or after judgments for debt, or damages or costs only, who shall take the oath in this Act mentioned, shall and may be relieved and discharged from their imprisonment, in such way and after such a manner as is directed by this Act. And in case such prisoner or prisoners coming before such justice or justices shall take an oath to this effect, viz., I (A.B.) do, upon my corporal oath solemnly profess and declare before Almighty God, that I have not any estate, real or personal, in possession, reversion or remainder, of the value of Ten pounds in the whole, or sufficient to pay the debt or damages for which I am in prison, besides what is mentioned and expressed in the Schedule which I have given in to the book-keeper for the use of my creditors, and that I have not, directly or indirectly, sold, leased, or otherwise conveyed, disposed of, or entrusted all or any part of my estate thereby to secure the same, to receive or expect any profit or advantage thereof, or defraud or deceive any creditor or creditors whatsoever to whom I stand indebted. Therefore, be it also enacted, that any person being in jail within the kingdom of England, dominion of Wales, or town of Berwick-upon-Tweed, upon his petition to any of the justices within the county, city, town or liberty where he or she is in prison, to be brought before him or them, and that he or she may have his or their certificate or summons gratis to summon his or her creditors that hath charged him or her in prison before him or them, and thereupon taking the said oath and giving in an account of their effects, if any, as in this Act is appointed, the creditor must detect him or her, or show just cause why the said justices or any three or more of them shall not discharge him or her from their imprisonment, which by virtue of this Act the justices at their next general sessions or meeting by adjournment or any three or more of them within their several counties, ridings, divisions, or precincts, are hereby authorised and impowered to put in execution all such powers, authorities and directions for the full release and discharge of all such persons as are in prison on the day of being the day on which his Majesty relieved us from popery and slavery.

§ viii. And whereas, in former charitable Acts the creditors had forty days notice to be left at their last abode, under the hand and seal of the justice of the county where such prisoner was in prison, which after proved of ill consequence to the creditors, for that the summoner neglected to perform the trust reposed in him by the prisoner, and though he dropt it, or left the notice carelessly, so that it never came to the hands of the creditors, yet the summoner made oath thereof, which caused many perjuries, to the damage of the creditor; For the prevention of which mischief for the future, Be it also further enacted, that the prisoner or prisoners shall leave a certificate in writing under the hand and seal of a justice of the peace giving notice to his or her creditor or creditors, or to his or their attorney or attornies, or at the last abode of the creditor, at whose suit he or she standeth charged or imprisoned, thereby appointing the said creditor or creditors, their executors or administrators, or his or their attorney, and the said prisoner to appear before the Justices at the next general quarter sessions to be holden for the same county, city, town or liberty where it shall upon oath appear, which oath the said Justices are hereby empowered to administer, that the said certificate was so served or left. And as to other persons and creditors to whom the prisoner is indebted, that they may not be deceived and give the prisoner new credit, or be kept in ignorance of his being in prison, the said book-keeper shall also cause to be printed a true and exact list of all prisoners' Christian and surnames, with additions of their quality, trade and mystery, who have entered their effects with the said book-keeper as aforesaid, which said list shall be sent to the several book-keepers in their respective counties before the sessions in discharge of the prisoners, as this Act directs, of which said list a sufficient number of printed copies may be had of the said book-keeper, at his office or some other convenient place or places whereof an advertisement shall be given in the London Gazette, where such lists are to be had for the use of the creditors, or any other person or persons who shall have occasion to peruse the same.

§ ix. And be it also further enacted, that after such oaths taken by the said prisoner, and not disproved by good testimonies of any credible person or persons upon oath, to be administered by the said Justices by virtue of this Act, then the said Justices being satisfied therein, shall direct their warrant under their hands and seals, commanding the said sheriff, jailer or keeper of prison, to set at liberty and discharge the said prisoner if imprisoned for the cause aforesaid, and no other, without paying anything for fee, or chamber rent, and that all bonds, judgments, statutes, recognizances, and all other securities whatsoever, given or entered into by any such prisoner or any other person or

House of Lords MSS.

1690.

persons bound for him to any jailer or keeper of prison for the payment of any fee or chamber rent, or for or upon any other condition or consideration whatsoever, shall be absolutely void, null and of no effect to all intents and purposes, as well in relation to such security as to the prisoner himself. And it is hereby provided, that such warrant as aforesaid shall be a sufficient discharge to the same sheriff, jailer, or keeper of prison, and that no action of escape or other action shall be brought against them or any of them for the same in any wise; and that upon any action of escape or other suit that shall be brought against any of the judges, justices of the peace, sheriff, jailer, or keeper of prison for any thing done in obedience to this Act, it shall and may be lawful to and for such judge or justice of the peace, sheriff, jailer or keeper of prison to plead the general issue and give this Act in evidence, which shall be a good and sufficient discharge, and shall save harmless every such judge, justice of the peace, sheriff, jailer, and keeper of prison pleading the same; And if the plaintiff in any such action shall be non-suited, or verdict pass against him, the defendant shall have double costs, to be taxed by the Court where such action is brought.

§ x. Provided always and be it further enacted that notwithstanding the discharge of the person of any such prisoner as aforesaid, all and every judgment had and taken against him or her, shall be and stand good and effectual in the law to all intents and purposes against the lands, tenements and hereditaments, goods and chattels. And every prisoner discharged by this Act, if required by any creditor to retain an attorney and appear for him and file common bail to every such action and plead thereunto, so that the plaintiff, if he pleases, may recover and enter judgment against such prisoner, to be executed and levied upon the lands, tenements, goods and chattels of such prisoner so discharged as aforesaid, his or her wearing apparel, furniture for his or her dwelling house, the said furniture not exceeding ten pounds in value, and his or her tools for his or her trade and occupation only excepted, but not upon the person of the prisoner, the persons of such prisoners being hereby for ever freed and discharged from imprisonment for anything hereunto relating contracted before the time of their discharge, having had notice as aforesaid.

§ xi. Provided always, and be it enacted that the discharge of any person or persons by virtue of this Act shall not amount unto, or be construed to free or discharge any other person jointly or severally bound and liable to answer the debt either as principal or security, but that such other person or persons shall be liable to answer the said debt to all intents and purposes as they were before the discharge of such prisoner.

§ xii. Provided also and be it enacted, that if any debtor to a prisoner discharged by this Act after his debt is entered with the book-keeper as aforesaid, shall pay any money due to such prisoner, that notwithstanding such payment, yet the said debtor shall be liable to pay the same to the creditors of such prisoner as if such payment had not been made at all.

§ xiii. Provided also, that no prisoner shall be discharged by this Act that hath not or shall not before such oath made have remained in prison by the space of six months.

§ xiv. Provided also that this Act shall not extend to any person or persons in execution for any fine, on him or her imposed, for any offence committed before the date hereof against their Majesties King William and Queen Mary.

§ xv. Provided also and be it enacted, that in case any sheriff, jailer or keeper of prison shall refuse or delay to bring or discharge any prisoner according to the order of the Justice or Justices of the peace to be made in manner as aforesaid, that then every such sheriff, jailer or keeper of prison shall forfeit and pay to the creditors of such prisoner detained contrary to such order, the sum of one hundred pounds, to be recovered by such creditors or any one of them, by action of debt in any of their Majesties' Courts of Record, and shall also be further subject to such fines and imprisonments as the said Justices shall, upon complaint, order and award.

§ xvi. Provided also that the Lord Chief Justices, Lord Chief Baron, the Justices of the peace in their several jurisdictions, and all Commissioners for charitable uses do use their best endeavours and diligence to find out the several legacies, gifts and bequests, bestowed and given for the benefit and advantage of the poor prisoners for debt in the several jails and prisons in this kingdom; and that they shall send for any deeds, wills, writings and books of account whatsoever, and for any person or persons concerned therein, and to examine them upon oath to make a true discovery thereof (which they shall have full power and authority hereby to do) and the same so found out and ascertained, then to be entered with the said book-keeper, and the said Judges and Justices of the peace and Commissioners for charitable uses, are hereby required and empowered to settle the same in some manner or way that the prisoner hereafter may not be defrauded, but receive the full benefit thereof, according to the true intent of the donors.

§ xvii. Provided also and be it enacted, that if any person discharged by this Act shall hereafter be arrested or held to bail for any debt contracted before the time of such discharge, that then the said Chief Justices, or any of the Justices of the court out of which the process came, or any Justice of the peace near to the place where the prisoner shall be in custody who shall, upon a petition to the said Judge or Justice, or either of them to that purpose, send for the said person before him, and upon his producing his duplicate or certificate of his discharge under two of the Justices' hands that discharged him, and witnessed and entered by the said book-keeper or his deputy, the said Judge or Justice shall immediately order his discharge. And if the plaintiff, notwithstanding such order, insist to imprison or detain him, he shall forfeit the value of his debt to be paid to the aggrieved party's creditors, to be recovered as aforesaid, and the party so arrested and detained, as aforesaid, shall likewise be at liberty to bring his action of false imprisonment against the plaintiff and all other persons concerned in the arrest or detained contrary to the intent and meaning of this Act.

§ xviii. Provided also that every book-keeper within any county, city, town or liberty within the kingdom of England, dominion of Wales and town of Berwick-upon-Tweed shall within after the release of prisoners by this Act, return up to the chief book-keeper's office, in or near London, the particular schedules of effects that was delivered to him with the books, deeds, writings and papers of accounts, there to be fairly entered, where the creditors may, by themselves or their agents, see how the estates of such debtors stand. And for the further benefit of the creditors, if there be any persons or prisoners that were discharged by a former Act made in the thirtieth year of King Charles the Second, entitled an Act for the further relief and discharge of poor prisoners for debt, by which Act they were to leave schedules of their effects with the clerks of the peace of the several counties, which was of no benefit to the creditors in such case, all such creditors have liberty to petition the Justices of the peace within their respective jurisdictions, or any two of them, for an order to any of the clerks of the peace to send a true copy of their effects, paying him for every such copy of any person's effects required to be delivered to the

House of Lords MSS. — 1690.

said book-keeper or his deputy, to be entered and sued for in manner aforesaid for the use of the creditors as the major part of them shall agree.

§ xix. Provided also, and be it enacted, that if any person be in execution and petition any Justices to be relieved by this Act, it shall and may be lawful for the sheriff, jailer, or keeper of prison to send with the prisoner a keeper to go before the Justice or Justices of the peace, and after he hath been examined and taken the said oaths and done what the Justices may require him to do by virtue of this Act, then the said keeper shall carry him back to the prison, which shall be a good and sufficient discharge, and shall save harmless every such Justice of the peace, jailer or keeper of prison pleading the same, in case any action of escape shall be brought against any of them for the same.

§ xx. Provided always, and be it enacted by the authority aforesaid, that no person or persons, who shall be discharged by virtue of the Act and shall give in a schedule of their effects as aforesaid, shall be deemed, taken or adjudged to be within any statute or statutes heretofore made against bankrupts, and that the execution of this Act shall not be crossed, hindered or obstructed, by colour or pretence of any commission or commissions of bankrupts already taken out or hereafter to be taken out against any person or persons who shall take the benefit of this Act as aforesaid, but that every such commission are hereby adjudged and declared to be null and void to all intents and purposes whatsoever, any law heretofore made to the contrary in any wise notwithstanding.

§ xxi. Provided always (and to deter all persons who are by the charitable intentions of this Act to be relieved from abusing the favour hereby to them intended) that if any person who shall in pursuance of this Act take his oath for any of the purposes hereby appointed, shall forswear or perjure himself, then such person being thereof lawfully convicted, shall beyond and over and above the penalties which may by the law now in being be inflicted, suffer imprisonment for the space of seven years without bail or mainprize. [Read 1a this day. L. J., XIV. 548. No further proceedings.]

323. Nov. 12. Williams' Estate Act.—Amended draft of an Act for the raising money out of the estate of Thomas Williams, Esq., deceased, by letting of leases and otherwise for the more speedy payment of his debts. [Read 1a this day; Royal Assent 20 Dec. L. J., XIV. 550, 601. Com. Book 17 Nov. 2 & 3 W. & M. c. 28 in Long Calendar.]

324. Nov. 13. Serle's Estate Act.—Amended draft of an Act for selling the estate of Henry Serle, Esq., deceased. [Read 1a this day; Royal Assent 20 Dec., L. J., XIV. 550, 601. 2 & 3 W. & M. c. 25 in Long Calendar.]

Annexed:—

(*a.*) 21 Nov. Lords' Amendments to the Bill, made in Committee this day. Com. Book.

325. Nov. 14. Petworth Parsonage Bill.—Draft of an Act for the uniting the parsonage of Petworth in the County of Sussex unto the Bishopric of Chichester. Whereas the King and Queen's Most Excellent Majesties, out of their princely care of the Church of England and all the interests thereof, are graciously disposed to advance the bishopric of Chichester in revenue by uniting thereunto the living of Petworth in the County of Sussex and diocese of Chichester, now in the patronage of the College Royal of the Blessed Mary of Eton, near unto Windsor in the County of Bucks, commonly called the King's College of Our Blessed Lady of Eton nigh or by Windsor in the said County of Bucks and the same College, And whereas their Majesties upon the humble petition of the Bishop of Chichester and by and with the consent of the said Provost and College, are willing to make recompense to the said Provost and College for their said living of Petworth; Be it therefore enacted by the King and Queen's most excellent Majesties, by and with the advice and consent of the Lords Spiritual and Temporal and of the Commons in this present Parliament assembled, and by the authority of the same, that the said rectory or parsonage of Petworth with all the chapels, members, rights and appertenances thereof or thereto belonging, or therewith used and enjoyed, and the perpetual advowson and right of patronage thereof, and all and singular the manors, messuages, lands, tenements, tithes, portions, oblations, rents, pensions, profits and hereditaments of what kind soever, parcel of the said rectory or thereunto belonging or therewith used and enjoyed, are hereby declared to be and immediately from and after the next avoidance of the said rectory or parsonage shall be united to the Bishopric of Chichester for ever. And the Bishop of Chichester and his successors in the said see of Chichester, shall be from thenceforth for ever parsons of the said Church of Petworth, to all intents and purposes, without any presentation, institution or induction to the said Church, and without any other ceremonies or any other act or thing whatsoever, save such as are or shall be from time to time requisite to the making of a Bishop of Chichester.

And be it likewise enacted and ordained, and it is hereby further enacted and ordained by the authority aforesaid, that the advowson and right of patronage of the Church of Clewer in the County of Bucks, near unto the said College of Eton, and the advowson and right of patronage of the Church of Farnham Regis in the County of Bucks, near unto the said College of Eton, and the advowson and the right of patronage of the church of Worplesdon in the County of Surrey near Guildford, and of all the chapels to the said last mentioned Churches respectively belonging, with all and singular the members, rights and appurtenances thereof or thereto belonging, or therewith used or enjoyed from henceforth, shall be settled in and upon the said Provost of the College Royal of the blessed Mary of Eton near unto Windsor, and the same College and their successors for ever. And the said Provost and College, in the right of their Corporation, shall be and are hereby declared and enacted to be the perpetual patron and patrons of the aforesaid respective advowsons of the Churches of Clewer, of Farnham Regis and of Worplesdon, and shall and may from and after the next avoydance of all or any of the said Churches, make such presentation and presentations thereunto as of right they have used heretofore to make to the Church of Petworth aforementioned, or to any other benefice whereof the right of presentation belongs to them in right of their Corporation. And further, that the said Provost and College shall and may have like remedies in all cases concerning their title to the said respective Churches hereby settled on them, as aforesaid, as if they had been actually patrons of the said Churches and had last presented to the same respectively.

And it is hereby further enacted and ordained by the authority aforesaid, that the advowson and right of patronage of the Church of Ford in the said County of Sussex, and the advowson and right of patronage of the prebend of Mardon in the said County of Sussex, both in the disposition and gift of the Bishop of Chichester, shall immediately from and after the next avoidance thereof respectively for ever hereafter, be vested and settled in their Majesties and their heirs and successors, and shall be from time to time disposed and disposable in such and the like manner to all intents and purposes as the aforesaid Churches of Farnham Regis and Clewer lately were, and as if their Majesties had been actually patrons of the said last mentioned Churches, and had last presented to the same respectively. And further, that the unions, annexations and several dispositions and settlements herein contained shall be firm as hereby meant and intended, the Statute of Mortmain or any other law, custom or thing whatsoever; saving unto their Majesties, their heirs and successors all the Tenths and first fruits of the said churches and chapels. And saving to their said Majesties, their heirs and successors all such right and title of and to the premises, or any part thereof, other than such as they have been pleased hereby to settle on the said Provost and College and their successors. And saving to all other persons and bodies politic their heirs and successors (other than the said Bishop and his successors and other than the said Provost and College and their successors) all such right, title, claim and demand as they or any of them have, or may have to the premises, or to any part thereof. [Read 1[a] this day. L. J., XIV. 552. In Committee the Provost of Eton consented on behalf of himself and the Fellows of Eton to the Bill, and the E. Rochester acquainted the Committee for the E. Nottingham that it was with the King and Queen's consent that the livings mentioned in the Bill should be applied as directed. (Com. Book 17 Nov.) The Bill was rejected on second reading in the Commons. C. J., X. 480.]

326. Nov. 14. Cudmore *v.* Lacy.—Copy writ of Error and transcript of record brought in this day, with tenor of judgment annexed thereto. The Plaintiffs, Thos. Cudmore, late of Kelvedon, co. Essex, Gent., Thos. Wilsheir and Thos. Argent, of Coggeshall, co. Essex, Yeomen, and William Adcock, of Boxsted, co. Essex, Yeoman, appeal from a judgment in an action brought by Thos. Lacey for ejecting him from Coggeshall Hall, which he held from Sir Gervas Elwes, Bart., for a term of 5 years unexpired. L. J., XIV. 552, 589.

327. Nov. 15. Writ of Summons (Duke of Schonberg).—Writ of Summons (dated 13 Nov.) to Charles, Duke of Schomberg. [Sat first in Parliament this day upon the death of his father. He signs his name "Schonberg" on the Test Roll (12th Report, Appendix, Part VI., No. **227**). L. J., XIV. 554.]

328. Nov. 15. Quakers' Affirmation Bill.—Amended* draft of an Act to prevent obstruction of Justice and other inconveniences occasioned by [many Protestant] *several of their Majesties'* subjects scrupling to swear in the form and manner now used. Whereas it is evident that there are [many of the King and Queens' Protestant] *several of their Majesties'* subjects, *commonly called or known by the name of Quakers,* who being [called] *summoned* in due course of law to give answers and evidence upon their corporal oaths in the several causes depending in their Majesties' Courts, or before Commissioners or persons empowered to tender an oath, do scruple to swear in that form and manner as is now ordained [or to give their answers and evidences or informations upon their oaths], by means whereof the proceedings in the said Courts and before such Commissioners and other persons so empowered are often obstructed and justice hindered and delayed from being done as of right it ought to be, and many times the truth of the

* The additions are shown by Italics, and the omissions by square brackets.

matters cannot legally be made appear, but suits and controversies are continued and prolonged to the great damage of their Majesties' subjects; For remedy whereof and that justice may have its due course, Be it enacted by the King and Queen's most excellent Majesties, by and with the advice and consent of the Lords Spiritual and Temporal, and the Commons in this present Parliament assembled, and by the authority of the same, That from and after the *five and twentieth* day of December, one thousand, six hundred and ninety, if any person or persons whatsoever being [Protestant] subject or subjects of the Kingdom of England, Dominion of Wales or town of Berwick-upon-Tweed, *commonly called Quakers, who shall first produce a certificate from the General Quarter Sessions of the Peace that he, she or they have made and subscribed the two Declarations in an Act in the first year of their Majesties' reign entituled An Act for exempting their Majesties' Protestant subjects dissenting from the Church of England from the penalties of certain laws,* shall be required to give answer or evidence, or to inform any Court, Commissioners or other person or persons empowered to tender an oath, or any Judge or jury in any matter, either between their Majesties and their subjects or between subject and subject, of the whole truth of the matter depending to the best of his or their knowledge, if such person or persons so called shall refuse to swear in the manner now used, That then [instead thereof] he, she [and] *or* they (*the men to be uncovered*), shall be required and admitted to make [a true and solemn answer as in the presence of Almighty God, according to the whole truth of the matter depending, according to the best of his, her and their knowledge] *answer or give evidence after having repeated the words following: I, A.B., do sincerely and solemnly declare in the presence of God that I will true answer make to all such questions as shall be asked me touching the matter in question, and that I will speak the truth, the whole truth and nothing but the truth, and I call God to witness and appeal to him as Judge of the truth of what I shall say;* And that such his, her [and] *or* their solemn answer, affirmation, denial or evidence shall be entered and be as valid and of the same force and virtue to all intents and purposes as if he, she or they had formally sworn according to the manner now used, and that thereupon verdict, judgment, sentence, determination or other proceeding shall be made and given as to justice and equity shall appertain, any law, statute, custom or usage to the contrary in any wise notwithstanding.

*And be it further enacted by the authority aforesaid, That if any person or persons so refusing to swear shall in his or their answer, information, affirmation, denial or evidence so solemnly given in any Court or place whatsoever or before any justice or justices of the peace, commissioner or commissioners or any other person or persons commissioned to tender an oath, wittingly and willingly falsify the truth by his, her or their said answer, information, affirmation, denial or evidence so given as aforesaid, That in such case, he, she or they so falsifying the truth, and being thereof duly convicted by the evidence of two or more credible witnesses, shall undergo such pains and punishments as are by law provided against perjured persons.† [Read 1ª this day L. J., XIV. 554. The Bill was sent to the Commons on 2 Dec., but was not read there. C. J., X. 491.]

---

* Compare with this clause the Act 7 & 8 Will. III. c. 34. sec. 3.

† Here it is noted to add Provisos A. B. and C. *See* Annexes *a*, *b*, and *c*.

HOUSE OF LORDS MSS.

1690.

Annexed:—

(*a.*) 29 Nov. Amended Proviso, marked A., viz., "Provided that if any such person being summoned to appear to *make answer*, give evidence or to testify his knowledge, shall refuse or neglect to appear *or to make answer* or to give evidence, [he] *such person* shall be subject to the same penalty as other their Majesties' subjects now are." [Agreed to as amended and ordered to be reported this day. MS. Min.]

(*b.*) 29 Nov. Amended Proviso, marked B.,* viz., "Provided that nothing in this Act shall be construed to enable any person to serve of any jury or in any public office, without taking the usual oaths and in such manner as by law is now used, *and that no Quaker shall suffer any penalty or forfeiture for refusing to serve upon any jury when summoned thereto.*" [On 25 Nov. it was proposed in C. W. H. that Quakers should not be of juries, and should have no privilege, but only give evidence. The above Proviso was agreed to, as amended, and ordered to be reported this day. (MS. Min.) This paper contains two other forms of the proviso, subsequently struck through, viz. (1) Provided that nothing in this Act shall be construed to enable any person to serve in Jury, give voice in elections or hold any public office further than they were qualified by the law before the making of this Act. (2) Provided that no Quaker shall have any more privilege or qualification to give voice in any election of Parliament men than they had before the making of this Act.]

(*c.*) 29 Nov. Amended Proviso, marked C., viz., "Provided always that nothing in this Act is intended to exempt [them Quakers] *any person or persons whatsoever* from taking the oath [in that case made and provided] *in the usual manner* at the election of Members of Parliament in that case made and provided." [Agreed to as amended and ordered to be reported this day. MS. Min.]

(*d.*) 29 Nov. List of Amendments made in C. W. H. and ordered to be reported this day. M.S. Min., Nov. 19, 20, 25, 29.

329. Nov. 15. Orphans of London Relief Bill.—Amended† draft of an Act for erecting a [Judicature for] *Court of Inquiry in order to* the relief of the [1400] distressed Orphans of the City of London. Whereas the Lord Mayor and Court of Aldermen of the [said] City *of London*, out of their deep sense of the deplorable condition of the State of the Chamber of the said City and the great debt from thence due to the said orphans, appointed a Committee to inspect and consider by what means any branch of its revenue may be improved, and earnestly desired them to proceed thereupon with utmost diligence and dispatch, And by their Order of the first of March 1687, [published in the Gazette,] did [firmly resolve and] declare that all improvements that could be made over and above the necessary charge of the City's government [shall] *should* be duly applied towards payment and relief of the said orphans, and that if any persons [can] *could* make any discovery how any part of the said revenue [may] *might* be improved,

* Compare 7 & 8 Will. III. c. 34. sec. 6.

† The additions are shown by italics, the omissions by square brackets. The whole of the enacting part was superseded by the clauses drawn by Mr. Justice Nevill. (Annex (*a.*) below.)

they [shall] *should* be recompensed for the same proportionably to such discovery: [And whereas several considerable discoveries have been made and are now ready to be demonstrated in pursuance of the said Order, and great numbers of the said orphans and their families must inavoidably perish if not speedily relieved]; *Now for the more effectual and speedy attaining the ends above mentioned*, May it [therefore] please your most [Sacred] *Excellent* Majesties, that it may be enacted, And be it enacted by the King and Queen's Most Excellent Majesties, by and with the advice and consent of the Lords Spiritual and Temporal and the Commons in Parliament assembled, and by the authority of the same, That [the said Order be and the said Order hereby is in all points ratified, established and confirmed.

And to the end that the said Order may be effectually prosecuted, Be it further enacted that the Right Honorable and , and the said Peers and honorable personages are hereby constituted a Court of Judicature for the Relief of the said orphans; and they are to sit in the Charter-House or where else their Lordships shall think more convenient; And such orders, leases, grants, compositions and decrees which shall be made by by any seven or more of them, are always to be Peers (*sic*) for the due improving of the said rights, revenues and discoveries, shall to all intents and purposes be held to be valid in law and shall be conclusive to all persons any ways concerned therein; and all persons any ways concerned are upon summons to give their attendance on the said Court, and to produce their accounts, titles, rentals, surveys, grants, leases and other writings relating to the premises; And the said Court is hereby empowered to administer an oath to such persons whom they shall think fit to examine touching any matter relating to the premises, and also to send such person or persons whom they shall find disobedient to them to such common goal within the County of Middlesex as to them shall seem fit, and the keepers of the said goals are hereby required to take and keep in their custody such person or persons as shall be so committed until they shall give obedience to the said Court or be delivered by due course of law; and the sheriff of the said County for the time being is to attend on the said Court when required, and diligently to execute such orders as their Lordships shall direct; and their Lordships are to appoint persons to attend on them and to give such allowances for their respective attendances as their Lordships shall think reasonable, and their Lordships are to examine concerning all receipts and disposal of the said orphan's moneys and concerning all the rights, customs, privileges, duties, liberties, offices, freedoms, fairs, gifts, grants, markets, tolls, vaults, waters, ways, wastes, profits and emoluments whatsoever relating or belonging to the said City, and also concerning all their lands, tenements, hereditaments and estate whatsoever, and about all causes, recognizances, pains, penalties, forfeitures and every other matter or thing relating to the premises or the improvement of them, whereby and by reason whereof the said orphans may be relieved, and to make such order as they shall think fit concerning the same. And after due provision made for paying the Lord Mayor of the said City for the time being the sum of per annum by quarterly payments, and to each of the sheriffs of the said City for the time being 500*l.* in like manner, and to and for the salaries of officers and the public charges of the said City the sum of yearly in like manner, to be disposed of as the Lord Mayor and Court of Aldermen for the time being shall appoint, all the rest and residue of the said profits which to their Lordships shall seem fit to be raised out of all or any part of the said premises shall, in such manner and methods as their Lordships

House of Lords MSS.

1690.

shall please to appoint, be paid out and disposed of to and for the satisfaction of the several portions due to every one of the said respective orphans or their respective executors or administrators, and afterwards to the payment of the other creditors of the said Chamber or their respective executors or administrators; and when any of them, or their legal representatives shall have received satisfaction for their respective debts, the respective bonds or other writings which any of the said orphans or other creditors have from the said Chamber, testifying the respective sums due to any of them, shall then be delivered up into the Court of Orphans or the said Chamber, and such acknowledgment of having received satisfaction thereupon shall then be entered as the said Court of Orphans and Chamber have anciently in such cases ordered to be done. And when satisfaction shall be made to the respective orphans and creditors to whom the said Chamber is at present indebted as aforesaid, the said Judicature hereby erected shall then utterly cease and be determined, And from thenceforth all the rest and residue of the said profits and premises not disposed of by the said Judicature, and all the advantages which can or may accrue by virtue of their Lordships accepting of the trouble of appearing on the said orphans', creditors' and City's behalf, shall redound, enure and be to and for the sole use, benefit and behoof of them the said Mayor, Commonalty and Citizens of the said City and their successors for ever, anything to the contrary thereof in any wise notwithstanding.

And for the better encouragement of all discoveries and proposals for the advancement of the public good of the nation, Be it likewise enacted that their Lordships shall have power to receive the same and to present such of them as their Lordships shall approve of to the next succeeding Sessions of Parliament, to the end that the respective discoverers and proposers may receive due recompense, in case the Parliament shall think fit to put any of them into execution].—[Read 1ª this day. (L. J., XIV. 554.) On the 21st it was read 2ª and referred to a Select Committee, with an instruction that the Committee, after hearing the Lord Mayor and Court of Aldermen, should add a clause for making void all contracts for compositions with any of the orphans. (*Ib.* 561.) The Committee met on Nov. 24 (Bp. of London, Chairman), Nov. 26 (V. Weymouth, Chairman), Nov. 28 (L. North, Chairman), and Dec. 1, 2, 3, 5, 6, 9, 13, 15, 16, (M. Halifax, Chairman). Their proceedings are thus recorded. On Nov. 24 *Ordered*, That the L. Mayor and Court of Aldermen and all persons concerned shall have notice and may be heard tomorrow. (Com. Book, 24 Nov.)—On Nov. 28 after reading the preamble, the parties were called in. *Mr. Common Serjeant* (for the L. Mayor) excepts to the word (" Gazette ") in the preamble, and says there has been no discovery made to the City, as is pretended. *Mr. Dobins* consents to leaving out the word. *Mr. Ward* (for the City): The revenue of the City of London is about 30,000*l.* per annum. Their debts to the orphans are about 500,000*l.* or 600,000*l.* *Mr. Lane* (for the City): There was such an order made by the City as in the Gazette. The order in the Gazette is read. The preamble is postponed. The first enacting clause is read. *Mr. Common Serjeant:* The said order has been complied with. The first clause was then read again and agreed to. (Com. Book Nov. 28.)—On 1 Dec. the parties are called in. The second enacting clause concerning Judicature is read. *Mr. Common Serjeant* (for the City): A Court of Judicature is to determine differences. We know of no differences between us and the City. The law directs that all differences be determined by a Jury. This Bill orders otherwise. They would have this Judicature determine without appeal to the Courts in Westminster Hall. *Mr. Ward* (for the City): This Bill directs the Judicature to sit in the Charter House. As the law now is, the citizens are not obliged to answer in Westminster Hall, nor out of the City. *Mr. Dobins* (for the Orphans): The Acts for making Rivers navigable direct such a Judicature. The City forced us to bring in our money. *Mr. Reding* produces an Order of the Court of Aldermen, dated 17 Jan. 1687–8, relating to the making discoveries for the payment of the Orphans, which is read. *Mr. Ward:* The City cannot compel Orphans to bring their money into the Chamber, but they may oblige them to give security. Since 1683 no money has been brought in by the Orphans, since which time the City have paid the Orphans above 90,000*l.* We have punctually observed the said Order. *Mr. Reding:* Not one house in ten that ought to pay to the City, pays anything. Improvements may be made at Radcliffe. 100 years purchase may be had for that. 100,000*l.* may be made of Upper Moorfields. The Officers, particularly the Comptrollers, have ten of the best houses near Cripplegate. *Mr. Dobins:* The City demands unreasonable security, and now necessitates the Orphans. There have been but 20,000*l.* paid to the Orphans and 1,000*l.* paid to the Lord Jeffreys. *Mr. Common Serjeant:* We will reduce everything to the City as far as the law will give us leave. Radcliffe is the King's and not ours. The encroachments on the Thames cannot be rented out; we are punishable if we should. There is an information against us by the Attorney-General for building the Artillery ground. There never was any reasonable security offered that we refused. All securities are proportionable to the money to be paid in. The penalty is double to the money lent. There is no wrong where there is an election in the party. The House being set, ordered that all persons attend to be further heard tomorrow. (Com. Book Dec. 1).—On 2 Dec. the Parties are called in. *Mr. Dobins* (for the Orphans): The City does not or cannot effectually improve the encroachments. The soil of the Thames is in the City of London. The City have done nothing these last seven years for the Orphans. They have not let leases nor sold lands. They ought not to be trusted with this estate any longer. They have been bankrupt these forty years. *Mr. Ward* (for the City): This clause is unlimited as to person, time and thing. We desire that all just recompense may be given to the Orphans. Interest has undone the City of London. *Mr. Common Serjeant:* The words in this clause are so general that we know not how to speak to it. There must be a limitation of the subject matter as well as of time. *Sir John Lawrence:* A great part of the City's estate is concealed. One Officer makes profit of our encroachments, though we can make none. We want powers to make the best of our estate. The City has the power of coal-meters; the chair has the disposing of them and the Chamber has no benefit of it. *Mr. Common Serjeant:* The Chamber has a part of it, and, besides, we have been about buying out the lives now in being and applying this to the Orphans. The last Coal-meter's place was sold and paid into the Chamber for the Orphans. The Tronage Office belongs to the City. It yields us nothing; at Amsterdam it yields 6,000*l.* a year. *Mr. Lane* (for the City): We have had many suits for Tronage, and were always cast. It costs the City great sums to sue every particular person for a small sum. The Orphans pray the City may allow them money for the carrying on this business. They withdraw. *Ordered,* That the Counsel on behalf of both sides meet this day and consider the point of Limitations, and be prepared to offer somewhat thereon tomorrow. (Com. Book 2 Dec.)—On Dec. 3 the parties are called in. The Counsel for the Orphans offer a clause,*

* This Clause is not among the Papers.

House of Lords MSS.

1690.

drawn in pursuance of the Order yesterday, which is read. *Mr. Common Serjeant* excepts to the words ("Bridgehouse") and ("Hospitals"). *Mr. Ward* says this Clause has no limitation of time. *Mr. Reding* (for the Orphans) proposes that the limitation of time may be from the year 1600. *Mr. Williams* (on the same side) proposes it may be from the year 1640. *Mr. Dobins* (on the same side) proposes from the year 1630. *Mr. Lane* (for the City): There are many things contained in this Bill, and they will require many times. The enacting clause is read. *Mr. Dobins:* We desire but the same power of discoveries that the King has in the like cases. *Mr. Ward:* There [is] but a Record to entitle the Crown. The subject may traverse it. In this case there can be no such thing. *Mr. Common Serjeant:* We understand not how far the words ("Rights and Discoveries") may extend; they are not bounded in our law. He excepts also to the word ("Premises"). Proposed that particular words may be inserted instead of ("Premises"). After ("penalties and forfeitures") add ("not pardoned by Act of Parliament"). For ("necessary charges") read ("reasonable charges"). The House being set, they withdraw. Ordered, that all persons attend tomorrow. (Com. Book 3 Dec.)—On Dec. 4 the Counsel are called in. *Mr. Ward* excepts to the word ("meliorations"). *Mr. Reding* (for the Orphans): The word is used in the Act for rebuilding the City. *Mr. Ward:* Every part of this Bill is founded upon a discretionary power. As to encroachments, we cannot make any benefit of them. An encroachment is a nuisance. This nuisance is pardoned by the Act of Grace. *Mr. Reding* (for the Orphans): 1,000*l.* a year is paid to the water-bailiff for encroachments. *Mr. Ward:* Money cannot by law be taken for encroachments. Though a nuisance cannot be rented, yet their common way is when a nuisance is presented to take perhaps 20*s.* fine, and so from time to time when presented, which makes the nuisances be still continued. *Mr. Baron Nevill* (*See* L. J., XIV. 576): Nuisances are generally pardoned in Acts of Grace unless particularly pardoned. *Mr. Justice Ventris:* The continuance of a nuisance is not pardoned. *Mr. Dobins* proposes that after ("nuisances") may be added ("other than such as have been pardoned by Act of Parliament"). *Mr. Common Serjeant:* We paid the Orphans interest till 1683, [the year] that the Quo Warranto was brought against us. Every Midsummer day a Committee is chosen and sworn to audit the accounts. *Mr. Dobins:* If the accounts were thus audited, it is the more inexcusable in the City, that so earnestly called for our money when they found they could never be able to repay us. This Court of Judicature may determine all this matter in six months. They withdraw. After debate, *Question*, Whether there shall be a Judicature established by this Bill? Contents, 11; Not-Contents, 0 (*sic*). Resolved in the Affirmative. (Com. Book 4 Dec.)—On 5 Dec. *Agreed*, That there be no retrospect. That the Judicature to be constituted by the Bill consist of 15 persons, whereof the L. Bishop of London, the two L. Chief Justices, the L. Chief Baron and the Dean of St. Paul's for the time being to be 5, 5 more to be chosen by the said persons on the behalf of the Orphans, and 5 others to be chosen by the Lord Mayor and Court of Aldermen. The place of meeting to be left to the said Judicature. The quorum to be five. The Judicature to have power to name Committees, but no final order to be made without one of the first five be of the quorum. That this Judicature shall have power by all legal ways and means to enquire, &c. Mr. Baron Nevill and Mr. Justice Ventris are desired to draw a clause to that purpose against tomorrow. (Com. Book 5 Dec.)—On Dec. 6 *Mr. Baron Nevill* gives in the clause, drawn in pursuance of the Committee's directions, which is read and given to the L. Bishop of Worcester, who is desired to show it and the Bill to Sir William Turner. After debate, adjourned. (Com. Book 6 Dec.)—On Dec. 9 the *L. Bishop of Worcester* acquaints the Committee that he has spoken with Sir William Turner, and he desires that the Committee will adjourn for two or three days, and in that time they will meet and make the best proposals they can to the Committee. (Com. Book 9 Dec.)—On Dec. 13 a Computation of the State of the Revenue belonging to the City of London and a brief of the Bridgehouse account from Michaelmas 1688 to Michaelmas 1688 (*sic*) are read and both taken back by the M. Halifax, who brought them in. *Mr. Reding* and *Mr. Sheppard* are called in and told that the Committee think that to turn the Judicature desired into a Commission of Inquiry, and they to give an account to the next Parliament, would be best for the Orphans. *Mr. Reding:* The Orphans will acquiesce in what your Lordships do. The Commission of Inquiry will plainly do the business if it be in good hands. *Ordered* to report that the Committee had voted there should be a Judicature erected, but upon further consideration, they were of opinion that a Commission of Inquiry to inquire into the state of the City of London will be more for the Orphans' advantage, but having so voted they are forced to resort to the House for their direction. (Com. Book 13 Dec.; L. J., XIV. 590.*)—On 15 Dec. *Proposed*, that the retrospect for inquiry be from the time of the Fire in London. *Proposed*, that before any report be made to Parliament, it shall be seen and approved by the Bishop of London, Dean of St. Paul's and three Chief Justices or the major part of them.† After amending the Bill as above noted, the Committee agreed on certain heads, and desired Mr. Baron Nevill to draw a Bill upon those heads and the debate of the Committee. (Com. Book 15 Dec.)—On 16 Dec. *Mr. Baron Nevill* brought a draft of a Bill on the heads agreed to, which was read entire and by paragraphs and ordered to be reported, (Com. Book 16 Dec.), and on the same day it was reported, ordered to be engrossed, read 3a and sent to the Commons, (L. J., XIV. 592). Two messages were sent to the Commons to remind them of the Bill (L. J., XIV. 604, 614), but they negatived the second reading on 2 Jan. 1690–1 by 68 votes to 52 (C. J., X. 533). The Bill was reintroduced in the Lords on 11 Nov. 1691 (No. **434**).]

Annexed:—

(*a*.) 16 Dec. Corrected‡ draft of an Act for erecting a Court of Inquiry in order to the relief of the distressed Orphans of the City of London. After a preamble agreeing with the amended one above, the Bill enacts, "That§ the Lord Bishop of London, the Chief Justice of the Court of King's Bench, the Chief Justice of the Court of Common Pleas, the Chief Baron of the Court of Exchequer and the Dean of St. Paul's for the time being, and ten other such persons as shall be nominated and chosen in manner

* The MS. Min. state that M. Halifax reported that the Committee, on consideration, thought that the Judicature "will have little to do." Mr. Baron Nevill and Mr. Baron Turton appear to have been first proposed instead of Mr. Justice Powell and Mr. Justice Dolbin. (MS. Min. 15 Dec.)

† This last proposal is struck through.

‡ The additions and omissions in this draft, shown respectively by italics and square brackets, are evidently corrections, not amendments, made in Committee, no mention being made in Com. Book of the draft having been amended. They indicate the differences between this draft and the two clauses below.

§ From ("the") to ("are hereby constituted") is left blank in the Bill of Nov. 1691 (No. **434**).

House of Lords MSS.

1690.

following, that is to say: five of them by the said persons before named *or any three of them* and the other five by the Lord Mayor and Court of Aldermen of the said City of London, are hereby constituted a Court of Inquiry for the relief of the Orphans of the said City, and for the better discovery and finding out all such ways and means as may best conduce to the payment and satisfaction of the said Orphans such sums of money as are now due and owing unto them from the said Mayor and Corporation of the said City.

And be it further enacted by the authority aforesaid, That the said* Lord Bishop of London, the said two Chief Justices, the said Chief Baron and the said Dean of St. Paul's for the time being, and such other person and persons as shall be so nominated and chosen as aforesaid, or any five or more of them, are hereby authorised and empowered to inquire and inform themselves, as well by examination of all and every such person and persons upon oath (which oath they are hereby empowered to administer) as they shall think fit to summon and call before them to give evidence touching and concerning the making any discovery as aforesaid, and by all other lawful ways and means which to them shall seem expedient, of and concerning all receipts and disposals of the said Orphans' money and of and concerning all the rights, customs, privileges, duties, liberties, freedoms, offices, fairs, gifts, grants, markets, tolls, vaults, waters, ways, wastes, encroachments, improvements, meliorations, contracts, concealments, frauds, fines, licenses, recognizances, pains, penalties and forfeitures, and of and concerning all the lands, tenements and hereditaments, estates, services, rents, profits and emoluments whatsoever of or belonging to the said Mayor, Commonalty and Citizens in right of the said City, And (if they shall think fit) cause and appoint any survey or surveys to be made of any of the lands, houses or tenements of or belonging to the said City. And the said persons, as above mentioned, are hereby authorized to send to prison such as shall disobey the order or orders which they are empowered to issue by virtue of this Act, and the Sheriffs of London and all other inferior officers belonging to the said City are hereby required to be aiding and assisting to the said Court in the execution of the powers given by this Act, And the said Court [shall have power] *is hereby empowered* to appoint such persons as they shall find necessary to act under them and [shall] *to* make them such reasonable allowances as they in their judgments shall think fit.

And be it further enacted that the said persons or any† five or more of them shall meet together on or before the‡ tenth day of January now next following in the Chapter House of St. Paul's in the City of London, in order to the putting this Act in due execution, and from thence shall adjourn themselves to such other time [and times, place and places] *and place* as to them shall seem most convenient, and so from time to time for and during the space of§ three months to be computed from the said

* From ("Lord") to ("are hereby authorised") is left blank in the Bill of Nov. 1691.

† The word ("five") is left blank in the Bill of Nov. 1691.

‡ From ("tenth") to ("in order to") is left blank in the Bill of Nov. 1691.

§ The words ("three months") and ("the said tenth day of January") are left blank in the Bill of Nov. 1691.

tenth day of January, unto which time the power and authority hereby given unto them is to continue and no longer.

And it is hereby also enacted that the said persons hereby authorized and empowered to make such inquiry as aforesaid shall make their Report thereof unto the Parliament* the first week after the next Session of Parliament that shall be held after the tenth day of April next, unless it shall happen that a Parliament shall be sitting at that time, in which case they shall make their Report unto the Parliament within a week after the said tenth day of April. Provided nevertheless that, if they shall think fit, they may make their Report at any time within the said three months, being the time wherein they are hereby empowered to act, if a Parliament shall then being sitting. And it is hereby further enacted, That every Report that shall be made by the said persons hereby empowered and authorized as aforesaid, shall be signed by† the said Lord Bishop of London, the said two Chief Justices, the said Chief Baron and the said Dean of St. Paul's, or three of them at the least [or otherwise the same is to be of no force or effect whatsoever]. *Endorsed* as reported and ordered to be engrossed this day. L. J., XIV. 592.

(*b.*) Rough draft of first portion of preceding, viz., from ("That the Lord Bishop of London") to ("belonging to the said City").

(*c.*) 15 Dec. Rough draft of concluding portion of annex (*a.*), viz., from ("And be it further enacted that said persons") to ("force or effect whatsoever"). *Dated* 15 Dec.

330. Nov. 18. Bullion Exportation Bill.—Commons' Engrossment of an Act against the exportation of Gold and Silver, and melting down the Coin of this Realm. "Whereas great benefit and advantage hath accrued to this kingdom by such Acts of Parliament heretofore made as have encouraged the importation of bullion and converting the same into the current coin of this realm, and whereas the said Acts have been found of late insufficient any longer to have the same good effect, because the price of silver abroad does exceed what the same will produce at their Majesties' Mint here at home, and does therefore cause and encourage the exportation of silver and the melting down of new milled and other weighty money, the same being of more value to be melted down and exported by near twopence per ounce than it goes for in money here, which, if not timely prevented, will inevitably cause the exporting of it, to the impoverishment of the nation and great damage thereof; for preventing of which, as well as for the encouragement of such as shall import Bullion into this kingdom; Be it declared and enacted by the King and Queen's most Excellent Majesties, by and with the advice and consent of the Lords Spiritual and Temporal and the Commons in this present Parliament assembled and by the authority of the same, That whereas the Master Worker of their Majesties' Mint within the Tower of London was and is obliged by Indenture between their most Excellent Majesties and himself to make and coin their Majesties' silver moneys to hold and be in value three pounds two shillings sterling the pound weight Troy with a Remedy of two pennyweight over or under upon the said pound weight Troy and to be and hold in fineness at the trial of the same eleven ounces and two penny-

* From ("the first week") to ("then be sitting") is left blank in the Bill of Nov. 1691.

† From ("the said") to ("of them at the least") is left blank in the Bill of Nov. 1691.

weight of fine silver and eighteen pennyweight of alloy in the said pound weight Troy as aforesaid, from and after the first day of September 1690, it shall and may be lawful to and for the Master and Worker of their Majesties' Mint for the time being, and the said Master and Worker of the said Mint for the time being is hereby empowered and enjoined to make and coin their said Majesties' silver money to hold and be in value three pounds five shillings sterling the pound weight Troy with the like Remedy of two pennyweight over or under upon the said pound weight Troy and to be and hold in fineness at the trial of the same eleven ounces and two pennyweight Troy as aforesaid, any law, statute, proclamation, order or usage to the contrary in anywise notwithstanding.

And whereas by one Act made in the fifteenth year of the reign of the late King Charles the Second, intituled An Act for the Encouragement of Trade, it is enacted That from and after the first day of August 1663, it shall and may be lawful for any person or persons whatsoever to export out of any port of England or Wales, in which there is a Customer or collector, or out of the town of Berwick all sorts of foreign coin or bullion of gold or silver, first making entry thereof in such Custom House respectively, by colour whereof several persons have exported gold and silver bullion manufactured in this kingdom; Now for the preventing thereof and for the better keeping in and increasing the current coin of this Realm, Be it declared and enacted by the authority aforesaid, that no gold or silver bullion shall or may be exported or put on board any ship, vessel or boat to be exported by virtue or colour of the said Act, but only in foreign coin and foreign bars and foreign bullion, under the penalty that every person or persons so exporting or putting on board any ship, vessel or boat to be exported shall forfeit the same, one moiety or half thereof to the King and Queen's Majesty and the other moiety or half to such person who shall sue for the same by action, bill, plaint or information, wherein no essoign, protection or wager of law shall be allowed, and that in case of a seizure on any parcel of gold or silver a doubt arises and a trial ensue, the proof thereof shall lie on the owner or claimer." *Parchment Collection.* [Brought from the Commons this day. L. J., XIV. 557. *See also* No. 353.] On 6 Dec. the Merchants and others were heard at the Bar. *Mr. James Houblon:* As this Bill is penned, it will not do. It will by no means prevent the exportation. We call now for more naval stores than otherwise. It will set the Mint on work and cut out all the heavy money in the nation. He delivers a Paper of observations on the Bill, which is read by the clerk. *Mr. Holles* (for the Bill): desires time to answer the objections in the Paper delivered by the Merchants. They withdraw. *Moved* for time to answer; *Agreed* to hear them. They are called in again and told the Lords have ordered a copy of the Paper and are willing to hear what they have to say to support the Bill. *Mr. Dormer:* 1 lb. Troy weight is 3*s.* 2*d.*; Bullion is now worth 5*s.* 4*d.* A Crown piece consists of 19 dwt., and (*sic*) These gentlemen that oppose the Bill are to get 5 per cent. by it. We have a computation of all the gold and silver that has been coined since 1672. In the guinea there is an alloy of 20 dwt., and that gives encouragement. Bullion was worth more by twopence in the ounce than the money coined. We hope we have gone a great way to justify the Bill. It will reduce money to a standard as our neighbouring traders (*sic*). *Mr. Holles:* We hoped we had good reasons before the Paper, and we hope we have now. What is clipt is here and that of weight is gone. The design of the Bill is only to bring it to that pass that it shall not be worth while to have it out of the kingdom. If you have it here, it is by tale, if beyond sea, by weight, and therefore the Merchants ought to keep it up. We desire a copy. *Mr. Dobins:* I am for the working Goldsmiths of the City, and we hope the second clause is very reasonable. *Sir John Houblon:* We do not come to speak against that part of the Bill that is for melting down the coin. It is the goldsmiths that melt it down. We will make it appear that 4*s.* 9*d.* will be melted down as well as the other and twopence per ounce gained. The exchange in Holland is now 34*s.*, and then it will be but 32*s.* All the trade we have in the world is on the intrinsic value. Speaks to the Portuguese case. *Mr. Houblon:* Gold and silver is a commodity and will be so, and let what law will be made, it will be ineffective. The matter arises upon the War. If we owe money above trade, we must pay it. The Act made for exportation of bullion is one of the best Acts that ever was made for trade. The Dutch export money. It is only the contingency of the War. We have less silver and more gold. They withdraw. One thing is observed, as the Merchants said concerning the exportation: that when this coin is lower, it will have the same effect as now and be as easily exported and with as much profit. Counsel called in again and told by the Speaker, that here is one thing affirmed by the Merchants, that they expect you will answer when heard, viz.: That when this coin is lower, it will have the same effect as now and be as easily exported and with as much profit. *Ordered* to be heard on Wednesday next. (MS. Min. 9 Dec.)—On 10 Dec. the Merchants and Counsel were called in. *Mr. Holles:* Speaks to the point laid down by the Merchants. This does not prohibit the exportation of money. Upon the importation of Irish cattle there are forfeitures made. Money is sent to Norway, and if it were less, it would not go there, as in rent it is the same thing. *Mr. Dormer:* Those that brought bullion to the Mint; the Act says the public, shall pay that. These gentlemen have said that if this Act pass, yet the same will be exported. This we deny. After this Act is passed, we carry the coined money nowhere. Foreign money will be exported. The bullion is one penny in the Crown better than money. Bullion receives its value from all parts of the world. I do not see that will be the consequence if this Act pass. They say it is the present War. That in fact is otherwise, for it has been at the same value for ten years last past as it is now. It cannot be to any man's prejudice, to any but those that export it. No standard for money has continued for above sixty years. *Mr. Dobins:* I am for the working goldsmiths for the sake of the last clause. They hope this Bill will pass, if it be only for that clause. It is melted down and carried out in bullion. 339,000*l.* exported in bullion and coin within sixteen months. The law in other countries is, that they may export as much bullion as they import. 17 Edw. IV. a Statute not printed. Coke's Reports. 5 Rich. II. a complaint that almost all the money of the Kingdom is gone. It is the Jews that export all the money. 2 Hen. VI. it is provided that Merchants should be pledges, one for the other. 17 Edw. IV., 15 Car. II. a law passed relating to trade. A particular clause, that it shall be lawful for all persons to export foreign bullion. There are trades that require bullion to be exported; East and Turkey. The bullion is brought from Spain in pieces of eight and some in bars. The Merchants owned that they got 10 per cent. by exportation. The Dutch manage their East India trade with our bullion, and their Turkey trade also. 9 Edw. III.; 4 Hen. IV.; 16 Rich. II.; 14 Car. II. c. 31. They melt it down in their cellars or other places. We hope this second clause is a very necessary clause. *Mr. Houblon* (for the Merchants): This clause will not reach the end pretended as it is penned. All the

House of Lords MSS. —— 1690.

endeavours that have been used could never prevent the exporting of it. The raising money in France will not do the end expected. He calls in his money, and in his Edict promises that when the money was come in [it should be] at 62 cents., and they that brought it not in (*sic*) it should be bullion. Now this did not do, and here was a fair standard, and he paid them it again at 66 cents. Now here we are to tax ourselves and have our rents paid us at 4*s*. 9*d*. instead of 5*s*. We are here to maintain that the Act of 15 Car. was a profitable Act for trade, and we have seen the effect of it; it is a commodity. The Exchange did in December begin to waver. As soon as we heard of his Edict, it fell to 55¼; 16 Dec., 55½, by sworn broker's account printed. I can bring the King of France's price. Bullion will rise accordingly; it will rise to 5*s*. 7*d*. per ounce. They will set at work to the prejudice of all that have rents. I am sensible it will not answer the end. *Sir James Houblon:* We apprehend that though this law be renewed, yet it will have no force. There are several laws in other countries, and yet they send out money. We say it is a commodity. I believe, though you call it a Crown, yet it will be but 4*s*. 9*d*., and this will be melted down as well as the other. The standard of silver is 5*s*. 2*d*., and the same coined is the same. By reason of wars and interruption of trade we have not the quantities of silver we had, and so bullion has risen. If this Act passes, you put bullion at 3*s*. per oz. It will rise to 5*s*. 7*d*. per oz. They shall get the same now as they did by the 5*s*. 2*d*. We have but 19*s*. for 20*s*. We cannot imagine that any will give us the same for 19*s*. as for 20*s*., and then they will give us but 32*s*., and they will carry it abroad and have the same advantage. Portugal was 40 years at other prices. As to the second head: the alteration of the coin from 3*s*. 2*d*. to 3*s*. 5*d*. will not do. This shall be valued no more than the other. We shall sell our goods for 20 per cent. [less] than before. They withdraw. Then the Bill was read a second time. *Moved*, not to go on with that clause where the coin is to be altered, and that a clause be drawn against the melting down the coin and preventing gold and silver lace.* The Bill was then committed, as in L. J., XIV. 584. (MS. Min. 10 Dec.)—On 11 Dec. in C. W. H., E. Huntingdon in the chair, after reading the first enacting clause, it was proposed to hear Mr. Neale on the point why the coin should not be brought to the same price as the bullion. Mr. Neale and the Merchants were then called in and told the point. *Mr. Neale* desires to be heard to the whole Bill, but is held to the point and heard. He says that there is no place in the world where the coin is not of more value than the bullion. There is 4*d*. better always. If a man has bullion and carries it to the Mint, he loses twopence per ounce. They withdraw. The first enacting clause for change of the coin is read again. *Proposed* to call in the Merchants to be heard, and ask them (1) how it comes to pass that the coin in Holland is of so great advantage and higher price than the bullion? (2) What they have to answer to Mr. Neale, viz., that when bullion is once at such a price it never falls? (3) What difference there would be if I carried 10 lbs. weight or carried 30*l*. into Holland, as to the difference of the exchange? (4) Whether if the Crown piece be reduced to 4*s*. 9*d*., then any place would not be twopence in the ounce more than now? (5) Whether if any foreign commodity be imported, it will not be of a higher price by twopence in the Crown? Mr. Neale and the Merchants are recalled and asked the questions. *Mr. Neale* is asked whether he laid it down that

* The entry of this motion is cancelled.

if it once came to a height it never falls? He is heard to it. The *Merchants* are heard: It rises and falls as other commodities do. You will lop all the loans to the Crown and reduce all into clipt money. The *Merchants* are asked the above questions. They answer: The coin in Holland is not always at a price. *Sir Francis Child* is heard. They withdraw. The first enacting clause was then rejected. The next clause read. The wasting and unnecessary consumption of gold and silver in this kingdom. A clause for melting down. A clause offered and read. E. Huntingdon then reported progress and added that the Committee were of opinion that two clauses should be added, (1) to prevent melting down coin, and (2) to prevent the wasting and unnecessary consumption of gold and silver; the clauses to be drawn by a Sub-Committee. (MS. Min. 11 Dec.; L. J., XIV. 586.) No further proceedings are recorded.]

331. Nov. 19. Lady Cornbury's Estate Act.—Amended draft of an Act to enable the Right Honourable Edward Lord Cornbury and the Lady Catherine, his wife, to settle, sell or otherwise dispose of divers manors, lands, tenements and hereditaments in the counties of Lincoln and Kent. [Read 1ª this day; Royal Assent (with amended title) 20 Dec. L. J., XIV. 558, 600. 2 & 3 W & M. c. 15 in Long Calendar.]

Annexed:—

(*a*.) 4 Dec. Petition of Sir Joseph Williamson, Knt., and the Right Honourable the Lady Catherine O'Brien, Baroness of Clifton, his wife. The Petitioner, Sir Joseph, having parted with large sums for the payment of the late Duke of Richmond and Lenox's debts, and otherwise under the said Duke's will, and having had conveyances pursuant to decrees in Chancery whereby he is greatly interested in the Estate, and the Lady Catherine having also a right for life in a considerable part of the Estate, pray to be heard before the Bill is committed. L. J., XIV. 578. [*Mr. Trevor* and *Mr. Ward* appeared for the Petitioners, and *Sir William Williams* for the promoters of the Bill. The latter stated that the Bill could not injure the Petitioners, as there was a saving clause in it. MS. Min. 5 Dec.]

(*b*.) 6 Dec. Power of Attorney by E. and Countess of Peterborough to give consent to the Bill.

(*c*.) 9 Dec. Proviso, marked A., disabling Lady Cornbury to sell till she is 21 years of age. [Agreed to be reported this day, having been drawn by Sir Francis Winnington pursuant to order of the 8th. Com. Book.]

(*d*.) 9 Dec. Proviso, marked B., for Sir Joseph Williamson. [Offered by Lady O'Brien's Counsel on the 8th, and agreed to be reported this day. Com. Book.]

(*e*.) 9 Dec. Amended Proviso, marked C., for Lady Katherine O'Brien. [Offered by Lady O'Brien's Counsel on the 8th, and agreed to be reported with an amendment this day. Com. Book.]

(*f*.) 9 Dec. Lords' Amendments in Committee. [Ordered to be reported this day. Com. Book.]

332. Nov. 19. Lucy's Act.—Amended draft of an Act for securing the portion of Elizabeth Lucy and breeding her up a Protestant, and for transferring the trust for that purpose. [Read 1ª this day; Royal Assent 20 Dec. L. J., XIV. 558, 601. The Bill was consented to by Sir Philip Meadows and Sir Richard Onslow. (Com. Book, Nov. 22, 24.) 2 & 3 W. & M. c. 26 in Long Calendar.]

Annexed :—

(a.) 24 Nov. Lords' Amendments in Committee, ordered to be reported this day. Com. Book Nov. 22, 24.

333. Nov. 19. E. Suffolk's Privilege (Price).—Petition of Edward Pryse and Simon Pryse. Petitioners are now in custody of the Black Rod, being wrongly charged with having disturbed George, Earl of Suffolk, in his quiet possession of a royal mine, &c. Pray to be heard by Counsel in defence and to have leave to attend as witnesses before the Committee of Elections of the House of Commons, whither they have been summoned. L. J., XIV. 557. [On 22 Oct. the House was informed of a breach of privilege committed against E. Suffolk in his silver mines in Cardiganshire. *Rice Vaughan*, sworn, asked if any Lord were in possession, he says, Yes. Is he disturbed ? Yes, by the Lady Price and others, and I employed horses to carry away the ore, and she came and took the bag away. *Ordered* that Price and John Floyd (*sic* in MS. Min.) be attached (MS. Min. L. J., XIV. 529). On reading the above Petition on 19 Nov. the House gave leave to the Prices to attend the Committee, on giving security to Black Rod to appear on the 26th, when counsel were ordered to be heard for Petitioners, as well as for E. Suffolk and their Majesties' Farmers of the Royal Mines (MS. Min. L. J., XIV. 557).—On 25 Nov. Sir John Brattle, Mr. Bolles, and Mr. Robinson, Assay Master, were ordered to attend to be sworn as witnesses, on the 27th (MS. Min. L. J., XIV. 565).—On 26th Nov., House moved that Petitioners may be at liberty upon the same bail as before (MS. Min. No entry in L. J.).—On 27 Nov. on motion made to the same effect, and for a postponement of the hearing, the House ordered Counsel to be heard on 1 Dec. (MS. Min. L. J., XIV. 568).—On 11 Dec. the Petitioners were again ordered to give security for their appearance on the 16th (MS. Min. L. J., XIV. 585), and finally, on 20 Dec. the House, on motion, ordered them to be discharged, there being an agreement made to try the title at law (MS. Min. L. J., XIV. 599).]

334. Nov. 20. Lawrence Maule.—Petition of Lawrence Maule and others, several tenants of divers messuages and lands within the manor of Notgrove, in the county of Gloucester. About 1663 Sir Clement Clarke, Bart., coming to be lord of the manor, and seeing that it was capable of great improvement by exchange and enclosure of the common field lands, induced the tenants to surrender their former estates and take new ones for lives or years. Several of these new leases were made in 1665 and some not till 1678, during all which time the tenants had no notice of any incumbrance on the premises except to George Skipp, Esq., who joined in all leases with Sir Clement. But in 1666 Sir Clement mortgaged the whole manor for 1,000 years to one Mr. Holman, who in 1669 assigned to Symon Bennet, Esq., who for further security took a conveyance of the fee in the name of one Russell, besides other securities from Skipp and Sir Clement for the money then lent. After these mortgages had lain dark for 14 or 15 years, the executors of Bennet and others claiming under him, pretending that the mortgaged premises were insufficient to pay the debt and interest in arrear, entered on the lands, and having found and bought in two recognizances acknowledged by Sir Clement in 1664 and taken extents thereupon, turned Petitioners, including those whose leases were made before the mortgage, out of their estates or obliged them to hold at several rack rents without regard to their leases or fines paid or surrenders made for the granting thereof, whereby Petitioners, being 17 in number, are utterly undone and Sir Clement is not responsible to make good the covenants contained in the leases which he granted. Petitioners have no remedy by the ordinary rules of Chancery, where, of late, mortgagees for valuable consideration have been allowed the buying in and keeping on foot any legal estate they can for the protection of their mortgages. Petitioners, however, hope they ought not to be involved in this rule, because the mortgagees, who could not but take notice of Petitioners renewing or taking new estates (the possession going constantly therewith), never gave the least notice of their mortgages to Petitioners to prevent their being ensnared by such renewings, nor were Petitioners in a capacity to discover, or even enquire after the incumbrances of their Lord, lest he should proceed to great severities for doing so. It would be of public mischief that a whole village of husbandmen should be ruined and swept away without any fault committed, and moreover the mortgagees are now actually possessed of the benefit of the exchanges and surrenders made by Petitioners to a much greater value than all the estates for lives were worth, might they be enjoyed to the purport of their leases. Pray for leave to bring in a Bill for their relief. L. J., XIV. 559.

335. Nov. 20. Salmon *v.* Hampton *alias* Lewis.—Petition of Anne Hampton, *alias* Lewis, John Williams, Richard Owen, Owen Edward, Jenkin Owen, Jane Verich and Hugh Prees, praying that a day may be appointed for hearing. L. J., XIV. 559.

Annexed :—

(*a.*) 1 Dec. Petition of John Salmon, Lessee of Robert Owen, Clerk, Hannah, his wife and Ellen Lewis, her daughter, praying that another day may be appointed for hearing. L. J., XIV. 573.

336. Nov. 20. Cecil *v.* E. Salisbury.—Petition of Robert Cecil, Esq., and other the younger children of James, Earl of Salisbury, deceased. Petitioners' father, having raised two trusts on his estate for payment of certain portions, annuities and legacies mentioned in his will, left Petitioners' brother, the present Earl, his executor. Petitioners and the legatees brought a Bill in Chancery in 1683 against the executor and trustees, and the Court in 1684 decreed an account of the late Earl's personal estate and of the trust lands and all other estates liable to the performance of the will. The present Earl then offered, if allowed to remain in possession of the trust estates, to add 1,500*l.* a year towards the discharge of Petitioners' portions, maintenance and all other annuities devised by the will, until the same should be fully satisfied. This offer was accepted by Petitioners and the trustees, and the Earl has had possession of the trust estates ever since, but has refused to make good his offer. Petitioners having applied to him two years since to waive his privilege and allow them to proceed in Chancery for an account and recovery of their portions, he agreed to do so provided the Earl of Carlisle and Sir William Forester, both parties to the Bills, would do the same, and this agreement (Annex (*a.*) below) was duly made and signed. The Earl, immediately taking advantage of it, brought a cross bill against E. Carlisle, Sir W. Forester, Petitioners and others concerned in the suits, thus obstructing Petitioners from proceeding in their causes, in regard to which he now stands on his privilege. Pray that the Earl may not be allowed to insist on his privilege in the said causes, having once waived it when it was for his advantage, and now taking it up again when he perceives that the causes are likely to go against him. *Signed* Rob. Cecill, Mary Forester, and Margaret Cecill. L. J., XIV. 559.

House of Lords MSS.

1690.

[On 24 Nov. a letter (Annex (*b.*) below) was read and Counsel being called in, *Mr. Trevor* (Counsel for E. Salisbury's youngest child) declared that his clients had agreed and were willing to waive their privilege. The House then ordered that the Earl should not insist on his privilege in the causes. L. J., XIV. 564. MS. Min.]

Annexed:—

(*a.*) 20 Nov. Agreement referred to in preceding petition, and appended thereto.

(*b.*) 24 Nov. Letter from E. Salisbury to Sir Robert Atkyns, Speaker of the House of Lords, to be by him communicated to the House. Having just received an Order of the House touching the waiving of his privilege, he acquaints his Lordship that he has never hindered the rents and profits of the trust estates from being applied accordingly, nor does intend it, although these incumbrances with his debts are computed to amount to above 130,000*l.* It is true he is endeavouring in Chancery to defend his other estates from being charged therewith, and has a cross bill there for that purpose, which cause he would willingly have had heard before they had proceeded further before a Master in Chancery in their endeavours to charge his other estates, and upon that occasion only he lately wrote a note, of which he encloses a copy. But finding that this note is now complained of by some few of the parties concerned to be an insisting upon his privilege which he once waived, not expecting such use would have been made of it, he is unwilling the House should have any trouble about his concerns, and therefore he entreats his Lordship, as Speaker of the House, to acquaint the House that he is willing to waive his privilege in all those causes, if their Lordships shall think fit to order him so to do, hoping that the like order shall be made as to M. Halifax, E. Leicester and E. Carlisle, who are parties in those suits, and that Sir William Forester, M.P., whose lady has subscribed the Petition to this House, will obtain the like order from the House of Commons. *Signed* Salisbury. *Dated* Hatfield, Nov. 23, 1690.—On the next page is written the note referred to above, dated Oct. 19, 1690, and directing one Sadler to tell all parties concerned that the writer expects they should not proceed any farther in the causes in Chancery wherein he is defendant until the Court has considered his Bill and given directions therein. This is so reasonable a matter that he supposes they will all comply readily, but if they will be pushing forward their suit first, he thinks he shall have just cause of resentment, and they know his circumstances. *Signed* Salisbury.

337. Nov. 21. Putt's Estate Bill.—Amended draft of an Act to enable the Executors and Trustees of Sir Thomas Putt, Bart., deceased, to lease several messuages, lands, tenements, and hereditaments during the minority of Sir Thomas Putt, Bart., son and heir of the said Sir Thomas Putt, towards the payment of 500*l.* apiece, legacies to his three sisters Margaret, Ursula, and Susannah Putt, as also the debts of the said Sir Thomas Putt, the father. The Lords' Amendments are marked on this Draft, and are all except one,* embodied in the later Act, (No. **435**) which, with this exception, is identical with this amended

* Viz.: "shall be applied towards the satisfaction of the said legacies [of five hundred pounds apiece to the said daughters in the first place, and afterwards of the said debts of the said Sir Thomas Putt the father] *portions and debts*, and if any surplusage." The Act retains the words in square brackets in lieu of those in italics.

draft. *See also* No. 344. [Read 1a this day; Question for passing the Bill negatived 28 Nov. L. J., XIV. 561, 570. Com. Book 27 Nov.]

338. Nov. 21. L. Ferrers *v.* Lady Ferrers.—Petition and Appeal of the Hon. Robert Shirley, Esq., and Anne, his wife, grandchild and heir of John Ferrers, Esq. John Ferrers, by his will in 1618, left Tamworth Castle, with his lands in Wareton, Warwickshire, worth 200*l.* a year, and the residue of his estate, after payment of certain legacies, to Lady Elizabeth Ferrers, mother of the Petitioner Anne, and appointed her his executrix and guardian of Anne. On the marriage of Petitioners, in consideration of Lady Ferrer's affirmation that Anne had lands in possession and reversion worth 2,000*l.* a year, the male Petitioner's father settled lands worth above 7,000*l.* a year upon her, but after the marriage and settlement Lady Ferrers claimed the possession of Anne's estate under the will until she was 21 years of age. Thereupon Petitioners and Lord Ferrers brought a bill in Chancery against her for an account and possession of the estate, and on 28 May 1690, the Court declared that the appointment for Lady Ferrers to have the custody of Anne's estate till she came to 21 was but a bare authority, which was determined by the marriage, and accordingly decreed possession to Anne's husband. This order was reversed on a rehearing on 17 Nov. 1690 by a majority of the Lords Commissioners. Appeal from this last order and pray that the previous one may be affirmed and Respondents ordered to answer. *Signed* by Appellants; *Countersigned* Ambrose Phillipps and Thomas Trevor. L. J., XIV. 560. [The Cause was heard, and the decree complained of reversed on 2 Dec., *Mr. Trevor* and *Mr. Finch* appearing for Appellants and the *Solicitor-General* and *Sir Charles Porter* for Respondents. L. J., XIV. 575. MS. Min.]

Annexed:—

(*a*.) 26 Nov. Answer of Dame Elizabeth Ferrers, the Hon Lettice Stanhope, Anne Stanhope, and Nicholas Parker. The Respondent, Lady Ferrers, claims possession of Anne's estate, not merely as a trustee for Anne until she comes of age, but also as a trustee for payment of John Ferrer's debts, of which there still remain owing above 1,000*l.*, and of the annuities charged upon the estate. The Lords Commissioners, upon a full hearing, declared that the possession is not a bare authority but an interest attended with a trust during the minority for the payment of debts, rent charges, and other securities. No breach or mismanagement of trust appearing, the possession ought never to have been altered, especially to an infant, the trust being personal to make leases, &c., and the Court decreed accordingly. Respondents refer to the will and codicil of John Ferrers, both of which were shown to Lord Ferrers on the marriage of Appellants. Pray that the Appeal may be dismissed with costs. *Signed* by Respondents. *Countersigned* Charles Porter and Alexander Stanhope. *Endorsed* as brought in this day.

339. Nov. 24. Vexatious Suits Act.—Amended* draft of an Act for preventing vexatious suits against such as acted for their Majesties' service in defence of the Kingdom. "Whereas in this present year of our Lord one thousand six hundred and ninety, about the time that the coasts of this Kingdom were invaded by the French, diverse Lords, Gentlemen and other good subjects, being Magistrates and officers or acting in pursuance of their orders, did for their Majesties' service and

* The additions are shown by italics, the omissions by square brackets.

House of Lords MSS — 1690.

the safety of the Kingdom apprehend and imprison several suspected persons, and did seize and use horses and arms and did cause [soldiers and others] *the greatest part of the Militia of this Kingdom to be raised, continued and maintained otherwise than is authorized by the Acts made in the reign of King Charles the Second in that behalf,* and to march and to be quartered in diverse places upon that occasion, all which proceedings were necessary in that extraordinary juncture and the parties concerned therein ought to be indemnified; Therefore for the preventing the trouble and charges which the said good subjects might be put to *by the prosecution of their Majesties their heirs and successors or* by the means of vexatious suits *of any person whatsoever* for and by reason of their actings and doings aforesaid, Be it enacted, &c., that all personal actions, suits, molestations and prosecutions whatsoever for or by reason of the premises or any matter or thing advised, commanded, [appointed, happened] or done *by their Majesties' Privy Council or any of them or by any officer or officers in the Militia or Justice of the Peace or by warrant or direction from them or any of them,* for their Majesties' service, the safety of their Government or the defence of their Kingdom, be and are hereby discharged and made void, And if any action or suit hereby declared [or intended] to be discharged *hath been or* shall be commenced or prosecuted, every person so sued may plead the general issue and give this Act and the special matter in evidence, And if the plaintiff shall become nonsuit or forbear further prosecution or suffer discontinuance, or if a verdict pass against him, the said defendant shall recover his double costs, for which he shall have the like remedy as in case where costs by law are given to Defendants." [Read 1ª this day; Royal Assent, 5 Jan. 1690–1. L. J., XIV. 563, 618. 2 W. & M. Sess. 2. c. 13. The amendments marked above were made in C. W. H. (MS. Min. 28 Nov.); the remaining amendments were added by the Commons.]

Annexed:—

(*a*) 28 Nov. Lords' Amendments to the Bill. [Made and ordered to be reported this day. MS. Min.]

340. Nov. 24. Bray's Estate Act.—Amended draft of an Act for the better enabling Jane Bray, widow, Relict and sole Executrix of the last Will of Reginald Bray, Esq., deceased, and others to the speedy raising of the portions already appointed for her daughters by the said Reginald Bray. *Endorsed:* Mrs. Bray's Bill. [Read 1ª this day; Royal Assent, 20 Dec. L. J., XIV. 563, 600. 2 & 3 W. & M. c. 24 in Long Calendar.]

Annexed:—

(*a.*) 28 Nov. Lords' Amendments to the Bill. [Reported from Committee and agreed to this day. L. J., XIV. 570. Com. Book 27 Nov.]

341. Nov. 25. Bishop of St. Asaph's Privilege.—Petition of William [Lloyd], Lord Bishop of St. Asaph. Petitioner about six years since, upon two trials, one at the Exchequer Bar and the other at Salop Assizes, obtained two verdicts and judgments for the rectory of Llanywllyn, in the County of Merioneth, as a presentation living in the gift of the Bishop of St. Asaph, against Peter Price, the pretended Impropriator, and Robert Wynn, Clerk, was accordingly put in possession and has enjoyed the living till September last, when, Parliament sitting and Petitioner attending it, at the prosecution of Thos. Price and Henry Mostyn, in the name of one Lewis Owen, lessee of Peter Price, the incumbent was ejected and judgment was obtained by default in the great Sessions for the County, notwithstanding Petitioner by his counsel insisted on his privilege of Parliament; and in October last, under pretence of a writ granted by Richard Green, William Wynn, under-sheriff of the County, with others, broke open the church door, and gave possession of the church and glebe lands to Edward Price. Prays that Robert Wynn may be restored to possession and the persons complained of ordered to answer the breach of privilege. L. J., XIV. 564. [The MS. Min. of 26 Nov. have the following: John Hooke, Randall Wynn, Hugh Griffith, Francis Evans, and John Price sworn for the Bishop of St. Asaph; John Williams, William Bold, and James Forster sworn for Mr. Price. The above Petition was read in Committee for Privileges on 28 Nov. and the parties called in, but no Counsel appearing for the Bishop, Counsel was not allowed for Price. *Thomas Price* said that if there was a breach of privilege, he only was guilty. There had been no such verdicts as was alleged in the Petition. *Sir William Williams* being present and prompting Price, *the Bishop* took exception to it. After reading the Standing Order of 28 May 1624, the Committee agreed to hear Counsel on both sides. On 1 Dec. *Mr. Finch* (for the Bishop) opened the case on the Petition. *Sir William Williams* (for Mr. Price) said the Bishop never in fact had a verdict, though Mr. Finch had confessed that the Bishop was at the charge of the suit. The Bishop had no possession and so could not be dispossessed by the parties complained of. When the Bishop had presented, the possession and inheritance was in Wynn, and while Wynn lived, the Bishop had nothing to do in the matter. The *officium et beneficium* is in Wynn, the incumbent. Mr. Price was never evicted by law out of anything but the glebe. He had been in possession ever since the 25th of Queen Elizabeth till within the last seven years. We brought our action against the Rector and not the Bishop. The latter is not concerned either in profit or loss. The Bishop has forty livings in his diocese in his gift. It were strange if no man shall bring an action of trespass against any of them without hurting the Bishop's privilege. *Mr. Dobins* (for Mr. Price) says Mr. Price was taken in custody by order of the House of Commons for this matter, a member of that House having rented the tithes of Wynn. *Sir William Williams:* The inheritance, the freehold, the profit and the possession is in the Rector, so the Bishop is not hurt. The Committee then resolved by 20 votes to 4 that the Bishop's privilege had been broken. (Priv. Book 28 Nov., 1 Dec.; L. J., XIV. 574.)]

Annexed:—

(*a*.) 3 Dec. Amended Order of the House this day. L. J., XIV. 577. *In extenso.* [The amendment was made on 3 Jan. 1690-1. L. J., XIV. 614.]

(*b*.) Affidavit of Robert Wynn that on 9 Dec. he was with Roger Jones when serving the Order of the House on Owen, who refused to yield up possession until advising with Counsel, and on David John Ellis, a tenant of part of the glebe land, who gave up possession as demanded. Deponent believes that no perfect obedience will be paid to the Order before particular directions be had from Thomas Price, who is principally concerned in the matter.

(*c*.) Affidavit of Roger Jones that he had served Owen and Ellis with the Order, and that the principal glebe house of the rectory is uninhabited and was locked up by Edward, brother of Thomas Price, when the Bishop's incumbent was turned out of possession by the Under-Sheriff.

House of Lords MSS.

1690.

342. Nov. 25. Protections (Horsfield *v.* Johnston).—Petition of Robert Horsfield and Thomas Thompson, Gent., and George Whichcot, Esq. Petitioners, being owed 200*l.* and interest on bonds by Dr. Nathaniel Johnston and his son Dr. Cudworth Johnston, who refused to pay, caused Nathaniel to be arrested, who, thereupon, insisted on a protection from the Bishop of St. David's, which the Bishop refused to revoke till Hilary term last, and on Petitioner then proceeding to law, Nathaniel insisted on another protection from the Earl of Ailesbury, and Cudworth insists on one from the Earl of Holdernesse. Petitioners hope that their Lordships will not conceive it reasonable that either Nathaniel, a Doctor of the College of Physicians, and near 70 years old, or his son Cudworth are any such menial servants as ought to be protected. L. J., XIV. 565.

Annexed :—

(*a.*) 23 Aug. 1689. Copy protection of Bp. of St. Davids. [Appended to preceding.]

(*b.*) 22 Jan. 1689–90. Copy protection of E. Ailesbury. [Appended to same.]

(*c.*) 23 Dec. 1690. Letter from E. Holdernesse to Sir Robt. Atkyns, Speaker of the House of Lords. He only received on the 15th inst. his Lordship's letter of 25 Nov. respecting Cudworth Johnston, who is his servant now actually employed in his affairs. He will write to Johnston and inquire what petition is against him, and dismiss him from his service, if necessary, for he will protect no servant from the payment of his just debts. *Dated* Aston, 17 Dec. *Endorsed* as received this day.

343. Nov. 27. E. Dorset *v.* Powle.—Petition of Charles, Earl of Dorset and Middlesex. Complains of a decree in Chancery giving to Respondent, who married Petitioner's mother when a widow, most of her personal estate and the rents of her land in arrear. L. J., XIV 563 and *ib.* 583 *in extenso.* [The cause was heard on 9 Dec. *Sir Charles Porter* (for Appellant): There was a writing under hand that he should have nothing to do with what she had, and a deed was drawn and Mr. Powle was a party to it. Upon these agreements the marriage took effect. She died and made a writing and disposed of all her personal estate to relations. *Mr. Finch* (for Appellant): Recites the several deeds and speaks to them. The agreement recites what she had at that time or should acquire hereafter. The deeds read. *The Solicitor-General* (for Respondent): The decree complained of consists of three parts. The case is on the two deeds; had they been alike, there had been no question. A letter proved in the cause will make appear the intention. There is a new title by the administration to Mr. Powle. *Sir Francis Winnington* (for Respondent): Mr. Powle never consented to her making a will and we have the record of the verdict. We shall read and leave it. The letter read, dated 20 June; it is proved in the cause. Some part may be secured for me. Some time after the marriage it fell out that Sir Thomas Clarges came. They read to the ninety interrogatories. They offer to read the verdict and the issue is read. Counsel for Appellant then replied and the House ordered as in L. J., XIV. 583. MS. Min. 9 Dec.]

Annexed :—

(*a.*) 4 Dec. Petition of Henry Powle, Esq., Master of the Rolls, for further time to answer. L. J., XIV. 578.

(*b.*) 6 Dec. Answer of Respondent. It had been tried and found by verdict that the supposed will of the Countess, Respondent's late wife, purporting to leave her estate to Appellant, had never been consented to by Respondent, who thereupon obtained administration, and brought a bill in Chancery against Appellant for discovery of the personal estate of the late Countess in his hands as executor. On a hearing on 15 Dec. 1687 the Lord Chancellor declared that the Countess had power to dispose of the personal estate, but not of the real estate, which the Respondent was declared at liberty to recover. This decree was affirmed on a rehearing before the Lord Chancellor on 3 May 1688. Prays that this decree may not be altered, all agreements for separate maintenance being against common rights and never favoured in any course of justice, and the agreements on Respondent's marriage being carried as far by the decree in favour of Appellant as the same could by any justice be extended to. *Signed* Thomas Vernon.

(*c*.) 19 Dec. Petition of Respondent for judgment to be amended. L. J., XIV. 598. *In extenso*. [The Petitioner, being heard to the point of the rents due after the deed of disposition, said, "By the marriage agreement she was not to receive her rents, but by my order. I am ready to restore as decreed. She died 20 April, and I presume those that were not received are in law vested in me." MS. Min. 19 Dec.]

344. Nov. 27. Putt's Estate Bill.—Lords' engrossment of an Act to enable the Executors and Trustees of Sir Thomas Putt, Baronet, deceased, to lease several messuages, lands, tenements and hereditaments during the minority of Sir Thomas Putt, Baronet, son and heir of the said Sir Thomas Putt, towards the payment of 500*l*. apiece legacies to his three sisters, Margaret, Ursula, and Susannah Putt, as also the debts of the said Sir Thomas Putt, the father. Identical with No. 337 as amended in Committee. *Parchment Collection* [Engrossment ordered this day. Bill rejected on the question that it do pass on 28 Nov. L. J., XIV. 567, 570.]

345. Nov. 27. Clifford Peerage.—Petition of Thomas, Earl of Thanet, cousin and next heir to George, Earl of Cumberland and Lord Clifford, deceased, together with the King's reference thereof to the House. L. J., XIV. 568. *In extenso*. [The Committee for Privileges began by reading the proceedings in the cases of E. Oxford and Mr. Longuevill. This entry (subsequently cancelled) then appears: "The opinion of the Committee is that the method of proceedings upon Petitions of this nature has been to hear the matter at the Bar of the House, for the Heralds to state the pedigrees and the Judges to deliver their opinions." The Committee then ordered to report the two cases above mentioned. (Priv. Book 1 Dec.; L. J., XIV. 574.) The House, on report, ordered Counsel to be heard on 14 Jan., but the hearing was prevented by the adjournment on 5 Jan.]

Annexed:—

(*a*.) 1 Dec. Paper of proceedings in the L. Willoughby's claim to the office of Lord Great Chamberlain. *Endorsed* as read in Committee for Privileges this day and again in the House on 2 Dec. Priv. Book 1 Dec.

(*b*.) 1. Dec. Paper of proceedings in Mr. Longuevill's claim to the title of L. Grey. *Endorsed* as preceding. Priv. Book 1 Dec.

(*c*.) 2 Dec. Petition of Elizabeth, Countess of Burlington and Cork, sole daughter and heir to Henry, late Earl of Cumberland and Lord Clifford, deceased, claiming the Barony of Clifford, and

HOUSE OF LORDS MSS.

1690.

praying for time to make good the allegations in her petition. L. J., XIV. 575. *In extenso.* [The MS. Min. contains an order to hear Counsel on both sides this day six weeks.]

(*d.*) 11 Dec. E. Thanet's Pedigree. *Endorsed* with date. No entry in Records.

346. Nov. 27. Williams *v.* Powell.—Agreement of both parties to withdraw the Petition of Appeal and Answer. An endorsement by the Clerk states that the Appeal and Answer were delivered back to the parties consenting. L. J., XIV. 567.

347. Nov. 28. Marshfield *v.* Weston.—Petition and Appeal of Thomas Marshfield. Petitioner, a gardener, having been arrested by Respondent, a seedsman, for money due for seeds supplied to him by Respondent, who was otherwise indebted to him, brought a bill in Chancery against Respondent for an account, and the Court on 11 July 1689 found a sum due to Respondent with costs. Respondent, refusing to pay, was arrested for contempt, but afterwards, taking advantage of the omission to file the report of costs, obtained a review of the report, and on 14 Oct. 1690 the Court discharged the costs taxed under the former decree, and ordered Petitioner to pay costs to Respondent. The Lords Commissioners refused a rehearing. Appeals from the last named decree. *Signed* by Appellant; *Countersigned* John Fryer and Thomas Brotherton, who certify to the Appeal, as Counsel. L. J., XIV. 570. Pet. Book 27 Nov. [The cause was heard on 15 Dec., *Sir William Williams* and *Mr. Dyer* appearing for Appellant, and *Sir Francis Winnington* and *Mr. Ward* for Respondent. MS. Min. L. J., XIV. 591.]

Annexed:—

(*a.*) 4 Dec. Answer of Francis Weston. Respondent having trade dealings with Appellant, who was his creditor on the whole account, desired an amicable settlement, but was forced to bring an action at law, as Appellant made fictitious claims against him. Appellant's proceedings in Chancery were irregular and purely vexatious, the proper remedy of both parties being at law. The matter of the Appeal is chiefly against costs, and the order complained of is in accordance with the constant practice of Chancery. *Endorsed* as brought in this day.

348. Nov. 28. Hutchinson. — Anonymous letter, addressed to Marquess of Carmarthen, as follows: "Sir, There is great cause to judge that there is a second Gunpowder Plot or some other such great mischief designing against the King and Parliament, by a frequent and great resort of notorious ill-willers, at most private hours, to the house of one Hutchinson, in the Old Palace, Westminster, situate very dangerous for such a purpose. Skilful builders may search, whether there be double walling, undermining, or vaults under the vaults that are there. This notice is only imparted to yourself, to the Earl of Monmouth, and to Sir John Lowther of Lowther, that so with privacy the enemies may be surprised in their design and not the nation in its execution. Now I have done my duty. 20 November 1690." L. J., XIV. 570, 571.*

* Luttrell, 28 Nov. 1690, has the following: "The cellars and vaults under the House of Lords have been lately searched, on intimation given by a letter of some design to blow them up; but nothing was found."

349. Nov. 28. Sedgwick *v.* Hitchcock and others.—Petition of Obadiah Sedgwick, Merchant. George Hitchcock and others, as creditors of Richard Slaney and Thomas Cudmore, against whom a Commission of Bankrupts was sued out for in February, 1684, brought a Bill in Chancery against Petitioner and others to set aside as fraudulent a distribution of Slaney's estate procured in August 1685 by Petitioner and some other of the creditors, and also a mortgage made to Petitioner of the manor of Lulsey, the estate of Slaney, for securing a sum of 2,200*l.* Petitioner brought a Cross Bill in support of the distribution, setting forth that the said sum was a *bond fide* loan from him to Slaney, made without any notice of the bankruptcy, on the security of a mortgage in fee of the manor, and a mortgage for 500 years of Slaney's estate made to one Minshall for 800*l.* and transferred to one Harris in trust for Petitioner; that the estate had been sold for 3,000*l.* and the proceeds fairly distributed according to law among all the creditors who had then come in; that, notwithstanding this, the late Lord Chancellor Jeffreys, without any Bill exhibited, had set aside the distribution and enforced a reconveyance of the estate to the assignees of the Commissioners of Bankruptcy, and ordered a new distribution to be made, admitting Hitchcock to the benefit of the Commission. On 28 May 1690 the then Lords Commissioners of the Great Seal, Sir J. Maynard, Anthony Keck, and Sir W. Rawlinson heard the cause, but before delivering judgment, they were changed; and both causes being heard by the present Commissioners on 23 July 1690, it was decreed by two of them that Petitioner should be paid the principal and interest only on Minshall's mortgage, the remaining proceeds of the sale to be distributed among the other creditors. Petitioner, who thus lost 1,400*l.* and interest, petitioned for a rehearing, but was refused, and on 22 Nov. the decree was enrolled. The mortgage made to Minshall and transferred to Petitioner's trustee, ought not to be redeemed without payment of all of Petitioner's loan with interest and costs. Appeals from the decree and prays that Respondents* may be ordered to answer and all proceedings stayed. *Signed* by Appellant; *Countersigned* by Geo. Treby and H. Finch. [Reported specially this day from the Committee for Petitions. (Pet. Book 27 Nov., L. J., XIV. 570.) The Appeal was first heard on 20 Dec. 1690. *Attorney-General* (for Appellant): His client was advised by Counsel to come in as a creditor.† . . . *Solicitor-General* (for Appellant): We have a distribution made to us by the Commissioners of Bankrupts. I cannot take this to be law. I am sure it is no equity. What equity is it that the last creditors should come in and defeat us, who are as good creditors as they? We had no notice; that is plain. The Commissions are taken out very clandestinely; nay, sometimes a friend of the bankrupt takes out a Commission fraudulently. He comes in and pays 15*s.* for his contribution. It will be insisted that a forfeited mortgage may be redeemed. But if you will redeem, it ought to be on the foot of both the accounts. A Court of Equity will never defeat anyone for finding out his right. Appellant has a legal interest to the money and has been secured for it. He having the law on his side and equity, they cannot take it from him. *Mr. Finch* (for Appellant): Appellant lends 2,200*l.* on the lands of Mr. Slaney. The Court of Chancery has taken away 1,400*l.* of it. Appellant took in Minshall's

* The Respondents' names are here given, being those in Annex (*a.*), and also William Pusdar and Francis Minshall.

† At this point the hearing was interrupted for a time by the arrival of the King.

House of Lords MSS.

1690.

mortgage, and so Slaney and Minshall make him a security for 2,200*l.*, and the Chancery will let him have but 800*l.* The point is, whether Appellant ought to lose this 1,400*l.* There are two points in this: whether Appellant be such a creditor as ought to come in and have the benefit of his security? The construction of the law is in the case. They say Appellant is no creditor within the meaning of the law. They say he cannot be an innocent purchaser, for that he has taken collateral security, and that he has taken notice of the Statute. They say the Court of Chancery has power to order all a Bankrupt's estate. This is contrary to all rules of equity. No man that is an innocent purchaser by conveyance ought to be destroyed, nor can he by law, and this rule the Chancery has followed in many cases. Cites *Gladwin* v. *Bullock*, Bridgman, the case judged by L. J. Hales. Appellant is an honest innocent purchaser. *Sir Ambrose Phillipps* (for Hitchcock): 2 March 1689 Sedg[wick] he is now no creditor. We cannot prove actual knowledge. There was no distribution at first. He has bought the estate of the bankrupt after we had petitioned the Lord Chancellor. As the bankrupt borrowed only this, he might have borrowed more, and the Chancery has only let us in. *Mr. Ward* (for Hitchcock): This depends upon the interpretation of several Acts of Parliament. The case of ordinary purchasers differs very much from this. Our case is upon Acts of Parliament. Cites Act of 13 Eliz. *Mr. Finch* and the *Attorney-General* having replied, the Speaker proceeded to report. *Question:* Whether the report shall be now made? Resolved in the Affirmative. The Speaker then reported what was said by Counsel on either side; and the House ordered the Decree to be reversed, and Slaney's estate to be sold, to satisfy Appellant his 2,200*l.* the overplus to go to Slaney's other creditors. (MS. Min. L. J., XIV. 601.)* For further proceedings, see notes to Annexes below.]

Annexed:—

(*a.*) 4 Dec. 1690. Answer of George Hitchcock, Esq., and Elizabeth, his wife; Anne Fountaine, her sister and widow of James Fountaine, executors to John Slaney, deceased; William Bird; Robert and Charles Mitchell; Richard Manlove and Mary, his wife; Robert Harvey; Thomas Yates, and Elizabeth Parr. Respondents were all creditors of Slaney when the Commission of Bankrupt was sued out, and duly prosecuted the Commission. If Appellant ever lent Slaney the 1,400*l.* besides the moneys he paid on the mortgage to Minshall, it was after Slaney had become a bankrupt and the Commissioners had assigned his estate, and more particularly the manor and lands in question, when Slaney had no power to charge his estate with the loan. Appellant by a feigned distribution and other methods endeavoured to defeat the other creditors. The Decree was just and reasonable. Pray that it may be confirmed, and the appeal dismissed with costs. *Signed* by Respondents; *Countersigned* by Ambr. Phillipps and Chas. Porter. *Endorsed* as brought in this day.

(*b.*) 20 Dec. 1690. Copy Order and Judgment of the House this day. L. J., XIV. 601. *In extenso.* [Appended to next paper.]

(*c.*) 2 Jan. 1690–1. Petition of George Hitchcock, Esq., Anne Fountaine, William Bird, Robert Mitchell, Chas. Mitchell,

* The case below is reported in 2 Vernon 158. *See also* Spence, Equit. Jur. of Court of Chancery, ii. 741, 742, ed. 1849.

Richard Manlove and Mary his wife, Robert Harvey, Richard March, Thos. Yates and Elizabeth Parr, widow, Creditors of Richard Slaney, Bankrupt, on behalf of themselves and others, the creditors of the said Bankrupt. Their Lordships' Order (annexed) reversing the Decree appealed from, mentions that the estate shall be sold to satisfy Appellant his debt of 2,200*l.*, thus barring Petitioners, unless explained, from any remedy taking any course at law to subject all the bankrupt's estate to the payment of his debts. Pray their Lordships to explain the Order accordingly. *Signed* by G. Hitchcock, Anne Fountaine, Will. Bird and Rich. Manlove. *Endorsed* as read this day; nothing done on it. MS. Min. No entry in L. J.

(*d.*) 12 Nov. 1691. Petition of George Hitchcock, Esq., William Bird, Merchant and several others, who are creditors of Richard Slaney, a Bankrupt. Refer to their previous Petition (Annex (*c.*) above), on which no order was made, owing to the pressure of public affairs and the near recess. Appellant has since their Lordships' judgment prosecuted Petitioners in Chancery, to compel them to join in a sale of the estate. Pray their Lordships to explain their Judgment of 20 Dec. 1690, that Petitioners may be enabled to proceed at law. *Signed* by G. Hitchcock, Anne Fountaine, Will. Bird, Rich. March, Rob. Michel, Chas. Michel, Rich. Manlove, Rob. Harvey and Eliz. Parr. [Read this day and referred to a Select Committee (MS. Min. L. J., XIV. 642).—On 17 Nov. this Committee, whose proceedings are not found to be recorded, reported their opinion, after hearing Counsel, that the Petition was not fit to be received. After a debate, temporarily interrupted by a Conference, the House, on motion, ordered to hear Counsel on both sides on the 21st on the point, whether the Petitioners ought to have liberty to try their title at law. (MS. Min. L. J., XIV. 649.)—On 21 Nov. Counsel are called in and told that they must keep to the point, whether Hitchcock ought to be at liberty to go to law. *Sir Thomas Powys* (for Respondents): States the case. We hope it is reasonable for us to go to law. *Mr. Ward* (for Respondents): This is a pure matter of law, and not of equity. *Attorney-General* (for Appellant): They have offered nothing why they should go to law. We have the decree to have our 2,200*l.* They do not pretend in this cause that the act of bankruptcy was before the mortgage. We have gone through all the law they would have us to be in. *Mr. Finch* (for Appellant): They pray the alteration of your Lordships' Order, and urge the case of *Dodd* v. *Burrows.** In that case, Burrows was entitled under the will, and brought his Bill. Burrows was willing that Appellants should take the legacies and release their right. Slaney's bankruptcy was unknown to Mr. Sedgwick. *Sir Thomas Powys* replies and the other side also. An Indenture read, being the distribution to which Appellant was a party. Counsel withdraw and Speaker reports. Order of 20 Dec. 1690 read. Question put to the Judges, Whether, if in this case the parties be left to law, the parties can afterwards come into Equity? *Holt, C. J.*: What cause there may be for equity in this case (*sic.*); otherwise they cannot. *L. C. Baron* [*Atkyns*]: I conceive they can only go to law on

* *See* 12th Report, App. Part VI., No. **192**.

HOUSE OF LORDS MSS.

1690.

the point whether Slaney was a bankrupt before this time or not. *Question:* Whether Hitchcock the Petitioner shall have liberty to go to law? Resolved in the *Affirmative*. After debate, *Question* put, whether any reasons shall be inserted in the Order. Resolved in the *Negative*. [The House then made the Order and Declaration set out in next paper. (MS. Min. L. J., XIV. 657.)]

(*e*.) 21 Nov. 1691. Order giving leave to Hitchcock, Bird and others to try their title at law, and cancelling the latter portion of the Order of 20 Dec. 1690 which directs the estate to be sold to satisfy Appellant's debt and the overplus given to Slaney's other creditors. L. J., XIV. 657. *In extenso*. [This Order was amended on 4 Dec. *See* Note to next paper.]

(*f*.) 23 Nov. 1691. Petition of Appellant. Their Lordships have been pleased to adjudge that Slaney's creditors shall have liberty to proceed at law. Prays to be heard by Counsel in answer to a deed put forward by Respondents in support of their application without notice to Petitioner, who can satisfy their Lordships that he is a just creditor in point of law, though he came in after the date of the Commission of Bankrupt. [The House, on reading the Petition this day, ordered that Appellant should be heard by Counsel to the point only upon the Deed (L. J., XIV. 658), and witnesses were ordered to attend on his behalf at the hearing (*ib.* 659).*—On 4 Dec. Counsel were called in. *Mr. Trevor* (for Appellant): It is a Deed of Assignment to Bird and Yates in trust for the creditors. The Deed, dated 14 Aug. 1685, is read. *Mr. Finch* (for Appellant): Can a man be guilty of contriving a fraud that knew nothing of it? He is a creditor to come in. *Sir Thomas Powys* (for Hitchcock) speaks to the Petition. *Mr. Ward* (for Hitchcock): We only ask the benefit of the law. The fraud consists in this, that Sedgwick was a creditor at the time of Slaney's becoming a bankrupt, and this was not true. Counsel heard to reply. Counsel withdraw and Speaker reports. *Question*, Whether the Deed of Disposition be fraudulent or not? *Question*, Whether the Deed of Distribution dated 14 Aug. 1685 was fairly obtained and made according to the course of law? The House then ordered the Order of 21 Nov. 1691 (Annex (*e*.) above) to be amended by adding the words ("And particularly whether the Deed of Distribution, dated the 14th day of August, 1685, was fraudulently obtained.") (L. J., XIV. 672. MS. Min.)]

(*g*.) 11 Feb. 1691–2. Petition of Appellant. Since their Lordships' Order of 21 Nov. last, giving Respondents leave to try their title at law to Slaney's estate and whether the deed of distribution of 14 Aug. 1685 was fraudulently obtained, Respondents have brought an ejectment, upon trial whereof, as Petitioner is advised, the matter directed by their Lordships touching the said deed cannot come in question or be tried, but only the matter of bankruptcy against the first mortgage to Minshall. Prays their Lordships to direct that both the said matters may be tried in proper issues for that purpose. [The House on reading the Petition this day, referred it to Mr. Justice Powell and Mr. Baron Powell to draw proper issues to be tried on the directions

* The MS. Min. of 25 Nov. have this entry: "Moved that the Cause be heard on Monday next," *i.e.* 28 Nov. The Order made was to hear it on 30 Nov., L. J., XIV. 662.

in the Orders of the House, and submit them to the House. L. J., XV. 71.]

(*h.*) 22 Feb. 1691–2. Issues in the Case Bird *v.* Sedgwick presented to the House this day by Mr. Baron Powell. [Read and agreed to this day, and ordered to be tried at the King's Bench by a Middlesex Jury. L. J., XV. 87.]

(*i.*) 4 Nov. 1692. Petition of Appellant. The Court of Chancery had proceeded on the original Order of 20 Dec. 1690, and a sale of the estate had been agreed on by Respondents, but before it was perfected, they petitioned the House a second time (*see* Annex (*d.*) above), and produced there for the first time the Commissioners' Deed of Distribution of 14 Aug. 1685, which they had had in their custody from the first, and insisting that the same was fraudulent, induced their Lordships to order that the question of fraud should be tried at law. Appellant, in obedience to the Order of 22 Feb. 1691, named a Defendant and an Attorney to accept the issues approved by the House and to take notice of trial, but Mr. Bird, one of the Respondents, who, being an assignee, acts for the rest, has refused to accept the Issues. Respondents admitted in their Answer to the Appeal that Minshall's mortgage preceded Slaney's bankruptcy, but now deny it. Their refusal to accept the Issues is merely for delay. The suit has already lasted seven years, and cost Appellant at least 550*l.* Prays their Lordships to revive* and establish their Order of 20 Dec. 1690. *Undated.* [It is evidently the Petition read this day, which Respondents were ordered to answer on the 9th inst. (*See* Annex (*k.*) below.) L. J., XV. 104.]

(i^1.) Affidavit of Obadiah Sedgwick, Junior, that, by direction of Appellant, he served a writing on Hitchcock, Yates, and Bird, on 5 April last, appointing Mr. Turbill as Appellant's Attorney to accept the Issues, and naming Appellant as Defendant, and also giving notice of trial; and that Mr. Bird refused to accept the Issues. *Sworn* 2 Nov. 1692 before Lacon W. Child. [Appended to preceding.]

(i^2.) Affidavit of William Turbill, one of the Attorneys of the Court of King's Bench, that on 4 April last he sent notice in writing to Mr. Wm. East, Clerk or Attorney in the Court of Common Pleas, who solicited the cause for the Defendants, that Deponent was appointed to appear for Appellant in the Court of King's Bench and was ready to receive the Issues directed by the House: but that no Issues had been delivered to Deponent. *Sworn* 3 Nov. 1692 before S. Keck. [Appended to Annex (*i.*).]

(*k.*) 9 Nov. 1692. Answer of George Hitchcock, Esq., and William Bird, on behalf of themselves and several other creditors of Richard Slaney, a bankrupt for 5,000*l.* and upwards. Respondents having obtained leave by their Lordships' orders of 21 Nov. and 4 Dec. 1691 to try their right at law, were advised to bring their ejectment, when Appellant, at the close of the last Session, without any notice to Respondents, petitioned their Lordships, suggesting untruly that the matters in question could not be tried by an ejectment, and their Lordships, without hearing Respondents on that point, referred it to Mr. Justice Powell and Mr. Baron Powell to draw proper Issues for trial. Appellant, taking advantage of Respondents' absence from town, presented

* Wrongly entered as "review" in L. J. XV. 104.

House of Lords MSS.
—
1690.

the Judges with Issues ready drawn, making Respondents admit several matters which they dispute, and on these Issues their Lordships directed the cause to be tried. Respondents petitioned against them, but the Prorogation happening that morning, their Petition was not read. Appellant has since called on Respondents to proceed to trial. Pray that the Issues may be referred back to the same or other Judges to be settled fairly between the parties. Here follow the exceptions taken to the said Issues. *Signed* by Respondents. [Brought in this day. The House referred this Answer and the Petition of 4 Nov. (Annex (*i.*) above), to the Committee for Petitions, whom Mr. Justice Powell and Mr. Baron Powell were ordered to attend. (L. J., XV. 106.) —On 12 Nov. the Committee met, M. Halifax in the chair. The Petition and Answer read. The two Judges give an account of the Issues directed by them. Orders of 11 Feb. and 22 Feb. 1691 read. *The Solicitor-General* opens the Petitioner's case and *Mr. Conyers* speaks to the Issues. *Mr. Finch:* What is now desired is to set aside all that your Lordships have done in this Cause. The ejectment will not try the Deed of Distribution. *Mr. Ward* (for Hitchcock): Your Lordships have not determined that Mr. Sedgwick shall have his money. These Issues are drawn with a preface which would make us own several things that we contest. They would have us admit that Sedgwick has paid 1,400*l.*, and that there has been a distribution of the bankrupt's estate, and that Sedgwick had 2,300*l.* due to him at Slaney's bankruptcy. The Issues drawn will never end the cause. *Sir Thomas Powys:* By these Issues we can never try the bankruptcy. There were no Issues settled by the Judges. *The Solicitor-General:* There is no reason to direct an Issue to try Minshall's bankruptcy. They withdraw. *Question*, Whether to refer back to the Judges to settle the proper Issues? Contents 8; Not-Contents 7. Resolved in the Affirmative. Ordered to report accordingly. (Pet. Book.) On 18 Nov. this Report was made, when the House, after hearing Mr. Justice Powell and considering several Orders made in the cause, disagreed to the Report and ordered the Cause to be tried in King's Bench on the Issues already delivered in (L. J., XV. 115).]

(*l.*) 22 Nov. 1692. Petition of Appellant. Their Lordships ordered a Commission to issue out of Chancery for examining Joseph Sedgwick, a material witness, then in the Isle of Wight. (L. J., XV. 117.) Petitioner finds that the method of issuing such a Commission would occasion by its delay the ruin of the said witness, by preventing his intended voyage to Jamaica. To avoid this Petitioner has sent for him to come up to London, and he is expected here this night. Prays that he may be examined either before a Judge of the King's Bench, where the cause is to be tried, or in the Examiner's Office in Chancery. L. J., XV. 121.

(*m.*) 14 Feb. 1692-3. Petition of Appellant. The Issues directed by their Lordships were tried at the Bar of King's Bench this term. Respondents proving acts of bankruptcy against Slaney in 1682 committed at Lisbon, where he resided, the Judges were of opinion that the Statutes of Bankrupts did not extend to him, being an English subject, and thereupon Respondents had a verdict on the first Issue. But Petitioners fully proving that he *bonâ fide* lent his money without any notice of Slaney's bankruptcy, and that he proceeded fairly in obtaining the distribution, obtained a verdict on the second issue. Prays that their Lordships' Judgment of 20 Dec. 1690 may be confirmed. [Read this day, and Respondents ordered to answer and Counsel to be heard on 27 Feb. (L. J., XV. 229.) On 8 March, Counsel were accordingly heard. *The Solicitor-General* (for Appellant): We cannot by law have the advantage of the Deed of Distribution. *Mr. Finch* followed. *Sir Thomas Powys* and *Mr. Ward* were heard for Hitchcock. After a reply, the Speaker reported and the House ordered that Appellants' claim should stand as it did before L. Jeffrey's order for cancelling the Deed, &c. as in L. J., XV. 281. (MS. Min.) *See* further Annex (*o*.) and note.]

(*n*.) 24 Feb. 1692–3. Answer of George Hitchcock, Esq., William Bird, Chas. Michel, Robert Michel, Thomas March, Merchant, and others, creditors of Richard Slaney, Respondents. Recite proceedings since the Judgment of 20 Dec. 1690. Pray that Appellant's Petition (preceding Paper) may be dismissed and Respondents as well as Appellant left to take their remedy at law. *Endorsed* as brought in this day.

(*o*.) 10 March 1692–3. Petition of Respondents, George Hitchcock, Esq., William Bird, Thomas March, Merchants and others, Creditors of Richard Slaney, a Bankrupt. Upon hearing the cause yesterday, upon the exposition of Mr. Finch, Appellant's Counsel, it was agreed by all parties that the Deed of Distribution should stand as if it had not been cancelled, and that no use or advantage should be made of the conveyance by the Assignees to Appellant or his reconveyance to them, and that each party should have liberty to proceed at law to try the validity of the Deed of Distribution. But in the minutes of the cause no mention is made that the conveyance as well as the reconveyance shall be set aside and not made use of. If the latter only is set aside, the former will be a bar to the assignees of the Commissioners and prevent them from bringing the validity of the Deed of Distribution into question. Pray that their Lordships' order may be amended accordingly. L.J., XV. 283. [On 13 March Counsel were heard on the point: whether as well the Deed of Conveyance from the Assignees of the Commissioners of Bankrupts as the Reconveyance to them should be set aside. *Sir Thomas Powys* heard for Appellant. *Mr. Finch* (for Appellant): An innocent purchaser ought never to be hurt by Equity. You have got the Distribution set aside, and will yet have the weapons in our hands set aside. Assignment was made to Sedgwick, and that must be set aside. No Court of Conscience ought to take away a man's right or disarm a purchaser. The House then dismissed the Petition and confirmed the Judgment of 8 March. (MS. Min. L. J., XV. 286.)]

(*p*.) 13 March 1692–3. Abstract of proceedings relative to the Appeal beginning 20 Dec. 1690 and ending this day. *Signed* and *certified* by J. Walker.

(*q*.) 13 March 1692–3. Copy of preceding Abstract.

(*r*.) 21 March 1695. Petition of George Hitchcock, Esq., Anne Fountaine, Widow, William Bird, Thomas March, Robert Michel, Charles Michel, Merchants, John Harvey and Elizabeth Parr, Widow, on behalf of themselves and others, Creditors of Richard Slaney, deceased. It having been found on the two

Issues directed by their Lordships, (1) that Slaney became a bankrupt in April, 1682, two years before the first mortgage, and (2) that the Deed of Distribution was not obtained by him by fraud, their Lordships on 8 Nov. 1692, on Appellant's Petition, ordered that his claim to an interest in the estate should stand as it was before L. Jeffrey's order, that what he or his trustee Noden had done in pursuance of the order should not be to his prejudice, and that a copy of the Deed should be admitted as evidence in lieu of the original, whereby Petitioners conceived they were at liberty to controvert the validity of the Deed in point of law, being advised that, if not fraudulent, it was insufficient to establish Appellant's claim. But by colour of the order, Appellant has got possession of the estate, and keeps in his hands 882*l.* beyond his pretended debt, as purchaser of the estate, which was repaid to him by Petitioners on his and his trustee's reconveyance. Pray for leave to controvert the validity of the Deed. *Signed* by above Petitioners except John Harvey. *Endorsed* as offered this day. [*See* next Paper.]

(*s.*) 21 March 1695. Petition of same. Identical with preceding one. *Signed* by G. Hitchcock, Anne Fountaine, W. Bird, Tho. March and Ro. Mitchell.* *Endorsed* as read this day: Ordered to consider what is fit to be done on it. L. J., XV. 714.

(*t.*) 18 March 1696. Petition of George Hitchcock, Esq., Anne Fountaine, Widow, William Bird, Thomas March, Robert Michel, Charles Michel, Merchants, John Harvey, Esq., Elizabeth Parr, Widow, and others Creditors of Richard Slaney, a bankrupt. Identical with Annex (*r.*) above. *Signed* by all of the Petitioners. *Endorsed:* Ordered to be rejected. L. J., XVI. 127.

(*u.*) Printed Case of same. To same effect as the last three Petitions and concluding with the same prayer. *Undated.*

(*w.*) 10 Jan. 1706-7. Petition and Appeal of George Hitchcock, Esq., Richard March, Surviving Executor of Thomas March, and Robert Michel and Charles Michel. Pray for the reversal of a Decree of the late L. Keeper Wright on 15 Nov. 2 W. & M. and an Order of the present Lord Keeper confirming the said Decree, and also for an explanation of the Order of the House of 8 March 1692. [Read this day, and referred to a Committee appointed to consider it and to state matters of fact in the case specially and report their opinion to the House. (L. J., XVIII. 193.) This Committee reported (*see* next paper) that the Petition was not fit to be received, as containing in substance the same matter that appeared in the Petition of 18 March 1696 (Annex (*t.*) above), which was rejected by the House. The House, on this report, finally rejected the Appeal, (L. J., XVIII. 202.)]

(*x.*) 22 Jan. 1706-7. Report of Committee appointed to consider preceding Petition, &c. L. J., XVIII. 200.

350. Nov. 29. French Trade Bill.—Draft of an Act for the more effectual restraining the Trade of France. § i. Whereas by an Act made in the first year of their Majesties' reign, entitled An Act for prohibiting all Trade and Commerce with France, it was enacted that from

* The autograph signature is spelt as here given; he signs his name also as "Michel." This is one of several instances of the same person found spelling his name in different ways.

and after the twenty-fourth day of August, Anno Domini 1689, no French Wines, Vinegar, Brandy, Linen, Silks, Salt, Paper or any other goods or commodities whatsoever of the growth, product or manufacture of any of the dominions or territories of the French King, or any goods, commodities or manufactures made of or mixed with Silk, Thread, Wool, Hair, Gold, Silver, Leather or other goods, or commodities being of the growth, product or manufacture of any of the dominions or territories of the French King should during or within the term of three years to be brought in by land or should be imported in any ship or ships, vessel or vessels whatsoever into any port, haven, creek or other place whatsoever in the Kingdoms of England or Ireland, Dominions of Wales or Town of Berwick-upon-Tweed, or Isles of Jersey, Guernsey, Sark or Isle of Man from any place or port whatsoever, either mixt or unmixt with any commodity of the growth or product of any other nation, place or country whatsoever upon such pain, penalties and forfeitures as in the said Act is contained. And forasmuch as it was the intent and meaning of the said recited Act that all goods and commodities whatsoever of the growth or manufacture of any of the Dominions or territories of the French King, which after the said twenty-fourth day of August and within the time limited in and by the said Act, should be taken and brought in as prize, should be subject and liable to all the penalties and forfeitures in the said Act contained; By reason whereof many Merchants and others forbore to send out any ships or vessels as privateers, and thereby the subjects of France did obtain a great freedom and liberty of trade, and the capers and privateers of that Kingdom became very numerous and much infested the coasts and ports of their Majesties' dominions, to the great prejudice and annoyance of the Merchants and others their Majesties' subjects; For the prevention therefore of such mischiefs for the future, and to the end such low rates may be set upon all French goods taken as prize as may prevent the importation of them by way of merchandize under colour of prize goods, and yet may give a due encouragement to their Majesties' subjects to fit out privateers, Be it enacted by the King and Queen's Most Excellent Majesties, by and with the advice and consent of the Lords Spiritual and Temporal and the Commons in this present Parliament assembled, and by the authority of the same, That all French Wines, Vinegar, Brandy, Linen, Silks, Salt, Paper and all other the goods and commodities whatsoever of the growth, product or manufacture of any of the dominions or territories of the French King, and all goods, commodities or manufactures made of or mixed with Silk, Thread, Wool, Hair, Gold, Silver, Leather, or other goods or commodities being of the growth, product or manufacture of any the dominions or territories of the French King, which since the twenty-fourth day of August have been taken and brought into any port, haven, creek or other place whatsoever in the Kingdom of England, Dominion of Wales or Town of Berwick-upon-Tweed, and are or shall be condemned as prize and which are not burnt or destroyed; And also all French Wines, Vinegar, Brandy, Linen, Silks, Salt, Paper and all other the goods and commodities aforesaid, which at any time hereafter shall be taken and brought into any port, haven, creek or other place whatsoever in the Kingdom of England [or Ireland],* the Dominion of Wales [and Town of Berwick-upon-Tweed],* and which shall be condemned as prize, such part or share of the said goods, commodities or manufactures (so already taken, brought in or con-

* The words in square brackets are cancelled.

demned as prize and which hereafter shall be taken, brought in and condemned as prize), which shall belong to the captors, shall be valued and rated at the rates and prices hereafter mentioned, that is to say: All Claret at 7*l.* for every tun; all St. Martin's white wine at 5*l.* for every tun; all other white wine at 7*l.* for every tun; all single Brandy at 10*l.* for every tun, all double Brandy at 15*l.* for every tun; all Vinegar at 5*l.* for every tun; all Rape at 3*l.* for every tun; all Black and Yellow Rosine at 4*l.* for every tun; all Common Turpentine at 6*l.* for every tun; all Oil of Turpentine at 20*l.* for every tun; all Cork at 8*l.* for every tun; all Prunes at 5*s.* for every hundred-weight; all Feathers at 5*s.* for every hundred-weight, and all Salt at 15*s.* for every weigh; And if any goods or commodities of the growth, product, or manufacture of any of the Territories or Dominions of the French King, or any goods, commodities or manufactures made of, or mixed with Silk, Thread, Wool, Hair, Gold, Silver, Leather or other goods or commodities, being of the growth, product or manufacture of any of the Dominions or Territories of the French King (other than the goods and commodities before specified and rated) have been, since the said 24th day of August, taken, brought in and condemned as prize (and not yet destroyed) or hereafter shall be taken, brought in and condemned as prize, the same and every part thereof shall at or within six days after the condemnation thereof, be rated by two of the sworn Appraisers of the Court of Admiralty at a fifth part of the value which the said goods shall be worth at the time of the appraisement thereof, and no more.

§ ii. And it is further enacted, by the authority aforesaid, that all the said goods and commodities already taken, or hereafter to be taken as prize and rated as aforesaid, and every part thereof, shall at the respective rates and prices before mentioned, be delivered to such Commissioner or Commissioners as shall be authorized by their Majesties on that behalf, such Commissioner or Commissioners, or such other persons, as shall for that purpose be directed and appointed by their Majesties, paying or securing to the captors of the said prize goods for their share, at the time of the delivery thereof, such sum and sums of money as the said goods, at the rates and prices before mentioned, shall and do amount to, which said Commissioners shall sell and dispose of the said goods and commodities, so from time to time delivered to them, to the best advantage they can for their Majesties' use and benefit, anything in this or the said recited Act to the contrary thereof notwithstanding.

§ iii. And be it further enacted by the authority aforesaid, that all and every person and persons whatsoever, which at any time or times hereafter shall take any ship or ships, vessel or vessels, or goods as prizes, such person and persons so taking the same, shall bring the ship or vessel and goods, so taken as prize, into the port, haven or creek within the Kingdom of England or Dominion of Wales, which is nearest to the place where such ship or vessel or goods shall be taken, and also shall within six hours after the bringing the same into any port, haven or creek, declare to the Chief Magistrate of the same place or, in the absence of such Chief Magistrate, then to the Constable or other Chief Officer of the said port, haven or creek, that the said ship and goods are taken and brought in as prize; And it shall not be lawful for such person or persons so bringing in such ship or goods as prize, to remove or convey the ship or goods so taken as prize, or any part thereof, out of or from the port, haven, creek or place whatsoever, without licence and leave in writing first had from the Commissioners to be appointed by their Majesties for the receiving the captors' shares as aforesaid.

§ iv. And be it further enacted by the authority aforesaid, that every Captain, Master or other chief officer of the ship or vessel that shall take and bring in any ship or vessel and goods as prize, shall within forty-eight hours after the bringing in the same into such next port, haven or creek as aforesaid, take an Oath before the Chief Magistrate of the town or before one of their Majesties' Justices of the Peace inhabiting in or near the said port, haven or creek into which the said ship and goods shall be so brought, that the said ship and goods were really and boná fide taken as prize; And if any ship or ships or goods which the captain, master or other chief officer as aforesaid, shall swear to be taken and brought in as prize, were not really taken as prize, but were fraudulently brought in and imported, by way of merchandise, in elusion of this and the said recited Act, that in every such case the said captain, master or other chief officer, being thereof lawfully convicted or attainted, shall for his or their said offence forfeit [*blank*].

§ v. And be it further enacted by the authority aforesaid, that if any person or persons, that shall take any ship or goods as prize, do not bring the same into the port, haven or creek next to the place where the said ship and goods were taken; or if they do not, within the space of six hours after the bringing such ship or goods into such next port, haven or creek, declare and swear in such manner as aforesaid, that the said ship and goods are taken and brought in as prize; or if the said person or persons, so bringing in such ship and goods as prize, shall or do land or put on shore, or cause or willingly permit to be landed or put on shore, any part of the said goods so taken and brought in as prize, before they have declared and sworn the same to be taken and brought in as prize in such manner as aforesaid, or after such declaration and oath made, shall or do without a license in writing to be obtained from the said Commissioners to be appointed by their Majesties as aforesaid, unship or put into any hoy, boat or vessel, or land or put on shore, or cause or willingly permit to be unshipt or put into any hoy, boat or vessel, or to be landed or put on shore, any part of the said goods so taken and brought in as prize, that then in every such case all the said goods so taken and brought in and every part thereof shall be deemed and taken to be French goods imported contrary to the said recited Act and liable to such seizure, penalties and forfeitures as in and by the said recited Act is directed and appointed, and the captain or master or other person taking care of the said ship or vessel, which shall take and bring in such goods as prize and which shall so unship or put into any hoy, boat or vessel or to be landed or put on shore any part of the said goods so taken and brought in as prize, and all and every the seamen, mariners, watermen, carmen, porters, labourers or other persons whatsoever assisting in the unshipping, landing, taking up, carrying or conveying of any of the said commodities either by land or by water, shall be subject and liable to the penalties and forfeitures in and by the said recited Act for that purpose imposed and enacted.

§ vi. And be it further enacted by the authority aforesaid, that it shall not be lawful for any derson or persons whatsoever to rent or farm or to take and accept of any grant or lease from their Majesties of the captor's share of the goods or commodities, which hereafter shall be taken as prize or any part thereof, or of the profits or advantage arising thereby, but all and every such letting to farm and grant shall be and is hereby declared to be null and void, and all and every person and persons so renting the same or which shall take any grant or lease thereof contrary to the true intent and meaning of this Act, shall forfeit [*blank*]. [Read 1ª this day, and, after debate, rejected. L. J., XIV. 571. The House was afterwards moved that a Bill be brought in for encouraging of privateers and that if they take a ship it shall be theirs, and that all privateers take a third part of their men landmen. MS. Min. 29 Nov. No entry of this in L. J. *See also* No. **379.**]

351. Dec. 1. Nathaniel Cox.—Petition of Nathaniel Cox. Complains that John Middleton, Gent., a Papist, with whose daughter Winfred, the Petitioner, a Protestant, has contracted to be married, designs to convey her away by force to some nunnery or other religious convent beyond the seas. Prays the House to interpose and prevent her removal. L. J., XIV. 573. [*Cox* being sworn this day at the bar, stated that the substance of his Petition was true; he had it from report, from one who had seen the woman that was to go with her, whose name was Anne Burket. On 3 Dec. *Middleton* was called in and asked if he intended to carry away his daughter to a nunnery. He said that Cox made several outrages upon his house. He hoped their Lordships would secure his daughter against him. He would bring her at any time. *A witness* deposed that a ring was bought. They gave her chocolate and stupefied her for 8 or 10 hours. The House then ordered as in L. J., XIV. 577 (MS. Min.).]

352. Dec. 1. L. Lovelace *v.* Alstone (Libel).—Printed sheet entitled "The Case of the Band of Gentlemen Pensioners," as follows: "The Band of Gentlemen Pensioners was first established in the reign of King Henry VII. By subsequent establishments and orders of Kings in Council it appears the power of the Captain of the Band is so restrained that he hath no authority to displace any Gentleman of the Band. It is evident, not only from the establishments before mentioned, but by constant experience and usage, that the Gentlemen of the Band have a right, esteemed equivalent to a freehold, for upon their admission their oath is to the King, his heirs and successors; and upon the death of any King, they have always continued as Gentlemen of the Band to the succeeding Prince, and never were removed unless for such offence as would have amounted in law to a forfeiture of an office for life. Every Gentleman of the Band hath always had liberty to dispose of his place, provided such person to whom such disposition was made, was first approved of by the King, as appears by an Order of King and Council. In consideration of the establishments and usages before mentioned, the Pensioners bought their places, and most of them paid 500*l.* for the same. Yet upon this happy Revolution, the Right Honorable the Lord Lovelace hath turned out above half the Band, without any cause assigned, to make way for friends of his own. Upon their Petition to his Majesty in Council, a day was appointed for hearing this case, but Mr. Attorney and Mr. Solicitor-General, being retained by the Petitioners as their Counsel, were prevented by Parliamentary affairs at that time from attending the Petitioners' case, whereby they did not profit by their Petition. At which time his Majesty was pleased to declare 'He wished each man's character was writ on his forehead,' from which it is apparent their misfortune proceeded from an ill character given of them. Kings in their grants may be deceived by misinformation, to the great damage of their subjects and their own prejudice; And we humbly hope, as Parliaments are the greatest Council and last Resort, they will think fit to mind the King of such deceits, and find him out a remedy to prevent the like for the future and some redress for the Petitioners, whose places were their only crimes, the Officer wanting them for his own friends, to the dishonour of his Majesty's Service. The general objection to our proceeding in this method is, *Objection:* That the King is at liberty to choose his own Household servants, otherwise he is denied that power which every private master hath and exerciseth in his own family. *Answer:* That the King hath and ought to have that power, is not to be denied; but all men condemn such stewards to private masters, who misrepresent old servants to bring in new ones for money, or otherwise to prefer relations, which servants, so retained, are more the Steward's than the Master's servants. No man's servant ought to be discharged but either as they are guilty of some offence or incapable to discharge the duty of their place, or as they are unnecessary. And if the Petitioners do not come within any of these exceptions, it is humbly hoped they shall not suffer under a particular hardship by misinformation only, and be the first instance of servants so discharged. For the first, if they stand charged with any offence, they are suitors for his Majesty's favour and to this Honourable House upon no other terms than as they can clear their innocence. For the second, as there is no great difficulty in the discharge of the duty, they think they may without breach of modesty affirm they are capable of it. As for the last, they humbly conceive they cannot be looked upon as unnecessary servants, the Band still continuing. We have the example of Ordinances of Parliament made in former reigns for the good government of the King's household servants, to prevent officers from abusing the King and his good subjects, and Parliaments to redress grievances, that old servants that have adapted themselves for, and spent the flower of their age in, offices and employments belonging to the Crown, and have honestly demeaned themselves therein, may not be removed without just cause, by the intrigues of officers to get money or prefer relations." L. J., XIV. 573. [The House being informed that there was one at the door who heard Alstone own the paper, the person, a *Mr. Hoard*, was called in and sworn. Asked if he knew the paper, he said he saw a man at the Commons' door, who confessed to Lord Lovelace that he owned the paper and that his name was Alstone. The House then ordered Alstone to be attached (MS. Min.). No further proceedings.]

353. Dec. 3. Bullion Exportation Bill.—Petition of several Citizens of London. The Bill proposes, amongst other things, to raise the standard of silver to 3*l*. 5*s*. the pound or 5*s*. 5*d*. the ounce, whereby the Crown piece will be coined 3 dwt. less in weight than now it is, which will be a manifest loss of five pounds per hundred on all the rents and moneys and will never answer the intended end of bringing in any greater quantities of silver, nor will it hinder the exportation, but will immediately stop all payments in weighty money, and nothing but clipt money will be current. It will obstruct the loans to his Majesty, and be an interruption in all trade, and it can be made appear the new Crown of 4*s*. 9*d*. may as well be melted down or shipped out as the former 5*s*. Petitioners, who are far less concerned in this affair than the nobility and gentry, that have great estates in lands and moneys, pray to be heard out of a public good before the Bill passes. *Signed* Jn. Houblon, Ralph Lee, Sam. Foote, Rob. Bodington, Abraham Dolins, Humphrey Cowins, John Moribin, Humphrey Willett. L. J., XIV. 576. *See also* No. **330**.

Annexed:—

(*a*.) 6 Dec. 1690. Observations on the Bill against the Exportation of Gold and Silver, and melting down the coin of the realm. The Bill designs to raise the standard of silver from 3*l*. 2*s*. to 3*l*. 5*s*. per lb. weight, whereby the 5*s*. piece thereby intended to be coined will be about threepence less in silver than the former 5*s*. piece. This raising the 5*s*. or other species of silver coin will not prevent the exportation of silver or the melting down of the new coined species of money, though it has less of silver in it by 5 per cent. For, as the Mint before yielded about 5*s.* 2*d.* per oz., with this alteration it will yield 5*s.* 5*d.* per oz., and if silver be in demand, it will rise above what the Mint will give, as it has done for these two years last past, standard silver having been sold for, and being now worth, 5*s.* 4*d.* per oz., so that there could be no coining any silver but at 3 per cent. loss. It is evident that as soon as this law shall be made, standard silver will rise to 5*s.* 7*d.* per oz., which will be twopence per oz. more than the Mint will give. By consequence, little or none of the new intended species will be coined; and, if so, there would be twopence per oz. profit to melt it down again into bullion, for the alteration of the exchange will soon cause this advantage on the bullion. Now, the true reason why silver is risen in price in England is from the interruption of our trade and commerce during the wars, for in time of peace it has been manifest that the trade and commerce of England have furnished us not only with necessaries and superfluities from all parts of the world, but also an overplus, which has been brought home in gold and silver, to the great enriching of this kingdom. And now it happens, by the interruption of the general trade, that from Flanders, Holland, Hamburg, and the East Country, where we have more frequent convoys, we import greater quantities of merchandise and naval stores than formerly, and by reason of the wars in Germany, Flanders, &c. they take off less of our manufactory and other goods than heretofore; for which reason, and for that also there has been an occasion to pay public moneys by exchange or otherwise in those parts, we become so much indebted to them that what our exports cannot answer in goods must be answered in bullion, and that has been the reason why ill men, for a gain of 3 to 4 p.c., have melted down our present 5*s.* and 2*s.* 6*d.* pieces and plate, and sent it abroad; And the same cause continuing, it is probable they may continue the same practice, notwithstanding any severe law to the contrary. In Spain, about three years since, they altered their coin, and have coined new pieces of eight, of 20 p.c. less in value, and in Portugal, since the year 1650, at three several times they have altered their Crusado or Crown from 4*s.* 4*d.* value to 2*s.* 5*d.*, yet so great a diminution (which was done to keep their money within those Kingdoms) has not in the least prevented it from going out, but is still exported from both the said Kingdoms, notwithstanding their severe laws of death and confiscation of estate upon that account. The ill consequence of the alteration of the value of the coin will be as follows:—(1.) A present stop in payment of all the former milled money and of all the weighty old money, so that none but clipt money will pass in payment, which will not only interrupt all trade and commerce, but obstruct the loans to their Majesties and alter the prices of exchange. (2.) It will be a manifest loss to all who have money owing them upon bonds or other debts, for if it be supposed there is in this Kingdom six millions of silver coin, and that one half thereof be weighty, then upon that three millions there will be 150,000*l.* gain to them that shall melt it down. (3.) It will be a loss on all debts, rents, annuities, pensions, &c. of 5 p.c., which will amount to an incredible sum. (4.) It will be a loss of 5 p.c. on all their Majesties' Revenue, Custom, Excise, &c. (5.) All foreign commodities will rise in value as the money is fallen, for call a piece of money by what name or denomination you will, yet it is the intrinsic value of the species of money that is the measure and rule of all commerce throughout the world, and 4*s.* 9*d.* will be but 4*s.* 9*d.*, though you call it 5*s.* (6.) As the silver is raised 5 p.c., so guineas will rise in proportion, and these alterations will put a profit into the hands of all the goldsmiths, refiners, and melters of silver and others, who have a quantity of gold and weighty coin by them, but will be a manifest prejudice to the King, and all the rest of his subjects, who have rents or money owing them.—And if it shall be objected that clipt money now passes as well as weighty money, it is to be noted that the said clipt money is not above one half of the current money; and clipt money is only current upon public faith, because it is now received in all public payments, but all contracts, bargains, and sales are made upon the intrinsic value of the weighty money, especially with foreigners, of which when there shall come to be a want, there will be a full stop of all trade of buying and selling, as it lately happened in Portugal, where the King was forced to call in all the money, it being all clipt, and promised to bear the loss himself, till afterwards, finding the loss too great, he coined the new money 20 p.c. loss in weight, and so delivered it out to his subjects, the owners of the said clipt money, whereby the loss fell upon them. [Delivered in by the Merchants and read in the House this day. MS. Min. *See* Notes to No. **330.**]

354. Dec. 4. Assistants of the House.—Petition of Henry Powle, Esq., Master of the Rolls. The Masters of the Rolls for the time being have, time out of mind, been summoned to attend in Parliament, as Assistants to the House of Peers. At the beginning of the present Parliament a writ was issued out under the Great Seal to Petitioner for that purpose to one Eddoes, a Messenger belonging to the Court of Chancery, who has refused to deliver it to Petitioner, pretending that it had lately been taken from him, though Petitioner has great reason to believe the writ still remains in his hands. Petitioner being very desirous to attend, according to the duty of his place, prays their Lordships to give directions for the delivery of his writ. L. J., XIV. 578. [In Committee for Privileges on 8 Dec. (L. North in the Chair), the *Master of the Rolls* was called in and brought the Pawn of the Petty Bag, where Writs of Parliament are entered, showing Writs of Assistance granted to his predecessors as follows:—

1 Jac. II. to Sir John Churchill.

13 Car. II.
30 Car. II.
31 Car. II.
32 Car. II. } to Sir Harbottle Grimstone.

15 Car. I. to Sir Charles Cæsar.

21 Jac. I.
1 Car. I. } to Sir Julius Cæsar.

In three Parliaments when Sir John Egerton was both Keeper and Master of the Rolls, he was not summoned as Assistant.

28 Eliz.
30 Eliz.
35 Eliz. } to Sir Gilbert Gerrard.

No records are extant between 28 Eliz. and 4 Philip and Mary.

4 & 5 Ph. & Mary to Sir William Cordell.
2 & 3 Ph. & Mary }
1 & 2 Ph. & Mary } to Sir Nicholas Hare.
1 Mary }
7 Edw. VI. to Sir Robert Bowe.
6 Edw. VI.

21 Hen. VIII. no mention of any summons.

36 Hen. VIII. to Sir Robert Southwell.

1 Edw. VI. the same person was summoned again as Assistant. (Priv. Book 8 Dec.) The Committee reported on 9 Dec. (L. J., XIV. 583), and on 10 Dec. *Mr. Pingry*, being sworn, attested the accuracy of the records produced by him in Committee. (MS. Min. 10 Dec. No entry in L. J.)]

355. Dec. 5. Arnold's (Reversal of Judgment) Bill.—Commons' Engrossment of an Act for reversing a Judgment given in the Court of King's Bench against John Arnold, Esquire, as follows:—Whereas this kingdom has of late years been most unhappily divided into parties and factions through men's different apprehensions of the public interest, and the prevailing passions and prejudices did so far bias and corrupt the Courts of Justice that the public administration thereof was become partial, and thereby divers persons, upon mistakes and small offences (wrested by innuendoes) were ruined, both them and their families, some by excessive fines imposed by the Court, and others by exorbitant damages given by juries; And Whereas such exorbitant and unreasonable fines and damages are against law, and so declared in the Bill of Rights; And Whereas a verdict was given against John Arnold, of Llanvihangell in the County of Monmouth, Esquire, for the sum of 10,000*l.* and 40*s.* costs and 98*l.* damages, in the term of St. Michael in the 35th year of the reign of King Charles II., in an action brought against him by Henry Duke of Beaufort in the Court of King's Bench at Westminster; And Whereas Judgment and Execution was sued out thereupon, and the said John Arnold continued a Prisoner thereupon for several years in the prison of the King's Bench, whereby he hath severely suffered both in his person and estate for words from which (suppose they had been spoken) the Duke of Beaufort did not suffer any real damage; therefore be it enacted by the King and Queen's most Excellent Majesties, by and with the advice and consent of the Lords Spiritual and Temporal and Commons in this present Parliament assembled, and by the authority of the same, that the said Verdict and Judgment given in the said action brought against the said John Arnold, and all executions and proceedings upon the same, shall be reversed, annulled and made void, and are hereby Declared and Adjudged to be reversed, annulled and made void to all intents and purposes whatsoever. *Parchment Collection.* [Brought from the Commons this day. L. J., XIV. 579. On 6 Dec., after the First Reading, the MS. Min. contain two expunged entries, one that the House was moved that D. Beaufort should be heard before the Second Reading, and the other, after mention of a debate concerning the ways and methods of this Bill, that it was ordered to be referred to the Committee for Privileges to consider of the nature of the Bill and the methods of its coming into this House. Then comes the entry for the adjournment of the debate whether the Bill shall be rejected, as in L. J. (MS. Min. 6 Dec.)—On 9 Dec., the motion to proceed with the debate was carried by 22 votes to 19, proxies equal. E. Thanet and E.

Stamford Tellers. Then the House went into the debate of the Bill, and concerning the nature of it, being an action for *Scandalum Magnatum* against a Peer; and this is a Verdict, and not an excessive fine. Ordered that the Bill be rejected. (MS. Min. 9 Dec.).]

356. Dec. 6. E. Cleveland's Estate Bill.—Draft of an Act for the continuing and reviving of several Acts herein-after mentioned for the better and more effectual payment of the debts of Thomas, late Earl of Cleveland and Thomas, late Lord Wentworth, his son, both deceased. Recites certain provisions of the Acts of 12, 13 and 18 Car. II. and enacts that all the clauses in the said Acts, as to all matters needful for paying to the Suppliant, Anne, Countess of Newburgh, the 4,000*l*., part of the 6,000*l*. in the second Act mentioned to be paid to Lady Anne Poole, Dorothy Withypoll and Lucy Withypoll, shall be in force and confirmed for paying the 4,000*l*. to the Countess, her heirs, executors, &c., and that any two Barons of the Exchequer may put in execution the same powers for raising and paying the 4,000*l*. as are contained in the former Acts. Provided that the lands of the Earl and his son, mentioned in those Acts and not excepted and whereof no sale has been made, shall be charged with payment to the Suppliant of the said 4,000*l*. provided to be paid to Lady Poole, and that neither the heirs, trustees or assigns of the said Earl or his son shall take any benefit by virtue of the Acts or otherwise in respect of those lands until the 4,000*l*. be paid to the Suppliant. The Barons may at their discretion during this session or for seven years after examine any matter touching the taking in of former mortgages or debts, or releasing or foreclosing the equity of redemption, and if it shall appear that any such mortgages have been bought in or the equity foreclosed by practice of anyone to defraud the creditors or lessen the remedy intended by the Acts, or that the mortgaged premises have been conveyed to or in trust for the heirs or assigns of the Earl or his son for less than the mortgage money really due, the Barons shall have power to take an account and charge the same with payment of the moneys in the schedule yet unpaid and also with the 4,000*l*. and interest, so far as the values thereof exceed the moneys really paid for the same by or on behalf of the said heirs or assigns or any in trust for them, allowing interest for the principal money and discounting the profits, and such charge on the premises shall be good in law and equity. [Read 1ª this day. L. J., XIV. 581. The Bill never reached a second reading.]

Annexed :—

(*a*.) Breviate of the Bill.

357. Dec. 8. E. Aylesbury's Estate Act.—Amended draft of an Act to enable Thomas, Earl of Aylesbury and Elizabeth, Countess of Aylesbury, his wife, to make provision for payment of debts, &c. and to make leases of their estates. The original preamble concluded as follows: "And whereas the said several sums of 15,000*l*. and 10,000*l*. have been already raised and by reason of the raising thereof in such manner as aforesaid, the said Thomas, Earl of Aylesbury, hath contracted great debts,* [which may be in danger to be lost, unless some provision may be made for the payment thereof, and therefore the said Thomas, Earl of Ailesbury and Elizabeth, Countess of Ailesbury his wife have agreed, That

* The portion that follows in square brackets was struck out, and superseded by the draft given in Annex (*b*.) below, amended by inserting 700*l*. as the amount of the rentcharge.

House of Lords MSS.

1690.

all and singular the manors, lordships, lands and hereditaments in the said Counties of York, Lincoln, Middlesex and Bedford in the said Indentures of Lease and Release bearing date the 23rd and 24th days of May 1678 contained, shall be conveyed to Trustees for the term of 12 years from the 25th day of March 1691, or until Charles, Lord Bruce, their eldest son, attain the age of one and twenty years, in trust for the payment of the debts of the said Earl, in manner herein-after mentioned, and after for the making some better provision for the younger children of them, the same Earl and Countess, than is already made; And that provision may be made for the maintenance and support of the said Charles, Lord Bruce, and in case of his death for such other son and sons of the said Thomas, Earl of Ailesbury and Elizabeth, Countess of Ailesbury his wife, as shall from time to time be their eldest son from the decease of the same Earl their father, during all such 12 years term or other estate as aforesaid, she, the said Countess of Ailesbury hath consented that the manors, lordships, lands and premises in the said counties of Berks, Wilts and Somerset in the said Indentures of Lease and Release, bearing date the said 10th and 11th days of July 1684, contained, shall from the decease of the said Thomas, Earl of Ailesbury and granting such 12 years term or other Estate as aforesaid, be charged with the yearly rentcharge or annual sum of (*blank*) for the maintenance and education of the said Charles, Lord Bruce, and in case of his death, of such other son and sons of the said Thomas, Earl of Ailesbury and Elizabeth, Countess of Ailesbury his wife, as shall from time to time be their eldest son, during the continuance of all such 12 years term or other estate as aforesaid, if he, the said Charles, Lord Bruce, or such other son or sons as aforesaid shall so long live; But the said Earl and Countess of Ailesbury his wife, being only tenants for life, cannot make any such lease of the said manors and premises in the said counties of York, Lincoln, Middlesex and Bedford for 12 years absolute, or charge the said manors and premises in the said counties of Berks, Wilts and Somerset with such yearly rentcharge or annual sum of (*blank*) for the maintenance of the said Charles, Lord Bruce, or such other eldest son as aforesaid, and the making of any such lease for 12 years, or granting any such rentcharge as aforesaid may be a suspending their power of granting estates within the said manors and premises, and so lose to them, the same Earl and Countess, the whole benefit thereof]; For remedy therefore in all and every the said premises," &c. The enacting clauses which are amended, run as follows :—" And be it further enacted by the authority aforesaid, That the said Thomas, Earl of Ailesbury, and the said Countess of Ailesbury his wife, shall and may, by writing indented under both their hands and seals, demise and lease the manors and premises in the said Indentures of Lease and Release, bearing date the said 23rd and 24th days of May, 1678, contained, every or any of them with their appurtenances for the term of 12 years *or any lesser term*, to commence and be accounted from the 25th day of March, 1691, *if they, the said Thomas, Earl of Aylesbury, and Elizabeth, Countess of Aylesbury his wife, or either of them, shall so long live* [or for any lesser term], without any rent or other thing to be paid for the same, in trust for the payment of such of the debts of the said Earl as he, the same Earl and the said Countess his wife shall by writing under both their hands from time to time nominate and appoint, *not exceeding in the whole the sum of 40,000l.*; and also the interest of the same debts grown and to grow due, in such order and precedency as by them, the same Earl and Countess, by such writing as aforesaid shall be directed:

House of Lords MSS.

1690.

[*And after the payment of all and (*sic*) the said debts and interest, for the making such further and better provision for the younger or other child or children of them, the said Thomas, Earl of Ailesbury and Elizabeth, Countess of Ailesbury, his wife (other than their said eldest son), as by them, the said Earl and Countess shall in that behalf be appointed.] *And after the payment of all the same debts and interest, then in trust to dispose the residue of the profits of the said premises so to be leased during the residue of such twelve years term, if the said Earl shall so long live, for the making some better provision for the younger children of the said Earl and Countess than is already made, equally to be divided amongst them, and for no other use or purpose whatsoever;* And that such lease and estate for twelve years, so to be made and granted as aforesaid, shall be good and available in the law against the said Earl and Countess of Ailesbury his wife, notwithstanding her coverture with the same Earl [and against the first and all the sons of the said Earl and Countess, and the heirs males of their bodies issuing, and all and every other person and persons claiming or to claim by, from or under any the limitations in the said Indenture of Release, bearing date the said 24th day of May, 1678, contained and mentioned], and that such lease for 12 years, so to be made by the said Earl and Countess as aforesaid, shall not be construed or taken to be any suspension or extinction of the power hereby granted to him the same Earl for the making any such lease and leases, demises and grants of the same manors and premises as afore are mentioned; but that the same Earl shall and may, during the said 12 years term and after the [expiration] *determination* thereof, make such lease and leases, demises and grants of the same manors and premises as afore are mentioned, the said term of 12 years or the making thereof, or any construction to be made thereupon, to the contrary notwithstanding; but the rents reserved upon such lease and leases, demises and grants, and the fines to be taken in respect of the making thereof, to grow due and be paid to the Trustees in such 12 years lease to be named during the continuance thereof, for the trusts aforesaid; *and the said Trustees are not to make any lease or leases of the same manors and premises.* And it is hereby declared, that from and after full payment made of all such debts of the said Thomas, Earl of Ailesbury as he, the said Earl and the said Countess his wife, shall from time to time appoint to have paid out of the said manors and premises so to be leased for 12 years as aforesaid, and also the interest of such debts [and such sum and sums of money as the same Earl and Countess shall direct to have raised thereout, as and for a further and better provision for their younger and other child or children (other than their eldest son) than is already made, raised and] satisfied, and the Trustees' charges reimbursed, that the said term and estate for 12 years so to be granted as aforesaid shall *from thenceforth* cease and be void. And be it further enacted by the authority aforesaid, That the said Charles, Lord Bruce, and, in case of his death, such other son and sons of the said Earl of Ailesbury and Countess of Ailesbury his wife, as shall from time to time be their eldest son, shall and may from [the decease of the said Thomas, Earl of Ailesbury, and granting such 12 years term or other estate as aforesaid, have, receive, take and be paid during all the continuance of such 12 years term or other estate as aforesaid] *his and their respective ages of sixteen years, during all the then remainder of*

* The omission of this paragraph in square brackets is one of the amendments made in Committee on 19 Dec., and given in Annex (*a*.) The words next following in Italics were added on recommitment. (Com. Book 23 Dec. and Annex (*e*.) below.)

HOUSE OF LORDS MSS.

1690.

the said term of twelve years, so to be granted as aforesaid, and after the determination thereof, during all the natural life of the said Thomas, Earl of Aylesbury, their father, in case he, the said Charles, Lord Bruce, or such other eldest son as aforesaid, shall so long live, *have, receive, take and be paid* out of the said manors and premises in the said Indentures of Lease and Release, bearing date the said 10th and 11th days of July 1684, contained, the yearly rent or sum of *seven hundred pounds* in good English money, for his and their maintenance and [education] *support,* to be paid at the feasts of St. Michael the Archangel and the Annunciation of the blessed Virgin Mary by equal portions, without any deduction or abatement for taxes by Act of Parliament, or any other taxes or payments whatsoever; the first payment thereof to begin and be made at the first of those Feasts next coming or happening after [the decease of the said Thomas, Earl of Ailesbury, and the making and granting] *he, the said Charles, Lord Bruce, or such other son and sons as aforesaid, shall attain his and their respective ages of sixteen years, and that such lease of twelve years shall be so made and granted of* the said manors and premises in the said Indenture of Release, bearing date the said 24th day of May, 1678, contained [for such term of twelve years or other estate] as aforesaid; And further, that, in case the said yearly rent or annual sum of *seven hundred pounds,* or any part thereof, shall be behind or unpaid by the space of one and twenty days next after either of the said Feasts herein-before appointed for payment thereof, That then the said Charles, Lord Bruce, and, in case of his death, such other son or sons of the said Earl and Countess his wife, as shall from time to time be their eldest son, shall and may enter into the said manors and premises whereout the same yearly rent or annual sum of *seven hundred pounds* herein-before is appointed to be issuing, and there to distrain, and the distress and distresses then and there found to take, carry away, impound, detain and keep until he, they and every of them of the said yearly rent or annual sum of *seven hundred pounds* and the arrears thereof, if any be, shall be fully satisfied and paid; *and the Earl of Aylesbury is to be discharged of the making the lease of Pilton Park and premises in Pilton for the benefit of the same Lord Bruce, as in an agreement heretofore made with the said Duke and Duchess of Beaufort for that purpose is mentioned.*"* After this, the original text concludes with the saving clause as in the Act. [Read 1° this day; Royal Assent 5 Jan. 1690–1. L. J., XIV. 581, 618; 2 & 3 W. & M. c. 38 in Long Calendar. On 16 Dec. Counsel were heard against the Bill at the Bar on behalf of the Duchess of Beaufort, M. Worcester and Robert Bruce, Esq., pursuant to order of the 8th. (MS. Min. L. J., XIV. 582.) *Mr. Trevor* (for the Duchess): The Bill recites several settlements. There is no extraordinary reason in the Bill to induce your Lordships to do this. There is 36,000*l.* paid out of the estate already. *Mr. Browne* (for the Duchess): We humbly conceive these settlements will not be undone. We are to offer the extraordinary sums of 30,000*l.* and upwards by sales and 20,000*l.* by fines. *Sir W. Williams* (for the Bill): Here are two settlements. We desire but the enlarging of the power. *Mr. Ward* (for the Bill): We hope your Lordships will pass the Bill. (MS. Min. 16 Dec.)—In Committee, on 17 Dec. *Mr. Foulks* (for the Bill) said the Bill is not to ask for an original power for his Lordship, but to enable him to make the best of

* Here are marked for insertion clauses A. and B. Annexes (*c.*) and (*d.*)

that power. We only pray he may fill up the estates as they fall. He can make leases in possession but not in reversion. *Mr. Browne* (for Duchess of Beaufort): Upon his Lordship's marriage it was agreed that he should make leases in possession but not in reversion. By the Bill no rent is to be reserved upon his Lordship's making a lease. If he or her Ladyship die within 12 years, then his son will have no rent upon these leases. Admits that his Lordship has such a power as is alleged. The compensation offered the heir is out of her Ladyship's estate, which, however, would come to him, if she died. *Mr. Foulks* proposes that his Lordship, for compensation to the heir, will bind himself from ploughing and cutting wood near the house. He may commit waste on the whole estate. *Agreed:* Lord and Lady Ailesbury to have power to make leases in possession and reversion of Lady Ailesbury's estate for 21 years or three lives or a term of years determinable upon one, two, or three lives, reserving the rents which, by the intent of the settlement, are to be reserved, except such as are excepted to be leased in the settlement. Lord Ailesbury to have the same power as to his paternal estate, reserving the rents in the settlement of that estate. Lord and Lady Ailesbury to lease the paternal estate for 12 years, if they live so long (and this not to suspend his Lordship's power of leasing that estate) for the payment of debts. The intended provision for the first son, in case his Lordship dies within the 12 years, to be out. The debt his Lordship would pay by this Bill shall not exceed 40,000*l.* Counsel withdraw. [His Lordship is willing that, if he have but one daughter, she may have 10,000*l.*, if two daughters, then 16,000*l.* betwixt them; if more daughters than two, then 20,000*l.* amongst them; the said sums to be raised equally out of my Lord and Lady's estates. The 1,500*l.* apiece already secured to them, to be taken away by this Act. My Lord is willing that his younger sons shall have 300*l.* a year apiece and 2,000*l.* apiece in money, to be raised equally out of his own and his Lady's estates. The Counsel are called in and the above-mentioned notes being read to them, it is *agreed* that no provision shall be made by this Bill for the above-mentioned younger child.] Counsel were called in and ordered to mend the Bill according to the notes above (omitting the portion in square brackets, which was struck through) and to compare the settlements with the preamble and bring the clauses, drawn, on the 19th. (Com. Book 17 Dec.)—On 19 Dec. the Bill was amended, several of the amendments agreed to, being offered by Mr. Anthony Ward. (Com. Book 19 Dec.)—On 22 Dec. *L. Newport* desired an amendment in the discharge of prices, and to the waiving of privilege. Agreed to. House informed that there is a clause in the Bill to which a peer takes some exception, and that it is desired that it may be recommitted as to the clause of the Lady Aylesbury's barring herself against the Earl, and that directions be given to the Committee that this clause be left out. (MS. Min.) Bill ordered to be recommitted accordingly. (L. J., XIV. 602.)—In Committee (on recommitment), on 23 Dec., *Mr. Browne* (for the Duchess) proposes that there may be a provision made for the younger children out of the residue of the term of 12 years after the debt of 40,000*l.* is paid. E. Aylesbury consents thereto. Counsel, after withdrawing to prepare a clause to that purpose, propose some words which are agreed to be added to the Bill. (Annex (*f.*) below.) Agreed to leave out the clause marked B. relating to Lady Aylesbury's barring the remainder. *Ordered* to report the Bill with these amendments. Com. Book, L. J., XIV. 603.]

Annexed:—

(*a.*) 20 Dec. 1690. List of Lords' Amendments to the Bill. [Agreed to in Committee 19 Dec. and reported this day. Com. Book. L. J., XIV. 599.]

(*b.*) Paper containing some of the Amendments referred to in preceding, among them the amendment superseding the concluding portion of the original preamble.

(*c.*) 20 Dec. 1690. Clause marked A., debarring the Earl from making waste on certain of the premises. [Agreed to in Committee 19 Dec., and reported this day. Com. Book. L. J., XIV. 599. It forms the last clause but one of the Act.]

(*d.*) 20 Dec. 1690. Clause marked B., as follows: "And be it further enacted by the authority aforesaid, that no recovery or recoveries, to be suffered by the said Elizabeth, Countess of Aylesbury after the decease of the said Thomas, Earl of Aylesbury her husband (in case she shall him survive) of the said manors and premises in the said Indentures of Lease and Release, bearing date the said 10th and 11th days of July 1684, contained, or any of them, shall in any manner bar and discharge the reversion or remainder in fee simple of such part and parts of the same manors and premises as in and by the same Indentures of Lease and Release are, in default of issue of the body of the said Elizabeth, Countess of Aylesbury begotten, limited to the said Thomas, Earl of Aylesbury and his heirs; but if such recovery and recoveries, if any shall happen, be so suffered as aforesaid as against the said Earl of Aylesbury as for and concerning his reversion and remainder in fee simple of and in the said premises, shall be void and of none effect, any law or statute to the contrary notwithstanding." [Agreed to in Committee 19 Dec., and reported this day. Com. Book. L. J., XIV. 599. Left out in Committee, on recommitment. Com. Book 23 Dec.]

(*e.*) 20 Dec. 1690. Lords' Engrossment of preceding clauses A. and B. and portion of the concluding saving clause. [It formed a skin, numbered 4, of the Act as first ordered to be engrossed this day, and was cut out on recommitment. Com. Book. 23 Dec. L. J., XIV. 599.]

(*f.*) 23 Dec. Amendment making provision for the younger children of the Earl and Countess. Begins ("*And after the payment*"); Ends ("*or purpose whatsoever*"). [Added in Committee on recommitment this day. Com. Book. It appears in the Act. *See* Notes above.]

(*g.*) Copy of the Act as passed. *Certified*, as correct, by E. Aylesbury.

358. Dec. 11. Dashwood *v.* Sir J. Champante.—Petition and Appeal of Sir Robert Dashwood, Knt. and Bart., Sir Samuel Dashwood, Knt., John Pery and Edward Noell, Esq., surviving Executors of the last will and testament of George Dashwood, Esq., deceased, in trust for minors and younger children of the said Mr. Dashwood. The House on 24 April 1690 (*see* 12th Report, Appendix, Part VI., No. 214) ordered the Court of Exchequer to examine Petitioners' witnesses as to the assignment and notice, which was done, but, notwithstanding that both were fully proved, the Court on 29 Nov. last ordered a trial at law of the issue whether Champante had notice of the assignment or not. Appeal from this Order, and pray that Champante may be ordered to answer. *Signed* by Appellants; *Countersigned* H. Finch and Sam. Dodd. [Reported this day from the Committee of Petitions (L. J., XIV. 586. Pet. Book 9 Dec.) On 13 Nov. 1691 this Appeal was heard and dismissed by 26 to 16. Tellers, L. Weymouth and L. Cornwallis. *The Solicitor-General* and *Mr. Finch* appeared for Appellants, and *Mr. Clerk* and *Mr. Ward* for Respondent. (MS. Min. L. J., XIV. 644.]

Annexed :—

(*a.*) 18 Dec. 1690. Answer of Sir John Champante. Similar to that in previous Appeal. *Endorsed* as brought in this day.

(*b.*) 6 Nov. 1691. Petition of Respondent for an early day for hearing. L. J., XIV. 635.

(*c.*) 6 Nov. 1691. Similar Petition of Appellants. L. J., XIV., 635.

(*d.*) 15 Jan. 1691–2. Petition and Appeal of Appellants, as above. Recites substantially the contents of the Appeal of 11 Dec. 1690. Pray that the issue for trial may be enlarged. *Signed* by above Appellants except Pery; *Countersigned* Rob. Sawyer, J. Soffiers, H. Finch and Sam. Dodd. L. J., XV. 32. MS. Min.

(*e.*) 13 Jan. 1692–3. Petition of Appellants. Pray their Lordships' directions, that Sir John Champante's accounts may be stated to the time he had notice of the assignment by Dashwood. L. J., XV. 181. Almost *in extenso*.

[The House ordered the Court of Exchequer to proceed with the account, notwithstanding the Appeal of "E. Ranelagh *v.* Sir J. Champante" (No. 243*), then depending before the House. *ib.*]

(*f.*) 17 Feb. 1692–3. Petition of Appellants. Petitioners having applied to the Court of Exchequer to have the cause set down to direct the account pursuant to their Lordships' Order of 13 Jan. last, Respondent has succeeded in delaying the hearing by pretending as an impediment, the privilege of E. Ranelagh, who is a member of the House of Commons, but who, in fact, has never insisted upon his privilege. Petitioners' defence to Respondent's demand is distinct from that of the Earl, their testator having assigned his interest long before the pretended stating of the accounts in question. Prays their Lordships' direction and relief. L. J., XV. 234.

(*g.*) 17 Feb. 1692–3. Petition of Respondent. The account in question is a joint account, in which E. Ranelagh is concerned, and the Earl as well as Mr. Bence, both members of the House of Commons, have insisted on their privilege, and the Court has allowed this objection to a hearing. Most of the vouchers have been destroyed in a fire. Prays their Lordships to suspend all further proceedings between Dashwood's Executors till they have heard the Appeal of the other Undertakers. L. J., XV. 234. [Counsel were heard on this and the preceding Petition on 24 Feb. They were told they were to speak to the point of hearing and stating the account before E. Ranelagh's Appeal be determined. *Mr. Finch* (for Appellants): We are told by the Court we cannot go on until L. Ranelagh's Appeal is heard. I cannot say what is the objection, why the account is not taken. *Mr. Dodd* (for Appellants) is heard. *The Solicitor-General* (for Respondent): The question is whether the Court of Exchequer shall proceed until the L. Ranelagh's Appeal be determined. Our account is an entire account, and the nature of it is so. Your Lordships have not judged whether L. Ranelagh's account be open or not. If L. Ranelagh prevails, then his account is open. *Mr. Ward* (for Respondent): L. Ranelagh did stand on his privilege. It is a joint account, and we cannot separate it. *Mr. Finch* heard in reply. Counsel withdrew, and the L. Speaker reported. *L. C. Baron* [*Atkyns*] heard as to their reasons in the Exchequer why the order was not pursued in the Exchequer. The Counsel for Sir J. Champante said they could not proceed because of the privilege. *Mr. Baron Powell:* There was Counsel on both sides there. It was urged that it was a joint account, and the other Barons said it was impossible to separate it. After debate, question put, Whether the Order to the Barons of the Exchequer shall be now repeated? Resolved in the *Negative.* Contents, 20; Not-Contents, 20. Tellers, E. Rochester and E. Bridgewater. The House then ordered the Appeal of E. Ranelagh *v.* Sir J. Champante to be heard on 1 March. *See* No. 243.* (MS. Min., L. J., XV. 247).]

(*h.*) 13 March 1692–3. Petition of Appellants. Their Lordships, on hearing Petitioners' Appeal on 24 April 1690 (*see* 12th Report, Appendix, Part VI., No. 214), ordered that the accounts in question should be understood by the Court of Exchequer to be open accounts as to Petitioner. Upon a trial at law, as ordered, a verdict was given for Petitioners that Sir John Champante had due notice of the assignment before 29 Sept. 1674. The Appeal of E. Ranelagh *v.* Sir J. Champante has been heard and the decree of the Court of Exchequer reversed. Prays their Lordships to order the Court of Exchequer to state the accounts between Sir John and Petitioners up to 29 Sept. 1674, to which time only Petitioners are accountable. L. J., XV. 286.

359. Dec. 13.* Privilege of King's Servant (Anthony Rowe).—Petition of Anthony Rowe, Esq., praying for redelivery of certain horses &c. seized by the Under-Sheriff of Gloucestershire. L. J., XIV. 589. MS. Min. of date.

Annexed:—

(*a.*) 13 Dec. Copy Order of the House on preceding petition. L. J., XIV. 589. *In extenso.* [Appended to next paper.]

(*b.*) 27 Dec. Petition of Benjamin Hyett, late Under-Sheriff of the County of Gloucester, recounting the circumstances of the seizure, and praying to be heard by Counsel at the Bar. L. J., XIV. 607. *In extenso.* MS. Min.

360. Dec. 15. Papists (Thomas Burdet).—Petition of Thomas Burdet, Gentleman, in custody of the Black Rod. Petitioner, being one of the Farmers of the Markets of the City of London and the principal manager of that affair, and there having been several petitions presented to the House of Commons praying that some regulations and alterations might be made touching the management of the said markets, Petitioner was by an order of the Court of Aldermen and divers summons from the House of Commons required to give his attendance; and there having been several hearings in the affair but the

* The MS. Min. of Dec. 12 contain the following entry, after the proceedings on the Appeal of Smith *v.* Blight: "House moved that the Committee for Privileges do consider the preventing the crowd of footmen in the out-rooms. Sir Thomas Duppa ordered to take care that no footmen be crowding at the door, and that they bid people stand by and be uncovered."

same not yet determined, Petitioner was waiting to speak with several members touching the same, when he was seized as transgressing their Lordships' Order against Papists resorting to either House of Parliament during this Session. Petitioner's attendance being necessary and he having always been a person of quiet and peaceable behaviour, he prays to be discharged without fees. L. J., XIV. 590. [On 8 Dec. *L. Lovelace* acquainted the House that as he was walking in the Court of Requests, one came and told him there was a Papist. I asked him how he had the impudence to be there? He said he would be heard. I then took him and put him into the custody of Black Rod. (MS. Min. 8 Dec. L. J., XIV. 582.) The Petition was read this day, but "Nothing done on it until the Lord Lovelace come, and he to have notice." (MS. Min.) On the 16th Burdet was ordered to be discharged. L. J., XIV. 692.]

361. Dec. 15. Campbell's Divorce Act.—Petition of Archibald, Earl of Argyll, in behalf of his brother James Campbell. A Bill being presented for the annulling and making void the marriage of James Campbell with Mary Campbell *alias* Wharton, his wife, to the prejudice of Petitioner's brother and high dishonour of Petitioner's family (the said brother being out of England), and Petitioner being well satisfied that the circumstances of the marriage are very much misrepresented and that in truth his sister was freely consenting to the marriage and well pleased therewith, and continued so for two nights and one day and more, even to the time when she was taken away from her husband, prays for the vindication of his brother and family to be heard by Counsel and witnesses at the Bar against the Bill. *Endorsed* as read this day; nothing done on it. MS. Min. of date. No entry in L. J. [*Sir Bartholomew Shower* was Counsel for the Bill. Evidence was given in Committee this day* to show that Mrs. Wharton, when on her way to her aunt's, had her coach stopped by three men, who knocked the coachman down, and was taken away forcibly by Sir John Johnston to the house of one Watson, a coachman in Westminster, where Capt. Campbell had taken lodgings and ordered supper, and where the parties were married by the Rev. Wm. Clewer, D.D.; Watson and his wife acting as witnesses and a Mrs. Collingwood, whom Campbell had invited to supper, providing the ring. *Dr. Clewer* deposed that Capt. Campbell came to him to Andrew's Coffee House, in Essex Buildings, on 14 Nov., to go with him about a marriage. He left me at Charing Cross and sent me to the coachman's. At 8 o'clock he brought in the lady and said "We are all agreed; do your office." The lady also, upon my asking, showed her willingness. I know not if I asked for a license. I never knew more willingness before, at or after marriage, in a woman than was in this lady She spoke more audibly than the Captain. She thanked those that wished her joy. The ring was too big. She refused to change it, saying it was not lucky to change. Sir John Johnston dictated the letter she sent her aunt. There was no force used. I had but two guineas for the marriage, and that was not till afterwards; and if I have done ill, Necessitas cogit ad turpia. Com. Book. The Bill received the Royal Assent on 20 Dec. L. J., XIV. 600. 2 & 3 W. & M. c. 17 in Long Calendar.]

* The following witnesses were sworn at the Bar on 12 Dec. to give evidence before the Committee, viz.: Anne Brierly, Anne Brierly, jun., Mary Wharton, Thos Prest, John Bull, Mary Watson, John Watson, Walter Boughton, and Robert Dolton. The circumstances of the abduction are given in Luttrell, Nov. 7, 21, Dec. 18, 23, 1690 and March 22, 1691-2. *See also* Ralph Hist. Eng. II., 233 *note*, and Clifford's History of Private Bill Legislation.

House of Lords MSS. — 1690.

362. Dec. 16. Privilege of King's Servant (Peter Stepkin).—Petition of Peter Stepkin, Esq., complaining of arrest and praying for relief. L. J., XIV. 592. *In extenso.* MS. Min. of date.

363. Dec. 16. Southwark Court of Conscience Bill.—Commons' Engrossment of an Act for erecting a Court of Conscience for the Borough of Southwark and parts adjacent. § i. Whereas it hath been found by long experience that the erecting of a Court of Conscience in the City of London for determining matters of debt and actions upon the case under forty shillings hath been of great benefit and advantage to the poorer sort of freemen and inhabitants of the said City, and hath prevented many great mischiefs and inconveniences that would otherwise have fallen upon them by the charges of arrests and other process and proceedings in law, in case the same should have been prosecuted against them in any of their Majesties' Courts at Westminster or other inferior Courts; But forasmuch as the jurisdiction of the said Court does not extend further than the said City of London and the liberties thereof; And whereas, since the establishment of the said Court within the said City and the Liberties thereof, the Borough of Southwark and other out-parishes of Surrey within the weekly Bills of Mortality are become very populous, and many poor artificers, labourers and others inhabiting therein, amongst whom, for want of the like good order and establishment, divers vexatious suits for several debts are daily commenced and prosecuted in the Courts at Westminster and the Marshalsea and other Courts, which are much more expensive to the parties than the respective debts and causes of action for which they sue, to the ruin of them, their wives and children, and filling the prisons with miserable debtors, and creating great charge to the several parishes where they were inhabitants for their support and maintenance; For remedy whereof, be it Enacted by the King and Queen's Most Excellent Majesties, &c., That there be a Court of Request or Conscience for the relief of the poorer sort of people in small debts erected and established in the Borough of Southwark and the parishes in the County of Surrey mentioned in the Bills of Mortality and hereafter named, that is to say, St. Saviour's, Southwark, Saint Olave's, Southwark, Saint Thomas', Southwark, Saint George's, Southwark, Rotherhithe parish, Lambeth parish, Christ Church, Saint Mary Magdalen, Bermondsey, and Saint Mary, Newington Butts.

§ ii. And be it further enacted, by the authority aforesaid, That there be sixty Commissioners named, and that the persons for that purpose hereafter named shall be Commissioners for hearing and determining of all such matters and causes as by this Act are appointed to be heard and determined in the said Court in the said County of Surrey, within the Weekly Bills of Mortality, that is to say, Jonadab Balam, of the parish of Saint Saviour's, Southwark, William Hester, of the same, Henry Hawkes, of the same, William Gray, of the same, carpenter, James Richards, of the same, William Smith, of the same, Thomas Cole, of Saint Thomas, Southwark, Edward Lane Esq., of the same, Sir George Megot, of Saint Olaves, Southwark, Francis Wilkinson, of the same, William Gibbs, of the same, Thomas Roffey, of the same, Samuel Hall, of the same, Anthony Rawlins Esquire, of the same, William Wheeler, of the same, Sir Peter Rich, of the parish of Lambeth, Walter Howland, Esquire, of the same, Thomas Wymondysall, of the same, Philip Foster, Esquire, of the same, John Blake, of the parish of Saint George's, Southwark, James Church, of the same, Crawley Vering, of the same, John Wood, of the same, John Mitchell, of Newington Butts, William Leeke, of the same, Samuel Atkinson, Esquire, of the parish of Rotherhithe, John Alwood, of the same, Samuel Lewin, Esquire, of Saint Magdalen,

Bermondsey, Edward Dimbleby, of the same, William Sherlock, of the parish of Christ Church, Henry Bartlett, of Saint Saviour's, Francis Prescott, of the same, Edward Goodman, of the same, Thomas Kentish, of the same, Ferdinando Holland, of the same, Daniel White, senior, of the same, Benjamin Tarrant, of Saint Thomas, Southwark, Dennis Herbert, of the same, Benjamin Cracker, of Saint Olave's, Southwark, John Hudson, of the same, John Ebbot, of the same, Joseph Chittey, of the same, Ralph Snow, of Lambeth, Esquire, Christopher Perring, of the same, Thomas Baker, of the same, Francis Stone, of Newington Butts, Thomas Tilsley, of the same, Richard Burton, senior, of the same, Benjamin Shove, of Saint George's, Joseph Sheppard, of the same, John Nicholls, of Rotherhithe, Peter Norborough, of the same, Jonas Fish, of the same, John Ball, of the same, William Baugh, of Saint Mary Magdalen, Bermondsey, William Alwood, of the same, William Steers, of the same, Thomas Kent, of Christ Church, John Sermon, of the same, John King, of the same, which said Commissioners or any three or more of them are hereby authorised and empowered to exercise the powers and authorities in this Act in such manner as is hereafter expressed; and the said Commissioners shall continue for six months from the 10th day of December in the year of our Lord 1690, whereof the first thirty named in this Act at the expiration of the said six months shall be discharged, and the remaining thirty, or so many of them as shall appear at the time of electing others in the place of those that are so discharged, shall chose thirty more of the ablest and best of the neighbours to serve for twelve months after, and at the end of six months thereof, the other thirty, the remainder of the first sixty, shall be discharged and the last chosen thirty shall elect thirty more in their room in the manner before mentioned, and so successively every six months after.

§ iii. And be it further enacted by the authority aforesaid, that before any of the said Commissioners shall execute the authorities of this Act, they shall take the oath following, before one of their Majesties' Justices of the Peace residing within the said county of Surrey, videlicet —I, A.B., do promise and swear that all such matters and causes as I shall order or determine, by virtue of this Act, I will order and determine with justice and equity, according to the best of my knowledge and understanding, so help me God.

§ iv. And be it further enacted by the authority aforesaid, that for the prevention of defrauding or oppressing the said poor, either plaintiff or defendant, that the costs of suit and number of the Officers to the said Court and the fees of the said Officers for dispatching the business of the said Court be such and no other than what are hereafter mentioned, that is to say; for every plaint, two pence; for every order, four pence; for every precept or warrant to commit to prison, six pence; for every search, two pence; for every satisfaction acknowledged on the order, four pence; for every warrant for levying the debt by sale of the goods, six pence; to the beadle or beadles attending the said Court for warning every person, four pence; for serving every precept or warrant, four pence, and to the gaoler, for every commitment by virtue of this Act, one shilling. And that Robert Weston, gentleman, is and is hereby nominated and appointed Register and Clerk, and Giles Hayward Armorer, beadle of the said Court of Conscience for the said borough of Southwark with the liberties thereof and parishes aforesaid, so long as they shall well and truly demean themselves in the execution of the offices. And in case of misdemeanor the said Commissioners for the time being, or the greater number of them may, and are hereby authorized and empowered to remove and displace the said Register or Clerk

House of Lords MSS.

1690.

and beadle for such misdemeanor, and appoint such other person or persons to execute and supply the said Office or place of him that shall so misdemean himself, And the said registrar or clerk and beadle are to nominate and appoint their deputies. And in case of removal upon lawful conviction of any misdemeanor or decease of either the said Register or Clerk and beadle, the said Commissioners upon any such removal or death, are to nominate and appoint some other person as they shall think fit for the supply of such vacancy as shall happen as aforesaid.

§ v. And be it further enacted by the authority aforesaid, that the said Commissioners or any three or more of them, so appointed as aforesaid, are hereby authorised and required to meet and assemble themselves together within the said borough on Wednesday and Saturday in every week, and oftener if the Commissioners shall think fit, and in such place as shall be appointed and ascertained by the said Commissioners for the time being, to hear and determine all such matters of debt and action of the case not amounting to forty shillings brought before them, according to the true intent and meaning of this present Act.

§ vi. And be it further enacted, that every person or persons inhabiting, or that shall inhabit within the said borough and parishes aforesaid, shall or may cause his, her or their debtor and debtors being under the value of forty shillings, by summons or other reasonable warning or notice to be given or left to or for the said debtor or debtors, at their dwelling houses, or places of abode, by the beadle of the said Court or his deputy, to appear before the Commissioners of the said Court. And that the aforesaid Commissioners, or any three or more of them, shall have power and authority by virtue of this Act from time to time to set down such order and orders to be made between such party and parties, complainants, and his and their debtor or debtors defendants, touching such debt, not amounting to the value of forty shillings before the said Commissioners as they shall find to stand with equity and good conscience in a summary way, with or without adjournment, not tying themselves to the exact forms and methods of the Common law or other Courts of Justice, which said order or orders shall be final and conclusive to all persons therein concerned, their executors and administrators, nor shall any writ of error, certiorari, or process of law or equity lie for the removal, stay or reversal of the same. All such their orders to be registered in a book or books fairly written, to be kept by the said Clerk or Register for the time being; and as well the plaintiff as defendant shall observe and keep the same in all points. And for the due proceeding therein, it shall and may be lawful for the said Commissioners or any three or more of them to administer an oath to the plaintiff or defendant and also to such witnesses as shall be produced on each party if the said Commissioners, or any three or more of them, shall so think it meet.

§ vii. And be it further enacted, that if any such creditor or debtor after warning given to him, her or them in manner and form before in this Act mentioned, shall, without some reasonable cause or excuse to be allowed by the said Court, refuse to appear in the said Court, that then it shall be lawful for the officer or officers of the said Court, by order of the said Commissioners or any three or more of them as aforesaid, to send and cause to be conveyed such party and parties to some prison within the said borough and parishes aforesaid, there to remain without bail or mainprise until he, she, or they perform or fulfil the order of the said Commissioners. And in case any creditor or debtor, plaintiff or defendant, do not or shall not obey or perform such order and orders or decree, as the said Court shall make, set down or direct in, for, or concerning such debt or debts, or the payment or allowance of any such costs or damages for or in respect of the same, that then it shall and may be lawful to and for the said officer or officers of the said Court by the order or orders, warrant or warrants of the said Commissioners, or any three or more of them, to levy such debt or debts, damages or money by the said Commissioners awarded or ordered to be paid by and out of the goods and chattels of such creditor or debtor, plaintiff or defendant, and by sale of the same, returning the overplus (if any be) to the party or parties upon whom they levied it. But if sufficient of the goods and chattels of such party or parties cannot be found within the jurisdiction of the said Court, whereby and whereout such debt or debts, costs or demages so awarded shall or may be levied, raised or satisfied, that then it shall be lawful for such officer or officers of the said Court, by the order or orders of the said Commissioners, or any three or more of them as aforesaid, to send and cause to be conveyed such party and parties to some prison within the said borough or parishes aforesaid, there to remain without bail or mainprize, until he, she, or they do or shall perform or obey such order or orders or decree of the said Court. And if any person or persons shall at any time after the said tenth day of December commence and prosecute any action in any of their Majesties' Courts at Westminster, or in any other Court, against any person inhabiting or residing within the said borough and parishes aforesaid, for any debt or sum of money due upon contract, promise, specialty, or otherwise, which upon the trial shall be found not to amount to the full sum or value of forty shillings over and above costs, no judgment shall be entered on record upon any such verdict, or if any judgment shall be entered thereon, then such judgment shall be and is hereby declared null and void. And also the defendant in every such action shall have his costs of suit, to be taxed by the said Court or their proper officer where such actions shall be tryed and paid him by such plaintiff in the said cause, any law or custom to the contrary in any wise notwithstanding.

§ viii. Provided always that this Act or anything herein contained shall not extend to any debt for rent upon any lease of houses, lands or tenements or to any other real contract, or to any fines or amerciaments in Courts Leet or Court Baron, nor to any debt that shall arise by reason of any clause concerning any testament or matrimony, or anything concerning or properly belonging to the Ecclesiastical Courts, albeit the same be under forty shillings, anything before contained to the contrary in anywise notwithstanding.

§ ix. Provided also and be it enacted by the authority aforesaid, that the town-hall within the said borough shall be the place and meeting of the said Commissioners for the execution of the matters in this Act contained, and that the prison commonly called the Compter, in the said borough, shall be the proper prison to which all persons inhabiting within the said borough shall be committed for any offence mentioned in this Act, if the Commissioners shall so think fit.

Parchment Collection. 12th Report. Appendix. Part VI. Nos. **195** and **198**. [Brought from the Commons this day, and rejected on First Reading. An entry in MS. Min. of this day, of a Petition from the inhabitants of Southwark being offered, preceding the entry of the rejection of the Bill, is cancelled. L.J., XIV. 592. *See also* next Paper.]

364. Dec. 16. Southwark Court of Conscience Bill.—Petition of the Inhabitants of the Borough of Southwark and parishes in the County

HOUSE OF LORDS MSS.

1690.

of Surrey within the Weekly Bills of Mortality. A Court of Conscience within the City of London being found by above 120 years' experience of great use and advantage to all the inhabitants of the said city, and to have prevented many thousand families from ruin; and the Borough of Southwark and parishes before mentioned being grown highly populous, and multitudes of seamen, watermen, handicraft and labouring men, with other poor inhabiting therein, who for want of the like good establishment are daily undone by suits in law for small debts, and their persons thrown into prison to the ruin of them and their families, the great decay of trade and a vast expense to Petitioners and other the inhabitants for their support and maintenance, Petitioners pray their Lordships to take their condition into consideration and to be pleased to pass an Act for erecting a Court for recovery of small debts in the nature of the Court of Conscience in the Cities of London, Bristol and Gloucester, Petitioners having more poor in their Borough than is in any of the said cities, and, by reason of the present war and taxes for the carrying on the same, less able to maintain them than heretofore they have been. [Offered in the House this day. MS. Min. (entry cancelled). No entry in L. J.]

365. Dec. 17. Bagenall's Estate Act.—Letter from Nicholas Bagenall to Robert Humphrys. Requests him to obtain from Mr. Bonithon the consent of the trustees, and to prosecute the Bill with vigour. Presents his humble service to Mr. Justice Dolben. *Dated* Dublin, 6 Oct. 1690. *Endorsed*: 17 Oct. 1690. One copy Act of Parliament left with Mr. Justice Dolben, and another with Mr. Bonithon to be perused. That returned with amendments. [Read in Committee this day, when evidence was given by Mr. Humphrys and Mr. Bonithon, the latter of whom stated that he had drawn the settlement of the Irish estate. Com. Book.]

Annexed:—

(*a*.) 17 Dec. Affidavit of Henry Pilkington, of Mulloghtee, in the County of Louth, Gent., deposing that one Richard White had taken possession of Deponent's house in Dec. 1688, and seized his goods for the use (as alleged) of Col. Dudley Bagenall, by order in writing from one Rowland White, who acknowledged to Deponent that he had given the order, in regard King James had granted Nicholas Bagenall's Estate in Ireland to the said Col. Dudley. Deponent adds that he had also been dispossessed of the lands of Mullabane and Ballyonane in favour of the said Col. Dudley. *Sworn* 6 Nov. 1690. [Read in Committee this day. Com. Book.]

(*b*.) Examination of Francis Chaddock, of Newry, in the County of Down. Deposes that some time before the end of June 1689, Examinant saw Dudley Bagenall, of the town of Newry, and with him a regiment of foot under his command, on their march towards Derry to serve the late King James in the siege of that city. Examinant also saw Rowland White, of Crowbane, in the County of Down, in the yard of an old castle belonging to Nicholas Bagenall, of Greencastle, in the same County, take a piece of earth into his hands, and in the presence of several witnesses, deliver it to the said Dudley and declare that he gave him thereby possession of the estate. *Sworn* 13 Aug. 1690. *See*. L. J., XIV. 592, 593.

366. Dec. 22. Mainwaring's Estate Act.—Certificate of consent of the trustees to the passing of the Bill for vesting certain lands (the estate of Thomas Mainwaring, Gent.) in trustees, to be sold for the payment of debts. *Signed* G. Booth and Thos. Hunt. [Produced and read this day before the Committee on the Bill. (Com. Book.) The Bill received the Royal Assent on 5 Jan. 1690–1, 2 & 3 W. & M. c. 40 in Long Calendar.]

367. Dec. 22. Jones *v.* Attorney-General.—Petition and Appeal of Herbert Jones. Sir Robert Sawyer, when Attorney-General, in 34 Car. II. exhibited an information in the Court of Exchequer against Petitioner and others, suggesting that several issues, sent in process against divers inhabitants of Monmouthshire (forfeited for not appearing to indictments for not repairing the highways), were constantly levied on the inhabitants by Petitioner as Under-Sheriff, who, instead of laying them out as the law required, by combination with the Justices of the Peace obtained certificates from them that they had received and paid the issues over to the supervisors of the highways and thus get allowances of the sums on passing his accounts, whereas he had retained them to his own use and was accountable for them to the King. Petitioner, in his answer as defendant, set forth that, as the issues came in charge at the request of the Justices and according to the Act 13 and 14 Car. II. cap. 6. he delivered copies of them to the Justices, who ordered the supervisors to levy them according to a pound rate upon the inhabitants for the repair of the highways, and gave Petitioner certificates that they were levied and applied accordingly. Petitioner had never levied more than what he returned. Out of 110*l.* 10*s.* levied when Mr. Luff was Sheriff, the Judges of Assize ordered Petitioner to have an allowance for getting the County discharged of the issues, and to pay the remainder to the persons mentioned in the order, and upon Petitioner's account before those persons there was remaining but 11*l.* Petitioner charged himself with the whole issues in his accounts in the Exchequer in regard he had the Justices' certificates for his discharge and upon no other account. The Court of Exchequer, on a hearing, disallowed the certificates for that the money was not paid on them, and decreed Petitioner to account for the whole moneys as they stand charged in the Sheriffs' accounts, ordering him to pay 829*l.*, notwithstanding the issues were not levied by him and notwithstanding his discharge by the certificates. Petitioner never received more than 126*l.* 10*s.* of the said issues, and charged himself in his accounts with the whole issues only in regard of the certificates and discharges, which method of discharge by certificates has ever since the said statute been the common method of passing the Sheriffs' accounts and discharging the country from the issues, or otherwise the country would be greatly oppressed in levying all issues set upon them. The Court, in disallowing the certificates and discharges, ought to have charged Petitioner only with what he had actually received, which on strict examination by several Commissions was not found to be more than 126*l.* 10*s.* The information was not exhibited until 34 Car. II., and the last Sheriff's account was for the year 1677, and the Appellant, having four years before the information brought respective *quietus ests* for the previous years, he was discharged according to the Acts of 21 Jac. I. c. 5 and 13 and 14 Car. II. c. 21. Appeals from the decree and proceedings in the Court of Exchequer and prays that the Attorney-General may be ordered to answer. *Signed* by Appellant; *Countersigned* by Robert Price and Sam. Dodd, who certify that there is just cause to appeal. [Reported this day from the Committee of Petitions as unfit to be received, and rejected by the House. Pet. Book 16 Dec. L. J., XIV. 602.]

House of Lords MSS.

1690.

368. Dec. 22. Myer and others *v.* Huddleston.—Petition and Appeal of Edmond Myer, Wm. Brockbank, Wm. Muncaster, Ferdinando Crowdson, John Fox, Ralph Ebbetson, John Smyth, Edward Jackson, Thos. Waters, John Lewthwaite, Hugh Atkinson, George Nicholson, Thos. Cragg, Eliz. Unter, widow, and divers other customary tenants within the several manors or lordships, or reputed manors and lordships of Millom Kirksanton, Satterton, Bootle, Corney, Whitcham, Whitbeck, and Ulpha, in the County of Cumberland, as well on their own behalf as on behalf of the rest of the tenants of the said several manors and lordships. The lords of the said manors having infringed the ancient customs, and imposed new duties, services, and fines, Petitioners in 1688 brought a Bill in Chancery against Respondent, the present lord, and others, to have their rights established, and for enforcement of a decree in Chancery of 4 Jac. I., in a suit brought by Petitioners' ancestors in the name of Anthony Fox and others against William Huddleston, Respondent's great grandfather, ordering that plaintiffs should be accounted tenants to defendant by the custom of tenant right, and should pay him, on every alienation or change of tenancy, the full yearly value of the tenement for a fine, and on every change of the Lord, half a year's value if by death, but no fine if by alienation. The Master of the Rolls, on 21 Nov. 1688, ordered Appellants to pay to Respondent *de bene esse* half a year's value, as ascertained by a Commission, for the fine due on the death of the late Lord, Ferdinando Huddleston, according to the former decree; and the Lords Commissioners, on 10 May 1689, confirmed this order, and further ordered them to pay him a full year's value for dropping fines due by change of tenants since Ferdinando's death. Appellants, after complying with this order, were afterwards sent to a trial at law on the issues, (1) whether the lord was entitled, on the death or alienation of a tenant, to a sum, not exceeding 20 years old rent, for a particular fine, of his successor, and (2) whether a lord, on the death of his predecessor, could demand a sum, not exceeding 15 years' old rent, for a general fine. A verdict having passed against Appellants, their Bill was dismissed on 27 Nov. 1690 after an *ex parte* hearing. Appeal against this dismission, the subject matter, which was to establish immemorial customs and prevent multiplicity of suits, being properly cognizable in Chancery, and the dismission not being warranted by the verdict, which related only to the fines payable by Appellants. Pray that Respondents may be ordered to answer. *Signed* by Appellants: *Countersigned* W. Williams and T. Vernon. [Ordered to be reported by the Committee of Petitions as unfit to be received (Pet. Book 16 Dec.) The House, however, on report, received the Petition this day, and ordered Respondents to answer. (L. J., XIV. 602.) The Appeal was heard and dismissed on 7 Nov. 1691, *Mr. Trevor* and *Mr. Finch* appearing for Appellant, and *Sir Thomas Powys* and *Mr. Dobins* for Respondents. MS. Min. L. J., XIV. 637.]

Annexed:—

(*a.*) 24 Oct. 1691. Answer of Joseph Huddleston, lord of the manor of Millom, in the County of Cumberland, and also of Richard Huddleston, Gent., and Thomas Benson. Respondent Joseph, on succeeding his brother Ferdinando in 1687, caused the general fine to be assessed at 15 years' old rent, according to custom. The tenants, about 400 in number, combined to resist him, and brought their Bill in Chancery. The decree of 4 Jac. I. directing only a half year's full value to be paid for a general, and a year's full value for a particular fine, was set aside by two subsequent orders in the same cause in 6 and 9 Jac. I., and ever since, the fines have been paid according to the ancient custom, viz. 15 and 20 years' old rent respectively. Appellants consented to the issues tried before Mr. Justice Powell and a special jury, and if they are aggrieved, they have their remedy at law. It has been the common usage in Cumberland and Westmorland, where most of the country consists of these kinds of manors, to set their fines by the old rent, unless otherwise agreed, and the practice is convenient, as the old rent remains the same, while the yearly value varies. The fines demanded by Respondent are not above a year and a half's value for a general, and two years' value for a particular fine, which are common fines in the adjacent manors, and in several of them much higher; and if the old rents are in some few particulars disproportionable with the rest, it is caused by the tenants' own fault, in parcelling their tenements without due regard to proportioning the old rents accordingly. The Court of Chancery, in directing a trial at law, has taken the usual method of ascertaining disputed fines. Appellants are seeking to weary out Respondent, who has already spent 700*l.* in law expenses. Respondent Richard is not concerned in the matter otherwise than as cousin and next heir of Joseph, in case of his death without male issue, and Benson only as steward of the manors. Pray that the Appeal may be dismissed without costs. *Signed* by Respondents; *Countersigned* Ambrose Phillipps and W. Marriott. *Endorsed* as brought in this day.

(*b.*) 27 Oct. 1691. Petition of Appellants for an early day for hearing. L. J., XIV. 628.

369. Dec. 22. Alnage Bill.—Commons' Engrossment of an Act for transferring the duty of Alnage to the Custom House.

§ i. Whereas the Office and Seal of the Alnager or Collector of the Subsidy or Duty of Alnage is no ways serviceable to the Woollen Manufacture of this Kingdom, and the manner of collecting the said Duties by Officers employed therein is found by experience to be not only very chargeable to your Majesties, but extremely oppressive and burthensome to your Subjects, and a great hindrance to the trade of the Woollen Manufactures. And whereas great disputes and controversies have arisen upon several kinds of Woollen Manufactures, whether any or how much duty are, or have been due for the same, for remedy whereof be it enacted by the King and Queen's most Excellent Majesties, by and with the advice and consent of the Lords Spiritual and Temporal and of the Commons in this present Parliament assembled and by the authority of the same, that from and after the second day of February, one thousand six hundred and ninety, the Office and Seal of the Alnagers or Collectors of the said duty and subsidy of Alnage, shall cease and determine, and that so much of every Act of Parliament as required or enabled the collecting the said duties by the Alnage officers shall hereby be and are repealed as to so much only as requires such collection.

§ ii. And to the end the duty thereby arising to your Majesties may be ascertained and brought in with little charge and trouble, Be it further enacted by the authority aforesaid, that from and after the said second day of February, one thousand six hundred and ninety, the duties and charges thereafter mentioned shall be collected and received by your Majesty's Officers of the Custom House, only upon the exportation of the several sorts of Woollen Manufactures hereafter named, according to such rates and proportions as are hereafter mentioned, over and besides what is now paid or payable for the said commodities at the Custom House, that is to say, for every long cloth sixpence; for every short cloth, according to the Book of Rates, sixpence; for every Minikin bay sixpence; for every double bay, threepence; for every single bay, twopence; for every pound weight of old and new drapery that is entered and pays by weight, half a farthing; for every dozen men's stockings a halfpenny; for every dozen children's stockings and ends of stockings, one farthing; for every hundred goads of cotton, sixpence; for every hundred yards of flannel, fourpence; for every hundred yards of freeze, eightpence; for every pair of blankets, a halfpenny; for every rug, a halfpenny.

§ iii. And it is hereby further enacted and declared, by the authority aforesaid, that for the better collecting the said subsidy or custom, the same shall be subject and liable to all the laws and statutes now in force for the better collecting and preventing frauds and concealments of subsidies and customs.

§ iv. Provided always and it is enacted and declared by the authority aforesaid, that the said duty of sixpence per cloth, payable by the merchant by virtue of this Act, be and shall be allowed by the respective clothiers upon the sale of every such cloth, and that it shall and may be lawful for the merchant or buyer of such cloth as is to be exported, to deduct the said duties out of the money he shall pay to the clothier for the same, anything herein-before mentioned to the contrary thereof in any wise notwithstanding.

§ v. Provided always that the several and respective duties and sums of money herein-before enacted to be collected and received by the said Custom House Officers shall be to the sole use and benefit of the Right Noble Frances Duchess Dowager of Richmond and Lenox, her executors, administrators or assigns, for and during so long time only and for so many years as the said Duchess had any right or title to the said duty or subsidy of Alnage hereby transferred, or to any rent reserved upon any lease or farm heretofore made thereof.

§ vi. And it is hereby enacted that the said officers shall from time to time pay all and every the said sums of money to be received by them or any of them, by virtue of the said Act to the said Duchess of Richmond, her executors, administrators or assigns or their order, and for such payment a receipt or acquittance under the hand of the said Duchess, her executors, administrators or assigns shall be a sufficient discharge against his Majesty, his heirs and successors, and against every other person whatsoever.

§ vii. And whereas the said Duchess of Richmond, for and in consideration of the sum of one thousand, one hundred, forty and eight pounds hath heretofore granted to Richard Seyes, of Lincoln's Inn in the county of Middlesex, Esquire, one annuity or yearly rentcharge of one hundred thirty and eight pounds to be paid and payable (in the first place and preferable to all other payments) out of the said subsidy or duty of Alnage, and out of the rents thereon then reserved for the term of twenty years and one half year, commencing from Christmas one thousand six hundred eighty-two to be paid by quarterly payments, of which term there are about thirteen years yet to come and unexpired. Be it therefore further enacted, declared and appointed, that out of such part of the said duty or subsidy hereby granted and appointed to be paid to the said Duchess of Richmond at the Custom House in London, the said annuity of one hundred thirty-eight pounds shall be paid unto the said Richard Seyes, his executors, administrators and assigns (in the first place and preferable to all other payments out of the same) by the said Officers who shall receive the said subsidy or duty hereby granted, the same to be paid yearly by quarterly payments (to wit) at the four several feasts of Christmas, Lady Day, Midsummer Day and Michaelmas Day, by equal portions for and during all the rest and residue of the said term of twenty years and one half year granted to the said Richard Seyes by the said Duchess of Richmond, yet to come and unexpired, the first payment thereof to be made at the feast of the Annunciation of the Blessed Virgin Mary, which shall be in the year of our Lord one thousand, six hundred ninety-one, anything in this Act contained to the contrary in any wise notwithstanding. *Parchment Collection.* [Brought from the Commons this day (L. J., XIV. 602), when the House was moved that the Lady Duchess of Richmond and Countess of Portland might be heard. Then the Petition (Annex *a.*) read. Then Ordered that the Petitioners be heard on Wednesday. Then on question that they be heard on Wednesday, resolved in the negative, and Friday fixed for the hearing as in L. J., XIV. 602. (MS. Min. 22 Dec.)—At the hearing on 26 Dec. *Mr. Trevor* (for the King) said the Duties of Alnage, or Subsidy, are distinct duties in themselves. *Sir W. Williams* (for the King): There is no branch of the King's revenue has a better establishment than this. It is not above 6*d.* a cloth, a very inconsiderable thing. The ancient office must be taken away. The reason of the seal is to give account what cloth has paid. Can there be a more equal provision than this is? It is standard not to be altered, a jewel in the Crown. This Bill repeals at least 40 Acts of Parliament. *Sir Wm. Thompson* (for the Duchess of Richmond): This is an ancient revenue of the Crown, and settled by 20 Acts of Parliament at least. The pretence they have to this is: the public is concerned. This is promoted by the greatest piece of Barratry in the world. This Revenue is established in Westminster Hall by verdicts and Decrees. The Duchess is settled in this by a legal conveyance. *Mr. Ward* (for Duchess of Richmond): There was a lease made to the Duke of Richmond. It is a duty vested by Act of Parliament. This Act is deficient in three things. In recompense, this cannot be a recompense, except a third part be as much as the whole. *Mr. Darnell* (for the Bill): This is only for altering the manner of collecting the Alnage, and is for the good of the subject. This Bill only makes a duty payable at a certain place. By this Bill the Patentee is to have five thousand pounds for three. *Mr. Dormer* spoke for the Bill. Counsel withdrew, the Speaker reported what they had said and the Bill was rejected; but a Committee was appointed to draw a new Bill. [MS. Min. 26 Dec. L. J., XIV. 604–5.]

Annexed:—

(*a.*) 22 Dec. Petition of Frances, Duchess Dowager of Richmond and Lenox, and others, Farmers of the ancient Duties of Subsidy and Alnage on Woollen Manufactures under the said Duchess and her Trustees. The Duchess has a legal right and title, in consideration as well of marriage as by purchase, to the said duties for long term of years yet to come, under a yearly rent payable to the Crown. The other Petitioners are farmers of the duties under the Duchess for a great fine and other valuable considerations, and a great yearly rent for part of the said term. The Bill proposes to abolish the ancient duties, and impose, as a recompense, duties on exports only. Petitioners desired to be heard at the Bar of the House of Commons, but were not heard. Hope to make it plain that the proposed duties will be inadequate compensation, and pray to be heard by Counsel against the Bill. *Signed* F. Richmond and Lenox. Joh. Hayes, John Eyles, H.

House of Lords MSS.

1690.

Stephens. [Read this day, and Counsel heard on 26 Dec. L. J., XIV. 602, 604. *See* Notes to Engrossment.]

370. Dec. 23. Rebels Attainder Bill.—Commons' Engrossment of an Act for attainting persons in rebellion in England and Ireland, and for applying their estates towards the charge of the present war.

§ i. Whereas great aids and supplies have been granted to their Majesties by the Commons of this realm for the reducing the kingdom of Ireland to the obedience of their Majesties; And whereas their Majesties, being desirous to ease their good subjects of this realm, are contented and pleased that all and every the forfeitures and confiscations whereunto their Majesties may be in any manner intituled for or by reason of the treason or rebellion whereof any of their Majesties subjects of the said kingdoms of England or Ireland, papists or others, have been guilty, should go and be applied towards the defraying the great charges of the war wherein their Majesties are at present engaged and otherwise in such manner as shall be hereafter appointed by authority of Parliament; The King and Queen's most excellent Majesties are pleased that it be enacted and be it enacted by the King and Queen's most excellent Majesties by and with the advice and consent of the Lords Spiritual and Temporal and Commons in this present Parliament assembled, and by authority of the same, that all and every person and persons who, on the thirteenth day of February in the year of our Lord one thousand six hundred eighty and eight, or at any time since have been or now are in rebellion against their Majesties in their Majesties' kingdoms of England or Ireland or elsewhere, or have levyed war against the King and Queen's Majesties, within their Majesties' realm of England or Ireland or elsewhere, or have willingly aided, assisted or abetted any person or persons in rebellion against the King and Queen's Majesties, or have invited, assisted, aided or abetted the French forces to invade, or in their invasion of the said kingdoms of England or Ireland, are and shall stand and be and by force and virtue of this Act are adjudged to be convicted and attainted of High Treason, as fully to all intents and purposes whatsoever as if they and every were expressly and particularly named or mentioned in this present Act and by name enacted and adjudged to be convicted and attainted of High Treason, and shall lose and forfeit to the King and Queen's Majesties their heirs and successors, all such estate, right, title, interest, use and possession which they or any of them or any other person or persons in trust or for the use or benefit of them or any of them on the said thirteenth day of February or at any time after had, or hereafter shall have of, in or unto any honors, castles, manors, messuages, lands, tenements, rents, annuities, reversions, remainders, uses, possessions, offices, rights, conditions, trusts or any other hereditaments whatsoever and wheresoever, and all judgments, statutes, recognizances, extents, right of action, right of entry or any other chattels real or personal of what name. nature or quality soever they be, and that all such right, title, interest, use or possession which they or any of them or any other person or persons in trust for them had on the said thirteenth day of February or at any time after shall have, or of right ought to have of, in or to the said honors, castles, manors, messuages, lands, tenements, rents, annuities, reversions, remainders, trusts, uses, possession, offices, rights, conditions or any other hereditaments whatsoever, and all judgments, statutes, recognizances, extents, rights of action, rights of entry, or any chattels real or personal shall be deemed and hereby are declared and adjudged to be vested, forfeited and settled, as from the said thirteenth day of February to and in their Majesties their heirs and successors, and to be in the real and actual possession and seizin of their Majesties, without any office or inquisition thereof found or hereafter to be found.

§ ii. Provided nevertheless that nothing in this Act contained shall extend or be construed to extend to convict or attaint any Protestant in the kingdom of Ireland, or shall vest or be understood or construed to forfeit to or vest in their Majesties their heirs or successors, or otherwise be prejudicial unto or take away any estate, honours, castles, manors, messuages, lands, tenements, rents, annuities, reversions, remainders, trusts, uses, possessions, offices, rights, conditions, or any other hereditaments whatsoever, or any judgment, statute, recognizance, right of action, right of entry, or any other chattel real or personal of what nature soever from any Protestant inhabitant or Protestant proprietors whatsoever in the said kingdom of Ireland, except only such Protestants as have acted in the Civil government under the late King James since the eighth day of July in this present year of our Lord, one thousand six hundred and ninety, in such place and station as is usually executed by Commission and except also such Protestant Officers who have actually borne arms in the Army of the late King James in Ireland from and under the said late King James since the tenth day of April in the year of our Lord one thousand six hundred eighty and nine in such place and station as is usually executed by Commission.

§ iii. And to the end that the said forfeited estates may be of the better value, It is hereby further enacted by the authority aforesaid, that wheresoever any forfeiture is by virtue of this Act vested, or to be vested in their Majesties, wherein the person attainted or to be attainted had any estate or trust in tail which was in his power to have barred and docked, every such estate and interest shall be and is hereby declared to be by virtue of this Act vested in the King and Queen's Majesties in fee simple absolutely, subject nevertheless to be disposed as by this Act is directed.

§ iv. And be it further enacted by the authority aforesaid, that all and every the honors, castles, manors, messuages, lands, tenements, rents, annuities, hereditaments and premises, which by virtue of this Act are or shall be forfeited to and vested in their Majesties, their heirs, and successors, and all the rents, issues and profits thereof shall be wholly and solely appropriated and applied towards defraying the charges of the present War and to such other uses as shall be hereafter appointed by authority of Parliament and to no other use or purpose whatsoever, any thing in this Act contained to the contrary thereof in any wise notwithstanding.

§ v. And to the end that the forfeitures so vested in their Majesties may not be aliened or any way diverted from the purposes aforesaid but remain in the Crown, and not be disposed, transferred, charged or incumbered otherwise than by authority of Parliament, it is hereby further enacted by the authority aforesaid, that all grants, dispositions and other Acts whatsoever made or to be made by their Majesties or either of them, whereby the said forfeitures or any part thereof (other than personal chattels) shall be diverted or hindered from being employed or disposed for the purposes aforesaid, shall be and are hereby declared to be null and void; and all and every person and persons and bodies politic are hereby disabled and made uncapable to accept any grant or disposition of all or any the said forfeitures (other than personal chattels) from their Majesties or either of them or to take any estate or interest by any such grant or disposition.

§ vi. Provided nevertheless that nothing in this Act contained shall extend or be taken or construed to extend to take away the benefit which any of the said rebels may have and claim by virtue of any proclamation or declaration published by their Majesties, whereof they did take the benefit, or make void any articles or terms which his

House of Lords MSS.

1690.

Majesty, or any of his general officers, or any by his authority hath already given or granted or hereafter shall give or grant to any persons in the said Kingdom of Ireland who were or are in arms and rebellion against their Majesties, but that such articles and terms are to be and shall be observed and performed as if this present Act had not been made, anything herein contained to the contrary in any wise notwithstanding.

§ vii. Saving nevertheless to all persons, bodies politic and corporate, their respective heirs, successors, executors, administrators and assigns other than the said rebels, their heirs, executors and administrators, and all and every person or persons claiming to their or any of their uses or in trust for them or any of them, and all and every person and persons claiming by, from or under them or any of them since the second day of November, one thousand six hundred eighty and eight, all such right, title and interest as they or any of them have or ought to have in, to or out of the said honors, castles, manors, messuages, lands, tenements, hereditaments or premises by this Act declared to be forfeited or any of them. *Parchment Collection.* [Brought from the Commons this day. (L. J., XIV. 603.)—On 30 Dec., in C. W. H., E. Fauconberg in the Chair, the Bill was read through. A number of Petitions (*see* No. 374) having been read, it was moved that one Counsel only be heard on each of them, and the Committee then ordered to report as in L. J., XIV. 609.—On 31 Dec. the Commons sent a message to remind the Lords of the Bill (*ib.* 611).—On 1 and 3 Jan. House again in Committee, E. Warrington in the Chair, Ordered to report as in L. J., XIV. 612, 614. No further proceedings. The House adjourned on 5 Jan. till 31 March (*ib.* 618).]

371. Dec. 23. False Musters (Navy) Bill.—Amended* draft of an Act to prevent false Musters at Sea and false payment of Seamen.

§ i. Whereas great abuses have been committed in the mustering of seamen and mariners that do serve on board their Majesties' ships of war, which hath occasioned great expenses to the Crown and been very oppressive to their Majesties' subjects; For remedy whereof and for reforming diverse abuses in the mustering of seamen and for provisions for the said seamen's wives and families in their absence, Be it enacted by the King and Queen's most Excellent Majesties, by and with the advice and consent of the Lords Spiritual and Temporal and Commons in this present Parliament assembled and by the authority of the same, That from and after the *twentieth* day of *January* next ensuing, no officer or seaman on board any of their Majesties' ships that now are or hereafter shall be employed in their Majesties' service, shall be paid any wages or salary but what shall be certified to the Commissioners of their Majesties' Navy under five of the officers' hands on board every such ship, whereof the Captain, Lieutenant or Purser to be two; And that whenever the Captain, Lieutenant, Purser or other officer on board any of the said ships shall give a false account to the Commissioners of their Majesties' Navy, and charge their Majesties with more seamen or more days than such seamen or any of them or other officers shall be living on board the said ship, that then such Captain, Lieutenant, Purser or other officer as shall by information upon oath of *two* or more witnesses be found guilty of any such fault, shall immediately be suspended, and upon due proof before any three of the said Commissioners of the Navy, lose his place and be for ever disabled to serve their Majesties in any office of trust,

* The only amendments are those marked in italics. They do not appear on the draft, but are recorded in MS. Min. of 3 Jan. as having been then made in C. W. H.

civil or military, whatsoever, and forfeit fifty pounds in money for every such fault or misdemeanour, which shall be equally divided amongst the Informers.

§ ii. And whereas many and further abuses are committed by sending seamen ashore and returning them to the Commissioners of the Navy to be very sick and ill, when they are many times in perfect health, Be it therefore enacted by the authority aforesaid that from and after the said *twentieth* day of *January* next ensuing no return or ticket of the seamen's being sent sick or ill ashore shall be allowed by the said Commissioners to be good, but what shall be signed by five officers' hands on board the said ship, whereof the Captain, Lieutenant, Purser, Doctor or Chirurgeon to be three, and that whenever any false return shall appear to be made upon oath of two or more witnesses, every such officer as shall be found guilty of any such fault shall be liable to the penalty as in this Act before mentioned.

§ iii. And whereas in trading voyages it hath been and is accustomed for Captains, Masters, Pursers, Officers and other Seamen on board their Majesties' ships as well as Merchant ships to pay the seamen by money or credit most of their wages before the said seamen come home to England, whereby their families are almost starved for want of subsistence; Be it therefore enacted by the authority aforesaid That if after the said *twentieth* day of *January* next ensuing, the Captain, Lieutenant, Purser or other chief officer on board any of their Majesties' ships or other Merchant ships shall pay any Seaman or Seamen belonging to any of the said ships more wages or salary by money or credit than two months in six and so proportionably for years, (and the remainder four months in six to whom the said Seamen shall appoint by Letter of Attorney or to the Executors, Administrators or Assigns of the said Seaman or Seamen), every such credit or payment shall stand for nothing and be void in law, anything in any former Act to the contrary notwithstanding. [Read 1ª this day. L. J., XIV. 604. The Select Committee, to whom the Bill was first referred (*ib.* 606), only met once, M. Halifax in the Chair, and then only to adjourn. (Com. Book 29 Dec.)—On 3 Jan., pursuant to order of the previous day (L. J., XIV. 613), the House went into Committee on the Bill, E. Bridgewater in the Chair. After amending the Bill by adding the words printed above in italics, the Committee moved the House to call in a person at the door, Mr. Sprigg, to be heard and to ask him what deficiency there is in the Orders of the Admiralty, and whether the Bill gave a supplement to them. *Mr. Sprigg* being called in, said he had reason to believe there were many false musters. House resumed and on report the Bill was referred to a Select Committee as before. (MS. Min. 3 Jan.; L. J., XIV. 614.) Nothing further recorded.]

372. Dec. 23. Protections.—(Dixon v. E. Lincoln).—Petition of William Dixon. Petitioner in July 1689, was seized by Robert Dickenson, Joseph Osborne, Anne Taylor, and Anne Lamb, Widow, and violently hurried into a house of the Earl of Lincoln's, where he was kept in a turret several weeks a close prisoner under strict guard, without being allowed candle, pen, ink, paper, or meat or drink but what he procured at his own charge to prevent being famished. Petitioner was thus used without any just cause or pretence of any legal warrant or process, only a paper was produced, pretended to be signed by the Earl and authorizing Petitioner's seizure and imprisonment until his Lordship's further order, for destroying his Lordship's gardens and other misdemeanours to that effect, a copy of which paper or of his commit-

House of Lords MSS.

1690.

ment Petitioner was not allowed to have. Petitioner, after several weeks confinement, was detained longer by one Joseph Taylor, husband of Anne Taylor, who was before in the country, and a writ was sued out against him at the suit of the Earl for 500*l.* debt and orders given to demand 1,000*l.* bail, and thereupon Petitioner was imprisoned in the County gaol for Lincoln for 18 weeks, when he was delivered, the action not being prosecuted. Petitioner's goods, papers, and writings of considerable value were seized on his imprisonment and are still detained, and Petitioner's health is much impaired and his estate ruined. Anne Lamb was chief contriver, and by her means Dickenson, Osborne, the two Taylors, and James Calvert brought about Petitioner's imprisonment and are liable, as he is advised, to his action and to answer damages. But Anne Lamb, though she keeps a common brewhouse, and Joseph Taylor, claim protection as the Earl's servants, so that Petitioner cannot proceed against them. Petitioner brought his action for part of his goods against Osborne and Taylor, but when it was ready to be tried, they produced a Protection under the Earl's hand, insisting on privilege of Parliament, and Petitioner has failed to procure the Earl's leave to proceed at law against them. Prays for relief. [Read this day. L. J., XIV. 604. On 13 Oct. the House, after reading the Order of 28 March 1690, declared all protections entered at the Parliament Office last Session to be null and void. (L. J., XIV. 521.) On 2 Dec. after reading the Protections entered in the Book, the House appointed a Committee to draw an Order for vacating all written or printed Protections for the future (*ib.* 576). The question led to an adjourned debate the next day (*ib.* 576), and on 5 Dec. the Committee was on motion revived. (*ib.* 580.) The proceedings of this Committee are not recorded, but on report, on 9 Dec., after a proposal made in the course of the debate, that all Lords who gave irregular Protections should be reprimanded by the House, the House ordered to go into C. W. H. the next day to consider of abuses in giving Protections and the remedies (*ib.* 583, MS. Min. 9 Dec.)—On 12 Dec., the House being put in Committee, it was proposed that the Lords be reproved in their places or sent to the Tower, and if they offend again, the liberty of protection taken away from them. House moved that the order for taking away written Protections may stand. *Question*, Whether the Lords that shall be found faulty shall be reproved? *Proposed*, That in case an Order be made, that where any persons be protected, it be made known that the people apply themselves to the House and the Peer defend it. *Question*, Whether all written Protections shall be taken away? House resumed. E. Bridgewater reported that the Committee desired to sit again. (MS. Min. 12 Dec.; L. J., XIV. 587.)—Nothing further occurred till 23 Dec., when the House was moved to consider of Protections and that something may be done to reform the abuse. *Moved*, That the Protections be read and the Lords summoned to attend that shall be found to have too many or such as be scandalous. The Book read. The above Petition of William Dixon being read, the debate was adjourned to the 26th, and all the Lords summoned to attend, the E. Lincoln in particular. (MS. Min. 23 Dec.; L. J., XIV. 601.)—On 26 Dec. the House was informed that E. Lincoln was sick and could not attend. The Protections were then read. A list is given of the Peers owning or disowning them. House moved to relieve Dixon upon his Petition. The order formally drawn by the Committee for taking away Protections is read. *Question*, Whether to agree with the Committee in taking away all written Protections? Debate adjourned to tomorrow, and D. Northumberland, E. Suffolk,

E. Lincoln, and L. Morley ordered to attend. (MS. Min. 26 Dec.; L. J., XIV. 605.)—On 27 Dec. the Orders concerning Protections and for D. Northumberland to attend are read. The Duke owns his Protections of W. Fanshaw and Peter Dugna; he recalls those of Thos. Potter, Rob. Gargrave, and Sir John Clayton, which he had ordered his Steward to vacate. E. Lincoln's Protections read, viz. Colney, Mrs. Barbara Roch, William Irons, Benj. Le Nud, George Breholt, and Knevet Hastings, Esq. L. Morley's Protection of Thomas Arnold, Butler, is read. He says there are three or four given, and for the future he will give no more and vacate these. *House moved that all Protections be vacated that the Lords declare they will never give more, but to their menial servants.** Ordered that all Protections be vacated of D. Northumberland, E. Lincoln, E. Suffolk, and L. Morley. House moved in Dixon's case against E. Lincoln that he may have his Petition granted and liberty to sue at law for his right. Ordered that the Petition be granted. After debate concerning vacating written Protections. *Question*, Whether any written Protection shall be granted? *Question*, Whether these words shall be added? Leave given to dissent to the Question (without leave of the House). *Resolved* in the negative. Contents, 24; Non-Contents, 41. Tellers, E. Warrington and L. North. Then the *Question* was put: Whether any written Protections shall be granted? *Resolved* in the affirmative. Contents, 43; Not-Contents, 25. Tellers, E. Warrington and L. North. The House then made the order for E. Lincoln to attend on the 29th. (MS. Min. 27 Dec.; L. J., XIV. 607.)—On 29 Dec. E. Lincoln was heard as to Dixon's Petition. He says he brought him to a place from 16*l.* a year to 40*l.* Dixon has destroyed his orange trees and all other things in his garden, and therefore he desires the Petition may be rejected. Dixon's Petition is read. (MS. Min. 29 Dec.) Nothing further recorded.]

Annexed:—

(*a*.) 31 Oct. 1689. Petition of John Newell. Petitioner was servant to E. Lincoln about 9 months, and having lent his Lordship 70 guineas, upon demand of his money was charged with robbery and committed to Newgate, where he lay 6 weeks until acquitted by a jury, after which he was taken up again in Lincolnshire on pretence of having broken goal. Petitioner might have prevented all this if he had given his Lordship 40*l.*, but he chose rather to suffer, trusting to his innocence. The Earl having made Petitioner's debt over to his steward, Joseph Taylor of Lincoln, Petitioner arrested Taylor, but finds him protected by his Lordship, and Petitioner and the Officers are liable to be arrested. Prays that there may be no proceedings against himself or the officer, and that Taylor may be left open to the law. [There is no reference in L. J. to this Petition; but the MS. Min. of this day contain the following: E. Lincoln complains that his servants have been arrested. Witnesses, George Selfe and Thos. Brooks called in and sworn. Asked if they knew of any servant of my Lord of Lincoln arrested, they replied "Yes, at the suit of Wood. They that arrested him said they did not value my Lord's privilege." What place was James Crosby in under my Lord? *G. Selfe* says he cannot well tell. *E. Lincoln* says he served him with wine, and he gave him sometimes a crown or so. The Roll of Orders read to

* The words in italics are cancelled.

HOUSE OF LORDS MSS.
—
1690.

this Privilege. This was waived. *E. Lincoln* complains that his steward in the country was arrested in the country. His name is Thomas (*sic*) Taylor. (MS. Min.).]

373. Dec. 26. Baldwin Leighton.—Petition of Colonel Baldwin Leighton. Charles II. in the 19th year of his reign, granted the office of Warden of the Fleet to Sir Jeremiah Whichcot in fee, upon condition that he should make Caroon House in Lambeth his prison for ever, but Sir Jeremy, contrary to his covenant, sold Caroon House from the Crown, and his Majesty's ancient prison of the Fleet to one Norwood, and he to one Bromhall, and Bromhall to Richard Manlove, the present Warden, who has committed several forfeitures, as appears by Inquisition duly returned and filed in the Petty Bag. His present Majesty in April last granted the office, so forfeited, to Petitioner, and the grant passed all offices till it came to the Great Seal, when it was stopped by Manlove and one Johnson, and although Petitioner had several orders for a hearing and attended often with 7 or 8 Counsel, yet he was put off till 17 July, when the Lords Commissioners declared that they did not think fit to determine the matter, till his Majesty's pleasure was known therein, and shortly after decreed the office to Johnson. His Majesty, soon after his return from Ireland, signified his further pleasure to the Lords Commissioners by several persons of quality that Petitioner's Patent should pass, but no notice being taken thereof, Petitioner petitioned his Majesty in Council, where it was ordered that the Lords Commissioners or one of them should attend the Board to give their reasons for not passing the Patent, and on 6 Nov. last the Lord Commissioner Hutchins attending, alleged that their reason was that the Estate was in Johnson not in Manlove (against whom the Inquisition was found), and they had decreed the office to Johnson, which has since been most justly reversed by their Lordships. Petitioner doubts the Lords Commissioners may, before Petitioner can be heard before their Lordships, quash the Inquisition, whereby his Majesty's title is in danger to be defeated, and Petitioner greatly damnified. Prays that a day may be appointed for hearing his Counsel in defence of his Majesty's title. *Signed* by Petitioner, *Countersigned* Humphrey Randall and R. Higgons. [Read this day and rejected. L. J., XIV. 605.]

374. $\frac{\text{Dec. 30.}}{\text{Jan. 1, 3.}}$ Rebels Attainder Bill.—Papers produced before the Committee of the whole House on the Bill (No. 370), viz.:—

(*a*.) 30 Dec. 1690. Petition of Thomas, Earl of Sussex, Henry Leonard, Elizabeth, Countess of Meath, and Elizabeth Coot. Elizabeth, late Countess of Sheppey, Grandmother of the Petitioner, Elizabeth Coot, and mother of the other Petitioners, devised her estate by will to her executors, Sir Charles Cotterell and Dr. Trumbull in trust to sell her lands in Suffolk and Gloucestershire for payment of debts and legacies (which were sold), and to settle one moiety of her lands on the Petitioner Henry and his heirs by any other after taken wife, with remainder to Francis Leonard and heirs, remainder to the first and all other sons successively of the Petitioner Thomas and their heirs male, remainder as to one moiety of the said moiety to the Petitioner, Countess of Meath and her heirs, and the other moiety of the said moiety to the Petitioner Elizabeth and Mary O'Bryan and their heirs; as to the other moiety of the whole premises unsold, to settle the same on Francis Leonard and heirs, remainder to Petitioner Henry and his heirs by other after taken wife, with like remainders over as is of the other moiety; and the said Will directs the Executors to take special care that in such settlements it should never be in the power of either Francis Leonard or the Petitioner Henry to dock the entail of either of the said moieties given them during their lives. The executors have made no settlement, but the estate in law remains in them under the trusts in the Will. Francis Leonard, to the great grief and sorrow of his friends, became a convert to the Popish religion, and was seduced and drawn into the rebellion in Ireland. If the Bill pass, the Petitioners Henry Leonard, the Countess of Meath, and Elizabeth Coot, and the said Mary O'Bryan and the sons of the Petitioner, the Earl of Sussex, are in danger of being barred of their several remainders, and the Petitioner, the Earl of Sussex, of the reversion in fee, he being heir at law to his mother. Petitioners are all Protestants, and have contributed as much as in them lay to this happy Revolution. Pray leave to offer a clause to the Bill for saving their respective estates and interests. *Numbered* 2. [Read in C. W. H. this day. M.S. Min.]

(a^1.) 1 Jan. 1690–1. Amended* Proviso marked A. as follows: "Provided always that this Act, or anything herein contained, shall not extend or be construed to forfeit, bar, *alter* or prejudice any estate, right, *title*, trust, or interest in law or equity in reversion, remainder or expectancy, which Thomas, Earl of Sussex, or any of his sons by him begotten or to be begotten, Henry Leonard, Elizabeth, Countess of Meath, brother and sister of the said Earl, the Lady Elizabeth Coot and Mary O'Brian, nieces of the said Earl, or any of them, have or hath, or could or might have or claim of, in or to any manors, lands, tenements or hereditaments in the Kingdom of England by the last Will and Testament of Elizabeth, late Countess of Sheppey, deceased [if this Act had never been made] *or the said Earl as heir of the said late Countess, his mother, if this Act had not been made.*" [Offered in C. W. H. this day by *Mr. Ward*, Counsel for E. Sussex, and agreed to. MS. Min.]

(a^2.) Parchment copy of same, before amendment.

(a^3.) Parchment copy of same as amended.

(b.) 30 Dec. 1690. Proviso marked B., for William Cecil and Charles Cecil, sons of James, late Earl of Salisbury,† as follows: "Provided that nothing in this Act shall extend to prejudice any pardon or pardons as to Life or Estate, that his Majesty shall grant to William Cecill, or Charles Cecill, sons of James, late Earl of Salisbury, being now infants, and conveyed privately to parts beyond the seas without the consent or knowledge of their guardians, if that the said William Cecill or Charles Cecil shall at any time before they do attain the age of eighteen years, bring a certificate to his Majesty's Courts of Chancery or King's Bench of his or their having received the Sacrament in any parish church, within the Bills of Mortality, according to the Church of England, and do then and there take the oaths, and subscribe the Declaration required and enjoined by an Act made in the first year of their Majesties' reign, entituled an Act for abrogating the oaths of Allegiance and Supremacy, and appointing other oaths. *Noted:* Agreed. [Offered in C. W. H. this day and again

* The additions are shown by italics and the omissions by square brackets.

† A proviso in their favour had been offered in the Commons on third reading (28 Dec.), but rejected. C. J., X. 523.

HOUSE OF LORDS MSS.

1690.

on 1 Jan. when it was agreed to. *Mr. Dolben* appeared as Counsel for the Cecils. MS. Min. of dates.]

(*b*[1].) Copy of same.

(*b*[2].) Another copy. *Noted*, in another hand, "Will[iam] 16, Ch[arles] 17. Are yet Protestants and willing to come over, but retained by " (*sic*).

(*c*.) 30 Dec. 1690. Petition of Elizabeth, Countess Dowager of Clancarty, in behalf of herself and of her three daughters. Petitioner, being appointed guardian of her son, an infant at the time of his father's death and now Earl of Clancarty, entered into a recognizance to Charles II. of about 30,000*l.* to bring him up in the Protestant religion, which she performed with great care by placing him first in the College of Dublin and afterwards at Christchurch, Oxford, under the care of Dr. Fell, then Bishop of Oxford, where he continued until he was by a letter from the said King removed from thence unknown to Petitioner. During Petitioner's guardianship, upon the marriage of the eldest of the said Earl's sisters, Petitioner gave security for payment of 4,000*l.* portion with her, part of which money she took up and stands still engaged for, and about 3,000*l.* principal and interest thereon remains yet unpaid, which Petitioner is engaged to pay; and Petitioner has also given her security for several other sums of money to the value of 4,000*l.*, which she engaged in for the clearing of Crown rents, arrears of quit rents and years value and several other incumbrances on the said estate, the profits of which were very inconsiderable by reason of two great jointures on the estate, so that Petitioner could not reimburse herself before the late troubles came on, since which time she has not received any rents thereout. Petitioner's husband, the late Earl of Clancarty, died suddenly in a fit of apoplexy, whereby he was incapable of making any provision for his daughters either by will or deed of settlement, so that Petitioner has three daughters whom she brought up in the Protestant religion and who are yet unmarried, and have no portion or maintenance, but what they depended upon to have out of the estate. Prays that some provision may be made in the Bill for securing to Petitioner out of the estate such part of her eldest daughter's portion as she stands engaged for and such other debts due out of the estate for which she has given her own security, and also for charging upon the estate such portions and maintenances for Petitioner's three unmarried daughters as may be suitable to their quality and may bear some proportion to the yearly value of the estate that their father and brother were possessed of. *Numbered* 1. [Read in C. W. H. this day. MS. Min.]

(*c*[1].) 30 Dec. 1690. Amended Proviso C., as follows: "Provided always that the estate in Ireland of Callaghan, late Earl of Clancarty, and now forfeited by Donough, Earl of Clancarty his son, shall stand charged with and subject to the payment of, and be it enacted that the same shall stand charged with and subject to the payment of, all and every such sum and sums of money which Elizabeth, Countess Dowager of Clancarty hath paid or advanced or stands bound or engaged for on account of the debts of her said late husband or son or of the said estate or of the portion of the Lady Ellen Colvill, eldest daughter of the said late Earl, *amounting to sixty-five thousand pounds*, as also with and subject to the payment of *four thousand* pounds apiece to each of the three unmarried daughters of the said late Earl, viz., *four thousand* pounds to the Lady Margaret MacCarty, *four thousand* pounds to the Lady Elizabeth MacCarty, and *four thousand pounds* more to the Lady Katherine MacCarty, for their portions all and every, which said sum and sums shall be raised and paid to the said persons, their executors, administrators, and assigns respectively; and as fast as the same can be raised by and out of the rents, issues, and profits of the said estate or otherwise, it shall and may be lawful to and for their Majesties, their heirs and successors, by and under the Broad Seal of England or Ireland, by mortgage of the premises or any part thereof, or by the sale of any part or parts of the premises to that value, to raise the said several sums of money, and to cause the same to be paid as aforesaid, anything herein contained to the contrary in any wise notwithstanding." *Endorsed:* Agreed. [A proviso on behalf of Lady Clancarty was offered in C. W. H. this day by *Mr. Stone*, her Counsel, and agreed to on 1 Jan. after hearing him, and filling up the blanks with the sums printed above in italics. MS. Min.]

(c^1.) 1 Jan. Engrossment of same, omitting the works in italics, for which blanks appear.

(*d.*) 30 Dec. 1690. Parchment Proviso, as follows: "Provided that nothing in this Act be construed to the prejudice or extend to the attainting the present Earl of Tyrone or the nulling of the settlements of his Estate made many years since by his father upon him." [A proviso was offered in C. W. H. this day, and agreed to on 1 Jan. as Proviso D. after hearing *Mr. Dolben*, Counsel for E. Tyrone. MS. Min.]

(*e.*) Petition of Sir John Ivory, of New Ross, in the Kingdom of Ireland. Petitioner, a Protestant and proprietor of lands in Ireland purchased by his father by his service againt the Irish in the former rebellion about forty years since or more, was dispossessed of the same by a late Act of the Irish Parliament, and put out of the government of Dungannon Fort, which he had purchased, by the consent of Charles II., at the cost of nearly 2,000*l.* Petitioner, upon the advance of William III. to Kilkenny, was commanded to summon in all the Protestants in those parts about Dungannon, and to block up the same until a general officer should come up with part of the army to summon the same, which he performed accordingly. Prays to be preserved in his Estate, either by means of a proviso or otherwise. *Undated. Numbered* 16. *Endorsed:* "E. Agreed." *See* next paper.

(e^1.) 1 Jan. 1690–1. Draft of Proviso, as follows: "Provided always that this Act or anything therein contained shall not extend nor be construed to extend to Sir John Ivory of New Ross, in the Kingdom of Ireland, Knt., or to any his Estate, real or personal, but that the said Sir John Ivory and his Estate, real and personal, shall be in the same case and no other than as if this Act had never been made." [A proviso was offered in C. W. H. by *Mr. Dolben* this day, and agreed to as Proviso E. MS. Min.]

(e^2.) Engrossment of preceding.

(*f.*) 30 Dec. 1690. Petition of divers creditors of the Lord Thomas Howard, deceased. The late Lord Thomas Howard, being indebted to Petitioners and divers other persons, by Indenture of 8 Dec. 1688, conveyed his Estate to Trustees for payment of his debts, which deed and the provision thereby made

Petitioners fear may be endangered by the Bill. Pray for a proviso saving to the creditors the benefit of the deed. *Numbered* 15. [Read this day. MS. Min.]

(f^1.) 30 Dec. 1690. Paper stating that the late Lord Thos. Howard, having undertaken to pay several debts of his brother the Duke of Norfolk, made over his estate, by deed of 8 Dec. 1688, to the Marquess of Worcester, Sir Robert Howard, Sir Rich. Onslow, and Sir Paul Ricaut, in trust for payment of his debts. The Bill of Attainder attaints of high treason all persons that are or have been in rebellion after 13 February 1688, and vests all their estates from that date in the Crown; and yet the rights of all persons claiming under any of the offenders since 2 Nov. 1688, are excepted from the benefit of the saving in the Bill, whereby the said deed of trust is in danger to be defeated. Prays that the Bill may be so amended as to make provision for the payment of Lord Howard's debts to his creditors; firstly, because forfeitures by attainders at common law relate only to the time of the fact done, nor can in reason be extended further, and the nature and intent of savings in Act of Parliament is to save and except what may be supposed to be forfeited by the body of the Act, and not to extend further than the body of the Act does; and secondly, because the debts were contracted long before the said 13 Feb. 1688, and it was impossible for the creditors to know then that Lord Thomas Howard would afterwards commit treason, nor is it reasonable they should suffer for his fault. *Endorsed:* "Memorandum for Lord Thomas Howard's creditors. Read 30 Dec. 1690. Agreed."

(f^2.) 1 Jan. 1690–1. Engrossed Proviso F., as follows: "Provided always and be it enacted by the authority aforesaid, that one deed or conveyance bearing date the 8th day of December, Anno Domini 1688, made and executed by the Lord Thomas Howard, since deceased, to the Right Honourable the Marquess of Worcester, Sir Robert Howard, Knt., Sir Richard Onslow, Bart., and Sir Paul Ricaut, Knt., upon trust for payment of the debts of the said Lord Thomas Howard and other trusts therein mentioned, shall not be impeached, defeated, made void, or frustrated by this present Act or by any means thereof; But that the same deed and the provision thereby made shall remain in full force and effect as for and concerning the payment of all debts then due and bonâ fide owing by the said Lord Thomas Howard to any person or persons whatsoever, this Act or anything herein contained to the contrary notwithstanding." [Offered in C. W. H. this day, and, after hearing Counsel, agreed to. MS. Min.]

(g.) 30 Dec. 1690. Petition of Anne, Viscountess of Clanmaleere. By the death of John Bermingham, Esq., Petitioner's brother, a moiety of his estate in Kildare descended to Petitioner as one of his sisters and coheirs. About 1676 this moiety, by agreement between Petitioner and her husband, was settled and secured for a separate maintenance for Petitioner, not to be controlled by her husband, and out of the profits thereof Petitioner purchased a lease of a small piece of ground in Dublin in the name of trustees for her use, and built a dwelling-house thereon. The income of the said moiety has also been the support of Petitioner, who has for the last five years constantly resided in Ireland, and continued not only quiet and submissive to the Government, but has been protected by the same and by the House by their

Lordships' order of 25 Dec. 1688. Prays for a proviso to secure her estate. [Read in C. W. H. this day. MS. Min.]

(g^1.) 1 Jan. 1690-1. Proviso G., as follows: "Provided always that Anne, wife to Maximilian, Lord Viscount Clanmalere shall hold and enjoy to her and her heirs all and every the lands, tenements, and hereditaments, reversion and remainders, which are descended or of right ought to descend unto her, the said Anne, as coheiress to her brother John Bermingham, of Dunforth, in the County of Kildare, in the Kingdom of Ireland, Esquire, deceased; and also a certain lease of a small piece of ground in the City of Dublin, which hath been by the said Anne, or in trust for her since purchased, and whereon she hath erected a dwelling-house, notwithstanding the said Anne's coverture, any other matter or thing in this present Act or any other Act, Statute, Ordinance, or Record to the contrary notwithstanding." [Offered in C. W. H. this day by *Mr. Stone*, Counsel for Petitioner, and agreed to. MS. Min.]

(g^2.) 1 Jan. 1690-1. Copy of preceding.

(h.) 30 Dec. 1690. Amended* draft of Proviso excepting E. Carlingford from attainder as follows:—"Provided always that this Act or anything therein contained, shall not extend [to disable their Majesties from granting any manors, lands, tenements or hereditaments, of which , late Earl of Carlingford was vested in fee simple or fee tail to , now Earl of Carlingford for such estate or estates as their Majesties in their Royal wisdom shall think fit to make] *to attaint or corrupt the blood of , late Earl of Carlingford, in the Kingdom of Ireland, deceased, but that all the honours, manors, lands, tenements, uses, titles, rights, of which the said late Earl was seised, shall descend, come, remain, and be unto Francis, now Earl Carlingford, as if this Act had not been made*." [The House was moved this day to add a proviso that nothing should corrupt the blood of the late E. Carlingford. Allowed. On 1 Jan. the proviso was read and agreed to as Proviso H. MS. Min. of dates.]

(h^1.) 1 Jan. 1690-1. Proviso H., being fair copy of preceding as corrected. *Endorsed:* "13, H. Agreed." MS. Min.]

(h^2.) 1 Jan. 1690-1. Engrossment of preceding.

(i.) 30 Dec. 1690. Amended* Proviso I., as follows: "Provided nevertheless and be it enacted by the authority aforesaid, That all Impropriations, Church leases, or any other revenues of right belonging to [the Church of Ireland] *any person or persons attainted by this Act*, be left entirely in their Majesties' power to dispose of for the advantages of [that] *the* Church *of Ireland*, as in their wisdom shall seem most necessary, anything in this Act [or any other] to the contrary notwithstanding." *Endorsed:* "L. Bp. London's Proviso I. Agreed." [Read in C. W. H. this day and again on 1 Jan. when it was agreed to as Proviso I. MS. Min. of dates.]

(k.) 1 Jan. 1690-1. Proviso K., as follows: "Provided nevertheless that if it shall hereafter seem good to their Majesties to extend their favour to Henry, Lord Dover,† and by Letters Patents under the Great Seal of England, express and declare their intention to have the said Lord Dover exempted or discharged from the

* The omissions are shown by square brackets and the additions by italics.

† A proviso to exempt Lord Dover had been rejected in the Commons on 19 Dec. by 119 votes to 112. C. J., X. 513.

HOUSE OF LORDS MSS.

1690.

attainder, penalties, and forfeitures by this Act made or imposed; That then and in such case the attainder, penalties, and forfeitures by this Act made or caused shall as to the said Lord Dover be annulled and discharged, and the said Lord Dover and his estate from the making of such Letters Patents be and continue to all intents and purposes in the same condition as he and it would or should have been if this Act had never been had or made." *Noted:* Agreed. [Read in C. W. H. this day and agreed to. MS. Min.]

(k^1.) 1 Jan. 1690–1. Engrossment of preceding.

(*l.*) 1 Jan. 1690–1. Proviso L., as follows: "Provided and it is hereby declared that this Act nor anything herein contained shall not impeach or in any manner avoid one Indenture Quadripartite dated the 21st day of January 1688, being an assignment of a house, stables, and coach-houses in the parish of St. James-in-the-Fields, in the County of Middlesex, from Henry, Lord Dover, Thomas, Lord Jermyn, Henry Poley, Thomas Coell, and Martin Folkes to James Ferne, in trust for Edward Horton, for several terms of years therein expressed, but that the same Indenture on Assignment shall be of such and the same force and effect as the same was before the making this Act, anything herein contained to the contrary notwithstanding." *Noted:* Agreed to. [Read in C. W. H. this day and agreed to. MS. Min.]

(l^1.) 1 Jan. 1690–1. Engrossment of preceding.

(*m.*) 30 Dec. 1690. Petition of Frances Arabella Bellew. Petitioner was married in 1686 to Walter, son and heir to John, Lord Bellew, and in consideration of 6,000*l.* for her portion, all the said Lord Bellew's estate in Ireland was settled after his death on her husband and heirs male, with provision for daughters and for payment of 700*l.* a year for the maintenance of Petitioner and her family during the said Lord Bellew's life, of which sum 150*l.* a year was to be paid to trustees for her pin money, and the whole 700*l.* was settled on Petitioner as her jointure, in case she survived her husband, during the joint lives of the said John, Lord Bellew, and his Lady, and 800*l.* a year after the death of either of them. Petitioner, who was born and bred a Protestant, has continued to reside in England, since her husband went to Ireland in December 1687, to take charge of a troop of horse. He has not since returned nor sent Petitioner anything for her subsistence since the War in Ireland, in which he and his father are unhappily engaged. Prays that a clause may be added to the Bill, reserving her right to so much of the estate as she is entitled to for her own and her daughter's maintenance as well as for her jointure, if she survives her husband and 4,000*l.* settled for her daughter's portion. *Endorsed* as dated.

(*n.*) 30 Dec. 1690. Petition of Richard Warburton, of Garrihinch, in the Kingdom of Ireland, Esquire. Petitioner, for subscribing the Association in England and adhering to their Majesties, had his real estate in Ireland, to the value of 800*l.* a year, and also his personal estate to the value of 2,000*l.*, seized by the Irish Papists, particularly by Sir Patrick Trant, Bart., who is now in rebellion. Petitioner held leases of several lands in the King's and Queen's Counties at the yearly rent in the whole of 169*l.* 10*s.*, of which divers years are yet unexpired, derived under the late E. Arlington, deceased, who sold the rent and reversion thereof to Sir Patrick Trant. Petitioner disbursed above 2,000*l.* in buildings and improvements in the leased lands, which for the most part are waste and yield nothing and may long continue of little value, and the rebuilding and planting thereof will be of great expense and cannot be undertaken without the encouragement of an additional term of years to be granted to Petitioner. Petitioner at his own cost maintains a garrison with some English in his house on the said lands, which is the only place in 24 miles from the Shannon that has held out against the Rapparies. Prays that an additional term of years to his leases may be granted. *Numbered* 9. [Read in C. W. H. this day. MS. Min.]

(n^1.) 1 Jan. 1690-1. Proviso as follows: "Provided always and be it further enacted by the authority aforesaid, That the lands, tenements, and hereditaments lying and being in the King and Queen's Counties in the said Kingdom of Ireland, which were held and enjoyed the 5th day of December 1688, by Richard Warburton, Esq., of Carryhinch, in the King's County aforesaid by one or more leases, by writing indented (from the late Earl of Arlington) for several years yet to come, at the rent of 169*l.* 10*s.* 0*d.* a year in the whole, the rent and reversion of which said lands were afterwards conveyed by the said Earl of Arlington, amongst many other lands, to Sir Patrick Trant, Bart., and his heirs, now or late in actual rebellion in that Kingdom, shall, in consideration of the said Warburton's present good service to the Government, in maintaining and keeping a garrison in Carryhinch aforesaid, by which the enemies are deterred from making incursions into and destroying the neighbourhood, and for his future encouragement, and of his great charge and improvements, and other costs and disbursements in and about the same, and the other land leased to the said Warburton, be and are hereby granted unto and settled upon the said Richard Warburton, his executors, administrators, and assigns, for and during the term of 51 years from the expiration or other determination of his said present leases respectively at and under the like yearly rents and covenants payable to their Majesties and their successors as in and by the said leases are expressed and reserved; and the said rent is hereby remitted unto the said Warburton, his executors, administrators, and assigns, for and until the said Kingdom of Ireland shall be by their Majesties declared to be reduced, and the war and rebellion there ended." *Endorsed* Rejected. [Read in C. W. H. this day and rejected. MS. Min.]

(n^2.) 1 Jan. 1690-1. Engrossment of preceding.

(*o*.) 30 Dec. 1690. Petition of Col. Charles Herbert. Petitioner's brother, Sir Edward Herbert, by deeds of 6th and 8th Dec. 1688 conveyed to Petitioner a farm called Oatlands Park and his Chambers in Serjeant's Inn, together with what goods he left behind him when leaving England. Petitioner has executed the consideration of the deeds by paying many of his brother's debts, but some of them still remain unpaid and will be avoided and Petitioner's right impeached unless provided for in the Bill. Prays that a Proviso may be added to save Petitioner's rights. *Numbered* 12. *Endorsed* as read this day and postponed.

(o^1.) 30 Dec. 1690. Proviso as follows:—"Provided that nothing in this Act contained shall be construed to debar or hinder their Majesties from granting or disposing of all their Majesties' right and interest of and in certain chambers or lodgings in the house or Society called Serjeant's Inn, in Fleet Street, within the City of London, to which their Majesties are entitled by virtue of an

House of Lords MSS.

1690.

attainder by outlawry for high treason of Sir Edward Herbert, Knt., Serjeant-at-Law; but that their Majesties may grant and dispose of all such their right and interest in and to the said Chambers, as if this Act had never been made, anything in this Act to the contrary in any wise notwithstanding.* *But this Act or anything herein contained is not intended or shall be construed to prejudice or alter the way or method of election or disposal of Chambers in the said Society, but to leave the aforementioned Chambers subject to such way and method as they would have been if this Act had not been made. Endorsed,* "Speaker. Read 30 Dec. 1690. 4." [*See also* Annex (*z.*) below.]

(*o*[2].) 30 Dec. 1690. Draft proviso as follows: "Provided always that this Act nor anything therein contained shall not extend or be construed in any sort to impeach or avoid any right, title, or interest, which Charles Herbert, Esq., hath in or to a farm called Oatlands Park in the County of Surrey or the Chambers in Serjeant's Inn, formerly belonging to his brother, Sir Edw. Herbert, or in or to any of his goods conveyed to the said Charles Herbert before the said Sir Edw. Herbert left this Kingdom, but the same shall be and remain as if this Act had never been made."

(*o*[3].) Engrossment of last Proviso.

(*p*.) 30 Dec. 1690. Petition of the Lady Anna Hume, Relict of Capt. George Mathew, late of Thomas-Town in the County of Tipperary, Ireland. Petitioner, a Protestant, being threatened by the Popish relations of her husband, who was also a Papist, for not conforming to their religion, and for warning her husband against concerning himself with Tyrconnel's Government, repaired for safety to England, where she lived without any support from her husband, for about three years before his death. On learning of his death soon after the victory of the Boyne, he never having been concerned in the Rebellion, she returned to Ireland to get the third part of his estate, but found that his daughter-in-law, whose husband is now a rebel, had got possession of the house at Thomas Town and converted his goods and chattels to her own use. Petitioner, at her marriage, had brought to her husband an estate worth about 10,000*l.*, which he promised should continue in her own name as a provision in case he should die before her, he having little or no estate of his own; but, nevertheless, he soon converted it all to his own use, changing all into his own name and that of others and making large purchases with her money. Prays their Lordships to consider her deplorable condition in her old age and to grant her a saving clause in the Bill. *Numbered* 7. *Endorsed* as read this day and rejected. [MS. Min. *See also* Annex (*t.*) below.

(*p*[1].) 1 Jan. 1690–1. Draft Proviso as follows: "Provided always that nothing in this or any other Act of Parliament contained shall in any wise extend or be construed to extend to prejudice or bar the Lady Hume from demanding, recovering, receiving and enjoying her dower and thirds of all and every estate and estates whereof her late husband Captain Mathew was seized or possessed at any time during his marriage with the said Lady Hume; any law, statute or custom to the contrary hereof in any wise notwithstanding." [Read this day and rejected. MS. Min.]

* The words in italics are added in the clerk's hand.

(p^2.) 1 Jan. 1690–1. Engrossment of preceding.

(q.) 1 Jan. 1690–1. Petition of Sir Maurice Eustace, Knt. Sir Maurice Eustace, late Lord Chancellor of Ireland, by deed in 1662 settled Castlemartin, the ancient family seat, and the estate thereto belonging on John Eustace, Esq., for life, with divers remainders in tail. All the precedent remainders being spent, that which is limited to Petitioner after the death of Sir Maurice Eustace of Castlemartin, who has no heirs male, and, as reported, is lately dead, is likely to be forfeited by his attainder in the Bill. The remainder or reversion of the manor of Portester, Meath, which the said Lord Chancellor purchased for 400*l.* or 500*l.* and was also confirmed to him by letters under the Great Seal of Ireland, and which he devised by will to Petitioner, to whom it was likewise confirmed, is likely to be vested by the Bill to the uses therein expressed. A great part of upwards of 20,000*l.* due to Petitioner in Ireland, is due from forfeiting persons and likely to be debarred by the Bill unless some provision is made to the contrary. Petitioner has already been a great sufferer by being attainted in Ireland and till of late deprived of the benefit of his estate of upwards of 4,000*l.* a year near Dublin, and his houses in Dublin and in Kildare have been destroyed and plundered, and his children turned out of doors so as to cause the death of one of them. Prays that a proviso on his behalf may be added to the Bill. *Noted:* Postponed. MS. Min.

(q^1.) 1 Jan. 1690–1. Engrossed Proviso as follows: "Provided always that this Act or anything therein contained shall not extend to vest in their Majesties, or to bar or hinder Sir Maurice Eustace, of Harristowne, in the County of Kildare, Knight, his heirs or assigns, of or from any remainder or remainders, reversion or reversions, or expectancy or otherwise, which he hath or ought to have in law or equity in or to any manors or lands in the Kingdom of Ireland expectant or descendant upon any estate or estates tail or for life, or other estate now or late in Sir Maurice Eustace of Castle Martin, or Maurice Eustace of Portlester, Gentleman, or any other of the said forfeiting persons, nor shall the same be hereby altered, devested, or prejudiced, but the same shall be and remain as if this Act had never been made. [Offered in C. W. H. this day by *Mr. Stone*, Counsel for Petitioner, and read and postponed. MS. Min.]

(r.) 3 Jan. 1690–1. Petition of Connor O'Brien, son and heir of Teolagh O'Brien, late of Drummore, in the County of Clare, in the Kingdom of Ireland. Petitioner's father being infirm and weak, and Petitioner being a minor, and bred in England and a Protestant, and attainted by James II. for his service to their present Majesties. Petitioner's father and grandfather were disseized of all their estate by Daniel O'Brien, Lord Viscount Clare, without any colour of right. Prays that his right in the said estate may be saved in the Bill. *Endorsed:* Read: agreed. MS. Min.

(r^1.) 3 Jan. 1690–1. Engrossed Saving clause as follows: "Saving always to Connor O'Brian, Esq., and his heirs, all his right, title and interest in law or equity in or to any manors, lands, tenements, or hereditaments now or late in the possession of Daniell, Lord Viscount Clare, in the Kingdom of Ireland, anything herein contained to the contrary thereof in any ways notwithstanding."

(s.) 3 Jan. 1690–1. Draft Proviso as follows: "Provided nevertheless that if his Majesty shall at any time hereafter be pleased by his Letters Patents to declare that the Lord George Howard shall be excepted out of this present Act, That then and from thenceforth the said Lord George Howard, his manors, lands, tenements, hereditaments, and estate, real and personal, shall be excepted and exempted out of this present Act, anything in this Act contained to the contrary thereof in any wise notwithstanding." *Endorsed:* Agreed. MS. Min.

(s[1].) 3 Jan. 1690–1. Engrossment of preceding Proviso.

(t.) 3 Jan. 1690–1. Petition of the Lady Hume. Petitioner some days since presented her Petition for a saving clause, which clause she offered yesterday, but the same was not admitted by reason, as Petitioner is informed, of some general words, which are now left out. Prays their Lordships to receive the clause as now engrossed. *See* next paper and also Annex (p.) above.

(t[1].) 3 Jan. 1690–1. Draft Proviso identical with (p[1]) above, except by omitting the concluding words ("any law, statute, or custom to the contrary hereof in any wise notwithstanding"). [Read in C. W. H. this day and agreed to. MS. Min.]

(t[2].) 3 Jan. 1690–1. Engrossment of preceding.

(u.) 3 Jan. 1690–1. Engrossed Proviso as follows: "And whereas William Whitmore, Esq., late deceased, by Indentures of Lease and Release, bearing date on or about the 26th and 27th days of November 1677, did convey several manors and lands in the Counties of Essex and Middlesex unto William, Marquess of Powis, William, Earl of Craven, Charles, Lord North and Grey, Francis, Lord Guilford and Sir Eliab Hervey, Knight and Baronet, and their heirs in trust to be sold and the moneys arising by such sale to be disposed as in the said Indenture of Release is mentioned; which said Francis, Lord Guilford and Sir Eliab Hervey afterwards released their said trust, and the said Marquess of Powis, Earl of Craven, and Lord North and Grey, the three other trustees, have sold the said manors and lands and disposed the moneys arising by such sales according to their said trusts other than and except the sum of 3,250*l.*, part of the sum of 3,750*l.* which was the parts and shares of William Whitmore, Katherine Whitmore, Anne Whitmore, and Dorothy Whitmore in the moneys so raised, which said 3,250*l.* was not paid to the said William Whitmore, Katherine Whitmore, Anne Whitmore and Dorothy Whitmore, they being all infants under the age of 21 years, And the said 3,250*l.* is in the hands of the said William, Marquess of Powis, and so will be inevitably lost unless provided for in this present Act; for prevention whereof Be it enacted and declared by the authority aforesaid, that the goods and chattels and the manors, lands and hereditaments of the said Marquess of Powis shall be and the same are hereby charged with and made liable to the payment of the said 3,250*l.* or such part thereof as is now unpaid to the said William Whitmore, Katherine Whitmore, Anne Whitmore and Dorothy Whitmore, their executors and assigns, with interest from the time the same 3,250*l.* was paid to him the said Marquess. And the Barons of their Majesties' Court of Exchequer may and are hereby authorized and directed to order the payment of the said 3,250*l.* or such part thereof as is now unpaid and interest as aforesaid unto the said William Whitmore, Katherine Whitmore, Anne Whitmore and Dorothy Whitmore out of the said goods and chattels and the rents and profits of the manors and lands of the said Marquess of Powis in the hands of any Sheriff or Sheriffs or other Officer or Officers, which shall at any time hereafter be charged with, or accountable for such goods and chattels or rents and profits before the same shall be answered and paid into their said Majesties' Receipt of Exchequer, and that previous to and before any other payments or applications to be made in pursuance of this Act, anything before in this Act contained or any law to the contrary notwithstanding." [Read in C. W. H. this day and agreed to. MS. Min.]

(*w*.) 3 Jan. 1690–1. Petition of Colonel Richard Ingoldesby. Petitioner, in right of his mother, has a good title to the manor of Hospitall, Co. Limerick, formerly the estate of his ancestors, but the possession of which was taken by one Col. Nicholas Browne, who claimed it in right of his wife. Petitioner, on coming of age about four years since, entered his claim, but was prevented from prosecuting it by the power and influence of the Papists. Browne is a notorious Papist and rebel and was outlawed for treason in England. Petitioner was early in arms for their Majesties and has suffered upwards of 11,000*l*. in the loss of his estate. He was in actual service at the Newry and once maintained a regiment at his own charge. Prays for a proviso to save his rights, and that the said manor and lands may be excepted out of the Bill. *Endorsed* as read this day and agreed.

(*w*[1].) 3 Jan. 1690–1. Engrossed Proviso as follows: "Provided always that this Act or anything herein contained shall not extend or be construed to extend to forfeit or vest or any ways to prejudice any the estate or interest, right, or title in law or equity, which Colonel Richard Ingoldsby hath unto the manor of Hospitall, with the lands, tenements, hereditaments and appurtenances thereunto belonging, or reputed as part thereof, or therewith enjoyed, in the County of Limerick, in the Kingdom of Ireland; but that the said Colonel Richard Ingoldsby, his heirs, executors, administrators and assigns, shall have and enjoy the same estate, right, title, and interest in law and equity of, in, and unto the said manors and premises and the said manors and premises remain subject and liable thereto, as if this Act had not been made, anything in this Act contained to the contrary notwithstanding. [Read in C. W. H. this day and agreed to. MS. Min.]

(*x*.) 3 Jan. 1690–1. Petition of Francis Mollineaux, Richard Rigby William Hudson and other the creditors of Allan Bellingham, Esq. Pray that provision may be made to save two conveyances of Allan Bellingham in trust to sell certain lands to pay his debts to Petitioners and other creditors. *Endorsed* as read this day and rejected. [Counsel for the Petitioners, *Mr. Ward* was heard, and stated that the debts were 2,500*l*. to tradesmen. MS. Min. 3 Jan.]

(*x*[1].) 3 Jan. 1690–1. Engrossed Proviso as follows: Provided nevertheless that this present Act or anything therein contained shall not extend to invalidate, impeach, or prejudice any the trust or trusts of and in certain manors, lands and hereditaments in the Counties of Lancaster, Westmoreland, Durham, and York, or any of them, vested and reposed in Charles Pigeon, Esq., and Robert Hilton, Gentleman, by Allan Bellingham, Esq., before the 13th day of February 1688, for the payment of the debts of the said Allan Bellingham, due to Francis Mollineaux, Richard

HOUSE OF LORDS MSS.

1690.

Rigby and William Hudson and other the creditors of the said Allan Bellingham, comprehended within the same trusts; But that the said creditors shall and may have the benefit of the said trusts for the payment of the said debts, and the said manors and lands remain subject and liable thereunto, as fully and effectually as if this Act had not been made, this present Act or anything therein contained to the contrary in any wise notwithstanding." [Offered this day and rejected. MS. Min.]

(y.) 3 Jan. 1690–1. Engrossed Proviso as follows: "Provided always that this present Act shall not prejudice or make void a grant or demise made by their present Majesties in the year 1689 to Thomas Preston, of Holker, in the County of Lancaster, Esq., of certain messuages and lands in Furness in the said County, lately the inheritance of Sir Thomas Preston, Bart., for the term of 21 years; but that the said Thomas Preston may hold and enjoy the same under the rents and covenants in and according to his said grant or lease, anything in this Act contained to the contrary notwithstanding." [Read this day and agreed to, after hearing Counsel, who stated that Sir Thomas Preston made a settlement of his estate in 1674. MS. Min.]

(z.) 3 Jan. 1690–1. Corrected Proviso as follows: "Provided always that this Act or anything therein contained shall not extend nor be construed to extend to forfeit, vest, impeach, or prejudice any estate, right, title or interest that Charles Herbert, Esq., had or hath by force and virtue of three deeds made by Sir Edward Herbert, Knt., to the said Charles Herbert, two of them bearing date the 6th, and the other the 8th day of December 1688, whereby the said Sir Edward Herbert did convey to the said Charles Herbert his house and the park and lands of Oatlands in the County of Surrey, and his chamber in Serjeants' Inn, in Fleet Street, and the goods belonging to him in trust for payment of the debts of him, the said Sir Edward Herbert, [nor] *as to* any provision for payment of debts thereby made, but that the said deeds and any of them shall for payment of the said debts that he owed to any person or persons at the time of the date of the said deeds, be of the same force and effect as if this present Act had never been made." [*See also* Annex (o.) above. After hearing Counsel, *Mr. Ward*, this day, the Committee ordered the Proviso before them to be rejected and another one brought in only to pay the debts. MS. Min.]

(z[1].) Engrossment of last Proviso, as far as the words ("debts thereby made") and without the correction of ("nor") for ("as to").

(aa.) 3 Jan. 1690–1. Petition of Thomas, Lord Jermyn. Henry, late Earl of St. Albans by deed and will settled a great part of his estate on Henry, Lord Dover, and heirs male, with remainder to Petitioner and heirs male. The Estate tail limited to Henry, Lord Dover, being forfeited by the Bill, Petitioner's remainder is thereby taken from him. Prays for a Proviso to preserve his remainder. *Endorsed* as read this day and agreed to.

(aa[1].) 3 Jan. 1690–1. Draft Proviso as follows: "Provided always that this Act or anything herein contained shall not extend or be construed to forfeit, bar, alter, or prejudice, any estate, right, title, trust, or interest in law or equity, in reversion, remainder, or expectancy, which Thomas, Lord Jermin, or any of his sons by him begotten, or to be begotten, or any of them have or claim of, in, or to any manors, lands, tenements, or hereditaments in the Kingdom of England, as if this Act had not been made." [Offered this day and agreed to. MS. Min.]

(*bb.*) 3 Jan. 1690–1. Petition of Robert Curtis, now in their Majesties' Service in the Kingdom of Ireland. Petitioner having in 1687 by bond and judgment a debt of 500*l.* with interest due from the E. Clancarty, lately in rebellion in Ireland, prays for a Proviso to save his right. [Read this day. MS. Min.]

(*bb*[1].) 3 Jan. 1690–1. Engrossed Proviso as follows: "Provided always that this Act nor anything therein contained shall not extend or be construed in any sort to impeach or avoid the right of Mr. Robert Curtis to a debt of 500*l.* with interest due by bond and judgment from the Right Honourable the Earl of Clancarthy, but that the said debt may be sued for and satisfied out of the estate of the said Earl, as if this Act had never been made, anything in this Act to the contrary thereof in any wise notwithstanding."

375. Dec. 30. Corn Spirits Act.—Petition of the Master, Wardens, Assistants and Commonalty of the trade, art and mystery of Distillers of London. Petitioners were many years since incorporated and their trade so increased that they are now and for several years have been one of the Livery Companies, and in all public solemnities and other occasions bear part of the charges with the other Companies, and are now become very numerous, and have several hundred apprentices, most of them being sons of country gentlemen and farmers. The Bill, as is pretended, is for encouraging the distilling of brandy and spirits from corn, and for laying duties on low wines or spirits of the first extraction. But, if it pass, it is impossible to effect the design of the consumption of corn, it not being possible to draw a spirit from corn without a mixture of some other material; and besides, it will considerably lessen their Majesties' revenue and also utterly ruin several thousands of their Majesties' subjects and the trade of distilling in England, to the enriching for a time such particular persons as have a quantity of French brandy in their hands. Pray to be heard by Counsel before the Bill pass. *Signed* by Wm. Harris, Dan. Wight, John Freeman, Thos. Jordan and Sam. Shephard. [Read this day. L. J., XIV. 609. Counsel were heard on this and the annexed Petitions on 31 Dec. *Sir William Thompson* (for Sugar Refiners): The Bill will not answer the ends designed. It will certainly lose the trade. It does not require molasses to be used. No spirits but in making will cost 4*s.* by this Act. It is but three. *Mr. Darnell* (for same): We draw a fine syrup from the sugar, called molasses. This [Bill] will diminish and not increase trade. *Mr. Ward* and *Mr. Palmer* are heard for the Distillers. *The Merchants* are heard: The Plantations are under very great hardships. (MS. Min.) The Bill for encouraging the distilling of brandy and spirits from corn, and for laying several duties on low wines or spirits of the first extraction, was brought from the Commons, and read 1[a] on 29 Dec. (MS. Min. No entry of this in L. J.);* and received the Royal Assent on 5 Jan. (L. J., XIV. 618.) 2 W. & M. Sess. 2, c. 9 in Fol. Ed.]

* The MS. Min. of 2 Jan. have the following entry: "House moved that the Bill for impositions on Brandy might be proceeded in." The Commons sent a message this day to remind the Lords of the Bill. L. J., XIV. 613.

House of Lords MSS.

1690.

Annexed :—

(*a*.) 30 Dec. Petition of the Merchants and Planters concerned in and trading to their Majesties' Sugar Plantations. The following mischiefs will ensue from the Bill. Their Majesties' Revenue will be diminished. The Sugar Plantations, which are already loaded with great duties and by the present War, and are brought to great distress, will be so much discouraged, that other nations, who rival us in the trade, and use all means to make it easy to their subjects, will have the advantage of us and in time beat us out of it. The West India Navigation, which breeds so many seamen and employs so great a number of ships, will be much abated. Many thousands, whose employment depends on refining sugars in England, will be ruined, and also many in the Sugar Plantations. The Act will not answer the ends proposed to increase the expense of corn, but will encourage the clandestine importation of foreign brandy. *Signed* by Thos. Hunt and 20 others. Pray to be heard before the Bill pass. [Read this day. L. J., XIV. 609.]

(*b*.) 30 Dec. Petition of the Refiners of Sugar. The Bill intends a total discouragement to the Distillers' use of molasses made in England, by an extreme and much higher duty to be laid upon low wines drawn from molasses than upon low wines drawn from corn, supposing thereby to promote the Distillers' consumption of corn. The Bill, if passed, will ruin the ancient, useful and beneficial trade of sugar refining in this Kingdom, and consequently lead to the ruin of many thousands of his Majesty's subjects concerned in and depending upon it, the demolishing many costly sugar works, the transplanting the trade to Holland, Hamburgh, and other foreign parts, where it is most studiously promoted and encouraged; the weakening the navigation of the Kingdom, and the abating to a very great degree of the revenue of the Crown. Pray to be heard by Counsel before the Bill pass. *Signed* by Thos. Eyre and 27 others. [Read this day. L. J., XIV. 609.]

376. Dec. 30. Navigation Act Suspension Bill.*—Draft of proceedings in Lords' Committee this day, with List of Amendments, as made this day in Select Committee, and re-amended on 2 Jan. in C. W. H. and on Report. [The Bill was referred on 29 Dec. to the Committee on the Bill to prevent false Musters at Sea. (L. J., XIV. 608.) *Sir Richard Haddock*, who was heard before the Committee this day, said that the Bill, as it was penned, would be very destructive to English seamen. (Com. Book 30 Dec.)—On report, the House was moved to hear Sir Richard Haddock to the Amendment in Sk. 1. Line 18, and as to whether, if the clause stood as it was, it would be for the advantage of the Fleet this summer. (MS. Min. 30 Dec.).—On 31 Dec., before calling in the Commissioners of the Navy and the Members of Trinity House, it was proposed to ask them what inconvenience there would be by half English seamen sailing with foreigners for one year. They were then called in. *Sir Richard Haddock* says there is such a clause passed already, and reads the clause in the Act. This gives discouragement to English seamen. He is asked whether manning ships for trade with half English and half others, will not hurt the manning of the Fleet. *Moved* to re-commit the Bill, and that care be taken that Danish ships may carry back corn. The Bill was then recommitted with directions

* The Bill itself is not among the records, having remained ultimately with the Commons.

to the Committee to draw a clause that nobody harbour seamen (Annex (*b*) below), a clause for encouraging seamen, and that if foreigners be allowed to sail in English ships, they take in part landsmen; and the Commissioners of the Navy and the members of Trinity House were ordered to attend the Committee. *Moved*, That an Address be made to the King that a month's advance be given to the seamen to encourage them to come in. (MS. Min. 31 Dec.; L. J., XIV. 611.)—On 1 Jan., in Committee (on recommitment), the Committee, after resolving by 7 votes to 5 to hear the Commissioners of the Navy and Members of Trinity House, adjourned till the next day. (Com. Book 1 Jan.) The House, however, on the same day, ordered that they should be heard at the Bar.* (L. J., XIV. 612.)—On 2 Jan. the Commissioners, &c. were called in and heard. *Sir R. Haddock:* Thinks it is a discouragement to our seamen and for that of corn. It will hinder shipping. Being asked what was proper to encourage English seamen, he says, that belongs to the Admiralty. They withdraw. A clause to be offered for deterring persons from harbouring seamen. The House then went into Committee on the Bill, E. Pembroke in the Chair. Agreed to begin with the Bill again. Title read and postponed. Preamble read and agreed to. A Proviso offered by L. Cornwallis for half landsmen. The Proviso read twice. Some Merchants at the door desire to be heard. Proposed to ask them whether landsmen are willing to serve, and whether the number of English will be disadvantageous to trade and a mixture. The Merchants were then called in and asked: Whether merchants did not give less wages to foreigners than other seamen. *Mr. Gardiner:* If we are obliged to sail with English seamen, except excempted from pressing, we lose our voyage. Two trades require it, West Indies and the Northern parts. Half landsmen is too many. We desire the time may be limited to the going out. The *Merchants* are heard to the Corn Clause. (*See* Annex (*d.*) below.) They withdraw. Reasons of the Trinity House read. Proposed that a fourth part be foreigners. [Proposed that a fourth part] be English. Question: Whether there shall be three parts foreign and one part English seamen, the Master and officers being English? Resolved in the *Negative*. Contents, 24; Not-Contents, 25. Tellers, E. Scarborough and L. North. Ordered, Half. The House in Committee then agreed to the remaining amendments of the Select Committee, and added a Proviso of E. Nottingham, (*See* Annex (*a.*) below) and a Clause for concealing Seamen (Annex (*b.*) below). The proceedings in the House on report are as in L. J., XIV. 613. (MS. Min. 2 Jan.) The Bill finally dropped in the Commons.]

Annexed:—

(*a.*) Amended† Proviso, marked A., as follows: "Provided always and be it further enacted by the authority aforesaid, That it shall and may be lawful at any time before the *tenth* day of December, which shall be in the year of our Lord 1691, to import any naval commodities in any foreign build shipping, although such commodities be not of the growth of that country where such ship was built, and although the master and three fourths of the mariners be not of that country, and although such commodities be not shipt or brought from the place or places, country or countries of the said growth, production or manufacture, or from those ports where the said goods and commodities can only or

* The MS. Min. state that the Order was that they should be heard "at the "Committee at nine o'clock," the House itself adjourning till 10 o'clock. (MS. Min. 1 Jan.) No further proceedings in the Select Committee, on recommitment, are recorded, nor do they appear to have ever reported.

† The additions are shown by italics and the omissions by square brackets.

House of Lords MSS.

1690.

are or usually have been first shipped for transportation." [Added to the Bill in C. W. H. on 2 Jan. (MS. Min.).]

(*b.*) Amended* Clause, marked B., as follows:—"*And whereas there is* [There being] no *sufficient* discouragement nor penalty upon such as *knowingly* conceal, *rescue* or hide seamen; be it further enacted *by the authority aforesaid* [for the future] that such person as shall *knowingly* conceal [or] hide *or rescue from being employed in their Majesties' service* any seaman, shall forfeit 10*l.*, one [half] *third part* thereof to the Informer, *one other third part to the poor of the parish*, and the other [half] *third part* to be paid into the Chest at Chatham; And for want of sufficient distress, the Party offending to be sent *by any one Justice of the Peace* to the House of Correction, there to be kept to hard labour for [six] *three* months." [Added to the Bill in C. W. H. on 2 Jan. (MS. Min.).]

(*c.*) Amended* clause as follows: "And whereas by the Act of Navigation, rosin and turpentine are prohibited from being imported into this nation from any other parts beyond the seas, except France, and whereas at this present there is a scarcity thereof in this nation, so that without a speedy importation their Majesties' Navy cannot be supplied, Be it enacted by the authority aforesaid That it shall and may be lawful for any of their Majesties' subjects *in English bottoms* to import the said commodities from Holland or any other parts, except France [during the present war] *until the said twenty ninth of September* anything in the said Act or any other Act to the contrary thereof in any wise notwithstanding." [A Clause for importing rosin and turpentine from Holland was read in Select Committee, *Sir Richard Haddock* saying it was a very necessary one, and then agreed to be added (Com. Book 30 Dec. and principal Paper above).]

(*d.*) Draft Clause as follows: "Whereas by an Act made in the first year of their now Majesties' reign, intituled an Act for the encouraging the exportation of corn, it is provided that every merchant or other person, who shall export any corn to parts beyond the seas in English shipping, the master and two thirds of the mariners at the least being their Majesties' subjects, shall receive the several sums of money mentioned in the said Act for encouraging the exportation of corn, when the price thereof is at the respective rates therein mentioned; And whereas the limiting the exportation of such corn to be on English shipping, whereof the master and two thirds of the mariners at least to be their Majesties' subjects, hath in this present time of war prevented the exportation of great quantities of corn, which otherwise would have been exported according to the intent and encouraging of the said Act, in case such corn might have been exported in any ships; Be it therefore enacted by the authority aforesaid, that every merchant or other person, that shall export any corn in any *such* foreign ship, *as shall come freighted with naval stores only, empowered thereunto, by the Act made in the twelfth year of the reign of King Charles the Second, intituled An Act for the encouraging and increasing of shipping and navigation*, or English ship navigated with foreign seamen during the limitation of this Act, according to the other directions of that Act, shall receive the several sums of money

---

* The additions are shown by italics and the omissions by square brackets.

that are appointed by the said Act to be paid upon the exportation of corn as effectually as if such corn had been exported in English ships whereof the master and two thirds of the mariners at least are their Majesties' subjects, anything in the said Act contained to the contrary in any wise notwithstanding." Underwritten is an amendment in Sk. 3, l. 20 of the Bill as brought from the Commons, marked above in italics, and inserted in the Bill in C. W. H. on 2 Jan. (*See* principal Paper above.)

377. Dec. 31. Parliamentary Elections Bill.—Commons' Engrossment of an Act for the speedier determining of questions touching elections of Members to serve in Parliament. § i. Whereas by experience it is found that many more Petitions are presented to the Commons in Parliament assembled in relation to elections then have been heretofore, and many of those Petitions upon causeless pretences, and likewise that pretences are frequently made of elections which are many times found to the contrary and made use only for persons to sit in Parliament when they had no right, which Petitions are of late so numerous that the deciding of them by a Committee doth hinder the business of Parliament and gives oppportunity to the abuse aforesaid; Be it enacted by the King and Queen's most excellent Majesties, by and with the advice and consent of the Lords spiritual and temporal and Commons in Parliament assembled and by the authority of the same, that from and after the determination of this present Parliament, all double returns and other matters relating to elections of members to serve in Parliament shall be heard and determined at the bar of the House of Commons before they proceed upon any other business than the taking the oaths and subscribing the declaration by law required, and no Petition shall be received touching any election or return of members to serve in Parliament unless the same be presented to the House the first day, or within three days after that the House shall sit and the Members then present shall have qualified themselves as aforesaid or within ten days in which the Parliament shall be actually sitting after such election made and declared.

§ ii. And be it further enacted that all and every person and persons intending to petition as aforesaid shall either in person or by his or their agent give notice in writing of such intent within two days after such election made and declared to the person or persons petitioned against, or to the officer or officers making return of the writ or precept respectively, or by leaving such notice at the house or most usual place of his or their respective abode, which election so to be made shall be publicly declared by the respective officer or officers within two days after the closing of the Poll. And all Sheriffs, Mayors, Bailiffs, Portreeves, Constables and other officers of counties, cities, corporations, boroughs, cinque ports and parishes are hereby required to permit the respective parties petitioning or petitioned against or his or their agents respectively upon request, to have and take copies of any polls, charters, parish books, rates or any other records, deeds or writings whatsoever whereby the right of election of such places respectively may be made appear. And all persons as shall be concerned in such cases as shall be found frivolous shall be punished according to the law and custom of Parliament.

§ iii. Provided always that if at any time this Kingdom shall be invaded by any hostile force, or that any insurrection or rebellion shall happen, it shall and may be lawful for the Commons in Parliament assembled to proceed on any business for the support and preservation of the Government and settling and securing the peace of the Kingdom, and to postpone the consideration and determination of all questions and causes touching elections and returns until such invasion be repelled or insurrection suppressed, anything in this Act to the contrary notwithstanding. *Parchment Collection.* [Brought from the Commons this day. L. J., XIV. 611. Committee and Third Reading were negatived on 5 Jan., *ib.* 617.]

1691.

378. Jan. 2. Prisoners for Debt Act.—Draft of concluding Proviso in the Act for relief of poor Prisoners for debt or damages, making the judgment still good, after discharge, against lands and goods. *Noted* as agreed to this day. [Added in Committee, L. Cornwallis in the Chair, on 31 Dec., and agreed to, with the other amendments, which are unimportant, on report this day. (Com. Book, L. J., XIV. 613.) The Bill received the Royal Assent on 5 Jan. (*ib.* 618); 2 W. & M. Sess. 2, c. 15 in Fol. Ed., 2 & 3 W. & M. c. 37 in Long Calendar.]

379. Jan. 3. French Trade (Prohibition) Act.—Petition of the Company of Vintners, London. A Bill has lately passed the House of Commons, enacting, among other things, that any person convicted after 1 Feb. 1690–1 of selling by retail, in any glass, bottle, or other retail measure not made of pewter, any kind of wine, shall forfeit 50*s.*, to be recovered by distress and sale of goods. This provision will encourage perjury, discourage trade, and ruin Petitioners. Pray to be heard by Counsel against the clause, which enacts a new way of conviction. *Signed* Rich. Kinsey and Mich. Waring. L. J., XIV. 615. [The Bill was read 1ª this day; Royal Assent 5 Jan. (L. J., XIV. 615, 618). 2 W. & M. Sess. 2. c. 14 (Fol. Ed.) In Committee, on 5 Jan., Counsel for the Vintners were heard against the clause in question. *Serjeant Thompson:* If the Vintners sell in quarts they can sell no wine out of doors. This will diminish the King's duty in wine licenses. This conviction before a Justice of Peace takes away the trial by jury. *Mr. Ward:* Speaks to the prices set for wines. The former Act sets no price on Spanish wine, and this Act directs it shall be sold according to prices set by that Act, whereas that Act sets no price; so Spanish wine cannot be sold at all. Italian wines come over in flasks, and cannot be sold by quarts. *Serjeant Thompson:* There is no appeal left from the conviction before the Justices. They withdraw. *Question:* Whether to agree to the second enacting clause as in the Bill? Contents 4; Not Contents 5; Resolved in the *Negative.* 2 Sk., 4 l. After ("by") add ("or"). *Question:* Whether to agree, with the clause so amended? Contents 6; Not Contents 2; Resolved. in the *Affirmative.* Ordered to be reported with the said amendment (Com. Book, L. J., XIV. 617.) See also No. **350.**]

380. March 31. Writ of Summons (V. Villiers).—Writ of Summons, dated 30 March, to Edward, Viscount Villiers. [Took the Oaths this day. L. J., XIV. 619.]

381. April 28. Writ of Summons (E. Sunderland).—Writ of Summons, dated 6 Feb. 1689–90, to Robert, Earl of Sunderland. [Took the Oaths this day. L. J., XIV. 619.]

382. May 26. Writ of Summons (E. Suffolk).—Writ of Summons dated May 19, to Henry, Earl of Suffolk. [Took the Oaths this day L. J., XIV. 620.]

383. May 26. Hall *v.* Fisher.—Writ of Error, brought in by Holt, C. J., this day. L. J., XIV. 620. *Parchment Collection.*

384. May 26. Hall *v.* Fisher.—Petition of James Caldwell, Bart. After great expense and delay, caused by William Fisher in contesting Petitioner's right to a horse, Petitioner obtained a verdict. Fisher moved five times in Chancery to stay execution, but failing, has brought a writ of Error merely to keep Petitioner out of possession. Prays that the writ of Error may not debar him from proceeding at law on the judgment. L. J., XIV. 620.

385. May 26. King's Servant's Privilege (Cockayne).—Petition of James Cockayne, servant to their Majesties and sworn Equerry in Ordinary. Petitioner was arrested and detained in prison since the last adjournment by Thomas Sheppard, John Wood and Francis Rouse, Attorneys, and Thomas Greenfield, — Kettleby, Francis Naylor and Cornelius Jones, Bailiffs, at the suits of Edward Basse, Robert Palgrave, Henry Warner, Tho. Maning and Robt. Watson, contrary to Privilege. Prays for release and that the offenders may be punished. *Endorsed* as read this day and be discharged. L. J., XIV. 620.

386. May 26. Prorogation.—Commission for proroguing Parliament to 30 June next. *Dated* this day. L. J., XIV 620. *In extenso. Parchment Collection.*

387. June 30. Prorogation.—Commission for proroguing Parliament to 3 August next. *Dated* this day. L. J., XIV. 622. *In extenso. Parchment Collection.*

388. Aug. 3. Prorogation.—Commission for proroguing Parliament to 5 October next. *Dated* this day. L. J., XIV. 623. *In extenso. Parchment Collection.*

389. Oct. 5. Writ of Summons (Archbishop of Canterbury).—Writ of Summons, dated August 3, to John [Tillotson], Archbishop of Canterbury. [Took the Oaths this day. L. J., XIV. 624.]

390. Oct. 5. Writ of Summons (Archbishop of York).—Writ of Summons, dated August 3, to John [Sharpe], Archbishop of York. [Took the Oaths this day. L. J., XIV. 624.]

391. Oct. 5. Prorogation.—Commission for proroguing Parliament till the 22nd instant. *Dated* this day. L. J., XIV. 624. *In extenso. Parchment Collection.*

392. Oct. 22. King's Speech.—His Majesty's Speech at the opening of Parliament this day. L. J., XIV. 625. *In extenso.*

393. Oct. 22. Writ of Summons (Bishop of Norwich).—Writ of Summons, dated Oct. 5, to John [Moore], Bishop of Norwich. [Took the Oaths this day. L. J., XIV. 625.]

394. Oct. 22. Writ of Summons (E. Westmoreland).—Writ of Summons, dated Oct. 20, to Vere, Earl of Westmoreland. [Took the Oaths this day. L. J., XIV. 625.]

395. Oct. 22. Clandestine Marriages Bill.—Amended* Draft of an Act disabling Minors to marry without the consent of their fathers or guardians and against their untimely marrying after the decease of their fathers and for preventing all clandestine marriages for the future.

* The additions are shown by italics, and the omissions by square brackets.

§ i. Whereas Minors are daily subject to be inveigled or forced away from their fathers or guardians, and thereupon do contract matrimony with persons unsuitable, before they are of years capable to dispose of themselves with that discretion which is requisite, and notwithstanding the severities of former laws, yet, there being no provision to annul such marriages, wicked persons presume they shall afterwards obtain the consent and reconciliation of friends, and are thereby encouraged to the said evil practices; And whereas clandestine marriages are and have been found to be of very pernicious consequence, and have given occasion to many wicked practices and disorders in families; Be it enacted by the King and Queen's Most Excellent Majesties, &c, That from and after the *thirtieth* day of *March in the year of our Lord* one thousand, six hundred, ninety [one] *two*, it shall not be in the power of any son, being under the age of [one and twenty]* *eighteen* years, nor in the power of any daughter, being under the age of [eighteen]* *sixteen* years, to marry him or herself, or to make any matrimonial contract of any kind whatsoever, except his or her father, in case he be then living, or his or her guardian or guardians, after the decease of the father, or the major part of them, if more than two, shall be present and consenting thereunto, or shall have given consent by writing, signed in the presence of two or more credible witnesses precedent to such marriage; but all such minors without such consent or being present are hereby made incapable and disabled to marry or make any matrimonial contract; and *therefore* all marriages and matrimonial contracts, that after the said *thirtieth* day of *March* shall be made without such consent or being present as aforesaid, shall be and are hereby enacted to be null and ipso facto void to all intents and purposes whatsoever.

§ ii. And be it further enacted, That after the death of the father it shall not be in the power of any son of such deceased father, being under the age of [eighteen]† *sixteen* years to marry himself or make any matrimonial contract, although with the consent of his guardian or guardians, nor shall it be in the power of any daughter of such deceased father, being under the age of [sixteen]† *fourteen* years, to marry herself or make any matrimonial contract, although with the consent of her guardian or guardians, but that, notwithstanding such consent, the marriage of such minors after the death of their fathers, under the said respective ages of [eighteen] *sixteen* years, if sons, and [sixteen] *fourteen* years, if daughters, shall be and are hereby enacted to be null and ipso facto void to all intents and purposes whatsoever.

§ iii. And be it further enacted, That in case of any pretended marriage had by such minor against the true intent and meaning of this Act, no right or title to any goods or chattels, or to any dower or tenancy by the curtesie, or to demand any benefit of any law or custom whatsoever, shall accrue by reason of any such pretended marriage, and it shall and may be lawful for the father or guardians, or any other friend of any such minor, to prosecute, in the name of any such minor,

---

* The amendment first proposed, but negatived without a division, was to substitute 16 and 14 for 21 and 18. (MS. Min. 30 Oct.)

† "*Question:* Whether the ages of (18) and (16) shall stand? Resolved in the *Negative*. Contents 17; Not-Contents 22. Tellers, L. Berkeley and L. Cornwallis. *Question:* Whether instead of (18) and (16), it shall be (16) and (14)? Resolved in the *Affirmative*. Contents 22; Not-Contents 17." (MS. Min. 2 Nov.)

or in his own name, in any Ecclesiastical Court where the matter may be conusable, any cause of jactitation of marriage or other suit, whereby to have such pretended marriage declared null and void, and without any let or contradiction of any such minor during such time as such minor shall continue under the respective ages wherein he or she are disabled to contract matrimony according to the true intent and meaning of this Act.

§ iv. And be it further enacted, that if any guardian shall be any way contriving, aiding, or consenting to any such pretended marriage or matrimonial contract of any minors contrary to the true intent and meaning of this Act, that thereupon such guardian shall be and is hereby declared for ever incapable of holding or enjoying any employment, profit, place, or office, either ecclesiastical or civil, and shall also forfeit the value of one third part of the estate, real or personal, of the minor to whose pretended marriage he hath been so contriving or consenting, and that the right, title, and interest to the custody or guardianship of any such minors shall remain and be in the other guardians or guardian that was not contriving, aiding, or consenting to such marriage, if there be any such, and if there be none such, then the said custody and guardianship shall come and be, and is hereby vested in the next of kin to such minor that is of full age, to whom the estate of such minor cannot immediately descend by course of inheritance; and the value of the said third part to be recovered in any of their Majesties' Courts at Westminster, by action of debt, bill, plaint, or information, wherein no essoigne, protection, or wager of law shall be allowed, the one moiety to the poor of the parish where the guardian or guardians so offending shall reside, which said moiety to be appropriated to the orphans and poor of the said parish, to the putting them apprentices, and the other moiety to the informer.

§ v. And be it further enacted, That in case any domestic or menial servant shall take upon him or her to make any pretended marriage or matrimonial contract between him or herself and any the children or pupils of his or her master or mistress during such their minority, or if any such servant shall seduce or betray, or be knowingly aiding and assisting to inveigle such child to marry any other in such manner as that the same is by this Act declared to be invalid, null and void, That then and in every such case, such servant, being lawfully convicted thereof, shall be committed to prison, there to remain by the space of three years in some House of Correction in the county where the said offence was committed, without bail or mainprize, and there to be kept to hard labour and receive correction in the same manner as rogues and vagabonds ought to have by course of law.

§ vi. And be it further enacted by the authority aforesaid, That whosoever, not being a household servant in the family, shall make any such pretended marriage or matrimonial contract, or be knowingly aiding or assisting to the same, or shall inveigle and marry any such minor, he or she so marrying, or being knowingly aiding or assisting to the same, shall forfeit one-third part of what he was [really] worth *in real and personal estate* at the time the fact was committed, one moiety whereof shall be to the informer, and the other moiety to the uses of the poor, as the other forfeitures are directed to be recovered, by action of debt, bill, plaint, or information in any of their said Majesties' Courts of Record, wherein no essoigne, protection, or wager of law shall be allowed, and shall also suffer three years' imprisonment in the common gaol, without bail or mainprize.

§ vii. And be it further enacted by the Authority aforesaid,* [That if any Chancellor, Commissary, or Official, or their Surrogates or any other person having or pretending to have power to grant Licences to marry, whether in places of ordinary jurisdiction, or in any exempt, peculiar, or privileged place] shall after the said *thirtieth* day of *March* grant any Licence for the marrying of any person (not being in the estate of widowhood, *or above the age of eighteen years if males, nor sixteen years if females*) whose [parents or one of them are] *father* is living, without the consent of such [parents or parent] *father* personally present or a certificate of such consent signed and sealed by such [parents or parent] *father* in the presence of a Justice of the Peace of the County where such [parents or parent] *father* shall then dwell, and attested by the said Justice of the Peace under his hand and seal and by the oaths of two credible witnesses, who have heard the [parents or parent] *father* declare [their or] his consent and seen the said certificate sealed and subscribed by [them or him] and the said Justice of the Peace, or shall grant any Licence for the marrying of any minor whose [parents are] *father* is dead, without full proof, upon the oath of two credible witnesses, that such minor is at least of the age of [eighteen] *sixteen*, if male, and [sixteen] *fourteen* if female, and likewise without the consent of his or her guardian or guardians personally present, or a certificate of his or their consent, signed and sealed by such guardians or guardian in the presence of a Justice of Peace of the county where such guardians or guardian shall then dwell, and attested by the said Justice of the Peace under his hand and seal and by the oaths of two credible witnesses, who have heard the guardians or guardian declare their consent, and seen him or them and the said Justice of the Peace subscribe and seal the said certificate, then every person aforesaid granting such license shall forfeit five hundred pounds, to be recovered and disposed of as the other forfeitures in this Act are directed, and shall also lose and forfeit his office, by reason or pretence whereof he was empowered to grant licenses of marriage, and all other ecclesiastical promotions, and be disabled for ever after to hold that or the like office or any other ecclesiastical or civil office, benefice, place or promotion whatsoever.†

[§ viii.] § ix. And be it enacted by the authority aforesaid, That any person in Holy Orders or pretending to Holy Orders, who shall marry or join in marriage such minor without such license as is directed by this Act, or without the publication of the banns in manner as is by law appointed, shall be and is hereby adjudged a felon, and shall suffer death as in case of felony without benefit of clergy, and that the father

---

* Here is marked for insertion Clause A, (Annex (*b.*) below), in place of the words immediately following in square brackets. With regard to Clause vii. the following notes appear. In C. W. H. on 6 Nov. after making all the amendments marked above, with the exception of the first one, on Question whether the Clause of disability shall stand, it was, after debate, Resolved in the Negative. Then on Question whether the 500*l.* forfeit shall stand, Resolved in the Negative. The Clause read without a penalty. House resumed. (MS. Min. L. J., XIV. 634.) On 9 Nov. in C. W. H. the whole of the Clause was agreed, after debate, to be postponed, and the Committee reported accordingly. (MS. Min. L. J., XIV. 639.) On 10 Nov. on consideration of the Report, a Clause (*see* Annexes (*b.*) and (*c.*) below) was offered and read, to be instead of the Clause postponed, and the House, on motion, recommitted the Bill. House adjourned during pleasure, and put into a Committee on the Clause. The Clause read. *Question:* Whether upon this part of the Proviso (*see* Annex (*c.*) below) the words ("Knowingly and wittingly") shall be part of the question? The Clause agreed to as amended. House resumed. Bp. Sarum reported as in L. J., XIV. 640. The Clause was then read and agreed to. (MS. Min.)

† Here is marked for insertion Proviso B. (Annex (*c*) below.

of such minor, and for want of such father, the mother, and if there be no father or mother, then the guardian not consenting to such marriage, and for want of such guardian, or in default of such prosecution by such guardian or any other person aforesaid, for the space of twelve months after such marriage, then the next of kin of such minor, shall have an appeal of felony against such person and persons in Holy Orders or pretending to Holy Orders, and shall have the suit to pursue the same to have them convict of life, wherein the Defendant shall not be received to wage battail, but that the truth of the matter shall be tried by inquisition of the country, neither shall any pardon be pleaded in bar of such suit or in stay of judgment or execution of the same.

[§ ix.] § x. Provided always that where the City of London or any other city or corporation have right to the guardianship or custody of any orphan, their consent in writing under their common seal to any marriage shall be sufficient within this law, according to the limitation of ages for minors before expressed.

* [§ x. Provided also that no marriage shall be impeached by virtue of this Act, where the parties shall cohabit until their respective full ages of five and twenty years, if males, and one and twenty years, if females, without any actual separation or suit commenced in some of their said Majesties' Ecclesiastical Courts for declaring the nullity of such marriage during such their minority, but that all such marriages shall be taken to be had with due consent according to the rules and provisions of this Act.]

§ xi. Provided also that, where the father of any minor shall by his last will or any other writing signed and attested as abovesaid, testify his approbation or consent to any marriage to be had by any of his children, and such marriage be accordingly had after his death, that such marriage shall be as valid as if he had been living and present and consenting thereunto.

† § xii. And for the preventing of all other irregular and clandestine marriages for the future, Be it further enacted, that if any parson, vicar or curate of any parish church or chapel, or the minister of any exempt, peculiar or privileged place, or any other person in Holy Orders, or pretending to be in Holy Orders, shall, from and after the said *thirtieth* day of *March*, officiate in the marriage of any persons without such publication of the banns as by law is required, or without license first had and obtained from such person as hath authority to grant licenses for marrying in the place where the parties to be married, or one of them, doth inhabit or reside, or shall officiate in such marriage at any other time or in any other place than by law is appointed, then every person so officiating shall for the first offence be suspended ab officio et beneficio, and be committed to the common gaol, there to continue for three years without bail or mainprize, and for the second offence shall be deprived of all his ecclesiastical benefices and preferments and be incapable of any such benefices or preferments for ever, and if he hath no such benefices or preferments, he shall be devested of his canonical habit and degraded from his ministry by the Bishop of the diocese, and be committed to the House of Correction for one year, there to be kept to hard labour and treated as rogues and vagabonds use to be.‡

[§ xiii.] § xiv. And be it further enacted by the authority aforesaid, That this Act shall be publicly read presently after Divine Service upon

* This Proviso was left out in C. W. H. on 9 Nov. (MS. Min.).

† This Clause was first left out in C. W. H. on 9 Nov., but afterwards reinstated, as appears from the Draft Bill itself, and from the List of Amendments in Annex (*a*.), where the amendment to omit it is struck through.

‡ Here is marked for insertion Clause φ (Annex (*d*.) below).

some Sunday before the said *first* day of January, *one thousand six hundred, ninety one*, in every Church and Chapel within the Kingdom of England, Dominion of Wales and Town of Berwick-upon-Tweed, *on the last Sunday in every month till the first day of January, one thousand, six hundred, ninety two*,* and shall also be read yearly in all Churches and Chapels the [last] *first* Sunday in Lent.

[Read 1ª this day. L. J., XIV. 626. After being considered in C. W. H. on Oct. 30 and Nov. 2, 6, and 9, the Bill was reported by the Chairman, the Bishop of Salisbury, with amendments (Annex (*a.*) below), and a postponed clause (§ vii.) concerning the grant of licences, in lieu of which another clause (Annexes (*b.*) and (*c.*) below) was offered on report, agreed to with amendments in C. W. H., on recommitment, and finally agreed to by the House on report. (L. J., XIV. 640. MS. Min. 10 Nov.) The Bill finally dropped in the Commons, though the Lords sent three messages to remind them of it. (L. J., XV. 13, 81, 88.).]

Annexed :—

(*a.*) 9 Nov. List of Amendments to the Bill. [Made in C. W. H. on Oct. 30, and Nov. 2 and 9, and reported this day. (L. J., XIV. 639.) *See* text above.]

(*b.*) 10 Nov. Amended Clause A. entitled "Clause for the Act of Clandestine Marriages, fol. 19." as follows "[And be it further enacted by the Authority aforesaid, That] from and after the 30th day of March, which shall be in the year of our Lord, 1692, no Licences shall be granted to dispense with the thrice open publication of Banns in the solemnization of matrimony, by any persons whatever exercising any ecclesiastical jurisdictions, or claiming any privileges or liberties in the right of their churches or otherwise, [But the same shall be granted] *except* by the persons hereafter named and by no other, *according to the Canons*, and in manner and form following; that is to say, From and after the 30th day of March aforesaid, all Licences for dispensation of the thrice open publication of the Banns of matrimony betwixt any persons shall be granted only by the Vicars Generals of the Archbishops of Canterbury and York for the time being, to the inhabitants of their respective Provinces, as well in places exempt as not exempt, or by some *one* person [or persons] deputed by the said Vicars Generals with the approbation of the said Archbishops respectively, and by the Commissary of the Archbishop of Canterbury (who is styled the Master of the Faculties) for the time being, or by some person deputed by him with the approbation of the said Archbishop, and by the Vicars Generals, who are styled the Chancellors, of the respective Bishops of each province for the time being, to the inhabitants of their respective Dioceses as well in places exempt as not exempt within the limits of their respective Dioceses, or by some *one* person [or persons] deputed by the said Vicars Generals *or Chancellors* with the approbation of their respective Bishops, and by the Commissaries of the Archbishop of Canterbury for the time being for his Diocese of Canterbury, and such Churches and parishes as are annexed to the Archiepiscopal See of Canterbury and lie in the City of London and in the counties of Kent, Middlesex, and Surrey, to the inhabitants of the said Dioceses and parishes only, or by some *one* person [or persons] deputed by the said Commissaries with the approbation of the said Archbishop, and by the Vicars Generals of the Guardians

* The Amendment first proposed was ("during the year 1692").

of the Spiritualities, and Commissary or Master of the Faculties in the vacancies of the respective Sees of the Archbishops and Bishops, or by some *one* person [or persons] deputed by them with the approbation of the said Guardians; and by the Dean of Windsor for the time being to the inhabitants within the Castle of Windsor only; And by the [Dean] *Commissary of the Dean and Chapter* of Westminster [or his Commissary] for the time being *or some one person deputed by him, with the approbation of the said Dean and Chapter*, to the inhabitants [of that part of] *within* the City of Westminster only [which lies within the jurisdiction of the Dean and Chapter of Westminster]; for which Licences no more shall be taken than the ancient accustomed Fee settled by the authentic and approved Tables within each respective office, which Fee shall be divided betwixt the officers, who are hereby authorized to grant the said Licences, and the Registers of the said Archbishops and Bishops of each Province, according to the said authentic and approved Tables: and if any question arise concerning the said Fee, it shall be determined by the said Archbishops and Bishops respectively; *And if any of the said persons hereby empowered to grant Licences* [*shall after*] . . . ." [Agreed to this day on report of C. W. H. after recommitment. L. J., XIV. 640. *See* § vii. of the Bill above.]

(*c*.) 10 Nov. Amended Proviso B. entitled "Proviso for the Deputies," as follows: "Provided and it is hereby enacted, That if any Deputies of the said respective officers aforesaid, who are hereby authorized and empowered to grant the said Licences for dispensation of the publication of the Banns of matrimony as aforesaid, shall by virtue or colour of their respective deputations [knowingly and wittingly] grant any such Licences as aforesaid contrary to the express rules and directions of this Act, That then the said respective officer or officers [only] as aforesaid, who deputed the said Deputy or Deputies so offending as aforesaid, shall be liable to the pains and penalties of this Act, [and not the said Deputy or Deputies as aforesaid;] Nor shall any Archbishop or Bishop be liable to the pains and penalties of this Act by reason of any approbation of the said Deputy or Deputies as aforesaid, anything in this Act to the contrary notwithstanding." [Agreed to this day on report of C. W. H., after recommitment, and added as § viii. to the Bill. *See* Note to § vii. of the Bill above.]

(*d*.) 11 Nov. Amended Clause ϕ as follows: "Provided always and be it enacted by the authority as aforesaid, That if any forged or counterfeited Licence shall be brought to any person *or minister* so officiating, he shall not incur the pains and penalties before mentioned, [but] if he hath notice that such Licence was forged; but he or they that shall *procure or knowingly* produce or deliver such forged or counterfeited Licence [or shall forge such Licence] or shall swear falsely to any certificate [for the obtaining of any such Licence or shall] *from the father or guardian of any such minor or shall* personate the father or guardian or affirm himself to be the father or guardian of such [child] *minor* for the procuring such Licence, every such offence shall be felony, and the person and persons so offending shall suffer death as in cases of felony without benefit of clergy, being thereof convicted or attainted upon an indictment or an appeal *to*

HOUSE OF LORDS MSS.

1691.

be brought by the persons in the manner as above mentioned.*" [On 10 Nov. a Clause concerning the forging of Licences, and another Clause, concerning Quakers' Marriages, were offered to the House, on report from C. W. H., and referred to a Select Committee. (L. J., XIV. 640. MS. Min., 10 Nov.) On 11 Nov. the Select Committee agreed to the Clause concerning forged Licences, but after reading the other Clause, left its consideration to the House. (Com. Book, 11 Nov.) The Clause concerning forged Licences was agreed to *eod. die* by the House on report, and added as § xiii. to the Bill. (L. J., XIV., 642. MS. Min., 11 Nov.) A Proviso for Quakers was offered to the House on the third reading on 21 Nov. and agreed to by 16 votes to 13, V. Longueville being Teller for the Contents and L. Culpeper for the Not-Contents.† (L. J., XIV. 656. MS. Min., 21 Nov.)]

396. Oct. 22. Whitaker *v.* Pawlin.—Petition and Appeal of Edward Whitaker, Gent. Petitioner, in 1682, being under the displeasure of the Government, was forced to withdraw himself, leaving 500*l.* for the support of his family in the hands of John Loggin, for which he took a Bond in the name of John Cooch in trust. Loggin afterwards joined his father and brother, Will. Pawlin and Will. Loggin, in the purchase of a lease from one Probee of certain ironworks and mills at Crawford, Kent, his contribution being 1,900*l.* In 1685 he became a bankrupt, and by a contrivance with his partners, on a pretended difference of accounts obtained an award from his uncle John Trinder, who had been appointed umpire to settle the affairs of the co-partnery, which award, though unjust, and defrauding his creditors of 1,900*l.*, was confirmed by a Decree in Chancery. Before the award was given, Loggin was proved a bankrupt before the Commissioners of Bankrupt, Thomas Goodinge, Esq., Robert Blayney, Esq. and John Cole, Gent., who assigned the mill to one John Smith, who undertook to sue for and recover the estate for the good of the creditors, who paid him a contribution for that purpose. This, however, by collusion with the partners, he refused to do, setting up the award and Decree in answer to Petitioner's Bill in Chancery to have an account of the Estate, and the Commissioners refused to force him to act. Petitioner's Bill was dismissed on 15 January last. Appeals against the dismission, and calls the Loggins, Pawlin, Cooch, Smith, the Commissioners, and one Wm. Newsame as Respondents. *Signed* by Appellant; *Countersigned* by Ambr. Phillipps and Jos. Washington. Read this day. L. J., XIV. 627. [The Appeal was heard on 18 Nov. 1691, *Sir Ambrose Phillipps* and *Mr. Finch* appearing for Appellant, and *Sir William Williams* for Respondent. MS. Min. L. J., XIV. 651. *See also* 2 *Vernon* 229.]

Annexed :—

(*a.*) 2 Nov. Answer of Thomas Goodinge and Robert Blayney, Esquires, and John Cole, Gent. Admit Petitioner's allegations, but pray to be dismissed as not being concerned in the dispute, otherwise than as Commissioners of Bankrupt. *Signed* by Respondents, and *countersigned* Fr. Tyton. *Endorsed* as brought in this day

* This amendment originally read: "*to be brought by the next kin to such minors as above mentioned.*"

† The engrossment of this Proviso was lost with the remainder of the Bill in the Commons, and no draft of it is found among the records.

(*b.*) 3 Nov. Answer of William Pawlin, William Loggin, William Newsam, and John Smith. John Loggin, who was to contribute 600*l.* to the partnership, contributed nothing, and was ordered by the award to pay 1,200*l.*, and 200*l.* towards losses. He was found to have defrauded present Respondents of over 72*l.* He further owes Pawlin 600*l.*, and Wm. Loggin 100*l.* over and above the award. Newsam was only a servant to the partners. Smith, the Assignee in Bankruptcy, has only 2*l.* of the contribution money in his hands. He is willing to be a party. The award and Decree were made before any steps were taken in the Bankruptcy. *Signed* by Respondents and *countersigned* Wm. Whitelocke. *Endorsed* as brought in this day. *See* L. J., XIV. 651.

(*c.*) 6 Nov. Petition of Appellant for a day for hearing, Respondents having answered, and that Mr. Carter, Pawlin's clerk in the Court of Chancery, produce at the hearing the Docket for the inrolling the Decree of 1685. L. J., XIV. 635.

(*d.*) 13 Feb. 1691–2. Petition of William Pawlin and Wm. Loggin. The Judgment of the House of 18 Nov. (L. J., XIV. 651) does not set aside the award or Decree, but leaves Appellant at liberty to charge Petitioners with any of John Loggin's Estate not comprised therein. Appellant had petitioned that Counsel might be heard in explanation of the Judgment, and a hearing had been ordered but not had. Pray that Counsel may be heard. Read this day. L. J., XV. 75.

(*e.*) 16 Feb. 1691–2. Petition of Appellant. Since his Petition of 30 Dec. last, praying for Counsel to be heard to explain the Judgment of the House, the Master in Chancery has proceeded on the Account, so that there is no further occasion to trouble their Lordships. Prays to withdraw his Petition. Read this day. L. J., XV. 79.

(*f.*) 23 Nov. 1692. Petition of William Pawlin and Wm. Loggin. The Court of Chancery had put off hearing exceptions to a Master's Report, that either side might apply to their Lordships for explanation of their Judgment of 18 Nov. 1691. Appellant had not renewed his application for that purpose. Pray that Counsel might be heard on the subject. Read this day. L. J., XV. 123. [Counsel were heard on 22 Dec. 1692 on this Petition and the answer thereto (Annex (*h.*) below), *Sir Thomas Powys* and *Mr. Filmer* appearing for Petitioners, and *Mr. Finch* and *Mr. Ward* for Respondent. (M.S. Min. L. J., XV. 161.)]

(*g.*) 30 Nov. 1692. Petition of Appellant. The Master has reported in Pawlin's and William Loggin's hands, of the Bankrupt's estate, 1,621*l.* 6*s.* 1*d.*, besides the interest in the iron mills. Pawlin and Wm. Loggin have filed exceptions for delay, but suggest no new matter. Prays that their Petition (preceding paper) may be dismissed. *See* L. J., XV. 130.

(*h.*) 30 Nov. 1692. Answer of Edward Whitaker to Petition of Pawlin and Wm. Loggin (Annex *f.*). The cause has been finally determined by the House, and there is nothing depending before it. *See* L. J., XV. 130.

397. Oct. 22. Browne *v.* Waight (Wayte).—Copy Writ of Error dated 14 Sept. 1691, &c. and transcript of record, with Issue joined by Defendant and Tenor of Judgment of the House noted at the end.

The Appeal is brought by Richard Browne against Ayloffe Wayte, executor of the late Edmund Wayte, who ejected Plaintiff in 1674 from the manor, &c. of Dauntsey, Wilts, which Plaintiff claimed under a lease for 7 years from 8 May 1674 from John Danvers, son and heir of Sir John Danvers, the brother and heir of Henry, E. Danby. Wayte admitted the ejectment, but claimed previous possession, on the ground that the said manors, having been in the possession of Sir John Danvers, who was specially exempted from the Act of free and general Pardon, were forfeited to the Crown, and were granted by Letters Patent of Charles II., dated 20 Sept. 1662, to James, Duke of York, who demised them to Edward Wayte for a term of years yet unexpired. Edward Wayte died before the appeal to the Court of Exchequer Chamber, which on 15 June 1689 affirmed the judgment of the Court of King's Bench,* finding Plaintiff guilty and awarding 150*l.* damages and costs. The Appeal is from this Judgment. [Brought in this day. L. J., XIV. 625. The Cause was heard on 23 Nov. 1691. *Sir Cresswell Levinz* (for Plaintiff): It was a judgment in the King's Bench against my client. The verdict found was that Sir John Danvers was in possession of the estate. The King grants this manor to the Duke of York, and Mr. Danvers brought an action *in ejectione firmæ*. Mr. Danvers brought his Writ of Error, and upon a division of votes the judgment was affirmed. *Mr. Finch* (for Plaintiff): The case is the exposition of the words in the Act of Pains and Penalties. Reads the words of the Act. *The Attorney General* and *Solicitor General* heard for Defendant. Debate and giving Judgment adjourned. (M.S. Min.)—On 25 Nov. the Judges gave their opinions. *Holt, C. J.:* Reads the words in the Act of Pains and Penalties. The question is, whether this manor of Dauntsey be forfeited. I am of opinion that the Judgments are well given and that the lands are forfeited by the words of the Act. *Athyns, C.B.:* I am of the same opinion with the Lord Chief Justice, that it is a forfeiture. *Dolben, J.:* I am of the same opinion. *Nevill, J.:* I was of opinion that the judgment given in this case ought to be affirmed. I am of the same opinion still, and that it is a forfeiture. *Powell, J.:* I am of the same opinion that these lands of Sir John Danvers are forfeited to the Crown. *Gregory, J.:* I am of the same opinion, that it is a forfeiture. *Lechmere, B.:* The case is rightly stated. The question is, whether by these general words in the Act an estate tail is forfeited. It is the first case that ever an estate tail has been forfeited by general words. The question is, whether the Statute *de donis* shall be repealed by these general words. The [estate] is not forfeited. *Rokeby, J.:* I gave my judgment in the Exchequer for affirming the judgment in the King's Bench, and I am of the same opinion still. *Eyre, J.:* I am of opinion that the judgments given below ought to be affirmed. *Turton, B.:* I was one of those two Judges that were of opinion it was not forfeited, and I see no reason to alter my opinion. *Powell, B.:* I am of opinion that it is a forfeiture. After long debate, Question put: Whether this debate shall be adjourned to Saturday next [28 Nov.]? Resolved in the *Negative*. Contents 36 (including 4 Proxies); Not Contents 36 (including 1 Proxy). Tellers, M. Halifax and E. Rochester. After debate, *Question* put: Whether to hear all the Judges before proceeding to judgment in this case? *Previous question* put: Whether this question shall be now put? Resolved in the *Affirmative*. Contents 39; Not Contents 27: Tellers, E. Warrington and V. Longueville. *Main question* put and resolved in *Affirmative*. Debate adjourned and all the Judges to attend. (M.S. Min.)—On

* 2 Mod. Rep. 130.

28 Nov. the MS. Min. contain the following cancelled entry: "House moved that the L. C. Baron give the House account whether it be not inconvenient for the Judges to attend on Monday next in the case of Browne v. Waight. *L. C. Baron* [Atkyns]: The next day after the term there are trials for Middlesex and London constantly. I intend to go into London on Monday to hear my causes." (MS. Min.)—On 30 Nov. the Judges were heard upon the whole case again. *Holt, C. J.:* I am of the same opinion, and am now confirmed in it, that this estate tail of Sir John Danvers is forfeited. *Atkyns, C.B.:* I am of the same opinion I was. *Dolben, J.:* I am of the same opinion, as before. *Nevill, J.:* I am of the same opinion as before, that it is forfeited. *Powell, J.:* I am of the same opinion as before, that it is forfeited. *Gregory, B.:* Of the same opinion as before. *Letchmere, B.:* 1 Edw. VI., c. 12. No forfeiture ought to be reversed. *Rokesby, J.:* I am of the same opinion, that the estate tail is forfeited. *Eyre, J.:* I am of the same opinion as before. *Turton, B.:* It depends only upon the Act of Pains and Penalties. I conceive that by that Statute it is not forfeited. *Powell, B.:* I am of the same opinion, that this estate tail of Sir John Danvers is forfeited. *Judges* asked, whether the general words will operate upon marriage settlements, and whether if Sir John Danvers had made a marriage settlement, it would not have hurt it? *The Judges* are of opinion that it affects not anything but what he was possessed of. *Question* proposed to ask the Judges: Whether the affirming the judgment in this case can in any manner affect the estates and settlements of any person not particularly named in the Act of Pains and Penalties or any marriage settlement? This it was agreed it could not. *Question* proposed and asked: Whether this is the first precedent of any judgment given upon general words that they forfeited an estate tail, and whether Judgments have been given formerly, whereby a forfeiture has been made, where there has not been a conviction or attainder? *Holt, C. J.:* I do not know whether ever there was the like case. As the cause was without precedent, so is the instance without precedent. The other Judges of the same opinion. *Moved*, that the case of *Adams v. Lambert** be argued by the Judges. *Holt, C. J.:* This was to keep up a superstitious use. It was judged that the estate tail was forfeited. This is a full case, an estate tail forfeited by general words. *Atkyns, C.B.:* Without express words the estate tail is forfeited. *Lechmere, B.:* This is not of the nature of estate tail for treason. I said there was no judgment of estate tail by general words. This was an estate tail by condition he was to receive no benefit by it. There is not one instance in my reading and observation of any estate tail forfeited by general words. [*Question*]: Whether general words have at any time disposed of an estate tail in case of treason? After debate, *Question* put to the Judges: Whether the word ("Interest") in Savill's case has not been adjudged to carry the estate tail? Coke's Reports. *Holt, C.J.:* The word ("Interest"), I take it, comprehends all manner of estates whatsoever. All [the Judges are] of the same mind. *Question* proposed: Whether this word ("Interest") would go, if a man makes a settlement with power of revocation, and becomes tenant for life? *Holt, C. J.:* If a man reserves a power of revocation by deed which is not annexed, it is forfeited. *Question:* How the difference is between the case of *Adams* v. *Lambert* and this? *Turton, B.:* That was for superstitious uses, and a nominal estate. There is no parity in the cases. The case read out of Coke's 4th Report. After debate *Question* put: Whether upon this Writ of Error the

* 4 Coke's Rep. 96, 104.

House of Lords MSS. — 1691.

Judgment given in the Exchequer Chamber shall be affirmed? Resolved in the *Affirmative*.* Contents 39; Not Contents 39: Tellers V. Newport and L. Chandos. Judgment affirmed. (MS. Min. L. J., XIV. 665.]

Annexed:—

(*a.*) Copy of issue joined by Defendant Ayliffe Wayte, Executor of Edmund Wayte, with draft of Tenor of Judgment of 30 Nov. at the end.

(*b.*) 23 Oct. Petition of Plaintiff Richard Browne. The Defendant Edmund Waight died since the Judgment. Prays the House to proceed to a Hearing upon notice to the Executor and the Tenants if they do not join issue. Read this day. L. J., XIV. 627.

(*c.*) 14 Nov. Petition of same. The Executor and tenants had joined issue. Prays for a day for hearing. L. J., XIV. 645.

398. Oct. 23. Smith *v.* Kellway. (In Error.)—Petition of Christopher Kellway, Gentleman, the Defendant. The Writ of Error was brought in simply for delay, to enable the Plaintiff, Richard Smith, Clerk, to have another year's profits by keeping Petitioner out of possession. Prays for a short day for hearing. L. J., XIV. 627 [The copy transcript of the Record is not extant. The Cause was heard, and Judgment affirmed on 30 Oct., *Mr. Staples* and *Mr Dobins* appearing for the Plaintiff, and *Mr. Whitelocke* for the Defendant. (MS. Min.)]

399. Oct. 27. Writ of Summons (Bp. of Peterborough.)—Writ of Summons, dated Oct. 23, to Richard [Cumberland], Bishop of Peterborough. [Took the Oaths this day. L. J., XIV. 628.]

400. Oct. 27. Writ of Summons (Bp. of Chichester).—Writ of Summons, this day, to Robert [Grove], Bishop of Chichester. [Took the Oaths this Day. L. J., XIV. 628.]

401. Oct. 27. Tuder *v.* King and Queen.—Copy Writ of Error, &c. and Transcript of Record brought in this day. L. J., XIV. 628. The Writ of Error is from a Judgment, on an information by the Attorney-General, convicting John Tuder, a scrivener, of perjury in respect of certain statements in his answer to two Bills in Chancery brought against him by a near relative John Tuder, of Stepney, Gent. The matters in dispute arose out of two loans on bond to Timothy Trigg, Clay Merchant, of Whitechapel, and John Wood, the bonds being given to William Manlove. [The Cause was heard and Judgment reversed on 19 and 20 Nov. the Judges being ordered to inspect the Record. *Mr. Darnell* appeared for the Plaintiff; no Counsel appeared for the Crown. (MS. Min. L. J., XIV. 653, 655).]

Annexed:—

(*a.*) Copy of issue joined by the Attorney-General.

(*b.*) 13 Nov. Petition of Plaintiff for a day for hearing. L. J., XIV. 644.

(*c.*) 20 Nov. Tenor of Judgment of this House this day. L. J., XIV. 655. *In extenso.*

402. Oct. 30. Hibbert *v.* Leech.—Petition of Mary Hibbert, widow and relict of Henry Hibbert, Doctor of Divinity, deceased, and her

* The MS. Min. entry is clearly wrong, and should have been: "Question, whether the Judgment &c. shall be reversed." Resolved in the Negative." A marginal note adds: Case of *Gore v. Rolt* read, Semper præsumitur pro negante, 31 March 1690. *See* Calendar, 12th Report. Appendix, Part VI. No. 179.

four daughters, Executrices of his last Will and Testament. William Hollingworth borrowed 100*l.* from Dr. Hibbert on the security of lands in Marple, Cheshire, which he conveyed to Ottiwell and Henry Higginbotham for 31 years in trust for Hibbert. Hollingworth then confessed a Judgment of 80*l.* and costs to one Wm. Smith. Hibbert, in ignorance of the Judgment, lent Hollingworth 340*l.* more, and took conveyance of the premises in his own name. Then one Nathan Leech, an Attorney, as principal creditor and administrator to Smith, obtained in the Exchequer a Judgment to redeem Hibbert's first mortgage, without paying off the second, Hibbert to account for the rents received and to have a conveyance of the premises from Leech. The Decree is unprecedented. Prays it may be reversed and proceedings below stayed. *Signed* by Mary Hibbert. *Countersigned* by Wi. Williams and R. Sawyer. L. J., XIV. 630. [The Cause was heard on 2 Jan. 1691–2, *Sir William Williams* and *Sir Robert Sawyer* appearing for Appellant and no Counsel appearing for Respondent. The *L. C. Baron* gave his reasons for making the decree in the Exchequer and stated the case. *Baron Turton* was heard, who was of a different opinion with the other Barons for Mr. Hibbert. The Decree was then reversed. (MS. Min. L. J., XV. 13).]

403. Oct. 30. Legh *v.* Aspinwall.—Petition and Appeal of Richard Legh, Esq., John Case, Thomas Cooke, and others. Sir Gilbert Ireland, deceased, being 2,500*l.* in debt, and having a great kindness for Henry Legh of Highlegh, Esq., since deceased, and the Appellants and others who are since dead, in April 1675 demised to them his lands in Cheshire and Lancashire, worth 300*l.* a year, in trust for 500 years, with power to make leases within the first 31 years after his death, to pay his debts, and to apply the surplus as directed in his Will, whereby he left his Lancashire estates to Gilbert Aspinwall and his heirs male. Aspinwall contended that the trust, which Petitioners consider gives them an absolute interest for 31 years, was only to pay Sir Gilbert's debts, legacies, funeral expenses and annuities, and brought a Bill in Chancery for an account of the rents and profits; but the Court being against him, he offered Petitioners 3,000*l.* for their interest. The Court ordered him to perform his offer, failing which the Bill to stand dismissed. He did not perform and his Bill was dismissed. He then brought another, without having paid the costs of the previous one, but nevertheless obtained a Decree that Petitioners should account with him, and a subsequent order that they should bring both the arrears of rent and the accruing rents into Court, though 14 years of the term of 31 are unexpired and 900*l.* of debt yet unraised, for which Petitioners are now liable, as they have given personal security for the same. Pray to be relieved and for stay of proceedings below. *Signed* by Appellants; *Countersigned* by Wi. Williams. L. J., XIV. 630. [The Cause was heard on 28 Nov. *Sir William Williams* (for Appellant): The Commissioners have made a decree against the express limitation in the Will. 30*l.* per [annum] is the value. In April 1675 he makes this deed and a settlement of his estate. *Sir Robert Sawyer* (for Appellant): The deed creates the trust and not the Will. The Chancery jumbles them together. Sir Gilbert Aspinwall recites the trust, and then he appoints that that surplus remain without account. The deed read. Several depositions read, testifying Sir Gilbert's steadiness in settling his estate. *Mr. Trevor* (for Respondent): I hope to show this is a very just decree. It was only a term for 31 years to make leases. *Sir William Whitelocke* (for Respondent) is heard. Depositions read of John Jeffreys and Geo. Maudsley, aged 34 years. Counsel for Appellant having replied, the

HOUSE OF LORDS MSS.

1691.

Speaker reported and the Decree was ordered to be reversed. (MS. Min. L. J., XIV. 664.)]

Annexed:—

(a.) 9 Nov. Answer of Gilbert Aspinwall, Esq. Sir Gilbert Ireland, Knt., deceased, Respondent's uncle, was only 500*l.* in debt, but was much persuaded and governed by Appellants, particularly Case and Cooke, his servants. He did demise to them his manors of Hutt and Hale in Lancashire and Croston in Cheshire for 500 years, in trust to raise and pay to his eldest sister Elianor, Respondent's mother, 50*l.* a year; to Case and Cooke 20*l.* a year for 21 years; his debts, &c., and the surplus as directed by his Will, which makes no mention of any term of 31 years. The Clause of the Will giving the lessees power to retain the surplus without accounting for it was held by the Court to be inconsistent with the Deed of Trust. The proposal to compromise for 3,000*l.* came from Appellants. Respondent would not comply as Appellants would not produce their books. He could not pay the costs of the first Bill, which amounted to 200*l.*, as he was a prisoner in the Fleet, and Appellants would not allow him to fell any of the timber, although tenant for life without impeachment of waste. Appellants have received 15,479*l.* from the estate, which is worth 500*l.* a year. Sir Gilbert's personal estate amounted to 1,500*l.* Prays that the Appellants may be ordered to perfect their Account before the Master, or that Respondent may be at liberty to compel them. *Signed* by Respondent and *countersigned* Wm. Whitelocke and Tho. Brotherton. *Endorsed* as brought in this day. *See* L. J., XIV. 643.

(b.) 10 Nov. Petition of Appellants, praying for a day for hearing which will enable them to be present, as they all live in Cheshire and Lancashire. *Signed* by Legh only. L. J., XIV. 640.

(c.) 12 Nov. Petition of Respondent, praying that Appellants may be ordered to produce their Rent Roll and Books of Accounts upon oath five days before the hearing. L. J., XIV. 643.

404. Oct. 60. Zouch *v.* Lady Wild and others.—Petition and Appeal of James Zouch, Esqre. John Colwall, Esqre., brother of Petitioner's wife Anne, who was living apart from him, had settled an annuity of 100*l.* upon her, and appointed his Executors to pay it. His mother Elizabeth, his only Executrix, transferred all his personal estate and her own to William Longueville and Charles Bonython, Esqres., and one Mr. Spour for the benefit of the infants Daniel, Thomas and Elizabeth Colwall. Thereupon Petitioner's wife, by her next friend, Lady Wild, brought a Bill in Chancery against John Colwall's Estate for the 100*l.* annuity. The Defendants contended that the 100*l.* a year was only payable in case of necessity, and that Anne was entitled to 250*l.* maintenance from Petitioner on a demise and redemise of some lands of his, executed between him and her father and brother Thomas and John Colwall, and they alleged collusion between Petitioner and his wife. Petitioner had kept back this allowance as a set off against the plate and other goods his wife had taken away with her; but the Lords Commissioners on 10 Feb. last decreed him to pay 812*l.* 10*s.* arrears, and Anne to restore whatever had not been expressly given to her. Appeals against the Decree because the 250*l.* was never sued for; because it was charged on his lands and he is made personally liable; because his wife need not have left him; because the payment of arrears was ordered in a suit in which he was not a party, and on other grounds, and prays that the parties below, viz., Dame Frances Wild, Anne Zouch, Daniel Colwall, Sir Thomas Pilkington, Knt., and others, and Daniel, Thomas and Elizabeth Colwall, infants, by their next friend, may be ordered to answer. *Signed* by Appellant and *countersigned* Creswell Levinz and R. Sawyer. L. J., XIV. 630. [The Cause was heard and the Judgment reversed on 8 Jan. 1691–2, *Mr. Finch* and *Mr. Ward* appearing for the Appellants; *Sir Ambrose Phillipps* and *Sir William Williams* for the Infant Respondents, *Mr. Trevor* for Mrs. Zouch, and *Mr. Serjeant Killingworth* for the other Respondents. (MS. Min. L.J., XV. 21.)]

Annexed:—

(*a*.) 14 Nov. Answer of Dame Frances Wild, widow, on the behalf of Anne Zouch, and of the said Anne Zouch. Anne had been forced by her husband's severities to part from him, and her brother, knowing him to be a hard man, settled 100*l*. a year on her. He made Daniel Colwall, his uncle, Sir Thomas Pilkington and his mother his Executors. Elizabeth Colwall paid the annuity for some time, but as she had settled all the estate on the children of Arnold (John's brother) and Susanna Colwall (Susanna being now the wife of Foot Onslow) her Executors ceased the payment, and Anne had been living on charity, though she had brought her husband a portion of 6,000*l*. Prays that both the 250*l*. and the 100*l*. a year with arrears may be decreed to her. *Signed* Frances Wild and Ann Zouch. *Endorsed* as brought in this day.

(*b*.) 28 Nov. Answer of William Longville and Charles Bonython, Esqres. and Richard Spoure, Gent. Appellant had 4,000*l*. a year. He settled the 250*l*. on his wife to prevent a sentence of the Spiritual Court for alimony against him, and paid it until his wife returned to cohabitation with him. Then they again separated, by collusion, in order to obtain payment of the 100*l*. a year, and Appellant threatened to put in suit a Bond for 2,000*l*., given him by his wife's father and brother to indemnify him against her acts. The Decree is just. *Countersigned* Ja. Smyth. *Endorsed* as brought in this day.

(*c*.) 7 Dec. Answer of Daniel, Thomas and Elizabeth Colwall, infants, by Foot Onslow, Esqre., their next friend. To same effect as preceding. *Signed* by Foot Onslow and *countersigned* Jo. Nowes. *Endorsed* as brought in this day.

405. Oct. 31. Hetley *v*. Hervey.—Petition and appeal of Carina Hetley, Elizabeth English and others, Executors and Administrators of Henry Cromwell *alias* Williams, deceased, and Richard Draper, deceased. Sir Robert Carr, late of Aswarby, Lincolnshire, Bart., long since deceased, and father of the last Sir Robert, also deceased, who was Chancellor of the Duchy of Lancaster, and of the Respondent, Isabella, settled, in March 1638, an Annuity of 20*l*. apiece on the two Appellants and Henry and Pembroke Cromwell and Anne, married to Richard Draper, the five children of Henry Cromwell, Esq. by the Lady Anne Carr, the elder Sir Robert's mother, the share of any of them dying to be divided among the rest. The Appellants alone survive. All his lands in Lincolnshire, except the jointure lands of the Lady Mary, his wife, were charged with this annuity, which continued to be paid until the war in 1641. In 1656 Appellants obtained a Decree in Chancery for the arrears, amounting to 1,463*l*., Fiennes and Lisle, the Commissioners of the Great Seal, finding that the Manors of Monkethorp, Steeping Magna and Steeping Parva, as well as the other lands charged, were liable, but not the person of Sir Robert. Immediately after the Restoration there were great lawsuits between Sir Robert Carr and Dame Mary and their son the late Sir Robert, who promised Appellants to pay them the annuity as soon as they were over. In 1664 an Act was past settling the Estate on the son, and three years later the father died. The son refused to pay the annuity. In 1676 Sir Robert obtained a Decree in Chancery reversing that of 1656, on the strength of two trumped up deeds that were not fully read in Court, for they in fact establish Appellants' rights. These very deeds were declared invalid four years ago in two suits brought to defraud Lord Holles and others. Appeal against the Decree of 1676, which was obtained by surprise, and pray that Isabella Carr, daughter and heiress of Sir Robert Carr, and John Hervey, Esq., her husband, may be ordered to answer. *Signed* by Carina Hetley and Eliz. English, and *countersigned* Edw. Hildeyard and Ro. Blayney. L. J., XIV. 630. [The cause was heard on 17 Feb. 1691–2, *Mr. Hildeyard* appearing for Appellant and *Mr. Ward* for Respondent. Counsel having agreed to take away the Statute, the House ordered as in L. J., XV. 80. (MS. Min.)]*

Annexed :—

(*a*.) 5 Nov. Petition of Respondents. The Appeal comes upon them by surprise. After fifteen years, they cannot easily get at the Agents or papers in the cause. Pray for further time to answer. *See* L. J., XIV. 634.

(*b*.) 19 Nov. Several Answer of John Hervey, Esq. and Isabella, his wife, daughter and heir of Sir Robert Carr, deceased. The Decree of 1656 was made by favour of the Usurper, who was nearly related to Appellants, and was executed by military force. Sir Robert died only in 1682 leaving his estate to Trustees, Isabella being then only twelve, and the Appellants might have proceeded against him or them. In 1676 Sir Robert borrowed 20,000*l*. on his estate, and after his death half the estate went to Mr. Fox, a member of Parliament, pursuant to the Act of 1664. The 20,000*l*. fell upon Respondent's half, from which also 500*l*. a year was sold to pay Sir Robert's debts; and the estate is also encumbered by a great debt due to Lord Holles, who is in possession of the lands securing it. There are several other incumbrances on the property. L. Holles and Mr. Fox are as much liable as Respondents, but are not made parties. Pray to be dismissed with costs. *Endorsed* as brought in this day.

(*c*.) 4 Dec. Petition of Appellants for a day for hearing. L. J., XIV. 672.

(*d*.) 2 Feb. 1691–2. Petition of same. Petitioners are very aged, and may not be living after the Session. Pray for a short day for hearing. L. J., XV. 60.

406. Oct. 31. Waring *v.* Plate.—Petition and Appeal of Richard Waring, Gent. Petitioner is the only son of the Respondent Dame Ann Plate by her first husband Sampson Waring, Merchant, who died when Petitioner was six years old, leaving a large personal estate. Dame Ann's third husband, John Twisleton, Esqre. settled upon her in jointure lands in Kent of the value of 300*l*. a year, and these she leased to Petitioner, under a yearly rent of 200*l*., in exchange for 500*l*. of his money which she had taken to make up a marriage portion of 2,600*l*. for his only sister Ann Waring. The lease was to be

* The MS. Min. of 18 Nov. have the following entry not in L. J.: "House moved, John Temple to enter into Recognizance for Mrs. Hetley. Ordered."

voidable on notice given to Edward Heighes, of Lincoln's Inn, since deceased. When Dame Ann contemplated marriage with Sir John Plate, Petitioner agreed with the latter to give up the lease for 500*l.*, but as Sir John was a man of no estate and could give no security, the agreement fell through. A subsequent agreement for 400*l.* fell through for the same reason. Then Sir John and Dame Ann obtained a Decree against Petitioner ordering him to give up the lease subject to a payment to him of 400*l.* Appeals against the Decree and prays for stay of proceedings below. *Signed* by Appellant; *Countersigned* by J. Somers and Mainwaring Davies. L. J., XIV. 631. [The Cause was heard on 8 Dec. 1691.* *The Solicitor General* (for Appellant): He looks upon Sir John Platt's bond as nothing, but by this bond it appears he had notice and so he had after, as appears by a letter. In the suit in Chancery they did not know what to insist upon. The decree is built on new foundation. *Sir Thomas Powys* (for Appellant): The question is, whether this lease is just and honest; what there can appear to a Court of Equity to make us deliver up this lease. This is her fourth husband. The question now is the agreement. There was such agreement, but Sir John Plate had no money for us. 18 Feb. 1670; the Will read. The lease read, 1672. *Sir Ambrose Phillipps* (for Respondent): There was an agreement to have 400*l.* down, and upon that the Court ordered the delivery of the lease. The gaining of this place was a surprise upon the Lady Plate. The agreement is good notwithstanding the Statute of Frauds and Perjuries. He acknowledges in his answer there was such an agreement. *Mr. Finch* (for Respondent): Depositions and letters read. Here we leave it to consider how this lease was gained. He recovered the rents all along in his mother's name. Counsel for Appellant having replied, the Speaker reported and the House ordered the decree to be reversed. (MS. Min. L. J., XIV. 678.)]

Annexed :—

(*a.*) 14 Nov. Answer of Sir John Plate, Knt., and of Dame Anne his wife. Appellant and his master, Edward Heighes, an attorney, on the day after the burial of John Twisleton, obtained the lease by practice and circumvention. Anne having borrowed 100*l.* from one Gregg, the Appellant repaid it with her money, and retained the Bond, which he threatened to put in suit. The Decree is more favourable to him than he deserves. *Signed* by Respondents; *Countersigned* by Wm. Stringer. *Endorsed* as brought in this day.

(*b.*) 18 Nov. Petition of Appellant for a day for hearing. L. J., XIV. 650.

(*c.*) 2 Feb. 1691-2. Petition of same. Since the Judgment of the House, the Court of Chancery had ordered a rehearing as to the account of the profits of the premises, which would annul the Judgment of the House. Prays for relief. L. J., XV. 60, 71. [In the Select Committee, to whom this Petition was referred, *Mr. Dobins* opened the case for the Appellant. Orders of Chancery of 12 and 19 Jan. 1691–2 read. *Counsel* for Sir John Plate: We having put several matters in our Petition to the Court, and the Court not having yet having declared on what point they will hear us, Mr. Waring comes too early to your Lordships. The order read is not drawn according to the Minutes. Lady Plate had a jointure of 300*l.* a year; she made

* "House moved to have an Order for witnesses to prove exhibits." MS. Min. 28 Nov. No entry in L. J.

her son a lease of it for 200*l.* a year. The question before your Lordships was that Waring should have the benefit of the lease. We submit to it. Your Lordships' intention was not that we should have the 200*l.* a year. There are 1,000*l.* arrears of this 200*l.* a year due to us. We ask no more than to be heard to the 200*l.* a year. The Defendant has drawn this order up contrary to the Minutes, and then applies to your Lordships. The Minutes in Chancery are read by the Register. The Order amended by the Court according to these Minutes is read. They withdraw. (MS. Min.) On report, the House ordered the Petition to be dismissed. (L. J., XV. 71.)]

407. Oct. 31. Fleetwood *v.* Fleetwood.—Petition and Appeal of Richard Fleetwood of Rossall, Lancashire, Esqre., and Ann, his wife. Appellant being seized of lands in Lancashire worth 800*l.* a year, employed Christopher Greenfield, Counsellor at Law, to draw his Will, leaving the same to his nephew Richard Fleetwood, and disposing of 5,000*l.* Greenfield drew a Lease and Release, which Appellant executed in ignorance, being near eighty years of age. Finding his mistake, he exhibited his Bill in Chancery to have the Deeds cancelled, but the Decree was given against him, with 90*l.* costs to his disherison. Appeals against the Decree and prays that the costs may be repaid to him. *Signed* by Appellants; *Countersigned* by W. Barnesley and John Radford. L. J., XIV. 631. [The Cause was heard on 12 Dec. 1691. *Sir Thomas Powys* and *Mr. Ward* were heard for the Appellant. *The Solicitor-General* (for Respondent): I am sure they have not made out anything, nor can make out anything. This woman being very earnest to get the deed, she pretended she had advised with Counsel. *Sir William Williams* (for Respondent): Shows the deed delivered by the Chancery. The deed executed read. *Agreed* That the deed was executed. The Speaker then reported and the House ordered the decree to be affirmed with 40*l.* costs. (MS. Min. L. J., XIV. 683.)]

Annexed:—

(*a.*) 23 Nov. Answer of Richard Fleetwood, Gent. It was not a Will, but a settlement, that was wanted, and it was properly drawn by Greenwood, [Greenfield] now a Member of Parliament,* and read over to Appellant before several witnesses. It appointed Christopher Parker, Robert Shawe, and William Werden, Trustees. The estate was worth 600*l.* a year. Appellant had docked an entail in the male line, else the estate would have come to Respondent, the son of Appellant's brother Francis, under an entail made by his grandfather Edmund Fleetwood, Esqre., under which Appellant had succeeded, to the exclusion of his elder brother Edmund's five daughters. *Endorsed* as brought in this day.

408. Oct. 31. Zouch *v.* English.—Petition and Appeal of James Zouch, Esqre. Appellant's late father by his Will left his daughter Dorothy a portion of 1,500*l.* charged on his lands, but, having a personal estate of 10,000*l.*, he declared the 15,000*l.* should be paid out of that, and made his wife Beatrix his Executrix. She, however, never paid the portion or the debts, but married again, and she and her husband, on pretence of her being Guardian, kept Petitioner out of his estate, and drew about 10,000*l.* from it. Petitioner lent his sister great sums of money to pay her extravagant debts, and, falling into bad hands, was induced, when

* Christopher Greenfield, returned as Member for Preston on 13 March, 1689-90.

drunk, to sign a Note promising to pay her 3,000*l.* when her uncle, the late E. Anglesey, should provide her with a suitable husband. His sister, sensible of the trick, released him from the Note in writing. Eventually she was married to Thomas English, a widower with five children, and with little or no unencumbered estate, but she deserted him the morning after the marriage, having been put to bed when she was unconscious. The fact that the 3,000*l.* was to be paid to the Earl or to Dorothy's aunt, Mrs. Baker, threw a suspicious light on the marriage. English sued Appellant for both the 3,000*l.* and the 1,500*l.*, and though L. Keeper North dismissed his Bill with regard to the 3,000*l.*, the Lords Commissioners, on a rehearing, decreed in his favour, unjustly charging the amount on Appellant's lands. Appeals against this last decree, and prays that English and Dorothy, his wife, may be ordered to answer. *Signed* by Appellant; *Countersigned* by J. Somers and Edw. Ward. L. J., XIV. 631. *See also* 7 Nov. 1693. [The Cause was heard on 10 Dec. 1691. *Mr. Trevor* (for Appellant): The thing carries all the practice in the world. *Mr. Finch* (for Appellant): This Note was given in 1668. There was no reason to make this decree. There was no reason for Mr. Zouch to give this Note. Depositions of witnesses read to prove Mr. Zouch was drunk when he gave the Note. *Mr Serjeant Tremaine* (for Respondent): I hope you will think fit to affirm this decree, notwithstanding what you have heard. *Mr. Trevor* (*sic*) (on the same side): It is part of the agreement that it shall stand. What disagreeableness is there in this? Let us see how this agreement is discharged. The release was obtained and kept afoot by fraud. She was threatened to be restrained if this be not released. This release discharged the original portion also. At law this release is an effectual bar, and therefore we could not go to law. We will show the marriage articles that she shall have the 3,000*l.* E. Anglesey's deposition read. The Note read. Counsel withdrew, and the Speaker having reported, the House ordered the decree to be reversed. (MS. Min. L. J., XIV. 681).]

Annexed :—

(*a.*) 10 Nov. Answer of Thomas English, Esqre., and Dorothy, his wife. Appellant's father never declared the 1,500*l.* should be paid out of personalty. Appellant obtained Dorothy's release as to the 3,000*l.* by very ill practices and threats. Deny other false statements in the Appeal. *Signed* by Respondents; *Countersigned* by Jo. Tremayne. *Endorsed* as brought in this day.

(*b.*) 21 Nov. Petition of Thomas English for a short day for hearing. L. J., XIV. 656.

(*c.*) 5 Dec. Petition of Appellant, praying that the Articles importing that the 3,000*l.* was to be paid to E. Anglesey and Lady Baker, produced by English at the trial before L. North, may be produced at the hearing. L. J., XIV. 647, almost *in extenso.*

409. Nov. 2. Bennet *v.* E. Salisbury.—Petition and Appeal of John Bennet, Esqre., and Grace, his wife. Symon Bennet, being possessed of a large real and personal estate, entailed his real estate on his two daughters Grace and Frances, and their issue, failing whom on Petitioner. He also, by Will, devised 20,000*l.* to each daughter, to be paid on her marriage after 16, or at the age of 25 if unmarried, and 200*l.* a year in the meantime, but if either of them married without the consent of her mother Grace, her father's cousin Ralph Lee, and his sister Lady Clifton, or one of them, she was to have only 10,000*l.* Petitioner married Grace in her father's lifetime, and the late E. Salisbury entered upon a treaty

HOUSE OF LORDS MSS.

1691.

of marriage between his son, the present Earl, and Frances, and demanded a portion of 60,000*l.* and 6,000*l.* a year, leaving all the real property to the other sister. These negotiations fell through, and after a treaty of marriage was entered into with L. Arlington, Symon and E. Salisbury died, and in July 1683 the present Earl married Frances when only 13, thereby violating the conditions of the Will. A portion of 10,000*l.* was therefore paid to the Earl, who obtained a Decree from the Lords Commissioners on 1 May 1691 declaring the 10,000*l.* to be a charge on the testator's personal estate in the first instance, and if that be not sufficient, the real estate to stand charged with the remainder, so far as the Court should afterwards direct. Appeals from this Decree. *Signed* by Appellants ; *Countersigned* by Tho. Powys, and Edw. Ward. L.J., XIV 633. [The Cause was heard on 20 Nov. 1691. *Mr. Finch* (for Appellant): Opens the case. Counsel withdraw. *Moved*, that E. Salisbury come in within the Bar. *Agreed.* Counsel called in again. *Mr. Finch:* She has married so as to lose the 10,000*l.* as she married before 16, which are the words of the Will. *Sir Thomas Powys* (for Appellant): We say the 10,000*l.* was never given by the Will, and the Court of Chancery has made the Will for Mr. Bennet. The words are : I give 20,000*l.* to my daughters so as such marriage is not before they attain the age of 16 and so as they marry with the consent of such and such persons, and if either of them marry otherwise, then only 10,000*l.* C. Baron Hale said in the case of *Fry* v. *Porter* he hoped it was fit your Lordships set bounds to the Chancery. *Mr. Finch* reads the words of the Will out of the Will. *The Solicitor General* (for Respondent): We come upon the point of construction. Originally Mr. Bennet intended 20,000*l.* each. It was a good gift, and if she had died presently after her father, the 20,000*l.* would have gone to her administrator. Mr. Lee and Mrs. Bennet consented. *Mr. Trevor* (for Respondent) : It is a strange construction to make a forfeiture. There is an express devise of the 10,000*l.* in the first place. 15 Car. II., case of *Lady Bellasis* v. *Erwin.** Case of *D. Southampton* v. *Bishop of Coventry and Lichfield.* The words were there "if she marry before 16." *Mr. Finch* replies. *Sir Thomas Powys* heard to the cases offered by Mr. Trevor. Swinburne has this whole matter in his treatise,† Counsel withdrew and the Speaker reported. Judges asked whether the words of the Will vest this estate in any other person or a devise over? [*Athyns*], *C. B.:* I agree there is no express disposal. *Dolben, J.:* No express disposal. *Gregory, J.:* It seems to me doubtful. I take it would have come to the administrator if she had died. *Nevill, B.:* I conceive here is no devise over to any other person. *Eyre, J.:* No devise over. House *moved*, that the reason that there is no devise over be the words of the Will (*sic*). *Ordered*, That the Appeal be dismissed and the decree affirmed. (MS. Min. L. J., XIV. 654.) See also 2 *Vernon*, 223 ; *Freeman*, 118.]

Annexed :—

(*a.*) 13 Nov. Answer of James, Earl of Salisbury and Frances, Countess of Salisbury, his wife. Symon Bennet vested all his property in London, and the Counties of Bucks, Leicester, Stafford, Derby, Notts, York, Middlesex, Warwick and Surrey in Ralph Lee, of London, Merchant, and Salathiel Lovell, Esqre., as Trustees. The treaty of marriage was only postponed, and the marriage was urged on by Mrs. Bennet and Lee, for fear Frances might be carried off by some less worthy suitor, and the Appellants

* 1 Cases in Chancery 22.

† Swinburne on Wills.

approved of the marriage and were present at it, and promised they would not oppose the whole 20,000*l.* being paid, out of gratitude for the late Earl having furthered Appellant's marriage with Grace, when there was a question of her marrying Respondent. The Earl left the country immediately after the marriage, and never bedded the Countess until she was over sixteen. The late Earl left a charge of 130,000*l.* on his estate. *Signed* Salisbury. *Endorsed* as brought in this day.

410. Nov. 2. E. Aylesbury's Estate Act.—Amended Draft of an Act for the making a twelve years' Lease made by the Earl and Countess of Ailesbury for payment of Debts (which was determinable on their deaths) to have continuance absolutely for those twelve years. [Read 1ª this day: Royal Assent 24 Dec. L. J., XIV. 633, 701. 3 W. & M. c. 5 in Long Calendar. Counsel were heard on 20 Nov. before the Second reading. *Mr. Browne:* I come to oppose a Bill brought in by E. Aylesbury. We hope you will give no more powers to the Earl than what he has. *Mr. Trevor* (for E. Aylesbury): The things desired in the Act are very reasonable nor is there any inconvenience to any person. My Lady has her life in it; it cannot hinder the issue. (MS. Min., L. J., XIV. 654.)—In Committee on 21 Nov. *Mr. Harcourt* stated that the Duchess of Beaufort did not consent to the Bill and desired it might not be passed to the prejudice of Lady Aylesbury or her issue. *V. Weymouth* acquainted the Committee that the Countess of Aylesbury had written to him to signify her consent to the Bill. *E. Rochester* acquainted the Committee that he had two letters from the Duchess of Beaufort, wherein she expressed a great dislike to the Bill, as conceiving it prejudicial to her grandchildren. *Ordered* to be reported with Amendments. (Com. Book.) The Lords' Amendments, which are inserted in the draft but not mentioned in Com. Book, are unimportant. The two amendments added by the Commons, which appear on the original Roll, are merely verbal corrections.]

Annexed :—

(*a.*) Abstract of the Earl and Countess of Aylesbury's Lease for 12 years made pursuant to an Act passed in the second year of W. & M. A *note* by A. Ward, dated Furnivals Inn, 9 Jan. 1691, states that E. Aylesbury desires the above paper to be printed and affixed to the Act.

(*b.*) 12 Nov. 1685. Order of the House this day, on report from the Committee for Privileges, declaring that no Privilege be allowed to Peers in cases where they are only trustees. *Signed* Matthew Johnson, Cler. Parliamentor. [Found with above papers.]

411. Nov. 2. Mathews' Estate Act.—Amended Draft of an Act for settling a jointure on Jane, the wife of Colonel Edward Mathews, daughter of Sir Thomas Armstrong, deceased. The two amendments are purely verbal. [Read 1ª this day. Royal Assent, 24 Dec. L. J., XIV. 633, 702. 3 W. & M. c. 11 in Long Calendar. See also Com. Book, 12 Nov.]

412. Nov. 2. Albyn *v.* Moyer.—Petition and Appeal of Benjamin Albyn, Merchant. Petitioner, as Factor at Smyrna of John Jolliff, a Turkey Merchant in London, being desired by him to dispose of certain cloths which were found unfit for sale at Smyrna, sent a parcel of them to Brusia [Brousa], at a cost of 500 dollars, and afterwards bartered with one Sheftogle, a Turk, for 50 bales of raw silk, costing 25,448 dollars

House of Lords MSS. — 1691.

(6,362*l.*), in return for which the Turk was to take 260 of Jolliff's cloths in part payment and the rest in money. Petitioner immediately sent the silk home to Jolliff. The Turk, however, finding the cloths not equal to the sample, as agreed, sent them back to Petitioner, who being in a strait to pay him and unwilling to borrow money for that purpose, as the rate of interest at Smyrna was two per cent. per month, and being driven out of Smyrna by the plague, sent 304 of Jolliff's and 100 cloths and other commodities of his own to Tauris in Persia, agreeing to pay the Turk out of the proceeds. Jolliff's cloths were sold for 6,977 dollars and 37 aspers less than the price offered by the Turk. Samuel Moyer and Dame Ann Dethick (since deceased), the executors of Jolliff, brought a Bill in Chancery against Petitioner, but were decreed on 30 Oct. 1685 to pay him 648*l.* and 5*l.* costs, no allowance being made for the 500 dollars spent by Petitioner. Moyer brought a Bill of Review, and on 25 Feb. 1689 the Lords Commissioners reversed the decree and upon another hearing on 4 May 1691 decreed Petitioner to pay back the 648*l.* with interest, and 6,977 dollars and 37 aspers in addition, in all 2,582*l.* 5*s.* 10*d.*, and Moyer has since prosecuted him for that sum upon a Commission of Bankrupt, to his utter ruin. Appeals against this last decree. *Signed* by Appellant; *Countersigned* by Edw. Ward and J. Darnall. L. J., XIV. 633. [The Cause was heard and after debate the decree reversed on 23 Dec.,* *Sir William Williams* appearing for the Appellant and *Sir Ambrose Phillipps* and *Mr. Vernon* for the Respondent. (MS. Min. L. J., XIV. 700.)]

Annexed:—

(*a.*) 11 Nov. Petition of same.—Respondent had caused some goods of Appellant's to be stopped in the hands of Captains John Haselwood, Jonas Cork, John Frost and Wakelyn, who refused to deliver them up to Respondent. A suit was therefore directed to be brought in their names against Appellant and Respondent. Prays for stay of proceedings. L. J., XIV. 642.

(*b.*) 13 Nov. Answer of Samuel Moyer, of London, Merchant, surviving Executor of John Jolliff, Esqre., deceased. Appellant acknowledged by a Letter of Advice that he had sold 280 of Jolliff's cloths at 55 dollars each. He had no right to send them to Persia, which is beyond the Turkey Company's limits, and should bear the loss. *Signed* by Respondent; *Countersigned* by T. Vernon. *Endorsed* as brought in this day.

413. Nov. 2. Hale *v.* Dashwood.—Petition and Appeal of Thomas Hale, Gent. Petitioner married Margaret, one of the daughters of Edw. Eltonhead, Esq., and in her right, under her father's Will, became entitled to 1,000*l.* marriage portion and a seventh of the residue of the estate, and to an annuity of 30*l.* until the portion should be paid. Petitioner owed Francis Dashwood 1,011*l.*, and made over to him his interest in his wife's estate as security, Dashwood covenanting to repay Petitioner the overplus after the debt was satisfied. Petitioner then brought a Bill in Chancery against Sir Samuel Dashwood, Knt. (who was also receiver of the rents of part of the estate) and Francis Dashwood, Executors of the said Francis Dashwood, deceased, for an account of his share of the estate. The Lord Chancellor on 12 July 1688 decreed accordingly, and the Master found 171*l.* 14*s.* due to Petitioner, including five years' arrears of the annuity. Upon hearing exceptions on 26 July 1690 an Order was made discharging this sum. Appeals

* A motion to hear the Cause on 30 Nov. was made in the House on 25 Nov. MS. Min. No entry in L. J.

against this Order, and prays for stay of proceedings. *Signed* by Appellant: *Countersigned* by J. Somers and W. Thomson. L. J., XIV. 634. [The Cause was heard and the Order affirmed on 1 Dec. 1692, *Sir Thomas Powys* and *Mr. Dodd* appearing for Appellant, and *Mr. Bowes* and *Mr Ward* for Respondent. (MS. Min. L. J., XV. 131.)]

Annexed:—

(*a*.) 19 Dec. 1691. Joint and Several Answer of Sir Samuel Dashwood, Knt., and Francis Dashwood, Executors of Francis Dashwood, Esq., deceased. Respondents never received the annuity claimed by Appellant, and ought not to be charged with it. Sir Samuel was appointed by the Court receiver of the Estates in Woolwich and Charlton, Kent. Sir Adam Oatley was the Master who made the Report. *Signed* by Respondents; *Countersigned* by Paul Bowes. *Endorsed* as brought in this day.

(*b*.) 7 Nov. 1692. Petition of Appellant for a day for hearing. L. J., XV. 105.

414. Nov. 6. Stephens *v.* Woollaston.—Petition and Appeal of Sir Richard Stephens, Knt., one of the Justices of King's Bench in Ireland. Petitioner in 1679 purchased of Richard Wollaston an estate then waste and untenanted at Wanford, Hants, for 2,000*l.* down, and 9,000*l.* payable at two terms, to be vested in Trustees to be sold, without Petitioner's consent, if the payments were not duly made. Petitioner, finding that Wollaston, who had bought the estate from Mr. Neal a year before for 7,500*l.*, had not yet completed his title by paying all the purchase, delayed payment of the first term, but ultimately paid Neal the unpaid balance, with Wollaston's consent, and borrowed 5,000*l.* of Mrs. Colwall, on mortgage of the estate, to pay the rest of the 9,000*l.* to Wollaston. Wollaston, however, on the ground of the delay, refused to levy the requisite fine or to receive the money. The result of cross suits between the parties was that Petitioner was ordered by the Lords Commissioners to pay Wollaston 5 per cent. on the unpaid balance. Appeals against this order, as the money had long been at Wollaston's disposal. Prays that John Wollaston, son and Executor to Richard Wollaston, deceased, may be ordered to answer. *Signed* by Appellant; *Countersigned* by Tho. Powys and Wm. Dobyns. L. J., XIV. 635. [The Cause was heard and the Appeal dismissed on 1 Dec. 1691. *Sir Thomas Powys* and *Mr. Dobyns* were heard for Appellant. *The Solicitor General* (for Respondent): The question is whether the agreement made 18 March 1679 is a good agreement and ought to be performed. It is the most reasonable agreement in the world. By the agreement he was to pay 6 per cent. *Sir Ambrose Phillipps* (for Respondent): Sir Richard Stephens is a purchaser who has not money. The lands were to be sold and Mr. Wollaston to have his 9,000*l.* Sir Richard takes possession. My client complains that the fine was not levied. (MS. Min. L. J., XIV. 668.)]

Annexed:—

(*a*.) 16 Nov. Answer of John Woollaston, Esq., Executor of Richard Woollaston, Esq., late of Wormley, Herts. The Orders appealed from were just and equitable. Prays to be dismissed with costs. *Signed* by Respondent; *Countersigned* by Ambr. Phillipps. *Endorsed* as brought in this day

(*b*.) 16 Nov. Petition of same. Appellant had traversed Respondent's father ten years in Chancery against a plain act and deed of his own. Prays for a short day for hearing. L. J., XIV. 646.

House of Lords MSS.

1691.

415. Nov. 6. Ewelme Hospital *v.* Town of Andover.—Petition and Appeal of the Master, Schoolmaster and 13 poor men of Ewelme Hospital, Oxon, William Drake Esq., and Constance, his wife, and William Goddard of Woodhay, Esq., Hants. William Delapole, Duke of Suffolk, in the time of Henry VI., settled on the Hospital the manor of Ramridge, Hants, on part of which, namely, Ramridge Down, belonging to Petitioners, as well as on some glebe lands of Weyhill rectory and a place, called Blissomer Hall acre, Weyhill Fair has been kept yearly about Michaelmas about 200 years. Petitioners got their chief support from the profits of pickage and stallage and sheep pens. In 43 Eliz. the town of Andover was granted the Out-hundred of Andover and a liberty to call and keep the fair at Weyhill, with a Court of Piepowder to determine differences, and license to take tolls, show money, &c., with intent that they should regulate disorders during the fair, but not with any power to remove the fair from Petitioner's land, which the town have been lately trying to do, and having got some interest by surrendering their charter in 1683, obtained a new one with power to hold the fair where they pleased on Weyhill, and removed it accordingly to Cholderton. Petitioners brought several Bills in Chancery to enjoin the town from removing the fair, pending which their right to have the fair held on their land was twice affirmed by special juries of Hampshire gentlemen, and obtained an injunction in Chancery to quiet their possession, a *Quo Warranto* brought against them in the time of James II. being set aside. Lord Jeffreys, however, having ordered a new trial, a verdict was found against Petitioners by a Middlesex jury, who were strangers to the place, and Petitioners were ordered to account for profits. On a Bill of Review the Lords Commissioners on 22 Nov. 1690 directed a new trial at the King's Bench bar by a Hampshire jury, who found in favour of Petitioners, which verdict was affirmed by the Lords Commissioners on 22 May last. Respondents, however, obtained on 22 September last an order from the Lords Commissioners, enjoining the Hospital from setting up pens, &c. on their own land otherwise than as the town should appoint; and having privately obtained a lease of the Glebe and Blissomer Hall Acre, the town set up all the profitable part of the fair there, and reserved Petitioners' lands for the empty waggons, the horse fair, and the hops, cheese, leather, and other unprofitable things. The fair, which is now one of the most considerable trading fairs in England, will be thereby diminished, to the great prejudice of the neighbouring counties; for no place is so convenient for the profitable part of the fair as Ramridge Down. *Signed* Wm. Drake; *Countersigned* J. Somers and Tho. Filmer. L. J., XIV. 635. Compare 1 *Vernon* 265. [The Cause was heard and the decree reversed on 4 Feb. 1691–2. Counsel for Respondents were told they may object to the insufficiency of the Appeal. *Mr. Trevor* (for Respondent): We have somewhat to offer. This is an Appeal from an Order and to explain that Order. *Sir Robert Sawyer* (for Respondent): I see not anything complained of in the decree. It is a very extraordinary one. I cannot tell how your Lordships should come to expound this verdict. I cannot tell what they would be at. Your Lordships never control verdicts. They are contented with one part of the decree, but pray the rectifying of the verdict. *Mr. Finch* (for Appellants): If the Appeal were as they say, it would be very strange. This order is in subversion of the decree we complain of. This fair was kept time out of mind where it is now ordered. The town of Andover are lords of the fair. The pickage and stallage is the profit. Now the question is whether the town of Andover can remove this fair and thereby prevent the Hospital from their pickage and stallage. The Order is quite to the destruction of the decree.

The Order of the King and Council and the decree are read. *The Solicitor General* (for Appellants) is heard. Then the Respondents' Counsel were heard. *Mr. Trevor*: I will show that this Order is just contrary to the decree which we complain of. They say: We will set up the booths on our land. The town then had the election to keep what part they will upon those places. If the town think fit, he has advantage; if no, he has no advantage. *Sir Robert Sawyer*: The matter is whether the order is contrary to the decree, which it is most certainly. (MS. Min. L. J., XV. 62.)]

Annexed:—

(*a*.) 23 Nov. Answer of the Bailiff, Approved Men, and Burgesses of Andover, and of James Grove, Will. Gaffion, Will. Barwick, Will. Cooper, Thos. Westcombe, Will. Dowling, and Edward Noyes [members of the Corporation]. King John, in his fifteenth year, granted to the good men of Andover, the then Corporation, the Manor together with the In-hundred and Out-hundred of Andover, reserving 100*l*. a year to the Crown. Ewelme Hospital was founded for superstitious uses, and, together with its lands, became vested in the Crown by 1 Edw. VI. c. 14, and so continued till 15 Jac. I., when it was granted to Oxford University, who presented the Master thereof. The fair was granted to the town in 41 Eliz. with a Court of Pypowders, stallage, piccage, fines, and all other profits, and has been ever since held by Respondents until disturbed by Mr. Drake and his father, who, during the late wars, infringed Respondents' rights, and erected booths, as did others also, without any advantage to the Hospital, which has no prescriptive rights in the matter. Both the Verdicts given for Appellants were certified by the Judges as being against right and evidence. There is no mention of the fair in Mr. Drake's lease from the Hospital, which does not receive a penny profit from it. *Countersigned* by W. Thomson and R. Sawyer. *Endorsed* as brought in this day.

416. Nov. 6. Griffin *v*. Lyngard.—Petition and Appeal of Edmund Griffin, Esq. Appellant in 1690 brought a Bill against Respondent for the redemption of certain lands in Bartherton, Cheshire, formerly mortgaged by Richard Griffin, his father, to Jeoffrey Minshall, and now in the possession of Respondent, who in 1683 had brought a Bill against Appellant's father, which he revived against Appellant, to redeem or be foreclosed, and by combination with one Collington, who formerly had an interest in the premises, assigned to one Whatton, who assigned to Respondent. An account being stated in 1687, the mortgage was overstated in order to defeat Appellant of his right of redemption. Respondent in his answer denied having had any notice of Appellant's father's right, before he lent the 1,000*l*. on the premises. On 14 Nov. last the Lords Commissioners, on hearing both causes, decreed the equity of redemption to Appellant, but ordered him to be concluded by the account stated between Collington and Respondent, and to pay the foot of that account, both principal and interest, with costs. Failing redemption on those terms, Appellant was not only foreclosed but ordered on 15 Dec. to convey to Respondent other lands not included in the mortgage. Appeals against this Decree. *Signed* by Appellant; *Countersigned* by Wi. Williams and Ambr. Phillipps, who certify that there is good cause to appeal. L. J., XIV. 685. [The Cause was heard, and the decree affirmed on 4 Dec. 1691. *Sir Thomas Powys* (for Appellant): We say the terms are unconscionable that we are to redeem on. Reads the answer to show that he had notice before lending the 1,000*l.* They had notice of the account stated. *The Solicitor General* (for Respondent): Reads letter of Richard Griffin the father, of 28 July 1683. *Mr. Finch* (for Respondent): Answers to the defeazance and reads several letters. *Sir William Williams* (for Appellant) heard to reply. They insist the conveyance was absolutely no defeazance. It is otherwise. We are ready to try the point of notice, dated 29 August 1657. In October after a fine levied. Counsel withdrew and the Speaker reported. *Moved* that it be referred to a trial at law whether notice or no notice. *Ordered*, that the Decree be affirmed and the Petition dismissed. *Question* put, Whether the Appellant shall pay 20*l.* costs? Resolved in the *Negative.* *Ordered* 10*l.* costs. (MS. Min. L. J., XIV. 672.)]

Annexed :—

(*a.*) 13 Nov. Answer of John Lingard [of London, Vintner]. The estate was mortgaged for 2,100*l.* by Appellant's father, who concealed some of the incumbrances. It is worth only 50*l.* a year, and has cost Respondent a great deal in paying off incumbrances and defending suits. The sum due to him upon it is 2,400*l.* Appellant would not offer more than 1,500*l.* *Endorsed* as brought in this day.

417. Nov. 6. Trials for Treason, &c. Bill. [H.L.]—Corrected Draft of an Act for [the better regulation of] *regulating the* trials *of all Peers and Peeresses and Commoners of this Realm.*

§ i. For the more equal and indifferent trial of [all the Peers] *every Peer, Peeress and every Commoner* of this realm in time to come, Be it enacted by the King and Queen's Most Excellent Majesties, by and with the advice and consent of the Lords Spiritual and Temporal and Commons, in this present Parliament assembled, and by the authority of the same, That for the trial of every person that now is, or hereafter shall be a peer or peeress of this realm, for any crime or crime for which he or she ought by the law of the land to be tried by his or her peers (a Parliament not then actually sitting), there shall be summoned, to be at and sit upon the said trial, sixty-one peers at the least, such as sate in the then last preceding sessions of Parliament, or were or ought to have been summoned to sit in the then last Parliament, whereof forty-four at the least appearing, the peer or peeress to be tried shall have liberty to challenge twenty of them peremptorily; and by the rest of them that shall remain after such challenge, not being under the number of twenty-four, the said peer or peeress shall be tried, and by the voices of the major part of them shall be acquitted or convicted, and not otherwise.

§ ii. Provided always, that during the being of a Parliament, every peer or peeress that shall be brought to his or her trial for any crime, shall be tried by the whole House of Peers according to former usage, and not otherwise; any law, custom or thing to the contrary in any wise notwithstanding.

§ iii. And be it further enacted, that in all cases of treason, other than concerning the King's coin, there shall be two witnesses of express overt acts of treason.

§ iv. And be it further enacted by the authority aforesaid, that no person shall be returned to serve upon the grand jury in any criminal case, nor upon the petit jury in case of high treason, unless the person so to serve have lands and tenements of some estate of freehold of the clear yearly value of twenty pounds at the least, nor to serve upon the petit jury in case of felonies, or in civil actions where the debt or damage amounts to twenty pounds, unless he have lands and tenements of some estate of freehold of the clear yearly value of ten pounds at the least, and that for want of such sufficiency of freehold such jurors may be challenged, and shall be set aside, except in case of trials in cities and towns corporate, where four hundred pounds clear personal estate shall satisfy in place of twenty pounds per annum, and two hundred pounds clear personal estate in place of ten pounds per annum.

§ v. And be it further enacted that if any peer summoned to be a Tryer or any person returned to serve upon the grand jury or petit jury in any criminal case, shall refuse to make the Declaration mentioned in the Statute of 30 Car II., entituled An Act for the more effectual preserving the King's person and Government by disabling Papists from sitting in either House of Parliament, being thereto required by the Court where such peer is to attend or juryman is to serve, which such Court is hereby required to tender to such grand juryman ex officio, and to such peer or peers or jurymen upon request of the defendant or defendants in such criminal cases, such peer, grand jury-man or jury-man shall be discharged and not suffered to serve in the said case.

§ vi. And be it further enacted, that every peer and peeress and other person that hereafter shall be indicted of any capital offence for which he or she shall be tried by his or her peers, or in the Court of King's Bench, shall have a copy of the indictment translated into English, whereupon he or she is to be arraigned, by the space of a week before such arraignment, and also of the panel by the space of two days before the trial, and in other inferior Courts a copy of the indictment the night before the arraignment, and a copy of the panel two hours before the trial.

§ vii. And be it further enacted, that Writs of Error, in all cases of treason, shall, upon petition of the heir or heirs of the person attainted to the Lord Chancellor, Lord Keeper or Lords Commissioners of the Great Seal for the time being, be granted of right and without delay.

§ viii. And be it further enacted, that in all cases of high treason, the defendant and defendants shall be admitted to have counsel to advise them before and at their trials, in matter of fact as well as law, which counsel, if the party demands it, shall be assigned by the Court.

§ ix. And be it further enacted by the authority aforesaid, that in all criminal cases, evidence shall be given upon oath for the defendant.

§ x. And be it further enacted, that in all criminal cases hereafter no proceedings or prosecution shall be by way of information, but only by way of indictment, and for the encouragement of the prosecution, the Court that gives judgment in the case, shall allow the prosecutor such part and proportion of the fine or forfeiture as he should have had, in case the prosecution had been by information. [Read 1* this day, and committed on 10 Nov. to a Committee of the Whole House. (L. J., XIV. 634, 639.)* No further proceedings. The original draft is identical with the Lords' Bill of 26 Feb. 1688-9 (Calendar, 12th Report, Appendix Part VI. No. 18) as sent to the Commons. The alterations marked above by italics and square brackets are evidently corrections not amendments, for the Bill was never considered in Committee.]

418. Nov. 7. Whiting *v.* Webb.—Petition and Appeal of John Whiting and Michael Pope, Sugar Bakers. Petitioners and Nehemiah

---

* A motion to commit the Bill "to the same Committee as the Bill for taking away [benefit of] Clergy" is expunged. (MS. Min. 10 Nov.)

Webb in 1682 signed Articles of copartnery for four years, if all of them should so long live, as sugar bakers at Bristol, each contributing 1,000*l.* Webb died the following year, whereby the partnership was at an end, and Appellants entered into a new partnership between themselves only, and tendered Webb's Widow, Joanna, 1,000*l.* with interest, as her share when the first partnership was dissolved. Joanna, however, claimed to be a partner for the whole term of four years, though she contributed nothing more to the business, and she obtained a Decree, on 18 June 1686, which, on her death, was revived by her Administrator Nathaniel Webb. Appeal against that Decree and pray for stay of proceedings. *Signed* by Appellants; *Countersigned* by Will. Killingworth and Mainwaring Davies. L. J., XIV. 636. [The Cause was heard and the Decree affirmed on 11 Dec. 1691, *Mr. Ward* and *Mr. Dobyns* appearing for Appellant and the *Solicitor General* and *Mr. Trevor* for Respondent. (MS. Min. L. J., XIV. 682.)]

Annexed:—

(*a.*) 13 Nov. Petition of same, praying for leave to rectify some small mistakes in the Appeal. L. J., XIV. 644.

(*b.*) 17 Nov. Answer of Nathaniel Webb, Administrator of the goods of Nehemiah Webb, deceased, not administered by Joanna Webb, deceased, and also of the goods of the said Joanna Webb. Appellants desired Respondent's mother, Joanna, to continue a partner after her husband's death, and not withdraw her capital. An agreement was entered into to that effect, and her being a partner was not questioned until the profits were found to be large. *Endorsed* as brought in this day.

(*c.*) 23 Nov. Petition of same for a short day for hearing. L. J., XIV. 659.

419. Nov. 7. Cony *v.* Terrill.—Petition of Appeal of Mary Cony, widow, Executrix of George Cony, of London, Merchant. George Cony sold the Manor of Shurt, Kent, to Samuel Tyrrill, Merchant, for 6,800*l.*, out of which Tyrill engaged to pay off a mortgage to Peter Calf for 500*l.*, and 2,000*l.* due by bond to Richard Vale. Vale and Tyrrill were partners in trade, and failed, paying 5*s.* in the £. Calf then arrested Cony on the public Exchange, and he remained in the Fleet for 13 years. Cony obtained 3,000*l.* damages from Tyrrill, but the latter alleged as a set off that Vale, his partner, had been employed by Cony and one Mathias Burnaby as their factor at Antwerp, and was owed large sums by them. Cony contended that Vale owed him 10,000*l.* Litigation had lasted for over 20 years, and Petitioner was forced to sue in formâ pauperis. Appeals against a Decree in Chancery of 2 May 1690 overruling her exceptions to a Master's report which charged Cony with 760*l.* on seven Bills of Exchange, and ordering the same to be applied towards satisfaction of Calf's mortgage money and the rest to the general account. It is usual among Merchants to draw Bills upon other men's accounts, and they ought not to be placed to the drawer's account without Letters of Advice or due proof of payment. The Decree also ordered Petitioner to acknowledge satisfaction of the 3,000*l.* *Signed* by Appellant; *Countersigned* by Hen. Darnell and Francis Browne. L. J., XIV. 636. [The Cause was heard and the Decree affirmed on 29 Dec. 1691, *Mr. Darnell* and *Mr. Browne* appearing for Appellant, and *Mr. Trevor* and *Mr. Vernon* for Respondent. (MS. Min. L. J., XV. 4.)]

Annexed:—

(*a.*) 17 Nov. Answer of Samuel Terrill. The Manor of Shur- had belonged to the Church of Canterbury, but had passed into

Cony's possession through an Act of the usurping powers. Respondent acted only as Vale's Agent in the matter. It was at Cony's request that the money destined to pay off Calf was diverted to pay Cony's Bills. The Manor reverted to the Church at the Restoration. It was proved to the Master that it is the custom at Antwerp to pay accepted Bills without taking receipts. *Signed* by Respondent; *Countersigned* by T. Vernon. *Endorsed* as brought in this day.

(*b*.) 19 Nov. Petition of Appellant, praying for a day for hearing and that she may prosecute in formâ pauperis, and Sir Francis Winnington and Francis Browne be assigned for her Counsel. L. J., XIV. 653.

(*c*.) 4 Jan. 1691–2. Petition of Appellant. The attested copy of a letter produced at the hearing by Haughton, purporting to be from Vale to Burnaby, to invalidate an account sent by Vale to Burnaby, on the strength of which letter the Appeal was dismissed, was a surprise to Appellant, who, upon searching the bundle of letters which were in proof before the Master, has found the original without any note or memorandum to show it was in evidence below. Prays for a re-hearing, such having been granted to one Sedgwick after an Appeal dismissed by a surprise upon the adversary's trumping up a deed not heard of before. L. J., XV. 15, 23.

420. Nov. 7. Howard *v.* Beaghan.—Petition and Appeal of Dame Elizabeth Howard, widow. Appellant was the daughter and heir of Sir Robert Newton, Bart., and on her marriage with her first husband, Sir John Baker, lands were conveyed to Sir Robert in trust to pay her, six months' after her husband's death, the 1,500*l*. in lieu of a jointure house, and 2,000*l*. apiece, and 50*l*. a year until payment thereof at the age of 17, to each of their daughters. Her husband's estate, worth only 2,000*l*. a year, was seized to pay debts amounting to 30,000*l*., and Appellant was forced to part with 450*l*. a year of her jointure. By a subsequent deed 400*l*. a year was secured to her for the separate maintenance of herself and her children. Sir John Baker died in 1660, leaving five daughters, whom Appellant maintained for several years. Sarah, the youngest, died in 1668; yet the estate was found insufficient to carry out the settlement. Edmond Beaghan married Anne, one of the daughters, who died leaving issue Anne, the infant Respondent. Beaghan obtained a Decree in Chancery for 50*l*. a year for his wife's maintenance until the age of 17, and 2,000*l*. then, with interest at the rate of 120*l*. a year, making no allowance to Appellant for her daughter's maintenance. Prays the Decree may be reversed, and proceedings below stayed. *Signed* by Appellant; *Countersigned* by Wm. Whitelocke and Tho. Trevor. L. J., XIV. 637. [The Cause was heard and the Decree affirmed on 21 Nov. 1691. *Sir William Whitelocke* (for Appellant) opens the case. *The Solicitor General* (for Respondent): This is a cause I thought we should never have heard of here, being the most frivolous of any I ever heard of. She received three or four times the value of the interest of that 200*l*. per annum. She complains of the collateral security; that is fully answered. She says she had no allowance for the wants of her daughter for 14 years, and yet she was in possession of the whole. *Mr. Ward* (for Respondent): She ought to pay exemplary costs in all Courts. (MS. Min. L. J., XIV. 656.)]

Annexed :—

(*a*.) 14 Nov. Answer of Edmund Beaghan, Esq., and Anne Beaghan, his daughter, an infant, by him, her Guardian. Appellant had

House of Lords MSS.

1691.

the bulk of the Baker Estate. Her daughter Anne had quietly enjoyed her share until her death, when Appellant caused the tenants to attorn to her. An arbitration was agreed to, Mr. Serjeant Pemberton and Mr. Martin Fokes being the arbitrators, and Chief Baron Montague the umpire; but, on its going against her, Appellant refused to abide by it, so the Respondents were forced to exhibit a Bill in Chancery. *Signed* by both the Respondents; *Countersigned* by T. Vernon. *Endorsed* as brought in this day. L. J., XIV. 656.

(*b.*) 16 Nov. Petition of same. Respondents had prosecuted the Appellant to a Sequestration, to avoid which she had fraudulently conveyed her estate to her son under age. Pray for a short day for hearing, and that Appellant produce the Deeds of Settlement at the hearing. L. J., XIV. 646.

421. Nov. 7. Swayne *v.* Jones.—Petition and Appeal of Wm. Swayne, Esq. Edwd. Souch borrowed 100*l.* of Bartholomew Lane, upon a mortgage to John Smith, in trust for Lane, of lands in Lamiate, Somersetshire, and Henry and Edw. Souch gave John Smith a bond for 200*l.* as collateral security. Henry Souch, being sued on the Bond, got Francis Summers to pay it, giving him a mortgage on his own land; and on payment by Summers, the mortgage to Smith in trust for Lane was assigned to him. The said mortgage has come by mean assignment to Petitioner. Richard Jones and his son-in-law Wm. Bray, pretending a subsequent mortgage of the same lands to them for 200*l.*, obtained in June last a Decree of the Lords Commissioners against Petitioner. Appeals against this Decree, and prays that service on Respondent's Clerk in Chancery may be sufficient service, appending an affidavit that he cannot serve them in person. *Signed* by Appellant; *Countersigned* by Wl. Williams and Wm. Dobin. L. J., XIV. 636. [The Cause was heard and the Decree affirmed on 9 Dec. 1691. *Sir William Williams* and *Mr. Dobin* appearing for Appellant, and *Mr. Trevor* and *Mr. Finch* for Respondent. (MS. Min. L. J., XIV. 679.)]

Annexed :—

(*a.*) Affidavit of John Pink, of St. Dunstan's in the West, Porter, that he had repeatedly tried to serve Respondents with process of the Court of Chancery without avail. Appended to preceding.

(*b.*) 7 Nov. Order of service on the Appeal. L. J., XIV. 636. *In Extenso.* Endorsed is the note of a motion for a week or ten days further time to answer.

(*c.*) 20 Nov. Answers of Richard Jones and Wm. Bray. The previous mortgage ought to have been cancelled when Summers paid off the debt. *Signed* Richard Joanes, William Bray. *Endorsed* as brought in this day.

(*d.*) 23 Nov. Petition of same for a short day for hearing. L. J., XIV. 659.

422. Nov. 7. Joyce *v.* Fowkes.—Petition and Appeal of Thomas Joyce. Appellant leased to one John Wills some lands in Barnet, Herts, for 132*l.* a year. The rent being unpaid, he distrained some sheep he found there, which were replevined by Richard Fowkes, Thomas Fowler, and Bryan Satterwaight, who said they were graziers and agisted their cattle on Appellant's land by inadvertency. Appellant obtained three Judgments at law against Fowkes and the others, but the Lords Commissioners on 10 Feb. 1689* ordered him to acknowledge satisfaction on

* *See* 2 *Vernon* 129.

his Judgments, and to pay the costs of the proceedings at law. He had paid 5*l*. for a rehearing, which was ultimately refused him. Appeals against this Decree, which would preclude him from recovering his rent, and prays for stay of proceedings. *Signed* by Appellant; *Countersigned* by Creswell Levinz and Nicho. Courtney. L. J., XIV. 637. [The Cause was heard and the Decree affirmed on 16 Dec. 1691, *Mr. Ward* and *Mr. Dodd* appearing for Appellant, and *Sir Thomas Powys* and *Mr. Row* for Respondent. (MS. Min. L. J., XIV. 689.)]

Annexed:—

(*a*.) 14 Nov. Answer of Richard Fowkes, Thomas Fowler, and Bryan Satterthwaite. The lands were those of the George Inn. The sheep remained there by Appellant's permission. The Judgments at Law were obtained by fraud. A rehearing was at first ordered in ignorance of the Order having been enrolled. The sheep suffered 40*l*. in value by having been impounded for three days. *Signed* by Respondents; *Countersigned* by J. G. Snow.

423. Nov. 7. Halton *v*. Williams (Privilege).—Petition of Timothy Halton, D.D., Archdeacon of Brecknock, and of Jno. Halton, B.D., his Lessee in trust, for leave to sue William Williams, Attorney-at-law, for 245*l*., the rent of the prebend, parsonage, rectory and tithes of St. David's in Llanvais in Brecon, which Williams refused to pay on the ground of privilege as a servant of the Bp. of St. David's. L. J., XIV. 637. Almost *in extenso*. [Read this day, and *ordered* that Williams may be sued. Then *Dr. Halton* being sworn stated that he was a common Attorney and Solicitor. *Ordered*, That it shall be understood that Attornies and common Solicitors shall not be privileged, upon oath made they are so. Referred to Committee for Privileges to draw an Order. Complaint having been made of a common Solicitor being privileged by a member of this House, which the House has not thought fit to allow of, it is referred to the Committee for Privileges to draw a general order in this case that no Attorney or common Solicitor shall for the future be allowed privilege, oath being made that he is so. *Ordered*, That it be referred to the Committee for Privileges to consider [upon the debate of this House concerning tradesmen being allowed privilege as noblemen's servants or to]* *of and* ascertain the privileges of the servants and agents of the Peers of this realm and members of this House. (MS. Min.) No proceedings are recorded in Priv. Book.]

424. Nov. 7. Punishment of Offenders (Benefit of Clergy) Act.—Amended draft of an Act to take away Clergy from some offenders and to bring others to punishment. The original draft contains the first four sections of the Act 3 W. & M. c. 9 (Fol. Ed.) with the variations noted below The Lords' amendments are as follow:—

§ i. Forasmuch as diverse wicked and ill-disposed persons are encouraged to commit robberies upon men's persons and in their houses and other felonies† by the privilege. . .

That all and every person or persons that shall at any time [hereafter] *from and after the first day of January in the year of our Lord one thousand, six hundred, ninety one*‡

* The words in square brackets are expunged and replaced by the words in italics, making the order read as in L. J., XIV. 637.

† The words ("and other felonies") are written in the margin of the draft. The words ("and other offenders") which replace them in the Act, were substituted by the Lords before engrossment, as is plain from the original Roll.

‡ This amendment was made by the Lords in Committee, and was amended by the Commons on third reading, by altering ("January") into ("March"), as in the Act. C. J., X. 646.

House of Lords MSS.

1691.

. . . or to break any dwelling-house or outhouse* thereunto belonging. . . . . . . although no person shall be within such dwelling-house or outhouse,* or shall counsel, hire or command any person to commit any burglary *or shall commit any offence against the Statute made in the twenty-first year of the reign of King Henry the Eighth, intituled Servants embezzling their Master's goods to the value of forty shillings or above, shall be punished as felony, or being a servant or servants of the age of eighteen years or upwards and no apprentice, shall steal any goods or chattel of the value of five pounds or more out of the house of his or her master,*† being thereof convicted. . .

§ ii. . . . to be of the Jury or shall be outlawed,‡ shall not be admitted to the benefit of his or their clergy.

§ iii. . . within this realm of England, *dominion of Wales or town of Berwick-upon-Tweed,*§ and thereof be convicted. . . .

[Read 1a this day (L. J., XIV. 636); committed on 9 Nov. to a Select Committee, assisted by C. J. Holt and Justice Eyre, with instructions to draw a Clause against servants running away with their masters' property. (*Ib.* 638.) The proceedings of this Committee are not recorded in Com. Book. They reported the Bill on 11 Nov. with some amendments, which were agreed to. (L. J., XIV. 641.) On the third reading on the 12th some further amendments were made at the table, and a Proviso was offered and read twice. Judges heard upon the Clause or Rider (Annex (*b.*) below), which was disagreed to after debate, and the Bill passed. (*Ib.* 642; MS. Min.) The Commons amended the first four sections as noted, and added Sections 5, 6, and 7 to the Bill. (C. J., X. 643, 646.) The Lords agreed to these amendments with an amendment in Section 6, adding the words ("*that is to say shall be burnt in the hand by the gaoler in open court and further be kept in prison for such time as the Justices in their discretion shall think fit, so as the same do not exceed one year's imprisonment*") to which the Commons agreed (L. J., XV. 54, 68; C. J., X. 653), and the Bill received the Royal Assent on 24 Feb. 1691-2. (L. J., XV. 92.)]

Annexed :—

(*a.*) 11 Nov. Lords' Amendments to the Bill. [Made in Committee and agreed to on report this day. L. J., XIV. 641. *See* notes to principal paper.]

(*b.*) 12 Nov. Draft Rider ‖ as follows:—"And forasmuch as diverse common thieves do frequently hire lodgings with a purpose to obtain an opportunity to steal the furniture or household goods being in such lodgings, be it therefore declared and enacted by the authority aforesaid that if any person or persons shall take away [or embezzle] any chattell, bedding, or furniture

* The words in the Act ("shop or warehouse") were substituted for ("or outhouse") by the Commons on Report. C. J., X. 643.

† These words in italics were added by the Lords in Committee but struck out by the Commons on Report, and are not in the Act. C. J., X. 643.

‡ The word ("thereupon") in the Act was inserted after ("outlawed") by the Commons on Report. C. J., X. 643.

§ This amendment was made by the Lords in Committee.

‖ The words in square brackets are struck out, and the word in italics substituted on the draft.

which by the contract or agreement he or they are to use, or shall be let to him or them to use with such lodgings, such taking [and embezzling] *away* shall to all intents and purposes be reputed, taken and adjudged to be felony and larceny, and the offender shall be punished as in case of felony. [Offered this day on third Reading, but rejected. *See* notes to principal paper above. Compare § 5 of Act, which was added by the Commons. C. J., X. 643.]

(c.) 12 Nov. Parchment Copy of preceding, adding the words "steal and" and "stealing and" before the words "take away" and "taking away."

425. Nov. 7. Beckman's Naturalisation Act.—Amended Draft of an Act for naturalising Sir Martin Beckman, Knt. and others. The Bill as introduced is to naturalise Sir Martin Beckman, Knt., Denis Dutry, Thomas Oulry, Nicholas Tourton, and Dr. Cornelis Noortwyck. The Lords' Amendment is a purely verbal one. (Com. Book. 10 Nov.) The remaining persons (10) naturalised by the Act were added by the Commons. (C. J., X. 581.) [Read 1a this day; Royal Assent 24 Dec. L. J., XIV. 636, 702. 3 & 4 Will. and Mary, c. 8, in Long Calendar.]

426. Nov. 9. Robert's Estate Act.—Amended Draft of an Act to vest certain messuages, lands and tenements in Thorpe Langton and elsewhere in the County of Leicester in Trustees to be sold for payment of the debts of Richard Roberts Esqre. and for raising portions for his Daughters. The one Amendment is purely formal.* [Read 1a this day. Royal Assent 31 Dec. L. J., XIV. 638; XV. 11. 3 W. & M., c. 13, in Long Calendar. *See also* Com. Book 24 & 25 Nov.]

427. Nov. 9. Stydolfe's Estate Act.—Draft of an Act for sale of the Manor of and lands in Wittering in the County of Northampton and the Advowson of the Church of Wittering aforesaid, late the inheritance of William Stydolfe, Esqre. deceased, late father of Sigismond Stydolfe, Esqre. Identical with Act. [Read 1a this day. Royal Assent 24 Dec. L. J., XIV. 638, 702. 3 W. & M., c. 10, in Long Calendar. *See also* Com. Book 13 Nov.]

428. Nov. 9. Barton *v.* Woodman.—Petition and Appeal of Amy Barton, George Willoughby and Joanna his wife, and William Taylor and Margaret his wife. Sir Thomas Badd, Knt. and Bart., conveyed to Edward Lord Noell, afterwards E. Gainsborough, and Thomas Sackville, Esqre., his manor of Cames or Camms Oysell, Hants, worth 500*l.* a year, in trust for the use of himself and his wife Dame Joan, and after their deaths to be sold and the money to be divided among his five daughters, Elizabeth, wife of Robert Blake, the Appellant Amy, Frances Dennis, widow, and the Appellants Joanna and Margaret, with a power to each of them, according to seniority, to take the lands on payment, within three months after the death of the father and mother, of 6,000*l.*, to be divided among the other sisters. By his Will shortly afterwards he gave this power of purchase to Frances, extending the time for payment to six months, and gave her all his lands within the manors of Fareham, Catesfield, and Porchester on that condition. On the last day of the six months Frances preferred a Bill for extension of time, and Robert Blake and his wife also preferred one to have the

---

* In L. J., XIV. 662 the Bill is stated to have been reported "with some amendments." Only one is marked on the draft and recorded in Com. Book.

HOUSE OF LORDS MSS.

1691.

estate conveyed to them on payment of the 6,000*l.* Frances died at Calais, and Joshua Woodman, a country attorney, as her executor, obtained a decree from the Lords Commissioners on 21 March last. Appeal from this Decree and pray that Woodman, Elizabeth Blake and Sackville may be ordered to answer. *Signed* by Appellants; *Countersigned* by Edw. Ward and Jo. Dalby. L. J., XIV., 639. [The Cause was heard and the decree reversed on 14 Jan. 1691–2. *The Solicitor-General* and *Mr. Ward* were heard for the Appellant. *Sir Ambrose Phillipps* (for Respondent): I agree the case is much as it is stated. *Mr. Filmer* (for Respondent): Col. Sackville stood on his privilege in this case. If the trustees will not accept of the money, we cannot help. S. Master's deposition read; he told Col. Sackville the money was ready. Mr. Pitt's Bill, 1688, produced. *Mr. Crisp* is heard for Elizabeth. (MS. Min. L. J., XV. 30.)]

Annexed:—

(*a.*) 13 Nov. Answer of Thomas Sackville, Esqre. Makes no objection to the Appeal. *Signed* Th. Sackevill; *Countersigned* Frac. Blower. *Endorsed* as brought in this day.

(*b.*) 25 Nov. Answer of Elizabeth Blake, widow. Frances not having tendered the money in time, and Respondent being ready to pay it, the surviving trustee should be compelled to convey the estate to Respondent. Prays for cost. *Countersigned* Robert Dormer *Endorsed* as brought in this day.

(*c.*) 10 Dec. Several Answer of Joshua Woodman, Gent. The reason why Sir Thomas Badd gave Frances a pre-emption (worth a double share) was that he had been guardian of her husband. Edward Dennies, Esqre., who died before his majority, had received the rents of his estate, about 700*l.* a year, for which he had never accounted, and owed it above 4,000*l.* Frances sued her mother for an account of Dennies' estate, but failed on the ground of the pre-emption given her of her father's estate. She had been ready to pay the 6,000*l* within the time, but could not get the trustees to receive it. She had made Respondent her executor for payment of her debts and 1,300*l.* legacies. Respondent was willing that the estate should be sold to the highest bidder, but Sackville, Appellant's uncle, resisted the sale, as he had been receiving the rents since Lady Badd's death, and insisted on his privilege of Parliament. *Signed* by Respondent; *Countersigned* by Ambr. Phillipps and Tho. Filmer. *Endorsed* as brought in this day. *See also* Calendar, 9th Report. No 259.

(*d.*) 4 Jan. 1691–2. Petition of Amy Barton, widow, that the Deed of Settlement, now lodged in the Court of Chancery, should be produced at the hearing. L. J., XV. 16.

(*e.*) 14 March 1698–9. Petition of Respondent Woodman. Frances died 3,000*l.* in debt. The reversal of the Decree by the House took away her right of pre-emption, but was not intended to take away her right to a fifth of the estate. The Court of Chancery cannot give any relief to the creditors of Frances in the face of the judgment of the House. Prays that the Appeal may be re-heard, with a view to giving the creditors some relief, and that Chancery may be directed how to proceed. *Signed* by Petitioner; *Countersigned* by Wm. Whitelocke and Ja. Master. L. J., XVI. 404, 408. [Counsel were heard on 19 April 1699 on this Petition and the Answers thereto (Annexes (*f.*) and (*g.*) below), *Serjeant Wright* and *Sir William White-*

locke appearing for Petitioner, and ***Sir Thomas Powys*** and ***Sir Bartholomew Showers*** for Respondents. (MS. Min.)]

(*f.*) 27 March 1699. Petition of Appellants George Willoughby and his wife, and Margt. Taylor. Amy Barton and William Taylor, the other Appellants, are dead. Pray for a week's further time to answer, as the papers are lost or mislaid. L. J., XVI. 420.

(*g.*) 4 April 1699. Answer of same. Woodman has acquiesced in the judgment of the House for seven years, and parts of the estate have been sold with the concurrence of the Respondent Elizabeth Blake. Woodman has advanced no new matter. *Signed* by these Appellants; ***Countersigned*** by T. Powys. *Endorsed* as brought in this day.

429. Nov. 9. Bromhall *v* Manlove.—Petition and Appeal of Thomas Bromhall, Infant, by his Guardian, Wm. Bromhall. Appellant's ancestor, Thomas Bromhall, in 1676 purchased the Office of Warden of the Fleet, thirteen houses thereto belonging, and all the shops of Westminster Hall, of Henry Norwood Esq., and mortgaged the same for the payment of 800*l.* per annum for fourteen years to Norwood as part payment. In 1687 [1677] Bromhall granted the said office and Mansion House only to Richard Manlove, Esqre., for life, for a payment of 800*l.* a year, and a deposit of 1,000*l.* without interest, to indemnify Bromhall against escapes and other damages. This 800*l.* a year was, at Bromhall's death, transferred to Norwood for the remainder of the 14 years which expired at Christmas last. Appellant, as heir-at-law of Bromhall, obtained a Decree in Chancery, giving him the Equity of Redemption. Appeals against the said Decree in so far as it decreed Appellant to pay Manlove's costs in defending the title of the Fleet, and awarded him interest for the 1,000*l.* *Signed* by Wm. Bromhall, father and guardian of the Appellant; *Countersigned* by Fra. Winnington and Gi. Duncombe. L. J., XIV. 639. [The Cause was heard on 2 Jan., 1691–2, ***Sir Thomas Powys*** and *Mr. Duncombe* appearing for Appellant, and ***Mr. Finch*** and ***Mr. Sloane*** for Respondent.—On 4 Jan. the *Lord* ***Commissioner Rawlinson*** attending, as ordered, the Lord Speaker stated the case to him. *Sir W. Rawlinson:* I have not seen any of the decrees. I thought the parties would have attended me with them. (He then gave the House an account of the case as it stood before the Commissioners.) The order is not definite nor any decree made. *Ordered*, That the Appeal be dismissed, the decree not being final, without prejudice to either party. (MS. Min.)]

Annexed:—

(*a.*) 16 Nov. Answer of Richard Manlove, Esq. Thomas Bromhall, Appellant's great uncle, gave 3,000*l.* for his purchase, and the office was granted to one Comerford in trust to secure the payment to Norwood, and afterwards to one Johnson in trust for Bromhall. The assignment to Manlove included the office of keeping the Palace at Westminster; but the 13 houses and the shops in Westminster Hall were added as security for the 1,000*l.* deposited by Respondent in Bromhall's hands to indemnify him for escapes. At Bromhall's death, 1,500*l.* of the 3,000*l.* and 80*l.* of the 800*l.* due to Norward remained unpaid, so Norwood resumed possession, and Respondent had to make a fresh agreement with him. Respondent has paid over 1,000*l.* of Bromhall's debts, besides 2,552*l.* 15*s.* 8*d.* to Norwood, but is

1,991*l.* 15*s.* 1*d.* in arrear in consequence of the profits of the office falling short. *Signed* by Respondent; *Countersigned* by James Sloane. *Endorsed* as brought in this day.

(*b.*) 18 Nov. Petition of Appellant for a speedy day for hearing, and for the production of documents. L. J., XIV. 650.

(*c.*) 19 Dec. Petition of Henry Johnson. Petitioner was a party in the Court below, but has not been made a party to the Appeal. Prays that the judgment may not prejudice his interest. L. J., XIV. 694, almost *in extenso.*

(*d.*) 9 Jan. 1691–2. Petition of Appellant. The Decree is not definitive as to the rent to be paid by Respondent since Christmas, 1690, and that rent is in abeyance until an account be stated. Prays that a final Decree may be made on the point, from which Appellant might appeal. Appellant owes Lady Lisle and others 4,000*l.*, and will be foreclosed of the Equity of Redemption if he does not pay Mr. Johnson's debt by a short day. L. J., XV. 22.

430. Nov. 11. Writ of Summons (D. St. Albans).—Writ of Summons, dated Nov. 10, to Charles, Duke of St. Albans. [Introduced and took the oaths this day. L. J., XIV. 641.]

431. Nov. 11. Gay *v.* Beaple.—Petition of Martha Gay. The circumstances of her lawsuit with Thomas Beaple are given in Calendar, 12th Report, Appendix, Part VI., No. **146.** Since the Judgment of the House Appellant has obtained Judgments against Andrew Edworthy and Andrew Corneall for 390*l.* for felling timber on the estate, and has recovered from Susanna Corneall an estate leased by Richard Gay, Petitioner's late husband, to Susanna's late husband Charles Corneall, for 65*l.* Thomas Beaple, though no party to these three judgments, had obtained an injunction to stay execution thereof. He has been found to owe Appellant nearly 1,000*l.*, and is insolvent. At the instance of Beaple, Edworthy and Corneall have been given leave by the Court of Chancery to cut down more timber. Appeals against these several Orders. *Signed* by Appellant; *Countersigned* by Jo. Tremayne and Edw. Ward. L. J., XIV. 641. [The Cause was heard on 9 Dec. *Serjeant Tremaine* (for Appellant): We think these orders are contrary to your Lordship's judgment. They have ordered him to cut more timber. *Sir Francis Winnington* (for Appellant): We separate these orders from other things. We will prove the Defendant Beaple has done us 500*l.* damage. This, we say, is a wrong. *Sir William Williams* (for Respondent): Here is an Appeal from five interlocutory orders, and this they appeal from before a final determination. Instances Wycherley's Case, 1680.* In this case, if you admit this, you may have five orders. The question before your Lordships on appeal was whether the right of redemption was in Richard or Martha Gay. *Another Counsel* is heard for Respondent. *Serjeant Tremaine* heard in reply. *Sir Francis Winnington* (in reply): Beaple is a beggar. We pray only, give us good security. *Ordered* that security be mutually given in Chancery as offered at the Bar. (MS. Min. L. J., XIV. 678.) For further proceedings *see* notes to Annexes (*d.*) and (*e*) below.]

Annexed:—

(*a.*) 21 Nov. Answer of Thomas Beaple. Richard Gay had willed to Respondent the estate leased to Charles Corneall. The

* *Wycherley* v. *Tylor*, L. J., XIII. 714. MS. Min., 13 Dec. 1680.

value of the timber felled had been applied to paying off the mortgage. Respondent had been ordered to account for the profits of the estate, and execution had been stayed till the account should be taken and Respondent's objections thereto heard. The Orders appealed from are only interlocutory, and Appellant should wait until a final judgment is given. *Endorsed* as brought in this day.

(*b.*) 23 Nov. Petition of Appellant for a day for hearing. L. J., XIV. 658.

(*c.*) 17 Dec. Petition of Appellant. Chancery refused to order any security (as ordered by the House on 9th Dec., L. J., XIV. 678), alleging they knew not what sum to fix, though Respondent has been certified to owe Petitioner over 1,000*l.*, besides 5,000*l.* owed to her by the estate. Prays that in default of security by the Respondent, the Orders appealed from may be reversed, and the felling of more timber forbidden. L. J., XIV. 691.

(*d.*) 9 Feb. 1691–2. Petition of Respondent. Far from being indebted to Appellant, she and the estate are indebted to him. Chancery did not refuse to fix a security, as untruly alleged by Appellant and her son-in-law, Mr. Ford, her solicitor, but deferred fixing it until Respondent's exceptions had been heard; upon hearing which a new account has been ordered. Chancery nevertheless has directed the security ordered by the House to be given. Prays that the taking of the security of 2,000*l.* may be respited till the account is taken, and that Gay and Ford may be summoned to answer for their mis-information. L. J., XV. 68, 75. [Counsel were heard and the Petition dismissed on 13 Feb. *Sir William Williams* (for Respondent): This Cause was heard in L. Nottingham's time. We desire these persons may be punished for their abuse. *Sir Francis Winnington* heard for Gay and Ford. *Mr. Dobyns* heard for Mr. Ford and Beaple. (MS. Min. L. J., XV. 75.)]

(*e.*) 12 Nov. 1692. Petition of Appellant. Has given security, but Respondent has not done so. Chancery would not on that account dissolve the Injunction, but only ordered the new Master to proceed with the account. Ford was sent to the Fleet for 10 days for his Petition to the House. Prays she may have the benefit of her judgments, as Respondent has not given security. L. J., XV. 109, 117. [Counsel were heard on this Petition on 19 Nov. 1692. *Sir Francis Winnington* (for Appellant) opens the case. *Sir William Thompson* (for Appellant) We come to support the honour of this Court. We desire the liberty the law gives. The Chancery have made several Orders that are not consistent with the Orders of this House. Order of 19 Dec. 1691 read. Order of 21 April 1692 read, for committing Mr. Ford. We pray we may have the effect of your authority in this Cause. *Mr. Gibbings* (for Respondent) is heard. *Sir William Williams* (for Respondent): The Chancery have fully performed your orders. *Sir W. Thompson* heard to show that they have given security pursuant to the Order of this House. *Ordered* that Martha Gay shall have the benefit of her verdicts and judgments at law. *Ordered* that the complaint as to Ford be referred to the Committee for Privileges, with power to send for the Lord Commissioner Rawlinson. (MS. Min. L. J., XV. 117.)—In Committee for Privileges on 7 Dec., E. Bridgewater in the Chair, Mr. Ford's Counsel are called in. *Serjeant Darnell* (for Petitioner) states the case. It was formerly heard

House of Lords MSS.
—
1691.

at the Bar whether Ford had slandered the Commissioners in Gay's Petition, and your Lordship's resolved he had not; but after the Prorogation the Commissioners imprisoned him and suspended him. *Sir Francis Winnington:* The reason why Ford was committed, was the presenting a Petition to this House. Reads the Order of Chancery for the suspension and imprisonment of Mr. Ford. No Court but this great Court ought to have done it. Cites L. Holles' Case, and Dr. Evan's Case upon an *Habeas Corpus* brought in the King's Bench for a contempt in Chancery, which the King's Bench refused to meddle with, it being a contempt in Chancery, which the Chancery itself was judge of. *Ordered* that the L. Commissioner Rawlinson attend.—On 12 Dec. *Sir W. Rawlinson*, attending, was placed on a chair at the end of the Table next the fire. *Mr. Darnell* (for Appellant): We complain that the Lords have not taken the security as ordered. The other [complaint] is committing our solicitor for petitioning your Lordships and slandering the Commissioners. He lies still under this suspension. *Sir Francis Winnington* (for Appellant) is heard as to the merits of the cause. We have your order for dissolving it. In my client's Petition we complain that the other [party] never could be got to give security. We offered undeniable security, and we ought not to go on until the other had given security. The cause of this man's confinement is [stated] in the Order; [namely] because he petitions. Order of Chancery of 21 April last read: Mr. Ford being present in Court and having greatly abused this Court in petitioning the House of Peers, &c. It falls out we have had your judgments. The wood-cutters have preferred a Bill, and for want of an answer, here is an injunction. *L. Commissioner Rawlinson:* The first complaint is that the Chancery have not obeyed by taking security. Order of Chancery of 16 January last read, wherein the Chancery directed security of 2,000*l*. We have directed it to be done, and we have directed a Master to take it. As for security in general, you not naming it, it is an act of judgment in us, and let me put the case. This cause was heard by the Lord North in 1684, I think. He states the case. On 11 May 1689 the cause was reheard. On 9 Dec. the injunction was confirmed, and the same day security in general is directed. Six days after Mr. Gay and Mr. Ford come to the Court of Chancery and move security to be taken, and move for 2,000*l*. The Defendant says but 200*l*. There was no conscience for 2,000*l*. We declared we would take security equal to the quantity of the demand. We ordered it the next day to be heard. Reads the Order of 15 Dec. The first day [of] exceptions, [which] was five days after, 17 Dec. Mr. Ford the same man with the order in their (*sic*) hands, comes with this Petition to this House. It was very scandalous to us, and particularly to me. It was as bad as calling me ill names or language. The Cause comes on to be heard [on] 21 [Dec.] before us. Then you directed it should be 2,000*l*., and thereupon we made the Order for 1,000*l*. On 16 January they came to us, and they had got a Report for 500*l*. Beaple to Gay and it appeared but 100*l*. due to Gay. The same 16 Jan. we ordered Ford to attend the Court in Hilary term. Then he did not attend nor bring the petition, so we ordered the first day of Easter term, and then, after four admonishments, he attends, and then we admonished him. Mr. Ford in Lady Mill's Case 1,400*l*.

(*sic*). The Order read, brought by Mr. Ford for his commitment; "false and scandalous Petition" are the words. The minutes of the Court read for committing Mr. Ford. We name the cause of *Sir William Gostwick* v. *Ashbolt* to him. For the abuse and contempt we made the salva et arcta custodia. He was not simply committed for that cause. Mr. Ford did not petition us till 30 April. We discharged him, but did not take his suspension; he never asked it. It is said we are reviving this injunction again. This I take upon myself; I sat for the Master of the Rolls. Reads the Minutes at the Rolls. In other names I have dissolved it, with a mark upon it. The order for commitment is signed Carew Gurdett, 30 April. Order read for Mr. Ford's discharge. Counsel and Sir W. Rawlinson withdrew. *Agreed*, that as to the first order for security in general, the Chancery did obey, and as to the 2,000*l.* security they did obey it also. *Moved* to send for Sir W. Rawlinson and say to him: "I presume you are satisfied (I am sure the Lords are) that the Register has issued an Order contrary to your directions, and the Lords hope you will take care to have him punished." *L. Commissioner Rawlinson*, being called in and directed to the chair, is told: "The Committee are very well satisfied with your Lordship, and will report it so to the House, but they are dissatisfied with the Register and his behaviour in this case, and suppose you are not less angry, and hope you will take care to have him punished as far as you can." *L. Commissioner Rawlinson:* I thank your Lordships for the great justice you have done us. The Register did not do well. As soon as we knew it, we admonished him, and we had then laid a mark of displeasure on him, but that it was depending before your Lordships; but now that it is over, we will censure him as it deserves. *Ordered* to report as in L. J., XV. 152. (Priv. Book.)]

(*f.*) 30 Nov. 1692. Petition of Edward Forde, the Appellant's solicitor. Was sent to the Fleet by the Commissioners of the Great Seal, for the same matter alleged against him two months before, which was heard and dismissed at the Bar. Has not yet been restored to his practice. Prays for a short day for hearing this matter by Counsel by the Committee for Privileges. L. J., XV. 130.

(*g.*) 8 Dec. 1692. Petition of Appellant. In spite of the Order of the House of 19 Nov. last, Edwerthy and Cornall have obtained a fresh Injunction in Chancery to stay proceedings, upon suggestion of a contempt for want of an answer. The Bill is signed by Mr. Gibbon, the Respondent's Counsel, and prosecuted by the Respondent's clerk in Chancery. Prays she may take execution in spite of the Injunction. L. J., XV. 138.

432. Nov. 11. George *v.* Godsalve.—Petition and Appeal of Rebecca George, late Godsalve, Relict and Executrix of Thomas Godsalve, deceased, and now wife of William George, Esq. Thomas Godsalve, Respondent's uncle, and Appellant's late husband, left 400*l.* a piece to John, Anne and Elizabeth, and 500*l.* to Thomas, payable out of Navy papers, supplemented by his personal estate. Appellant joined in a friendly suit, in order to have the money placed at interest for Respondent's benefit and her own indemnity, and a Decree was pronounced against her by the Lords Commissioners on 30 October last, for the amount of the legacies with interest and costs. Appeals against the

Decree as regards the interest and costs, as she had not herself made use of the money, but had kept it ready for Respondents, and as the suit was a friendly one. *Signed* by Appellant and her husband; *Countersigned* by Wm. Whitelocke and Tho. Filmer. L. J., XIV. 611. [The Cause was heard and the Decree affirmed on 5 Dec. 1691, *Sir William Whitelocke* and *Mr. Filmer* appearing for Appellant, and *Sir Ambrose Phillipps* and *Mr. Trevor* for Respondent. (MS. Min. L. J., XIV. 674.)]

Annexed :—

(*a*.) 20 Nov. Answer of John, Thomas and Elizabeth Godsalve, infants, by Christopher Godsalve, their father and next friend. Thomas, their father's only brother, was a Clerk in the Navy Office, and acquired an estate of 6,000*l.* by his own industry. Appellant did receive interest for the legacy money, and the suit was not a friendly one. *Signed* by Christopher; *Countersigned* by Rich. Hetford. *Endorsed* as brought in this day.

(*b*.) 20 Nov. Petition of the above Respondents (with the addition of Anne, an infant) for a short day for hearing. The Appeal was brought only for delay. L. J., XIV. 654.

433. Nov. 11. Peacock *v.* Spooner.—Petition of Thomas Peacock. On his way from Stortford, Herts, where he lives, to present his appeal, he fell sick and thus allowed the time for bringing appeals to elapse. Prays for leave to present his appeal under the circumstances. L. J., XIV. 641. *See* Notes to next paper.

Annexed :—

(*a*.) 13 Nov. Petition and Appeal of same. Humphrey Aylett, in 1600 demised to James Collins the lands of Caldycott in Leaden Roothine, Essex, for 1912 years at a peppercorn rent. The lease, after mean assignments, came to Robert Long, who assigned it as a jointure to Samuel Pigbone and John Smith in trust for Long's son Robert and his wife Mary, Pigbone's daughter, and for the heirs of her body by Robert Long. The Longs had three daughters: Mary, wife of Henry Spooner, Elizabeth, wife of Samuel Smith, and Frances, wife of Thomas Freeman. On Robert Long's death Appellant married his widow, since deceased, and now claims the estate as her administrator, for an estate for years cannot be limited to the heirs of the body, but must go to the Administrator. His late wife's daughters, however, pretending a title to the estate, Appellant gave the title deeds to Thomas Wheeler to show them; but by confederacy with Wheeler, they got possession of them and refused to restore them, and got the tenant to attorn to them. The estate in Law was in Mary Smith, executrix of the trustee John Smith, who survived Pigbone; but she refused to allow Appellant to bring an ejectment in her name. Appellant therefore brought a Bill in Chancery against the daughters and their husbands and Wheeler, to compel them to assign their estates and deliver back the deeds to him, and having obtained a decree from Lord Jeffreys,* was put in possession of the premises. This decree was reversed on a rehearing by the Lords Commissioners,† who ordered Appellant to reassign the premises and title deeds. Appeals against this last Decree. *Signed* by Appellant; *Countersigned* by Will. Monington. L. J., XIV. 644. [The Cause was

* 2 Vernon, 43.

† *Ibid.* 195, and note thereto, giving an extract, made by Mr. Coxe, of the MS. Min. entry of the Judge's opinions in the House on Appeal.

House of Lords MSS.

1691.

heard on 15 Feb. 1691–2, *Mr. Holles* and *Mr. Dodd* appearing for Appellant, and *Mr. Trevor* and *Mr. Row* for Respondent. One 17 Feb., the Speaker having reported, the judges were heard. *Atkyns, C. B.:* The point was agreed in the case of *D. Norfolk* v. *Howard*. [The estate] is not good. *Nevill, J.:* I differ from the L. Chief Baron. The estate to Mary and the children is a good estate to them. The first settlement is in consideration of marriage. *Gregory, J.:* I take it, if this had been a limitation to a man and his issue, then no other person could take it. This would be a perpetuity, which the law abhors. I am of opinion Peacock and his wife are well entitled, and he had from the L. Justice Holt that the Appellant had a good title. *Lechmere, B.:* The cases mentioned do not come to this. Here is no limitation. It is a singular case. He will run away with the whole subsistence of his wife's father. The case has no precedent. Peacock has not a good title. *Rokeby, J.:* I differ from my brother that spoke last. Thomas Peacock has a good interest in this term. His wife had the whole, and so he comes in. *Powell, B.:* This is a point in law. Terms and inheritances have different terms in law. I am of opinion that L. Jeffrey's decree is good, and that this decree of the Lords Commissioners is not good. *Turton, B.:* I am of opinion that the Appellant Peacock is well entitled as administrator to his wife. The Decree was then affirmed. (MS. Min. L. J., XV., 77, 80.)]

(*b*.) 14 Dec. Joint and Several Answer of Henry Spooner and Mary his wife, Samuel Smith and Elizabeth his wife, Thomas Freeman and Frances his wife, and Mary Smith, widow, and Thomas Wheeler. Appellant, when delivering over the deeds on the death of his wife, was satisfied with Respondent's right, and only pretended a title, by virtue of the letters of administration. The Lords Commissioners ordered his Bill to be dismissed, in case he failed to reassign and deliver up the deeds by a certain time, and he reassigned, though not decreed to do so, in order to have the costs remitted. *Signed* by Respondents; *Countersigned* by Tho. Powys. *Endorsed* as brought in this day.

434. Nov. 11. Orphans of London Relief Bill [H. L.].—Amended Draft of an Act for [erecting a Court of Inquiry in order to] the relief of the distressed Orphans of the City of London. The Draft, before amendment, is identical with the Bill of 15 Nov. 1690,* except in leaving blanks where indicated in the notes to that Bill. The amendments, which are appended to this Draft, consist in omitting the words in the above title, included in square brackets, and in substituting the amended clauses given in Annex (*p*) below, for the rest of the Bill, after the words ("proportionably to such discovery") in the Preamble.

[Read 1ª this day (L. J., XIV. 641), and referred on the 12th to a Select Committee† (*ib.* 642. Annex (*a*) below.) The subsequent proceedings are thus recorded:—

14 Nov. (In Committee.) First enacting clause read. The Orphans called in and told that they would be heard on the 18th inst., the

* *See* No. **329** and Annex (*a*) thereto.

† *See* Annex (*a*) below. The Chairmen of this Committee were as follows:—Bp. of Worcester, Nov. 14 and 18; E. Bridgewater, Dec. 11 and Jan. 12, 23, and 25; E. Rochester, Dec. 12, 15, 17, 22, and Jan. 2, 5, 9, 13; V. Weymouth, Dec. 17 and 22, Jan; L. Cornwallis, Jan. 19; and Bp. of London, Jan. 22. On Dec. 11 and 11. 21, Jan. 22, and 23 the Committee met only to adjourn. (Com. Book.)

HOUSE OF LORDS MSS.

1691.

Lord Mayor and Aldermen meantime to have a copy of the Bill. (Com. Book.)

18 Nov. (In the House.) Petitions of Lord Mayor, &c. and of Orphans* read, and Counsel ordered to be heard on the 24th inst. (MS. Min.).

Eod. die. (In Committee.) Enquiry is made at the door, whether any attend to be heard, and none attending for the City, *Mr. Reading* (for the Orphans) acquaints the Committee that the Bill is the same that was formerly before their Lordships,† and prays that another peremptory day may be appointed for the City to attend, and for an order for witnesses. *Ordered*, That the Lord Mayor, &c. attend with Counsel on the 23rd inst., and that the following witnesses should attend to be sworn at the Bar, viz.:—

Leonard Robinson.	Sir Hugh Chamberlain.
John Goodfellow.	Sir Peter Pett.
Joseph Lane.	—— Hales.
Sir John Lawrence.	Robert Murray.
John Johnson.	Sir John Sparrow.
John Midgley.	Phillip Oddy.
Samuel Kendall.	Sir Peter Daniell.
Thomas White.	Sir Peter Rich.
John Oliver.	Sir Patience Ward.
James Cumber.	John Borret.
Sir Humphrey Edwin.	Henry Crisp.
Alderman Wildman.	William Middelton.

(Com. Book.)

24 Nov. (In the House.) Counsel called in. *Counsel for the City* say that the City have agreed to settle 8,000*l.* a year, all the City revenue.‡ *Mr. Dobyns* (for the Orphans): They are very sensible for the House's kindness to them. They pray the Bill may not fall, and if the City be in earnest, they are willing to rest in it. *The City* leaves the time to the House, and *both sides* submit to it. *Ordered* to be heard on the 30th inst. (MS. Min.)

9 Dec. (In the House.) Select Committee revived. (L. J., XIV. 678.)

12 Dec. (In Committee.) First enacting clause read. *Agreed*, that the inquiry to be made by the Commissioners to be appointed by the Act shall not be beyond the Act of Indemnity in 1660; that the Commissioners shall not be empowered to examine any man against himself; that there shall be no imprisonment, but what shall be bailable; and that the Commissioners shall have no other power as to imprisonment than what the Commissioners of Bankrupts had. (Com. Book.)

15 Dec. (In Committee.) Instead of ("shall make their Report thereof unto the Parliament")§ read ("shall make their Report thereof unto the King and both Houses of Parliament"). *Agreed*, that the Commissioners shall consist of 15 persons, whereof the Bishop of London, the two Chief Justices and Chief Baron and the Dean of St. Paul's for the time being to be five, and five more to be chosen on behalf of the Orphans, and the remaining five by the Lord Mayor and

---

* Annexes (*b*) and (*c*) below.

† *See* Annex (*d*) below.

‡ The Corporation informed the Commons also of this resolution in a Petition on 27 Nov., praying for leave to promote a Bill. C. J., X. 562-3.

§ For the context *see* the amended Bill of 1690. No. 329, Annex (*a*).

Court of Aldermen. *Agreed*, that a reward be given to anyone that shall make a discovery, as in the preamble of the Bill. *Ordered*, that the L. Mayor and Court of Aldermen be sent for to propose five persons to be part of this Judicature. *Mr. Reading* is called in and directed to propose at the next meeting five on behalf of the Orphans,* and to have copies of the Heads agreed on by the Committee, and to prepare Clauses. (Com. Book.)

17 Dec. (In Committee.) The parties being called in, *Mr. Reading* offers some clauses† drawn pursuant to the Heads agreed on. *The Common Serjeant* (for the City): Mr. Reading showed the L. Mayor a copy of the order, but would not leave it with him, though desired. The L. Mayor appointed some of the Aldermen and myself to wait on your Lordships to desire it, for he, not having it till last night, durst not take upon himself without the Aldermen to name any persons as Commissioners. *Ordered*, that Mr. Reading deliver to the L. Mayor a copy of the order, and that on the 22nd the L. Mayor and the Orphans each propose five persons as Commissioners. (Com. Book.)

22 Dec. (In Committee.) Enquiry is made at the door, whether any attend from the L. Mayor. The Clauses drawn by Mr. Reading in pursuance of the order of 17th Dec. are begun to be read. *Mr. Reading* is called in, and says that the L. Mayor was served with the order for attending this day. *John Dowse* says he served the L. Mayor with the order of the Committee on the 19th inst., and that the next day he met the City Solicitor, and asking him if he had named the five Commissioners, he said "We will follow the Bill in the House of Commons." *Ordered*, that the House be acquainted therewith and moved that John Dowse may be sworn.‡ *The Common Serjeant, Sir John Moore, Sir Patience Ward*, etc. being at the door, are called in. *The Common Serjeant* says the L. Mayor and Aldermen would have complied with the order for naming Commissioners, if they had been capable, but considering the purport of the Bill, to imprison and to enquire into freeholds, and having but a limited power, they think it too hard for them, and therefore submit to their Lordship's wisdom. *Ordered* that the House be acquainted herewith. Adjourned to 5 Jan. (Com. Book.)

31 Dec. (In the House.) Report made from Committee by E. Rochester,§ recommending that the Court of Inquiry should be 15 in number, and that the Bishop of London should be one; but that the Committee did not know what to do on these proposals without directions from the House. *Moved* that the Committee may nominate such as they shall think fit, and that the Committee be revived. (MS. Min., L. J., XV. 10.)

2 Jan. 1691–2. (In Committee.) *Mr. Reading*, being called in, offers a Paper,‖ which he proposes may be shown to the Committee of Council. The same is read. (Com. Book.)

9 Jan. (In Committee.) Mr. Reading's clauses, offered on the 2nd inst., are read again. *Mr. Reading* is called in and asked for the Order of 20 Nov. last. The same is produced and read. *Ordered* that Mr. Goodfellow attend on the 12th and bring a true copy of the

---

* *See* Annex (*e*) below.

† *See* Annex (*f*) below.

‡ This Order is struck through.

§ The Committee had been twice ordered to report, viz. on Dec. 23 and 29. L. J., XIV. 700; XV. 4.

‖ Annex (*g*) below.

HOUSE OF LORDS MSS.

1691.

Order. The clause beginning in the 9th line* of Mr. Reading's Papers is postponed. *Ordered* that the L. Mayor and Aldermen be sent for to give account what sum the particulars mentioned in the Bill yearly amount to, and to what uses it is applied. *Question:* Whether the Conservancy of the rivers Thames, Medway, and Lee shall be one of the particulars to be enquired of the L. Mayor? Contents 2; Not-contents 7. Resolved in the *Negative.* Here follows the Order to the L. Mayor and Aldermen, directing them to give the Committee on the 12th inst. "An account in writing to what uses the particulars underwritten are applied, and what are the several yearly values of the same, viz., the Office of Keeping the Beam, and of weighing of wool and all other merchandises and commodities whatsoever, which anciently have been and now ought to be weighed, and the office of measuring and surveying all merchandises and commodities whatsoever, which anciently have been and now ought to be measured and surveyed, and the offices and duties of baillage, paccage, scavage, portage, tolls and markets, and of the public waters to the said city belonging, and the profits of the Lombard office and the several offices of out-roper, gauger, garbler and sewager, and of the green-wax duties, and by licensing of brokers, factors, alehouses, barges and lighters,† [and the laws relating to the premises and government of the streets, passages, pavements and sewers in the said City and liberties thereof, and the pains and forfeitures which shall be incurred for transgressing the same]." (Com. Book.)

13 Jan. (In Committee.) *The Common Sergeant* says that the L. Mayor and Aldermen could not possibly prepare the account since the receipt of their Lordships' Order, and it being Sessions week, where they are to be daily, he prays a longer time. *Ordered* that they give in their account on the 19th. *Mr. Goodfellow* offers two Orders of 20 and 23 Nov. 1691,‡ which are read. The Committee are of opinion that the Order of 23 Nov. 1691 is that which is to be mentioned in the Bill. *Mr. Goodfellow* is directed to send to the Clerk a copy of the L. Mayor and Aldermen's Petition to the House of Commons.§ (Com. Book.)

19 Jan. (In Committee). All parties called in. *The Common Sergeant* offers the L. Mayor and Aldermen's answer to the particulars in the Order.‖ The Paper is read. (Com. Book.)

25 Jan. (In Committee.) *Mr. Reading* is called in, and offers a new Bill, which he calls an Amendment,‖ the Preamble of which is compared with the Preamble of the Bill depending. It is returned to him again. (Com. Book.)

27 Jan. (In Committee). *Mr. Reading* is called in and offers Amendments to the Bill,¶ which are read. He withdraws. The Committee then amended the Bill as stated above; and ordered it to be reported as amended. (Com. Book.)

The Report was made on 28 Jan. by E. Rochester, who stated that there was nothing in the Bill now but the common funds, which the L. Mayor and Aldermen had offered for a security for the orphans. Further debate adjourned till the next day. (MS. Min., L. J., XV. 53.)

---

* *See* the clause following the words ("shall be committed for") in Annex (*g*) below.

† What follows in square brackets is struck through. Compare Annex (*p*) below.

‡ Annexes (*l*) and (*m*) below.

§ Annex (*n*) below.

‖ Annex (*o*) below.

¶ Annex (*p*) below.

On 29 Jan. the amendments were read again and agreed to, and the Bill ordered to be engrossed. (L. J., XV. 54.) In the Commons, after a reminder from the Lords (*ib.* 74), it was rejected on 20 Feb. on second reading by 116 to 58. (C. J., X. 682).]

Annexed :—

(*a.*) 12 Nov. 1691. Draft Order appointing a Select Committee on the Bill. It contains the following names in addition to those in L. J., XIV. 642, viz., D. Ormond, M. Halifax, E. Bridgewater, E. Westmoreland, E. Marlborough, E. Warrington, Bp. of St. David's, D. Clifford and L. Stawell.

(*b.*) 18 Nov. Petition of the Lord Mayor and Court of Aldermen of the City of London. Petitioners, who have received an Order to attend the Committee and also a copy of the Bill, conceive that the Bill purports the taking away divers jurisdictions and privileges enjoyed by the City of London time out of mind, and which they hope to show are necessary to the good government of the City and fit to be continued. Pray to be heard at the Bar before the Bill is further proceeded with. L. J., XIV. 651. [*See* Notes above, Nov. 18 and 24.]

(*c.*) 18 Nov. Petition of about 1,400 distressed Orphans of the City of London. Since their Lordships' last session, Petitioners, with great submissiveness and prejudicial attendances, have importuned the Lord Mayor and Aldermen, their guardians, not to suffer them to perish for want of their respective portions, which, under pain of imprisonment, were forced into the Chamber of London, especially since so many proposals had been offered then for relief, and several Reports thereupon had been made long since; notwithstanding which, they cannot prevail to have a Common Council called for establishing the same. Their Lordships' Committee having summoned the said guardians to be heard, Petitioners on the 18th inst. have endeavoured to see several orders and accounts relating to the receipts and disbursements of their portions, and to obtain some part of their own moneys, to carry on their relief before their Lordships, but they are denied the same, and their guardians, well knowing that they have neither money to pay the fees of the Bill, nor to fee their Counsel, have declared that they will petition their Lordships to be heard at the Bar against relieving them. Pray for leave to inspect the said orders and accounts, and that they may have some of their own moneys to prosecute their relief. *Signed* by Ann Symonds, Susanna Butler, Mary West, Sarah Browne,—Stanton, Hannah Hickes, John Walsh, Robert Chevall, John Sheppard, Nath. Newdigate and John Dowse.

Endorsed as read this day, MS. Min. No entry in L. J. [*See* Notes above, Nov. 18 and 24.]

(*d.*) 18 Nov. 1691. Breviate of the Bill. States, after giving a summary of its contents, that it is no other than a transcript of the Act sent from the House of Lords to the House of Commons last Session, with blanks for the persons, places and times in the former Act mentioned. And the condition of the poor Orphans is now much more deplorable, by reason that the former Bill did not pass the Commons. [Probably delivered in this day to the Committee by *Mr. Reading*, Counsel for the Orphans.* *See* Notes, under date, to first Paper above.]

* The House in 1689 ordered "brevials" to be made of all Bills. (L. J., XIV. 410.) Breviates of Private Bills had been ordered in 1661. (L. J., XI. 335.)

HOUSE OF LORDS MSS.

1691.

(*e.*) 15 Dec. Names of persons desired by the Orphans to be Commissioners, viz., Sir John Lawrence, Sir William Pritchard, Sir Joseph Herne, Samuel Westerne, Esq., Col. Francis Griffith, Sir Thos. Vernon. [*See* Notes to first Paper above, Dec. 15 and 17.]

(*f.*) 17 Dec. Draft Clauses. Identical with Clauses 1 and 2 in Annex (*g*), except in the particulars stated in the notes thereto. [*See* also Notes to first Paper above, Dec. 17.]

(*g.*) 2 Jan. 1691–2. Draft Clauses (4) as follows:—

"1. Provided always and be it further enacted, That the said Commissioners shall not make any inquiry into any of the particulars before-mentioned, save only from and since the date of the Act intituled The King's Majesty's most gracious, free and general Pardon, Indemnity and Oblivion, which passed in the 12th year of the reign of the late King Charles the Second, nor shall they examine any person against himself. Neither shall they have or execute other powers concerning imprisoning any person as aforesaid, save such persons only which the Commissioners authorised by the Statutes against Bankrupts are enabled to execute;* nor shall any person they commit be continued in prison, in case he finds sufficient sureties to answer what he shall be committed for.

2. And be it likewise enacted by the authority aforesaid, That the Order which was made in the Court of Common Council of the said City upon the 20th day of November last past, for charging the sum of 8,000*l.* per annum upon the lands and all other the estate and revenue now belonging, or which shall hereafter belong, to the said City, for and towards the payment of the said orphans, be established, ratified and confirmed accordingly; and the Chamberlain of the said City for the time being is hereby required and empowered to issue forth and pay the said 8,000*l.* per annum by equal quarterly payments, and to begin to pay the first 2,000*l.* thereof from and after the † day of next, and to distribute the same ‡ amongst the said Orphans or their legal representatives, according to the respective sums due to each of them respectively, and in such manner as the present or former Chamberlains of the said City have accustomed to do, deducting out of the same such § allowances as are hereafter mentioned; and that one moiety of the reward or recompense which the said Commissioners or any five of them shall conceive fit to be given to any person or persons, who shall make any of the said discoveries, whereby any branch of the said City's rights and revenues may legally be improved above what they now are as aforesaid, as also of the salaries aforesaid and other allowances and charges relating to the attendance on the said Commissioners, shall from time to time be paid by the said Chamberlain out of the said 8,000*l.* per annum belonging to the said Orphans as aforesaid; and that the other moiety of the said reward or recompense, and of the said salaries, allowances and incidental charges, shall in like manner be paid by the said

* From ("nor shall") to ("committed for") at the end of this Clause is wanting in Annex (*f*).

† Annex (*f*) reads ("25th day of this instant December, 1691").

‡ Annex (*f*) inserts here ("proportionably").

§ Annex (*f*) inserts here ("moiety of").

Chamberlain out of those moneys which shall be raised and brought into the said Chamber by reason or prosecution of the said discoveries and improvements, and that the acquittance or acquittances of the persons receiving the said moneys shall be held and taken to be a good discharge to the said Chamberlain in that behalf.

3. "And to the intent" &c. This Clause is identical with the rejected Clause (originally § ii.) in Annex (*p.*) below, with the following exceptions:—

After ("now ought to be weighed") this Draft reads ("and the office of measuring and surveying the merchandises and commodities whatsoever, which anciently have been, and now ought to be measured and surveyed, and the offices and duties of Baillage, Paccage, Scavage, Portage, Tolls, and Markets, and those of the Conservancy of the Rivers of Thames, Medway, and Lea, and of the rights and privileges of the said City to the due improving of the same, and of the public waters to the said City belonging and appertaining, and likewise the profits of the Lombard Office, and of the several offices of Out-Roper, Gauger, Garbler, and Searcher, and of the Greenwax Duties, and by the licensing of Brokers, Factors, Alehouses, Barges, and Lighters, and all the wholesome laws relating to any of the premises and to the good government of the streets, passages, pavements, and sewers of and within the said City and the liberties thereof, and the reasonable pains and forfeitures which hereafter shall be incurred for transgressing the same").

Before the words ("or their legal representatives") this Draft reads ("and shall be disposed of in such manner and method among the said Orphans").

4. "And for the recovering of the trade of the citizens of the said City, which hath been of late exceedingly invaded and decayed by great numbers of Hawkers and unfree persons trading contrary to the rights and laws of the said City in that behalf. Be it further enacted, That the said rights and laws be confirmed and duly prosecuted, and the same are hereby confirmed and ordered to be put in execution accordingly." [*See* Notes to first Paper, Jan. 2 and 9.]

(*h.*) 2 Jan. 1691-2. Printed paper (appended to Annex (*g.*) as follows: "To the Right Honourable the Lord Mayor, Aldermen, and Commons of the City of London, in Common Council assembled. We, whose names are subscribed, in obedience to an Order of this Honourable Court, bearing date the third day of February 1690, appointing us to be a Committee to consider of the Petition of several Orphans, and to receive the proposals of the said Petitioners, or any others, and to report our opinions concerning the same to this Honourable Court, do humbly certify, That we have had several meetings, and have published the general day of our meeting (Thursday in the afternoon) in several Gazettes, and have received all such proposals as were by any persons tendered to us; and have also considered among ourselves of several matters not proposed from abroad, which may contribute towards the payment of the Orphans' Debts; and have had laid before us the several particulars of the City's Receipts and Disbursements; and do think it reasonable, as well for the honour of this City, as for the satisfaction of this

HOUSE OF LORDS MSS.

1691.

Honourable Court, and of the said Orphans, humbly to offer our opinions as follows, viz.:—

	£
That the Revenues of the City's lands formerly agreed on, with the improved value thereof, amounting at *per annum* - - - -	3,000
That the Revenue of the Markets, being valued at -	3,000
The Farm of Garbling and Packing, let at - -	1,500
The Aqueducts and improvements thereof, valued -	500
Total per annum - -	£8,000

be appropriated and settled, free of all charges, by Act of Common Council, towards payment of 4*l.* per cent. per annum for the present relief of the Orphans (the Committee having taken great care to find out ways for the support of the Government); And we humbly propose, That this Fund be offered to be confirmed in Parliament, and that application be made to that most Honourable Court for such further aid, as they in their great wisdom shall think fit, whereby a fund of 24,000*l.* per annum may be vested in the Mayor and Commonalty and Citizens of London, for satisfaction of the debts due to the present Orphans, and as a future security for all Orphans' Money that hereafter shall be paid into the Chamber of London. All which, notwithstanding, we humbly submit to the better judgment of this Honourable Court. *Dated* the 11th day of May 1691.

Aldermen.	Commoners.
Sir William Turner.	Sir Thomas Vernon.
Sir William Pritchard.	Sir Ralph Box.
Sir John Moore.	Arthur Barron.
Sir Samuel Dashwood.	John Morris.
	Francis Griffith.
	John Johnson.
	John Midgley.
	Thomas Blackmore.

(*i.*) Five other printed copies of preceding.

(*k.*) Notice, partly printed, as follows: "Sir,—Your worship is desired to be at a Court of Aldermen at Guildhall on Monday next, at eight of the clock in the fore-noon, being the eleventh day of January 1691, to consider of an Order come from the House of Lords upon extraordinary business. Your answer to be returned on Tuesday morning next." [Evidently between 5 and 10 Jan. 1691.]

(*l.*) 13 Jan. 1691-2. Order of the Court of Common Council of 20 Nov. 1691 charging 8,000*l.* per annum on the estate and revenue of the City of London towards the payment to the Orphans of the yearly sum 4*l.* per cent., and directing the Committee lately appointed by the Court, to whom the consideration of the Orphans' Petition was referred, to draw up, together with Mr. Recorder, a Petition to Parliament praying that the same may be settled by Act of Parliament, and such other aids for payment of the 4*l.* per cent. to the Orphans and other creditors of the City as Parliament shall think fit. *Signed* Goodfellow. [*See* Notes to first Paper above, Jan. 9 and 13.]

(*m.*) 13 Jan. 1691-2. Minute of proceedings in the Court of Common Council on 23 Nov. 1691, confirming the Order of the

20th inst., and declaring it to be the Order of the Court. *Signed* Goodfellow. [*See* Notes to first Paper above, Jan. 9 and 13.]

(*n.*) 13 Jan. 1691–2. Petition of the Lord Mayor, Aldermen, and Common Council of the City of London, to the Honourable the Knights, Citizens, and Burgesses in Parliament assembled. By the general troubles in and after the reign of Charles I. the Mayor and Commonalty and Citizens of the City of London lost divers great sums of money. By reason thereof, by the payment of interest, by the destruction of the greatest part of their estate in the Fire, and by the very great but necessary expenses thereupon, and the losses and charges by reason of the late *Quo Warranto* illegally prosecuted against them, their debts to the Orphans of the City of London amount to a sum vastly greater than they are able to pay without the assistance of this Honourable House. Petitioners have employed their utmost endeavours to raise money, and from time to time have paid the same towards the relief of the most pressing exigencies of the Orphans. After many and serious considerations of the best ways and means of satisfying the said debts as far as possible, without destroying the government of the City, Petitioners have in Common Council agreed that the sum of 8,000*l.* per annum shall be charged upon the lands and all other the estate and revenue belonging to the City, towards paying the Orphans 4*l.* per cent. per annum. But since so vast debts cannot be satisfied by all the estate or powers of the City, and many of the Orphans will be ruined and the government of the City destroyed unless some further provision be made for the same, Petitioners pray the compassionate assistance of the House in these necessities for raising and settling a sufficient fund for an annual payment to be made in lieu of the said debts. *Signed* Goodfellow. [*See* Notes to first Paper above, Jan. 13, and C. J., X., 563.]

(*o.*) 19 Jan. 1691–2. Answer of the Lord Mayor and Aldermen of the City of London, as follows: "In obedience to your Lordships' Orders of the 9th and 13th of this instant January, requiring an account in writing what are the yearly values of the particulars therein mentioned, and to what uses the same are applied, we humbly lay before your Lordships the state thereof as followeth:

(1.) That there are two Beams, viz., the King's Beam and Iron Beam, to which the City conceive they have a right by prescription and Charters, and that Merchants' goods sold by Avoirdupois weight, ought to be weighed at the said Beams, and that there are certain ancient fees according to a Table hereunto annexed. The City also have from time to time appointed officers to weigh the said goods, and to collect the said Duties, upon account, but since the late troubles arose in England the Merchants have for many years taken the advantage of the distractions and frequent revolutions of Government, and most of them have refused to weigh their goods at the said Beam, and others, whose goods have been and ought to have been weighed, refuse to pay the duty to the City, being advised that the ancient Orders of Common Council for distress of the goods would not now be justified in the Courts of Judicature, and not thinking it reasonable to bring such a multitude of actions at law for such small sums as those Duties for weighing. By these means there hath been scarce so much profit made by

House of Lords MSS.

1691.

the said Beams as hath defrayed the charges about the same, excepting such moneys as remain in the Merchants', Weighers', and Porters' hands, which are due and cannot yet be recovered. For these reasons the City have from time to time made their humble application to the Commons in Parliament, to be enabled to recover the said Duties more certainly and easily, without which the said ancient Duties are likely to be utterly lost.

(2.) The profit of weighing of wool is not separately collected nor let, but, together with the weigh-house housing for wool, was in the year 1666 let for 31 years at 30*l*. per annum.

(3.) There are distinct officers for the measuring several commodities and merchandises, and the same are granted for good behaviour or life, without rent or fines, the fees thereof being accounted but sufficient to answer the labour of the officer, saving four of the coal-meters do pay to the City 80*l*. per annum each, and ten others pay each of them the like rent to the Lord Mayor for the time being for maintenance of the City officers, attending his Lordship about the affairs of this City, and in his household have by long and constant wage been paid, and by several Acts of Common Council continued and confirmed for that purpose, the office of measuring of coals being always to be executed by the Lord Mayor, his Deputy or Deputies, saving also that the Measurer of Woollen pays 40*l*. per annum.

(4.) The Duty of Bailage is divided into foreign and inland, both which Duties were anciently among other things granted to the City by the Crown, and a fee farm rent of 300*l*. per annum reserved, payable by the Sheriffs; But about the year 1683 judgment in a *Quo Warranto* was given against the City as to the foreign Duty, against which they hope to be relieved by your Lordships' Judicial power or by Bill in Parliament, and a Bill in the Commons' House for that purpose among other things was depending in the last Parliament. The Inland Water Bailage is divided into two collections, the one eastward of Billingsgate, with the moiety of Billingsgate, the other westward, with the other moiety of Billingsgate, each of which is let for 26*l*. per annum, payable to the Sheriffs for the time being, to the answering the fee-farm afore-mentioned, but the said Duties have often been disputed and much money expended to maintain the right thereunto, and notwithstanding many verdicts have been obtained for the City's right therein, yet lately in a trial at the King's Bench Bar a verdict was given against the same, and the payment of the rent is thereby obstructed.

(5.) The profits by Paccage, Scavage, and Portage were let in the year 1687 to one Richard Peirce for 14 years yet to come, for the yearly rent of 1,200*l*. which had always heretofore been let for less than a third part of that sum.

(6.) The Tolls of Smithfields and places adjacent therewith usually let are at present leased to Mr. Stephen Sedgewick for 99 years, determinable upon the death of James Burgess at 260*l*. per annum.

(7.) The tolls of Aldgate and places adjoining are let to Joseph Smart, Esq., for 20*l*. per annum, which tolls and other duties issuing out of the same have always been answerable to the Sheriffs in aid of the fee-farm above-mentioned.

(8.) The Toll or Duty of Wheelage of London Bridge was let to Mr. Blagrave in 1678 for 21 years at the yearly rent of 335*l*. 13*s*. 4*d*., which never before was let for above 80*l*. per annum, but belong[ed] to the Bridge-house for repair of the bridge.

(9.) The Tolls of Fleet Channel, settled by a late Act of Parliament, were let in 1681 for 12 years and a half at the yearly rent of 100*l.*, but by the said Act are appropriated to the support of the Channel.

(10.) The Tolls of Leather-Fair in Smithfield, worth *communibus annis* 40*l.* which does not answer the charge.

(11.) The Tolls of Paccage and Stallage in Bartholomew Fair were lately let at 100*l.* per annum, which heretofore yielded no profit to the Chamber. The profits of the markets were for many ages past collected by several officers of the Lord Mayor as Clerk of the Markets and were applied to their uses, in compensation whereof, by condescension of the Lord Mayor for the benefit of the City, several annual sums are paid to the Lord Mayor and his officers, as appears by the Reprisals following:—

(12.) But since the Fire of London, much ground being brought in by the City for market-places and greater conveniences for the market people made than formerly, the City have endeavoured to improve the profits of those markets for the use of the Chamber, and have let the same to farm by lease for divers years to come at the yearly rent of 3,600*l.*, but the farm being outed by judgment at law of some part of the Duties let to them, thereupon 500*l.* per annum have ever since been suspended, so that now there is yearly paid to the City but 3,100*l.*

(13.) The public waters were brought from several springs to the City of London and conduits erected and given by benefactors for the common use of all the inhabitants and not for a public revenue to the body corporate, and many legacies were given by benefactors to maintain the said watercourses and conduits for the use aforesaid, and divers of their lands charged for the same, and for that reason the intention of the Donors hath been observed and no annual or other profit made to the City by the same, but have been and are a great yearly expense to the City, nor can they be improved without a vast sum of money, which the City is not able to disburse.

(14.) That there never was such an office as a Lombard Office in the City.

(15.) The office of Outroper was anciently exercised by the Common Cryer and chiefly for the benefit of Orphans in the sale of goods of citizens deceased, where the Executors refused to accept them at the priced value, but public sales of goods becoming more frequent, in hopes of improvement, it was let to Mr. John Puckle for the term of 12 years (viz.) for the first three years of the said term for one-third of the clear profits, for the next four years one-half of the said profits, and for the residue of the said term for two-thirds of the clear yearly profits, and for all which sums he is to be accountable, but as yet no profit is either made or received.

(16.) The Lord Mayor is Gauger and accounts to the King for the profits in their Majesties' Court of Exchequer yearly.

(17.) The office of Garbling was let in 1686 to Mr. Stewart for 61 years at 300*l.* per annum determinable upon his death.

HOUSE OF LORDS MSS.

1691.

(18.) All the Searchers and Sealers of Leathers pay only 10*l.* per annum.

(19.) There is no such Duty as the Greenwax Duty, but all recognizances and issues upon jurors are estreated into the Exchequer, upon which the King's process goes out, commonly called the process of Greenwax, the profits of which are granted by the Crown to the City for the ease and benefit of the citizens, who are always admitted to compound the same according to their several abilities, and the defaulters being generally poor, no profit hath been made thereof, neither can any certain profit be from that expected, and 25*l.* per annum being paid to the Clerk of the Estreats, besides the charges of the several officers for managing the same.

(20.) The Brokers upon the Exchange are and ought to be licensed by the Lord Mayor and Court of Aldermen, and are sworn and do give bond with sureties to the Chamberlain for the due and faithful execution of their office between party and party concerned, but there is no settlement of any fines or annual payment from them to the City, they being generally poor and decayed citizens and freemen.

(21.) Factors never were licensed or paid anything to the City.

(22.) Alehouse keepers are licensed as in other Counties, but pay nothing to the City.

(23.) Barges and lighters are neither licensed nor pay anything to the City for liberty to work, save only there was a tilt boat or ferry from Billingsgate to Gravesend, which anciently was licensed by the City.

Out of these several profits aforesaid there are these Reprisals following:—The Moiety of the Duties of Package, Scavage, and Portage, being by ancient and continued usage and by Acts of Common Council due to the Lord Mayor. 173*l.* 6*s.* 8*d.* have been by Acts of Common Council given yearly instead thereof, and 150*l.* paid to the Sheriffs towards the payment of the fee-farm before mentioned.

Out of the annual Rents of the Markets there is payable yearly, viz.:—

	£	*s.*	*d.*
To the Lord Mayor - - - - -	100	0	0
To the three Clerks of the Markets at 3*l.* per week each - - - - - -	468	0	0
To the Under Water Bailiff at 5*s.* per week -	13	0	0
To the four fruiterers, 10*l.* per annum each -	40	0	0
Interest of 1,550*l.* deposited as a security for the due payment of the Rent at 6*l.* per cent. per annum, which is annually paid, and the principal to be deducted at the last year's payment, which is to be allowed in the last half year of the term granted - -	93	0	0
To the Company of Vintners: Rent for tenements in Lime Street, parcel of the Market at Leadenhall - - - - -	12	0	0
To the Company of Skinners for ground in the Herb Market in Gracechurch Street -	16	13	4

	£	s.	d.
To Mdm. Margaret Jarmin, an Annuity by Contract for ground laid into Woolchurch Market - - - - - -	42	6	8
To Sir John Cropley for ground in Woolchurch Market - - - - - -	30	0	0
To the parishioners of St. Dunstan East for a quit rent issuing out of Leadenhall Market -	4	0	0
To the Minister of St. Mary Woolnoth for glebe land and tithes in Woolchurch Market	18	13	4
For the tithes of Hony Lane Market - -	15	19	0
To the Minister of St. Peters, Cornhill, for tithes out of Leadenhall - - - -	4	0	0
To the Minister of St. Austins for tithes out of Newgate Market - - - - -	8	0	0
For the poor of St. Faith out of the said market - - - - - -	9	15	0
For the poor of Miclestreet [? Michael Street] out of the market - - - -	3	6	8
For the poor of Hony Lane out of the said market - - - - - -	5	4	0

In answer to your Lordships' demand unto what uses the several profits of the premises are applied, we humbly acquaint your Lordships that all and every the profits of the premises, together with the revenue of the City's lands and all other their income whatsoever are paid into the Chamber, as the Common Treasury of the City, and are thence issued only by the Orders of the Court of Aldermen or Common Council, in the first place, for the payment of all those sums that have anciently been given for charitable uses, which are many, and in the next place, for many rents due from the City, and for repairing the public buildings and great quantities of public pavements, taxes, tithes, and rates to the poor, and maintaining public watercourses, pipes, and conduits, salaries, wages and liveries to the officers, customary liveries to the chief officers of State, Judges and others, defraying the charges of the several prisons, the charges of suits in law and equity, together with many other constant necessary expenses and charges incident to the support of the Government, the particulars whereof are too many to be here enumerated and cannot be ascertained, being some years more and others less, as occasions require. And whatever sum or sums of money from time to time have been received or brought into the said Chamber from any revenue whatsoever, certain or contingent, more than have been annually expended as aforesaid, the same hath been from time to time paid to the Orphans and other Creditors of the City, since the judgment given in the *Quo Warranto* against this City, amounting to upwards of 100,000*l*. And we do humbly insist that we have done and do still use our utmost endeavours to find out all concealments of the City's rights, and believe ourselves sufficiently instructed in the interests and concerns of the City from whence any profit can possibly arise to the Orphans; and that there can neither be justly objected against us any failure of our duties therein or the least waste or mis-employment of any part of the City's income, or that there has been any defect in giving reasonable encouragement to any persons, who can do any further service for the Orphans. *Signed* Goodfellow.

House of Lords MSS.

1691.

The Ancient Table of Tronage or the King's Beam in the Paper mentioned.

	s. d.		s. d.		s. d.
From 14 lb. weight to 4 cwt. - -	0 6	Whereof to Weigher	0 2	To Porters -	0 4
" 4 cwt. to 5 cwt. - - -	1 0	"	0 4	" -	0 8
" 5 cwt. to 8 cwt. - - -	2 0	"	0 8	" -	1 4
" 8 cwt. to 10 cwt. - - -	3 4	"	1 4	" -	2 0
" 10 cwt. to 12 cwt. - - -	4 8	"	2 0	" -	2 8
" 12 cwt. and above - -	0 8	"	2 8	" -	4 0
Mall Madder, the bale, both parties -	1 4	"	0 8	" -	0 8
Copporis, the butt - - -	1 4	"	0 8	" -	0 8
Hops, the sack, being 4 cwt. or above	1 4	"	0 8	" -	0 8
Mall Madder, weighing under 4 cwt. -	0 6	"	0 2	" -	0 4
Copperis in small barrels under 4 cwt.	0 6	"	0 2	" -	0 4
For a fother of lead - - -	0 10	"	0 4	" for rebast	0 1
		Clerk for sealing -	0 1		
The Porters to have at the Cart at every time - - - - - -					0 8
And for every pitch from one place to another - - - - - -					0 8

Endorsed. Paper relating to the Orphans' Bill. For the Lords Committees, 19 January 1691. [Delivered in to the Committee this day by the Common Sergeant. *See* Notes to principal Paper above under date and Jan. 9 and 13.]

(*p*.) 27 Jan. Amended * Draft entitled "Amendments to the Orphans' Bill." It proposes (1) to leave out the words ("erecting a Court of Inquiry in order to") in the preamble, and (2) after the words ("proportionately to such discovery") in the preamble to leave out all the rest of the Bill, and substitute the following:—

§ i. . . . "And whereas the Lord Mayor, Aldermen, and Commons of the said City, upon the 23rd day of November last past, in their Court of Common Council assembled, did then order that the sum of 8,000*l.* per annum should be charged upon the lands and all other the estate and revenue then belonging, or which hereafter shall belong to the City of London, for and towards the payment of the Orphans of the said City, and that the Committee lately appointed by the said Court, to whom the Petition of the said Orphans was referred, together with Mr. Recorder, should forthwith draw up a Petition to the Honourable and High Court of Parliament, thereby praying to have the same settled by Act of Parliament, [and a Petition was drawn up accordingly]; Now for the more effectual and speedy obtaining the ends above mentioned, May it please your Majesties that it may be enacted, and be it enacted by the King and Queen's Most Excellent Majesties, by and with the advice and consent of the Lords Spiritual and Temporal and the Commons in Parliament assembled, and by the authority of the same, That both the said Orders and every point and article in each of the said Orders contained, so far as they relate to the payment and satisfaction of the said Orphans, be ratified, established, and confirmed *and put in execution* accordingly.

[§ ii. And to the intent that some further provision may forthwith be made for the said distressed Orphans, many of whom,

* The Amendments are shown, in the case of omissions, by square brackets, and, in the case of additions, by italics. This Draft, consisting of two sheets, is appended to the Bill as originally introduced, and forms with it the text of the engrossment, which was sent to the Commons, where it remained.

by reason that their portions were forced into the said chamber, have been reduced to a perishing and most calamitous condition; and to the end also that the rights and privileges belonging to the said City, both by prescription and divers Charters confirmed by sundry Acts of Parliament, for receiving several profits and emoluments by the offices, duties, and means hereafter mentioned, may not be prejudiced by having been neglected, but be put beyond all question for the time to come, and be confirmed and duly managed for the future, and that the several profits arising thereby, and the known fees and perquisites to the same respectively appertaining, may be established, appropriated, and improved to and for the relief of the said Orphans, and for the preserving of the government of that renowned City from being torn in pieces by the multitude of actions, which the pressure of the said debt may expose it to; Be it further enacted, and it is further enacted by the authority aforesaid, That the office of keeping the Beams, and of weighing of wool and all other merchandises and commodities whatsoever, which anciently have been and now ought to be weighed, and the offices and duties of * , be confirmed and appropriated as aforesaid, and the same, together with the respective Tables of Rates and Fees, which anciently have been allowed and paid for any of the said duties, are hereby confirmed and appropriated accordingly, and shall from and after the day of next be collected, managed and received to and for the relief of the said Orphans or their legal representatives; and in case any persons concerned in payment of any the aforesaid duties or profits shall refuse to pay the same towards so pious and charitable a work, Be it likewise enacted that the legal and ancient ways and means for collecting and gathering the same shall be, and the same are hereby ratified, established, and confirmed.]

[§ iii.] § ii. And be it likewise enacted, That a Committee of Aldermen and Commoners be yearly appointed and chosen in the Court of Common Council of the said City [for prosecution of the said discoveries, and for the full performance and execution of the several matters and things in this Act before mentioned] *to take care that this Act be duly executed and performed*, in order to the speedy and effectual relief of the said distressed Orphans, and that particular books be fairly kept of all proceedings thereupon, to the end it may appear what relief hath hereby been given to the said Orphans, [in order to their being further relieved.]" [*See* Notes to first Paper, Jan. 25 and 27.]

(*q.*) 28 Jan. 1691-2. Lords' Amendments to the Bill. [Made in Committee 27 Jan. and reported this day. Com. Book. L. J., XV., 53.]

435. Nov. 11. Putt's Estate Act.—Draft of an Act to enable the Executors and Trustees of Sir Thomas Putt, Baronet, deceased, to lease several Messuages, Lands, Tenements, and Hereditaments during the minority of Sir Thomas Putt, Baronet, son and heir of the said Sir Thomas Putt, towards the payment of five hundred pounds apiece, legacies to his three sisters Margaret, Ursula, and Susannah Putt, as also the debts of the said Sir Thomas Putt the father. Identical with Act. [Read 1a this day; Royal Assent 24 Dec. L. J., XIV. 641, 701. 3 W. and M. c. 7 in Long Calendar, Com. Book, 7 Nov. *See also* No. **337.**]

* As to this blank, compare the proceedings in Committee on Jan. 9 and 19, given in the notes, under dates, to first Paper above. *See also* Annex (*o.*).

House of Lords MSS.

1691.

436. Nov. 12. Goodwyn's Estate Bill.—Amended draft of an Act for the enabling of Thomas Goodwyn, the younger, Gent., to sell lands in Radway, in the County of Warwick, for the payment of his debts. Thomas Goodwyn, of Radway, a trader in grazing, settled in 1685 on his son Thomas, on his marriage with Elizabeth Wainwright, in consideration of her marriage portion of 1,000*l.*, certain lands known as Radway Grange, in the parish of Bishop's Itchington, together with the closes thereto belonging, and the tithes arising therefrom, which had been purchased by his father, William, from John Danvers and John Washington; but after inducing his son to become bound for him in sums amounting to 1,600*l.* and upwards, he absconded, leaving debts amounting to 3,000*l.* beyond the value of his real and personal estate, for which the creditors threaten to prosecute his son, the Suppliant for the Bill. The estate limited to Suppliant is so strictly settled, that he cannot sell any part or make any security or mortgage for those of his father's debts for which he is liable, or for his own, amounting to 500*l.*, and is unable to provide maintenance for his wife and children. The Bill, therefore, vests the said premises in Thomas Bouchier and Thomas Fetherstone, the Trustees under the marriage settlement, in trust to sell them and apply 2,000*l.* of the purchase money in discharge of Suppliant's debts. [Read 1ª this day. (L. J., XIV. 642.) Reported 7 December, and after debate, rejected on question whether it should be engrossed, by 21 to 14. L. Cornwallis was Teller for the Contents, and L. Brooke for the Not-Contents. MS. Min., 7 Dec. L. J., XIV. 676.]

Annexed:—

7 Dec. Lords' Amendments in Committee. [Made and ordered to be reported this day. Com. Book, Dec. 1 and 7. These two amendments are wholly unimportant.]

437. Nov. 12. Mountagu's Estate Act.—Draft of an Act for the vesting and settling divers lands in Gloucestershire in Trustees, to be sold for the paying of the remaining portions to the children of George Mountagu, Esquire, deceased. [Read 1ª this day; Royal Assent, 24 Dec. L. J., XIV. 642, 702. 3 W. and M. c. 9 in Long Calendar. Com. Book, 19 Nov.]

438. Nov. 13. Court of Chancery &c. (Bills of Review) Bill.—Amended* draft of an Act for the better [determining] *reviewing* of Causes [on Bills of Review] in Chancery and other Courts of Equity.

Whereas in a long tract of time there have been found many inconveniences in the [methods of the practice] *proceedings* of the Court of Chancery and other Courts of Equity very fit and necessary to be redressed and regulated by authority of Parliament for the good of all the subjects of England, when there shall be a fitting time duly to weigh and consider the same, and whereas amongst other great inconveniences in the [said methods of practice] *proceedings* it does manifestly appear that the practice of the Courts of Equity upon Bills of Review is one of the greatest inconveniences [in the practice of the said Courts], and not of sufficient efficacy and remedy to their Majesties' subjects, not only because such Bills of Review are brought before the same person or persons that decreed in the same Cause before, but also that such Bills of Review have been restrained and confined of late to Error appearing only upon the face of the Decree, without looking into the proofs taken in the Cause,† which ought to be the ground of the Decree,

---

* The omissions are shown by square brackets, and the additions by italics.

† *See* Case of *Mellish* v. *Williams* (1683), 1 Vernon 166, and Smith's Chancery Practice, i. 811.

in cases where the matter of fact was not tried by jury; which is most fit and necessary without further delay to be redressed by authority of Parliament, and therefore be it enacted by the King and Queen's Most Excellent Majesties, by and with the advice and consent of the Lords Spiritual and Temporal and Commons in this present Parliament assembled, and by authority of the same, That [from and after the day of Bills of Review may be brought upon all Decrees in all Courts of Equity in all same Court where such Decree shall be made, as well for injustice in the Decree as for Error appearing upon the face thereof, and when any cause upon a Bill of Review is ready for hearing, either upon demurrer or otherwise, the same upon motion in Court shall be adjourned into the Exchequer Chamber before the judges for the time being of the Courts of King's Bench, Common Pleas and Exchequer, who are hereby required to attend the same]* upon every Tuesday, Thursday, and Saturday in the afternoon in term and every day for the next [six] *fifteen* days together that is not Sunday after every term, if occasion shall require, [which said Judges, or any seven of them, whereof the Chief Justice of the King's Bench or Common Pleas, or Chief Baron of the Exchequer for the time being to be one, shall hear and determine all such Causes upon Bills of Review as shall be adjourned before them as aforesaid]† and they, having regard to the Common Law and Statutes of this Realm, shall and are hereby empowered to reverse [or] affirm *or alter* the said Decree and Decrees, *Order or Orders of Dismission*, and shall make such further order and decree therein as shall be agreeable to justice and equity, *and shall give costs upon the affirmance of such Decree or Decrees, Order or Orders of Dismission, or for want of prosecution thereof against the said Petitioner or Petitioners*, and after such Decree drawn up and signed by the major part of the Judges present at the hearing of the Cause [upon the Review], the same shall be remitted to, and enrolled and put in execution in and by, the Court where the first decree in the Cause was made, and *every decree or order upon every* such Review *or rehearing* shall be final and without any rehearing unless upon appeal in Parliament [or in cases where it is necessary some matter of fact be referred to a trial at law]‡ *to which the Party or Parties grieved, if he, she, or they think convenient, may resort, either before or after such review or rehearing, anything in this Act contained to the contrary in anywise notwithstanding*. Provided nevertheless that the Lord Chancellor, Lord Keeper or Commissioners for the custody of the Great Seal for the time being may be present at the hearing of the Cause upon every such [Bill of] Review *or rehearing* to give his or their opinions, but not to have any vote in the judgment to be given upon the same.

[§And be it further enacted that Bills of Review adjourned from the Court of Exchequer as aforesaid, that Court being a Court of Equity as

* In lieu of the above words in square brackets, there are marked in the margin for insertion the amended Clauses marked with an asterisk and given in Annex (*a.*) below.

† The words here included in square brackets were first amended by inserting after ("shall") the words ("*hereby and by the authority aforesaid have full power and authority to*"), and reading ("*by way* of Review") instead of ("upon Bills of Review"). Com. Book, 3 Dec. This amendment was afterwards superseded by omitting the bracketed portion, as in the text.

‡ First amended by retaining the words in square brackets and adding after ("trial at law") the words ("*before any final Order or Decree can be made on such rehearing*"). Com. Book, 3 Dec. This amendment was superseded apparently on recommitment, by the one in the text. It does not appear among the amendments in Annex (*d.*) below.

§ Here, in place of the portion following in square brackets, are marked for insertion Clauses A. *See* Annex (*b.*) below.

HOUSE OF LORDS MSS.

1691.

well as of Law, neither the Chief Baron of the Exchequer nor any other Baron or Judge of that Court shall have any vote in the judgment to be given in the Bill of Review adjourned from the said Court of Exchequer as aforesaid, but that such order and decree upon any Bill of Review shall be made as aforesaid by the Judges for the time being of the King's Bench and Common Pleas, or any five of them, whereof the Chief Justice of the King's Bench or Common Pleas shall be one, anything in this Act contained to the contrary in anywise notwithstanding.] Provided nevertheless that the Chief Baron and Barons of the Exchequer for the time being, or any of them, may be present at the hearing of the Cause upon every [Bill of Review adjourned from the Court of Exchequer as aforesaid] *such review or rehearing* to give their opinions but not to have any vote in the judgment to be given upon any [Bill of] *such* review *or rehearing* adjourned as aforesaid from the Court of Exchequer, anything in this Act contained to the contrary in anywise notwithstanding.* [Read 1a this day. (L. J., XIV. 643.)† The motion on 19 Nov. for the House to go into Committee on the Bill was negatived by 17 (including one Proxy) to 15. Teller for Contents, E. Stamford; for Not-Contents, E. Monmouth. (MS. Min.)—On 21 Nov. the Bill was referred to a Select Committee, assisted by L. Commissioner Rawlinson, C. Justice Holt, Justice Eyre, and Justice Rokeby. (L. J., XIV. 656.) The proceedings of this Committee are thus recorded. On Nov. 23 after the Bill was read through, the *L. Commissioner Rawlinson* was heard. He said that the matter of the Bill was new to him, so he could not say much to it on a sudden. The method and grounds of the practice in Chancery have been that when a Cause has been heard in Chancery, before the enrolment, the Cause may be reheard, and all the proofs are again read upon the merits. After that, it is drawn into a formal decree and signed by the L. Chancellor, &c. After this, a Bill of Review may at any time be brought upon the matter in the body of the record, or upon new matter of fact, if it has come to knowledge since. This Bill gives the Judges the same power that your Lordships have upon an Appeal. The consequence will be, that if this be not meant to be final, it will both increase the expense and be of greater delay, because they may afterwards come to your Lordships. It is therefore better to come to your Lordships only. This intermediate judicature will be very hard to get together, seven being to be the quorum. If all proceedings must in the meantime stop, many accidents of consequence may happen by the death of the plaintiff or defendant. There is no time set when this Bill of Review shall be brought. The Judges by their oaths are to judge according to the law. Whether it is not fit they ought not to have an oath to judge according to equity and conscience, having regard to the law as well as the Commissioners? *Ordered*, That L. Commissioner Rawlinson and the other Assistants have each a copy of the Bill. *Eyre, J.*: This proceeding will lessen the expense. This is a subordinate judicature. Your Lordships have done the same thing in Writs of Error in the Exchequer Chamber. Your Lordships hold the scales between these two Courts. (Com. Book, 23 Nov.)—On the 27th the *L. Commissioner Rawlinson* says the other two Lords Commissioners have the same thoughts that he had, when he last attended. The Bill is in a great measure unnecessary. This new Court will have the same jurisdiction that the House of Peers have. This, being not final, will increase the trouble and vexation to

* Here are marked for addition Clauses B. (Annex (*c*.) below).

† The MS. Min. of 13 Nov. have the following entry not in L. J.: "House moved to receive a Bill for regulating the Court of Chancery."

the people, as well as prove troublesome to the Judges. The Bill, instead of lessening the charge and delay in Chancery suits, will *re verâ* be grievous to the people. It makes two Appeals, whereas the people will acquiesce in one before your Lordships. *Holt, C. J.:* The preamble of the Bill recites the reason of this new Appeal. The rehearing is before the same persons that make the decree, which is seldom successful. It is no more charge to the people to be heard before the Judges in the Exchequer Chamber than upon a Review in Chancery. Though this will be a trouble to the Judges, and though without recompense, yet being for a public good, though I am not fond of this new jurisdiction, yet I will cheerfully submit to it. Our oaths bind us as well to observe all laws to be made, as well as already made. The Committee then considered the Bill by paragraphs, and after reading the first enacting Clause, *Holt, C. J.*, offers a Clause (instead of the first enacting Clause) which is read. *L. Commissioner Rawlinson* says this Clause is new, and desires a copy of it to show his brethren. *Holt, C. J.*, is directed to mend the Clause according to the debate, touching giving security to perform the decree and paying costs and prosecuting within a certain time, and to send it to the Clerk to be remitted to L. Commissioner Rawlinson. (Com. Book, 27 Nov.)—On 3 Dec., after Mr. Justice Eyre had offered some amendments, the Committee proceeded to consider and amend the Bill. *L. Commissioner Rawlinson* said the Commissioners did not consent to the Bill, it being dispensable to the King and prejudicial to the people, and might make difference between the two Houses. He should not speak to any part of the Bill, because he was against the whole. He conceived the Bill to be unnecessary. The people acquiesced well in Appeals to their Lordships. The Chancery was the King's Court, and it was the King's conscience that was exercised there. The King could in intervals of Parliament appoint Lords and others to receive Appeals. The intermediate Court not being to be final, the delay would be greater and more chargeable than now. This is to invert the Court and course of Chancery that has been many years. It is an invading the King's prerogative. *Eyre, J.:* The same thing that is done by this Bill with the Chancery, has been done by your Lordships with the King's Bench and Exchequer. The expense will not be so great as now. A clause may be added to prevent the abatement of the suit by the death of any of the parties, as is done upon Writs of Error. (Com. Book, 3 Dec.)—On Dec. 7 the *L. C. Justice* and *Mr. Justice Eyre* offered some amendments to the first enacting Clause, which were agreed to, and the Committee amended the Bill to the end. (Com. Book, 7 Dec.)—The Committee after being twice ordered to report (L. J., XIV. 679, 681) reported on 11 Dec. (*ib.*, 683.)—On 12 Dec. the Committee, on recommitment, reported the Bill with two further amendments, which had been offered to them that day by the Judges and agreed to. (*Ib.*, 684; Com. Book, 12 Dec.) The Bill finally dropped in the Commons.]

Annexed:—

(*a.*) 11 Dec. Amended Clauses marked with an asterisk, as follows:—[That instead of Bills of Review, that have been formerly used] when any decree or dismission of any Bill shall be pronounced in the Chancery or any other Court of Equity in the Kingdom of England, or Dominion of Wales (except the Court of Exchequer), and [the] *such* decretal order or orders of dismission be entered, the party or parties who shall conceive himself, herself, or themselves to be thereby grieved, may within *fourteen days* exhibit a Petition to the Justices of the King's

HOUSE OF LORDS MSS.

1691.

Bench and Common Pleas and Barons of the Exchequer of the degree of the coif for the time being, requesting them to review and rehear the cause so decreed or dismissed; and from and after a certificate made by any three of the said Justices and Barons to the Lord Chancellor, Lord Keeper, or Lords Commissioners for the custody of the Great Seal or any other Judge or Judges of any other Court of Equity, of any Petition exhibited to rehear or review a cause decreed, and after two sufficient securities, to be approved of by the Lord Chancellor, Lord Keeper, or Lords Commissioners for the custody of the Great Seal or other Judge or Judges of any other Court of Equity where the decree shall be made, have entered into a recognizance or obligation [to the plaintiff or plaintiffs] in such Court of Equity in double the sum or value of the thing decreed, to prosecute his or their Petition with effect, and to perform the decree or such part thereof as shall be affirmed, and also to pay such damages and costs as shall be adjudged against the Petitioner or Petitioners, either upon the affirmance of the decree or dismission of his or their Petition for not prosecuting the same, all further proceedings upon such decree shall be wholly *suspended and* superseded until the cause shall be heard and determined or the Petition dismissed for want of prosecution; *And be it enacted by the authority aforesaid that the said Justices and Barons or any five of them, whereof the said Chief Justice of the King's Bench, Chief Justice of the Common Pleas, or Chief Baron of the Exchequer shall be one, shall have power and authority, and are hereby required to rehear and review all and every such cause and causes wherein there shall be any decree or dismission, upon a Petition to be exhibited in manner as aforesaid, and in order thereunto shall assemble themselves in the Exchequer Chamber or some other convenient place.** . . [Offered in Committee 3 Dec. (Com. Book), and, after amendment, reported this day. L. J., XIV. 683.]

(*b*.) 11 Dec. Amended† Clause A., as follows:—And be it further enacted by the authority aforesaid, That when any decree or dismission of any cause shall be pronounced in the said Court of Exchequer, the party or parties thereunto who shall conceive him, her, or themselves to be thereby grieved, may within the time aforesaid, and in manner as aforesaid, petition the Justices of the King's Bench and Justices of the Common Bench for the time being, to review and rehear the said cause so decreed or dismissed, which Petition being received, and a certificate thereof made by the said Justices or any two of them to the Chancellor or Barons of the said Court of Exchequer, and security given in manner as aforesaid by the party or parties so petitioning, all proceedings on the said decree or dismission shall be thereupon wholly suspended and superseded, and the said Decree or Order of dismission shall be reheard and reviewed, in manner as aforesaid, before the said Justices of King's Bench and Common Pleas aforesaid, and the said Justices or any five of them, whereof the Chief Justice of the King's Bench or Chief Justice of the Common Pleas shall be one, are hereby and by authority of this

* The MS. Min. of 3 Dec. when this amendment was made, add the words "*to be set down in the said certificate.*"

† The Amendment at the end, which appears in Annex (*c*.) but not in Annex (*d*.) below, was apparently made on recommitment.

present Parliament empowered and required to take such order and to proceed, hear, determine, reverse, affirm, or alter the said Decree or Order of dismission as the said Justices and Barons, or any of them, may, by virtue of this Act, upon decrees or dismissions in the said Court of Chancery or other Court of Equity, which affirmance, reversal, or alteration of the said Decree or Decrees shall be remitted into the said Court of Exchequer, to be there executed in manner as aforesaid, which said Decrees and Orders shall be final and conclude all parties without any rehearing, unless upon Appeal in Parliament, [or where it is necessary to have some matter of fact tried at law before any final decree or order can be made on such review and rehearing as aforesaid], *to which the party or parties grieved may resort either before or after such rehearing, in manner as aforesaid.* [Offered in Committee and agreed to, as amended 7 Dec. (Com. Book) and reported this day. L.J., XIV. 683.]

(c.) 11 Dec. Clauses B. as follow:—And for avoiding of all delays, which may be any ways occasioned by such reviews or rehearings, Be it further enacted by the authority aforesaid, That where any Decree, Order or Orders of Dismission shall be pronounced in the said Courts of Chancery, Exchequer or other Court of Equity, from which any Appeal shall be made to the said Justices and Barons or any of them as aforesaid, the death of any or either of the parties, plaintiff, or defendant, after the pronouncing of such Decree, Order and Orders of Dismission, and before the enrolment thereof, or of such other decree or order which shall be made on such appeal, shall noways abate or determine the said suit, but the same may, after such death or deaths so happening, be enrolled and put in execution in the same manner as if all the parties to the said suit had been living at the time of the enrolment thereof. Provided always that this Act nor anything herein contained shall not extend or be any ways construed to give the said Justices of the King's Bench, Common Pleas, and the said Barons of the Exchequer, or any of them, any power or jurisdiction to receive or rehear any cause decreed or dismissed in any Court of Conscience or Equity established by authority of Parliament since the reign of their present Majesties King William and Queen Mary, but that all causes now depending, or hereafter to be commenced and prosecuted in the said Courts and every of them, may be proceeded in, decreed and determined in every of the said Courts without any appeal from the same, anything in this Act contained to the contrary thereof in anywise notwithstanding. [Offered in Committee and agreed to 7 Dec. (Com. Book) and reported this day. L. J., XIV. 683.]

(d.) 11 Dec. Lords' amendments to the Bill. [Made in Committee on Dec. 3 and 7 (Com. Book) and reported this day. L. J., XIV. 683.]

(e.) 12 Dec. Two additional amendments, not in preceding. [They are the two amendments noted above as having apparently been reported on re-commitment. Com. Book, 12 Dec. L. J., XIV. 684.]

439. Nov. 17. Writ of Summons (Bishop of Gloucester).—Writ of Summons, dated Oct. 5 to Edward [Fowler], Bishop of Gloucester. [Took the oaths this day. L. J., XIV. 649.]

HOUSE OF LORDS MSS.

1691.

440. Nov. 17. Shore *v.* Billingsly.—Petition of Dame Sarah Shore, widow, executrix of the last Will and Testament of Sir John Shore, Knight, deceased, and also surviving residuary legatee and administratrix, with the Will annexed, of Mary Shore, unadministered by the said Sir John Shore. Mary Shore, by her Will in 1659 left 300*l.* to her brother Sir John Shore, on condition of his paying 12*l.* yearly to her mother, and left 400*l.* to Elizabeth Taylor, an infant (who afterwards married Mr. Lewis Billingsly), at the age of 18, and gave some other legacies, devising the rest of her personal estate of 1,500*l.* to Lady Wheeler, her executrix and to her said brother. On her death in 1660, Lady Wheeler possesed all her personal estate but never proved the will, and died in 1670, leaving all her own real estate, together with 500*l.* in one Mr. Dixie's hands, to Elizabeth Taylor, whom she made her executrix, and desired Sir John Shore and Dr. William Denton to be overseers of her Will. Sir John, being Elizabeth Taylor's uncle, administered her estate during her minority, and took her under his custody and tuition, and obtained letters of administration of his sister's personal estate, unadministered by Lady Wheeler. In 1672 Elizabeth Taylor, by Roger Taylor, her next friend brought a Bill in Chancery against Sir John and others for an account of the personal estates of Mary Shore, Lady Wheeler, and one Margaret Cole, and for payment of her legacies of 400*l.* and 500*l.*, and in June 1674 the Lord Keeper Finch decreed an account and directed a trial as to the 500*l.*, which Sir John, had denied being the money of Lady Wheeler. A verdict passed against Sir John, who was ordered to pay the said 400*l.* and 300*l.* as far as assets of Mary Shore. The Master, however, who was directed to take an account, made no report, and the suit abated on Elizabeth Taylor's marriage with Mr. Billingsly, and again on Sir John's death in 1680. Petitioner, as his widow and executrix, proved his Will and obtained letters of administration of the personal estate of Mary Shore, unadministered by Sir John, and as residuary legatee of the said Mary Shore, and in 1681 brought her Bill against Mr. Billingsly for an account of the estates of Lady Wheeler and Sir William Wheeler and of Mary Shore's that came into Lady Wheeler's hands, and to be paid the legacy of 300*l.* The Court in Jan. 1684 decreed an account to be taken upon both Bills. The suits again abated on Elizabeth Taylor's death in Jan. 1686, but not before the account was taken, and in 1687 and 1689 the Master made reports, to which Petitioner and Billingsly both excepted. Petitioner sets forth the grounds of her exceptions, and appeals against the said decrees, orders, and proceedings, and prays that further proceedings may be stayed and Billingsly ordered to answer. *Signed* by Appellant; *Countersigned* by Ambrose Phillipps, T. Powys, and P. Bowes. [L. J., XIV. 649. The Appeal never came to a hearing.]

Annexed :—

(*a*.) 17 Nov. 1691. Copy order of service on preceding Petition. *Signed* Math. Johnson, Cler. Parliament. L. J., XIV. 649. *In extenso.*

(*b*.) 28 Nov. 1691. Petition of Charles Ballett, Gent., and Francis Gregg, Gent. L. J., XIV. 664 almost *In extenso.*

(*c*.) 12 Jan. 1691–2. Answer of Lewis Billingsly, Esq. Respondent, in right of his late wife, and by virtue of several letters of administration and decrees and orders in Chancery is justly entitled to 400*l.* legacy out of Mary Shore's estate, to one-half of the rest of her personal estate, to all the personal estate of Margaret Cole, to 500*l.* legacy out of Lady Wheeler's estate, and to the rest of the Lady Wheeler's personal estate. Admits that

Appellant is entitled by the decrees and orders to 300*l.* legacy out of Mary Shore's estate, to the other half of her personal estate, to 140*l.* for Sir John's sojourning Lady Wheeler, and to 50*l.* due to him out of Lady Wheeler's estate, by virtue of an administration to his mother; but none of these sums, except the moiety of the surplus of Mary Shore's personal estate, ought in justice to have been decreed to Appellant. The money in Dixy's hands was found at the trial to belong not to Sir John Shore but to Lady Wheeler. The Master's reports showed a balance due to Respondent on the accounts, as they stood at the death of Lady Wheeler in 1670, of 2,764*l.* Prays that the Appeal may be dismissed with costs, as vexatious, and the final order and decree confirmed. *Countersigned* William Dobyns. *Endorsed* as brought in this day.

441. Nov. 17. Oath of Supremacy Abrogation (Ireland) Act.—Amended* draft of Clauses marked A. Seven pages. They form the Clauses added by the Lords, as finally amended and ordered to be engrossed this day. The engrossment of these Clauses is annexed to the Roll as a separate Schedule marked A., and, with the later amendments of the Commons, forms Sections viii. to xi. inclusive of the Act 3 W. & M. c. 2. (Fol. Edit.) The contents of this draft are as follows:—

Pages 1 (marked A.) and 2 † are identical, as amended or corrected with Sect. viii. of the Act. The passages amended or corrected are the following:—

§ viii. Line 1 sqq. (Fol. Edit.). And be it enacted by the authority aforesaid, that all and every Archbishop . . . . that [are now residing within this realm of England and] shall [reside] *happen to be* in this realm *of England* the first day. . . .

Line 9 . . . in the said Kingdom of Ireland in the morning *and between the hours of nine and twelve*, where the same . . .

Line 10 . . . and if any such [Bishop] *Archbishop* or [Bishops] *Bishop* or other person . . .

Line 12 . . . [residing] *happening to be* within this realm . . .

Line 15 . . . dignities and promotions [also made] *and* incapable . . .

Line 16 . . . every other person *or persons* having any office. . . .

Line 20 . . . first day of *the said* Hilary term . . .

Line 22 . . . and in case such *other* person . . .

Line 23 . . . and if such *other* person or persons so residing or inhabiting in *the realm of* England. . . .

Page 3.‡ as amended first by the Lords, and afterwards by the Commons, forms Section ix. of the Act (Folio Edit.). The Lord's amendments are shown in the first column, the Commons' amendments (L. J., XIV. 681) in the second, viz.:—

---

* Additions are shown by italics, omissions by square brackets.

† Pages 1 and 2 appear to have been drawn by C. Justice Holt, in substitution for the cancelled Proviso on pp. 6–7, and reported on 16 Nov. together with pp. 5–6 as "Clauses marked A."; then recommitted to a Select Committee, and agreed to, on their report, on 17 Nov.

‡ Pages 3 and 4, which are in different handwritings, appear to have been added in the House on 17th Nov., after agreeing to the Report of the Select Committee. *See* L. J., XIV. 649.

HOUSE OF LORDS MSS.

1691.

Amended Draft.	Sect. ix. of Act.
Provided always that this Act . . . shall not extend to hinder or disable any person or persons who [on] *at any time before* the third day of October in the year of our Lord one thousand, six hundred, ninety [and] one, *submitted to their Majesties' government, or on the said third of October* were inhabiting or residing in Limerick . . .	Line 1. Provided always that this Act . . . shall not extend to hinder or disable any person or persons, who [at any time before the third day of October in the year of our Lord one thousand, six hundred, ninety one, submitted to their Majesties government, or] on the [said] third of October *one thousand, six hundred, ninety one*, were inhabiting or residing in Limerick . . .
. . . then in being or before that time treated with . . .	Line 6. . . . then in being or [before that time] *were then* treated with . . .
. . . or practicer of law, physic or other science, but they may freely use . . . . . to the contrary notwithstanding; [Yet so that such person and persons shall be liable and compellable to take the said Oath to bear faith and true allegiance to their Majesties under the penalties hereafter in this present Act mentioned.]*	Line 9. . . . or practicer of law or physic [or other science], but they may freely use . . . . . to the contrary notwithstanding. *Provided nevertheless that every such barrister at law, Clerk in Chancery, or Attorney or practicer of law or physic, who shall claim any benefit hereby to be exempted from taking the Oaths, and making, subscribing and repeating the Declaration in this Act mentioned, in the Court and in the manner hereby appointed, shall make out his claim thereunto, according to the respective qualifications hereinbefore expressed, before the Court of King's Bench in Ireland, in open Court there in term time, between the hours of nine and twelve in the morning, on or before the last day of Michaelmas term next, to be there allowed and recorded; for the entry whereof upon record there shall be one shilling paid and no more; and in default of such claim made, to be excluded from the same.*

Page 4 is identical, as amended or corrected, with Sect. x. of the Act. (Fol. Edit.). The amendments or corrections are as follows:—

§ x. Line 1. Provided [always] *nevertheless and be it enacted*, that . . .

Line 5. . . . in any of their Majesties' Courts *of Record* in Ireland . . .

Line 7. . . . such person so [practising] *using or exercising his profession or calling* shall be adjudged . . .

Pages 5, 6 (originally numbered 1, 2) and 7 (not numbered) contain two Clauses.† The first of them, as amended by filling in the penalty upon the third refusal to take the Oath, vizt, from the words ("*danger and penalty of Præmunire*") to ("*take the said Oath*"), is identical with Section xi. of the Act (Fol. Edit.), with two verbal exceptions, vizt. ("as the said Justices") instead of ("as they, the said Justices"),

* This passage, before being struck out, was amended to read as follows: "Yet so that such person and persons shall be incapable and disabled to exercise their respective professions, trades, and callings, before he or they shall have taken the said Oath to be faithful and bear true allegiance to their Majesties, and shall be liable to all the penalties in this present Act mentioned."

† These two Clauses appear to have been drawn originally by the Judges for the Committee of the Whole House, pursuant to Order of 14 Nov., and the first of them to have been reported on 16 Nov., together with the clause on pages 1 and 2, as "Clauses marked A."

and ("held for such County") instead of ("holden for such County"). The second of them, which is struck through, reads as follows :—

[Provided always and be it enacted by the authority aforesaid, that if any Archbishop, bishop, officer or other person, hereby required to take the said Oaths, and to make, repeat and subscribe the said Declaration in the King's Bench in Ireland (*blank*) shall reside and continue in England until (*blank*), he or they may take the said Oaths, and make and subscribe the said Declaration in the Court of Chancery or King's Bench in the Kingdom of England before (*blank*), which shall be as good and effectual as if such archbishop, bishop, officer or other person had taken the said Oaths, and made, repeated and subscribed the said Declaration in the King's Bench in Ireland within the time first before mentioned, and such person shall be exempted and discharged from incurring any of the penalties, forfeitures and disabilities before-mentioned for not taking the said Oaths, or making, repeating, and subscribing the said Declaration in the King's Bench in Ireland before (*blank*).]

Endorsed on p. 7. "Clauses added to the Bill of Oaths for Ireland. 17 Nov. 1691."

[The Bill, embodying originally only §§ i–vii. and § xiv. (Fol. Edit.) of the Act, was brought from the Commons on 11 Nov. (L. J., XIV. 641). There is no entry either in L. J. or MS. Min. of its first reading. The subsequent proceedings were as follows :—

14 Nov. House in Committee, E. Rochester in the chair. The Bill is read through.

Title and Preamble read and agreed to.

First enacting Clause (§ i.) read and agreed to.

Second enacting Clause (§ ii.) read. Statutes of Ireland ordered to be sent for, and some of the Judges sent for. The Clause postponed.

Next Clause (§ iii.) read.

The Irish Statute read. The postponed Clause (§ ii.) read, and after debate, *Question* [proposed]: Whether to agree to the paragraph ending within five lines of the second Press?* *Question* put: Whether this Clause be postponed? Resolved in the *Affirmative*. The latter part of the paragraph† read and agreed to.

The next Clause read and postponed from ("and") in Press 3, line 5, to ("and") in Press 4, line 4.‡

The next Clause § read and agreed to.

The Clause for Peers to take the Oaths (§ iv.) read and agreed to.

The Declaration (§ iv.) read. In Press 5, lines 15 and 16, leave out the words ("of the Church of Ireland").‖

The next paragraph read to the forfeitures of those that shall refuse the Oaths and Declaration (§ v.). Press 6, line 17, postponed from the word ("and") to the word ("And") in Press 7, line 16.¶

The next Clause, as to the Oaths, (§ xvi.) read and agreed to.

Press 8, line 3 (§ vii.) after ("factory"), add ("or to any chaplains in their Majesties' Service, by sea or land, out of the Kingdom of Ireland").**

* This Question is expunged. The paragraph here referred to, as appears from the Roll, is the one in § ii. ending with the words ("one shilling and no more").

† From ("And if any Archbishop") to ("place or cure whatsoever") in § ii.

‡ This postponed portion begins with ("And all and every other person") in § ii. and ends with ("Court of Record or not of Record") in § iii.

§ Namely, the rest of § iii.

‖ These words, which are erased on the Roll, but supplied in C. J., X. 566, occur in the Declaration, viz. :—"As they are commonly understood by Protestants [of the Church of Ireland] without any evasion."

¶ This postponed portion forms the whole of § v.

** These words are interlined on the Roll. *See* C. J., X. 566.

HOUSE OF LORDS MSS.

1691.

Mr. Harbord's Clause (§ vii.) read and agreed to.*

The last Clause (§ xiv.) read. Postponed.

A general Clause to be prepared, to exempt such from the penalty in the Act who shall take the Oaths in the King's Bench here. [*See* pp. 6-7 of Draft.] To empower the civil officers in Ireland to tender the Oath of Fidelity to such persons as they shall suspect, upon such pains and penalties as are in the Act here. [*See* pp. 5-6 of Draft, § xi.]

House resumed. *E. Rochester* reported as in L. J., XIV. 645 (MS. Min.).

16 Nov. House in Committee, E. Rochester in the chair.

First postponed Clause (§ ii. to line 21) read and agreed to.

The next relative Clause (§ ii. line 22 *ad fin*, and § iii. to line 7) read and agreed to.

The postponed Clause, Peers to take the Oaths (§ v.) agreed to.

The Clauses drawn by the Judges, read. Then the first Clause (§ xi.) read again. The blank filled out of the Statute 3 Jac.† The last Clause read. *The L. Chief Justice* [*Holt*] desired to draw two Clauses, one relating to the Bishops and Clergy, and the other to Officers. [*See* pp. 1-2 of Draft.] The Clauses drawn by the Judges read twice and agreed to.

The last Clause in the Bill postponed (§ xiv.) read and agreed to.

Last Press, line 26, after ("notwithstanding")‡ add the Clauses marked A.

House resumed, *E. Rochester* reported that the Committee had gone through the Bill with some amendments and two Clauses,§ which were read. The Amendments were read again. *Ordered* that the two Clauses ["two first clauses" in L. J.] drawn by the Judges be recommitted to a Select Committee, with C. J. Holt to assist. *Proposed* to leave out the words ("Barrister-at-law, Physicians, and Clerks in Chancery"). The Articles of Capitulation in Ireland‖ are read. House moved to adjourn (MS. Min., L. J., XIV. 646).

17 Nov. In Select Committee, *E. Rochester* in the chair. *C. Justice Holt* offers the Clause prepared, which is read and agreed to, and ordered to be reported (Com. Book.).

Eod. die.—*E. Rochester* reported from the Select Committee the Clauses drawn by the Judges. The Clauses were read. Then the first Clause was read and agreed to. The next Clause was read and agreed to. *Ordered* that the Clauses be engrossed.

Then the House went into debate whether Lawyers and Physicians should be left out in the Bill. A Proviso¶ offered in this case was read, read again and agreed to, and ordered to be engrossed.

---

* It had been added in the Commons on third reading. C. J., X. 549.

† *See* the Amendment in p. 6 of the Draft (§ xi.), which is taken from the Act for the better discovering and repressing of Popish Recusants, 3 Jac. I. c. 4 sect. 9. (Fol. Edit.)

‡ Namely, at the end of § vii.

§ Presumedly sect. viii. on pp. 1-2, and sect. xi. on pp. 5-6 of the Draft. The former section is numbered 1 in the margin of the Draft on p. 1, and the latter is numbered 2 on page 5.

‖ L. J., XIV. 647-8. *In extenso.* The objection to the Commons' Bill, as violating the Treaty of Limerick, appears to have been raised by E. Nottingham. Pulteney's MS. Letters to Cole, 17 Nov. 1691, quoted in Grey's Debates, 30 Nov. 1691.

¶ The Journal entry (L. J., XIV. 649) specifies "a Clause for exempting Attornies, Clerks in Chancery and Physicians, who were in Limerick at the Capitulation, from some of the penalties of this Act," namely, the first portion of sect. ix. (p. 3 of Draft), but does not mention this Proviso, which is apparently sect. x. (p. 4 of Draft).

House moved that the last Clause in the Bill (Sect. xiv.) may be left out. *Agreed* to be left out. (MS. Min., L. J., XIV. 649.)

On 18 Nov. the Bill was read 3d, and the next day it was returned with the amendments to the Commons (L. J., XIV. 650, 653).

1 Dec. Conference desired by Commons as to Lords' Amendments, agreed to and Reporters named.* Conference had. *D. Bolton* reported that the Commons had agreed to the first two amendments,† and to Section viii., disagreed with Reasons to the two Provisos [Sections ix. and x.], agreed to Section xi. with the addition of Clause B., namely Sections xii. and xiii., relating to Quakers, and disagreed to the omission of Section xiv., forbidding the Act to be dispensed with. (MS. Min. L. J., XIV. 667.)

3 Dec. Commons' Amendments and Reasons considered. Sections ix. and x. insisted on, and Committee appointed to prepare Reasons for insisting. The other amendments of the Commons agreed to. (MS. Min., L. J., XIV. 671.)

4 Dec. In Committee. E. Rochester in the Chair. Part of the Articles of Limerick are read. Reasons to be given at a Conference are agreed and ordered to be reported. (Com. Book.)

Eod. die. Lord's Reasons for insisting reported and agreed to, and Conference desired with Commons thereon. (MS. Min., L. J., XIV. 673.)

5 Dec. Conference had. *E. Rochester* reported that he had delivered the Lords' Reasons for insisting. (MS. Min., L. J., XIV. 674.)

10 Dec. Conference desired by Commons; agreed to and had. *D. Bolton* reported that the Commons had agreed to Sections ix. and x. with amendments, including the addition of Clause C. Said amendments agreed to. (MS. Min., L. J., XIV. 680, 681.)

The Bill received the Royal Assent on 24 Dec. (L. J., XIV. 701.)]

442. Nov. 18. Trials for Treason Regulation Bill.—Commons' Engrossment of an Act for regulating of Trials in cases of treasons *and misprision of treason*.‡ Identical, as amended, with Sections i., ii., v., vii., viii., and xi. of the Act of 1695–6 (7 & 8 Will. III. c. 3. Fol. Edit.), except where quoted in the second column below, viz. :—

Engrossment as amended.	Act of 1695–6 (Fol. Edit.)
Preamble.	Sect. i.
. . . that [prosecutions] *persons prosecuted*§ for high treason . . .	
. . . whereby the liberty, lives, honour . . .	Line 2. . . . whereby the liberties, lives, honour . . .
. . . [For remedy whereof]. *In order thereunto*§ . . .	
. . . persons [indicted] *prosecuted*§ for high treason . . .	

* The name of V. Weymouth appears in MS. Min. as one of the Reporters originally proposed.

† Namely those in sections iv. and vii.

‡ This and the other Amendments of the Lords are taken from Annex (*a*.) below, the additions being shown by italics, and the omissions by square brackets.

§ Agreed to on 11 Dec. by the Commons (C. J., X. 582), and retained in the Act of 1695–6.

Engrossment as amended—*continued.*	Act of 1695–6—*continued.*
Clause 1.*	
. . . the King and Queen's most excellent Majesties . . .	. . . the King's most excellent Majesty . . .
. . . from and after the first day of January, one thousand, six hundred, ninety one . . .	Line 8. . . . from and after the five and twentieth day of March in the year of our Lord one thousand, six hundred, ninety six . . .
. . . corruption of blood may or shall be made to any the heir or heirs of any such offender . . .	Line 9. . . . corruption of blood may or shall be made to any such offender or to any the heir or heirs of any such offender . . .
. . . shall have a true copy of the whole indictment delivered unto him or them ten days at the least before he or they shall be tried for the same . . .	Line 11. . . . shall have a true copy of the whole indictment, but not the names of the witnesses, delivered unto them or any of them five days at the least before he or they shall be tried for the same . . .
. . . to advise with counsel thereupon, his or their attorney . . .	Line 13. . . . to advise with counsel thereupon, to plead and make their defence, his or their attorney . .
Clause 2.	
. . . or witnesses, *who shall then be*† upon oath [or otherwise] for his and their just defence . . .	
Clause 3.	
. . . and in case [any Councillor-at-law shall refuse to appear and plead at any Court on the behalf of any person or persons so accused or indicted] *upon the arraignment of any person or persons so accused or indicted, such person or persons shall desire Counsel,*‡ the Court before whom such person shall be tried, *or some Judge of that Court,*† shall, and is hereby authorized and required to, assign [such or other Counsel]† to such person and persons *such and so many Counsel, not exceeding three, as the person or persons shall desire, ten days at least before such person or persons shall be tried,*† to whom such counsel shall have free access at all seasonable [times] *hours,*† any law or usage to the contrary notwithstanding.	Line 20. . . . and in case any person or persons so accused or indicted shall desire Counsel, the Court before whom such person or persons shall be tried, or some Judge of that Court, shall and is hereby authorized and required, immediately upon his or their request, to assign to such person and persons such and so many Counsel, not exceeding two, as the person or persons shall desire, to whom such Counsel shall have free access at all seasonable hours, any law or usage to the contrary notwithstanding.
Clause 4.	Section ii.
. . . from and after the said first day of January, no person . . .	Line 1. . . . from and after the said five and twentieth day of March in the year of our Lord one thousand, six hundred, ninety six, no person . . .
. . . shall be indicted, arraigned, tried, convicted, outlawed, condemned or attainted . . .	Line 2. . . . shall be indicted, tried or attainted . . .

* The Clauses are numbered here in accordance with the notes of proceedings in MS. Min. below.

† Agreed to on 11 Dec. by the Commons (C. J., X. 582), and retained in the Act of 1695–6.

‡ Agreed to on 11 Dec. by the Commons, C. J., X. 582.

Engrossment as amended—*continued.*	Act of 1695–6—*continued.*
. . . any corruption of blood may or shall be made to any the heir or heirs of any such offender . . .	Line 3. . . . any corruption of blood may or shall be made to any such offender or offenders, or to any the heir or heirs of any such offender . . .
. . . of two lawful witnesses to the same treason, unless . . .	Line 5. . . . of two lawful witnesses, either both of them to the same overt act, or one of them to one, and the other of them to another overt act of the same treason, unless . . .
. . . confess the same, *or shall stand mute, or refuse to plead*, or peremptorily challenge above the number of five and thirty of the jury.*	Line 7. . . . confess the same, or shall stand mute or refuse to plead, or in cases of high treason, shall peremptorily challenge above the number of thirty five of the jury, any law, statute or usage to the contrary notwithstanding.
———	Section iii.
———	Section iv.
Clause 5.	Section v.
. . . from and after the said first day of January, no person . . .	Line 2. . . . from and after the said five and twentieth day of March in the year of our Lord one thousand, six hundred, ninety six, no person . . .
. . . indicted, arraigned, tried or prosecuted . . .	Line 3. . . . indicted, tried or prosecuted . . .
. . . or for any misprision of such treasons, *that shall be committed or done within the Kingdom of England, Dominion of Wales, or town of Berwick-upon-Tweed after the said first day of January,** unless the same indictment be begun, preferred and prosecuted within three years next after the treason or offence done and committed, and not afterwards.	Line 4. . . . or for misprision of such treason, that shall be committed or done within the Kingdom of England, Dominion of Wales, or Town of Berwick-upon-Tweed, after the said five and twentieth day of March in the year of our Lord one thousand, six hundred, ninety six, unless the same indictment be found by a Grand Jury within three years next after the treason or offence done and committed, and that no person or persons shall be prosecuted for any such treason or misprision of such treason committed or done, or to be committed or done within the Kingdom of England, Dominion of Wales or Town of Berwick-upon-Tweed before the said five and twentieth day of March, unless he or they shall be indicted thereof within three years after the said five and twentieth day of March.
———	Section vi.
Clause 6.	Section vii.
. . . accused, indicted and tried . . .	Line 1. . . . accused, indicted or tried . . .
. . . after the said first day of January, shall have . . .	Line 2. . . . after the said five and twentieth day of March in the year of our Lord one thousand, six hundred, ninety six, shall have . . .

* Agreed to on 11 Dec. by the Commons, C. J., X. 582.

House of Lords MSS.

1691.

Engrossed as amended—*continued.*	Act of 1695–6—*continued.*
. . . indicted of any such treason . . .	Line 5. . . . indicted for any such treason . . .
. . . to compel any witnesses to appear against them.	Line 7. . . . to compel witnesses to appear against them.
Clause 7.	Sect. viii.
And be it further enacted by the authority aforesaid, that . . .	And be it further enacted, that . .
———	Sect. ix.
———	Sect. x.
Clause 8.*	Sect. xi.
Provided always, and it is hereby declared, that this Act nor anything herein contained, shall any ways extend to, or be construed to extend to [any proceedings in Parliament upon any impeachment or impeachments in any kind whatsoever] *limit any time for impeaching in Parliament any person or persons for high treason or misprision of such treason, yet nevertheless the person or persons so to be impeached shall have Counsel, witnesses sworn and process for them, copies of the said impeachments, and like means of defence, and in such manner as any other persons indicted for the said offences are hereby allowed to have and enjoy.*†	Provided always that neither this Act nor anything therein contained shall any ways extend to, or be construed to extend to any impeachment or other proceedings in Parliament in any kind whatsoever.
———	Sect. xii.

Parchment Collection. Endorsed: Lost upon the Lords adhering, 28 Jan. 1691–2. [The Bill was brought from the Commons this day (L. J., XIV. 650). The subsequent proceedings were as follows:—

24 Nov. In Committee of the whole House, the Bill was read through.

Title and Preamble read and postponed.

Clause 1. First enacting Clause read. *Question:* Whether this Clause shall pass without any amendment? *Question:* Whether the L. Chief Baron [Atkyns] shall be asked as to this Clause? Resolved in the *Negative. Question* put: Whether this paragraph shall be part of the Bill without any amendment? Resolved in the *Affirmative.*

Clause 2 read. *The L. C. Baron* heard to the words ("upon oath or otherwise"): It refers to writings or deeds.

Press 1, line 40. After ("witnesses") add ("who shall then be").

" 2, " 1. Leave out ("or otherwise").

Clause 3, concerning assigning Counsel, read. Agreed to ("And") in Press 2, line 2. House resumed. *L. Cornwallis* reported as in L. J., XIV. 661. (MS. Min.)

* The whole of this Clause was originally left out in Committee of the whole House (MS. Min., 2 Dec.). On report, after debate, it was first recommitted to C. W. H., and then referred to a Select Committee, who amended it as above, in which shape it was agreed to by the House (MS. Min. and Com. Book, 3 Dec. L. J., XIV 671). The Commons on 11 Dec. agreed by 208 votes to 153 to amend it by inserting ("and") before ("copies"), and leaving out all the words in italics after ("impeachments") (C. J., X. 582 and Annex (*e.*) below), to which amendments the Lords, at the second Conference, agreed (L. J., XV. 5).

† Here is noted to add Clause A. *See* Annex (*a.*) below.

26 Nov. House again in Committee, V. Weymouth in the Chair.

Clause 3 considered. *The L. C. Baron* offered a Clause to force Counsel assigned to plead and attend. The Clause read. Another clause drawn, read; a Clause concerning the assigning Counsel.

Press 2, line 2. After ("and in case") leave out to ("indicted") inclusive in line 5, and insert ("Upon the arraignment of any person or persons so assessed or indicted, such person or persons shall desire Counsel").

line 8. Leave out ("such or other Counsel") and insert ("such and so many Counsel, not exceeding three, as the person or persons shall desire, ten days at least before such person or persons shall be tried").

line 6. After ("tried") read ("or some Judge of that Court"). The Clause agreed to as amended.

Clause 4. The Clause of corruption of blood by witnesses is read.

Press 2, line 23. After ("same") add ("or shall stand mute or refuse to plead"). Judges to be asked upon the words ("two lawful witnesses to the same treason"). Agreed to Press 2, line 11 [*i.e.*, to ("contrary notwithstanding") the end of Clause 3].

Clause 4, beginning ("And") in Press 2, line 11 postponed.

Clause 5 read.

House resumed. *V. Weymouth* reported as in L. J., XIV. 664. Ordered that the Judges attend on 1 Dec., and have a copy of the Bill as amended. (MS. Min.)

2 Dec. House again in Committee, L. Cornwallis in the Chair.

Clause 4. Judges heard whether ("two witnesses to the same treason") will make any alteration in the law. *L. C. Baron* [*Athyns*]: I take it to be the law now that there must be two witnesses to prove the death of the King, that is, treason, and so in other treasons. All the Judges of the same opinion. *Agreed to.*

L. C. Justice [*Holt*] presented an Amendment. The Clause read, as amended, and agreed to. [Probably Clause 5 above.]

Next Clause read and agreed to. [Probably Clauses 6 and 7 above.]

Clause 8.—Press 3, line 16. Leave out from ("whatsoever") to the end of the Bill.

Moved that a Clause be added, that upon the trial of a Peer, the whole number of Peers shall be summoned. That the whole body be summoned, and no exceptions to be made. *Question* proposed: Whether there shall be any exceptions? A Clause proposed to regulate the trial of Peers. *Question:* Whether there shall be a liberty of exceptions to be put in the Clause that shall be framed for the trial of a Peer? Resolved in the *Negative*. [*Moved*] That upon the trial of any Peer or Peeress, all the Lords that have a right to sit and vote in Parliament shall be summoned.* *Agreed to. Proposed:* a penalty if any Lords be summoned and do not attend. *Agreed* to be left out. *Proposed:* a number. *Agreed* that all that come shall have votes. Provided that, before any such Peer shall sit or vote upon any such trial, the Lord High Steward shall administer the Oath and Declaration to him. *The Judges* withdrew to draw the Clause.

The Title postponed is read. The words ("and misprision of treason") to be added.

The Preamble postponed is read.

Press 1, line 11. For ("indicted") read ("prosecuted").

The Clause read as amended ("In order thereunto").

* The words first proposed, and here expunged, were as follows: "That upon the trial of any Peer or Peeress all the Lords shall be summoned, that are capable of sitting, and that are compelled to take the Oaths."

HOUSE OF LORDS MSS.

1691.

The Clause drawn by the Judges was brought in and read twice, and agreed to be added at the end of the Bill.*

House resumed, *L. Cornwallis* reported as in L. J., XIV. 670. (MS. Min.)

3 Dec. Bill reported with the amendments. The Clause concerning impeachments, after debate, recommitted. House again in Committee accordingly. The Clause read. House resumed. Select Committee appointed to prepare a Clause upon the debate (MS. Min.; L. J., XIV. 671).—In this Select Committee, L. Cornwallis in the Chair, a Proviso was drawn and agreed to be offered to the House (Com. Book, 3 Dec.) This Proviso was reported, as an amendment to the Clause, and agreed to by the House the same day, together with the other amendments to the Bill† (MS. Min.; L. J., XIV. 671).

5 Dec. Bill read 3ª and returned to the Commons (MS. Min.; L. J. XIV. 674).

17 Dec. *Duke of Norfolk* reported from the Conference this day that the Commons had disagreed to certain of the Lords' amendments, including Clause A.‡ Committee appointed to prepare reasons for insisting (L. J., XIV. 691.)§

23 Dec. Message from Commons to remind the Lords of the Bill (L. J., XIV. 700).

24 Dec. The Committee appointed to prepare reasons, ordered to meet on the 28th inst. (*ib.* 702).

28 Dec. The Committee met, V. Halifax in the Chair, and after reading the Commons' Reason for not agreeing to Clause A. (L. J., XIV. 691. *In extenso*), agreed to report some Reasons for insisting on the Clause (Com. Book).

29 Dec. The Committee reported these Reasons (L. J., XV. 3. *In extenso*),‖ and the House, after agreeing to them, sent a Message to the Commons to desire another Conference (L. J., XV. 4), which was accordingly held the same day, and the Lords intimated their agreement to the Commons' Amendments to the Clause concerning Impeachments, and communicated their Reasons for insisting on Clause A. (*ib.* 5).

31 Dec. The Commons, on considering the Report of the last Conference, resolved by 186 votes to 120, to insist on disagreeing to Clause A.¶ and ordered a Message to be sent to the Lords to desire a free Conference (C. J., X. 604).

4 Jan. The Lords agreed to a Free Conference the next day (L. J., XV. 15), and appointed as Managers the Committee who had prepared the Reasons for insisting on Clause A. (*ib.* 16).

5 Jan. Free Conference had and reported, and further debate on the Report adjourned till the 7th (*ib.* 18).

7 Jan. Adjourned debate resumed. After debate, the House resolved to insist on Clause A., but instructed the Managers of the Free Conference to acquaint the Commons, "that they may explain any words in the Clause, if they think it necessary, in relation to the Bishops not sitting upon trials of Peers out of Parliament, and if the Commons think it material that all the Lords should be present at the

---

* Clause A. in Annex (*a.*) below.

† Annex (*b.*) below.

‡ Annex (*c.*) below.

§ Annex (*d.*) below.

‖ *See also* Grey's Debates, X. 217–8. These reasons are not printed in the Commons' Journal.

¶ Annex (*e.*) below.

trial of any Peer, their Lordships will be willing to receive any expedient that shall be thought proper to oblige all the Lords to attend at every such trial."* A Message was then sent to the Commons to desire another Free Conference (L. J., XIV. 20). After this, the MS. Min. contain the following entry, not in L. J. :—"Lords Committees appointed to draw what shall be entered on the Books upon this intimation to be delivered at the Free Conference concerning a penalty upon such Peers as shall not attend, being summoned, upon the trial of any Peer," (MS. Min.)

Eod. die. The Commons, on receiving the Lords' Message, resolved by 139 votes to 110 not to agree to a present Free Conference, but ordered a Message to be sent the next day agreeing to one (C. J., X. 615).

8 Jan. The Message sent to the Lords, who appoint the next day for the Free Conference (C. J., X. 617).

9 Jan. Free Conference had and reported (L. J., XV. 23; C. J., X. 618).†

13 Jan. The Commons, after considering the Report made by their Managers of the last two Free Conferences, resolved to agree to Clause A. with certain Amendments,‡ and ordered a Message to be sent to the Lords the next day, to desire another Free Conference (C. J., X. 627).

14 *Jan.* Free Conference agreed to and had. Report made, that the Commons had agreed to Clause A. with amendments. Select Committee appointed to inspect Commissions for Lord High Stewards§ (L. J., XV. 29).

15 Jan. In Select Committee, E. Mulgrave in the Chair, *Mr. Pingrey*, Clerk of the Petty Bag, being called in, says he has no Records concerning Commissions for Lord High Stewards, and that he has been to the Clerk of the Crown, who, he believes, makes entries of them. He is directed to go back to the Clerk of the Crown, and send him with such entries as he has of such Commissions. *Mr. Johnson* produces two forms of Commissions for Lord High Stewards in the cases of L. Audley and L. Morley, which are read. The Commission for the Lord High Steward at E. Strafford's trial, 30 Dec. 1680, is read. *Ordered*, that the *Custos Brevium* of the King's Bench bring this day, at or before 1 o'clock, the Record of D. Buck's trial in the time of Hen. VIII., and all such others since that time out of Parliament as he shall find before 1 Jac. II. The Committee then adjourned during pleasure (Com. Book).

Eod. die, E. Mulgrave, reported as in L. J., XV. 32. The *Custos Brevium* was called in, and delivered some records to the House, who ordered him to attend the Committee the next day with what others he had in his custody. Then the House, after reading the Commons' Amendments to Clause A., and agreeing to the first of them, ordered the Select Committee to meet again the next day and report on the

---

* The latter part of these Instructions originally ran as follows: "And if the Commons think it material that all the Lords *shall attend upon a penalty, the Lords will agree to the alteration of the Clause with such penalty as shall be thought fit.*" The words in italics are struck through.

† The Bill was delivered to the Commons at this Free Conference (L. J., XV. 23), and returned to the Lords at the Free Conference on 14 Jan. (C. J., X. 627).

‡ C. J., X. 627, and Annex (*f.*) below.

§ The list of Lords first proposed for this Committee, as given in MS. Min. adds to the names in L. J., XV. 29 that of E. Marlborough and omits those of M. Halifax and V. Weymouth.

HOUSE OF LORDS MSS.

1691.

18th, till which day the debate was adjourned (MS. Min.; L. J., XV. 32).

16 Jan. In Select Committee, E. Mulgrave in the Chair, *Mr. Bolt* brings in an Abstract of several trials of Peers before L. High Stewards, which is read. *Ordered* that Sir Samuel Astrey bring on the 18th the Records of L. Morley's, L. Delamere's, and L. Cornwall's trials. Adjourned to the 18th (Com. Book).*

18 Jan. Report made from Select Committee (L. J., XV. 35. *In extenso.*) After debate, Declaration agreed to, That all Peers were directed to be summoned to the trial of every Peer. Debate of Commons' Amendments to Clause A. adjourned till to-morrow. (MS. Min.; L. J., XV. 35.)

19 Jan. Debate adjourned till to-morrow. (MS. Min.; L. J., XV. 35.)

20 Jan. After debate, some of the Commons' Amendments to Clause A. agreed to, and others disagreed to.† Message sent to H. C. to desire another Free Conference. (MS. Min.; L. J., XV. 40.)

21 Jan. Free Conference agreed to by the Commons, had and reported. (MS. Min.; L. J., XV. 41, 43.)

25 Jan. The Commons, on considering the Report of the last Free Conference, after refusing by 125 votes to 120 to put the Question for insisting on their Amendments to Clause A., and rejecting by 127 to 106 a motion to adjourn the debate, resolved, without a division, to adhere to their disagreeing to the Clause, and ordered the Resolution ‡ to be delivered to the Lords at another Free Conference. (C. J., X. 641.) This Free Conference was had on the 27th, and the Lords, on considering the Report the next day, resolved after debate to adhere to Clause A. (L. J., XV. 51, 53.) The Bill accordingly was lost.]

(*a.*) 3 Dec. Lords' Engrossment of Clause A. added as an amendment to the Bill and afterwards amended by the Commons.§—Identical with Sect. x. of Act of 1695–6, except where quoted in the second column below:—

Clause A., as amended.	Act of 1695–6. Sect. x.
	And whereas by the good laws of this Kingdom, in cases of trials of Commoners for their lives, a jury of twelve freeholders must all agree in one opinion before they can bring a verdict either for acquittal or condemnation of the prisoner; And whereas upon the trials of peers or peeresses a major vote is sufficient either to acquit or condemn;
And be it further enacted by the authority aforesaid, That upon the trial of any *temporal* peer or peeress	Be it further enacted by the authority aforesaid, That upon the trial of any peer or peeress . . .
for any such treason or misprision of treason as aforesaid, that [all] *not less than six and thirty of* the *temporal* peers who have a right to sit and vote in Parliament, shall be duly summoned twenty days at	. . . that all peers who have a right to sit and vote in Parliament shall be duly summoned twenty days at least before every such trial, to appear at every such trial,

* No further proceedings of this Committee are recorded

† These Amendments are specified in L. J., XV. 40. The Question whether the penalty should be 2,000*l.* was negatived by 45 votes to 31. Tellers, E. Bridgewater and L. Berkeley. (MS. Min.)

‡ Annex (*h.*) below.

§ The Commons' Amendments are shown by italics and square brackets. The Clause as first sent to the Commons is printed in C. J., X. 584. *In extenso.*

least before every such trial, upon *the pain of forfeiting of one thousand pounds for every such peers not appearing after due proof made of such summons, and no reasonable excuse showed and allowed by the Court for such his default,* to appear at every such trial, and that [every peer so summoned and appearing on such trial] *at least three and twenty of the peers so summoned, and not under that number,* shall vote in the trial of such peer or peeress so to be tried, he and they first taking the Oaths mentioned in one Act of Parliament made in the first year of [King William and Queen Mary] *their Majesties' reign,* intituled an Act for abrogating the Oaths of Supremacy and Allegiance and appointing other Oaths, and also subscribing and audibly repeating the Declaration mentioned in an Act of Parliament made in the thirtieth year of the late King Charles the Second, intituled an Act for the more effectual preserving the King's person and government by disabling Papists from sitting in either House of Parliament.	and that every peer so summoned and appearing at such trial, shall vote . . . . . . in the first year of the reign of King William and Queen Mary, intituled . . . . . . mentioned in an Act for the more effectual preserving the King's person and government by disabling Papists from sitting in either House of Parliament, and made in the thirtieth year of the reign of the late King Charles the Second.

(*b.*) 3 Dec. Lords' Amendments to the Bill. C. J., X. 582. *In extenso.* [Reported from C. W. H. and agreed to this day. (L. J., XIV. 671.) They are embodied in the text above.]

(*c.*) 17 Dec. Commons' Resolutions on the Lords' Amendments, agreeing to the Clause concerning impeachments, with amendments, disagreeing to Clause A., and agreeing to the remaining amendments. [Agreed to by the Commons 11 Dec. (C. J., X. 582), and communicated at the Conference this day.]

(*d.*) 17 Dec. Draft Order of the Lords appointing a Committee to draw Reasons for insisting on Clause A. The List of the proposed Committee contains the names of E. Stamford* and E. Rochester, in addition to those given in L. J., XIV. 691. The Order is dated 18 Dec., but the Committee was appointed on the 17th.

(*e.*) 5 Jan. 1691–2. Commons' Resolution insisting on their disagreement to Clause A. [Agreed to by the Commons on 31 Dec. (C. J., X. 604), and communicated at the Free Conference this day.]

(*f.*) 14 Jan. Commons' Amendments to Clause A. [Agreed to by the Commons 13 Jan. (C. J., X. 626. *In extenso*), and communicated at the Free Conference this day.]

(*g.*) 20 Jan. Lords' Resolutions this day, agreeing to some of the Commons' Amendments to Clause A., and disagreeing to others. L. J., XV. 40.

(*h.*) Jan. 27. Commons' Resolution adhering to their disagreement to Clause A. [Agreed to by the Commons 25 Jan. (C. J., X. 641. *In extenso*), and delivered at the Free Conference this day.]

443. Nov. 18. State of the Nation (Intercepted Letters).—Letter from Sir Ralph Delaval to E. Nottingham. *Endorsed:* Delivered

* E. Stamford's name appears also in MS. Min. of date.

HOUSE OF LORDS MSS.

1691.

19 Nov. 1691.* L. J., XIV. 652. *In extenso.* [Read in the House this day. On 16 Nov. the House of Commons, being acquainted that Mr. Bridges, a member, could give an account of an information given him by a captain of the Fleet, that Sir Ralph Delaval had lately taken a French boat going for Ireland, with papers of dangerous consequence to the Government, ordered Mr. Bridges to name the person who gave him the information, whereupon he named Lord Danby. Sir Ralph was ordered to attend the next day with the papers. The Commons refused by 186 votes to 66 to appoint a Committee to repair to the Earl of Danby and desire his information in the matter, but resolved to send a message to the Lords for a Conference on matters relating to the safety of the Kingdom. (C. J., X. 554.)—On the 17th the Lords agreed to the Conference, which was held the same day, after which *D. Bolton* reported the statements made to the Commons, adding that, among the papers seized, there was one entitled "A true copy of General Ginkel's Letter to Sir Ralph Delaval," and another entitled "A true copy of L. Nottingham's Letter to Sir Ralph Delaval." The House then ordered L. Kiveton† to attend the next day (L. J., XIV. 649).—On 18 Nov. *L. Kiveton* attended and gave the House an account, which he afterwards put into writing (L. J., XIV. 651. *In extenso*). His Information being read, it was moved to ask him, if he asked the Master of the vessel where he had these papers. He replied: "I had no discourse with the man after I saw the papers. The Captain was taken, I believe, on the 25th of last month." *Moved* to send for Sir Ralph Delaval and papers and the prisoner. *E. Nottingham* having informed the House that he had received a letter from Sir Ralph by the hands of one John Ward, together with a bundle of papers, which he had ordered Ward to bring unopened to the House, *Ward* was called in and delivered the parcel, which was opened by the Clerk, and the 18 papers it contained (*See* Annexes below) were marked by him and read by the Bishop of Salisbury. Then, after reading the above letter from Sir Ralph Delaval to E. Nottingham, the House ordered Sir Ralph Delaval, Capt. Martin, Mr. Batten, Capt. Gillam, and the French prisoner who commanded the French vessel, to attend with all convenient speed, and sent a message to the Commons for a Conference,‡ the Managers of which were ordered to deliver at it L. Kiveton's Information, and Sir Ralph Delaval's letters and papers received from him. (MS. Min., L. J., XIV. 652.) The Commons referred the examination and translation of the papers to a Select Committee (C. J., X., 556).—On 23 Nov. the House, being informed that Sir Ralph Delaval and others attended at the door, sent a message to the Commons to desire to have the papers returned, and ordered L. Kiveton to be sent for. *Mr. Edward Batten* was then called in and sworn. Q. Were you with Sir Ralph Delaval at Spithead? A. Yes. Q. Have you discoursed with Sir Ralph Delaval concerning a packet? A. I took some papers wherein General Ginkel was named and something about his own order. Q. Did you hear Sir Ralph Delaval say anything of other Orders? A. I heard so (*sic*). [The letter he wrote (L. J., XIV. 658. *In extenso*) were then read.] I believe that is what I wrote. I think it was the last information I got. Q. What had you from Sir Ralph Delaval? A. I would refer myself to Sir Ralph. Q. Did Sir Ralph tell you what was in his postscript? A. I wrote as news, not

* The endorsement is in the same hand as the endorsements on the 18 papers annexed.

† The Earl of Danby, Caermarthen's son, had been called up, by writ, 19 March 1689, by the title of Baron Kiveton.

‡ For Reports of this Conference, *see* L. J., XIV. 653; C. J., X. 555.

that Sir Ralph told me so. Sir Ralph did say that there was something of Ginkel and orders. Q. What did Sir Ralph say to you upon the papers or letters? A. Sir Ralph told me there was a letter of General Ginkel, wherein were things relating to his orders. I had the other as news, and not from Sir Ralph Delaval. *Ordered*, That L. Kiveton, Sir Ralph Delaval, Capt. Gillam, Capt. Martin, and the French Captain attend to-morrow. (MS. Min.; L. J., XIV. 658-9).—On 24 Nov. the Papers were returned by the Commons, and the House examined Sir Ralph Delaval and the French Captain, L. Ashburham acting for the latter as interpreter. (MS. Min.; L. J., XIV. 660-1).—On 25 Nov. the House ordered L. Kiveton to attend on the 28th (L. J., XIV., 661), on which day he was ordered with Capt. Martin and Capt. Gillam to attend on 5 Dec. (*ib.* 664); and on 1 Dec. Capt. Beaumont and Capt. Mundon were also ordered to attend on the 5th (*ib.* 668).—On 5 Dec. *Capt. Martin* was first examined, and stated the tenor of the letter from General Ginkel and the copy of the letter from the French Governor of Limerick, Dusson to Mons. Chateaurenaud. L. Kiveton's Information being read, Capt. Martin was asked what he could say to it? A. "The papers were brought on board, and I took a memorandum of them, which I have in my pocket. [Takes it out and reads it.] I never heard of E. Nottingham's name in any paper but this. Asked whether or no, when he came on board, he did not read along with me (*sic*) in reading some part of it? A. I remember L. Danby sent for me. They were reading; but what paper he was reading I know not. Some words my Lord scrupled at. I never saw among the papers any paper entitled "A Copy of my Lord Nottingham's Letter to Sir Ralph Delaval." He withdraws. *L. Kiveton* was then heard in his place, and said: "I think it a great misfortune for any man to affirm anything that may be doubted. I think a man ought to acknowledge the mistake. I told your Lordships, as my paper says, it was upon a postscript of a letter. I assure your Lordships that what I did say I did verily believe. I did see it, as I see any of your Lordships. Since I have talked with worthy men, I have great reason to think I am mistaken. There is L. Nottingham's name in the letter. In that hurry I might take up another of the same, and so might mistake. I have great reason to know Sir Ralph Delaval, who is so worthy that he would not hide anything against the kingdom. My Lord Nottingham I have had a good opinion of and of his goodness. I have great reason to suspect and doubt my own opinion in this. I had no ill design to deceive your Lordships or any other whatsoever. I confess to your Lordships I am for these reasons most apt to believe I am mistaken." The House then appointed a Select Committee to draw up what should be entered in the Journal on this business. (MS. Min.; L. J., XIV. 675.) This Committee, E. Rochester, chairman, met on Dec. 12 (only to adjourn) and on Dec. 14, when an entry to be made of what L. Danby said in the House was agreed to and ordered to be reported. (Com. Book.) The Report, stating the opinion of the Committee, that there was not a copy of any letter from E. Nottingham to Sir Ralph Delaval taken on board the French vessel, was made and agreed to on 14 Dec., when the Lords sent a message to the Commons for another Conference (L. J., XIV. 685), which was had the next day, and E. Rochester reported that they had delivered the Papers, as commanded. (*Ib.* 687.) The matter was thus concluded.] The 18 Papers are as follow, each being endorsed with the number and with these words: "J. W. D[elivere]d 19 Nov. [16] 91."*

* The J. W. is, no doubt, John Ward. But the date would appear to be wrong, for the papers were delivered in and marked by him on the 18th (MS. Min.; L. J., XIV. 652).

House of Lords MSS.

1691.

Annexed:—

(1.) Statement (in French) of provisions for the Grandmont, "galiote du Roi," Capt. Partarieu, with a crew of nine men and master, commissioned for 30 days. Underwritten is a receipt for the same from M. Verdier, Garde Magazin General des vivres de la Marine at Brest, signed by Partarieu. *Dated* Brest, 31 August 1691. *Endorsed:* No. 1. J[ohn] W[ard]. Delivered 19 Nov. 1691.

(2.) Statement (in French) of provisions for a three months' voyage of the Grandmont of Bayonne, Capt. Partarieu. Underwritten is a receipt for the same, signed Partarieu. Rochefort, 7 June 1691. *Endorsed:* No. 2. J. W Delivered 19 Nov. 1691.

(3.) Cover addressed "À Monsieur le Comte de Chateau-Regnaut, Lieut.-General des armées navales du Roi, ou à celui qui commande la flotte de sa Majesté. A son bord." *Endorsed:* No. 3 J. W. Delivered 19 Nov. 1691.

(4.) 19 Nov. 1691. Paper stating as follows:—" Nous sousignants nous avons convenu ensemble pour ce qui s'ensuive, savoir, moi, Monsieur de Rivage de charger dans monnavire 'Le Grandmont' trois tonnes de vin de grave, huit barils de sel, pour porter en Irlande au premier port ou Dieu me conduira pour être vendu tier à tier de profit entre nous, comme aussi le retour des dites marchandises en France et de trente pistolles en argent au cas qu'elles soient employés en achat de quelques marchandises que je ferai avec le Sieur De La Mar, ainsi que nous sommes convenus à Brest, Le 6ième Septembre, 1691, et sera payé au Sieur de Rivage tant de ce qui doit venir pour le frais de ces marchandises, de la manière que nous conviendrons ensemble à l'amiable. Le 5 Janvier." *Endorsed:* No. 4. J. W. Delivered 19 Nov. 1691.

(5.) Letter from Nicolas d'Ordelin as follows:—Valencia. Le 10ième Octobre, 1691. Mon frère, Je viens de recevoir la votre à 6 heure du matin. J'ai bien vu que le temps ne vous a pas permis de sortir. J'en suis bien faché. Le navire est encore à Ventry. Les pacquets sont arrivés d'avant hier. Mais il fait un temps de diable; l'on ne peut pas prendre la mer d'un temps comme il fait, ni même sortir d'un port. Je m'en vais remettre à terre à l'heure que je vous ecris, pour donner une autre fois de suif à l'égal du cuir à Dingle. Il m'a conté 6 sh. en troc de vin et eau de vie; c'est de bonne marchandise. Je l'ai vendu le dernier voyage 14 sh. la livre. Si vous en trouvez, prenez en plûtot que de la laine. Il y a plus de profit. Si vous veniez en ce lieu, vous trouveriez cuir et laine, et si vous avez vin ou eau de vie (quant aux lames [?] de (*illegible*), je ne les ai pas vendu une seule). Si vous me mandiez de vous les envoyer, je les donnerai à votre courier. Mais je n'en ferai rien, attendu que sont des gens à qui l'on ne peut rien fier. J'ai recu une lettre de M. de Fumeron, qui est du 27ième de Septembre. Il ne me marque rien de ce qui se passe à Limerick. Il ne m'a point envoyé de courier. Celui qui a apporté les pacquets, m'a dit que tout va fort bien à Limerick, et qu'il croit qu'ils n'ont plus de bombes à jeter, et meme il croit qu'ils leveront le siege. L'on m'a dit que O'Nelson (*sic*) est prisonnier; on l'a accusé et plusieurs autres. Les soldats sont fort bien payés. L'eau de vie ne leur manque point. Les ennemis avaient fait un pont pour passer la rivière, et meme ils avaient passé du côté de Clare trois mille cavaliers; mais ils ont été bien aise de se retirer.

Si vous étiez en ce lieu, je pourrais bien vous accommoder de pain. Vous seriez bien plus paré en ce lieu, et l'on pourrait vous donner des vivres; l'on m'a donné jusqu'à de la bierre. Croyez moi, si le capitain [?] vous permet de loisir de venir, nous ne manquerions jamais le navire la. Ils sont à demi morts. Ils ne vivent que de cocoa. Mon frère, mon fils vous saluent et moi, qui suis de tout mon cœur votre serviteur *Nicholas d'Ordelin.* *Endorsed:* No. 5. J. W. Delivered 19 Nov. 1691.

(6.) Letter from Nicolas d'Ordelin as follows:—"Valencia. Le 3ième Octobre, 1691. Mon frère, J'ai recu la votre en date du 30ième, par laquelle j'ai appris que vous étiez en parfaite santé. Je suis bien faché de ce que vous n'êtes pas venus en ce lieu, parcequ'il ne me manque aucun vivre, et si vous voulez venire, le navire dont je vous ai parlé, qui est à Ventry (ce n'est pas Bantry), il est encore à l'heure qu'il l'est dedans le port. C'est un Hollandais, d'environ cent tonneaux. Si vous voulez faire diligence, et que vous le pouviez faire, ne tardez point. Cela nous sera immanquable. Je tacherai de sortir du premier beau temps pour le siege, attendant les paquets, et, si je vois, je donnerai à bord. Il n'a que 5 pièces de canon et 18 hommes, conforme le rapport qu'on m'en fait, parcequ'ils ont envoyé un bateau à bord, qui a tout vu, parcequ'il passait pour Protestant. Il est chargé de sucre et des oranges en panniers. Je crois qu'il aura quelque orge, monnaie et perroquets. Il vient de Surinam. Tachez de venir. Il vient d'arriver un bateau de Dingle à 5 heure, et je vous écris à l'heure qu'il l'est, si vous venez pour entrer par le chenal des escaliers, je veux dire du côté des dix escaliers, il faut ranger l'ile du côté de babord et mouiller au dedans d'un vieux chateau, qui est du même côté, et mouiller au dedans de la pointe de tribord au dedans du dit chateau. Il y a fort bon mouillage et à l'heure à 7 ou 8 brasses d'eau, parcequ'au dedans il y a quelques basses, et vous apprendrez le chenal. Étant mouillé, vous verrez le passage. Ne vous étonnez pas pour ne voir pas l'entrée, parcequ'il y a trois îles, qui vous bouchent le chenal. Rangez l'ile à donner la main à terre. Vous ne rencontrerez rien. Le courier part à 7 heure pour vous aller trouver. Mon frère, je ne doute pas, qu'on ne vous donne des vivres, mais il y a Monsieur Connell, qui a ordre d'en fournir de la part de Milord Chief Baron. Mon frère vous salue, mon fils et moi, qui suis votre frère et serviteur. *Nicolas d'Ordelin.* Nous n'avons point aucune nouvelle de Limerick, ni de Monsieurd de Chateau-renaud. Je prie Dieu qu'il vous l'amene." On the last page is written a table of figures of no importance. *Endorsed:* No. 6. J. W. Delivered 19 Dec. 1691.

(7.) Letter from T. Gillam to Sir Ralph Delaval, Vice-Admiral of the Blue, as follows:—"This vessel did belong to the King of France, and came out of Brest last Thursday at 8 in the morning. He was sent to look for Monsieur Chateau-renaud, who is here to westward with 20 men-of-war, and he was ordered to sail first W.S.W. 15 leagues from Scilly, and if he could not find him in that station, then he was to find him towards Limerick, and yesterday morning he took your fleet for Monsieur Chateau-renaud's. He says that he did not believe any ship could have out-sailed him. Sir, he waits on you with the French captain as soon as possible. Sir, from your very humble Servant T. Gillam." *Dated* Chester, Sunday, 25 Oct. 1691. On the last sheet is written in the same hand: "Sir, This vessel

House of Lords MSS.

1691.

belongs to the King." *Endorsed:* No. 7. J. W. Delivered 19 Nov. 1691.

(8.) Paper as follows:—"Le Marquis Dusson, Lieutenant General et Commandant en Chef de l'Armée du Roy en Irelande. Nous prions tous Commandants des vaisseaux Anglois et Hollandois de laisser librement passer les vaisseaux de Sa Majesté très Chretienne, qui viendront sur les cotes d'Irelande, ou à l'emboucheur de la rivière de Limerick, suivant le traité qui a été fait entre M. Le General Ginkell et nous, pour transporter les troupes Irelandoises en France, comme il paroit par la copie de lettre de ce General cy jointe à M. Le Chevalier De La Vall à Limerick. Le 18/8 Octobre, 1691. Dussou." *Endorsed:* No. 8. J. W. Delivered 19 Nov. 1691.

(9.) Copy letter from General Ginkell to Sir Ralph Delaval, commanding their Majesties' squadron on the coast of Ireland:—"Monsieur. Je suis adverti par My Lord Nottingham que vous devez venir avec l'Escadre que vous commandez sur ces costes, ce qui fait que je vous advertis que nous sommes entrés en traité avec la ville de Limerick et l'armée Irelandoise, et que nous en sommes venus à une conclusion. En attendant nous faisons cessation d'armes par terre, et avons arresté que la mesme chose se feroit aussi par mer sur les costes de ce Royaume, ayant à transporter plusieures des troupes Irlandoises, et devons pour cet effet nous servir de vaisseaux Francois aussi bien qu'Anglois. Pour cette raison je vous prie de ne pas empecher tous les vaisseaux Francois de transport d'entrer dans le Shannon, non plus que la reste de leur flotte dans la Bay de Dingle. L'intendant Francois ici a ecrit de son côté à l'escadre de leur vaisseaux de guerre, qu'ils attendent, et nous assure qu'aucune hostilité ne sera commise par eux, et je vous prie d'observer la meme chose de votre côté, laquelle chose est fort necessaire pour finir promptement les affaires que nous avons en main, à quoi je suis sur que vous contribuerez autant que vous pourrez. Monsieur, Votre très humble &c." *Endorsed:* No. 9. J. W. Delivered 19 Nov. 1691.

(10.) Letter from the Marquis D'Usson to "Monsieur le Comte de Chateaurenaud, Lieutenant-General des armées navales du Roi ou celui qui commande la flotte de Sa Majesté en mer," as follows:—"Nous avons deja eu l'honneur de vous écrire, Monsieur, qu'il y avait une cessation d'armes entre l'armée ennemie et nous. Nous donnons avis presentement qu'elle continue, et que la capitulation a été signée le treize de ce mois. A moi, Monsieur, vos vaisseaux de charge peuvent entre librement dans la rivière de Limerick, et le General Ginkell ayant envoyé une lettre dont vous trouverez cy joint une copie, afin que nos vaisseaux et ceux qui les ennemis nous fournissent pour aider au transport des troupes qui passent en France, ne trouvent nul empechement ni depart ni d'autre, comme c'est une chose qui convient au service du Roi. Nous avons cru, Monsieur, que vous voudriez bien y consentir; on ne peut avec plus de passion que nous sommes, Monsieur, vos tres humbles et tres obeissants serviteurs, D'Usson, Le Chevalier de [*Illegible*]." *Dated* Limerick, le 14 Octobre 1691. *Endorsed:* No. 10. J. W. Delivered 19 Nov. 1691.

(11.) 19 Nov. 1691. Cover marked "Lettres d'Irlande pour Monsieur de Chateauren[aud]." *Endorsed:* No. 11. J. W. Delivered 19 Nov. 1691.

(12.) Copy letter from General Ginkell to Sir Ralph Delaval. *Signed* D'Usson. Identical with No. 9. *Endorsed:* No. 12. J. W. Delivered 19 Nov. 1691.

(13.) Another copy of same. *Signed* D'Usson. *Endorsed:* No. 13. J. W. Delivered 19 Nov. 1691.

(14.) Letter from the Marquis D'Usson to the Commanders of the English and Dutch ships. *Signed* D'Usson. Identical with No. 8. *Endorsed:* No. 14. J. W. Delivered 19 Nov. 1691.

(15.) Letter from Stephen Rice to M. de Rivage, commanding the "Kenmare," as follows:—"Monsieur. Le Courier qui a eu charge les pacquettes que vous avez porté, est ici de retour, n'ayant pas encore trouvé apropos de rien risquer à present; mais je crois qu'en deux jours il partira, et je ne puis pas dire quand est ce qu'il arrivera, ou que vous aurez vos depeches. Le siege continue, et on entend le bruit des canons tous les jours, mais la garrison est en bon état, et, j'espère, qu'ils se soutiendront bien jusqu'au temps de l'arrivée de la flotte avec les secours. Monsieur Cotter qui commande tous les troupes qui sont de ce côté de Limerick me mande que l'ammunition lui manque, et ne pouvant pas en espérer de Limerick, il vous prie de grace de lui fournir de quelque poudre et balles de plomb, et moi qui suis fort sensible de la grande necessité d'en avoir, et de la consequence qu'il serait pour incommoder les ennemis au siege, que ses troupes soient en état de les attaquer (ce qu'ils ne peuvent pas faire à cause de la disette d'ammunition), je vous prie de lui fournir autant que vous pourez. S'il serait àpropos de nous offrir ou d'argent ou du cuir (*illegible*) laine, bœuf ou aucune autre marchandise qu'on peut trouver en eschange (*illegible*) je suis certain que Monsieur Desclusseaux vous en aura bon gré, et tous les honnêtes gens de ce pays vous en auront une grande obligation et particulièrement Monsieur votre très humble serviteur Stephen Rice.—Je vous prie de donner votre response a Monsieur Haas, qui est officier des droits du Roi." *Dated* Ross Castle, $\frac{11}{21}$ Sept. 1691. *Addressed* to Monsieur de Rivage, Commandant la Corvette Kenmare. *Endorsed:* No. 15. J. W. Delivered 19 Nov. 1691.

(16.) Duplicate of No. 10. *Signed* D'Usson. *Endorsed:* No. 16. J. W. Delivered 19 Nov. 1691.

(17.) Letter from Brigadier Cotter to M. de Rivage, Captain of the Kenmare, as follows:—"Par le Brigadier Cotter, Gouverneur des Countés de Kerry, Cork et Limerick. Monsieur Du Longe, le porteur de ces presentes, ayant affaire de passer en France pour le service du Roi, mon maître, au plûtot par la première corvette ou pacquet-boat qui part, je supplie le Capitaine de la corvette ou pacquet-boat qui est à present dans la rivière de Kenmare de lui laisser passer en France sur son vaisseau avec le premier pacquet. Faite à Ross, le premier jour d'Octobre, 1691. *Signed* J. Cotter. Pour le Sieur de Rivage, Capitaine de la Corvette à present dans la riviere de Kenmare." *Endorsed:* No. 17. J. W. Delivered 19 Nov. 1691.

(18.) Letter as follows:—"Je vous envoye, Monsieur, le porteur pour vous informer que nous sommes convenus par la capitulation de Limerick avec le General de l'armée Anglaise, qu'il y aurait une cessation d'armes non seulement entre son armée et la notre, mais encore entre votre flotte et la flotte Anglaise qui est dans la rivière de Limerick, afin que nous puissions embarquer les troupes qui doivent passer en France sans aucune empêchement,

HOUSE OF LORDS MSS.

1691.

et pour cet effet il a été arresté que vous vous tienderiez avec les vaisseaux de guerre que vous commandez dans la bay de Dingle, et qu'il n'y aurait que des vaisseaux de charge qui pouraient entrer dans la rivière de Limerick pour prendre les troupes que nous devons passer en France. M. Dusson et M. le Chevalier de Lessé vous informent aussi ce traité par ce porteur afin que vous puissiez prendre sur cela les mesures qui conviendront à votre sureté et au service du Roi avec le commandant de la flotte Anglaise, avec lequel il me parait necessaire que vous conveniez aussi de la même chose. Je vous supplie très humblement de nous avertir du parti que vous avez pris afin que nous puissions nous regler la dessus pour notre embarquement. J'ai l'honneur d'être avec bien du respect, Monsieur, votre très humble et très obéissant serviteur, Fumeron.—Depuis ma lettre écrite j'ai appris que la Bay de Dingle n'est pas extrèmement bonne, mais que celle de Ventry, qui en est proche à l'ile de Valencia étaient des endroits fort surs pour se mettre à couvert des grands vents que pour le mouillage." *Dated* à Lymerick, 9 Octobre 1691. *Endorsed:* No. 18. J. W. Delivered 19 Nov. 1691. [Comp. C. J., X. 587.]

444. Nov. 21. Burton's Estate Act.—Amended Draft of an Act for the enabling Sir Thomas Burton, Baronet, to sell lands for payment of debts. [Read 1ª this day; Royal Assent, 24 Feb. 1691-2. (L. J., XIV. 656; XV. 93.) 3 & 4 W. & M. c. 22 in Long Calendar.]

Annexed:

(*a.*) 7 Dec. Lords' Amendments to the Bill. [Made in Committee 5 Dec. (Com. Book) and reported this day. (L. J. XIV. 676.)]

445. Nov. 23. Writ of Summons (Bishop of Bristol).—Writ of Summons, dated Oct. 27, to John [Hall], Bishop of Bristol. [Took the Oaths this day. L. J., XIV. 657.]

446. Nov. 23. E. Rochester's Privilege (Cruse *v.* Wilkins).—Petition of Oliver Langton, complaining that John Wilkins of Wootton Bassett, Attorney-at-law, had arrested Charles Cruse, bailiff there to E. Rochester, on 2 Nov. last, during the privilege of Parliament. L. J., XIV. 658. *In extenso.* [*Langton*, being sworn this day at the Bar, said that he [Wilkins] knew that Cruse was the Earl's servant; Deponent told him he was so before the second and third times of arresting, and that Wilkins said that what he had done he was able to answer. *Ordered* that Wilkins be attached. (MS. Min.)—On 1 Dec. Charles Skull, bailiff at Wootton Bassett, as well as Hugh Jones the Elder, and Hugh Jones the Younger, at whose suit Cruse was arrested, were also ordered to be attached, (L. J., XIV. 667.) *Cruse*, who was sworn that day at the Bar, on presenting his Petition (Annex (*a.*) below), having said that they knew he was the Earl's servant. (MS. Min. 1 Dec.)—Wilkins was discharged, on his submission, on 11 Dec. (Annex (*b.*) below.)—On 28 Nov. 1692. Skull and the two Joneses, who had insisted on Black Rod's discharging them after the Prorogation, were again attached. (L. J., XV. 127 and Annex (*c.*) below.)—On 24 Jan. 1692-3, William Hill, who had been employed by Black Rod, to serve the Order of attachment, and had been arrested in consequence by Jones the Elder, on a charge of false imprisonment, was ordered to be discharged from his arrest. (L. J., XV. 197; MS. Min.)—On 17 Nov. 1693, *V. Weymouth* having moved "that there had been an arrest on E. Rochester's [servant] sent by Hugh Jones, &c." the House ordered the last order to be renewed and the parties to be attached. (L. J., XV. 300; MS. Min.)—On 5 Dec. 1693 the House being moved on behalf of the Earl, and an affidavit by Hill (Annex (*d.*) below) being read, the sheriff of Wilts was ordered to secure Jones the elder and deliver him to Black Rod. (L. J., XV. 314; MS. Min.)—On 23 Feb. 1694–5, a Petition of the two Joneses to be discharged (Annex (*e.*) below) was rejected, and they were ordered to be continued in custody. (L. J., XV. 504. No entry in MS. Min.)]

Annexed :

(*a.*) 1 Dec. 1691. Petition of Charles Cruse, complaining of his arrest by Wilkins, at the suit of Hugh Jones the elder and Hugh Jones the younger, of Bowden, co. Wilts, yeomen. L. J., XIV. 667. *In extenso.*

(*b.*) 11 Dec. 1691. Petition of John Wilkyns. Petitioner voluntarily submitted himself on 1 Dec. to the Usher of the Black Rod. He is sorry if he has offended the Earl, to whom he has made his submission and who, as Petitioner is informed, is satisfied with it. Prays to be discharged. L. J., XIV. 682.

(*c.*) 28 Nov. 1692. Petition of Sir Thomas Duppa, Gentleman Usher of the Black Rod. On complaint made of breaches of privilege, several persons have, at Petitioner's great charge, been taken into custody by the Orders annexed, but Prorogations happening before they were discharged, they threatened Petitioner if he detained them longer, and left him without paying their fees. Prays their Lordships' directions. L. J., XV. 127.

(*c*[1].) 25 Nov. 1689. Order of date to Black Rod to attach Mr. Bayspoole and others. *Signed* Jo. Browne, Cler. Parliamentor. L. J., XIV. 353. *In extenso.* [Appended to preceding.]

(*c*[2].) 1 Dec. 1691. Order of date to same to attach Hugh Jones the Elder, Hugh Jones the Younger, William Wilkins and Charles Skull. *Signed* Matth. Johnson, Cler. Parliamentor. *Underwritten* is the following: "I appoint William Hill, John Doleman, Thos. Holister, Thos. Squire, Roger Brinsden, Will. Brewer, John Tanner, Thos. Shirley* to execute this order. Thos. Duppa, Black Rod." [Appended to (*c.*) above.]

(*c*[3].) 1 Dec. 1691. Copy of last Order. [Appended to (*c.*) above.]

(*d.*) 5 Dec. 1693. Affidavit of William Hill, of the parish of St. Mary's, in the town of Marlborough, yeoman. Deponent, in Dec. 1691 was deputed with others by Sir Thos. Duppa, Black Rod, to execute a warrant of the House for attaching Hugh Jones the Elder, and Hugh Jones the Younger. On his attaching the latter, Jones' brothers threatened to shoot him, if he came again for their father, and Deponent's prisoner, being brought as far as Twyford on the way to London, made his escape. In April 1692 one William Brewer, also a deputy of Sir Thos. Duppa, attached Hugh Jones the Elder, who would have shot him, had not he struck the pistol out of his hand, and who threatened to shoot Deponent also, and who shot two bailiffs about a month since, and now stands upon his guard with arms, so that no officers can go near him without danger of their lives. *Sworn* 4 Dec. 1693 before Miles Cooke. *Signed* by Deponent his mark. L. J., XV. 314.

(*e.*) 23 Feb. 1694–5. Petition of Hugh Jones, Senior, and Hugh Jones, Junior. Petitioners have a long time lain under the

* Shirley's name is struck through.

House of Lords MSS.

1691.

displeasure of the House. They beg pardon of the House and of the Earl and are sorry for their great offence. Pray to be discharged. L. J., XV. 504. *Endorsed* as read this day and rejected.

(e^1.) 23 Feb. 1694–5. Draft Petition of same. Petitioners are heartily sorry for their offence in causing the Earl's servant to be arrested, by occasion whereof their creditors have fallen upon them, so that they dare not, though willing, appear in person. Their creditors daily work to apprehend them for debts, and commit them to gaol, which they hope to prevent, if discharged. Pray to be discharged. [Appended to preceding. This is a rough draft, partly corrected, and written apparently in the Clerk's hand.]

447. Nov. 23. Watts v. Sir John Hoskins. (Privilege.)—Petition of William Watts, Bachelor in Divinity and Rector of the Rectory of Dere, in the county of Hereford, praying for leave to proceed at law for the recovery of tithes from certain tenants of Sir John Hoskyns, a Master in Chancery, who claims privilege as attendant on their Lordships' House. L. J., XIV. 658. [*Sir J. Hoskyns* was heard at the Bar on the 24th and stated that the lands were monastery lands. The tenants were tenants at will, and he was in possession. (MS. Min.) In Committee of Privileges, to whom the matter was referred, he stated further that he presumed the lands never paid any tithes. (Priv. Book, 14 Dec.) The House, on report, ordered that no privilege should be allowed in suits for tithes. (L. J., XIV. 687.)]

448. Nov. 24. Ashton *v.* Ashton.—Petition and Appeal of Sir Edmund Assheton, Bart. Petitioner, having an ejectment brought against him by Respondent for the manor of Downham and other lands in Lancashire, of the yearly value of 300*l.*, brought a Bill in Chancery to discover writings and to have a decree for the estate if the writings were lost, but prayed no injunction to stay proceedings. The matter of the title arising upon evidence in the trial was drawn into a case for the opinion of the judge, Baron Powell, against whose judgment the Appellant brought a Writ of Error, and Respondent having meanwhile taken out execution, the Court of King's Bench ordered restitution of possession to Appellant. The cause in Chancery being heard on 30 Oct. 1689 by the Lords Commissioners, before restitution was made, Appellant obtained a decree for some writings detained by Respondent, but the Court declared that the title was a matter for determination of law. Appellant thereupon assigned errors in the judgment and took out a writ of restitution and was restored to possession. Against this the Respondent in July 1690 complained to the Lords Commissioners, who committed Appellant to custody for violation of an order made by the Court in May 1689, and granted Respondent an injunction to restore and quiet the possession, and on 6 Nov. 1690 decreed costs against Appellant, which were taxed at 80*l.* Appeals against these orders and injunctions of the Court of Chancery, which had itself declared the matter in question proper for law. *Signed* by Appellant; *Countersigned* by William Williams and C. Greenfield. L. J., XIV. 660. [The Appeal was heard on 18 Jan. 1691–2. *Sir William Williams* (for Appellant): We say the Court had not power to do what they have done. *Sir Thomas Powys* (for Appellant): All men's freehold's ought to be determined at the Common law. Mr. Ashton brought his action of ejectment in 1686. The Order in Chancery we complain of is that of 2 May, contrary to the King's Bench. The

Decree and Rule of King's Bench are read. *Mr. John Lee* sworn to the truth of an affidavit. *Sir John Somers, Solicitor-General* (for Respondent): They complain of an interlocutory order, and nothing more. Sir Edmund Ashton brought two Bills in Equity, not my client. *Mr. Ward* (for Respondent) was heard. Counsel having replied and the Speaker reported, the House dismissed the Appeal. (MS. Min.; L. J., XV. 35.)]

Annexed :—

(*a.*) 7 Dec. 1691. Petition of Richard Assheton, Esq., Respondent, for further time to answer. *Endorsed* as brought in this day. L. J., XIV. 677.

(*b.*) 15 Dec. 1691. Answer of Respondent. The lands belonged to Respondent, as heir-at-law of the late Sir Ralph Assheton, Bart. The case was drawn up for the Judge on the importunity of Appellant's Counsel, who objected to a deed of revocation given in evidence at the trial by Respondent, and it was made, by consent, a rule of Court that execution should meantime stay on the verdict and that no writ of error should be brought. The Judge having decided in favour of Respondent, the injunction prayed for and obtained by Appellant in his supplemental Bill of 10 Feb. 1687, was dissolved, and Respondent took possession in November 1688. The Court of Chancery on 2 May 1689 allowed Appellant to go on with his Writ of Error, but ordered that Respondent should not be removed from his possession till the Court was further moved therein. Appellant procured his writ of restitution in violation of this order and of the previous rule of Court made on consent, and was guilty of a flagrant contempt of Court. Appellant has no title to the estate, and, if he has, the Orders in Chancery in no way bar him from his proper remedy at law. Prays that the Appeal may be dismissed with costs. *Signed* by Respondent. *Endorsed* as brought in this day.

(*c.*) 20 Jan. 1691–2. Petition of Appellant for leave to prosecute his right at law. L. J., XV. 30.

(*d.*) 14 Dec. 1694. Petition of Appellant. Recites the proceedings ending with the dismissal of Petitioner's appeal by the House. Prays for explanation of their Lordships' judgment, the effect of which is to exclude him from all means of reversing the judgment in ejectment and proving his title at law. L. J., XV. 444. [The Petition was referred this day to a Select Committee; and dismissed on 10 Jan. 1694–5 on their report (*ib.* 457). The proceedings in Committee are thus recorded. *Mr. Atwood* (for Petitioner) opens the case. The merits of the cause were never heard in any other Court. Cites *Nicol v. Kegwin*, 21 Feb. 1692; *Chetham v. Humphry*, 10 March 1692. The Petitioners were only dismissed; *Selwyn v. Blackston and Herne*, 9 Dec. 1667. The Order amended in material words: *Englefield v. Englefield*, 21 June 1692. Cause reheard, 21 Jan. 1692. *Trosse v. Pierce, Davy v. Courtney*, 5 Jan. 1692; *Hitchcock v. Sedgwick*, 20 Dec. 1690. Issue directed, 21 Nov. 1691; Order altered 23 Nov. 1691. Their Lordships had relieved against their own orders. *Mr. Dodd* (for Mr. Ashton): This appeal was heard three years ago, and no explanation was ever desired till now. They have since gone to law, and there is a special verdict depending. The Order your Lordships have confirmed is only that they should not take possession without leave of the

House of Lords MSS.

1691.

Chancery. The Chancery can give leave. *Ordered* to report as in L. J., XV. 457. (Pet. Book.)]

449. Nov. 25. Moore's Estate Act.—Draft of an Act for enabling Francis Moore, Esq., to sell the Manor of Bayhouse and lands in West Thorock, in the county of Essex, and to purchase other lands in lieu thereof. [Read 1a this day; Royal Assent, 24 Feb. 1691-2. (L. J., XIV. 662; XV. 93.) 3 & 4 W. & M. c. 31 in Long Calendar. Com. Book, Dec. 1 and 10.]

450. Nov. 25. Shatterden's Estate Act.—Amended draft of an Act to vest the Estate late of Henry Drax, Esq., deceased, in Thomas Shatterden, Gent., and to enable the said Thomas Shattenden and others, to whom the said estate is devised, to make a Jointure. The Lords' Amendments are to enable Thos. Shatterden to appoint to his wife during her life any part of the premises not exceeding 1,000*l.* a year, and to limit all the Jointures in being to 1,500*l.* a year. (Com. Book.) [Read 1a this day; Royal Assent, 24 Feb. 1691-2. (L. J., XIV. 662; XV. 63.) 3 & 4 W. & M. c. 43 in Long Calendar.]

Annexed:—

(*a.*) 15 Dec. Lords' Amendments in Committee. [Made and reported this day. Com. Book. L. J., XIV. 687.]

451. Nov. 28. Albury and North Mims Act.—Amended draft of an Act for enfranchising several copyhold Lands and Tenements holden of the manors of Albury and North Mims in the county of Hereford. [Read 1a this day; Royal Assent, 24 Feb. 1691-2. (L. J., XIV. 664; XV. 93.) 3 & 4 W. & M. c. 17 in Long Calendar. The Amendment is purely clerical. *Mr. John Duncombe* for the copyholders and *Mr. William Vernon* for the L. President prayed the passing of the Bill. Com. Book, 5 Dec.]

Annexed:—

(*a.*) Breviate of the Bill.

452. Nov. 30. Pote *v.* Pote and another.—Petition and Appeal of Thomas Pote, Gentleman. Complains of a Decree of the Lords Commissioners of 14 Nov. 1691* giving to Elizabeth Pote for life certain lands called Gannacott and Blagdon, in the county of Devon, settled on her as a jointure by her late husband Leonard, Petitioner's elder brother. Petitioner claims under an entail, the said Leonard having died without issue. *Signed* by Appellant; *Countersigned* by J. Somers and William Williams. [Read this day. Cause heard and Decree affirmed 7 Jan. 1691-2. L. J., XIV. 665; XV. 20. The proceedings at the hearing are not recorded in MS. Min.]

Annexed:—

(*a.*) 14 Dec. Answer of Elizabeth Pote, Widow, and John Raw, Gent. Appellant's father was seized of the estate not in tail but in fee, and granted Appellant an annual rentcharge out of it of 12*l.*, which he has continued to receive since his father's death. The estate was settled on the Respondent Elizabeth, the eldest daughter of Edward Pyne, Esq., on her marriage with Leonard Pote, in consideration of her portion of 700*l.* and upwards, and Appellant, who engrossed the very marriage settlement, never pretended any entail to hinder its effect. Leonard, who was a barrister, well knew his title, and often declared there

* 2 Vernon, 239.

was no entail. By his will he devised the entire inheritance to the Respondent Raw, who has paid the legacies charged upon the estate, and has since, on his marriage with Mary, the daughter of Thomas Kelly, Esq., settled the inheritance on the issue of that marriage. Appellant obtained a verdict at the trial on the ejectment by means of a pretended deed of entail, alleged to have been made on his father's marriage. Prays that the Decree for confirming the jointure may be established, and the Appeal dismissed with costs. *Signed* by Respondents. The countersignature of Nicholas Hooper is copied. *Endorsed* as brought in his day.

(*b*.) 16 Dec. Petition of Appellant for an early day for hearing. L. J., XIV. 689.

453. Nov. 30. Shepheard *v.* Wilkins and others.—Petition and Appeal of Samuel Shepheard. The Respondent Wilkins, the Master and part owner of the "Ann and Mary," agreed to ship Petitioner's wines at Bordeaux at a freight of 3*l.* per tun, but on arriving there, he took advantage of the fear of a war with France, and demanded a rate of 10*l.* After two unsuccessful actions by Wilkins on his return, Petitioner brought a Bill against him in Chancery to discover the agreement, and the Court, on 9 Nov. 1689, having ordered a trial at law on the single point whether there was an agreement for the lower or the higher rate, a verdict was twice found for Petitioner, with which verdicts the Court, on a Bill being brought by Wilkins, refused to interfere. The other owners then brought a new Bill against Petitioner, and, for a colour, made Wilkins a defendant, falsely suggesting that he had made but a faint prosecution, and the Lords Commissioners pronounced a decretal order for a new trial at the King's Bench in a new action to be brought in Wilkins' name on the point already tried. Prays that this decretal Order may be reversed. *Signed* by Appellant; *Countersigned* by W. Thompson and Wm. Whitelocke. L. J., XIV. 665. [The Cause was heard, C. Justice Holt having been ordered to attend (L. J., XV. 23) on 15 Jan. 1691–2. *Serjeant Thomson* (for Appellant) opened the case. *Mr. Finch* (for Appellant): We appeal from the decree upon the action to be tried in the King's Bench, whether 3*l.* per tun or 10*l.* per tun in January 1688, which was the rate all over the Exchange. We show our verdicts; that is a flat bar. We are sent to this trial after our witnesses are dead. *The Solicitor-General* (for Respondents): We had a proper Bill in Chancery, and this direction for a trial was just and equitable. The Master has a proper remedy at law for the freight. The owners have no recovery in law but in equity. *Mr. Trevor* (for Respondents): There was no such agreement in writing. We have writing to show there was no such agreement. We have another writing that exactly falsifies his answer under his own hand by two witnesses. They offer to prove a Paper read in Chancery, but could not for Wilkins (*sic*). Counsel withdrew. *Ordered* that the Decree shall be reversed. (MS. Min.; L. J., XV. 31.)]

Annexed:—

(*a*.) 14 Dec. Answer of Samuel Stanier, John Morgan, Abel Ward, John Pettit, and Richard Meriwether and Naomi, his wife. No such agreement for 3*l.* per tun was ever made with Appellant by the Respondents Stanier and Morgan, who repudiated it in a letter to Wilkins and instructed him to get the highest freight he could. Respondents brought their Bill against Wilkins and the Appellant and the other freighters, not having been parties to the suits between Wilkins and Appellant, and fearing they should be defrauded of their parts of the freight, according to the account as made up. Their cause was heard by the Lords Commissioners together with that in which Wilkins was Plaintiff against Appellant, with whose previous verdicts the Court declared itself dissatisfied. The order complained of is just, Respondents never yet having had any trial with Appellant for their shares of the freight. Pray that the Appeal may be dismissed with costs. *Signed* by Respondents; *Countersigned* by J. Somers.

(*b*.) 14 Dec. Answer of Michael Wilkins. Respondent, having a previous account with Stanier and Morgan, on a voyage to Sally, still unsettled, and being anxious to go to Bordeaux, to secure the high freights there caused by the rumour of a French war, agreed to ship Appellants' wines at the same freight that Appellant should obtain, on his behalf, from Stanier and Morgan, who were delaying payment of their debt. On reaching Bordeaux he heard that Appellant had never come to any agreement with Stanier and Morgan for 3*l*. per tun, as Appellant falsely informed him he had, and accordingly he had it inserted in the Bills of Lading, to pay freight according to agreement, and, if no agreement, at 10*l*. per tun, being the rate then ruling. On Respondent's return, Appellant at first did not insist on any such pretended agreement, but the account was made up at the higher rate. Prays that the Appeal may be dismissed with costs, as vexatious. *Signed* by Respondent (by his Attorney Edward Ames) and by Robert Otterburne.

454. Dec. 1. Bishop of Ely's Estate Act.—Amended draft of an Act for settling a Fee-Farm rent of 100*l*. per annum upon the Bishop of Ely and his successors, to be issuing out of Hatton Garden, in the County of Middlesex and the messuages thereupon erected, and for settling and assuring the same, subject to the said rent, upon Christopher, Lord Viscount Hatton, his heirs and assigns for ever. The Lords' Amendment (Com. Book, 3 Dec.) is a purely verbal one. The Commons' later Amendments are given in C. J., X. 584. [Read 1ª this day; Royal Assent, 24 Dec. (L. J., XIV. 667, 701.) 3 W. & M. c. 6 in Long Calendar.]

Annexed:—

(1.) 3 Dec. Lords' Amendment to the Bill. [Made in Committee and reported this day. Com. Book; L. J., XIV. 671.]

455. Dec. 1. Curtis' Estate Act.—Amended draft of an Act for the more speedy payment of the debts of Elizabeth Curtis, Widow, late deceased, and performance of an agreement touching the same, made between Charles Curtis in his life time and Edward Earle, according to a Decree in the High Court of Chancery. The Amendment is to add the Saving Clause at the end. [Read 1ª this day; Royal Assent, 24 Feb. 1691–2. (L. J., XIV. 667; XV. 93.) 3 & 4 W. and M. c. 30 in Long Calendar. Com. Book, Dec. 4, 5, 14, 17.]

Annexed:—

(*a*.) 17 Dec. Letter from Mr. Appleton, dated 7 Dec., consenting to the passing of the Bill. [Read in Committee this day. Com. Book.]

456. Dec. 2. Burton *v*. Muschamp.—Petition and Appeal of Philip Burton, Gent. Complains of an Order of 17 Dec. 1690 and other orders of the Court of Chancery, setting aside the enrolment of certain decrees made in Petitioner's favour and confirmed on a Bill of Review. Prays that Respondent, now a prisoner in the Fleet, may be ordered to answer, and that the said Orders may be reversed. *Signed* by Appellant; *Countersigned* by Wm. Whitelocke (whose signature is copied) and H. Finch. L. J., XIV. 669. [The Cause was heard on 19 Dec. 1691. *Sir William Whitelocke* (for Appellant): There were three causes depending in 1676. On 14 May 1678 they were all heard. *Mr. Finch* (for Appellant): What we complain of is an Order of the Commissioners for opening the enrolled Decrees. The Chancery had no power in this matter, and yet they have taken upon themselves to do it. This was signed and enrolled in a former Chancellor's time, and yet they say, We will open the cause. The Order is 17 Dec. 1690. The L. North confirmed (*sic*). Order of 11 Nov. 1678, the L. Jeffreys confirmed that order and ordered it to be enrolled. *Sir William Williams* (for Respondent): This enrolment was made but in 1685, and not confirmed by three Chancellors, as they say. We have the Minutes here. *Sir Thomas Powys* (for Respondent) is heard. *Counsel* are heard in reply and read Orders for examining the cause as to the fraud in obtaining the enrolment. Counsel withdrew, the Speaker reported and the House ordered the Decree and Orders to be set aside. (MS. Min.; L. J., XIV. 684.) *See also* under 14 Nov. 1692.]

Annexed:—

(*a*.) 10 Dec. 1691. Answer of Henry Muschamp. The orders complained of are just and consistent with the practice in Chancery, the enrolments having been defective and irregular. Prays that the Appeal may be dismissed with Costs. *Signed* by Respondent. *Endorsed* as brought in this day.

457. Dec. 2. Old Governors of Birmingham School *v.* New Governors of Birmingham School. Petition and Appeal of Samuel Carter, Esq., Isaac Stanton, George Wyrley, William Colmore, William Doley and Thomas Rowney, the Old Governors of the Free Grammar School of Birmingham in the county of Warwick, on the behalf of themselves and the other Governors of the said School, that have by them been duly elected Governors of the said School. Complain of a Decree in Chancery of 10 July 1691, ordering the enrolment of a surrender to Charles II. of the old Charter of the School, granted by Edward VI., which surrender had been signed by some of the then Governors, on the requirement of the King, but had not been enrolled. The new Charter granted by James II. made the person who had procured the surrender a Governor, although he was not an inhabitant of the town, and reserved the right to remove the Governors and Master at the King's pleasure. The Old Master, who had acquitted himself to the satisfaction of the town, has been removed, and some school land let for building a Popish chapel, much to the inhabitants' disgust. The enrolment is invalid, not having been made in the reign of Charles II. No breach of trust can be alleged against Appellants, who, on the contrary, with their predecessors, have increased the School revenue from 20*l.* to 300*l.* a year, besides having built lodgings in Katherine's Hall, Cambridge and there allowed 70*l.* a year to poor Scholars bred up in the School. Pray that the Decree may be reversed. *Signed* by all Appellants except Doley and Rowney; *Countersigned* by J. Somers and Ja. Stedman, whose signatures are copied. L. J., XIV. 669. [The Cause was heard on 9 Jan. 1691–2. *Mr. Trevor* (for Appellants) opens the Cause. *The Solicitor-General* (for Appellants): The cause is new and without precedent. Reads the Grant of 5 Edward VI. *Mr. Finch*

HOUSE OF LORDS MSS.

1691.

(for Respondents) is heard, and reads the new Charter and Depositions. A Deposition offered to be read. *Counsel* heard in reply. Counsel withdrew. After debate whether the witness that was proposed to be read, which was read in Chancery [be read]. *Counsel* called in again and told that they had liberty to read John Cotterell's Deposition. Then the Deposition was read by the Defendants. They withdraw. After debate, it was *proposed*, that the Judge's opinions should be asked whether King James could grant a new Charter till the surrender of the old Charter was enrolled? *Previous Question* put: Whether that Question shall be put? Resolved in the *Negative*. *Question* put: Whether the Decree shall be reversed? Contents, 27; Not-Contents, 22. Resolved in the *Affirmative*, and Ordered accordingly. (MS. Min.; L. J., XV. 22.)]

Annexed:—

(*a*.) 12 Dec. Answer of the Right Hon. William, Lord Digby, Baron of Geoshell in the Kingdom of Ireland, Sir Charles Holt, Bart., and Sir Henry Gough, Knt. King Edward VI.'s Letters Patent gave the Governors no power to apply the school revenues, with the consent of the Bishop of the Diocese, to any other purpose than the support of the Master and Usher. The Old Governors took little care to supply the school with able masters. In 1682 they made a shoemaker an usher, and scarcely ever placed any tolerable master there, except one Brooksby, now dead. The improvement of the revenue is due, not to their industry, but to the expiration of long leases and the great increase of trade in the town, and when the revenues were by such means advanced, several of the Governors, being then of mean degree and estate, made leases to one another of the School lands much under value, and on some Governors of better quality endeavouring to check the abuse by procuring with much difficulty an order that no Governor should be a tenant of the School estate, they evaded it, like the Appellant Colmore, by making leases to their children or to friends. The exhibitions at Cambridge were diverted to the benefit of relations or friends, two of whom, Baldwin and Turton, had fathers quite able to provide for them at the University. These abuses having become notorious and being complained of by the inhabitants, Sir William Dugdale in 1684 represented them to Charles II., who, conceiving himself concerned as a patron of the School, resolved to take the management out of the hands of such mean, necessitous persons and vest it in others whose quality and fortunes placed them above the temptation of misemploying the charity, and accordingly sent a letter, signed by himself and countersigned by the Secretary of State, demanding the surrender of the Charter. Sir Charles Holt, on receiving this letter from the Secretary of State, presented it to the majority of the then Governors, in meeting assembled, of whom 16 out of 17, without any threats or insinuation, as is falsely alleged, signed an order for surrender. Charles II. on having the old Charter presented to him, immediately cancelled it and directed a new one to be drawn, with sundry beneficial provisions. His Majesty dying after this Charter was prepared, but before it had passed the Great Seal, it was granted by James II., within 14 days after his accession, without any alteration, and the new Governors entered on their trust. Mr. Brooksby, the master, was not removed by them but resigned of his own accord; and Mr. Jos.

Hickes, a Fellow of Magdalen College, Oxford, who was afterwards deprived by his fellowship by James II., was appointed in his place. The school has since flourished; especial care has been taken of the town boys, and the revenues have been raised to the extent of 30*l.* a year. No part of the revenues, however, have been employed for the maintenance of poor scholars at the University, the new Governors being advised that to do so would be a breach of trust, and conceiving it more for the public good to educate poor boys to reading and writing than to increase clergymen, who are already more numerous than preferments are for them. The new Governors have executed their trust at their own private charge, and to the satisfaction of all the sober and substantial inhabitants of Birmingham. The Appellants have sought to harass them, finding their hope of making further profit out of the school rents now gone. The new Charter, from the time of its first delivery, was left with the Attorney-General to be enrolled. Respondents, having suffered a judgment by default, in an action of ejectment from the Schoolmaster's house, brought their Bill to avoid further trouble. The Lords Commissioners unanimously declared that the surrender having been executed as far as it could be by the old Governors, might be enrolled at any time, but refused to allow it to be enrolled then, for want of some formality in its delivery, but directed the new Governors to proceed in Chancery by way of Information in the Attorney-General's name. Respondents petitioned for a Bill in Parliament, but were refused leave to introduce one, and were left to proceed at law or equity. They accordingly proceeded, as directed, by Information in the Attorney-General's name and obtained the Decree appealed from. As to the Popish Chapel, it was erected by one Randolph, a popish priest, on land rented by him from John Ensor, assignee of George Fentham, to whom the Governors had leased the land. They could not prevent it. *Signed* by Respondents; *Countersigned* by Tho. Powys and Arthur Onslow. *Endorsed* as brought in this day.

(*b.*) 19 Dec. Petition of Respondent for a day for hearing. Appellants are delaying to prosecute the Appeal, whereby Petitioners may be obstructed in performing their Trust, and the stock of the school is wasted. Pray also that Appellants may in the meantime enter into Recognizance. L. J., XIV. 695.

(*c.*) 22 Feb. 1691–2.—Petition of the Old Governors of the Free Grammar School in Birmingham, in the County of Warwick, of the foundation of King Edward VI. Petitioners, having obtained from their Lordships a reversal of the decree in Chancery appealed from, intended to take out execution upon a judgment in ejectment against Mr. John Hicks, the Schoolmaster under the new Charter. But one Moreton Slaney, the solicitor of the New Governors, with four of the New Governors who were Relators in the suit in Chancery, on pretence that since their Lordships' judgment they have as Old Governors appointed Hicks, have brought their Bill in Chancery in his name and obtained on 11 Feb. an injunction to stay proceedings, whereby Petitioners are still kept out of possession, and will be wholly deprived of the benefit of their Lordships' reversal, the ejectment lease expiring in March next. These proceedings of

Slanley and the others are merely an artifice, to elude their Lordships' judgment. Pray that the injunction may be dissolved. *Signed* Sam. Carter, William Colmore, Geo. Wyrly, and Thomas Rowney. L. J., XV. 88. [No further proceedings, the Prorogation being on the 24th.]

458. Dec. 2. Gawdy *v.* Sir W. Scroggs.—Petition and Appeal of Anthony Gawdy, Esq. Mary Bonfoy, of London, Widow, lent 350*l.* in 1664 to Richard, late Earl of Carbery, for repayment whereof he and Sir Anthony Browne, as his surety, confessed two Judgments of 700*l.* each to one Robert Shaw, in trust for Mrs. Bonfoy. About four years afterwards Sir Anthony sold the manor of Southweald and other lands in Essex subject to this judgment, on which 400*l.* then remained due, to Sir William Scroggs, who had notice of the judgment and an allowance of 400*l.* in his purchase towards satisfying it. Sir William neglecting to pay both principal and interest, Mrs. Bonfoy in 1671, being then Shaw's administratrix, at Sir Anthony's request extended the manor and other lands, against which extent Sir W. Scroggs brought a Bill in 1672 against E. Carbery, Mrs. Bonfoy, and one Wm. Dickenson, suggesting that Dickenson, who was her agent and put out the 350*l.* for her, was a co-surety with Sir Anthony, and ought therefore to pay a moiety of the debt. The Defendants denying all the equity of that Bill, Sir William surceased further proceedings upon it, and in 1673 stated an account of the debt, paid 200*l.* down and covenanted to pay 340*l.* more in six months, besides interest and charges at law, and in equity. Before this account was stated, Dickenson, at Mrs. Bonfoy's request, and to put her at ease, she being disturbed at Sir William's suit, gave her another security in exchange for Sir Anthony's judgment, but continued to transact with Sir William in her name. Dickenson dying soon after, Sir William paid 100*l.* more of his debt to Mrs. Smithsby, his executrix, and gave a judgment in ejectment to secure the residue. Mrs. Smithsby wanting money, Petitioner purchased her whole interest in the debt. Thereupon Sir William brought a fresh Bill for the same matters, and the L. Chancellor Nottingham stayed all proceedings at law on the extent and judgment in ejectment and Sir William's deed of covenant, and assigned to Sir William the Earl of Carbery's judgment and that of Sir Anthony, or the latter to be vacated. Sir William dying before the decree was executed, his son, the present Sir W. Scroggs, sold the extended lands to Erasmus Smith, Esq., who thereupon brought a Bill for the same matters against Petitioner and others, and the present Sir William brought a Bill to revive the former proceedings and decree obtained by his father; and on hearing both causes, the Lords Commissioners confirmed L. Nottingham's decree of 1682 and stayed all proceedings against Erasmus Smith and his estate purchased as above. Appeals from these decrees. Petitioner, a stranger to all the former transactions, purchased the extent on the credit of the account stated by Sir William, and his covenant to pay the money. Even if Dickenson were a co-surety, it is unjust that Petitioner should assign E. Carbery's judgment to Sir William, to re-imburse him the 300*l.* he paid. Prays for relief, and that all proceedings on the decrees may be stayed. *Signed* by Appellant; *Countersigned* by Ambrose Phillipps and J. Somers. L. J., XIV. 669. [The Cause was heard on 5 Feb. 1691–2. *The Solicitor-General* (for Appellant): We claim a sum of money due upon the estate of Sir Anthony Browne in 1664. Speaks as to the death and debts. *Sir Ambrose Phillipps* (for Appellant): Upon making up Mr. Bonfoy's account with Dickenson, they say there was no more due. Sir William

Scroggs was of opinion the money was due to us. Reads Sir Anthony Browne's letter of 2 Aug. 1669. Sir William Scrogg's Articles of 25 June 1673 recite the Judgment. There are other letters wherein Sir W. Scroggs offers to pay the money. *Mr. Finch* (for Respondent): This was drawn up by Mr. Dickenson's clerk. Recites it, and reads several Depositions. *Sir William Williams* (for Respondent) is heard. Counsel withdrew and the Speaker reported. *Question:* Whether the Decree shall be reversed? Resolved in the *Negative*. Contents, 9; Not-Contents, 12. Tellers E. Westmoreland, L. Delaware. Decree affirmed. (MS. Min.; L. J., XV. 63).]

Annexed:—

(*a*.) 4 Jan. 1691–2. Answer of Sir William Scroggs, Knt., son and heir of Sir William Scroggs, Knt., deceased. Sir Anthony Browne informed Respondent's father, on selling him Weald Hall, that Dickenson (who was E. Carbery's agent and commonly bound with the Earl in all securities) was also a co-surety for the debt, and that the Earl had given him, Sir Anthony, a counterbond, drawn by Dickenson's directions, to indemnify him against the judgment, wherein it was recited that Dickenson had given a warrant of attorney to confess the like judgment from Dickenson as Sir Anthony had confessed to Shaw; and thus Sir Anthony prevailed with Respondent's father to allow it to be inserted in the articles that the latter should indemnify Sir Anthony against the judgment as far as 400*l*. Shaw dying, Mrs. Bonfoy took out letters of administration as to this debt, and assigned the judgment to Dickenson. Respondent's father, not knowing of this assignment, and being unable to find any judgment entered from Dickenson to Shaw, and Dickenson keeping himself close in the Temple and not to be arrested, and Respondent's father's purchased lands being extended by Benfoy, paid 200*l*. in 1673 and 100*l*. more afterwards to Benfoy. Dickenson died and made Anne Smithsby his executrix, and Respondent's father, having discovered that Dickenson had paid off Mrs. Bonfoy and taken an assignment of Sir Anthony's judgment in 1672, and also that, although no judgment was actually entered from him to Shaw, had sealed a warrant for confessing judgment at the same time when Sir Anthony sealed a warrant, and, being entrusted by Bonfoy to take what security he thought fit, had fraudulently omitted to cause the judgment to be entered against himself, brought a Bill against Smithsby, Bonfoy, and Appellant (who pretended to have an assignment of the judgment from Smithsby against Sir Anthony), and L. Nottingham pronounced the decree set forth in the Petition, being fully satisfied that Dickenson was co-surety with Sir Anthony, and that Respondent's father had the same equity as Sir Anthony had, and that, since the debt was come to be claimed by Dickenson's Executrix, and since Respondent's father had paid his full share of the debt, Dickenson's Executrix or Assignee ought not to have any further satisfaction from Respondent's father, but ought to bear the other moiety themselves, as the Respondent's father had done on his part. The Lords Commissioners, on a rehearing, were of the same opinion and confirmed the decree. Prays their Lordships to confirm the same with good costs against Respondent. *Signed* by Respondent; *Countersigned* by Mat. Smith. *Endorsed* as brought in this day.

House of Lords MSS.

1691.

459. Dec. 3. L. Widdrington *v.* E. Derby.—Petition of William, Lord Widdrington, Baron of Blankney, Executor of the last Will and Testament of William Stanley, Esq., deceased. Petitioner's testator, by virtue of a settlement made on the marriage of Sir Charles Stanley with Jane, daughter of William, Lord Widdrington, his father and mother, was entitled after his father's death in 1676 to an annuity of 600*l.* a year, chargeable on the estates of the Earl of Derby. The Earl refusing to pay, he brought a Bill in Chancery, and obtained a judgment in 4 Jac. II., but the Lord Chancellor proposed, as an amicable compromise, that the Earl should pay at the rate of 500*l.* a year for arrears due from Sir Charles's death, one-thousandth part thereof to be paid on the next Bartholomew day, and the rest, with interest, within six months after; but ordered, that if the Earl should refuse to accept, or fail to comply with this compromise, he should account for the arrears and continue future payment at the rate of 600*l.* a year. The Earl not signifying his consent, the Order was ultimately made absolute. The testator has devised by will to Petitioner the arrears of the annuity and also the manor of Thurlby and divers lands in the county of Lincoln, subject to the payment of 9,000*l.* debts and 2,000*l.* legacies. Prays that, if their Lordships refuse him leave to revive the suit, he may be allowed to prove the will in Chancery, to enable him to pay the said debts and legacies. L. J., XIV. 670. [In Committee for Privileges, to whom the Petition and Answer were referred, the order of 3 July 1678 was read for examining witnesses *in perpetuam rei memoriam.* *Sir Bartholomew Shower* (for Appellant): We only desire to prove the Will, to keep our witnesses and, in case of death, if an ejectment be brought, the witnesses may be preserved, otherwise privilege will be an extinguishment. The Statute of Frauds requires a great many circumstances as to witnesses. *E. Derby:* I am not prepared in this thing. All the difficulty I find is, that there were such practices made in the obtaining these wills, and I had not time to consider of it. *Ordered* to report as in L. J., XIV. 687. (Priv. Book, 14 Dec.).]

Annexed:—

(*a*.) 10 Dec. 1691. Answer of E. Derby. As to the rent-charge, Respondent is advised that the first settlement thereof is liable to material legal exceptions, and although Respondent and his father did not endeavour to avoid it, in respect of their near relationship to Sir Charles Stanley and his son, yet Respondent's father and his trustees alienated many years ago the manor of Childwall, and paid so much money to Sir Charles or for his use that he was able to purchase therewith a great part of his Lincolnshire lands, and on that consideration 150*l.* a year of the rent-charge of 600*l.* was discharged. William Stanley, a few days before he died, had drunk wine in excess to the deprivation of his reason, and was carried into a brandy cellar and then to his lodgings, where he had frequent delirious fits. One Dr. Conquest, his physician, was a Papist, and introduced several of his persuasion, and these got one of the Queen Dowager's Chaplains to induce Mr. Stanley, who all his life was extremely averse to the Romish religion, to become a Papist on his deathbed. Amongst them was one Mrs. Panton, his late wife's mother, whom in his health he could not endure to see, nor had he, till so introduced, seen for several years. The day before her coming, he had been prevailed, as is said, to make a will, at which time he seemed to have a raving passion for his late wife's sister, who is said to be a minor in France and supposed to be a recluse in a monastery there, and being asked who should be his executor, he named her. After Mrs. Panton's coming, the Protestants with him were desired to withdraw, and the priest, it is supposed, gave him extreme unction. Mrs. Panton having got to the will and finding nothing for herself, contrived with one Gardner, a solicitor, to persuade the distempered Mr. Stanley to have another Will made (which was done in another room), making L. Widdrington executor. These are the Wills to devest Respondent, who is heir of Mr. Stanley, of all Mr. Stanley's lands and otherwise encumber him with clamorous reflections and a chargeable suit; and which of these wills L. Widdrington will insist on, Respondent desires to know. L. J., XIV. 681.

460. Dec. 3. Pember's Estate Bill.—Draft of an Act to enable Thomas Pember, Gent., to sell his estate to pay his debts and make provision for his daughter. Whereas Thomas Pember, Gent., late of Ellesdon and now of Kington, in the county of Hereford, has agreed to sell to William Whitmore, Gent., all his lands in Ellesdon and the Moor and in the parish of Lyonhalls in the said county, of the yearly value of 80*l.* or thereabouts; and whereas the said Thomas Pember and his wife have mortgaged part of the lands for 250*l.* and interest, and have limited the lands, after satisfaction of the mortgage, to the use of themselves for life, then to Alice, their daughter in tail, and in default of issue by her, to the use of Thomas Pember's heirs and assigns, and, having no other issue but Alice, have agreed to dispose of 500*l.*, part of the purchase money, for the benefit of Alice, as an equivalent for the estate tail, which, by reason of her minority, cannot be effected without the authority of Parliament; the Bill, therefore, enacts that the estate tail shall be barred, and, that, as satisfaction to Alice, the 500*l.* shall be paid, on completion of the purchase, to Sylvanus Vaughan, of the Court of Hergest, and John Edwards, both of the parish of Kington, clerks, and their executors, &c. (on payment whereof, Whitmore shall stand discharged of that amount of the purchase money) on trust to invest for Alice Pember, paying her the principal when she reaches the age of 21 or marries, with the consent of her parents if under 21, and till then, paying her 12*l.* yearly out of the interest for her maintenance, the rest of the interest to be employed in increasing her portion. The Bill concludes with the usual saving clause. [Read 1[a] this day. Question for Engrossment negatived on 22 Dec. (L. J., XIV. 671, 698.) In Committee on 18 Dec., E. Cornwallis in the Chair, *Mr. Price* said the estate was liable to 250*l.* debts and 6 years' interest. The infant would have an equivalent. She would have 700*l.* The mother was provided for with 400*l.* The father would have but 200*l.* to dispose of. The father was not 40 years old, and might mortgage the estate for his life and son's. Letter read from Mr. Pember to Sir Thos. Duppa giving his consent to the Bill. Certificate of Mr. and Mrs. Pember's consent to the Bill read. (Com. Book.)]

Annexed:—

(*a*.) 22 Dec. Lords' Amendment to the Bill. [Made in Committee 18 Dec. and reported this day. (Com. Book. L. J., XIV. 698.) It is purely clerical.]

461. Dec. 4. D. Norfolk (Office of E. Marshal).— Petition of Henry, Duke of Norfolk, Earl Marshal of England, &c. Petitioner is rightfully vested in the office of Earl Marshal of this kingdom by inheritance, and sole judge of the Court of Constable and

House of Lords MSS.

1691.

Marshal in the vacancy of a Constable, as has been declared by the Patents of divers Kings and practice of the said Court ever since the 13th of Henry VIII., and is thereby empowered in the ancient laws and statutes of this realm to hold a Court and take cognizance of such matters as belong to the said Court. It is provided by 13 Ric. II. cap. 2 that if any will complain that any plea be commenced before the Constable and Marshal, that might be tried by the Common law of the land, the same plaintiff shall have a Privy Seal of the King without difficulty, directed to the Constable and Marshal, to surcease in that plea till it be discussed by the King's Council, if that matter ought, or of right pertaineth to that Court, or otherwise to be tried by the Common law of the realm, by any other method than which neither Petitioner nor any other Constable or Marshal for above these three hundred years last past were ever stopt in their proceedings that can anywhere be found. Nevertheless, in certain cases prosecuted in Petitioner's said Court against Charles Domville, Thomas Powell, and William Lambe, the Barons of the Exchequer have granted Prohibitions to stop proceedings in the said Court (which Prohibitions are hereunto annexed), contrary to the said statute and the constant practice thereupon, as may appear by ancient records. Petitioner appeals against the said Prohibitions and prays that their Lordships will declare them null and void. [Read this day and referred to the Committee for Privileges (L. J., XIV. 672), whose proceedings were as follows: *Dr. Walter* (for Petitioner): His Grace thinks there can be no such Prohibitions, because there have not been any so many hundred years. *Dr. Oldys:* There were several Acts before this 13 Rich. II. that limit the power of the Earl Marshal, and if there had been any remedy in Westminster Hall, they need not have had the Act made. 8 Rich. II. A Privy Seal will examine whether the Cause belongs to this Court or to the law. We pray the Prohibitions may be declared void. The *Solicitor-General:* It is a rule that all Courts assert their jurisdiction. The Earl Marshal asserts his. The Exchequer ought to have theirs. For many years there was no Prohibition. We cannot find that before the sitting of this Court or since there were Prohibitions until now. We can show a Privy Seal has been taken out, but we cannot discover that there was ever a Prohibition. The Court of Chivalry has been as apt to go beyond its bounds as any, and yet we can find no Prohibition or one instance in our books or histories. Counsel withdrew. The Judges were heard. *Baron Lechmere:* The matter is as to Prohibitions granted out of the Exchequer upon the Court of Chivalry. Of the judges that then were, there are but two here. I have looked over the Prohibitions and the Libel. There was a libel that several had provided and marshalled funerals. The reason of the Prohibition was, if these persons have invaded the office of Sir Henry St. George, then they had a remedy at Common law. Sir William Dugdale had the same beyond Trent. One Homes marshalled the funeral, and Sir William brought his action. He had a trial and a verdict for him, and we thought it our duty to grant Prohibitions in this case. This right we cannot deny. It is a *jure rege conservand.* This is the case, and how could we do less? The Statute has not abrogated the Common law. In E. Macclesfield's case your Lordships have declared it cannot come *per saltum. Ordered* to report the difficulty the Committee finds in this case, and the state of the matter to the House. (Priv. Book, 11 Dec.)—On 12 Dec., the House, on receiving this report, gave leave to D. Norfolk to produce precedents before the Committee for Privileges at their next sitting. (L. J., XIV. 684.) The Priv. Book contains no further entry of proceedings.]

Annexed :—

(*a*.) 4 Dec. 1691. Prohibition of the Court of Exchequer, referred to in preceding, and addressed to William Oldys, "legum doctori in curia Henrici, Ducis Norfolk, Domini Comitis Marescalli Angliæ militari advocato, nostro, sive aliquo ab indies in hac parte competenti." Recites that Charles Domville had complained to the Court of Exchequer that, contrary to Magna Charta, William Oldys had preferred certain Articles against him in the Court of Chivalry, on behalf of Henry, Duke of Norfolk, setting forth that, whereas the cognizance of arms and pedigrees and the marshalling of funerals belonged to Sir Henry St. George, Clarencieux and King at Arms, Domville had marshalled certain funerals, viz., of the wife of Barkstead at Chelsea, and of Elizabeth, daughter of Michael Godfrey of Woodford, Essex, at St. Swithin's parish church, London, in August 1691, and of William Sprignoll at Highgate in September 1691, and had exhibited before his shop, to attract custom, coats of arms and funeral emblems, which Articles the Duke, without proper authority, had compelled Domville to answer. Stops all further proceedings in the Court of Chivalry. *Signed* Robert Atkyns, 11 Nov. Anno primi nostri regni. [This and the two next Annexes are appended to preceding.]

(*b*.) 4 Dec. 1691. Similar Prohibition on the complaint of Thomas Powell, charged with having marshalled the funerals of William Painter, of Lime Street, London, in August 1691: of Gardner, of Haddon, Herts, in June 1691; and of Hammond, of London, in August 1691.

(*c*.) 4 Dec. 1691. Similar Prohibition on the complaint of William Lamb, charged with having marshalled the funerals of the daughter of Denn, of Bread Street, London, and of Cann, widow, of Brentwood, in March and July 1691.

462. Dec. 4. Smith's Estate Act.—Amended draft of an Act to enable trustees to sell the estate of Edward Smith, Esq., deceased, to raise money for the payment of his debts and to make provision for his children, who are infants. The Lords' Amendments (Com. Book, 10 Dec.) are unimportant. [Read 1ª this day; Royal Assent, 24 Feb. 1691-2. (L. J., XIV. 673; XV. 93.). 3 & 4 W. & M. c. 36. in Long Calendar.]

Annexed :—

(*a*.) 10 Dec. Lords' Amendments to the Bill. [Made in Committee and reported this day, Com. Book; L. J., XIV. 680.]

463. Dec. 5. E. Stamford *v*. E. Suffolk.—Petition of Thomas, Earl of Stamford. Sir John Maynard, late first Lord Commissioner of the Great Seal, left by will 10,000*l*. to one of his grandchildren, Petitioner's present wife, to be paid on her marriage, and died on 8 Oct. 1690 leaving a very plentiful personal estate, and making Lady Mary Maynard, his wife, executrix of his will in trust, after payment of debts and legacies, to lay out the residue of his personal estate for the sole benefit of his grandchildren and their issue. Lady Mary proved the will, and was possessed of the personal estate, and Petitioner, on marrying his present wife, brought a Bill in Chancery against Lady Mary for the legacy of 10,000*l*. and (to remove all doubts of her not having assets) to discover testator's personal estate. Lady Mary in her answer neither denied nor confessed assets. The Court, on

House of Lords MSS.

1691.

17 July last, directed her to account for the personal estate, in order to pay Petitioner the legacy, but, in kindness to her, ordered her only to give a note with particulars of the said estate in two months' time, and if it did not appear that she had not sufficient assets to pay the legacy, she was to be examined on interrogatories to make a full discovery. Lady Mary failing to give any such note or make any discovery, Petitioner on 30 October moved the Court, on whose order interrogatories were exhibited before the Master for her examination. The Court on 13 Nov., allowed her a week's further time to be examined, and in default ordered her to be committed. She has not, however, yet been examined, and her agents have given notice to Petitioner's agents that she is married to the Earl of Suffolk, which marriage was solemnised only two days before the time for her examination expired. Petitioner, though conceiving that by the Standing Order of 12 Nov. 1685, concerning trustees having no privilege, he may proceed against the Earl and Countess of Suffolk, yet out of regard to the privileges of the House, prays their Lordships' determination. L. J., XIV. 674. [In Committee for Privileges, to whom this Petition and the subsequent Petition of Elizabeth Maynard (*ib.* 682) were referred, the following proceedings are recorded. *Mr. Trevor* (for E. Stamford): The question is whether Lady Suffolk is a trustee. She is executrix to Mr. Serjeant Maynard. An executrix is by nature a trustee, even by law. This is expressed in the will. There are great legacies given away. She has a legacy given her. *Mr. Bowes* (for Mr. Maynard): The Lady Suffolk is as bare a trustee as may be. *The Solicitor-General:* There are two sorts of estate: the real and personal. As to the real estate she is a trustee, intended so at this time she is no trustee at all. It had been done before now. The Bill was drawn; then they would not allow her to be an executrix. From the end of June last they say there is delay. As to the real estate, the Lady Suffolk is to have during her life, so as to that estate she is not a trustee; only as to the other, she will be a trustee when the E. Stamford will allow her to be so. The E. Stamford stands upon his privilege in one case. *Mr. Ward* (for Lady Maynard): She is not only a trustee. The real estate is in dispute and stopped by privilege. The personal estate was kept under difficulty till June last, so she had no power, the Chancery having laid their hands on the deeds. *Mr. Trevor* (in reply): The E. Stamford demands no account but for the personal estate. After debate, ordered to report as in L. J., XIV. 684 (Priv. Book, 11 Dec.). With regard to Elizabeth Maynard's Petition, the Committee, being informed that E. Suffolk would waive his privilege, ordered to report as in L. J., XIV. 687. (Priv. Book, 14 Dec.)]

Annexed:—

(*a*.) 11 Dec. 1691. Petition of Elizabeth Maynard, widow and administratrix of Joseph Maynard, Esq., late deceased, the son and heir of Sir John Maynard, Knt., late deceased. Sir John, on Petitioner's marriage with his son, agreed not only to settle on her an annuity of 400*l*. a year, but also to invest 10,949*l*. with several years' interest he had received in trust for his son, in the purchase of an estate to be settled upon her. But before the same was effected, Joseph died, and Petitioner, as his administratrix, became entitled to the 10,949*l*. with interest, but in regard to her late husband's debts, she offered to let Sir John administer; but Sir John persuaded her to administer, and informed her that the administration would prove to her advantage, he having another way settled portions for his granddaughters. About 12 months since, Sir John died, and though in all former wills he charged his estate with no less than 400*l.* a year, to Petitioner for life, yet by the duplicate he signed (which he willed to be his will in case his will should miscarry), no more is left to Petitioner than 350*l.* a year, and of that nothing has been paid to Lady Maynard (who is Sir John's only acting executrix, and has proved his will). Petitioner in consequence brought a Bill in Chancery for an account and satisfaction of the 10,949*l.* and annuity; but the Lady Maynard being about a fortnight since married to E. Suffolk, Petitioner is advised not to proceed till their Lordships' pleasure is known in respect of privilege. Through the non-payment of the money, Petitioner cannot pay her husband's debts nor maintain herself and family. Prays for leave to proceed in Chancery against E. Suffolk and his Countess, notwithstanding privilege. [Read this day and referred to the Committee for Privileges. L. J., XIV. 682.]

464. Dec. 5. Lougher *v.* Prichard and others.—Petition and Appeal of Richard Lougher, Esq. Petitioner about twelve years ago gave a bond to one Morgan Jenkins for a loan of 100*l.*, and paid him interest for several years thereon. After Jenkins' death, the Respondents claimed the debt under the will of Katherine Williams, for whom, as they alleged, Jenkins was only a trustee, and on Petitioner insisting on a discharge from Jenkin's executors or administrators, they set up one Harry Evans to procure administration *de bonis non* of Jenkins and to sue Petitioner at law upon the Bond, which he did, and obtained judgment, and Petitioner paid Evans the debt. Evans refusing to pay any of the money to Respondents, they brought a Bill in Chancery in 1681 against Petitioner and Evans, and on Evans' death, revived the suit against his administrators, and on 24 July last the Lords Commissioners decreed payment of the debt with interest. Prays that this decree may be reversed, and Respondents ordered to answer. *Signed* by Appellant; *Countersigned* by Thos. Trevor and J. Lowes. L. J., XIV. 674. [The Appeal was heard and the decree reversed on 13 Feb. 1691-2. (L. J., XV. 75.) *Mr. Trevor* and *Mr. Finch* appeared for Appellant, and the *Solicitor-General* and "another Counsel" for Respondent. (MS. Min.)]

Annexed :—

(*a*.) 19 Jan. 1691-2. Answer of Joan Prichard, Jane Prichard *alias* Steed, James Steed, her husband, and Thomas Roberts. The 100*l.* was lent by Katherine Williams, who held the bond, and for whom Jenkins was only a trustee. After her death, the Appellant offered payment if Respondents would give him a general release, but they refused, as it would discharge Appellant of another debt of 14*l.* due by him and his wife to the said Katherine. Respondents chose Evans, as being Jenkins' nearest kinsman, for the sole purpose of putting the bond in suit against Appellant, and undertook to defray his expenses. Evans having obtained judgment in the Court of the Great Sessions of Wales, held at Cowbridge, Appellant by fraud procured him to acknowledge satisfaction, though he was only a formal party to the action, in order to defeat Respondents of their debt. Evans, in Chancery, did not disown the trust, as Appellant falsely alleges, and Appellant himself confessed that the money belonged to Mrs. Williams and that he had paid her interest till her death in 1682. The fraud fully appeared when the cause was heard, and the Court on 26 Nov. 1691, and not on the day stated in the Appeal, finally decreed payment to Respondents of principal and interest, amounting altogether to 288*l*. Appellant has brought no Bill of Review, and his Appeal is merely for delay. Pray that it may be dismissed with costs. *Signed* by Respondents, except Roberts; *Countersigned* by Rich. Turner (signature engrossed). *Endorsed* as brought in this day.

465. Dec. 7. Penry and others *v.* Walker.—Petition of Elizabeth Penry, widow of Rice Penry, deceased, Charles Penry, Elizabeth Penry, and Mary Penry, the children of Rice Penry and under age, by their guardians Sir John Powell, Knight, one of the Justices of the Court of Common Pleas, Charles Hughes and John Walters, Esquires, trustees for the said children. Hoe Games, having in fee copyhold property in the County of Brecon, worth 48*l*. a year, mortgaged it to Jane David as security for a loan of 546*l*., and paid interest at 8 per cent. Games was succeeded in his interest by his son John, and the latter by his three sisters and co-heirs—Elizabeth, wife of Thomas Walker, Esq., Katharine and Florence, wife of Richard Lucy, Clerk, the Respondents. Jane David's interest went first to Hugh Penry and John Powell, in trust for Magdalen Penry, then to Magdalen's son, Rice Penry, who paid his mother's debts in expectation of continuing to receive the 8 per cent. interest, and, in default of payment, entered in 1676 on the premises, which he devised to the Petitioners, Powell, Hughes, and Walters, in trust to be sold for portions for his children. The co-heirs then brought a Bill in Chancery, claiming under 12 Car. II. to pay only 6 per cent., the other 2*l*. to go to a sinking fund, and on 3 May 1688 the L. Chancellor Jeffreys decreed that the 8 per cent. paid before Rice Penry's entry should stand, the interest to be 6 per cent. thereafter.* On a Bill of Review, brought by Respondents, on 1 July 1690, the Decree was reversed by the Lords Commissioners,† and the interest was decreed at 6 per cent. from the date of the Act, which will deprive Petitioners of about 250*l*. Appeal against the second Decree. *Signed* by Elizabeth Penry only; *Countersigned* by J. Sŏmers and Ge. Pauncefoote. L. J., XIV. 676. [The Appeal was heard and dismissed on 9 Feb. 1691-2 (L. J., XV. 68). *Mr. Trevor* and another Counsel (for Appellants) contended that the Statute did not make existing contracts void. *Sir Ambrose Phillipps* and *Mr. Finch* appeared for Respondents. (MS. Min.)]

Annexed :—

(*a*.) 17 Dec. 1691. Answer of Thomas Walker, Esq., and Elizabeth, his wife, Katherine Games and Florence Lucy, widow. Respondents add that the L. Chancellor on 12 May and 17 July 1680 had decreed interest at 6 per cent. from the date of the Act. *Signed* by Thomas Walker for himself, his wife, and the other Respondents. *Endorsed* as brought in this day. MS. Min.

466. Dec. Penny and others *v.* Keymer.—Petition and Appeal of Edward Penny, Gent., and Henry Moore and Thomas Moore, infants under the age of 21 years, by the said Edward Penny, their Guardian. Respondent's father, Francis Keymer, having had a lease for 99 years, determinable on three lives, of an old ruinous tenement in Yeovil, granted him by the Port-reeve, on condition of rebuilding it in two years, assigned the lease to Henry Moore, father of the infant Petitioners, who laid out nearly 400*l*. in building, and died in 1679, leaving

* 2 Vernon, 42, 78. † *Ib.*, 145.

the Petitioner Penny administrator of his will during his sons' majority. Penny received the profits for their use till 1686, when Keymer, having got himself into the Charter House, and designing to defraud the infants of a debt of 350*l.* due to their father by himself and his son Elias, filed a Bill in Chancery in the names of his daughters Mary and Joan, claiming for them, as pretended assignees for 10*l.* of the first lease, an equity to the benefit of the second lease to Moore, whose outlay, amounting, as alleged, to only 280*l.*, he swore to have recouped by assigning to him for 12 years an estate at Hasselbury, worth 60*l.* a year. His evidence failed to satisfy the L. Chancellor Jeffreys or the jury by whom a trial at law was directed, but, on a rehearing, the Lords Commissioners on 3 July 1691, on a bare presumption that 280*l.* was all that had been laid out on building, and was part of the 350*l.* otherwise secured, decreed Petitioner to deliver up possession, and assign the lease to Moore, and account for profits, and by subsequent orders the Court has directed him to pay costs both at law and in Chancery. Moore's outlay was no part of the consideration of the articles concerning the Hasselbury estate, which were entered into by Francis Keymer and his son Elias as security for 350*l.* due by them to Moore and 120*l.* due to Mrs. Anne Cary, and not for one penny due by Mary and Joan Keymer. If Mary Keymer had any equity of redemption, she ought not to have been let in to redeem without paying principal, interest, and costs. Prays that the Decree may be reversed with costs, and Respondent ordered to answer. *Signed* by Appellant; *Countersigned* by Will. Guiddit, L. J., XIV. 676. [The Appeal was dismissed on 10 Jan. 1693–4 for want of prosecution. L. J., XV. 338.]

Annexed:—

(*a.*) 14 Dec. 1691. Answer of Mary Keymer, Spinster. The lease was first assigned to Respondent, who afterwards assigned it to Moore, for satisfaction of whose charges, amounting to 280*l.*, Respondent's father, the original lessee, by articles of 1 July 1674, made over to him his Hasselbury estate for 12 years, worth 70*l.* a year. Thereupon Moore delivered over possession, but died without assigning the lease, though he and Penny received the rents of the said estate for the whole 12 years. The Court of Chancery on 18 May 1688 referred to a trial at law the issue whether the money mentioned in the said articles was distinct from the money laid out by Moore in building the house. Appellant, by contrivance with one Acourt, his son-in-law and solicitor, who was for that purpose named a bailiff, arrested one of Respondent's principal witnesses, on his way to the Court, for a pretended debt 23 years old, and obtained a verdict, by producing a bond for 400*l.*, which had been given only to save Moore harmless from being bail in Yeovil Court for Respondent's father. The cause being reheard, the Master, who was ordered to examine how much money was laid out on building, and how the 350*l.* became due, reported that the 280*l.* was part of the 350*l.*, and that a balance, on the account, of 40*l.*, remained due to Respondent, and this Report was confirmed by consent of Appellant's own counsel. The house, after all Respondent's expenses, is now let for only 12*l.* a year. Prays that the Appeal may be dismissed. *Signed* by Respondent: the countersignature of James Stedman is engrossed. *Endorsed* as brought in this day.

(*b.*) 20 Jan. 1691–2. Petition of Respondent, that the Appellant may be ordered to find security in a week and set down the

HOUSE OF LORDS MSS.

1691.

Cause for hearing, or that the Appeal may be dismissed with costs. L. J., XV. 40.

(*c*.) 8 Jan. 1693-4. Petition of Respondent. Appellants have never found security. Prays that the Appeal may be dismissed. L. J., XV. 336.

467. Dec. 7. Stickland *v.* Coker.—Petition of John Stickland [Strickland], Thomas Green and Mary his wife. The Cause, which was appointed for hearing in Dec. 1685, not having been heard, pray that it may stand revived and be heard on an early day, and that certain deeds, evidences, and writings produced by Respondent in Chancery, by order of the Court, and left in a Master's hands, may be left with their Lordships' Clerk for production at the Bar. *Unsigned.* L. J., XIV. 676. [The Cause never came to a hearing. *See also* 11th Report, Appendix, Part II., No. **322.**]

Annexed:—

(*a*.) 5 Feb. 1691-2. Petition of Appellants that Respondent may be ordered to deliver to them a true copy of a certain deed. *Unsigned.* L. J., XV. 64. *In extenso.*

(*b*.) 5 Feb. Notice referred to in preceding Petition, as appended thereto. *Signed* Ja. Groundman, Solicitor for Respondent. *Dated* 27 Jan. 1691. *Endorsed* as read this day.

ACCOUNTS COMMISSIONERS.

House of Lords MSS.

1691.

468. Dec. 7. Accounts Commissioners—Book entitled. A brief Revenue from the 5th day of November 1688, to the 29th of Sep- tuted by one Act of Parliament made in the second year of their Commissioners to examine, take and state the Public Accounts

Folio 1. Receipts.

	£ s. d.	£ s. d.	£ s. d.
Out of Customs and Coinage, viz.:—			
Remained in their Majesties' Exchequer, 5 Nov. 1688 on said account - -	8,174 7 1		
Received from several Collectors of the same between 5 Nov. 1688, and 1 January following, on the behalf of the then Prince of Orange - - - -	10,117 2 11¾	19,291 10 0¾	
Remained 5 Nov. 1688 in the hands of Richard Kent, Esq., the then Receiver-General, viz.:			
On moneys proper to the year's account ending Michaelmas 1688 -	678 10 6		
And on the subsequent year - -	2,320 0 5		
	2,998 10 11		
Received more by him for Customs between 5 Nov. 1688 and 29 Jan. following, which was due before Michaelmas 1688	15,316 15 7		
Received more by him between 5 Nov. 1688 and 25 March 1689 - - -	165,525 0 0½	183,840 7 3½	
Received by Thos. Fox, Esq., Receiver-General, viz.:			
From Lady Day 1689 to Michaelmas following - - - -	367,226 14 7		
And from Michaelmas 1689 to Michaelmas 1690 - - - -	350,671 12 10¾		
Received more by him for Customs and Coinage from Michaelmas 1690 to Michaelmas 1691, as arrears by his quarterly accounts - - £535,645 12 10			
And to 3 October, that was due before Michaelmas last - - £6,301 8 5½			
Received more by him for Coinage within the said time - - £10,889 3 0½	558,604 4 4½	1,278,028 11 10	1,470,764 9 2
Out of New Impositions on Silks and Linens, viz.:—			
Received by the above Richard Kent, Esq., from the 5th of Nov. 1688 to the 25th March 1689 - - - -	19,329 9 11¾		
By the above Thos. Fox, Esq., from the 25th of March 1689 to Michaelmas following - - -	29,168 9 11	48,490 19 10¾	
Out of New Impositions on Wines and Vinegar, viz.:—			
Received by the aforesaid Richard Kent, Esq., from the 5th of Nov. 1688 to the 25th March 1689 - - - -	75,403 4 4¾		
And by Thos. Fox, Esq., from the 25th of March 1689 to Michaelmas following - - - -	107,655 16 11½	183,059 1 4¼	

STATE of the INCOMES and ISSUES of their MAJESTIES' PUBLIC tember 1691, with MEMORANDUMS made by the COMMISSIONERS consti- MAJESTIES' reign, entitled An Act for appointing and enabling of the KINGDOM.

PAYMENTS. Folio 2.

		£ s. d.	£ s. d.	£ s. d.
For the Army, viz.:—				
To the Right Honble. Richd. Earl of Ranelagh, viz.:—				
Paid his Lordship out of the Exchequer between the 5th of Nov. 1688, and the 29th Sept. 1691, as by Sir Robt. Howard's account - £2,854,527 5 0½				
More which Sir Robt. Howard saith was paid before, but upon examination appears to have been paid since the said 5th of Nov. 1688 -	12,000 0 0	2,866,527 5 0½		
More as by his Lordship's voluntary Account in folio 13 - - -		615,058 1 7½		
		3,481,585 6 7½		
Out of which is to be deducted so much his Lordship paid the Lord Falkland, and is charged to the Navy in that Lord's account - - - -		3,000 0 0	3,478,585 6 7½	
To the Right Honble. Wm. Harbord, Esq., viz.:—				
Paid him out of the Exchequer during the time of his being Paymaster-General of the Irish Army, besides what he received from the Earl of Ranelagh which is not mentioned, to prevent a double charge - - -		1,073,268 12 7½		
More for the amount of his voluntary account as in folio 11 appears at large -		28,768 11 6¼	1,102,037 4 1¾	
To Charles Fox and Thomas Coningsby, Esq., viz.:—				
Paid them out of the Exchequer from the time of their being Paymasters of the Irish Army to the 29th of Sept. 1691 - - - - - -		1,260,607 1 0½		
More by the voluntary charge of Charles Fox, Esq., as in folio 11 appears at large - - - £7,456 12 3				
More for the amount of the voluntary charge of Thomas Coningsby, Esq., as in folio 11 - - -	79,096 12 6¾	86,553 4 9¾	1,347,160 5 10¼	
To Col. Thomas Hill for the forces in the Leeward Islands - - -		—	1,100 0 0	
To Monsr. Vandereeck, Paymaster of the Dutch Forces which he hath been required to give an account of, but as yet the Commissioners cannot obtain it		—	20,000 0 0	

House of Lords MSS.

1691.

Folio 1. Receipts—*cont.*

	£ s. d.	£ s. d.	£ s. d.
…of New Impositions on Tobacco and Sugars, viz.:—			
Received by the aforesaid Richd. Kent, Esq., from the 5th of Nov. 1688 to Lady Day 1689 - - - - -	16,498 13 9½		
And by Thos. Fox, Esq., from Lady Day 1689 to Michaelmas following - - - - -	91,045 6 2¼	107,544 1 11¾	
Transported - - - -	—	—	1,470,764 9 2

Folio 3.

	£ s. d.	£ s. d.	£ s. d.
Customs and Coinage transported -	—	—	1,470,764 9 2
New Impositions transported - -	—	329,064 3 2¾	
Out of New Impositions on Silks and Linens, viz.:—			
Received by Thos. Fox, Esq., from 29th Sept. 1689 to 29th Sept. 1690 - -	14,482 8 1½		
Out of New Impositions on Wines and Vinegar, viz.:—			
Received by Thos. Fox, Esq., from 29th Sept. 1689 to 29th Sept. 1690 - -	61,891 18 10¼		
Out of New Impositions on Tobacco and Sugars, viz.:—			
Received by Thos. Fox, Esq., from 29th Sept. 1689, to 29th Sept. 1690 - -	75,689 10 11½	152,063 17 11	
Out of New Impositions on Silks and Linens, viz.:—			
Received by Thos. Fox, Esq., from 29th Sept. 1690 to 29th Sept. 1691 £108,311 19 8			
And more to the 3rd of Oct. 1691, that was due before the said Michaelmas - 800 0 0	109,111 19 8		
Out of New Impositions on Wines and Vinegar, viz.:—			
Received by Thos. Fox, Esq., from 29th Sept. 1690 to 29th Sept. 1691 £104,810 12 10¾			
And more to the 3rd of Oct. 1691, that was due before Michaelmas last - - 805 0 0	104,581 12 10¾		
Out of New Impositions on Tobacco and Sugars, viz.:—			
Received by Thos. Fox, Esq., from the 29th Sept. 1690 to the 29th Sept. 1691 £99,475 7 7¾			
And more to the 3rd of Oct. 1691, that was due before Michaelmas last - - 740 1 3	100,284 8 10¾	313,838 1 5	865,006 2 6¾

House of Lords MSS.

1691.

Payments—*cont.*

Folio 2.

	£ s. d.	£ s. d.	£ s. d.
Memorandum. Since the closing of this Account Mounsr. Vandersch hath been with us, and from the King acquainted us that the above 20,000*l.* was paid him for Secret Service, and that no part thereof was distributed to any Member of Parliament.			
	Transported -	—	3,948,202 16 7½

Folio 4.

	£ s. d.	£ s. d.	£ s. d.
For the Navy, viz.:—			
To the Right Honble. Anthony Ld. Viscount Falkland, viz.:—			
Paid his Lordship out of the Exchequer during the time of his being Treasurer of the Navy - - - -	198,068 0 1		
More for his Lordship's voluntary charge, folio 11, being the balance of his cash, remaining the 5th of Nov. 1688 - -	6,976 8 2		
More paid his Lordship by the Earl of Ranelagh, in his account of contingencies - - - - -	3,000 0 0	208,044 8 3	
To the Right Honble. Edward Russel, Esq., viz.:—			
Paid him out of the Exchequer to the 29th of Sept. 1691 - - - -	2,911,706 2 10½		
More for the amount of his voluntary charge, as in folio 11 appears at large -	1,249 14 4	2,912,955 17 2½	
To Sir Dennis Ashburnham and others, Victuallers, for the surplusage of their accounts - - - - -	—	1,086 12 4½	
More for what was in Cash the 5th of Nov. 1688 in the hands of Anthony Sturt, jun. Esq., Treasurer to Sir Richard Haddock, Sir John Parsons, and others, the then Commissioners of the Victualling - - - - - - -	—	4,010 10 2½	3,126,097 8 0½
For the Ordnance, viz.:—			
To the Honble. Charles Bertie, Esq.:—			
Paid him out of the Exchequer from the 5th of Nov. 1688 to the 29th of Sept. 1691 - - - - - -	660,202 11 11½		
Paid him out of the Customs, 17 May 1689, and omitted to be charged by Sir Robt. Howard - - £883 14 0			
Paid him by Sir Robert Howard, who mentions it for Salary - 120 0 0	1,003 14 0	661,206 5 11½	
More for the amount of his voluntary charge, as in folio 11 appears at large -	6,023 11 2		
More for so much paid him by Philip Ryley, Esq., Surveyor of the Forests South, than is charged in the above voluntary account - - -	4,023 10 0		

House of Lords MSS.

1691.

Folio 3. Receipts—*cont.*

	£ s. d.	£ s. d.	£ s. d.
Out of the Excise, viz.:—			
Received from several collectors of the same between the 5th Nov. 1688, and the 1st Jan. following on the behalf of the then Prince of Orange - -	11,384 11 8¾		
Remaining in Cash the 5th of Nov. 1688, and received from that time to the 29th of Sept. 1689 - - - -	598,606 16 6		
And for strong Waters and Brandy in said time - - - -	66,292 5 1½	676,283 13 3¾	
Received out of Old Excise from 5th Nov. 1688 to the 29th of Sept. 1690 - -	621,288 17 1		
And for Brandy in said time - -	7,417 1 7¾	628,705 18 8¾	
Received out of Old Excise from 29th Sept. 1690 to the 2nd of Nov. following -	59,649 2 3		
And out of ½ Excise to the 29th of Sept. 1691 - - - -	173,191 7 6¾		
And out of Hereditary and ½ Temporary Excise in said time - -	288,763 13 1¾	521,604 2 11	
Received out of the Additional Excise from the 24th July 1689 to the 29th of Sept. 1690 - - - - -	156,092 5 1½		
And from 29th of Sept. 1690 to the 29th of Sept. 1691 - - -	181,559 16 6¼	337,652 1 7¾	
Received out of Double Excise to the 29th of Sept. 1691 - - - -	—	412,921 4 11	
Received for Low Wines to the said time - - - - - -	—	5,100 0 0	
Received more by Sir Robert Howard by Tallies of Assignment the 11 of Sept. 1691, payable to Her Majesty the Queen Dowager which was not paid the 29th of Sept. 1691 - - -	—	3,072 8 9½	2,585,340 10 3¾
Transported - - - -	—	—	4,870,120 2 6¾

Folio 5.

	£ s. d.	£ s. d.	£ s. d.
Transported - - - -	—	—	4,870,120 2 6¾
Out of Hearth Money, viz.:—			
Remained the 5th of Nov. 1688, in the hands of the Four Tellers of the Exchequer, as appears by accounts before us - - - - - -	2,107 0 0		
And in the hands of Charles Duncomb, Esq., the Cashier - - -	3,816 13 9	5,923 13 9	
Received by the said Charles Duncomb, Esq., to the 3rd of Oct. 1689 - -	33,368 1 5		
And by Thos. Hall, Esq., the Cashier, to Michaelmas 1691 - - -	191,578 3 4¼	224,946 4 9¼	

Payments—*cont.* Folio 4.

	£ s. d.	£ s. d.	£ s. d.
More paid him by Richd. Kent, Esq., being paid to John Pitch, for the fortifications at Hull - - - -	250 0 0	12,307 1 2	
		674,103 7 1¾	
To the Executors of the Duke of Schomberg paid out of the Exchequer for the said Duke's arrears of Salary as Master of the Ordnance - - - -	—	219 17 11	
To the Executors of Christopher Musgrave, Esq., paid out of the Exchequer for the arrears of his Salary, as Clerk of the Deliveries - - - -	—	170 12 6	674,493 17 6¾
Transported - - -	—	—	9,743,434 2 2¼

Memorandum.

Besides the above account there is 48,[illegible]l. 16s. 1d. paid by way of Imprest before, and vacated since the 5th of Nov. 1688. Besides, there is not included what money he hath had from Mr. Russell and Mr. Fox, neither of whose accounts are yet stated.

Folio 6.

Transported - - - - -	—	—	9,743,434 2 2¼
For Secret Service, viz.:—			
To several Secretaries of State. Paid them out of the Exchequer for Intelligences - - - - -	—	12,505 12 0	
To Henry Guy, Esq., as per his voluntary Account before the 5th Nov. 1688 in Folio 13 appears at large £9,551 17 1¼			
More paid him out of the Exchequer from the 5th of Nov. 1688 to the time of William Jephson, Esq. - £7,013 11 5			

House of Lords MSS.

1691.

Folio 5. Receipts—*cont.*

	£ s. d.	£ s. d.	£ s. d.
Received from several Collectors of the same, between the 5th of Nov. 1688, and the 1st of January following, on the behalf of the then Prince of Orange	—	3,206 2 2	234,066 0 1¼
Out of Letter Money, viz.:—			
Remained the 5th of Nov. 1688, in their Majesties' Exchequer - - -	—	485 6 0½	
Received by Stephen Lilly, Esq., Receiver General, viz.:			
From — The 1st of Nov. 1688 to the 25th of March 1689 - - -	28,548 7 9		
The 25th of March 1689 to the 25th of March 1690 - -	75,284 15 5		
The 25th of March 1690 to the 25th of March 1691 - -	73,127 0 10		
The 25th of March 1691 to the 29th of September following -	39,925 14 11	216,885 18 11	
Received from several Post Masters between the 5th of Nov. 1688 and the 1st of January following, on the behalf of the then Prince of Orange - -	—	253 17 2	217,625 2 1½
Out of Small Branches and Casualties, viz.:—			
Tenths.—Remaining in the Exchequer the 5th of Nov. 1688 - - -	48 0 3½		
Received from the 5th of Nov. 1688 to the 29th of Sept. 1691, viz.:			
By Moneys paid into the Exchequer - £17,334 14 8			
By Tallies of Assignment levied - 15,004 11 0	32,339 5 8	32,387 5 11½	
First Fruits. Received as appears by the Account of the Remembrancer of the same - - - - -	16,177 19 10		
More by Sir Robt. Howard's Account in Money and Tallies - -	5,647 2 10	21,825 2 8	
Temporalities. Remaining in the Exchequer the 5th of Nov. 1688, and received from that time to the 29th of Sept. 1691, out of the dioceses of Canterbury and York - - - -	6,301 1 0½		
More received out of the diocese of York, between the 5th of Nov. 1688 and the 1st of January following, on the behalf of the then Prince of Orange - - - -	253 8 7	6,554 9 7½	
Goods seized. Remaining the 5th of Nov. 1688, and received since, as by Account from Sir Robt. Howard - -	—	14,372 1 3	
King's Bench Fines. Remaining in the Exchequer the 5th of Nov. 1688, and since received as by Account from Sir Robert Howard - - - -	—	2,037 5 4½	
	Transported -	77,176 4 10½	3,321,800 4 3½

Payments—*cont.* Folio 6.

HOUSE OF LORDS MSS.

1691.

	£ s. d.	£ s. d.	£ s. d.
Out of which is to be deducted what Mr. Guy paid (by Order from the Lords Commissioners of Irish Affairs) unto and which is charged upon Charles Bertie, Esq., Treasurer of the Ordnance - - 600 0 0 — 7,013 11 5	16,565 8 6½		
More paid him out of the Exchequer from the 3rd July 1691 to the 29th of September following - - -	10,411 11 4		
	26,976 19 10½		
To Wm. Jephson, Esq., as appears by his account - - - - -	242,778 4 8½	269,755 4 7	
		282,258 16 7	
For the Privy Purse, viz.:—			
To James Graham, Esq. - - -	2,253 0 0		
To the Right Honble. Wm. Earl of Portland, besides what his Lordship hath had for the servants of King Charles the Second - - -	76,906 0 0	79,160 0 0	361,418 16 7
For Her Majesty the Queen Regnant. Paid to the 29th of September 1691 -	—	106,550 0 0	
For Plate. Paid to the said 29th of September 1691 - - £38,387 2 4			
For Jewels. Paid to the said 29th of September 1691 - - - 24,092 6 8	62,519 9 0		
For Gardens. Paid to the said 29th of September 1691 - - £34,300 0 0			
For Works. Paid to Thomas Lloyd, Esq., Paymaster, to the said 29th of September 1691, besides what was paid him for the servants of King Charles the Second 125,719 13 8	160,019 13 8	328,339 2 8	
For the Cofferers, viz.:—			329,780 2 8
To Sir Peter Apsely, late Cofferer, for the amount of his voluntary charge as in folio 13 appears at large - -	7,086 18 0		
More out of the Exchequer from the 5th of Nov. 1688 to the 10th of August following - - - -	36,786 18 2¼	43,873 16 2¼	
To the Right Honble. Francis Lord Viscount Newport, out of the Exchequer from the time of his being Cofferer, to the 29th Sept. 1691 - - -	216,615 4 0¼		
More for the amount of his Lordship's voluntary charge, folio 13 - -	819 14 4	217,734 18 4¼	
			261,608 14 6½
	Transported -	—	10,739,290 16 0¾

House of Lords MSS.

1691.

Folio 7. Receipts—*cont.*

	£ s. d.	£ s. d.	£ s. d.
Transported - - - - -	—	—	5,320,809 4 3½
Out of Small Branches and Casualties transported - - - -	—	77,176 15 10½	
Wine Licences, Received from the 5th Nov. 1688 to Lady Day 1691, as by an account from Wm. Young, Gerald Russell and others, Esqrs., the then Commissioners - - - - -	26,624 7 9½		
Received more from Sir Stephen Evance and others the present Commissioners, as by an Account from Sir Robert Howard - - - - -	31,500 0 0		
Received more between the 5th of Nov. 1688, and the 1st of Jany. following, on the behalf of the then Prince of Orange	15 0 0	58,139 7 9½	
4½ per Cent. in the Barbados and Leeward Islands, Received from the 5th Nov. 1688 to Michaelmas 1691 - - -	—	10,830 9 0½	
Fines and Forfeitures in the Barbados, Received from 5 Nov. 1688 to Michaelmas 1691 - - - - - -	—	1,300 0 0	
Alienations, Remaining in the Exchequer the 5th Nov. 1688, as by an Account from Sir Robt. Howard - - -	400 0 0		
Received since, to the 24th of June 1691, as by an Account from the Commissioners - - - - -	9,899 3 4		
Received by Sir Robert Howard, by a Talley of Assignment, since the 24th of June 1691 - - - - -	250 0 0	10,549 3 4	
Post Fines, Received from the 5th of November 1688 to 29th Sept. 1691, as by Sir Robert Howard's Account - - -	—	10,548 18 7	
Duchy of Cornwall, as by Account from the Honble. Wm. Harbord, Esqr., besides the Arrears in the tenants' hands -	—	32,911 3 1½	
Fines of Leases - (Remaining the 5th of Nov. 1688, and received since to the 29th of September 1691, as by Sir Robert Howard's Account -)	—	8,682 17 2	
Rents on Grants -		4,987 18 4½	
Rents of Lands -		696 8 7½	
Sheriffs of Counties - (Received from 5th Nov. 1688 to 29th Sept. 1691, as by Sir Robert Howard's Account - -)	—	3,350 13 9	
Sheriffs of Cities -		231 18 3	
Redemption of Lands		2,000 0 0	
Lands seized - -		0 13 4	
Baronets, Received in money and talleys from the 5th of Nov. 1688 to the 29th Sept. 1691, as by Account from Sir Robert Howard - - - - -	—	5,682 14 10	
Sale of Fee Farm Rents (Received from 5th Nov. 1688 to the 25th of Dec. 1690, as by Sir Robert Howard's Account - -)	—	117 0 6	
Issues of Jurors -		10 0 0	
Compositions - -		14 2 0	
Imprest Money Repaid, Received to the 29th of September 1691 - - -	—	1,271 18 8	

Payments—*cont.* Folio 8.

	£ s. d.	£ s. d.	£ s. d.
Transported - -	—	—	10,702,250 16 0½
To the Treasurers of the Chamber, viz.:—			
Lord Griffin, late Treasurer, out of the Exchequer, from the 5th of Nov. 1688, besides what his Lordship had in his hands at that time, of which no account is yet given - - -	—	3,849 15 0	
Sir Rowland Gwin, the present Treasurer to the 29th of Sept. 1691, besides what he hath had for the servants of King's Charles the Second - -	—	87,184 11 8½	
			91,034 6 8½
For the Wardrobe, viz.:—			
To the Ld. Viscount Preston, late Master thereof - - - - -	—	675 15 3	
To the Right Honble. Ralph Earl of Montague, the present Master of the same, to the 29th of September 1691 -	—	74,856 18 2¼	
		75,532 13 5¼	
For the Robes, viz.:—			
To the Right Honble. Henry Ld. Sidney, late Master thereof, in the time of King Charles the Second, in part of a greater sum due for the service of his said Office, besides what his Lordship had that was given to the inferior servants of the said King Charles - - - - -	5,130 1 3		
To Mons. Zuylestein, the present Master to the 29th of Sept. 1691 - -	11,351 3 0		
		16,481 4 3	
To the Master of the Horse, viz., Monsr. Ouerquerck, besides what he received from the Cofferer by the Establishment of the Household - - -	—	13,000 0 0	
For the Gentlemen and Grooms of the Bedchamber to the 29th of Sept. 1691 - -	—	88,107 10 3¾	
For the Band of Pensioners, to Wm. Smith, Esqr., Paymaster to the 29th of Sept. 1691 - - - - -	—	15,000 0 0	
			143,171 5
For Her Majesty the Queen Consort to the late King James - - - -	—	—	1,332 3 4¾
Transported - -	—	—	10,942,788 14 1¼

House of Lords MSS.

1691.

Folio 7. Receipts—*cont.*

	£ s. d.	£ s. d.	£ s. d.
Profit on Tin Farthings and Half Pence, Received to the 29th of Sept. 1691 -	—	12,685 2 6	
Sale of Woods, Remaining in the Exchequer the 5th of Nov. 1688, as by Sir Robert Howard's Account - -	175 0 0		
Received from said time to the 29th of Sept. 1691, by Philip Riley, Esqr., Surveyor of the Forests South - -	9,539 2 10		
		9,714 2 10	
Forfeitures for Treason, Received to the 29th of Sept. 1691 - - - -	—	308 2 9	
Hanaper Office. Received by Tallies of Assignment to the 29th of Sept. 1691 -	—	111 13 9	
Arrears of Old Taxes, Granted in the two last Reigns, viz.:—			
Remaining in the Exchequer the 5th of Nov. 1688 - - - - -	1,298 1 6¾		
Received from said time, to the 29th of Sept. 1691 - - - - -	1,006 17 6		
		2,304 19 0¾	
Transported - - -	—	260,482 4 1¾	5,321,809 4 3½

Folio 9.

		£ s. d.	£ s. d.	£ s. d.
Transported - - - - -		—	—	5,321,809 4 3½
Out of Small Branches and Casualties transported - - - -		—	260,482 4 1¾	
Receivers General, Received from 5th of Nov. 1688 to 26 June 1691, as by Sir Robert Howard's Account - -		—	800 0 0	
Lotteries - -	Remaining in the Exchequer the 5th Nov. 1688, as by Sir Robt. Howard's Account.	—	857 0 0	
An Interloper -		—	3,161 0 2	
Old Irish Farm -		—	441 13 5	
His Majesty's Dividend of Hudson's Bay - - -		—	150 0 0	
Money paid for Conscience Sake -		—	200 0 0	
4s. per Chaldron on Coals - -		—	2 13 9	
Hackney Coaches -		—	365 4 7	
Benevolence for Redemption of Captives - - -		—	1,958 12 4	
Sir George Downing's Surplus - -		—	0 0 0¾	
Loans remaining the 5th of Nov. 1688, in the Exchequer on several accounts, viz.:—				
Lemuel Kingdome, Esq. - -		8,371 1 0½		
Excise - - - - - -		412 4 2¾		
French Linens and Tobacco - -		19 12 11½		
French Linens - - - - -		317 4 5½		

House of Lords MSS.

1691.

Payments—*cont.*

Folio 8.

	£ s. d.	£ s. d.	£ s. d.

Folio 10.

	£ s. d.	£ s. d.	£ s. d.
Transported - - - -	—	—	10,942,788 14 1
To Ambassadors, Envoys, Residents, and Consuls, viz.:—			
The Right Hon. Earl of Carlingford, Envoy for King James to Spain - - - -	1,000 0 0		
The Marqs. d'Abivile, Envoy from the same to Holland - -	1,300 0 0		
Bevil Skelton, Esq., Envoy from the same, to France - -	1,290 0 0		
John Robinson, Esq., Agent from the same to Sweden - -	457 0 0		
John Stafford, Esq., Envoy from the same to Spain - - -	250 0 0		
Charles Scarborough, Esq., Envoy from the same, to Portugal -	500 0 0	4,797 0 0	
The Right Hon. the Earl of Pembroke, Ambassador to Holland -	3,514 17 0		
The Right Hon. the Ld. Dursley, Envoy to Holland and Plenipotentiary at the Hague - -	7,365 6 0	10,880 3 0	
The Right Hon. the Ld. Paget, Envoy to Germany - -	5,218 4 0		
Hugh Hughes, Esqr., employed in Germany - - - -	558 6 3	5,776 11 0	
Alexr. Stanhope, Esqr., Envoy to Spain - - - -	4,492 15 6		

HOUSE OF LORDS MSS.

1691.

Folio 9. Receipts—*cont.*

	£ s. d.	£ s. d.	£ s. d.
Tobacco and Sugars - - -	176 17 3¼		
Wines and Vinegar - - -	18,156 11 2	21,453 11 10½	
Prizes.—As by the Treasurer's Account of Receipts, from the 1st Nov. 1689 to the 3rd of July 1691, inclusive - -	—	21,715 10 9	
Wrecks at Sea—Remaining in Cash, the 5th of November 1688, at the Exchequer	—	20,760 17 5	332,388 7 9½
	Transported -	—	5,654,107 11 11¾

Folio 11.

Transported - - - -	—	—	5,654,107 11 11¾
By the Voluntary Charges, viz.:—			
Of the Honoble. Wm. Harbord, Esq.:—			
Deduction for one day's pay - -	263 14 0¾		
The Same for 12s. in the Pound - -	12,916 3 8		
Gained by guineas in his account -	4,107 18 10		
Received in Ireland on the account of the Revenue there - - -	11,420 15 0	28,708 11 6¾	

Payments—*cont.*

Folio 10.

	£ s. d.	£ s. d.	£ s. d.
To Andrew Eckart, Esq., Resident at Brussels - - - -	2,191 13 8		
		6,084 9 2	
Wm. Duncombe, Esq., Envoy to Sweden - - - -	—	6,250 6 11	
Robt. Molesworth, Esq., Envoy to Denmark - - - -	—	5,591 1 11	
James Johnson, Esq., Envoy to the Duke of Brandenburgh - -	5,294 2 6		
Gregory King, Esq., sent with the Garter to the said Duke - -	437 4 6		
		5,731 7 0	
The Right Hon. the Ld. Lexington, Envoy to the Duke of Brandenburgh and Ambassador to Spain - - - -	—	4,963 3 0	
Sir William Dutton Colt, Envoy to the Dukes of Brunswick - -	—	5,455 5 6	
Edmd. Pooley, Esqr., Envoy to the Duke of Savoy - - -	—	963 0 0	
Thos. Cox, Esqr., Envoy to the Swiss Cantons - - -	4,738 10 0		
Philip Hervart, Esq., Resident at Geneva - - - -	1,587 8 2		
		6,325 18 2	
Sir Paul Ricaut, Resident at the Hans Towns - - -	—	2,076 18 5	
Jno. Methwyn, Esqr., Envoy to Portugal - - - -	—	955 0	
Sir Thomas St. George, carrying the Garter to the Duke of Zell -	—	300 0 0	
Nathaniel Lodington, Esq., Consul to Tripoli - - - -	—	1,140 0 0	
John Erlisman, Esq., Consul at Algiers - - - -	570 0 0		
Thos. Baker, Esq., Consul at the same - - - - -	1,398 7 0		
		1,968 7 0	
			70,180 11 1
	Transported -	—	11,012,969 5 ¼

Folio 12.

Transported - - - -	—	—	11,012,969 5 2¼
For Salaries to Ministers of State, Judges, Officers, &c. :—			
The Right Hon. the Earl of Sunderland, President of the Council to the late King James	—	375 0 0	
The Right Hon. the Marqs. of Carmarthen, the present President, besides 3,500*l.* p. annum paid till lately out of Secret Service and now out of Letter money - - - -	—	3,166 5 0	

HOUSE OF LORDS MSS.

1691.

Folio 11. Receipts—*cont.*

		£ s. d.	£ s. d.	£ s. d.
Of Charles Fox, Esq. :—				
Gained by guineas, poundage and one day's pay to the 30th of April 1691, as by his account - - - -		5,070 0 3½		
More on said accounts, to 30 Aug. 1691 - - - - -		1,677 11 11½	7,406 12 3	
Of Thomas Coningsby, Esq. :—				
Received of the Revenue in Ireland -		63,831 11 3½		
Profit on Exchange - - - -		867 15 3		
Profit on guineas - - - -		9,945 14 10		
For forfeited goods in Ireland - -		123 12 0		
Brass money of King James's - - -	£12 10 3			
Money of King James's in the Mint - - -	641 10 4¾			
209,220 French Sous Marqs. found in the Treasury, and sold at a halfpenny each piece - - -	435 17 6	1,090 16 1½		
Wool licenses - - - -		554 7 4		
Poundage deducted - - - -		2,243 3 3		
For so much short cast in 40,705 guineas at several rates - - - -		439 12 6	79,006 12 6¾	
Of the respective Treasurers of the Navy, viz. :—				
The Right Honble. Anthony Ld. Faulkland for what remained in his Lordship's hands the 5th Nov. 1688 -		6,976 8 2		
Anthony Sturt, Jun., Esq., cashier to Sir Richd. Haddock and others the Commissioners of the Victualling, remaining with him, 5 Nov. 1688 -		4,010 10 2½		
The Right Hon. Edwd. Russell, Esq., for ships and other materials sold to the 27th March 1691 -	£180 8 0			
More he received for freight of goods brought home in men of war to the 22nd of June 1691 - - -	1,060 6 4	1,240 14 4	12,226 12 8½	
Of the Hon. Charles Bertie, Esq., Treasurer of the Ordnance :—				
Remaining in his cash, the 5th of Nov. 1688 - - - - -		3,486 4 6		
For so much he owns to have received more than Philip Ryley, Esq., chargeth to have paid him, viz.:— He owns to have received £7,395 16 8				
Mr. Ryley chargeth to have paid him but -	6,023 10 0	1,372 6 8		
More received of Henry Guy, Esq., by order from the Lords Commissioners for Irish affairs - - - -		600 0 0		

Payments—*cont.* Folio 12.

	£ s. d.	£ s. d.	£ s. d.
To The Right Hon. the Lords Commissioners of the Great Seal	—	9,505 9 6	
The Rt. Hon. the Marqs. of Halifax and others, Commissioners of the Privy Seal	—	3,567 10 0	
The Rt. Hon. the two Secretaries of State on their old fee of 100*l.*, and their new fee of 1,850*l.* p. ann.	—	9,137 10 0	
The Rt. Hon. the Lords Commrs. of the Treasury	—	21,600 0 0	
Sir John Nicholas (Clerks of the Council)	625 0 0		
Charles Montague, Esq. (Clerks of the Council)	464 18 0		
Richd. Cooling, Esq. (Clerks of the Council)	464 18 0		
Wm. Blathwait, Esq. (Clerks of the Council)	589 18 0		
		2,144 14 0	
Wm. Blathwait, Esq., as attending the Committee of Trade	—	2,779 14 7½	
Benjamin Cooling, Esq. (Door Keepers of the Privy Council)	148 5 0		
Nathaniel Cox, Esq. (Door Keepers of the Privy Council)	148 5 0		
		296 10 0	
The 12 Judges of England	29,390 4 0		
Eleven Masters in Chancery	2,575 0 0		
The Attorney General	183 0 0		
The Solicitor General	137 10 0		
Sir Thos. Pinfold, besides what paid him from the Commrs. of Prizes	45 0 0		
		32,330 14 0	
The Rt. Hon. the Ld. Lovelace, Chief Justice in Eyre	—	333 6 8	
The Rt. Hon. the El. of Macclesfield, as President of the Council of Wales, viz., out of the Exchequer	200 0 0		
More out of the Revenue of South Wales, besides what his Lordship hath had out of North Wales	2,306 13 4		
		2,506 13 4	
Several Welsh Judges and others paid out of South Wales	3,983 3 1		
Sir John Trenchard, Chief Justice of Chester	1,250 0 0		
Littleton Powis, Esq., another Judge of the same Circuit	400 0 0		
		5,633 3 1	
Sir John Trevor, Speaker of the House of Commons	[illegible]35 0 6		

HOUSE OF LORDS MSS.

1691.

Folio 11. Receipts—*cont.*

	£ s. d.	£ s. d.	£ s. d.
More for money lent the Office by the Duke of Schomberg, in the name of Mr. Thomas Goddard, merchant -	1,000 0 0		
More he received of the Patentees for ensuring houses from fire for 2 years ¾ to Midsummer 1691, at 60*l.* per annum - - - - - -	165 0 0	6,023 11 2	
Transported - - -	—	134,182 0 2¼	5,054,197 11 11¼

Folio 13.

	£ s. d.	£ s. d.	£ s. d.
Transported - - - - -	—	—	5,054,197 11 11¼
By the Voluntary Charges transported -	—	134,182 0 2¼	
Of Henry Guy, Esq.:—			
Received before the 5th of Nov. 1688, but most of it paid since upon the account of the late Government -	3,651 17 1¼		
Received more since the 5th of Nov. 1688, as by Mr. Lownde's account, of which Sir Robert Howard takes no notice - - - - - -	5,900 0 0	9,551 17 1¼	
Of the Receiver General of South Wales, as by his account - - - -	—	7,179 13 4¼	
Of Sir Peter Apsely, the Cofferer:—			
Remaining in his hands the 5th of Nov. 1688, as by his account - - -	6,485 16 8		
Received by him of several, as by said account - - - - - -	581 1 4	7,066 18 0	

Payments—*cont.* Folio 12.

	£ s. d.	£ s. d.	£ s. d.
Sergt. Topham attending the Speaker	150 11 3		
The Door-Keepers of the House of Commons	80 0 0	1,135 11 3	
Sergt. Harsnet, attending the Speaker of the House of Lords	366 10 0		
The Door-Keepers of the House of Lords	150 0 0	516 10 0	
Sir Thomas Duppa, Usher of the Black Rod	—	300 0 0	
Sir Charles Cotterel, master of the Ceremonies	900 0 0		
John Dormer, Esq., Deputy Master of the same	365 0 0		
Richard Le Bass, Marshal of the Same	300 0 0		
The seven Sergeant at Arms	1,555 16 3	3,120 16 3	
The Rt. Hon. the Lord Lucas, for safe keeping of Prisoners	1,881 13 9		
Sir Algernon May; for two years' Salary as Keeper of the Records of the Tower	1,000 0 0		
The Rt. Hon. Sir Henry Goodrick, Lieutenant of the Ordnance, besides what paid him out of that office	100 0 0	2,981 13 9	
Transported	—	102,765 7 5½	11,012,969 5 2¼

Folio 14.

Transported	—	—	11,012,969 5 2¼
For Salaries to Ministers of State, Judges, Officers, &c., transported	—	102,765 7 5½	
Symon and Bryan and Mary his wife keepers of Kensington Palace	375 0 0		
Ralph Keine, Esq., his Majesty's Closet Keeper	400 0 0		
John Jones, apothecary to the Household	333 6 8		
The Rt. Hon. the Countess of Monmouth, as Maid of Honour to the Queen Dowager	113 6 8	1,221 13 4	
The Bishop of Salisbury, as Chancellor of the Garter	—	1,368 3 0	
Thomas Shadwell, Esq., Poet Laureate, 2 years' salary	—	600 0 0	
Symon Smith, Otter Hunter	79 2 11		
More to him as Harbinger	524 9 1		

HOUSE OF LORDS MSS.

1691.

Folio 13. Receipts—*cont.*

	£ s. d.	£ s. d.	£ s. d.
Of the Rt. Hon. Francis Ld. Viscount Newport, Present Cofferer.			
Received of several, as by his Lordship's account - - - - - -	—	819 14 4	
Of the Rt. Hon. Wm. Harbord, Esq., in a particular account.			
Received of the Ld. Waldgrave's servant, so much had been collected by the said Lord in the West for Trophy money -	—	250 0 0	
Of Govrn Corbin, remaining in his hands of the Revenue of the Forests North, besides what is in the hands of the Executors of Mr. Corbin - - -	—	20 0 0	130,130 3 8½
By the particular Voluntary Charge of the Right Hon. Richd. El. Ranelagh—			
His Lordship allows as received before the 5th of Nov. 1688, because he brings in his account from the 1st of January preceding, that being the time of his last declared Account.			
By the balance in his Lordship's hands upon the last declared account - -	—	3,065 13 6½	
Received from the Exchequer upon a Privy Seal, the 26th of Jan. 1687-8 -	—	603,104 9 11	
Received more from thence, on another Privy Seal of the 18th of Oct. 1688 -	—	294 11 4	
Received more from Ireland and Scotland, and several other Receivers in England not issued out of the Exchequer - - - - - -	—	20,673 6 8	
		627,068 1 7½	
Out of which must be deducted what Sir Robert Howard makes paid before the 5th of Nov. 1688, but appears, by an Account received from Mr. Lowndes to be paid his Lordship since, as is accordingly charged on him in the Account of the Army - - -	—	12,000 0 0	615,068 1 7½
Transported - - - - -	—	—	6,425,373 16 7½

Payments—*cont.* Folio 14.

	£ s. d.	£ s. d.	£ s. d.
More to him for prosecuting Sir Wm. Doyley's debt - - - - -	35 4 10		
		679 10 10	
Christopher Tanchard, Esq., master of the Harriers - - - - -	—	750 0 0	
Thomas Felton and Wm. Chiffinch, Esqs., masters of the Hawks, on 10s. p. diem, 30s. p. mensem, 100l. p. annum part of the time, and afterwards increased to 800l. per annum - -	—	2,002 0 5½	
Peter Guimon Beaubuisson, keeper of the Bows - - - - -	—	237 7 6	
Philip Ryley, Esq., surveyor of the Forests South - - - - -	929 8 3		
Walter Laycock, surveyor of the Forests North - - - - -	62 10 0		
Col. Wolseley, two years and a half for the Officers of the Forests of Dean -	525 0 0		
John Barnard, Riding Forester in New Forest - - - - -	13 13 0		
		1,530 12 0	
Richard Welbeck, Keeper of the Stables at Reading - - - - -	—	30 10 0	
Thomas Pullen, Esq., Master of the Studs	—	300 0 0	
Sir Christopher Wren, Surveyor of the Works - - - - -	—	22 16 5	
John Fitch, Esq., Master Worker of the Fortifications - - - -	—	130 0 0	
John How, Esq., Keeper of the Pall Mall - - - - -	—	200 0 0	
Col. Edwd. Stead, Governor of Barbados	1,380 0 7½		
Isaac Richier, Esq., Governor of Bermuda - - - - -	120 0 0		
		1,500 0 7½	
The Master of the Rolls, on a Fee of 10l. p. ann., and 27l. 4s. 7d. for 2 Chaplains	—	111 13 9	
Solomon Foubert, Esq., in part, as Equerry Extraordinary to King Charles the 2nd - - - -	—	180 5 4	
The Countess of Newbourg, for the rent of Bagshot Park - - - -	—	25 0 0	
Bernard Greenvile, Esq., rent for Moore Park - - - - -	—	75 0 0	
The Rt. Hon. Sir John Earnley, as Chancellor, and Under Treasurer of the Exchequer - - - - -	—	100 0 0	
The Rt. Hon. Richd. Hampden, Esq. Chancellor and Under Treasurer of the same - - - - -	—	200 0 0	
Transported - - - -	—	115,135 16 5¾	11,018,969 5 2¼

Folio 15. Receipts—*cont.*

	£ s. d.	£ s. d.	£ s. d.
Transported	—	—	6,428,373 16 7½
From the several following Aids, viz.:—			
Of the 6/ms or Present Aid (To 29 Sept. 1691)	—	400,657 6 9½	
1st Poll	—	255,396 14 10½	
Review of the said Poll, and Additional Poll	—	21,692 13 1½	
1st 12d. Aid	—	404,073 9 7	
2nd Poll	—	234,120 15 9½	
3s Aid	—	906,172 13 2¼	
Additional 12d.	—	406,086 5 8¾	
12/ms Tax	—	733,369 16 0	3,083,449 15 6¾
By the Public Loans to their Majesties, viz.:—			
On French Linens and Tobaccos	—	35,800 0 0	
New Impositions to pay the Dutch	—	120,000 0 0	
Customs in General, by Thos. Fox, Esq.	50,000 0 0		
By the Ld. Lumley	3,000 0 0		
⅔ Custom	500,000 0 0		
⅓ Custom, by Thos. Fox, Esq.	20,000 0 0	573,000 0 0	
Excise in General, by the Citizens of London	185,675 0 0		
½ Temporary Excise	250,000 0 0		
Hereditary and ½ Temporary Excise	240,670 17 1		
By Whitfeild Hayter	40,000 0 0		
Scawen and Cornish	26,458 6 3		
Charles Duncomb, Esq.	20,000 0 0		
Earl of Montague	7,000 0 0		
Reiliff Cratchrood and other Clothiers	8,500 1 0	787,304 4 4	
On Hearth Money	15,000 0 0		
Letter Money	21,300 0 0		
Duchy of Cornwall	2,300 0 0		
By Sir Boucher Wray	300 0 0		
Jno. Black and other Clothiers	350 0 0		
On Exchequer in General £237,023 13 10½; Wine Licences 30,000 0 0	267,023 13 10½	267,675 13 10½	

Besides 3,500*l.* which Mr. Twitty saith was borrowed more on the Exchequer in General, and that the whole of that debt was repaid with interest, though Sir Robert Howard chargeth nothing thereof as paid, either principal or interest.

Payments—*cont.* Folio 16.

		£	s.	d.	£	s.	d.	£	s.	d.
	Transported	—			115,133	16	5¾	11,012,960	5	2½
For Salaries, Incident Bills, and Taxes for Commissioners and Inferior Offices of Several Branches of the Revenue, viz.:—										
Of	Customs	140,204	5	11½						
	Excise	72,184	4	2¾						
	Letter Money	27,060	16	4						
	Hearth Money	7,867	5	4¾						
Small Branches, viz.:—										
Of	Alienation Office	2,787	1	6						
	First Fruits	715	4	0						
	Wine Licences	5,846	10	1						
	Duchy of Cornwall; Pensions there included	15,719	8	9						
	Receivers of South Wales	889	16	11½						
	Survey of the Forests South	960	9	8						
					274,996	11	10½			
For Salaries, Incidents, &c. of the Exchequer Officers, viz.:—										
To	Baron Bradbury	345	0	0						
	Sir Robert Howard	1,320	8	4						
	Auditor Auldworth	1,050	0	0						
	Auditor Bridges	1,093	6	8						
	Auditor Done	333	6	8						
	Auditor Thales, viz.—600*l.* charged by Sir Robert Howard, and 400*l.* which is not charged by him	1,000	0	0						
	The Hon. Wm. Harbord, Esq.	1,200	0	0						
	Agents for Taxes	2,004	7	1						
	Several Receivers of Taxes in Reward	6,404	10	2						
	Sir John Osburn, Treasurer Remembrancer	246	17	3½						
	Geo. Backwell and Jno. Taylor, Secondaries there	93	13	4						
	Arnold Squib, Clerk of the Nitches	50	0	0						
	Sir Nicholas Steward, Jno. Loo, Pr. Le Neeve, and Philip Hillard, Esqrs., besides what paid them, together with the Officers of the Receipt	462	3	4						
	Mr. Jno. Packer, Usher of the Receipts	4,821	17	8½						
	Wm. Parks, Porter of the same	55	0	0						
	Officers, Clerks, and Ministers of the Receipt	1,874	3	8						
	Messengers	3,918	10	8						

HOUSE OF LORDS MSS.

1691.

Folio 15. Receipts—*cont.*

		£ s. d.	£ s. d.	£ s. d.
On	8/ms or Present Aid - - -	373,775 13 2		
	1st Poll - - - -	238,283 9 7		
	1st 12d. Aid - - - -	771,113 10 0¾		
	2s Aid - - - - -	602,432 0 6¾		
	Additional Aid - - -	430,751 18 2		
	2nd Poll - - - -	65,000 0 0	2,481,356 11 6	
	The 12/ms Tax to 28 Sept. 1691 -	1,534,732 14 9		
	New Impositions on Silks and East India Goods - - -	306,550 9 10		
	Continued Impositions - -	700,100 0 0		
	½ Additional Excise - - -	995,225 0 2½	3,536,608 4 9½	7,883,704 14 6
		Transported -	—	17,997,530 6 7¾

Folio 17.

	£ s. d.	£ s. d.	£ s. d.
Transported - - - - -	—	—	17,997,530 6 7¾
Of George Kaynton, Esq. for what he had formerly received for the Servants of King Charles the Second - -	—	20,000 0 0	
By the following Credits, viz.:—			
Philip Ryley, Esq., Surveyor of the Forests South, the balance of his account overpaid - - - -	84 15 7		
Richard Kent, Esq., Receiver General of the Customs, due to him for the balance of his account overpaid - -	971 0 4	1,055 15 11	21,055 15 11
	Transported -	—	18,018,586 2 6¾

Payments—*cont.* Folio 16.

	£ s. d.	£ s. d.	£ s. d.
Jno. Walker, Usher of the Exchequer - - - -	2,799 17 9		
Thos. Cole and Walter Wallinghar, Secondaries - - - -	40 0 0		
Wm. Warder, Esq., Clerk of the Pells - - - - -	654 0 0		
Jno. Pottinger, Comptroller of the Pipe - - - - -	120 0 0		
Serjt. Ryley - - - -	301 2 0		
Jno. Aysley, Clerk of the Talley Court - - - -	5 0 0		
The Officers of the Talley Court -	830 10 6		
Timothy Whitfeild, Clerk of the Estreats - - - -	145 0 0		
Robt. Russell, Esq., Clerk of the Pipe - - - - -	134 0 2½		
Jno. Hastings, Clerk of the Foreign Estreats - - - -	96 13 4		
Jno. Norrice, Serjt. - - -	39 3 4		
Henry Villars, Serjt. - -	39 3 4		
Henry Ayliff, Esq., the King's Remembrancer - - -	1,273 5 0		
Wm. East, Clerk of Estreats at the Common Pleas- - -	55 0 0		
		35,215 0 4½	425,317 8 8¾
For Debentures, Portage Bills, Allowances, &c., at Custom House.			
Paid from the 5th of Nov. 1688 to the 29th of Sept. 1691 - - - -	240,177 5 5		
More to Mr. Thrale, to defray the charge of the Duty of 4½ p. ct. - -	2,093 2 2		
		242,270 7 7	
For the Charges of the Packet Boats -	—	25,421 10 7	
			267,691 18 2
	Transported -	—	11,706,008 12 1

Folio 18.

Transported - - - -	—	—	11,706,008 12 1
For Pensions and Annuities, viz.:—			
To Her Majesty, the Queen Dowager, out of Excise - - - - -	38,076 16 8½		
More out of Letter Money - - -	1,700 0 0		
More out of Loan on Q(ueen)'s Aid - -	4,500 0 0		
More out of Duchy of Cornwall - -	1,500 0 0		
More as by Sir Robt. Howard's account, 11 Sept. 1691, by a tally on the Excise though not actually paid the 29th of said September - - - -	3,052 8 9½		
		48,829 5 6	

House of Lords MSS.

1691.

Folio 17. Receipts—*cont.*

	£ s. d.	£ s. d.	£ s. d.
Memorandum. Whereas Mr. Kent's Money above is brought in to be as a credit to him, yet, in the Weekly accounts of the Customs, it appears that he was possessed of several Bills of Exchange to a greater sum, which was not delivered over to Thomas Fox, Esq., his successor.			

Payments—*cont.* Folio 18.

	£ s. d.	£ s. d.	£ s. d.
To Their Royal Highnesses the Prince and Princess Ann of Denmark -	—	124,000 0 0	
To The Duke of Southampton - -	—	3,425 0 0	
To The Duke of Grafton and Duchess	—	13,900 0 0	
To The Duke of Northumberland -	—	6,750 0 0	
To The Duke of Norfolk - -	—	1,500 0 0	
To The Duke of Ormond, besides what his Grace had out of Secret Service and privy purse - -	—	625 0 0	
To The Duke of Schomberg - -	—	4,000 0 0	
To The Duchess of Richmond and Lennox - - - -	—	520 0 0	
To The Duchess of Buccleugh, besides 5,336*l.* out of Secret Service -	—	15,084 0 0	
To The Duchess of Cleveland - -	—	4,700 0 0	
To the Earls of Bath, besides 3,000*l.* per annum paid his Lordship out of the Duchy of Cornwall -	—	12,750 0 0	
To the Earls of Derby, for Preachers in the Isle of Man - - -	—	300 0 0	
To the Earls of Litchfield - - -	—	300 0 0	
To the Earls of Oxford - - - -	—	5,500 0 0	
To the Earls of Peterborough - - -	—	200 0 0	
To the Earls of Rochester - - -	—	5,200 0 0	
To the Earls of Sunderland - - -	—	2,750 0 0	
To the Earls of Warrington, besides what his Lordship had out of Secret Service - - - -	—	1,000 0 0	
To the Counts of Bristol - - - -	—	5,500 0 0	
To the Counts Marshall - - - -	—	300 0 0	
To the Counts of Plymouth - - -	—	8,150 0 0	
To the Counts of Portland - - -	—	1,090 0 0	
To the Lord Chenie - - - -	—	600 0 0	
To the Lady Barham Allhone and Richd. Graham, Esq., for her - -	—	187 10 0	
To the Lady Mary Howard's Executors -	—	650 0 0	
To the Lady Price - - - -	—	200 0 0	
To Sir Wm. Killigrew - - -	—	1,500 0 0	
To Sir Thomas Windham, on 600*l.* per annum - - - -	—	3,000 0 0	
To Sir Saml. Morland & Son - -	—	250 0 0	
To Wm. Dockwra, Esq. - - -	—	60 0 0	
To Gregory Alford - - -	—	60 0 0	
To Ann Baker - - - -	—	350 0 0	
To Dr. Braddy - - - -	—	40 0 0	
To Robt. Bertie - - - -	—	130 0 0	
To Ludowick Bray - - -	—	110 0 0	
To Jane Browning - - -	—	90 0 0	
	Transported -	275,160 15 0	11,706,008 12 1

House of Lords MSS.

1691.

Folio 19. Receipts—*cont.*

	£ s. d.	£ s. d.	£ s. d.
Transported - - - - -	—	—	18,018,586 2 6¼

Payments—*cont.* Folio 20.

		£ s. d.	£ s. d.	£ s. d.
	Transported - - - - -	—	—	11,706,006 12 1
	For Pensions and Annuities transported -	—	273,160 15 6	
To	Samuel Clerk, Esq., or, 300*l.* per annum - - - -	—	823 0 0	
	Daniel Child - - - -	—	32 5 0	
	Joan and Ann Ellesden - -	—	150 0 0	
	Eliza Elliot - - - -	—	300 0 0	
	Thomas Fairfax - - -	—	80 0 0	
	Ann Goulding - - -	—	220 0 0	
	Charles Gifford - - -	—	375 0 0	
	George Gunter - - -	—	150 0 0	
	Dr. Gibbon - - - -	—	225 0 0	
	Mrs. Hamilton and her Children -	—	3,712 10 0	
	Amias and Juliana Hext - -	—	550 0 0	
	Wm. Levett - - - -	—	450 0 0	
	Ann Lawson - - - -	—	412 10 0	
	Charles Mansel - - -	—	150 0 0	
	Nicos. Needham - - -	—	120 0 0	
	Francis Reynolds - - -	—	150 0 0	
	John and Ann Rogers - -	—	60 0 0	
	Dr. Sherlock, Master of the Temple	—	93 6 8	
	George Tuthill - - -	—	225 0 0	
	Rachel and Francis Windham -	—	700 0 0	
	Nicholas Yates - - -	—	225 0 0	
	Cambridge University and Emanuel College - - - -	170 0 0		
	Margaret Professor at Oxford -	50 0 0		
	Reader of the Civil Law at Cambridge - - - -	130 0 0		
	Eaton College - - -	126 0 0		
	Southwell School - - -	30 0 0		
	Lancashire Preachers to the Bp. of Chester - - - -	100 0 0		
	Dean and Chapter of Westminster, for the Savoy French Ministers -	240 0 0		
	The Vicar of the Tower - -	56 13 4		
	The Vicar of Lichfield, besides what is paid out of the Duchy of Cornwall - - - -	45 0 0		
			947 13 4	
To the Poor.	Of St. Magnus Parish - -	63 14 0		
	" St. Michael, Cornhill - -	30 10 0		
	" St. John the Baptist, Walbrook	7 13 4		
	" St. Botolph, Aldgate - -	26 15 0		
	" St. James, Westminster - -	150 0 0		

Folio 19. Receipts—*cont.*

	£ s. d.	£ s. d.	£ s. d.

Folio 21.

	£ s. d.	£ s. d.	£ s. d.
Transported from folio 17 - -	—	—	18,028,586 2 6½

Payments—*cont.* Folio 20.

	£ s. d.	£ s. d.	£ s. d.
Of St. Martin's - - -	300 0 0		
„ St. Margaret's Westminster, and King Charles the 2nd Hospital - - - -	200 0 0	888 12 4	
To Christ Church Hospital, for the Mathematical School - -	—	1,111 10 0	
To the Corporation Of Berwick - - - -	200 0 0		
„ Dartmouth - - -	120 0 0		
„ Hull - - - -	18 0 0		
„ Lyme - - - -	250 0 0		
„ London - - - -	193 4 0		
„ Yarmouth - - - -	480 0 0	1,261 4 0	198,335 6 10
	Transported -	—	11,204,543 18 11

Memorandum.

There are some Questions to about 3,600*l*. concerning three or four of these pensions, which cannot yet be cleared.

Folio 22.

Transported - - - - -	—	—	11,204,543 18 11
For Parks and Forests, viz.:—			
To Wm. Clerk, for Hay for the Deer at Windsor Forest - - -	60 0 0		
To Robert White, for the same at New Park - - - - -	1,750 0 0		
To Wm. Harbord, Esq., for St. James's Park - - - - -	500 0 0	2,310 0 0	
For Prosecution of Law Suits, viz.:—			
To Philip Burton and Richard Graham, Esq. - - - -	631 4 6		
To Aaron Smith, Esq. - - -	5,200 0 0		
To Samuel Hemming for discovering Rents - - - -	74 0 0	5,905 4 6	
For the Mint, viz.:—			
To Thomas Neal, Esq., the Master Worker - - - -	18,000 0 0		
To Philip and Joseph Rotiers the two Gravers - - - -	1,125 0 0		
To the Commissioners for making and coining Tin farthings and halfpence - -	3,942 11 3	23,067 11 3	
To the Commissioners of Accounts and George Tolici, Esq., to Michaelmas 1691 -	—	4,850 0 0	

House of Lords MSS.

1691.

Folio 21. Receipts—*cont.*

	£ s. d.	£ s. d.	£ s. d.

Payments—*cont.* Folio 22.

	£ s. d.	£ s. d.	£ s. d.
For Gifts and Charges for Services, viz.:—			
To James Spratt - - - -	100 0 0		
Derick Stort - - - -	92 10 0		
Henry Killigrew, Esq. - -	500 0 0		
Carol du Lysle - - -	419 12 0		
The Earl of Bath, for two Journeys	500 0 0		
Several Baronets each 1,095*l.* -	5,475 0 0		
Sir Scroop How - - -	2,000 0 0		
Dr. Wake - - - -	600 0 0		
Lady Montroth [Montrose?] -	300 0 0		
Thomas Pottinger - - -	50 0 0		
Susannah Woozencroft and eight others - - - -	320 0 0		
Eleanor Needham - - -	75 0 0		
James Clifton and Ambrose Holland, for discovering Highwaymen - - - - -	20 0 0		
Col. George King and Lieut. George Murrel - - -	100 0 0		
French Protestants - - -	3,000 0 0		
Thos. Howard, Esq., for Mr. Kingsmill* - - - -	50 0 0		
The Ladies Coot, Shane and Bartley	250 0 0		
George Barrel, Charnock Heron, Percival Brumskil, and Wm. Parsley - - - -	100 0 0		
Christr. Gibbon, Joseph Teron, Lady Newcomen, and Joseph Whitle - - - -	80 0 0		
Sir Pr. Rich, Chamberlain of London, Soliciting and receiving loans - - - - -	500 0 0		
Leonard Robinson, Esq., the same, his reward and charges - -	2,898 11 1		
	17,314 13 1		
To the Hanaper Office, Paid into the same, out of Alienations - - - -	5,479 17 0	22,794 10 1	56,297 5 10
For Redemption of Captives, Paid to Robert Squib, Esq. - - - -	—	—	500 0 0
To Several Receivers and Accountants for Surplusages due to them - - -	—	—	7,467 13 3½
By Defalcations to the Farmers of the Post Fines - - - - -	—	—	10,543 18 7
	Transported -	—	12,069,397 16 7¼

* See Grey's Debates, 3 Dec. 1691.

House of Lords MSS.

1691.

Folio 23. Receipts—*cont.*

	£ *s.* *d.*	£ *s.* *d.*	£ *s.* *d.*
Transported from folio 17 - -	—	—	18,019,586 2 0¾

Payments—*cont.* Folio 24.

		£ s. d.	£ s. d.	£ s. d.
Transported		—	—	12,009,287 10 7½
For the Servants of King Charles the Second		—	—	50,890 14 3½
To the States General of the United Provinces		—	—	600,000 0 0
For the Service of His Highness the Prince of Orange in the West and North between the 5th of Nov. and the 1st of January following, viz.:—				
To Joseph Bosoo, carrying Ordnance from Exeter		284 13 0		
To Col. Gibson carrying the Artillery		200 0 0		
			484 13 0	
To several out of Deviated Customs		16,117 2 11½		
" Deviated Excise		11,284 11 8½		
" Deviated Hearth Money		3,596 2 2		
" Deviated Letter Money		253 17 2		
" Deviated Small Branches:—				
Temporalities	£253 8 7			
Wine Licences	15 0 0			
Deviated Voluntary for charge:—				
Trophies	£50 0 0			
		318 8 7		
			31,570 2 7	
				32,054 15 7
For Interest on Several Loans, viz.:—				
To Richard Kent, Esqr. on the Customs		473 8 3		
To Thomas Fox, Esqr., on the same		4,134 12 6		
To Lord Lumley		250 0 0		
To Several on Letter Money		647 9 7		
To Several on French Linens and Tobacco		3,784 9 3½		
To Charles Duncomb, Esqr.		2,223 6 6¾		
To Sir Peter Rich for the Citizens Loan of 185,875*l.*		8,069 13 9½		
To Whitfield Hayter on 40,000*l.*		488 4 3½		
To Scawen and Cornish on 26,458*l.* 6*s.* 3*d.*		402 15 3		
To Cratchrood and other Clothiers		300 7 10¼		
To Bankers and their Assignees		828 11 2		
To Lenders on the Hereditary and Temporary Excise		7,255 10 6		
To Commissioners of Excise for their Loan to the Dutch		1 296 3 2¾		
To Lenders of Hearth Money 13,000*l.*		1 307 13 7		
To Several for Interest paid out of small branches, though no mention made to whom, or for what sum paid		20 8 6		

House of Lords MSS.

1691.

Folio 23. Receipts—*cont.*

	£ s. d.	£ s. d.	£ s. d.

Folio 25.

Transported from Folio 17 - -	—	—	18,018,386 2 6½

HOUSE OF LORDS MSS.

1691.

Payments—*cont.* Folio 24.

	£ s. d.	£ s. d.	£ s. d.
Monsr. Vansittars, out of Low Wines, though no mentioning for what - - - -	909 16 0		
Joseph and Nathaniel Horneby -	1,037 8 2		
Sir Basil Firebrace, Interest and Discount - - - -	89 1 2		
Samuel Heron - - - -	545 16 8		
		34,812 16 5¾	
On 6/ms, or Present Aid - -	4,095 19 8		
On First Poll - - - -	1,838 9 0		
On First 12d. aid - - -	14,618 8 4		
On 2 sh Aid - - - -	23,695 9 8		
On Additional 12d. - - -	14,571 14 4		
On Second Poll - - - -	42 18 0		
On Continued Imposts - - -	14,201 16 2		
		73,064 15 2	
			107,877 11 7¾
	Transported -	—	12,909,200 18 1½

Folio 26.

Transported - - - -	—	—	12,869,200 18 1½
For Loans of Money lent before the Revolution, viz.:—			
To Richard Kent, Esq. - - -	—	15,000 0 0	
To Charles Duncomb, Esq. - -	—	20,000 0 0	
To Joseph and Nathaniel Horneby -	—	25,000 0 0	
To Citizens of London - - -	—	272 7 5	
To The Lenders on the Register on French Linens and Tobacco -	—	83,412 19 9	
To Commissioners of Wine Licenses -	—	12,628 11 11	
			156,313 19 1
For Repayment of Loans to the present Government:—			
The Lenders on French Linens and Tobacco - - - -	—	35,800 0 0	
The same on Excise by Sir Pr. Rich and others - - -	—	185,675 0 0	
Whitfield Hayter - - -	—	40,000 0 0	
Seawen and Cornish - - -	—	20,458 6 3	
Charles Duncomb, Esq. - -	—	90,000 0 0	
The Earl of Montague - -	—	7,000 0 0	
Crutchroad and others - -	—	8,500 1 5	
The Lenders on the New Impositions to pay the Dutch - -	—	150,000 0 0	

House of Lords MSS.

1691.

Folio 25. Receipts—*cont.*

	£ s. d.	£ s. d.	£ s. d.

Folio 27.

Transported from Folio 17 - -	—	—	18,018,586 2 6¾
To Balance this account there is more paid than received - - -	—	—	1,816 19 11¼
Which is supposed to happen in the difference between the Tallies given to pay money and the money actually paid upon the Revenue before it comes into the Exchequer.			18,020,403 2 6

(Signed)
Benjamin Newland (L.S.)
Sam. Barnardiston (L.S.)
P. Colleton (L.S.)

Payments—*cont.* Folio 26.

	£ s. d.	£ s. d.	£ s. d.
To The same on the Hereditary and Temporary Excise - - -	—	174,670 17 1	
To The same on the ½ Temporary Excise - - - - -	—	163,038 1 1	
To The same on Wine Licenses -	—	30,000 0 0	
To The same on the Duty of Hearth Money - - - -	—	15,000 0 0	
To The same on the Duchy of Cornwall - - - - -	—	2,500 0 0	
To The same on Letter Money -	—	21,800 0 0	
To Sir Boucher Wray - - -	—	500 0 0	
To The Ld. Lumley, on Customs -	—	3,000 0 0	
To Thos. Fox, Esq., on Customs -	—	20,000 0 0	
To Jno. Black and others - -	—	250 0 0	
To the Lenders on the 6/ms, or present Aid - -	373,775 13 2		
To the Lenders on the First Poll -	228,223 9 7		
To the Lenders on the First 12d. Aid -	771,113 10 0½		
To the Lenders on the 2s Aid - -	692,451 19 6½		
To the Lenders on the Additional 12d. -	450,751 18 2		
To the Lenders on the Second Poll -	65,000 0 0	2,581,316 10 6	
Memorandum.			
Mr. Lowndes makes 30,000*l.* borrowed of Thos. Fox, Esq., cashier of the Customs, and most of it repaid, but Sir Robt. Howard takes no notice thereof, now Mr. Fox, except to allow himself the Interest.			
Further, Mr. Twitty saith, paid on Exchequer in general 271,122*l.* 13*s.* 10½*d.*, besides Interest but no more appears in account than to Capt. Ingram - -	—	5,000 0 0	
To the Lenders on Continued Imposts, Principal - - - - -	—	500 0 0	
Transported - - - -	—	3,411,008 15 11	13,025,514 17 2½

Folio 28.

	£ s. d.	£ s. d.	£ s. d.
Transported - - - -	—	—	13,025,514 17 2½
For repayment of Loans to the Present Government transported - -	—	3,411,008 15 11	
For Repayment of Principal and Interest on Several Loans mixed, which the Commissioners have not yet had time to separate, viz.:—			
To the Lenders On ½ Custom - - -	207,934 15 4		
To the Lenders East India Goods - -	97,174 1 9		
To the Lenders ⅔ Additional Excise - -	37,381 11 1		
To the Lenders Land Tax - - -	832,907 16 5		

HOUSE OF LORDS MSS.

1691.

Folio 27. Receipts—*cont.*

	£ s. d.	£ s. d.	£ s. d.
Ro. Harley (L.S.)			
P. Rich (L.S.)			
Tho. Clarges (L.S.)			
Paul Foley (L.S.)			
Robt. Austen (L.S.)			

Folio 29. AN ABSTRACT of the PRECEDING

Receipts.	£ s. d.	£ s. d.
Customs and Coinage - - - - Folio 1	1,479,764 9 2	
New Impositions - - - - Folio 3	805,006 2 6¾	2,284,770 11 8¾
Excise: From all the several parts thereof Folio 3	—	2,586,309 10 3¾

Payments—*cont.* Folio 28.

	£ s. d.	£ s. d.	£ s. d.
On account of the several 12th Aids, paid more than the First Principal borrowed, with Interest, comes to, in satisfaction of their Loans being transferred to those Funds - - -	151,522 4 1	1,380,199 8 8½	4,791,249 4 7¼
For the Account of Prizes, Paid by and to the Commissioners thereof, as by the Treasurer's Account thereof appears, viz.:—			
Paid: John Dyve, Esq. - - -	—	2,065 6 0	
For Salaries - - -	—	11,253 15 4	
For Salaries and Incidents mixed - - - -	—	2,798 7 5	
For Fees to the Office of the Admiralty - - -	—	1,448 19 2	
To Mr. Middleton - -	—	75 0 0	
To Dr. Oxenden, the Civilian -	—	50 0 0	
For Freights - - -	—	938 6 10	
For Rewards 50*l.* and other Incidents 1,810*l.* 5*s.* - -	—	1,860 5 0	
To Wm. Jepson, Esq. - -	—	300 0 0	
To the Ship Gift - - -	—	200 0 0	21,038 19 9
			17,837,783 1 7
1691, Sept. 29th. *Resting in the Exchequer and with the Persons following*, viz.:—	--	—	182,620 0 11
			18,020,403 2 6
Exchequer - - - - -	63,152 5 4¾		
Receiver of the Excise - - -	37,485 5 0		
Thos. Fox, Esq., Receiver of the Customs on the balance of his Account - -	75,423 12 0		
Receivers of the Hearth Money - -	164 14 7½		
Receivers of Cornwall - - -	2,451 5 7		
Alienation Office - - - -	252 4 10		
Receiver of the First Fruits - -	157 3 4		
Commissioners of Wine Licenses - -	1,475 8 8		
Receivers of Wood Sales - - -	1,281 10 6		
The Treasurer to the Commrs. of Prizes -	696 11 0		
Mr. Gowen Corbin, on account of the Revenue of the Forests North - -	50 0 0		
	182,620 0 11		

Receipts and Payments. Folio 30.

Payments.		£ s. d.	£ s. d.
For the Army - - - - -	Folio 2	4,948,902 16 7¼	
For the Navy - - - - -	Folio 4	3,106,027 8 0½	
For the Ordinance - - - -	Folio 6	674,403 17 6¾	8,719,434 2 2¼

House of Lords MSS.

1691.

Folio 29. Receipts—*cont.*

			£ s. d.	£ s. d.
Out of	Hearth Money	Folio 5	—	234,036 6 1½
	Letter Money	Folio 5	—	217,025 2 1½
	Small Branches and Casualties	Folio 9	—	332,288 7 8¾
	Voluntary Charges	Folio 13	159,120 3 0½	
	The Particular Voluntary Charge of the Earl of Ranelagh		615,058 1 7¼	774,178 4 7¾
	The several Aids	Folio 15	—	5,683,419 15 6¾
	The several Loans	Folio 15	—	7,885,704 14 6
Of George Bayntoo, Esq.: Repaid what formerly paid him for the Servants of King Charles the Second		Folio 17	90,000 0 0	
By Credits for over-payments of Accountants		Folio 17	1,655 15 11	91,655 15 11
				18,018,586 2 6¾

House of Lords MSS.

1691.

Payments—*cont.* Folio 30.

	£ s. d.	£ s. d.	£ s. d.
For the Civil List, viz.:—			
Secret Service and Privy Purse - -	Folio 6	361,418 16 7	
Her Majesty - - - Folio 6	106,250 0 0		
Plate and Jewels, Work and Gardens -	223,539 2 8		
		329,789 2 8	
Cofferers - - - - -	Folio 6	281,608 14 7¼	
Treasurers of the Chamber - -	Folio 8	91,634 6 8½	
Wardrobe - - - - -	Folio 8	75,532 13 5½	
Robes - - - - -	Folio 8	16,481 4 3	
Master of the Horse, besides what in the Establishment of the Household - - - - - -	Folio 8	13,660 0 0	
Gentlemen and Grooms of the Bedchamber - - - - -	Folio 8	28,107 10 3¾	
Band of Pensioners - - - -	Folio 8	15,000 0 0	
Queen Consort to the late King James -	Folio 8	1,332 3 4¼	
Ambassadors, Envoys, Residents and Consuls - - - - -	Folio 10	70,180 11 1	
Salaries to Ministers of State, Judges, Officers managing the Revenue, Exchequer Officers, &c. - - -	Folio 16	422,347 8 8½	
Pensions and Annuities - - -	Folio 20	288,535 6 10	
Mint and Commissioners of Tin Farthings Folio 22	23,067 11 3		
Parks and Forests - - Folio 22	2,310 0 0		
Prosecution of Law Suits - Folio 22	5,935 4 6		
Commissioners of Accounts - Folio 22	4,250 0 0		
Bounties and Charges for Services and the Hamper - - - Folio 22	20,794 10 1		
	56,357 5 10		
Defalcations to Farmers of Post Fines Folio 22	10,548 18 7		
		66,906 4 5	
		2,044,294 2 11¾	
Debentures, Portage Bills and Allowances on Customs and Charges on Packet Boats - - - - -	Folio 16	267,691 18 2	
			2,311,986 1 1¾
For Extraordinaries, viz.:—			
Loans in the late King James's time -	Folio 20	136,313 19 1	
Servants of King Charles the Second -	Folio 24	59,880 14 5¼	
States General - - - -	Folio 24	600,000 0 0	
Service of the Prince of Orange in the west and north - - - -	Folio 24	32,064 15 7	
Charges on Prizes - - - -	Folio 28	21,018 19 9	
Surplus of Receiver's Accounts - -	Folio 22	7,467 13 3½	
Redemption of Captives - - -	Folio 22	500 0 0	
Interest of Loans - - - -	Folio 24	107,877 11 7½	
			985,113 13 7½
or Loans, with the Interest mixed and undistinguished - - - Folio 28	—	—	4,791,289 4 7½
			17,537,783 1 7

House of Lords MSS.
1691.

Folio 31. Receipts—*cont.*

	£ s. d.	£ s. d.

Payments—*cont.* Folio 32.

	£ s. d.	£ s. d.
An Account prepared by Wm. Jephson, Esq., while living, and after his death, delivered to us by Robt. Squib, Esq., of Pensions, Salaries and Bounties, Paid out of Secret Service Money to Members of Parliament, viz.:		
To Henry Powle, Esq., Speaker of the House of Commons, on his allowance - - - -	1,575 0 0	
To Sir Jno. Trevor, for equipage and allowance as Speaker - - - - - -	2,465 0 0	
To The late Duke Schomberg, Free Gift - -	3,000 0 0	
To The Duke of Ormond, Free Gift, and on Pension of 2,500*l.* - - - - - - -	5,690 17 0	
To Capt. Philip Howard, Free Gift and on Pension of 130*l.* - - - - - - -	1,660 0 0	
To Philip Darcey, Esq., Free Gift - - -	200 0 0	
To John Lord Culpeper, Bounty - - - -	100 0 0	
To Thomas Lord Morley and Monteagle, Bounty -	400 0 0	
To Lord Willoughby of Parham, Bounty - -	350 0 0	
To Ralph Lord Eure, Bounty - - - -	100 0 0	
To Marqs. of Carmarthen, on a Pension of 3,500*l.* per annum - - - - - -	3,873 19 0	
To Thomas Howard, Esq., for himself, besides what he received for Mr. Kingsmill - - - -	100 0 0	
To Earl of Oxford, Free Gift - - - -	4,000 0 0	
To Sir Henry Fane, Free Gift - - - -	400 0 0	
To The Earl of Warrington, Bounty - - -	500 0 0	
To Sir Charles Porter, for his Equipage into Ireland -	1,000 0 0	
To Sir John Lowther, of Lowther - - -	600 0 0	
To Thomas Frankland, Esq. - - - -	800 0 0	26,814 16 0
More paid by Henry Guy, Esq., out of Secret Service—		
To Henry Powle, Esq., Speaker - - - -	140 0 0	
More paid out of Privy Purse—		
To The Lord Fitzharding in payment of part of the arrears of the Duke of Southampton's pension - - - - - -	300 0 0	
To The Duke of Ormond, for his Equipage to go into Flanders - - - - - -	1,000 0 0	1,440 0 0

MEMORANDUM.

That this Account is as exact as we have been able to make, up to this time, and the reasons why it is not more perfect, according to the directions of the Act, by which we are empowered, are—

There is a doubt not yet cleared, upon the account of Thomas Fox, Esq., late Receiver General of the Customs, viz., whether he is not doubly charged with divers sums, amounting to about Twenty Thousand Pounds, which hath happened, because he hath not delivered to us a distinct account of bonds given for Customs, he sometimes charging himself therewith and afterwards allowing in his weekly accounts several sums to be received upon bonds, without distinguishing whether the said bonds were old or new; and such sums as upon examination, appear to be doubly charged, will lessen the Receipt of Customs in this account, and take off from the balance that the said Thomas Fox is charged with in folio 28.

We can get no Account from the Treasurer of the Chamber to the late King James, who is presumed to have great sums remaining in his hands on the fifth of November, one thousand, six hundred, eighty eight, and therefore cannot be included in this account.

We have yet no account of the receipts and payments of the Revenue of North Wales.

The Account of Tenths is brought in to us but in part, the usual time for accounting for that Revenue being by the Statute, to be about Christmas, and therefore this account contains only the net receipts paid into the Exchequer.

The Account of the Irish Army, as to the part thereof, under the charge of Thomas Coningsby, Esq., one of the Paymasters, is brought in but to the 11th day of March 1690.

That the Account of the produce of Forfeited Goods seized in Ireland, and Forfeited Lands let there, and provisions and stores there taken, is, as yet, but in a very small part, and lately brought to us; though that account (as we are informed) is very considerable.

That the accounts of principal and interest paid, are undistinguished, and intermixed; and the Loans upon the several credits of them so often transferred, without the Accountants taking notice thereof, upon such accounts, or explaining them to us (though desired) that we have not been able to offer, at this time, a more perfect state of them than is now delivered.

That the great accounts of the Army, Navy and Ordnance, have not yet been fully brought into us in the manner and time as by our precepts, pursuant to the said Act have been appointed, whereby we have not been hitherto able to examine and make a perfect state of each of them, as the nature of the same requires, divers great sums therein being to be transferred from one account to the other, and money imprested to other persons whose accounts are not yet before us.

That the Accounts of Stores particularly referred to us by the said Act, are so voluminous, consisting of above ninety volumes in folio, besides those yet to come in to complete the same, that many of the offices concerned therein allege they have not been hitherto able to prepare perfect accounts for us; and the ledger of the Office of the Ordnance could not be transmitted to us until since the Order we received for making up this account.

This Account of the Incomes and Issues of the Public Revenue, is as exactly made as it could be, to the time appointed for delivering it in, which would have been more answerable to the scope and intention of the Act, whereby we are empowered, if we had had time sufficient for examining and stating of all the other accounts of those accountants to whom the said Revenue hath been distributed, which (as to the most important of them) are so voluminous, that it will require much more time to examine and state than is limited in the said Act for the same.

Benjamin Newland (L.S.)	R. Rich (L.S.)
Sam. Barnardiston (L.S.)	Tho. Clarges (L.S.)
P. Colleton (L.S.)	Paul Foley (L.S.)
Ro. Harley (L.S.)	Robt. Austen (L.S.)

[On 2 Dec. 1691, the House being moved that the Commissioners of Accounts be sent for to give an account, the Clause in the Act* was read. *Ordered*, That the Commissioners send an account in writing forthwith of their examinations and proceedings how the public treasure, revenues and other things mentioned in that Act have been disposed of (MS. Min.; L. J., XIV. 668.) The above Book of Accounts, bound in vellum, was delivered to the House this day (7 Dec. 1691) by *George Talbot*, Secretary to the Commissioners of Public Accounts, who, being sworn, stated that it was the same he had from them. On motion that a day should be appointed for reading it, the House ordered to read it the next day (L. J., XIV. 677; MS. Min.).—On 8 Dec. the Book being read, *Moved*, That a day be appointed to consider it. *Moved*, to send to the Commissioners that the House has received the Book of Accounts and that the House supposes they have made some remarks and observations upon them, and, if so, that they be desired to send them. *Ordered* accordingly (L. J., XIV. 678; MS. Min.).—On 12 Dec. the Observations of the Commissioners (Annex (*a.*) below), were delivered in by their Clerk (L. J., XIV. 684; MS. Min.), and on 14 Dec. the House, on motion, ordered to read them the next day (L. J., XIV. 686; MS. Min.).—On 15 Dec. the Observations being read, *E. Warrington* acquainted the House with the particulars of the moneys received and

---

* 2 W. & M. Sess. 2, c. 11, An Act for appointing and enabling Commissioners to examine, take and state the Public Accounts of the Kingdom. The proceedings on this Bill in the House of Lords were as follows:—It was brought up from the House of Commons on 26 Dec. 1690 (MS. Min. Entry omitted in L. J.), and read 1ª on the 27th (L. J., XIV. 606).—On the 29th, after a second reading, it was proposed that at the Committee the persons named for receiving the public accounts in the Bill should be left out and others named that are of neither House, and but three. *Moved*, That the Commissioners named in the Bill may give an account to both Houses. *Ordered*, That the Bill be committed to a Committee of the whole House. *Question*, Whether directions shall be given to the Committee to name some Lords to be added to the Commissioners named in the Bill? [Ralph (ii. 252) states that E. Rochester was the author of this motion.] *Previous Question*: Whether this question shall be now put? Resolved in the *Affirmative*. *Main Question* put and resolved in the *Affirmative*. *Ordered*, That four Lords only shall be named by the Committee to be added to the Commissioners in the Bill, and that it be done to-morrow morning by way of balloting box. (MS. Min.; L. J., XV. 608).—On 30 Dec., the ballot being taken, E. Bridgewater, E. Stamford, E. Rochester, and L. Cornwallis were reported as having been chosen. (MS. Min.; L. J., XV. 610).—On 31 Dec. in C. W. H. the Bill was amended by adding the names of the four Lords, and also a Proviso against the acceptance of any office by the Commissioners, which was carried by 28 to 23. Tellers, E. Huntingdon and E. Warrington. On report, *eod. die*, *E. Rochester* thanked the House for the honour they had done him in choosing him. He did not go by any affectation to decline this matter, but he desired to be excused from being a Commissioner. *Moved*, To appoint a method to choose another, if one be excused. The three other Lords also desired to be excused. The Amendments were then disagreed to, and the Bill read 3ª. (MS. Min.; L. J., XV. 611.) It received the Royal Assent on 5 Jan., 1690–1. (*ib.*, 618.)

House of Lords MSS.

1691.

mentioned in the Book of Accounts.* House *moved* that a day be appointed for considering the Book. First Head of the Observations read again. House *moved*, That the Secretary to the Commissioners attend on the day when the accounts are considered. *Ordered* that the House be put into Committee on Friday, the 18th inst., to consider the Book of Accounts and Observations thereon, the Committee to have power to name a Sub-Committee to examine such things as they shall think fit.† *Ordered*, That the Commissioners send the names of such persons as they find to be material to give any light to the House upon the First Head, and also whether they have made any discovery of any officers of the Revenue who have bought tallies (L. J., XIV., 688).

18 Dec. House in Committee. Heads 1 and 2 of the Observations read. *The Secretary to the Commissioners* was called in to the Bar and delivered a Paper from the Commissioners of Accounts (Annex (*b.*) below) which was read by the Clerk. Asked whether the Commissioners did not examine Toll before he died? A. One of the first precepts that was sent out [was] to the Lord Ranelagh, and it is come in very lately. *Mr. Talbot* is asked if he knew who sold those tallies? He says he knows not who bought or sold the tallies. The *L. President* and *L. Godolphin* informed the House that, as to the 200,000*l.*, there was necessity to allow tallies before the actual receipt of money. The second part of the Paper delivered this day was read. *The Secretary to the Commissioners* is called in, and the last Observation read, which was brought in this day. Asked why they were called "fictitious tallies"? A. I have no order to explain anything for the Commissioners. I take them to be tallies that are now given, the money not yet paid. Asked if he knew anyone that had lent one sum of money to include another debt? A. I desire the Commissioners may be asked this. I cannot speak to it. *Moved* to send to the Commissioners of Accounts: 1. To explain what is meant by "fictitious tallies." 2. Whether the money that tallies have been struck for was all actually lent, and whether part of some of them were not old debts included in the said tallies; and if there are any such, to give the House an account of them. *Agreed to.* Report made by E. Fauconberg, and *Ordered* accordingly. (MS. Min.; L. J., XIV. 693.)

19 Dec. House in Committee. E. Fauconberg in the Chair. *The Secretary to the Commissioners of Accounts* was called in and delivered a Paper. (Annex (*c.*) below.) The Order made yesterday was read, and then the Paper delivered in was read. Then the Secretary withdrew. *Moved*, that the tallies and loans from 20 March 1689 to Michaelmas after be sent to this House by Mr. Lowndes by the Lords of the Treasury. *Ordered* accordingly. *Moved*, that the Act for the present assessment may be read. *Moved*, that an Address be made to his Majesty that he will give leave to the Commissioners of the Treasury to give the House an account of such things as the House shall have occasion for relating to the public accounts now before this House.

---

* Luttrell (17 Dec. 1691) has the following: "The Lords read the public accounts on Tuesday (15 Dec.) and the Lord Warrington, finding his name therein, declared he never received any for secret service, but 500*l.* one time and 1,000*l.* another, for money due to him; on which the Lord Halifax moved that each Lord might, as his name occurred, stand up and justify himself in the same."

† Between this and the next Order the MS. Min. have the following: "Commissioners Treasury, Toll's executor, Toll's successor. The Clerk to the Commissioners of the P. Seal; that they send the Privy Seal." The Privy Seal had been put into Commission (19 Feb. 1689–90), on the retirement of L. Halifax, the Commissioners being Wm. Cheney, Esq., Sir John Knatchbull, Bart., and Sir Wm. Pulteney, Knt. *Ralph* ii., 192 and *note*.

Moved, that the House will consider further of the two Heads of the Observations. *Ordered*, that the further consideration of these two Articles in the Observations is hereby deferred until the whole be considered of. Head 3 in the Observations read, and the Clause in the last Act of Assessment read out of the Statutes. *Moved*, that the Commissioners send an account whether there have been any anticipations or tallies of anticipation of *pro* struck upon the last Land tax? Whether they find that any tallies of *pro* or anticipation have been struck upon the last Land Tax contrary to the Act intituled An Act for granting an Aid to their Majesties? *Ordered* to report the Address to the House and the directions to the Commissioners of Accounts. House resumed. *E. Fauconberg* reported as in L. J., XIV. 695. The Report was agreed to, and the House ordered accordingly (*ib.*). (MS. Min.)

21 Dec. The *L. Chamberlain* reported the King's Answer to the Address, stating that he was pleased to comply with the desires of the House. (MS. Min.; L. J., XIV. 696). . . . *Moved*, that the Resolution of 18 Dec. for going on *de die in diem* be revoked. *Ordered* accordingly. [*Moved* that the House may go presently upon the Observations and nothing to intervene]* . . . *Moved* to go upon the Accounts and Observations. House in Committee. Then, after considering the Observations, the Committee, through E. Fauconberg, reported progress upon Heads 5 to 9 inclusive, and that Mr. Charles Toll's executors and successor be sent for to attend, to which the House agreed. (MS. Min.; L. J., XIV. 697.)

22 Dec. House in Committee. Order of 19 Dec. read. *The Secretary to the Commissioners of Accounts* was called in and delivered a Paper (Annex (*d.*) below), pursuant to that Order, which was read. The remaining Heads, 10 *ad fin*, considered. House resumed. E. Fauconberg reports progress. House to be again in Committee on 29 Dec., and Mr. Toll's executors and successor to attend. (MS. Min.; L. J., XIV. 699.)

29 Dec. House *moved* to go on the Book of Accounts after the Conference. *Ordered* accordingly. . . . House in Committee. The several Heads read. *Ordered* to report that the Committee have agreed upon several Queries to the Commissioners. House resumed. E. Fauconberg reported that the Committee desire a time may be appointed for the Report. *Ordered* that the Report be made to-morrow. (MS. Min.; L. J., XV. 5.)

30 Dec. E. Fauconberg reported the several Queries which were agreed to. (L. J., XV. 7–8 *In extenso.*)† *Ordered* that the Commissioners send particular Answers in Writing on 2 Jan. (*ib.*)

2 Jan. *The Secretary of the Commissioners* was called in and intimated that the Commissioners were preparing their answers and would speedily send them. (MS. Min.; L. J., XV. 14.)

---

* These words in square brackets are struck through. The House disposed of some other business before resuming this subject.

† These Queries will be found also on the Paper containing the Commissioners' Answers (Annex (*e.*) below). The MS. Min. contain some additional information not given in this Report, as follows: "Head 17th, Concerning Customs and Hearth money sums in arrear and the Lord Bishop of London. Head 18th, Pensions charged upon the Customs and Post Office. *Defer to further consideration. A List of the pensions.* [These words in italics are struck through.] Vide Book Accounts. Head 28th, Concerning the Paymaster of the Army. Referred to a further consideration. Head 29th, The rest [*i.e.*, except the names of the Muster Masters] referred to a further consideration. Head 30th, Danish officers. *To know who withheld their pay from them.* [These words in italics are struck through.] Referred to further consideration." (MS. Min., 22 Dec.)

House of Lords MSS. — 1691.

12 Jan. *The Secretary of the Commissioners*, being called in, delivered a Book (Annex (*e.*) below) as their Answer. (MS. Min.; L. J., XV. 25.)

15 Jan. *Moved* that the House be put into a Committee to-morrow to consider the Commissioners' Answers. *Ordered* accordingly. (MS. Min.; L. J., XV. 32.)

16 Jan. House in Committee. Head 1 read. This is disagreed to and deserves further consideration. Head 2 read. To be considered this first part. Second and third parts to be considered. Fourth part to be considered as to the verbal order of 1,500*l.* per annum to Sir Robert Howard.* William Herbert's business and allowances to be further considered. [In Margin: To 7th Head.] House resumed. E. Fauconberg reports progress. House to be again in Committee on 18 Jan. (MS. Min.; L. J., XV. 33.)

18 Jan. Nothing recorded.

21 Jan. House to be in Committee on the Answers on 25 Jan. (MS. Min.; L. J., XV. 41.) No further proceedings.]

Annexed :—

(*a.*) 12 Dec. 1691.—Observations made by the Commissioners appointed by Act of Parliament to examine, take and state the Public Accounts of the Kingdom, upon the Accounts brought in before them, so far as they have been able to examine the same, to the 29th of September 1691; as follows:

1. In the Account there is paid above 150,000*l.* in satisfaction of money lent before 5 Nov. 1688, and the only warrant appearing to us for the same is a Privy Seal, dated 25 March 1689, to repay money lent to the late King James with interest, not exceeding 6 per cent.; Whereas part of the said sum was lent in the time of King Charles II., and so not authorized to be paid by the said Warrant, and above 80,000*l.* was paid upon a credit raised by Letters Patents of the late King James, where we find the loans made upon that credit were chiefly by those who had the public money of the Kingdom in their hands, and particularly Mr. Charles Toll, Servant to the Paymaster-General of the Army, did lend thereon above 100,000*l.*, which being presumed not to be his own money, makes it doubtful whether the loans and repayments were real or fictitious.

2. That the striking of Talleys upon credits given by the late Acts of Parliament for Aids, before the Money is actually borrowed, increases the interest very much above the rate allowed by the law; and these Talleys being struck to several Paymasters for great sums, may prove a temptation to delay the application of them to the uses intended for the advantage of the interest due upon them.

That the great gains made by buying of Talleys doth tend very much to lessen the public credit of the kingdom.

3. That great sums of money have been taken up upon Loans, notwithstanding the Customs, Excise, Letter Money, and (after the first quarter) the Land Tax have come in weekly.

4. That whereas the Parliament gave to the Dutch 600,000*l.* upon divers branches of the Revenue, to be paid them as the money came in, 150,000*l.* upon that Act was taken up beforehand, and the King charged with the interest thereof.

5. That several persons, who have very great salaries, do now make the King pay the charge of passing their Patents and

* See Head 6 in Annex (*e.*) below.

Accounts (which amounts to a great sum of money) though formerly such charges were defrayed by the officers themselves.

6. That of late years, those that have great Salaries, have upon slight pretences got them increased, and extraordinary Bills of incident charges seem to have had very easy allowance.

7. That several Salaries, granted upon special reason, are still continued, though the reasons cease.

8. Divers great sums of money have been borrowed from the Receivers of the Public Revenue, and interest allowed them for the same, whereas, at the making up of their accounts before us it appears that they have had sums of the Public money in their hands.

9. We, being directed to enquire into and demand an account of all the Pensions, Salaries and Sums of money paid or payable to Members of Parliament, out of the Revenue or otherwise (not excluding such payments out of monies paid to their Majesties' Privy Purse or for Secret Service), we have not been able to get a full account thereof, on allegation to us that some sums of money have been paid to Parliament-men for matters relating to the State fit to be concealed; but taking ourselves to be obliged by the Act to have that Account, did often press Mr. Jephson,* late Receiver of the Money for Secret Service, for the same, and immediately on his death, required it from Mr. Robert Squib, who had his papers, and have also made application to the Lords Commissioners of the Treasury for an Account thereof; the final answer whereunto was brought us by the said Mr. Squib the 20th day of this instant November, in writing, as he said, by order of the said Lords Commissioners in these words following, viz., That there were other payments made by Mr. Jephson to several Members of Parliament for services relating to the State, the nature of which payments are of great concern and importance to the Government, and are neither for Pensions, Salaries nor Bounties, nor in any sort disposed to them with regard to their being Members of Parliament, and therefore, the secrecy of them being so absolutely necessary, his Majesty does believe that the House will not desire the Particulars of them.

10. That in the late Act for the King and Queen's most Gracious, general and free Pardon, several great sums imprested to divers persons before 25 March 1673, to the value of several hundred thousand pounds, have been thereby pardoned, whereas the arrears of Fee-farm and other small Rents, some of them of very inconsiderable value, are excepted from Pardon.

11. That excessive Fees are exacted and taken by officers, that have great Salaries allowed them for the execution of their places, for which no legal precedent appears to justify the same.

12. That there are great quantities of Plate in the hands of late Ambassadors, officers and others, not returned to the Jewel House, or brought to any account.

13. That in the State of an Account of the late farmers of the Revenue in Ireland, there appears to be due to their Majesties on the 5th of November 1688 the sum of 75,553*l.* from the said farmers, whereof some of them are very responsible.

* *See* Grey's Debates, 3 Dec. 1691.

House of Lords MSS.

1691.

14. That the Revenue of the Duchy of Lancaster is all distributed in payments to officers, which may be reserved to their Majesties, if the same be, by Act of Parliament, put under the survey of the Exchequer.

15. That the Royal Oak Lottery, which the late King James granted by Indenture dated 9 July, in the third year of his reign, with *non-obstantes* of Dispensation to several Acts of Parliament, which made all the like Grants to be illegal, has been lately renewed.

16. The Charge of the Civil List is increased by Pensions and Allowances to persons discharged of their offices.

17. That upon the Customs, Excise, Hearth-Money and Tenths, and several other branches of the Revenue, great sums are in arrear; and in particular, William Tempest, Esq., of the Bishopric of Durham, is returned to us to stand indebted to the King's Majesty in the sum of 3,572*l.* 14*s.* 2*d.*, for so much as he has received upon the Hearth-Money; and though often written to by the Commissioners of that Duty, to pay the same, will neither pay the money, nor return any answer. And the present Lord Bishop of Winchester is returned to us, to be indebted to the King's Majesty in the sum of 1,628*l.* 2*s.* 6¾*d.* for public monies received by him, when he was Bishop of Bath and Wells.

18. That upon the Customs, Excise and Post Office many pensions are charged, some of which do not appear to us to be paid, unless out of Secret Service money; which we suppose may have been, because since Mr. Jephson's death divers sums are paid at the Exchequer, of which we have had no notice before. And we observe the Post Office is clogged with pensions, old and new, that take away from the Crown a very great part of that revenue.

19. That some accounts have been passed by virtue of Privy Seals only.

20. That the Duplicates of Taxes and Aids given have been so irregularly brought in from the office where they ought to be of record, that we are informed no account thereof has been made up for divers years past.

21. That the Commissioners and Receivers General of the Excise have charged the King with what taxes were laid upon them by Act of Parliament in respect of their Salaries.

22. Many payments are made at the Custom House, Excise and Post Office for pensions and other public payments, besides yearly salaries and incidents, of which there is no notice taken in any of the accounts of the Exchequer; so that no one general account of the Receipts and Issues of the Public Revenue is kept in any one place; and such like anticipations by warrants, before the money comes into the Exchequer, renders it not only difficult to find out how the public money has been distributed, but if those who were entrusted to make such warrants were so disposed, it were very easy for them to waste the treasure of the kingdom.

23. That upon examination of some complaints of defrauding of their Majesties in their Revenue, it appeared before us that upon a contract to pay 100 guineas to Mrs. Susan Willis, she did undertake, and accordingly a Captain's place was procured for the command of one of their Majesties' Men-of-War; and the Captain, who paid the same, said if it were further exa-

mined, it would appear other Captains had paid greater sums than he had done.

24. It appears in Establishments in the Army of King Charles II. that it was a standing direction therein, that nothing should be offered for the Royal Signature for alteration of the Establishment, but what should first be approved by the Lord Treasurer, the Captain-General of the Army for the time being, and the Secretaries of State, or two of them, whereof the Treasurer or General to be one. But it does not appear to us that the like method is now observed, by reason whereof many warrants have been obtained to pay the Army beyond the number of effective men; and in cases not extraordinary, and the present establishment, proportionable to the numbers, is higher than in any former time or reign. And, moreover, some Commissaries of the Masters, by direction from the officers, have made up the Muster Rolls not according to effective men and for longer time than the said Rolls ought to have been closed. We further observe the first enlarging of Establishments, as to numbers and pay, began in the time of the Lord Clifford's Ministry, and was augmented in the reign of the late King James.

25. That whereas in the time of King Charles II. and the late King James, the Forces kept in Scotland were paid out of the Scotch Revenue, yet, of late, the Forces in Scotland have been paid out of the Revenue of England.

26. That the Agency to Regiments is a thing lately brought into practice; and many of the Agents giving great sums of money for their places, make their profits by deductions from the soldiers; and money is paid for Debentures or Certificates of the Paymasters of pay due to the Regiments, and gratuities to such Paymasters and their under officers, although the same is taken away by Act of Parliament.

27. That many of the Contracts for clothing the Army in Ireland have been at much greater rates than for which they might have been provided.

28. That the Paymaster-General of the Army in England, in an account of the disposition of poundage, deducted from the soldiers' pay, by him very lately exhibited to us, delivered us a Paper, entitled A Copy of the State of the Paymaster's Office, presented to the late King James by Sir Stephen Fox, on the 19th of October 1685, which he has since laid before the King's Majesty, and is (without any Warrant or Order produced to us) observed by him in the distribution of a third part thereof, amounting to the yearly sum of - - £10,000 0 0

Whereof he distributes yearly to the Clerks and other officers - - -	£6,386	1	8
And keeps in remain to himself, as Pay Master - - - - -	£3,613	18	4
Whereout, he says, he has a verbal direction from the King to pay to Sir Robert Howard the yearly sum of - - -	£1,500	0	0
which he has accordingly paid: whereas it appears not in any of the allowances of the Pay Master and his Clerks, by any of the establishments of the late King Charles II. or King James, there is any more allowed than the yearly sum of - - -	£366	0	0

29. That we, judging it necessary to the public service, and the execution of the trust reposed in us, to have an exact account of the true number of the Forces in Ireland, before they took the field the last Summer, did issue out our Precept to the Commissary-General of the Musters there, to take a Muster of all Forces, according to such directions as we had given him for the better discharging the said Service, and did also recommend the forwarding the said work to the Lord Justices; but the Muster-Master did not comply with our directions, and alleges for excuse, he had not the assistance from those in authority, without which it was impossible for him to perform what was required by us.

30. That, by complaint of some of the Danish Officers, it has been certified to us, that they have received very little money, although they find great sums charged by the Treasurer at War there, as paid for the use of those Forces, which was one cause of the plunder and spoil of the Protestant inhabitants.

31. That in the Accounts brought to us, there are several miscastings, which we have not yet had time thoroughly to examine; and, in particular, in the account of Charles Fox, Esq., Paymaster to the Army in Ireland.

These Observations are the most considerable which have occurred to us at present, upon making up A State of the Income and Issues of the Public Revenue, committed to our examination, within the time appointed for it, which would have been more answerable to the scope and intention of the Act, whereby we are empowered, if we had had time sufficient for the examining and stating of all the other accounts of those accountants, to whom the said Revenue has been distributed; which (as to the most important of them) are so voluminous, that it will require much more time to examine and state than is limited in the said Act for the same. *Signed* R. Rich, Tho. Clarges, Benjamin Newland, Paul Foley, Math. Andrewes, P. Colleton, Rob. Harley, Sam. Barnardiston, and Rob. Austen. *Endorsed:* Book of Observations from Commissioners of Accounts. Brought in 12 Dec. 1691. L. J., XIV. 684.

(*b.*) 18 Dec. 1691. Paper stating as follows: "The first Observation takes notice (1) of several debts contracted before the Revolution, paid since, without any warrant appearing to us, the particulars of which are:—

	£ s. d.	
In Nov., Dec., and March 1688, to Richard Kent, Esq., late Receiver-General of the Customs, besides interest - - -		15,000 0 0
In Jan. 1688 to Charles Duncomb, Esq., besides interest - - - -		20,000 0 0
In Jan. and March 1688 to Mr. Joseph and Mr. Nathaniel Horneby, on several talleys struck in 33, 35, and 36 Charles II., in full of 70,000*l.*, originally Bankers' Debt - - -	20,000 0 0	
More to Nathaniel Horneby, Esq., 22 March 1688, on a talley struck the 16th of the said month -	5,000 0 0	
- -		25,000 0 0

	£ s. d.	£ s. d.
To the citizens of London and the Commissioners of Wine Licenses, as appears by the Account delivered in, folio 26, viz. :—		
To the citizens - -	272 7 5	
To the Commissioners of Wine Licenses - -	12,628 11 11	
		12,900 19 4
		72,900 19 4
(2.) That a Privy Seal, dated 25 March 1689, was procured and produced to us for repayment of money lent to the late King James, with interest not exceeding 6 per cent. —The Commissioners observe there was borrowed on credit made by Letters Patents, 15 Oct. 1686 the sum of 353,798*l.* 6*s.* 9*d.*, of which above two-thirds was lent to King James by his own cashiers and officers, and particularly 111,150*l.* was lent by Mr. Charles Toll, Servant to the Paymaster of the Army, of which debt, on this credit, the sum of 83,412*l.* 19*s.* 9*d.* is charged in the Account, since 5 November 1688, to be repaid in satisfaction of the said credit; But the Commissioners, though they have required it, cannot get an account to whom the same was paid; which matter (considering how unlikely it was for Mr. Toll to lend so much of his own money) they therefore lay before the Parliament, to satisfy themselves therein - -		83,412 19 9
		156,313 19 1

The second Observation relates to the striking of Talleys of loan before the money is actually lent, which was observed, because the Acts which create those credits, do provide, that neither directly nor indirectly, more interest shall be given than those Acts respectively allowed, whereas by this course more interest is paid. This was the rather noted, because such Talleys are struck, not only on credits which would be a long time coming in, but upon the Land Tax, the best security that can be given. It appears to the Commissioners that such kind of fictitious Talleys have been struck to the Paymasters of the Army, Treasurers of the Navy and Ordnance, and other officers, and by them assigned and afterwards sold to great loss; but who bought the same does not appear to us. By the Account, Folio 16, there was lent on the Acts for East India Goods, continued imposts and ⅔ additional Excise, the sum of 1,995,875*l.* 10*s.* 0½*d.*, more than one-half of which, viz., 1,091,391*l.* 16*s.* 8*d.*, were fictitious Talleys, struck to the Hon. Edward Russell, Esq., Charles Fox, Esq., The Right Hon. the Earl of Ranelagh and the Hon. Charles Bertie, Esq., besides other loans, put upon the Judges and other officers for money due to them, the greatest part of which, being on sale about the town, is supposed greatly

House of Lords MSS.

1691.

to hinder Loans to the Exchequer, and therefore submitted to the consideration of the Parliament." *Signed* P. Colleton, Math. Andrewes, Paul Foley, Sam. Barnardiston, and Thos. Clarges. *Endorsed* as brought in by the Secretary to the Commissioners of Public Accounts this day, No. 1.

(*c*.) 19 Dec. 1691. Paper stating as follows: "In answer to your Lordships' order of 18 Dec. 1691, the Commissioners of Accounts do mean by '*Fictitious Talleys*' such as were struck without the money being actually paid, that being the term by which they are called by the Exchequer officers, as they have informed us, and appear to us to be of two sorts: 1. Such as were struck in order to be afterwards delivered to the Treasurer of the Navy or other Paymasters, that so they might dispose of them for the principal money, with the advantage of interest, from the date of the Talleys, besides what was due from the actual payment of such moneys; of which sort there was the last year struck to the value of near 1,500,000*l*. principal money. 2. Another way was to strike Talleys unto persons to whom money was due for salaries, pensions, or on other accounts, who did not advance any money on loans, otherwise than taking such Talleys for their debt.—As to the next Enquiry: *Whether all the moneys the Talleys were struck for, were actually lent?* By what is above, it appears, that the moneys the Talleys were struck for, were either due to the persons to whom the Talleys were struck, or paid by those who bought the same of the officers to whom they were given, at the time of such sale, though not at the time of striking the Talleys.—Third Query: *Whether part of the money for which the talleys were struck, were not old debts included in the said talleys?* We find in January 1688, as we have before observed to your Lordships, Charles Duncombe, Esq., was allowed a debt of 20,000*l*., due to him upon an account made up in October 1688, for which he had talleys, to be paid with interest; And thereupon the said Mr. Duncombe did lend, 10 January 1688, 20,000*l*., for which he had interest paid him to the 20th of December following, when the principal was repaid.—March 11, 1690, the Right Hon. the Earl of Bath is charged in account to be paid on his annuity out of loans on the unappropriated Excise 10,000*l*. The same day, in the account of loans on unappropriated Excise, his Lordship is said to lend 10,000*l*., which seems to us to be the same debt due to him. What other particulars of this nature are in the accounts, we cannot set forth for want of time to examine them." *Signed* Sam. Barnardiston, R. Rich, Paul Foley, Rob. Austen, Math. Andrewes, and P. Colleton. *Endorsed* as brought in by the Secretary to the Commissioners of Public Accounts this day. No. 2.

(*d*.) 22 Dec. 1691. Paper stating as follows: "In answer to your Lordships' order of the 19th of December 1691, the Commissioners do not know of any Talleys of Pro. or Anticipation on the late Aids given, which are Talleys struck to receive money before it comes into the Exchequer, but there are many Talleys of Pro. or Anticipation struck on the hereditary and ½ temporary Excise, for payment of principal money borrowed thereupon, with the interest thereof, as it became due, and the like Talleys have been struck on the same and other branches of the Revenue, to pay several Pensions and other payments. Also, Thomas Wharton, Esq., received from the several Collectors of the Excise, of Nottinghamshire, Shropshire, Oxfordshire, Berks, and Hertfordshire, several sums, amounting to 3,000*l.*, and from the Collectors of the Taxes of Bucks and Berks several sums of money, amounting to 1,700*l.*, by way of anticipation; but it appears not to them whether by Talley or by what other Warrant. But they find in the Accounts before them fictitious Talleys, which are, as explained in their last Paper, to the sum of 1,432,682*l.* 6*s.* 2*d.*, viz.:

	£	*s.*	*d.*
On the Act for granting an Aid to their Majesties of 1,651,702*l.* 18*s.* 0*d.*, the sum of - - - - - - -	341,290	9	6
On the Acts for East India Goods, and new Impositions, the sum of - -	295,135	11	5½
On the Act for ⅔ Additional Excise, the sum of - - - - - -	796,256	5	2½
	£1,432,682	6	2

Of which Talleys,

	£	*s.*	*d.*
The Treasurer of the Navy had to the sum of - - - - - - - -	957,090	9	6
The Paymaster of the Army in Ireland -	299,028	6	5¼
The Paymaster of the Army in England	135,631	5	0
The Treasurer of the Ordnance - -	40,932	5	2¾
	£1,432,682	6	2

The interest of these Talleys was paid from the date thereof, though the money borrowed, given or allowed thereupon, was not till some time afterwards.—The next Enquiry: Whether the residue of the 600,000*l.* was not paid to the Dutch by advance, and the interest thereon placed to the King's account, as well as the 150,000*l.* in the Observation mentioned?—The Commissioners find no other money advanced but that 150,000*l.*, but besides the interest mentioned therein, they find 1,150*l.* 14*s.* 6*d.* was paid the Ambassador from the States of Holland for the interest of 140,000*l.* part of the said 600,000*l.*, from the respective days when the same was brought into the Exchequer to the 10th of June 1691, when the same was lent at interest, by consent of the States, upon the Act for continuing the new Impositions." *Signed* Paul Foley, Math. Andrewes, Benj. Newland, R. Rich., Robert Austen, P. Colleton, and Sam. Barnardiston. *Dated* 22 Dec. 1691. *Endorsed* as brought in by the Secretary to the Commissioners of Public Accounts this day. No. 3.

(*e.*) 12 Jan. 1691–2. Book containing Particular Answers of the Commissioners of Public Accounts to the Queries made by the Lords on Heads V. to XXXI. inclusive on 30 Dec. 1691, as follows: Head V. Concerning persons who have Salaries, and the King hath paid for passing their Patents and Accounts. Q. Whose Patents and Accounts they are that the King was at the charge of, and the names of those persons that claimed it, and that allowed the Account.

HOUSE OF LORDS MSS.

1691.

Passing Patents.

	£	s.	d.
Paid Mr. Noel, Solicitor to the Excise Office, by allowance of the Lords Commissioners of the Treasury, Oct. 10, 1689, for the charge of passing the Excise Commission in April 1689 for Sir Henry Fane, Sir Henry Ashurst, Sir Humphry Edwin, Thomas Frankland, Francis Parry, John Danvers, and John Wilcox, Esq., to be Commissioners of the Excise - - - - - - -	153	8	0
Paid the said Mr. Noel by allowance, as above, his charge in passing the Excise Commission in October 1689, for Sir Henry Ashurst, Sir John Mordyn, Sir Samuel Dashwood, Sir Humphry Edwin, Stephen Evance, Wm. Strong, and John Foche, Esqrs., to be Commissioners for the Excise, and Charles Duncomb, Esq., to be Cashier -	176	10	2
In Mr. Noel's Bill; paid to the Chief Baron's Clerk, for swearing the Commissioners twice -	2	16	0
Paid Sir Edmund Jennings, for expenses in passing the Commission for Prizes - - -	68	7	8
The Commissioners for tin farthings were allowed by the Lords Commissioners of the Treasury, being the charge of passing their Patent, because of the profit that they had made to the Crown by their Office - - - - - - -	58	0	0
	£459	2	4

Passing of Accounts.

Customs.

	£	s.	d.	£	s.	d.
Paid by Richard Kent, Esq., Receiver-General of the Customs, for passing his account from the 5th Nov. 1688 to Lady Day following - -	417	4	5			
Paid by the same, to Auditor Bridges, for examining and passing the accounts of the Customs and New Impositions for one half-year ending at Lady Day 1689 - - - - - -	455	0	0			
				872	4	5
Paid by Thomas Fox, Esq., Receiver-General of the Customs, for passing his account for the half year ended at Michaelmas 1689 - -	156	19	3			
Paid by him more, for Fees in passing his account for the year ended at Michaelmas 1690 - - -	271	8	10			
Paid by him to Auditor Bridges, for passing the account of the Customs and Impositions, as above - -	405	0	0			
				833	8	
				1,705	12	6

Excise.

	£	s.	d.
Among the Incident Bills allowed to the Excise Office, from the 25th December 1688, to the 24th June 1689, there is allowed charges for passing the Commissioners account for one year, from the 24th of June 1684 to the 24th June 1685, the sum of -	73	3	5

Since which time, as we are informed, the Commissioners have passed but one account, viz., for the year 1686, but are now passing the account for the year 1687. The Commissioners have not before them the charges of passing that account for 1686, which is supposed to be contained in Mr. Noel's bill for law charges, which have not yet been laid before us.

Letter Money.

	£	s.	d.	£	s.	d.
Paid Wm. Auldworth, Auditor, in full for three years' and three quarters' salary at 200*l.* per annum - -	750	0	0			
Paid Henry Ballow, for joining 110 talleys. at 1*s.* each - -	5	10	0			
Memorandum, the Customs is charged but 4*d.* per talley.						
Paid John Tayleur, for entering three years' accounts in the Treasurer's Remembrancer's Office - -	24	0	0			
Paid Walter Wallinger, for a quietus, in passing three years' accounts -	122	7	4			
Memorandum; this seems to be more, according to proportion, than is charged for the Customs.						
Paid Thomas Hall, entering three years' accounts in the King's Remembrancer's Office - - -	40	0	0			
Memorandum, for the Customs is paid but 6*l.* 9*s.* per annum.						
Paid Fees at the Treasurer and Chancellor of the Exchequer declaring the account - - - -	25	10	0			
Carrying of Money, passing of Accounts and fees for Talleys - -	47	15	6			
				1,015	2	10

Navy.

	£	s.	d.
Paid John Tayleur, Accountant-General to the Treasurer of the Navy, for defraying the charges of the account, as per his receipt the 23rd of Dec. 1690 - - - - - - -	350	0	0

Memorandum: This is what appears to us, there having [been] no account for the Navy passed for many years.

The Right Honble. Anthony, Ld. Viscount Falkland acknowledgeth to remain in his hands the 30th April 1689, the sum of 3,318*l.* 12*s.* 9*d.*, which he keeps for passing that and several other preceding accounts.

HOUSE OF LORDS MSS.

1691.

Ordnance.

	£ s. d.	£ s. d.	£ s. d.
Paid usual Fees in passing a Privy Seal for money - - -		50 15 9	
Paid for an Imprest Roll - -		10 14 6	
Paid Thomas Hall entering the same in the King's Remembrancer's and a Pipe Office - - - -		41 14 6	
Paid the Auditors, for auditing and passing the accounts, for the years ending June 1688, 1689, 1690 -		720 0 0	
Paid the Barons of the Exchequer and Auditor of the Imprest, their ordinary fee, for 9 years past, to the 30 June 1690, at 15*l.* 6*s.* 8*d.* per annum - - - -		138 0 0	
			961 4 9

Cofferers.

	£ s. d.	£ s. d.	£ s. d.
Sir Peter Appesly, paid the Auditor's fee for his account from the 5th of November 1688 to the 19th July 1690 - -	60 0 0		
Script. Compūt. -	42 0 0		
		102 0 0	
The Right Honble. Ld. Viscount Newport, paid Auditor's fee - -	45 0 0		
Script. Comput. -	31 10 0		
		76 10 0	
			178 10 0

Works.

	£ s. d.	£ s. d.	£ s. d.
Paid by Thos. Lloyd, Esq., master thereof, to the Auditors of the Imprest, on account of the Ordinary Service -		45 0 0	
Paid a yearly reward to the officers of the said account - - -		19 4 0	
			64 4 0

Mint.

	£ s. d.	£ s. d.	£ s. d.
Paid by Thomas Neal, Esq., to the Auditor - - - -		84 0 0	
And to the Pell Office - -		2 0 0	
			86 0 0

Hearth Money.

	£ s. d.
Paid Auditor Auldworth, in part, for examining and perfecting five years' accounts of that Revenue	300 0 0

Tin Farthings and Half-pence.

	£ s. d.
Paid the Auditor for passing the account -	12 0 0
	£4,745 17 6

Head VI.—Concerning those that have great salaries, and have got them increased. Q. To explain and give instances to whom and how much?

The Secretary at War the beginning of Charles 2nd's reign had 10*s.* per diem; afterwards it was increased to 20*s.*, and now advanced to 3*l.* per diem.

There was at first one Commissary-General and six deputy Commissaries. Now there is one Commissary-General, a Chief Deputy Commissary and seven other Deputy Commissaries.

The Commissary-General had 17*s.* 6*d.* per diem.

The Deputy Commissary had 13*s.*, and is now advanced 10*s.* more.

The other seven had 5*s.* per diem each, and are now advanced to 10*s.* per diem.

The Reason of that increase is assigned, because King James was resolved to have Musters every month, whereas they formerly had them but once in two months; and though now Musters are less frequent, yet, notwithstanding, their additional pay is kept up.

Richard Kent, Esq., late Receiver-General of the Customs, had, since this Revolution in the last half year of his time, some allowance for his additional trouble of receiving the new Impositions, which were granted in the time of the late King James, though nothing was allowed him, besides his salary of 1,000*l.* per annum, till after the Abdication. Thomas Fox, Esq., who succeeded him in that place, had, besides his salary of 1,000*l.* per annum, allowed him on account of those new Impositions, 300*l.* per annum. More, the said Thomas Fox, Esq., had allowed him for loss in receiving and paying of money 200*l.* per annum, which was 100*l.* per annum more than was used to be allowed on that account, notwithstanding in the year in which he first had that additional allowance, much less was received than in the year preceding, which (with other allowances) appear in particular, as follows:—

	£	s.	d.	£	s.	d.
Charges of money paid into the Exchequer, for ½ year to Michaelmas, 1689 - -	122	4	4			
Expenses in receiving Bills of Exchange, porterage, waterage, and other incident charges - - -	38	9	2			
Loss in receiving 550,432*l.*	100	0	0			
Collecting the new Impositions - - - -	150	0	0			
				410	13	6
More for the year ended at Michaelmas 1690:—						
Charges [for] paying money into the Exchequer - -	99	9	2			
Expenses in receiving bills of exchange, &c., as before -	57	7	2			
Loss in receiving 538,031*l.* 10*s.* 0*d.* - - -	200	0	0			
Collecting the new Impositions - - - -	300	0	0			
				656	16	4
				£1,067	9	10

House of Lords MSS.

1691.

Memorandum.

By a reference made by the Lords Commissioners of the Treasury the 16th of January 1688 (on a bill of charges brought in by the Cashier of the Excise), to the consideration of the Auditor and Comptroller of the Excise, they, in their report, give it as a reason why the Cashier of the Excise should be allowed 100*l.* per annum, and no more, (as he claimed) for brass and short money, because the Treasurer and Cashier of the Customs was then allowed for the like but 100*l.* per annum.

The Receiver-General of the Excise, since the Revolution, hath these extraordinary allowances, over and above 1,500*l.* per annum salary, for himself and clerks (which is more by 400*l.* per annum than any of his predecessors had) and an addition of about 220*l.* per annum for new Clerks, since the double Excise, viz.:—

	£	s.	d.
For brass and short money 100*l.* per annum, which was allowed him February 1688–9, for eight years and a half backwards, that being the time of his first coming in, to the 14th of Nov. 1688; though neither he nor any of his predecessors had any allowance thereof in the reigns of King Charles or King James - - - - -	850	0	0
He had also, at the same time, an allowance of 4*s.* 6*d.* for every thousand pounds paid into the Exchequer, viz.:—			
For 3,876,937*l.* 13*s.* 8*d.* to the 14th of Nov. 1688, the sum of - - -	759	16	0
	£1,609	16	0

There has been allowed in two years and a half to the Excise Office, in Bills of Incidents, besides what is above noted:—

	£	s.	d.	£	s.	d.
The Stationers and printed ware - -	3,271	16	6			
Law Charges - -	338	1	10			
For fees in Talley Court, for paying the public money into the Exchequer - -	24	7	8½			
For Mr. Farmer's bill for writing books - -	206	1	6			
To the door-keeper, for coffee, newspapers, gazettes, and letters, to Sir Roger L'Estrange, and other incidents - - - -	518	12	10½			
To the Clerk of the Register for expenses - -	30	19	0			
To Porters, for carrying money - - - -	97	0	0			
For money bags - -	229	19	6	6,159	5	7¼
To boat-men - -	22	0	10			
For strong waters and distillers' incidents - -	153	12	10½			

House of Lords MSS.

1691.

	£	s.	d.
For Coffee incidents	219	19	9
To the Deputy housekeeper	166	4	0
To the Yard-keeper	3	15	0
To the Woodmonger	501	12	6
To the Chandler	127	12	8
To the ironmonger, smith, glazier, upholsterer, bricklayer, joiner, carpenter, plumber, and mason, plasterer	174	14	8¾
For wages to the accountant of beer exported	42	17	4

Besides the rent of the office,

And (which is observed under another head) the charges of passing the Commissions, and the Commissioners passing their accounts.

There is an increase of salary to Mr. Felton and Mr. Chiffinch, as appears at large in the Account, folio 14.

Memorandum.

There is an account of 200*l.* per annum to Sir Robert Howard, particularly expressed under the head of excessive fees.

The Pay-Master of the Army by the establishments in the reign of King Charles the Second (still continued in the succeeding establishments) is to have 20*s.* per diem for himself and clerks; but from the time that the 12*d.* in the pound was deducted from the soldiers' pay, he has taken to himself besides the established allowance per annum - £3,613 18 4

And for his Clerks per annum - - 1,460 0 0

Besides 4,926*l.* 1*s.* 8*d.* per annum distributed by him for New Year's gifts, and other payments into the Exchequer; over and above what he has had when the payment to the Army has exceeded 600,000*l.* per annum. Only of late he has paid by a verbal order, to Sir Robert Howard, an annuity of 1,500*l.* per annum: all which payments have been made without any Privy Seal or account.

	£	s.	d.
Allowed the Right Honble. Wm. Harbord, Esq., as Paymaster to the Army in Ireland, from the 25th of March 1689 to the 5th of June 1690, for himself, besides what was allowed for his Clerks	7,000	0	0
More, he gives himself credit in the account of the Duchy of Cornwall, for three years' salary to Michaelmas 1688, as Surveyor-General	600	0	0
More, in the said account, as Auditor	420	0	0
More, paid him at the Exchequer, the 15th of May 1689, for extraordinary services to that time performed as Surveyor (besides 85*l.* 17*s.* for reward of making a new head to Slade Pond, in New Park, and repairing the island in the said pond)	1,114	3	0
	£9,134	3	0

House of Lords MSS.

1691.

Head VII.—Concerning Salaries continued, though the reasons cease :—Q. To send a List of the names and Salaries, and what employment they were, or are in.

The Salaries formerly allowed to the Commissioners of Excise were 500*l.* per annum to each: afterwards, because the Hearth-money revenue was also put under their management, the Salaries were increased to 1,000*l.* per annum each; which was continued till lately it is reduced to 800*l.* per annum; but the Commissioners are now increased in number to nine. It appears in the accounts before us, that the Salary and other allowances, heretofore established for the President and Council of Wales, to the value of 2,306*l.* 13*s.* 4*d.* per annum, is continued, though the Court of the President of Wales is taken away by Act of Parliament.

In the time of the late Government before the return of King Charles the Second, Mr. Hutchinson, the Treasurer of the Navy, had for himself, cashier, paymaster, and all the clerks of that office, per annum - - - - - £1,500 0 0

In the year 1660—

	£	*s.*	*d.*
Sir George Carteret was made Treasurer of the Navy, and claimed and received 3*d.* in the pound out of all payments by him made.			
The Earl of Anglesea succeeded to the like.			
Sir Thomas Osborn, now Marquess of Carmarthen, and Sir Thomas Littleton succeeded, and had each of them 1,000*l.* per annum for all the charge of the office, which was per annum - - - - - -	2,000	0	0
Sir Edward Seymour succeeded, at the salary per annum, for himself and clerks, of -	2,000	0	0
He, afterwards, being Speaker of the House of Commons, procured an addition to that office, of per annum - - - - -	1,000	0	0
And after that procured for a Paymaster 400*l.* per annum, and the like for a Cashier; for both - - - - - -	800	0	0
The Lord Falkland had the like, viz., with an addition of 8*s.* per diem for clerks to write the Sea Books, and 10*d.* or 12*d.* per diem to each clerk, for riding charges -	3,800	0	0
Mr. Russell now succeeds to the like salary, for himself, cashier, paymaster, and clerks, per annum - - - - - -	3,800	0	0
The 8*s.* per diem procured by the Lord Falkland to a Clerk for the Sea Books, was retrenched, in the Lord Falkland's time.			

The Fee Farm Rents, and some other rents of the Crown, were sold by an Act of Parliament, entitled, An Act for advancing the sale of Fee Farm Rents and other rents, made in the 22nd of King Charles the Second, and because that by the sale of those rents, the fees and perquisites legally belonging to the Auditors of the Revenue were extinguished, as to those rents; by warrant from the Treasury, the sum of 200*l.* per annum was, for the reason aforesaid, allowed to such of the said officers, as were then in being, and was to be a recompense to the said Auditors; but though some of them are since dead, new grants have been made to new Auditors, and the like salary yet continued, though the reason for the first granting of the same is ceased.

House of

1691.

We do find allowed to five Commissioners of Appeal in the Excise Office, for causes in London, 200*l.* per annum each, besides allowances to inferior officers belonging to them; but we do not find that they have sat for many years, or that there is any occasion for them, because all complaints of that nature are determined by the Commissioners of Excise.

The Hearth-Money duty expired the 25th March 1689, and yet the salaries on the account of the said duty are charged to Lady Day, 1691 - - - - - 4,983*l.* 16*s.* 4*d.*

	£	*s.*	*d.*
The Commission for Sir Richard Haddock, Sir John Parsons, Anthony Sturt, Senr., and Nicholas Fenn, Esqrs., for Victualling the Navy, ceased the 25th of Nov. 1689, and after the said Commissioners had charged the full salaries due to them and their officers, to the 25th of December following, they again charge one half year's full salary for themselves, from Christmas 1689 to Midsummer 1690 - - - - - -	800	0	0
And for the salary of their Cashier, for one year from Christmas 1689 to Christmas 1690 -	150	0	0

And yet it appears not to us that he paid any money after the 25th of March 1690; his employment ceasing when the new commission took place, the 25th of Nov. 1689.

The Honble. Henry Savile, Esq., late Vice-Chamberlain, had, upon special reason, an increase of salary of 600*l.* per annum, which has since been procured to be paid to his successor.

Head VIII.—Concerning several sums of money borrowed of the Receivers of the Public Revenue and interest for the same. Q. Who they were that had those sums, and what the said sums amount to?

The Commissioners, in viewing the accounts, took notice the Receivers of the Customs, the Cashiers of the Excise and Hearth money, had advanced money upon loans, and had interest allowed them for the same, as appears by the account delivered in folio 24.

		£	*s.*	*d.*
To	Richard Kent, Esq., for Interest - -	473	8	3
	Thomas Fox, Esq., for the same - -	4,131	12	6
	Charles Duncomb, Esq., for the same -	2,223	6	6¾
	Thomas Hall, Esq., Receiver of the Hearth money, for the same - - -	1,367	13	7

The Accounts at first brought in to the Commissioners wer half-yearly or yearly accounts, till, about Ladyday last, that they came in weekly, and so they could not tell thereby, whether at the time of loan the respective Cashiers and Receivers had the King's money in their hands, to the value of their loans. But it appeared to them, upon making up of their accounts at

House of Lords MSS.

1691.

Michaelmas last, that there was owing by Thomas Fox, Esq., Receiver-General of the Customs, very near the sum he lent, which was 50,000*l.*; and that there was in cash at the Excise Office, as appears by the account in folio 28, 37,485*l.* 5*s.*; therefore the Commissioners finding, upon making up of the accounts, money in the hands of the said Receivers, who formerly had lent money, and had interest for the same, made the Observation mentioned in this Head as fit for further examination, though they could not directly charge them to have had so much money in their hands at the time of the loans.

Head IX.—Concerning moneys having been paid to Parliament men out of Secret Service Money. Q. What the payments to Parliament men, whose names are not mentioned, amount to upon this Head?

The Commissioners having been refused an Account of what sums of money were paid out of Secret Service Money to Members of Parliament, can give no other account than what they have already observed, which is contained in the account folio 31, that being the account Mr. Jepbson, late Receiver of the Secret Service Money, drew up when he desired to be excused from giving any further account.

Head X.—Concerning great sums to divers persons which have been pardoned, and small Fee-farm rents excepted from pardon.—Q. To have a particular what the pardoned sums were, and by whom they should have been paid?

An account was brought to the Commissioners from Auditor Done, one of the Auditors of the Imprest, of such sums of money as appeared in his office to have been imprested upon account, to any person or persons, either out of the Exchequer, or by the Commissioners of the Navy, or Officers of the Ordnance, since the year 1660, and before the 25th of March 1673, and not accounted for, or their debt answered to the Crown.

The Account is very long, the Abstract of which is—

	£	*s.*	*d.*	£	*s.*	*d.*
The supers upon the Accounts of the Treasurers of the Navy - - -	351,448	14	11			
The debt upon the foot of Sir George Carteret's Account -	2,271	0	2			
The debt upon the foot of the Earl of Anglesey's Account	17,311	13	4¼			
The debt upon the foot of Sir Thomas Littleton's Account	18,119	2	10¼	549,257	19	2
The debt upon the foot of Sir Dennis Gauden's Account -	35,138	3	1¼			
The imprest to his Grace, George, late Duke of Albemarle - - -	5,000	0	0			
The supers on the account of the Treasurers of the Ordnance - - -	24,692	3	7½			
The imprests out of the Exchequer unaccounted for -	95,277	1	1¾			

After the said Abstract by him delivered, he exhibits the following Memorials, expressed in these words, viz.: There may be some of these imprests accounted for and cleared by Mr. Auditor Bridges, in accounts depending in his office, that I have not examined, or been acquainted with, and therefore do humbly refer you to the comparing this with his certificate.

Upon the account of the Remembrancer of First Fruits, there remains in super, upon Lawrence Steel, formerly the Receiver of that Revenue, the sum of 9,424*l.* 7*s.* 1*d.* And upon Sir Jno. Pretyman, Baronet, who succeeded the said Mr. Steel in that Office, the sum of 19,864*l.* 9*s.* 9*d.*, which sums, I am humbly of opinion, are likewise discharged by the Act of Grace.

I have been informed that Sir Jno. Pretyman's estate was extended for this debt, and that the whole, or greatest part thereof, was satisfied thereout, but this never appeared to me, or any of my predecessors, in such manner as to authorise me to discharge the account of the said debt.

I do further acquaint your honours, that since the delivery of Sir Thomas Littleton's last ledger into my Office, and before the passing the late Act of Grace, the now Sir Thos. Littleton did inform me, that he had found several Navy bills and vouchers, and was in hopes of finding sufficient to have discharged all, or the greatest part of the foregoing debt, had not the Act of Grace pardoned the same.

J. DONE,
Auditor.

Mr. Bro. Bridges, the other Auditor, of the Imprest, brought to the Commissioners some collections from the General Imprest Rolls, entered in his Office, of such sums of money as appear to have been imprested upon account before the 25th of March 1673, and are yet, for ought appears to him, unaccounted for, and which are as follows:—

The Right Honble. Arthur, late Earl of Anglesey, upon his account as Treasurer of the Navy, ended the 6th of Nov. 1668 (long since declared) remains indebted the sums of 17,311*l.* 13*s.* 4½*d.*, of which sum, upon a hearing before his then Majesty and several of the Privy Council, met for that purpose, the 14th of March 1684–5, at the Treasury Chamber, it was agreed, that 10,901*l.* 5*s.* 6¼*d.* (part of his demands) should be allowed him; but no Privy Seal, or other sufficient authority having yet been brought to me, for discharge thereof, the whole remains yet a debt upon his account.

There was also imprested to Sir Thomas Osborn (now Marquess of Carmarthen) and Sir Thomas Littleton, as joint Treasurers of the Navy, between the 6th of Nov. 1668, and the 14th of October 1671, several great sums of money, amounting (as by the general certificates) to 1,235,252*l.* 11*s.* 9¼*d.* whereof (Sir Thos. Osborn being discharged by Letters Patents) the executors of Sir Thos. Littleton have passed accounts for so much thereof as was imprested before the 31st of Dec. 1670, and are thereupon in superplus, 106,054*l.* 7*s.* 9¾*d.* But the account from the said 31st of Dec. 1670 to the 14th of October 1671, (which is before Mr. Auditor Done) not being finished, I cannot certify the balance of it.

Samuel Pepys, Esq., late Treasurer for Tangier, had several sums imprested to him for the service of that garrison, between

HOUSE OF LORDS MSS.

1691.

the 4th of Nov. 1664, and the 30th of April 1680, amounting (as by the said imprest certificates) to 852,537*l.* 1*s.* 0*d.*, and upon his last declared account, ended the 31st of December 1671, is indebted 16,712*l.* 5*s.* 7½*d.* His subsequent accounts for that service are not prosecuted.

John Jervice, Esq., had 2,341*l.* 17*s.* 11½*d.* imprested to him in the years 1670 and 1671, for the use of the President and Council of the Marches of Wales, which I do not find accounted for.

Peter de Mouline, late Secretary to the Council for Trade, has 700*l.* imprested to him for the service of the said Council, before the 25th of March, 1673, which I do not find accounted for.

Besides the particulars above mentioned, there are very many sums which remain as imprests upon sundry persons, in the accounts of the Navy and Ordnance, which I have not particularly mentioned. BRO. BRIDGES.

These are the sums returned to us to be imprested before the 25th of March, 1673, to which time all sums of money are pardoned by the Act of Grace, but how much was due to the Crown, in case the accounts have been made up, cannot appear to us, the Act of Grace preventing any further accounting.

Head XI.—Concerning excessive fees not to be challenged by law. Q. An Account of what fees, and by whom such fees have been received, for which there is no legal precedent to justify the same?

A List of excessive fees exacted and taken by officers, that have great salaries for the execution of their places, for which no legal precedent appears to justify the same:—

	£	s.	d.
The Office of Writer of the Talleys and Counter Talleys in the Exchequer is of late erection, he being properly the Clerk of the Lord Treasurer, or Commissioners of the Treasury, in which office there appears not to have been more than six persons from the first institution thereof.			
In the time of King James the first (as by a general charge of the Government then made) there was allowed to that officer the yearly sum of	91	13	4
And for a Clerk per annum - - -	9	0	0
In all - -	100	13	4
Which continued to the time of Sir Robert Long's being by the Earl of Southampton invested in that office, who had also a grant in reversion of the same, by Letters Patent of King Charles the First, under the great Seal of England, dated at York, the 6th of August in the 18th year of his reign, with the yearly salary for life, of - -	316	13	4
And the house in the Cloisters, which had formerly belonged to Sir Walter Mildmay, Chancellor of the Exchequer, and Under Treasurer thereof.			
This office is now possessed by the Honble. Sir Robert Howard, knight, by virtue of two Commissions, one from Lord Clifford and the other from Lord Viscount Osborn, now Marquess			

	£	s.	d.
of Carmarthen, late Lord Treasurer of England; and by Letters Patent of King Charles the Second, dated the 30th day of March in the 25th year of his reign, he has the like yearly salary as Sir Robert Long, of - - - - - -	316	13	4
And the house which was granted to the said Sir Robert Long, is also to him granted for life, with the augmentation of his salary, by the present Lords Commissioners of the Treasury, for extraordinary attendance, the yearly sum of - -	200	0	0
In all - -	516	13	4
But the said Writer of the Talleys, notwithstanding this salary, claims and takes several fees, upon the receipts and issues of the public revenue, as Auditor of the Receipt, which appears not to be any office now in being. And as Writer of the Talleys and Counter Talleys (which is the only office granted to him) to a great value, as may appear by the particulars subjoined; and by comparing the payment of such fees with the receipts and issues, whereby they arise, they amount in one year to more than, per annum -	6,000	0	0
Besides other payments for the entries of letters patent, privy-seals, warrants, certificates, and imprest accounts.			
And besides a yearly pension paid to him by the Paymaster of the Army by verbal order, out of money deducted from the soldiers' pay, the sum of - - - - - - -	1,500	0	0
And besides a yearly New Year's Gift, paid by the said Paymaster of the Army, 120 guineas, computed, at 20*d*. to the guinea - - -	130	0	0

Fees received by the Auditor of the Receipt of their Majesties' Exchequer :—

		£	s.	d.	
The Navy - -	per cent.	—			A gratuity 120*l*. (Navy and Victuallers)
The Victuallers of the Navy - -	„	—			
The Ordnance -	„	0	1	3	
The Forces - -	per £	0	0	0¼	$\frac{588}{1000}$
The Cofferer -	per cent.	—			Gratuity 60*l*.
The Treasurer of the Chambers -	„	—			Gratuity 24*l*.
The Robes - -	„	0	6	3	
The Wardrobe -	„	0	2	6	
The Works - -	„	0	2	0	
The Master of the Horse - -	„	0	6	3	
The King's Goldsmith	„	0	6	3	
The King's Jeweller	„	0	12	6	
Secret Service -	„	0	12	6	
The Mint - -	„	0	1	6	
The Privy Purse -	„	—			Gratuity 20*l*.

House of Lords MSS.

1691.

		£	s.	d.	
Tower Bills -	- per quarter	1	6	8	
Judges of Wales -	per cent.	0	12	6	
Lords Commissioners of the Great Seal -	"	0	12	6	
Commissioners of the Privy Seal -	"	0	12	6	
Ambassadors and Envoys for Equipage -	"	0	18	9	
For their ordinary entertainment -	"	0	12	6	
Pensions, Annuities, and Free Gifts -	"	1	5	0	
Band of Pensioners -	"		—		Gratuity 54*l*.

Fees as Writer of the Talleys, on which depend many particular services, and perpetual attendance:—

		£	s.	d.
Annuities and pensions -	- per cent.	0	18	10
Talleys upon sale of lands	-	0	5	6
Talleys on redemption of land	-	0	5	0
Talleys for Custom and Excise, upon every 1,000*l*. -	-	0	0	6
Talleys for Receivers General	-	0	0	6
Sale of wood, defective titles, fines of leases -	-	0	1	6
Alum works, pre-emption of tin, Receivers of Recusants	-	0	2	6
Sheriffs and Remanente Comps, sale of Recusant's goods, First-fruits, and all other Talleys -	-	0	0	6
Each search in the Records of the Talley Court -	-	0	1	0

Fees for Entries:—

		£	s.	d.	
All Letters Patent, per skin	-	1	0	0	
All Privy Seals -	-	0	4	6	
All Warrants, &c. -	-	0	2	6	
All Certificates - -	-	0	2	6	
All Imprest Accounts -	-		—		According to their length.

Fee by Patent (as is before observed) - £316 13 4

John Dyves, Esq., is, by Letters Patent of their present Majesties, constituted Secretary to the Prize Office, at the yearly salary of - - - - - - £500 0 0

Besides which salary, he charges and takes the fees following, viz.:—

	£	s.	d.
Upon all ships restored by decree of the Court of Admiralty, for an order of discharge - -	2	10	0
For the constitution of the Sub-Commissioners in the Out-ports, being ten in number, for their commissions and instructions, of each - -	6	0	0

For all Officers constituted by the Principal Commissioners under their hands and seals, for their commissions and instructions, viz.:—

Of the inferior officers - - - one guinea.

And of the other - - - - two guineas.

There be many other fees claimed by great Officers of the Crown, who have great salaries, but they having not been yet before us, we cannot specifically describe the same.

And there be many more officers of the Exchequer who take and claim fees, as the Tellers of the Exchequer, and others, but in regard they have but moderate salaries, we do not specifically mention the same, but humbly submit it, whether there can be any such legal prescriptions for fees out of the Exchequer, as are now required out of the Receipts and Issues of the Public Revenue; which, as to the greatest branches thereof, is of very modern existence; and whether any fees can be legally taken by Officers that have salaries for the execution of their offices; or any sort of fees in any kind demanded, which are not warranted by immemorial prescription, or constituted and authorised by Act of Parliament, of which there are many precedents in all times.

Head XII.—Concerning great quantities of Plate kept out of the Jewel House. Q. To have a List of the Plate sent in, and the names of the persons that retain it?

In answer to this, the Commissioners subjoin a State of all that is before them relating to this Head.

Plate in the hands of the Ambassadors of King Charles the Second and the late King's, and also in the hands of some great Officers of the late King's, and of other Officers, standing charged in the books of the Jewel House, viz.:—

	oz.
Earl of Sandwich, ambassador to Spain, from King Charles the Second - - - -	5,229
Lord Montague, ambassador to France, from the said King - - - - -	6,959
Earl of Sunderland, ambassador to Spain, for the said King - - - - -	6,959
Earl of Carlisle, ambassador to Sweden, from his said Majesty - - - - -	219
Sir Wm. Lockhart, ambassador to Holland, from the said King - - - - -	5,893
Earl of Castlemain, the late King's ambassador to Rome - - - - - - -	8,305
Sir Joseph Williamson, Secretary of State to King Charles the Second - - - -	2,433
Earl of Mulgrave, Lord Chamberlain to the late King - - - - - - -	1,161
Earl of Sunderland, Secretary of State to the late King - - - - - -	1,005
Lord Dartmouth, Master of the Horse - -	1,011
Earl of Peterborough, groom of the Stole to the late King - - - - - -	1,065
Lord Yarmouth, master Treasurer to the late King -	1,002
Lord Waldgrave, Comptroller - - -	1,015
Countess of Peterborough, groom of the Stole to the late Queen - - - - - -	1,009
Mr. St. Amand, their late Majesties' Apothecary -	1,150
Earl of Bath, groom of the Stole to King Charles the Second - - - - - - -	3,185
Earl of Bath, received from the bed-chamber, back-stairs and barbers to King Charles the Second -	4,151

House of Lords MSS.

1691.

	oz.
Sir Thomas Williams, chemist to King Charles the 2nd - - - - - - -	347
Lord Dartmouth - - - - - -	929
Lord Waldgrave - - - - - -	462
Mr. Thomas and Mr. Lesserteur, her late Majesty's cooks - - - - - - -	834
Jno. Peach, yeoman of the field to the late King -	30
John Bayley, yeoman of the field to the late King -	29
Mr. Point, of the cellar - - - - - -	4
Mr. Crofts, page of the bed-chamber to the late Queen - - - - - - -	146
Mrs. Dawson, dresser to the late Queen - -	62
Mr. Rondise, keeper of the late Queen's chapel -	329
Mr. Bell and Mr. Pedly, of the late Queen's chapel -	120
Mr. Horn, page of the backstairs to the late Queen -	45
Mr. Dufour, page of the bed-chamber to the late King - - - - - - -	4
Countess of Powis - - - - - -	783
Mr. Henry FitzJames - - - - -	2,447
	oz. 58,322

Signed:
Fra. Lawley.
Jno. Brydall.

To the Honble. Commissioners
of the Public Accounts.

Head XV.—Concerning the Royal Oak Lottery, with *non-obstantes* to several Acts. Q. Whether this Patent be passed with *non-obstantes*, as the other in King James's reign, and what essential difference there is between them?

The Commissioners find the Patent passed in the said King James's time to be with *non-obstantes* to the Statutes of

33rd of Henry the 8th,
2nd and 3rd of Philip and Mary,
39th of Queen Elizabeth,
1st of King James the first,
16th of King Charles the 2nd, or any other law, statute, act, ordinance, provision, proclamation, restriction, prohibition, or other matters or things whatsoever, in any wise to the contrary notwithstanding.

The Commissioners have not seen the new Patent, but, as they are informed, it is passed without any *non-obstante*. But in regard that the late King's learned Counsel took it to be requisite to have such *non-obstantes* to the said several Acts, to warrant such a Patent, and that since that time all power of dispensation is by Act of Parliament taken away, therefore the said Commissioners doubt how this present Patent can subsist, as to the legality thereof.

And they further observe that the mischief of that farm in debauching of apprentices, and other servants has been so much complained of, that they thought it incumbent on them to take notice thereof, and leave it to the wisdom of the Parliament to judge of the consequences of such a grant.

Head XVI.—Concerning persons discharged of their offices, and yet their pensions continued. Q. A List of such persons' names?

It appears by the Account, in folio 31, what is paid out of Secret Service money to the Earl of Warrington, Sir Henry Fane and Thomas Franckland, Esq., which is supposed to be upon the account of the offices from whence they were removed.

And, by the account of the Paymaster of the Irish Army, there is more paid, a standing allowance to the said Sir Henry Fane of 200*l.* a quarter.

And it further appears in the Account delivered in, folio 18, that the Earl of Sunderland's pension of 1,000*l.* per annum, granted to him by Patent in May 1680, is continued to be punctually paid, though of late it has been charged as paid to Mr. Charles Toll, lately deceased, as assignee of the said Earl.

Other instances of this kind appear in the paper now delivered, under the Head of Salaries granted upon special reasons, and continued, though the reasons are ceased.

Head XIX.—Concerning accounts that have been passed by Privy Seals only. Q. To mention particular cases, where accounts have been discharged by Privy Seals only?

In August, 1690, a Warrant, by Privy Seal, to the Exchequer was issued, directing the Officers thereof to state and pass, according to the course of the Exchequer, the account of the Right Honble. Wm. Harbord, Esq., for several sums received and expended from the 11th of Nov. 1688, to the 15th of December following, and to cause an allowance to be made to him, in a succeeding account, for the sum of 9,793*l.* 4*s.* 8*d.*, to be allowed him on his account as Paymaster-General of their Majesties' Forces in Ireland. In Aug. 1690 the like Warrant, by Privy Seal, was issued to the Officers of the Exchequer, for the Right Honble. Thomas Wharton, Esqr., for moneys received and expended by him, for carriages and horses and other contingent charges, for their Majesties' service in Ireland, between the 23rd of Jan. 1689 and the 24th of June 1690, charging him in the said account 19,717*l.* 8*s.*, and against the same to allow and discharge him the sum of 21,504*l.* 2*s.* 8*d.*

Sir John Guise, late Colonel of a regiment of foot, is charged with several sums of money, paid him by several Receivers in the West, between the 12th of Nov. 1688 and the 6th of January following, amounting to 1,380*l.* 2*s.*, and craving an allowance for 1,388*l.* 6*s.* 8*d.* by him paid for the said regiment, is discharged thereof, by virtue of a Privy Seal, dated in June 1691. In the Establishment of their Majesties' Land Forces and garrisons in England, commencing the 1st of May 1689, is a Warrant signed by his Majesty, subscribed by the Commissioners of the Treasury and Chancellor of the Exchequer, bearing date the 25th of August in that year, in which there is an allowance to the Paymaster of the Forces, of the deduction of a third part of one shilling, to be paid to him without account, for himself and Exchequer fees, whereof it appears not, by the said Establishment, that there is granted to him therein more than the yearly pay of 365*l.*; so that if the pay of the Army amounts to 600,000*l.*, there will remain the sum of 9,635*l.* yearly to be applied to Exchequer fees, and, as the Army is now increased, that deduction may

House of Lords MSS.

1691.

amount to more than twice that sum. But whether the Commissioners of the Treasury have examined and stated the Exchequer fees, appears not to us.

Head XX.—Concerning the duplicates of Particular Accounts. Q. What accounts, and by whom such accounts have been brought in?

Concerning the neglect in bringing in the several duplicates of the sums assessed upon the respective counties, the Commissioners found it to be so great, that it was a great hindrance to them in making up the account. And besides, they found it a usual practice in the Exchequer not to call for duplicates, where the sum, in the Aid given, was expressed, how much every county should pay, by which means whatever was raised on the county more than the sum given (which has been often practised) or by fines, or otherwise, was never accounted for in the Exchequer. And this was the rather observed, because there are agents who have a yearly salary and other allowances, to the end they may hasten in those accounts; but by their omission it has not been possible to make up a general account of any Aid given for many years.

Head XXI. — Concerning Commissioners and Receivers General. Q. A list of the names of such persons?

Payments of Taxes charged upon the King by those who have salaries.

Excise.

By the Commissioners of Excise, for the following taxes on the salaries of themselves and Cashier, viz.:—

	£	*s.*	*d.*	£	*s.*	*d.*
24 January, 1689, on the 12*d.* Aid	425	0	0			
9 July, 1690, on the 3*s.* Aid	1,275	0	0			
15 Oct., 1690, on their Poll Tax	425	0	0			
8 April, 1691, on the 12ms. tax, for the first quarterly payment	118	15	0			
				2,243	15	0

Memorandum.

These sums were paid by orders from the Commissioners of the Excise

In the account from the Commissioners of Excise, for the taxes of the salaries of the inferior officers, viz.:—

	£	*s.*	*d.*
26 September, 1689, on the Poll tax	441	6	2¼
15 October, 1689, on the same to Anto. and Hen. Seagar	6	0	0

	£ s. d.	£ s. d.	£ s. d.
5 February 1689-90 on the 12*d.* Aid	224 7 0		
August 1690 on the 3*s.* Aid	961 19 0		
		1,633 12 2½	
			3,877 7 2½

Memorandum.

That by several orders from the Lords of the Treasury, the above taxes were paid for the inferior officers of the Excise in London; besides what was paid for all other inferior officers in the several counties, which is supposed amounted to a very great sum, though the particulars are not yet brought in to the Commissioners.

Note.

The 1st order of the 23rd of January, 1689, was to pay the taxes for under officers, whose salaries did not exceed 70*l.* per annum.

The order of the 31st July, 1689, was to pay the taxes to under officers, whose salaries did not exceed 80*l.* per annum.

The order of the 7th of July, 1690, was to pay the taxes for salaries of under officers not exceeding 100*l.* per annum.

All which were paid, by virtue of the said several orders from the Lords Commissioners of the Treasury.

Memorandum.

The order for the repayment of taxes, on the salaries of the inferior Officers of the Customs and Letter Office, was to those who had but 60*l.* per annum.

Customs.

By the Commissioners of the Customs, for the taxes charged on several inferior officers, whose salaries did not exceed 60*l.* per annum - 2,405 6 10

Letter Office.

By the Masters of the Letter Office, for the taxes charged on several officers, whose salaries did not exceed 60*l.* per annum. - - 162 18 0

Prizes.

The Commissioners for Prizes charge the King for taxes of the salaries of themselves and Secretary, 300*l.*, which they have since, in their account, allowed back again, excepting - 22 10 0

£6,468 2 0½

Head XXIII.—Concerning Susan Willis procuring a Captain's place. Q. To send the Captain's name?

The Captain's name appears by the Affidavit signed by himself, copy whereof is as follows:—

28th September, 1691.

Captain John Venner, late Commander of the Samuel and Henry, of London, in their Majesties' service, attended the Board, and being asked what he gave for his commission to command that ship, saith, that he became acquainted with my Lady Newport, and upon discourse of having a commission, she asked him what he would give her to procure a commission for him? He said he would give one hundred guineas; and she brought him acquainted with one Mrs. Susan Willis, whom he met by appointment, at one Mr. Tassel's, a goldsmith, in Lombard Street, at the sign of the Bunch of Grapes. And he saw her likewise at other times, and he said to her he would give her a hundred guineas to have a commission. Admiral Russel wrote a letter on his behalf to the Admiralty, and went afterwards with him himself to the Board. And he had a commission, and when he had it, he gave one hundred guineas to Mrs. Willis, in the presence of my Lady Newport, in the lodgings of the said Mrs. Willis, in Scotland Yard. And he paid about five or six guineas to the Clerks of the Admiralty, which he took to be the customary fees. John Venner.

Head XXIV.—Concerning Establishments of the Army, and that nothing used to be offered for the Royal Signature, but under the hands of certain persons therein named, and its beginning in the Lord Treasurer Clifford's time. Q. Who the Officers were that gave the directions to the Muster Masters, and who those Commissaries of the Musters were, and what it appears to them the King paid by such Rolls, more than if he had paid effective men?

The Commissioners are informed upon oath, that in the Muster at Dundalk, Major-Gen. Kirk, Brigadier Steward, and Sir John Hanmore prevailed with the General, by verbal order, to have their Rolls closed for 6/ms, although, upon examination of their accounts, they ought to have been for 5/ms.

The Commissioners likewise had an account, that Lieut.-Genl. Douglas, in December 1689, took a review of the forces in Ireland, upon which there appeared to be between eleven and twelve thousand men; besides 1,192 which, upon the officers' word and honour, were allowed to be absent by reason of sickness. But when the Muster Rolls, for that time, were returned to the Commissioners, those Rolls make 8,106 to be absent by sickness.

The Commissioners examined Mr. Abraham Yarner, Commissary General of the Musters in Ireland, how the difference came to be between the Rolls and Major-General Douglas's review? His answer was that he believed there were very few of those returned sick in being. But the Commissaries, upon the assertion and certificate of the Officers (from whom likewise at every Muster, as we are informed, they usually take money) made up the Rolls accordingly.

The Commissioners have likewise had brought to their Board a copy of an order signed by Major-General Thos. Talmash, to the effect following:—

These are to direct and require you to pass the battalions and regiments undermentioned, complete upon the Muster Rolls, from the 1st of Nov. last to the last of February following, viz.:

One battalion of the 2nd Regiment of English Guards, of 7 Companies.
One battalion of Scotch Guards, in 7 Companies.
The Royal Regiment in two battalions, 26 Companies.
Col. Hodges' Regiment in Thirteen Companies.
Col. D'Offarel's Regiment in Thirteen Companies.

For which this shall be your Warrant. Dated at Ghent.

THOS. TALMASH.

To Mr. Richard Uthwat,
Commissary of the Musters.

The Commissioners cannot say how much the King would have saved, if the Army had been paid only for effective men, because it is not possible for them to know how far the orders of the respective Commanders in Chief, and certificates of the Officers, have prevailed with the Commissaries to fill up their Rolls with men not in being.

And besides, there have been many warrants procured to pay several regiments of the army, as if full, without regard to the Muster Rolls, though they have been so ill made up.

But by the best computation they can make, upon the examination of witnesses, they are of opinion that one-third part (at least) of the charge might have been saved if the Army had been always paid according to the effective men.

Head XXVI.—Concerning Agency to Regiments. Q. The names of the Agents that have given money for their places, and what regiments they belong to; and to whom they gave it, and who those Agents are that keep money in their hands?

The Commissioners do not in their Observations charge the agents with keeping money in their hands, otherwise than what they claim and deduct from the soldiers as fees to themselves. But for further answer to this Query, the relation of such of the agents themselves, as have appeared before us, being examined upon oath, is as follows:—

Mr. Newdigate Owsley, agent to Col. Matthew's regiment of Dragoons, gave to the said Colonel for his agent's place 200*l*.

Mr. William Walley, agent to the Lord Brandon's regiment of horse, gave his Lordship 50 guineas for the Agency, and was to give 150 more if the regiment stood twelve months.

Mr. Edward Ridley, agent to Sir John Fenwick, gave the said Sir John Fenwick for his place 200 guineas.

Mr. Molines, agent to the fourth troop of Guards, commanded by the Lord Dover, gave his Lordship 500 guineas for his place, to be paid out of the first money coming to him, out of the profits arising as agent of the said troop.

Mr. Richard Harnage, agent to Col. Danl. Deering's regiment, gave to Sir Edwd. Deering 50 guineas.

House of Lords MSS.

1691.

Mr. William Wallis gave 50*l.* for the agency of Col. Leveson's regiment; 50*l.* to another Colonel; to the Earl of Oxford 200 guineas; about the same sum for Lieut.-General Kirk's; and 50 guineas for Major-Gen. Trelawny's.

Mr. Thomas Richiers, agent to the Earl of Marlborough's regiment, gave to the said Earl, after he had been two years agent, 150 guineas; and paid to Sir Theophilus Oglethorp, to be agent to his regiment, 200 guineas.

Mr. John Clancy, agent to Col. Roger McElligot, gave to the said Colonel for his employment 300 guineas.

Mr. Adam Cardonnel gave for his agent's place, to Col. Hales, 200*l.*

The agents of the regiments of horse generally take 2*d.* per pound each muster for themselves, which, at six musters in the year, is 164*l.* 5*s.* per annum for a regiment.

The agents for the foot regiments generally stop 40*s.* each muster, out of each company, and reckon six musters every year, whether they are so often mustered or not, which is 12*l.* per annum for each company; and for each regiment of 13 companies, is 156*l.* per annum.

Besides their profits of 1*s.* in the pound for money advanced to the officers and soldiers on their pay before it comes due, all which, excepting the money advanced to the officers, goes out of the soldiers' pay. And several did own that they made considerable advantages from tradesmen who furnished the Army with clothes, shoes, &c., though some others have nothing of that advantage, the officers clothing their companies themselves.

Memorandum.

The whole Army formerly paid six shillings for every troop and company, at each respective muster, for Debenture Money, which (being lately taken away by Act of Parliament) is notwithstanding, by direction of the respective officers, continued to be given as a gratuity to the clerk at the Pay Office.

There is also stopped, by the several agents, out of the soldiers' pay, one day's pay, and 12*d.* per pound for the use of Chelsea College, &c.

Head XXVII.—Concerning buying of clothes. Q. To give instances where the rates of clothing were excessive?

The Commissioners offer these following instances, how the matter of clothing appears to them, as they have been able yet to examine the same :—

The Right Honorable Wm. Harbord, Esq., late Paymaster of the Forces in Ireland, charges shoes bought for the Army not at more than 3*s.* 6*d.* per pair. Mr. Mathew Ingram, who was appointed by the Right Honourable the Lords of the Committee for the Affairs of Ireland, to contract for clothes and accoutrements for several regiments there, charges the like sum of 3*s.* 6*d.* per pair. But Col. Charles Godfrey (who furnished clothes for above twenty regiments) in his account charges shoes at 4*s.* 6*d.* per pair, notwithstanding great quantities were bought by each of the three before-mentioned persons of the same shoemaker.

The Commissioners have not seen any patterns of the hats, shirts, cravats, and stockings, which have been by him furnished

House of Lords MSS.

1691.

to the soldiers; and those being of different goodness, by consequence are of different prices too, therefore they cannot judge of the reasonableness of what they are charged at, but take notice that Mr. Ingram charges nine pounds in the hundred less to the King, in his account of clothing, than the said Col. Godfrey does for the same things; but whether they differ in goodness, and to what degree, they cannot relate.

Mr. Richard Harnage and Mr. Richard Acton, did contract to furnish 10,000 surtouts for the Army in Ireland, and though they refused to give such an account to the Commissioners, as they required from them, yet, upon examination of the workmen by them employed, it did appear, that according to the greatest rates they gave, both for materials and making, they gained about forty pounds in the hundred by their contracts.

Head XXIX.—Concerning Irish Musters. Q. To send the names of the Muster-Masters?

The Commissioners sent their Precept to Mr. Abm. Yarner, Commissary-General of the musters of the Army in Ireland, to whose direction all the inferior Muster-Masters are subjected, which was dated the 12th of March 1690; and therein he was required not only to give an account of former musters, but to make exact musters of all the forces then in Ireland, on or before the 1st day of May 1691, that we might thereby know the state of the Army at that time, and to make a return thereof by the 1st day of June following. And the said Mr. Yarner, in a letter dated the 8th of May, acknowledged to have received the said Precept on the 23rd of March 1690, and in that and several other letters sent to us afterwards by him, he signified to us that he could not comply with our Precept, without the order of the General and Lords Justices, to whom he had applied himself for the same; but instead of obtaining an order to do it within the time required of him, three of his Commissaries were sent to Cork, Waterford, and Belfast, to attend the recruits coming from England, and he could get no order from the said General for making the said musters till the end of May, the General saying he would write to the Commissioners to satisfy them. After this, an Order was obtained from the General to muster the Army, dated about the end of May, but that muster was very long in taking, it being directed by the General's order, that at the taking thereof all the officers should take the oath of fidelity to their Majesties, whereby, and by reason that many of the forces were in garrison, as was alleged, in the midst of the enemy's quarters, no muster was completed till after the Army had been in the field, and in a great measure recruited; and not returned to the Commissioners before the 20th of September 1691. Since which time we have had the Commissary-General of Ireland before us, and examined him at our Board to all the particulars above mentioned, and cannot find that the fault of not pursuing our Precept, in the time therein limited, is to be imputed to him.

Head XXXI.—Concerning miscasting accounts, and particularly Mr. Fox. Q. In what particular this miscasting was?

As to miscasting of accounts in general, it has given the Commissioners a great deal of trouble, many of the accounts brought before them being greatly faulty herein.

House of Lords MSS.

1691.

In particular, as to what concerns Charles Fox, Esq., that mistake has been rectified since the Account delivered into the House of Commons, as appears by the entry in their Minute Book, dated the 2nd of December, 1691.

John Knight, Esq., Receiver General of the Customs, having obtained leave of the Commissioners to amend some mis-countings in the accounts of Charles Fox, Esq., Paymaster of the Army in Ireland, attended the Board, and rectified the following errors, viz.:—

An error of 1,300*l*. in the account of July and August, 1691.

A like mistake in the account of May and June for 5,000*l*.

And, in the same account, a mistake of 2,000*l*., making in all 8,300*l*.

In regard the Account, with the Observations of the Commissioners, was before that time delivered into the House of Commons, the Commissioners thought it best for them to deliver to your Lordships a true transcript of what they had before sent to the House of Commons, that being pursuant to your Lordships' order.

Memorandum.

There are many other particulars brought into us relating to salaries increased, and extraordinary bills of Incidents easily allowed, which we have not yet had time to examine and state.

Tho. Clarges.
Math. Andrewes.
Sam. Barnardiston.
P. Colleton.
Benj. Newland.
Paul Foley.
Ro. Harley.

Endorsed: Brought in 12 Jan. 1691–2, by the Secretary, Mr. Talbot, to the Commissioners of Public Accounts.

469. Dec. 9. Sir F. Penyston *v.* Lady Read.—Petition and Appeal of Sir Fairmedow Penyston, Baronet. Sir Compton Read, father of Petitioner's late wife, left her, as a portion, 4,000*l*. charged on his estate, and intended to leave her 1,000*l*. more, but abstained from so doing on his wife, the Respondent, who had an estate of her own worth 300*l*. a year, and was to have 400*l*. a year more on his death, undertaking to raise the 1,000*l*. out of her own estate. Respondent renewed this assurance to Petitioner, on marrying her daughter, and on the faith of it, Petitioner settled a jointure of 500*l*. a year on his wife. After the marriage, Respondent repeatedly promised to pay him the money, and offered to assign to him a security of 1,300*l*., which offer, however, he declined, having other expectations from her, as she boarded in his house, and expressed great affection to him and his wife. Petitioner having received some of Respondent's rents, by her directions, and also expended other sums on her behalf, gave her an account on 11 November 1685, showing a balance of 563*l*. in hand, which, with her consent, he retained in part payment of the 1,000*l*. Respondent afterwards acquiesced in his retaining further sums, amounting to 248*l*. and, though demurring to the payment of interest on the debt, never pretended that these sums so retained were for any other purpose but in part payment of the 1,000*l*., until Petitioner brought a Bill in Chancery to recover what remained unpaid, when Respondent for the

first time alleged that the sums in question were paid on a general account for her use, and so brought a bill in Chancery against him for an account and to have the money repaid, and on 22 July last the Lords Commissioners decreed that he should account to her for what he had received, but should not be allowed on such account any part of the 1,000*l*. Prays that this decree may be reversed, and Respondent ordered to answer. *Signed* by Appellant; *Countersigned* by Thos. Powys, William Pudsey, and Thomas Filmer. L. J., XIV. 679. [The Petition was ordered to be withdrawn with costs on 13 Feb. 1691-2. L. J., XV. 74.]

Annexed:—

(*a*.) 21 Dec. 1691. Answer of Dame Mary Read, widow. Denies that her late husband, who left two daughters, of whom Appellant's wife was the younger, ever intended to have charged his estate with the additional 1,000*l*., which was more than the estate would bear, or that Respondent ever gave such assurances as pretended. Appellant married without the consent of Respondent, who objected to the marriage, understanding how small and incumbered was Appellant's own estate. So far from being privy to the marriage, she did not know it had taken place till three days after. The marriage articles stipulated only for 4,000*l*. portion as consideration for a jointure of 500*l*., and when the conveyance came to be drawn, it was found that the lands settled by Appellant on his wife were incumbered by a jointure to his mother and by portions to nine brothers and sisters, and would only bring in about 300*l*. a year. Respondent never offered Appellant a security of 1,300*l*., or authorised him to pay himself out of her rents. She went to live with Appellant and his wife at their own request, and Appellant, in his accounts given to her, charged her 150*l*. a year for the maintenance of herself and three servants, two of whom ploughed and did other work for him. Appellant being in great want of money, Respondent allowed him to receive her rents, but never on account of the 1,000*l*. Appellant, so far from desiring a retainer of the moneys in his hands towards the 1,000*l*., brought his Bill to have satisfaction for the whole, and not merely part of that amount. Respondent never gave him any note in writing for the 1,000*l*., and, when the cause was heard in Chancery, his own counsel were so well satisfied with the invalidity of the pretended promise, as contrary to the Statute of Frauds, that they offered, with Appellant's consent, to pay Respondent 250*l*. in Court, in case she would discharge him from the account. Respondent's Bill was not to have the Appellant pay back any moneys he pretends to have received in part of the pretended 1,000*l*., but to have a general account of all the moneys which he and his agent received and paid for her. Appellant, in his accounts, has charged Respondent with several sums expended for his own use. Prays that the Appeal may be dismissed with costs. *Signed* by Respondent; *Countersigned* by Ambrose Phillipps. *Endorsed* as brought in this day.

470. Dec. 9. Swynock *v*. Sutton.—Petition and Appeal of Samuel Swynock, Merchant. An Agreement was made on 17 April 1690 between the Corporation of White Paper Makers, represented by Col. Norton (since deceased), the Governor, Petitioner, the Deputy Governor, Roger Gillingham, the Treasurer, and John Turner, Richard Sprigg, Nicholas Duplin, and John Dunston, Members of the Corporation, of the one part, and the Respondent, William Sutton, of Byfleet, Surrey, of

House of Lords MSS.

1691.

the other part, and subscribed by Petitioner, Norton, Duplin, and Sprigg, to the following effect:—Sutton was to assign George Hagar's Patent for making white paper to the Corporation within 14 days after the passing of an Act then in agitation, the passing of which Sutton was to use his interest and diligence to promote, in return for which the Corporation, within seven days after the passing of the Act, were to admit him as a member and assign to him four out of the 400 original shares. Sutton, whether the Act passed or not, was to lease his paper mills at Byfleet to Dunston and Peter Delanoy for 21 years from Midsummer next, at a rent to be settled by one or two referees, jointly chosen, and in case of their disagreeing, by a third, whom they should choose. By way of fine, the Corporation were to advance Sutton 100*l.*, half to be paid him on sealing the lease, and the remainder two days after the Act was passed, the first half to be deducted from the first year's rent, in the event of the Act not passing. To enforce performance of this agreement, Respondent brought a Bill into the Court of Exchequer, and the Court on 29 June 1691 decreed in his favour, giving him arrears of rent from Midsummer 1690. Petitioner, to avoid commitment, procured for Respondent his admission and his four shares, and named one Joseph Allen to settle the rent with Hagar, the nominee of Respondent. These two disagreeing, and failing to appoint a third referee, the Court referred the question of rent to Baron Turton, who fixed it at 150*l.* a year. Appeals from this Decree. The Court should have left the parties to their mutual actions at law; first, because Sutton had no right to assign Hagar's Patent, the same having been previously assigned to one Paris Slaughter on a Statute of Bankrupt; secondly, because Petitioner only acted for the Corporation, and Delaney and Dunston are no parties to the suit; and thirdly, because the Court had no right to go beyond the agreement and delegate the settlement of the rent to a person not chosen by the two original referees. Prays that the Decree may be reversed. *Signed* by Appellant; *Countersigned* by Ambrose Phillipps. [Reported this day from the Committee for Petitions, who decided by 4 to 2 that it was first to be received. (Pet. Book, 8 Dec. L. J., XIV. 679.) The Appeal was heard and dismissed on 16 Jan. 1691-2. (L. J., XV. 33.) *Mr. Darnell* (for Appellant) opened the case. *Sir Ambrose Phillipps* (for Appellant): The other part of the agreement is independent. This business or patent was not worth anything, but was a cheat to Col. Norton. *Sir Thomas Powys* and *Mr. Brydges* were heard for Respondent. (MS. Min.)]

Annexed:—

(*a*.) 19 Dec. 1691. Answer and Case of William Sutton, Gent. Respondent, who holds his mills, known as the King's Mill, by virtue of several leases from the Crown, obtained from the Commissioners of Bankrupts in 3 Jac. II. an assignment of a Patent for making white paper by sizeing of it in the morter, which Hagar had held for fourteen years from 10 August 34 Car. II. Petitioner and others, about April 1690, got a Bill introduced into the Commons for establishing the Corporation and excluding others from making White Paper, against which Respondent petitioned, in the name of Hagar, but having subsequently made the agreement referred to, he informed the Committee on the Bill of the fact, and the Bill was passed. Respondent did his best to perform the agreement, but as the Corporation refused to do their part, he was forced to bring a Bill into Exchequer, being unable to let his mills to anybody else. Since the Bill was exhibited, they allege falsely that they offered to value the mills and sent two persons for that purpose, but that Respondent did not send anyone to represent him. As to Delanoy and Dunston not being parties, the Corporation themselves moved the Court to strike their names out of the Bill, in order to correct the mistakes in their answers, and it was with their consent that Respondent continued to work the mills pending the completion of the agreement. The reference to Baron Turton was made on their own motion, and the rent he settled was what was to have been given, had the Bill not been introduced into Parliament. Appellant, since presenting his Appeal, has brought a Bill in Chancery, in the name of Paris Slaughter and Edward Highmore, against Respondent and Hagar and the Corporation, claiming the patent for Slaughter and Highmore, as creditors of Hagar. Prays that the decree in Exchequer may be confirmed with costs. *Signed* by Respondent; *Countersigned* by Edw. Brydges. *Endorsed* as brought in this day.

(*b*.) 21 Dec. 1691. Petition of Respondent for an early day for hearing. L. J., XIV 697.

(*c*.) 11 Jan. 1691–2. Petition of Appellant. The Appeal was to be heard this day, and Petitioner has feed his Counsel, the Solicitor General and Mr. Ward. But neither can attend; the former being Chairman of the Committee in the Commons appointed to sit this day on Supply, and the latter being engaged about the D. Norfolk's Bill. Prays for another day for hearing. L. J., XV. 23.

471. Dec. 9. Verdon and another *v.* Cooke and another.—Petition and Appeal of Sarah Verdon, widow, and James Verdon, an Infant. Cyriac Cooke, brother of the Respondent Roger Cooke, having borrowed 100*l.* in 1665 of Appellant's late husband, Samuel Verdon, mortgaged to him, in the name of Henry Ossant, the reversion in fee of certain lands in Beeston, Norfolk, expectant on the estate for life of Thomas Bishop, which Samuel afterwards purchased for 600*l.*, together with Bishop's life estate, worth 60*l.* a year. In 1671 Roger Cooke and Anthony Freston, pretending to be creditors of Cyriac, obtained from him a conveyance of the lands in trust to pay his debts, and their own claims in the first place, and in 1674 brought a Bill in Chancery against Samuel and Ossant to redeem the mortgage and have the purchase deed set aside as fraudulent. The Court on 31 Jan. 1682 decreed in their favour, but no proceedings were taken on the decree till after Samuel died, leaving the lands to the Appellant Sarah, his widow, to be sold for payment of his debts, and the surplus for portions for his children, when the Cause was revived against Petitioners, and on 3 Dec. 1690 the Lords Commissioners decreed against them, as against Samuel, without allowing them to prove the purchase deed at a trial at law. Pray that this decree may be reversed and Roger Rooke and Freston ordered to answer. *Signed* by Sarah Verdon; *Countersigned* by Ambrose Phillipps and Jo. Warkhouse. L. J., XIV. 679. [The Cause was heard on 2 Dec. 1692. *Sir Ambrose Phillipps* (for Appellant): There was no room for equity to interpose in this case. The Court put it to a trial. We go upon it there was no proof. *Sir Thomas Powys* (for Appellant): I will put it upon that point. This is a title at law or nothing. We have a title by twenty-four years' possession. They have decreed our deed to be set aside. *Mr. Holles* (for Respondent): They would not appear to hear judgment. Counsel withdrew, and the Speaker reported. *The Judges* heard:—Fraud or not fraud, ought to be referred to a trial at law, and the Chancery ought to have it referred to a trial. *Ordered* that the Decree be reversed. (MS. Min., L. J., XV. 132.)]

House of Lords MSS.

1691.

Annexed:—

(*a.*) 19 Dec. 1691. Answer of Roger Cooke and Anthony Preston. Samuel Verdon got the papers relating to the lands into his custody, under pretence of being Cyriac Cooke's solicitor. Cyriac confessed in his answer below that Samuel Verdon only paid him 40s. consideration for the purchase, for which he afterwards made Cyriac debtor in some accounts between them. Respondent Cooke was prevented from prosecuting the decree by being committed to the Fleet for debts, for which he was bound for his brother Cyriac, and Samuel Vernon died immediately after his release. The Master reported that the 100*l.* and interest due on the mortgage to Ossant was satisfied by mesne profits with an overplus of 533*l.*, and this report was confirmed by the decree of 3 Dec. 1689 (*sic*). Bishop died in 1676, and Respondents have been prosecuting the cause in Chancery for 16 years at the cost of over 300*l.* and are disabled from making any defence at law, as the Appellants detain all the papers. Appellants never moved the Court of Chancery for a trial at law. Pray that the appeal may be dismissed with costs. *Signed* by Respondents. *Endorsed* as brought in this day.

(*b.*) 4 Jan. 1691–2. Petition of Respondents for an early day for hearing. L. J., XV. 15.

472. Dec. 14. E. Salisbury's Estate Act.—Amended draft of an Act for the better securing the portions, debts, and legacies given and owing by James, late Earl of Salisbury. The Lords' Amendments, besides those which are either drafting or verbal ones, are to add the Clause, offered by Mr. Dobyns, for determining the terms of 99 years limited by James, late Earl of Salisbury to the Earls of Devonshire, Burlington, and Cork and Wm. Montagu. The Commons' later Amendment (C. J., X. 631) is a verbal one. [Reported from Committee for Petitions on 9 Dec. as fit to be received (Pet. Book, 8 Dec.; L. J., XIV. 679). Read 1ª this day; Royal Assent 24 Feb. 1691–2 (L. J., XIV. 680; XV. 92). 3–4 W. & M. c. 12 in Long Calendar.]

Annexed:—

(*a.*) 21 Dec. 1691. Lords' Amendments to the Bill. [Made in Committee 16 and 18 Dec. (Com. Book), and reported this day. (L. J., XIV. 696.)

(*b.*) 21 Dec. 1691. Amended clause, marked A. [Added in Committee 16 Dec. (Com. Book) and reported this day. (L. J., XIV. 696.]

(*c.*) 21 Dec. 1691. Clause marked B. [Offered by Mr. Dobyns to Committee and agreed to on 18 Dec. (Com. Book), and reported this day. (L. J., XIV. 696.)]

(*d.*) Lords' Amendment to the Bill. [It is marked on the Draft Bill, but is not among the amendments in Annex (*a.*), nor is it mentioned in Com. Book. On the other side of this paper is written "Mr. Relfe. Pray procure Pember's Committee to be adjourned till to-morrow morning. Your servant J. Allen."]

473. Dec. 10. Mason *v.* Woodroffe.—Petition of Nicholas Mason, Gent. Since Petitioner brought his Appeal, the then Respondents, viz., Sir George Woodroffe, Sir Arthur Onslow, and Richard Sims, Executors in trust of Roger Duncomb, are all dead. Sir G. Woodroffe has left George, his son, and Mary Langley, his daughter, his executors; Sir A. Onslow has left his son, Sir Richard, his executor, and Sims has left his son, Thomas, his executor, and George Duncomb, heir at law, is in possession of the estate. Petitioner's demand is only for performance of a trust, and by a Standing Order of the House of Commons of

2 Nov. last* no privilege is allowed to any member of that House in cases where, as is the case with Sir Richard Onslow, they are only trustees. Prays that a day may be appointed for hearing. L. J., XIV. 680. [The Appeal never came to a hearing. For earlier papers in this Cause see Calendar, 11th Report, Appendix, Part II., No. 450.]

474. Dec. 10. E. Winchelsea's Estate Act.—Amended Draft of an Act for the enabling the Right Honorable Charles, Earl of Winchelsea, to settle a jointure upon any wife he shall marry during his minority. The Lords' Amendments are either verbal or drafting ones. (Com. Book.) [Reported from Committee for Petitions on 9 Dec. as fit to be received (Pet. Book, 8 Dec.; L. J., XIV 679). Read 1ª this day; Royal Assent 24 Feb. 1691-2. (L. J., XIV. 680; XV. 92.) 3-4 W. & M. c. 15, in Long Calendar.]

Annexed:—

(a.) 19 Dec. 1691. Consent of Heneage Finch, Thomas Finch, Leopold William Finch, and Lesley Finch, uncles of the E. Winchelsea, to the passing of the Bill. *Dated* 13 Dec. 1691. [Delivered in to the Committee this day. Com. Book.]

(b.) 21 Dec. 1691. Lords' Amendments to the Bill. [Made in Committee 19 Dec. (Com. Book), and reported this day. (L. J., XIV. 696.)]

(c.) Unamended draft of the Bill.

475. Dec. 10. Martyn's Estate Act.—Draft of an Act for the sale of the Manor of Manworthy, with the appurtenances, in the County of Devon, being the lands and estate of Nicholas Martyn, Esquire, by Trustees herein-after named, for the payment of the debts of the said Nicholas Martyn. The two Amendments (Com. Book, 21 Dec.) are purely clerical. [Reported on 9 Dec. from the Committee for Petitions (L. J., XIV. 679), who resolved by 6 votes to 1 that it was fit to be received. (Pet. Book, 8 Dec.) Read 1ª this day; Royal Assent 24 Feb. 1691-2. (L. J., XIV. 680; XV. 93.) 3-4 W. & M. c. 27 in Long Calendar.]

476. Dec. 11. Sir J. Mordaunt *v.* Keck.—Petition and Appeal of Sir John Mordaunt. Respondent, having obtained two judgments from Robert Mordaunt, Appellant's uncle, one of 600*l.* and another of 200*l.* in the name of Richard Rabon, for payment of 323*l.* and 100*l.* respectively, brought his Bill in Chancery against Robert Mordaunt and Petitioner, who, as he alleged, had got his uncle's estate into his hands and promised to be bound with him in a bond for the debts. Petitioner denied this promise, and pleaded that he had more than satisfied what he had received on account of his uncle, by paying three of his bills to Sir Francis Child, and others for 1,600*l.*, and 166*l.* to Braylesford and Chester on their assignment of certain judgments, and also interest on a mortgage of 700*l.* to Charles Mordaunt, leaving his uncle indebted to him for 1,497*l.* The Court on 2 May last decreed Appellant to pay Respondent's claim out of his uncle's estate in his hands, in case his uncle did not pay, and Respondent has since obtained an injunction to stay all proceedings at law on writs of error to reverse the two judgments. Prays that the decree and injunction may be reversed, and Respondent ordered to answer. *Signed* by Appellant; *Countersigned* by William Whitelocke and Jam. Stedman. L. J., XIV. 682. [The Appeal was heard and dismissed on 19 Feb. 1691-2 (L. J., XV. 85), *Sir William Williams* and *Mr. Finch* appearing for Appellant, and the *Solicitor-General* and *Mr. Trevor* for Respondent. (MS. Min.)]

---

* C. J., X. 544.

Annexed:—

(a.) 24 Dec. 1691. Answer of Samuel Keck. Robert Mordaunt employed Respondent as his attorney, to defend the will of one Bassett Cole in his favour, which was disputed by Cole's widow, and being in want of money on his return from Holland, borrowed large sums from Respondent, by whose means he succeeded in recovering an estate of above 10,000*l*. Appellant was appointed to receive the rents of this estate, under trust to pay his uncle's debts, and never disputed Respondent's claim, till Respondent's house was burnt down and his papers destroyed. It was proved at the hearing that Appellant had enough money in his hands to pay Respondent, whose debt was certified by the Master to amount to 869*l*. Robert Mordaunt, since the proceedings, became and still is a prisoner, and Respondent is not likely to have any part of his debt paid by him. Prays that the Appeal may be dismissed with costs as vexatious. *Signed* by Respondent; *Countersigned* by William Squibb. *Endorsed* as brought in this day.

477. Dec. 11. Hungerford and others *v.* Pollard.—Petition and Appeal of Jane Hungerford, Anthony Withers, Matthew Boucherett, and Sarah his wife, executors of Sarah Pollard, deceased, Nicholas Hughes, son and heir of Nicholas Hughes, deceased, William Downe, John White, John Bidder and Joane Withers. John Pollard, the great uncle of the Respondent, Thomas Pollard, being seized in fee of certain lands in Middlesex, Devonshire, and Cornwall, settled them in 19 Car. II. on William Withers and Nicholas Hughes, in trust to mortgage or sell for payment of his debts, the surplus to go to Sarah Pollard, his widow, during her life, with remainders for life successively to the heirs of his body, to Thomas, the grandfather, and Richard, the father of Appellant, and to Richard's first son, namely, the Respondent. John Pollard died in 1667 without issue, and the trustees and Sarah, by their directions, paid his debts and sold part of the estate. Respondent's grandfather and father then brought a Bill in Chancery against Sarah and Hughes, the surviving trustee, for an account, but on receiving one to their satisfaction, they proceeded no further. All the parties to this suit having died, Respondent, by his guardian, brought a Bill against Appellants for an account and conveyance of the surplus of the land, and the Court on 16 June, 4 Jac. II., having directed a Master to take an account, he reported charging Appellants with all the receipts set forth by Sarah and Hughes in their answer to the former Bill, and the Lords Commissioners, on hearing the exceptions to this report on 17 Nov. 1691, refused to allow Appellants the sum of 728*l*., paid by Sarah and the trustees for John Pollard's debts. Pray that their decretal order may be reversed and that the account of Sarah Pollard and Hughes may stand. *Signed* by the Appellants, Jane Hungerford, Anthony Withers, and Nicholas Hughes; *Countersigned* by William Williams and J. Darnell. L. J., XIV. 682. [The Cause was first heard on 5 Feb. 1691-2. *Sir William Williams* (for Appellant): We have every particular of his receipts and payments. The question is an answer seventeen years before the Cause heard. An account was annexed and all the items are in the account. *Mr. Finch* (for Appellant): This 700*l*. is an item in the account of 16 years since, and we depend upon that account as stated; but because his account was not adjusted, there is another 300*l*. allowed us, but not the whole, which is Stephens' debt. Addington acknowledged payment, and we ought to have it allowed. *Mr. Trevor* (for Respondent): The account was not fairly kept, and goes backward and forward. We have proved what they received. *Sir Thomas Powys:* The Court upon the Master's Report [found] there is a release from Addington, and one Coppleston is brought out of gaol for this. The Court thought him so ill a man that he was fit for prison again. A deed from Hughes and Sarah to E. Aylesbury, and no mention of the deed amongst those mentioned. They read 29 Sept. a note under John Pollard's hand. They read the rental of the debts to any in E. Aylesbury's deed. *Counsel* heard in reply on both sides. Counsel withdrew and the Speaker having reported, it was referred to a trial at law in King's Bench on a feigned issue whether the whole sum of 728*l.* 5*s.* was a real debt or not, or how much was so, and whether it had been really paid. (MS. Min., L. J., XV. 63.)—On 17 Feb. the House, on a Petition of the Appellant, Jane Hungerford (Annex (*b.*) below) gave her leave to try the title to the estate at the next Assizes for Devon. (L. J., XV. 80.)—On 7 Nov. 1692 the Appellants having petitioned for a day for hearing on the equity reserved (Annex (*c.*) below), and the Respondent for a rehearing on the merits (Annex (*d.*) below), the House referred both Petitions to the Committee for Petitions (L. J., XV. 105), who after hearing Counsel and reading an Affidavit of Mr. Stephens, another of John Cane, and a Deposition of Lancelot Copleston (Priv. Book, 19 Nov.), reported that a new trial be appointed upon the new evidence, which the House accordingly ordered to be had at King's Bench. (L. J., XV. 117.)—On 25 Nov. a Commission was granted on a Petition of the infant Respondent's guardian (Annex (*e.*) below) for examining Henry Stephens and Ursula Pollard. (L. J., XV. 125.)—On 24 Jan. 1692–3 a Petition of the Appellant for a reference to one of the Judges to settle the issue (Annex (*f.*) below) was rejected (L. J., XV. 197), and the next day, on a Petition of the Respondent (Annex (*g.*) below), the Appellants were ordered to appoint an Attorney to accept of an Issue, otherwise the Respondent to proceed in Chancery. (L. J., XV. 200.)—On 20 Feb. the Respondent, who had obtained a verdict in King's Bench, petitioned to have the Appeal dismissed. (Annex (*h.*) below, L. J., XV. 237.)—On 23 Feb. the House heard Counsel on this Petition. *The Solicitor General* was heard for the Appellant. *Mr. Darnell* heard for Petitioner. *Sir Bartholomew Shower:* We differ upon the issue directed by your Lordships. We did not know when Pollard died or Addington died. *Holt, C. J.:* We conceive we can give you an account of the business. *Mr. Gibbins* (for Appellant): It was tried upon the merits of the cause. *Holt, C. J.*, was heard. Counsel withdrew. A new trial ordered at King's Bench on a feigned issue to be settled by C. Justice Holt, and Appellant to pay Respondent 20*l.* costs. (MS. Min., L. J., XV. 246.)—On 2 March the House, on motion, gave leave to William Downe to pay certain money, not comprehended in the Appeal, to Margaret Cave, guardian to the infant Respondent. (*Ib.* 256.)—On 10 Nov. 1693, Appellant, having gained a verdict in King's Bench, petitioned for a hearing on the equity reserved. (Annex (*i.*) below. L. J., XV. 297.) In the Committee for Petitions, to whom this Petition was referred, the following proceedings are recorded:—Nov. 14. Petition of Thos. Pollard given in.* Their Lordships being called into the House, *Ordered* that both sides be heard on the 17th inst.—Nov. 17. E. Stamford in the Chair. Petitions of Jane Hungerford and of Thos. Pollard read. Order of 5 Feb. 1691 read. *Ordered* that the books be brought over at the next meeting. L. C. Justice Holt to be spoken with. *Eodem die*, E. Bridgewater in the Chair. The two Petitions read. *Holt, C. J.*, says he never directed a jury. He always leaves it to their consideration. The verdict was

* This Petition is not among the Papers.

HOUSE OF LORDS MSS.

1691.

grounded on strong evidence. The Parties are called in. The paragraph in Pollard's Petition reflecting on the L. C. Justice is read. *Mr. Gibbins* says he knows nothing of it; he never saw the Petition till this morning. He should have been ashamed, and should have asked my Lord's pardon, if he had done anything in it. *Mr. Hooper* (for Hungerford) desires they may be heard at the Bar as to the equity, a verdict having been found for them. *Mr. Gibbins* desires Downe may produce the deed in his hand. *Mr. Hooper:* The deed was produced at the trial at Exon. They withdraw. *Ordered* to report that Appellant's Petition is fit to be received, that the House be moved that Thos. Pollard should make his submission to C. Justice Holt, and that the matter of the Deed should be left to the House. (Pet. Book of dates.)—On 18 Nov. the House, on this report, ordered a rehearing in Chancery, and that the Deed should be then produced. *Thomas Pollard*, being called in, asked pardon of the House and was ordered to do the same of C. Justice Holt. (MS. Min., L. J., XV. 302.)]

Annexed:—

(*a.*) 29 Dec. 1691. Answer of Thomas Pollard, an Infant, by his guardian. Sarah Pollard concealed her husband's deed of trust from Respondent's grandfather and father, and having many poor kindred of her own, pretended great debts due to them and others from the estate, and sold a great part of it, in collusion with the trustee Hughes, who was her brother-in-law and of her own nomination. Respondent's grandfather and father offered to secure what debts were proved in order to save the estate, but she refused. They were never satisfied with her account, but were prevented from contesting it by the death of the grandfather, and because Respondent's father could not proceed by way of revivor. There was no proof that the 728*l.* was a debt within the trust. The Appellant, Sarah Boucherett, is some years since dead, and Downe, White, Bidder, and Joane Withers have given no authority for bringing the Appeal. Prays that the Appeal may be dismissed with costs. *Countersigned* by John Niccolls and William Lowther. *Endorsed* as brought in this day.

(*b.*) 17 Feb. 1691–2. Petition of Appellants, that a trial may be directed at the next assizes in Devonshire, and that Respondent may be obliged to receive a declaration and join issue, or that the issue may be taken *pro confesso*, the Appellant, Jane Hungerford, being near 77 years of age, and having defended the cause at her own charge for the benefit of the poor legatees. *Signed* by Jane Hungerford only. L. J., XV. 80.

(*c.*) 7 Nov. 1692. Petition of Appellants. In pursuance of their Lordships' order of 17 Feb. last, Appellants carried down a Record to be tried at the assizes in Devonshire, on the issues directed, and the Petitioner Hungerford has obtained a verdict, finding that the 728*l.* 5*s.* was a real debt and bonâ fide paid by her and Withers and Hughes. Pray for a day for hearing on the equity reserved. L. J., XV. 105.

(*d.*) 7 Nov. 1692. Petition of Thomas Pollard, an Infant, by his Guardian, Respondent. Appellants' only material witness at the trial was one Lancelot Coppleston, her nephew, who had been proved to have forsworn himself in Chancery, and whose evidence is contradicted on affidavit by Stevens. The whole pretence of the debt is a fraud and contrivance. Prays for a rehearing on the merits and on the Affidavits annexed. L. J., XV. 105.

(*d*[1].) Affidavit of George Blinch, of Buckland, co. Devon, Brewer, that Henry Stevens, of Deponent's parish, was unable from illness to attend the assizes at Exeter. *Sworn* 29 Jan. 1692 before S. Keck. *Examined* 4 Nov. 1692, P. J. Poynter. [This and the following Affidavits are appended to preceding Petition.]

(d^2.) Affidavit of Henry Stevens, of Buckland, Brewer, that John Pollard, late of Langley, co. Devon, deceased, was in no way indebted at his death to Deponent, nor has Deponent since his death received of either his widow, or Withers, or Hughes any sum in discharge of any debt from Pollard. *Sworn* 19 May 1692 before [E.] Rosier. *Examined* 4 Nov. 1692, P. J. Poynter.

(d^3.) Affidavit of John Cave, of St. Dunstan's parish, West London, Garnisher, that he has seen it recorded in the Register Book of Braunton, co. Devon, that Thos. Addington died there on April 4, and was buried April 6, 1668, as appears by the annexed extract, subscribed by the Parish Clerk. *Sworn* 3 Nov. 1692 before S. Keck. *Examined* 4 Nov. 1692, P. J. Poynter.

(d^4.) Extract from Parish Register of Braunton, referred to in preceding Affidavit. *Signed* George Berry, Parish Clerk. *Examined* 4 Nov. 1692, P. J. Poynter.

(d^5.) Affidavit of Henry Pethybridge, of Atherington, co. Devon, Yeoman, that John Pollard was buried at Yarnescombe, in the said county, on 16 Nov. 1667, as appears by the annexed extract from the Register Book. *Sworn* at Torrington, 22 Aug. 1692, before E. Rosier. *Examined* 4 Nov 1692, P. J. Poynter.

(d^6.) Extract from Parish Register of Yarnescombe, referred to in preceding Affidavit. *Signed* by John Pyne, Vicar, and Anthony Oatway, Parish Clerk. *Witnessed* by H. Pethybridge, before E. Rosier. *Examined* 4 Nov. 1692, P. J. Poynter.

(*e*.) 25 Nov. 1692. Petition of Margaret Cane, Guardian to the Respondent Pollard, that a Commission may issue for the examination of witnesses. L. J., XV. 125. *In extenso.*

(*f*) 24 Jan. 1692-3. Petition of Appellant. Their Lordships ordered a new trial between the parties at King's Bench, by a Middlesex jury at Nisi Prius, without limiting any time. It rests on Petitioner's part to prove the 728*l.* a real debt, but one Lewes Vicary, D.D., a most material witness, lives in Devonshire, and being nearly 80 years old, cannot come to London until the days are longer and the ways better, and without his evidence Petitioner will be utterly undone. Prays that it may be referred to one of the Judges to settle the issue to be tried, and for leave to examine Dr. Vicary by a Commission. *Signed* by J. Hungerford only. [Read this day and rejected. L. J., XV. 197.]

(*g*.) 25 Jan. 1692-3. Petition of Respondent. Appellants obtained a verdict by false evidence and surprise. Petitioner's Attorney prepared an issue for a new trial, but Appellants' Attorney refused to accept it. Pray their Lordships to order Appellant forthwith to appoint an Attorney to accept the same, or, in default thereof, for leave to prosecute Appellant on the Decree in Chancery. *Signed* Margaret Cane and Thomas Pollard. L. J., XV. 200.

(*h*.) 20 Feb. 1692-3. Petition of Respondent to dismiss Appeal, and direct the Chancery to allow the money now appearing due to him, with interest and costs. L. J., XV. 237.

(*i*.) 10 Nov. 1693. Petition of Appellant. At the last trial at Nisi Prius before Chief Justice Holt, Respondent obtained a verdict owing to a mistake in the issue, and not, as Chief Justice Holt himself declared, on the merits. Their Lordships, on

23 Feb. last, ordered a new trial in the Court of King's Bench on a feigned issue to be settled by the Lord Chief Justice. This new trial has been had, and a verdict found for Petitioner. Prays for a day for hearing Counsel at the Bar on the equity reserved by their Lordships after the trial at law. L. J., XV. 297.

478. Dec. 12. Hall *v.* Ayres (In Error).—Copy Transcript of Record, with tenor of Judgment of the House (L. J., XV. 70. *In extenso*) affixed thereto. The Plaintiff, John Hall, had ejected Defendant, William Ayres, from some lands in Chilton, Bucks, which the latter had leased from John Ayres. Defendant obtained costs and damages in the Court of King's Bench, from which judgment Plaintiff appeals. [Writ of Error brought in this day. (L. J., XIV. 683.) At the hearing on 10 Feb. 1691–2, no Counsel appearing for Defendant, *Mr. Carter*, for Plaintiff, prayed exemplary costs. Standing Order read, and Judgment affirmed with 20*l.* costs. (MS. Min., L. J., XV. 70.)]

Annexed:—

(*a.*) 5 Jan. 1691–2. Petition of Defendant for an early day for hearing. L. J., XV. 18.

479. Dec. 12. Briggs *v.* Clerke (In Error).—Copy Transcript of Record, with tenor of Judgment of the House (L. J., XV. 36. *In extenso.*) affixed thereto. Maria Cooke, the Defendant, obtained a judgment for a debt of 201*l.* 3*s.* and 12*l.* 1*s.* damages and costs against Thomas Cooke, Deputy Marshal of the Marshalsea under Mr. Philpot, and on Cooke failing to pay more than 23*s.*, caused him to be arrested for the balance, namely, 212*l.* 1*s.*, and Philpot kept him in custody. William Briggs, the Plaintiff, having succeeded Philpot as Marshal in June 1690, let Cooke escape. Defendant then brought an action against him for the debt, and obtained a verdict and judgment, which was confirmed by the Exchequer Chamber. Plaintiff appeals from this Judgment. [The Writ of Error was brought in this day. L. J., XIV. 683. The Cause was heard on 18 Jan. 1691–2. No Counsel appearing for Plaintiff, *Counsel* for Defendant moved for costs. Judgment affirmed with 20*l.* costs. (MS. Min., L. J., XV. 36.) *See* Shower's Cases in Parliament, p. 110.]

Annexed:—

(*a.*) 31 Dec. Petition of Plaintiff for an early day for arguing the errors. L. J., XV. 11.

480. Dec. 14. Salt (Naval Prize) Act (3 W. & M. c. 4.)—Account of Spanish and Portugal Salt, viz.:—

						£	s.	d.
From Lady Day	1684	to Lady Day	1685,	Weys	1,429¾ -	90	11	0
Do.	1685	do.	1686,	,,	1,067¾ -	67	12	6
Do.	1686	do.	1687,	,,	862½ -	50	16	6
Do.	1687	do.	1688,	,,	394 -	24	19	1
From Michaelmas	1688	to Michaelmas	1689,	Weys	224 -	14	3	9
Do.	1689	do.	1690,	,,	457 -	28	18	9
Do.	1690	do.	1691,	,,	1,156 -	73	4	3

By discourse with several Merchants that have been employed in victualling, and one that was an agent for Merchants for Ireland, that have tried all salts, Spanish and Portuguese, French and English, [they] say that the French is the best for the victuallers, for the English is too weak and the Spanish and Portuguese too piercing. *Noted:* We certify to Outports double increase of price. *Endorsed* as brought in by Commissioners of Customs this day. [The Bill for preserving two ships lading of Bay Salt, taken as prize, for the benefit of the Navy, &c., was brought from the Commons on 5 Dec., and read 1ª on the 7th, when the House ordered to hear the Commissioners of Customs and of the Victualling Office. (L. J., XIV. 673, 676.)—On 14 Dec. the *Victuallers of the Navy* were called in, and informed of the Bill. *Mr. Papillon:* I was a Victualler in 1672 and 1673. We have experience that this salt is most useful, and no other does so well, and last year we had great experience from Dover; great quantities of meat were lost. (Reads a letter that it was from the want of French salt.) We have made all experiments of salt, and we would encourage our manufacture. The Portugal salt pierces and eats up the meat. We have tried all sorts of salt. There is at Liverpool something that does well. There is something in the matter of price, and we think we ought to be as good husbands as we can. I do not urge the necessity, of French salt, but from the necessity of this accident. For merchants' ships, where it is well looked after, it may do, but in the King's ships it is not so well looked after. I have had experience for 30 years, and the Spanish salt breeds scurvy. It is of late lessened, for more of that salt that is lost; and the men's health depends upon it. The year before we came in, there were victuals to 200 or 300 pieces defective, just when we were to use it . . . . *The Commissioners of Customs* called in, and asked what quantities of salt there are imported from beyond the seas. *Sir Patience Ward:* I have made an abstract of what has been formerly imported. Asked if there be any Nantwich salt in the Ports? I do not think it worth their while to bring it. *Mr. Booth:* We had not time to have an abstract of things or particulars. *Moved:* That the Commissioners of Customs give an account to-morrow what ships of salt there are in the River Thames. *Merchants* called in: There are none. Then, after some time spent in debate on the Bill, the question was put for the second reading, and resolved in the affirmative by 39 to 26. Tellers, E. Bridgewater and L. Chandos. (L. J., XIV. 685, MS. Min.) —In Committee, to whom the Bill was referred, V. Weymouth sat Chairman on Dec. 17 and the Bishop of Salisbury on Dec. 18, on which days the Committee met only to adjourn. On Dec. 19, E. Bridgewater in the Chair, the Act prohibiting trade with France was read. The Victuallers are called in. *Mr. Papillon* says that no Nantwich salt comes to London but in baskets. There is neither Newcastle nor Nantwich now in London. For want of this salt, we cannot salt our hogs, and so are forced to shut them up. We desire no more than will serve the King's occasions. The takers of this salt may carry it out after condemnation; but, if they land it, it must be burnt. Then, on the second enacting clause was carried (on question) by 8 to 2. (Com. Book.) On 21 Dec. the Bill was reported without amendment. (L. J., XIV. 697.) Royal Assent 24 Dec. (*Ib.* 701.)]

Annexed:—

(*a.*) 14 Dec. Account of French Salt, viz.:—

From Lady Day	to Lady Day	Weys.	£	s.	d.
1684 -	- 1685 -	0 -	0	0	0
1685 -	- 1686 -	813¼ -	39	9	8
1686 -	- 1687 -	992¼ -	47	2	7½
1687 -	- 1688 -	1,437 -	68	5	2
1688 -	- 1689 -	618 -	29	7	1

Noted: More than double in Outports. [See Notes above.]

House of Lords MSS.

1691.

481. Dec. 14. L. Waldegrave's Estate Act.—Amended* draft of a Bill to enable Trustees of the Right Hon. James, Lord Waldegrave, to make leases and grant copyhold estates for the payment of the [debts] *arrears of annuities* of Henry, Lord Waldegrave, his father deceased. The Lords' Amendments (Com. Book, 21 Dec.) besides those in the Title, were to add the Schedule (Annex (*d.*) below), and to alter the Preamble accordingly, the debts of Henry, L. Waldegrave having been originally stated as ("8,000*l.* and upwards"). The Commons' later Amendments (C. J., X. 619) are unimportant. [Read 1ª this day; Royal Assent 24 Feb. 1691-2. (L. J., XIV. 684; XV. 93.) 3-4 W. & M. c. 18 in Long Calendar.]

Annexed:—

(*a.*) 21 Dec. Affidavit of Charles Waldegrave, that he has the free consent, and is appointed by Henrietta, Lady Dowager Waldegrave guardian of the Right Hon. James, L. Waldegrave under age, and others who have jointures and annuities charged upon his Lordship's lands in Somersetshire, to endeavour to obtain an Act to empower trustees to grant leases of the lands during L. Waldegrave's minority, and that all the parties concerned are in favour of an Act being passed for that purpose. *Sworn* 16 Dec. before Lacon Wm. Childe. [Read this day in Committee (Com. Book)].

(*b.*) 21 Dec. Affidavit of James Keith, of St. Giles'-in-the-Fields, Gent., that he has been employed for more than seven years in paying the annuities charged on L. Waldegrave's estate, and that the following sums are due on that account for arrears, viz., 500*l.* to Henrietta, Lady Dowager Waldegrave, 887*l.* 14*s.* 6*d.* to the Lady Helena Waldegrave, 434*l.* 10*s.* to Sir Wm. Waldegrave, 150*l.* to Mr. Henry Waldegrave, 257*l.* 17*s.* 2*d.* to Mr. Charles Waldegrave, 750*l.* to Mr. Edward Waldegrave, and 750*l.* to Mr. Francis Waldegrave. *Sworn* 16 Dec. before Lacon Wm. Childe. [Read this day in Committee (Com. Book).]

(*c.*) 29 Dec. Lords' Amendments. [Made 21 Dec. (Com. Book) and reported this day. (L. J., XV. 3.)]

(*d.*) 29 Dec. Schedule of arrears of Annuities, marked A. [Added 21 Dec. (Com. Book) and reported this day. (L. J., XV. 3.)]

482. Dec. 15. Traitorous Correspondence Act.—Amended* draft of an Act against [adhering to] *corresponding with* their Majesties' enemies. For preventing of traitorous correspondence *and commerce* with the French King or his subjects, and supplying them with warlike or other stores or commodities, by means of which they may be any way aided or comforted in carrying on their war against their Majesties;† [Be it enacted by the King and Queen's Most Excellent Majesties, etc. That if, during the war between their Majesties and the French King, any of their Majesties' subjects shall without their Majesties' license hold, maintain and keep correspondence and intelligence with the said French King or any of his subjects or other persons in his service and employment, or shall send, convey or deliver, or ship or lade any lead, coal or other commodities, with intent or to the end

* The omissions are shown by square brackets, and the additions by italics.

† The remainder of this draft was superseded in C. W. II. by Annexes (*a.*) (*b.*) and (*c*), which, together with the above title and preamble, formed, as ultimately amended, the Act.

that the same may be delivered or come to the hands or use of the said French King or any of his agents, officers, subjects or other persons in service or employment under him, or shall without license as aforesaid voluntarily go or repair into France or any dominions of the French King, or come thence into any of their Majesties' realms or dominions, every person so offending, being thereof lawfully convicted, shall be and is hereby adjudged to be guilty of High Treason, and shall incur and suffer such pains, penalties and forfeitures, as in case of High Treason are usually inflicted.]—[The above Bill, which was brought in by Lord Newport,* was read 1a this day. (L. J., XIV. 687.) On 21 Dec., in C. W. H., the Bill was read through. House *moved* to know how the Common Law stands as to holding correspondence with their Majesties' enemies. The *L. C. Baron* [*Atkyns*], *Mr. Justice Nevill*, and *Mr. Baron Powell* were heard. *Moved:* That none shall go into France without license. That the Act be not evaded by anyone's going into Flanders to go into France. *Moved:* That the Judges draw a Bill upon the debate. *Moved:* a Clause for the conviction of those that have *estates in England*† and are now in France and have their estates sent over to them. 1. To give aid or comfort to the King's enemies to be declared High Treason, and the Judges to describe it by sending goods or information. That the French Protestants shall hold no correspondence with France, without a license from a Secretary of State. *Moved:* That a short day be appointed for hearing all the Judges upon the Bill. *Ordered* to report as in L. J., XIV. 697. (MS. Min., 21 Dec.)—On 30 Dec., in C.W.H., *the Judges* were heard whether the sending over any commodities to France is treason? If anyone send over or trade with France, if this be not aiding in the war? [*Holt, C. J.*]: This will require further time to answer. I think sending gunpowder or bullets into an enemy's country is treason. *L. C. Baron* [*Atkyns*]: To send over every or anything to them, with intention to promote the war, that I take to be high treason; but if it be only to enrich him that sends it, then it is a misdemeanour. *Nevill, J.*, is heard. *Lechmere, B.:* Of the same opinion. *Eyre, J.:* I take high treason to be in the heart (*sic*), and there must be an overt act, and some things speak the intent, as powder and bullets; but if a man only trade for himself, this is a great misdemeanour. *Powell, B.:* Of the same opinion. Sending over horses is adhering to their Majesties' enemies. *Moved:* That the treason shall go no further than for powder and bullets; yet in another case it might not only be liable to a fine, but that the time for imprisonment be put in the Bill. *Moved:* That the Judges draw a Clause or Bill upon the debate. Judges heard whether they may imprison. *Holt, C. J.:* We may imprison in some cases, and [it] must be suitable to the offence. *Proposed* whether it shall not be capital to carry goods. *Question proposed:* Whether all trading with France shall not be capital? *Proposed* that all trading with France shall be and incur a Præmunire, which are (*sic*) not already treason. *Proposed* that those goods which are High Treason already be enumerated, and all other goods to be a Præmunire that shall be carried to France. *Agreed:* That the Judges bring in a clause specifying what goods shall be High Treason to be carried into France, and another Clause to make it a Præmunire to carry or send to France any other goods and commodities whatsoever which are not specified in the first Clause. *Proposed*, a third Clause

* Luttrell, 22 Dec. 1691.

† The words "revenues from the Government," which are struck through, stood originally in place of these words in italics.

House of Lords MSS.

1691.

declaring it treason for any person to go into France or come thence without his Majesty's leave. House resumed. *V. Newport* reported the two Heads upon which the Judges are to draw Clauses. *Ordered* that the Judges draw two Clauses accordingly. House to be again in Committee to-morrow. (MS. Min., L. J., XV. 7.)—After two orders, on 31 Dec. and 4 Jan., putting off the Committee (L. J., XV 11, 16), a peremptory order was made, on motion, on 11 Jan. for the House to be put into Committee on 13 Jan., and that the Judges and all the Lords be summoned to attend. (*Ib.* 23.)—On 13 Jan. House in Committee. *V. Newport* in the Chair. The Clauses drawn by the Judges were read. *Agreed* that pitch, tar, hemp, saltpetre, lead, cordage, masts, iron and coal be put in the first Clause.* *Proposed* that there may be a time limited for persons that reside in France to return. First Clause agreed. House resumed. *V. Newport* reported progress. House to be again in Committee on 18 Jan. and Judges to attend. (MS. Min., L. J., XV. 28.)—On 19 Jan. House *moved* to go into Committee on the 21st. *Ordered* accordingly. (MS. Min., L. J., XV. 38.)—On 21 Jan., *Ordered* that the Bill be proceeded with to-morrow the first business, and all the Judges to attend. (MS. Min., L. J., XV. 43.)—On 22 Jan. House in Committee. *L. Cornwallis* in the Chair. The second Clause drawn by the Judges* was read and agreed to.

Sheet 1, line 11. After ("or")† read ("And be it also enacted by the authority aforesaid, that all and every person and persons who"). *Agreed* that whosoever shall go into France, or embark with intent to go thither, shall be guilty of High Treason. That all their Majesties' subjects that shall after   come out of France without their Majesties' leave shall be guilty of (*sic*)." *Question* put: That any person, who is their Majesties' subject, that after   shall come into England or any of their Majesties' dominions from France or any of the French King's dominions in Europe without their Majesties' leave, shall be guilty of High Treason. Resolved in the *Negative*. Contents 24; Not Contents 32. Tellers, D. Norfolk and E. Mon. (*sic*).‡ *Question* put: That any person who is their Majesties' subject, that after   shall come into England or any of their Majesties' dominions from France or any of the French King's Dominions in Europe without their Majesties' leave, shall be liable to suffer imprisonment§ without bail or mainprize. Resolved in the *Affirmative*. Cont. (*sic*).‖ 1st February for going into France. 25th March for coming out into England.

Title read, and instead of ("adhering to") read ("corresponding with").

Preamble read. Line 1, after ("correspondence"), read ("commerce").

The Clause drawn by the Judges against going into France¶ read and agreed to. The other Clause** agreed to, and the whole Bill agreed. After some time spent therein, the House was resumed (MS. Min.; L. J., XV. 45).—On 26 Jan., *Ordered* that the Bill be reported tomorrow, and that L. C. Justice Holt and Mr. Baron Powell attend.

* *See* Annex (*a*.) below.

† Namely, after the words ("in his service and employment or"). This amendment was superseded by the omission of the Clause.

‡ Either E. Monmouth or E. Montague.

§ As first drawn it was "shall be imprisoned without," &c.

‖ No division is recorded.

¶ Annex (*b*.) below.

** Annex (*c*.) below.

(MS. Min.; L. J., XV. 50).—On 2 Feb. *L. Cornwallis* reported the Bill with the amendments, which were agreed to, and the Bill ordered to be engrossed (MS. Min.; L. J., XV. 59).—On 22 Feb. it was returned from the Commons agreed to with amendments,* to which the Lords agreed (*ib.* 88), and the Bill received the Royal Assent on the 24th (*ib.* 92). 3 W. & M. c. 13, Fol. Ed.]

Annexed:—

(*a.*) 2 Feb. 1691-2. Draft Clauses (2) marked ✠, being § i., without the Preamble, and § ii. of the Act. [Offered in C. W. H. by the Judges, agreed to after adding the words ("*pitch, tar, hemp, masts, cordage, iron, coals, lead or saltpetre*") and reported this day. L. J., XV. 59.]

(*b.*) 2 Feb. Draft Clause, marked A, being (with the Commons' amendment†) Section iii. of the Act. [Offered in C. W. H. by the Judges, agreed to, and reported this day. L. J., XV. 59.]

(*c.*) 2 Feb. Draft Clause, marked B, being (with the Commons' Amendment‡) Section iv. of the Act. [Offered in C. W. H. by the Judges, agreed to, and reported this day. (L. J., XV. 59.) The draft is altered by substituting ("the 25th of March 1692") for ("the 25th of March next ensuing") and by omitting after ("closely kept") the words ("without permitting any person to come to him or them").]

(*d.*) 2 Feb. Lords' Amendments to the Bill. [Reported from C. W. H. this day. They are to add the words in italics in the Title and Preamble above, and to substitute Annexes (*a.*) (*b.*) (*c.*) for the remainder of the original Bill.]

483. Dec. 15. E. Suffolk's Estate Act.—Amended Draft of an Act to enable the Trustees of James, late Earl of Suffolk to sell the manor of Hadstock in Essex, for discharging several other manors and lands of the said late Earl from 5,000*l.*, remainder of 10,000*l.* by him formerly charged thereon. The Lords' Amendments (Com. Book, 29 Dec.) are either verbal or drafting ones. [Read 1ª this day; Royal Assent, 24 Feb. (L. J., XIV. 687; XV. 92.) 3-4 W. & M. c. 13 in Long Calendar.]

Annexed:—

(*a.*) 5 Jan. 1691-2. Lords' Amendments to the Bill. [Made in Committee 29 Dec. (Com. Book), and reported this day. (L. J., XV. 18.)]

(*b.*) Clause marked A, vesting certain rentcharges in the Rector of Radstock in lieu of another annual payment. [Marked on the Draft Bill for insertion before the concluding Saving Clause, where it appears in the Act. The amendment is not noticed in Annex (*a.*).]

484. Dec. 15. Sir D. Cullum's Estate Act.—Draft of an Act for enabling Sir Dudley Cullum, Bart., to raise monies to pay his brother and sisters portions. [Read 1ª this day; Royal Assent, 24 Feb. 1691-2. (L. J., XIV. 687; XV. 93.) 3-4 W. & M. c. 23 in Long Calendar. Com. Book, 22 Dec.]

---

* Wrongly described in L. J., XIV. 88, as "an amendment." See C. J., X. 682.

† Namely, to substitute ("tenth day of March") for ("first day of February"), C. J., X. 682. The date on the draft was originally left blank.

‡ Namely, to add the concluding words ("for any time not exceeding twelve months"), C. J., X. 682. The draft makes the Clause nonsense by omitting the words ("he or they") before ("shall be committed to prison"). The mistake is repeated in the Act itself."

House of Lords MSS.

1691.

485. Dec. 15. Vernon's Estate Act.—Draft of an Act for the better assuring to George Vernon and his heirs and assigns four acres of land in Ebisham, in the County of Surrey. [Read 1ª this day; Royal Assent, 24 Feb. 1691–2. (L. J., XIV. 687; XV. 93.) 3–4 W. & M. c. 29 in Long Calendar. Com. Book, 15 Jan. 1691–2.]

486. Dec. 16. Shelton's Estate Act.—Amended Draft of an Act to enable the sale of several lands for the payment of the debts and legacies of Maurice Shelton and others, and for settling other lands instead of them. The Lords' Amendments (Com. Book, 18 Dec.) are merely to fill up two blanks with the words ("24th of March"). [Read 1ª this day; Royal Assent, 24 Feb. 1691–2. (L. J., XIV. 688; XV. 93.) 3–4 W. & M. c. 33. in Long Calendar. The Bill was reported with amendments on 21 Dec. (MS. Min. No entry in L. J.), the Committee having been revived on the 18th (MS. Min.)]

487. Dec. 16. E. Derby's Estate Bill.—Draft of an Act for the restoring of William George Richard, Earl of Derby, to the Manor of Mould and Mouldsdale, and the castle and manor of Hawarden, and the advowson of the church of Hawarden, in the County of Flint, the manor of Bidston in the County Palatine of Chester, and the manor of Broughton and the Bailiffwick of Loynsdale, in the County Palatine of Lancaster. "Whereas, James, late Earl of Derby, grandfather of William George Richard, now Earl of Derby, in the time of the late unhappy wars and usurpation in this Kingdom, for his loyalty and allegiance to their late Majesties King Charles I. and King Charles II., of ever blessed memory, was in the month of October 1651, murdered and put to death by the late usurpers, and all his estate, whereof he was seized in possession, reversion or remainder on the 20th of May 1642, or at any time after, by a pretended Act of the then usurping powers, declared and enacted to be forfeited and sold for treason pretended against those usurpers; in pursuance whereof the same was accordingly seized upon, sequestered, and sold, and in particular the manors and lordships of Mould and Mouldsdale, Hope and Hopesdale, and the castle and manor of Hawarden, otherwise Harden, and the advowson of the church there, all in the County of Flint, the manor of Bidston in the County Palatine of Chester, and the manor of Broughton, and the Bailiffwick or Wapentake of the hundred of Loynsdale, in the County Palatine of Lancaster (being the possessions and the inheritance of the said James, late Earl of Derby, at the time of his death) were for small considerations, for the most part paid by doubled bills of soldiers' Debenters (usually bought at 54 or 55 per cent. or under) to the then usurped Powers, sold and conveyed to the several persons hereafter named, by pretence of and according to the direction of, those pretended Acts, by colour whereof the pretended purchasers being in possession, and Charles, late Earl of Derby, father of the now Earl and son and heir of the said Earl James, thereby reduced to very great straits and necessities, he, the said Earl Charles, was, for very small consideration, viz., for about a year's real value of some of them, and under a year's value of others of them, received by him, prevailed upon, through such his sad circumstances, to make several deeds of release and further conveyances of the said manors and premises to the respective purchasers and their heirs and assigns, viz., of the said manors of Mould and Mouldsdale, Hope and Hopesdale, and of the castle, manor, and advowson of the church of Hawarden to George Twissleton, Andrew Ellis, Humfrey Ellis, Sir John Trevor, and John Glynn, Serjeant-at-law, afterwards Sir John Glynn, knight, some or one of them or others in trust for them, some or one of them and their heirs respectively, the said Sir John Glynn claiming by some contract by him made or the said manor and premises in Hawarden with the said Trevor,

Andrew and Humphrey Ellis, and Twissleton, some or one of them, the first purchaser or purchasers thereof from the usurpers, and of the manor of Bidston to William Steele, Esq., and his heirs, and of the said manor of Broughton and Bailiffwick of the hundred of Loynsdale to Edward Lee and his heirs, and all the said manors and premises noware, and ever since the said pretended purchases have been, enjoyed under the same conveyances and releases (save only the manor of Hope and Hopesdale from Lady Day 1683, of which the now Earl of Derby about that time obtained the possession, by virtue of a recovery thereof at law by him in Hilary Term 1682, obtained as heir in tail thereof, the reversion thereof being still in the Crown), and the same conveyances from the said Earl Charles being obtained for so small considerations in the time of the late troubles, while the said Earl Charles lay under such great necessities and oppressions, and not in any condition to relieve and help himself, and by the favourites of those rebellious times, who took advantage thereof against him, there is great justice that the said purchasers should content themselves with the receipt of their purchase moneys and interest for the same; and that (upon satisfaction thereof, either upon a discount of the profits of the said premises or otherwise) the said manors and premises should be restored to the now Earl: And to that end, that the said respective purchases should be accounted only in the nature of mortgages;" The Bill, on the prayer of the said William George Richard, Earl of Derby, enacts that the manors and lordships of Mould and Mouldsdale, and Hawarden, *alias* Harden, and the advowson of the church of Hawarden, *alias* Harden, and the manors of Bidston and Broughton, with the Bailiffwick or Wapentake of the hundred of Loynsdale, sold and enjoyed with the said manor of Broughton, as existing at the death of the said James, Earl of Derby, shall be vested in (*blank*) and their heirs, to pay, out of the rents or if necessary, the sale thereof, to the heirs, &c., of the said George Twissleton, Andrew Ellis, Humphrey Ellis, Sir John Trevor, Sir John Glynn, William Steele, and Edward Lee such sums as upon account in any suit in Chancery, to be preferred for that purpose by either party within (*blank*) next after the end of the present session, shall be found to have been actually paid to the late usurping powers and the said Charles, late Earl of Derby, for the purchase of the respective premises, with interest and a discount of all the moneys, rents, and profits, as well constant at casual, received by Twissleton, &c., or their heirs, &c., thereout, as shall appear to be due to them, and an allowance for all taxes and quit rents or chief rents paid, and moneys laid out on repairs or improvements; and so much of the purchase money as they paid in doubled bills, is to be computed according to the then value of those bills; and the purchase money paid on contract is to be looked upon in the accounts as satisfied by such moneys as have been paid by Sir John Glynn, so far as the same will extend, and Sir John Glynn is to be looked upon as the person originally advancing the same, and to have allowance for the same accordingly, and the said premises, or the now Earl not to be doubly charged by reason thereof; And after payment to Twissleton, &c., of all sums found due on the account, the persons in whom the premises shall be vested as above, shall stand seized thereof as trustees for the now Earl and heirs, &c., to whom they are empowered to convey them for ever. Provided that if in such accounts it shall appear that more money has been raised out of lands since their purchase from the usurping powers than will suffice to discharge the purchase money with interest, none of the purchasers or their heirs, &c., shall be compelled to refund any part thereof to the Earl. The Bill concludes with the usual saving clause. [Read 1a this day (L. J., XIV. 689). On 25 Jan. 1691–2, Counsel were called in. *Mr. Dormer* (for Petitioners against the Bill*): This is an Act of resumption, and there never was such an Act for a subject before. You have all sorts of interests—femmes coverts, purchasers, &c.; all sorts of titles here will be destroyed. This is a new Bill, except the manor of Mould, and I think the reason of it cannot be imagined after 30 years. *Sir Thomas Powys* (on the same side): I am for divers other persons. He is heard to the settlements of the several manors. It was referred to the King, who dismissed the reference as not fit to be done. No fraud was ever made out here. The Earl of Derby could not be surprised in this, for it was deliberately done, and if, after 40 years' possession, the estate be stricken, then all the line of fines, &c., will be overthrown. They read the Report of the Lords referred in this case and the King's of 14 June 1664. *Sir William Thompson* (for E. Derby): I question not but I shall show the Bill is very reasonable. It is rather a Bill of restitution or an equity of redemption than anything else. For 20*l*. Sir J. Glynn made 16,000*l*. of the woods. He hopes now his Bill will have its effect, he having brought it so soon as he knew the particulars of it. We will pay you principal and interest for all moneys paid. There is no time too late to do justice. We will submit to all; your Lordships shall make it what you please. On purchasers it would be hard, but they shall have principal and interest. *Sir William Williams* (for the Bill): These gentlemen speak as to part of the Bill, but not one as to the whole Bill. The question is whether the Earl of Derby has not an equity and justice in this case to receive such a Bill. He had an equity in 1664; where, then, is your line? Counsel withdraw. A Paper offered and read, signed W. Rawlinson. (Annex (*c*.) below.) The Speaker then reported, and, after debate, the second reading was negatived. (MS. Min.; L. J., XV. 48.)]

Annexed:—

(*a*.) 22 Dec. 1691. Petition of John, Lord Cutts, Sir William Glynne, Bart., John Twisleton, Esq., Edward Sayer, and William Lightfoot, on behalf of themselves and divers others interested in opposing the passing of the Bill. Petitioners only had notice of the Bill yesterday, and having no copy of it, are unprepared to oppose it. Their writings, witnesses, &c. are in Wales and other remote counties. Pray for a reasonable day to be heard against the Bill. L. J., XIV. 699.

(*b*.) 31 Dec. 1691. Names of witnesses for E. Derby, ordered this day to attend on 19 Jan. L. J., XV. 11. *In extenso*.

(*c*.) 25 Jan. 1691–2. Proposal made by Colonel Sawrey to E. Derby, as follows: As to the Manor of Broughton and Bailiffwick of Loynsdale in Lancashire, if the Earl pleases, there shall be some person at the Bar to inform the House that Col. Sawrey, who is concerned in the above Manor and Bailiffwick, being satisfied with the justice of E. Derby's claim, has submitted himself to the Earl and so does not contest the matter, and thereupon the Earl has frankly offered to leave him out of the Bill; or, if the Earl pleases, some of the peers shall have a copy of this paper, and inform the House of this. *Noted*: The original of this paper was given to Mr. Greenfield, E. Derby's Counsel, and approved of and accepted by the Earl, and returned to Mr. Greenfield, with directions to get one of the peers to acquaint

* *See* Annex (*a*.) below.

the House therewith. *Underwritten* is the following: "My Lord, I pray therefore on Col. Sawrey's behalf, that you will take an opportunity, when the debate about the Earl of Derby's Bill is over, or during the debate (if you find it more proper) to inform the House of the Proposal above mentioned and to get some order or note taken by the Clerk attending the House of Peers, that the manor of Broughton and Bailiffwick of Loynsdale may be left out of the Earl's Bill accordingly. I am with all sincerity, your Lordship's most humble servant, W. Rawlinson." [*See* Notes above.]

488. Dec. 16. Grantham's Estate Act.—Draft of an Act for the enabling Vincent Grantham, Esq., to lease part of his manor of Goltboe, in Lincolnshire, for the raising moneys to pay portions and debts charged thereupon. [Read 1ª this day; Royal Assent, 24 Feb. 1691-2. L. J., XIV. 689; XV. 93; Com. Book, 8 Jan.] 3-4 W. & M. c. 41 in Long Calendar.

Annexed:—

(*a.*) 8 Jan. 1691-2. Consent of Sir Thomas Fanshawe to the passing of the Bill. *Dated* 4 Jan. *Attested* by Robt. Rayner and M. Wyndham. [Read in Committee this day. (Com. Book.)]

(*b.*) 8 Jan. Consent of William Osbaldeston. *Sworn* 7 Dec. 1691 before George Prickett, Master in Chancery. [Read in Committee this day. (Com. Book.)]

(*c.*) Copy of Act.

489. Dec. 16. Sir W. Halford's Estate Act.—Amended draft of an Act to vest divers manors, lands, and tenements in the county of Leicester in Trustees, to be sold for the payment of the debts and legacies of Sir William Halford, Knt., deceased, and for payment of the other debts of Sir William Halford now living, prior to his marriage settlement with the Lady Frances, his now wife. The Lords' Amendments, omitting verbal and drafting ones, are to except, at the end of the Preamble, such incumbrances ("as are to be intended to be kept on foot for protecting of the jointure lands of the Lady Frances not hereby directed to be sold")*; to add to the estate to be vested in the Trustees ("the trusts created by the will of the said Sir William Halford, deceased, and vested in Dame Elizabeth Burton *alias* Halford, Henry Halford, and Thomas Atkins, Esquires"); to add ("Matthew Johnson, Esq., Clerk of the Parliaments") to the Trustees; to amend the Clause† immediately before the concluding Saving Clause, by adding the words following in italics, viz. ("And be it enacted by the authority aforesaid that all mortgages, statutes, judgments and incumbrances precedent to the aforesaid marriage settlement of such of the jointure lands of the said Lady Frances as are intended to remain unsold, *together with such assignments as have been made of any of the said mortgages or incumbrances*, shall be transferred, assigned, and kept on foot for the better protection of the said jointure and settlement from all other incumbrances whatsoever"); and in the Saving Clause to add the names of ("Dame Elizabeth Burton *alias* Halford, Henry Halford, and Thomas Atkins"). The Commons' later Amendments are given in C. J., X. 679. *In extenso.* [Read 1ª this day; Royal Assent, 24 Feb.

* These words were erased by the Commons (C. J., X. 679).

† The whole of this Clause was erased by the Commons, who substituted Clause A. (C. J., X. 679), which is annexed as a separate Schedule to the Act.

House of Lords MSS.
—
1691.

1691–2. (L. J., XIV. 689; XV. 93.) 3–4 W. & M. c. 25 in Long Calendar.]

Annexed :—

(a.) 2 Jan. 1691–2. Lords' Amendments to the Bill. [Made in Committee Dec. 22 and 24 and reported this day. Com. Book, 24 Dec. The proceedings of the 22nd are not in Com. Book.]

(b.) 2 Jan. 1691–2. Another copy of preceding, adding notes of proceedings in Committee on 22 Dec.

(c.) Letter from Mr. Parker to the Clerk of the Parliaments, declaring his consent to the Bill. Begs, if any obstruction occur for want of Sir Richard Atkins' and Mr. Verney's consents, who are trustees in the settlement of Lady Frances with her brother, Mr. Cecil, for raising 6,000*l.* for daughters, in case of no sons, that he will satisfy the Committee that there will remain above 10,000*l.* worth of land unsold, liable to raise the money, so (as Sir Anthony Keck is clearly of opinion) there is no need of their consents, there being no injury done to the daughters by the Bill, in case of the sons dying without issue. *Dated* Kibworth, 26 Dec. 1691. *Addressed* to Matthew Johnson, Esq., Clerk in Parliament to the House of Lords, at his Chamber in the Middle Temple [Mr. Johnson was added in Committee to the Trustees in the Bill.]

490. Dec. 17. Mrs. Wallwyn *v.* E. Monmouth.—Petition of Mary Walwyn, Widow, Relict of John Wallwyn, late of Helens, in the County of Hereford, Esq., deceased. Petitioner's late husband, being tenant for life of an estate of 400*l.* a year in the County of Hereford, and having two sons, both idiots, and two daughters by Petitioner, obtained on 26 June 1684 a Patent to Petitioner, Mr. Serjeant Geeres and Robert Dobyns, Esq., for the custody of the persons and estate of the said sons, the better to enable Petitioner after his death to pay his debts and to make some provision for herself and the other children out of the remainder of the profits of the estate. The Patent was renewed by the same patentees in the reign of James II., but being made only during pleasure, it became void by the demise of James II., whereupon, one of the sons being then dead, the same patentees obtained a new order from the Lords Commissioners of the Great Seal for renewing the Patent as to the surviving idiot, but before the Patent was passed, the Earl of Monmouth petitioned the Lords Commissioners for the custody to be granted to him. This Petition being, after a hearing, refused, he procured a Warrant from the King, and the Lords Commissioners on 29 Jan. 1689, in obedience to the King's command, directed that Petitioner should have the keeping of her son, and be allowed 200*l.* a year out of the estate, for maintaining him and herself and daughters, the surplus of the profits to be paid to E. Monmouth, and, with these directions, ordered a grant to be passed the Great Seal for committing the custody to the Earl, which grant accordingly passed *durante bene placito*, as is usual. On 5 April 1690 the Earl obtained another Warrant for passing a new Patent to himself for the custody *durante idiociâ*, which accordingly was passed by the Commissioners, but subject, in all other respects except the duration of the Patent, to their previous order. The Earl then sent his agents to collect the rents of the estate and arrears due before his Patent, but took no care for the maintenance of Petitioner and her son and family, as directed; and therefore Petitioner and the tenants of the estate refused to deliver up possession or to attorn tenants to him. Thereupon the Earl in 1690 petitioned the Lords Commissioners for a Writ of Assistance to put him into possession, but their Lordships declared the case was one of great compassion and that Petitioner should have what had been ordered her, and appointed a day for hearing, which the Earl afterwards declined, and by reason of his peerage, Petitioner could not proceed before the Commissioners to have their former order performed. So matters rested till 11 August 1691, when the Earl, with a large number of attendants, forcibly entered the capital messuage of the estate, called Hellens, where Petitioner then lived with her son and his sisters and their husbands, and having put the said husbands under a guard, seized the son and carried him away, and forced most of the tenants to attorn to him and pay his rents and arrears, out of which he left Petitioner only 100*l.*, although above 400*l.* was then due to her. Petitioners can obtain no relief from the Lords Commissioners, owing to the Earl's privilege. Prays to be allowed the provision intended for her maintenance by the Patent of Charles II., renewed by James II. L.J., XIV. 692. [In Committee for Privileges, to whom, after reading the Earl's answer (Annex (*a.*) below) the matter was referred on 21 Dec. (*ib.*, 697) the proceedings were as follows: On 4 Jan. 1691–2, L. Ferrers in the chair, Counsel called in. *Mr. Trevor* (for Mrs. Wallwyn) being asked what they had to say concerning the Earl's having insisted on his privilege, says that his Lordship's Agent, Mr. Penington, threatened them with breach of privilege. *Sir Thomas Powys* says the Earl's agents, both in town and country, wished them to have a care of his Lordship's privilege. *Thomas Marriatt* (sworn) says that in August 1690 Mr. Penington brought the Earl's Petition to the Commissioners. Mrs. Wallwyn desired them that the Commissioners would clear the matter, which they did, but they told me afterwards they could not. Mr. Hooks, the Earl's Agent, said he could not consent. Mr. Penington often bade us have a care what we did. *John Noble* (sworn), says that Mr. Penington told him "You do finely. Have a care what you do. We will have you punished for breach of privilege." *Mary Wallwyn* (sworn), says that the Earl, on her waiting on him, told her that he knew of no order made by the Commissioners concerning money to be paid her, and if she gave him any further trouble, she should have nothing. *Thomas Penington* (sworn), says: On 13 August last, after Mr. Noble disturbed the tenants, I bade him have a care he break not the Earl's privilege in disturbing his tenants in possession. I have told it generally that the Earl never would insist on his privilege as to any suit. They withdraw. *E. Monmouth* declares that he did and does waive his privilege as to any suit. *Counsel* are called in and told that the Earl never insisted on any privilege, and has declared that he always did and does waive his privilege as to any suit, but complains that his privilege has been broken by forcible entry on his estate. *Sir W. Williams* (for the Earl), says Mr. Shepheard, among others, attorned tenant to the Earl, after which, the Earl setting his woodward in September to cut underwood, Shepheard discharged him and assaulted him. In August last, the Earl's agents, that were in possession, were used with great violence by Noble and Shepheard; and one Rawlins, who had attorned tenant and paid 40*l.* rent, had his cattle seized by these men and driven away. *Colonel Jeremiah Babb* (sworn), says that Mr. Richard Wallwyn lived with him; that he endeavoured to have had something out of the estate, being next in remainder, but Mrs. Wallwyn, being a great Jacobite, got the custody of the idiot; but the Earl, after getting custody of the idiot, allowed him 120*l.* a year. The tenants afterwards all attorned to the Earl, and afterwards, Mr. Shepheard falling out with his mother, Mr. Wallwyn, he gave possession of Hellens to Mr. Wallwyn, as agent to the Earl. Witness has heard Mr. Richard

HOUSE OF LORDS MSS. — 1691.

Wallwyn often say that, he being the last in remainder, intended, if ever he had possession of the estate, he would give the Earl the reversion. The attornment of the tenants under their hands to E. Monmouth is *read*. *Thomas Penington* says that Mrs. Wallwyn and he took the attornments on 23 and 24 June. On 23 August following, Lady Monmouth went to Hellens, but could not be admitted into the house. Noble, Shepheard, and Mrs. Wallwyn had threatened the tenants so that I got but 60*l.* rents; she called me rogue, villain, &c. In June last, the Earl went down. Rawlins gave me 40*l.* They were all extremely civil, and expressed great satisfaction in the Earl's civility, and the Earl gave Mrs. Shepheard's child three guineas every morning for diet, while his servants were there. Mrs. Wallwyn went with the idiot to the Bath in the Earl's coach, and said, though the coach broke, she would not go back. The Earl received about 100*l.*, and gave it to Mrs. Wallwyn, who expressed the greatest satisfaction. The Earl allowed to the tenants whatever money she had of them. *Richard Hooper* (sworn), says: In August 1690, Mrs. (*blank*), who had attorned tenant, dying, I took possession of the house for the Earl; but Mrs. Wallwyn called me rogue and rascal, and Shepheard broke down the door, and I for my own safety escaped out of the house with the key. *William Ferris* (sworn), says: In August last I was sent by the Earl before his Lordship to Hellens. As soon as I was in, Noble asked me what I did there? I told him I was there from the Earl, who was coming. He set the gun to me, but I took it from him, just as the Earl came in, and while the Earl was there, all things were quiet, and some time after, the idiot was carried away in the Earl's coach, and his mother with him. *Mr. Trevor:* It does not appear that we disturbed the Earl's possession by anything that has been said. *Sir Thomas Powys:* This is a case of the greatest calamity. The custody of idiots has scarcely ever been granted to strangers, but always to relations. The Order of Chancery of 3 April 1690 for Mrs. Wallwyn's custody of the idiot, is *read*, whereby she is to have 200*l.* a year out of the estate. The Grant, reciting this Order, wherein the Earl covenants to perform that Order, is *produced*. *John Noble* (sworn), says that he supplied for a long time his mother Mrs. Walwyn with money for the maintenance of the idiot. He never was with her otherwise than on a visit. Ferris coming into the house with a birding piece, the Earl, with four or five others, came in and held pistols to Shepheard's head, after which we were taken away, and kept under guard with two pistols. The next day, Mr. Penington came, and sent for the tenants and threatened them for their rents and for money they had paid Mrs. Wallwyn, which he swore they should pay again. The house was guarded from the Earl's coming to the time of the taking away the idiot. Mrs. Penington told me the Earl would not take away the idiot. *Margaret Noble* (sworn), says: On 11 August last, the Earl put a pistol to my breast, and commanded me to show him the door where the idiot was; and I, finding an armed guard on, my brother Shepheard desired he might be released, which was done. In Whitehall, when my mother desired what the Court had ordered, the Earl told her he had nothing to do with the Order, and if she insisted on it, she should have nothing, nor see the child any more. *Mrs. Wallwyn* says (being asked) that the Earl said he would refer the matter to Sir John Somers and Mr. Dobyns. She has received nothing these last three years, since the Earl's Patent, save 100*l.* *John Shepheard* (sworn), says that in August last Ferrers [Ferris] came to Hellens, stood in the door, with his pistol cocked, and immediately came by the Earl with several others, with pistols cocked. The Affidavit of Elizabeth Baker, relating to the Earl's breaking open the door where the idiot was, is *read*.* The Affidavits of Elizabeth Wynington to the same purpose Annex (b^1) below), and of Frances Shepheard (Annex (b^2) below), are *read*. *Mary Wallwyn* (sworn), says that on the 11th August she was in the room with the idiot, when the door was broken, and the child seized and a guard set. The Earl kicked my sister and threatened to run her through, and calling me, he would have the child to the Bath, and I doubted not but to have had him back, which made me willing to go. I saw the child once since at Parson's Green. Since that, the Earl told me I should never see the child more, which has been a great trouble to me. The following Affidavits *read*, viz., of William Clarvo, of Margaret Tomkins, of John Lewis, of Richard Hodges, and of John Rawlins (Annexes (b^3) to (b^9) below). *Louis Duplessy* (sworn), says that he was with the Earl at Hellens on 11 August, and all things were very quiet. The attornment of Shepheard, dated 13 Aug. 1691, to the Earl is *read*. *Mr. Trevor:* Rawlins was under-tenant to Bowen, and when Bowen came to demand the rent of Rawlins, he told him he had paid it to the Earl, whereupon Bowen gave Noble a letter of attorney to distrain Rawlins' cattle, which he did in Bowen's right. *John Shepheard* says: It was reported by everybody that the Earl would turn me out, and Parson (*blank*) telling me the Earl would be very kind, and make me a Captain in his regiment, so between hope and fear I attorned. Consideration of the matter adjourned to the 8th. (Priv. Book, 4 Jan.) —On 8 Jan. V. Weymouth in the Chair, Mr. Penington for the Earl, and Mr. Mason for Mrs. Wallwyn are called in. *Mr. Mason* says there has been a waste made upon the estate by the Earl. Mr. Trevor has been told, since the last meeting of the Committee, by the Earl that he would join with the Solicitor-General and Sir Thomas Powys to make an end of this matter, but he was now in waiting, and he could not look after it this week. *Mr. Penington* says that the Earl has spoken to the Solicitor-General to join with those gentlemen about composing the matter, and they have appointed to meet about it on the 12th inst., for sooner the Solicitor-General cannot. Further consideration adjourned to the 11th. (Priv. Book, 8 Jan.)—On 11 Jan. the business was further adjourned till the 18th. (Priv. Book, 11 Jan.) —On 19 Feb. E. Stamford in the Chair, *Mr. Penington* and *Mr. Mason*, being called in, severally delivered writings drawn in pursuance of the Earl's proposals. (Annexes (*d.*) and (*e.*) below.) The Solicitor-General's letter of proposals to Mrs. Wallwyn's Counsel touching the idiot is *read*. (Comp. (Annex (*c.*) below.) The writing given in by Mr. Penington is *read*, as also part of the paper delivered in by Mr. Mason. (Priv. Book, 19 Jan.) Nothing further recorded.]

(*a.*) 21 Dec. 1691. Answer of Charles, Earl of Monmouth. The matters complained of are cognisable in the inferior courts in Westminster Hall, where Respondent has always been, and is ready to answer, never having insisted on privilege, and being willing to waive it. Respondent, out of kindness to Richard Wallwyn, Esq., who was next heir in remainder to Fulk Wallwyn, the idiot, and was very poor, procured about April 1690 a grant from the King of the custody of the idiot and his estate. Conceiving he might trust the idiot's keeping with his mother, Respondent, while the said Richard, his uncle, was living, consented, though not compellable thereto, that she should keep him, and have 200*l.* out of the estate, being

* This Affidavit is not among the Papers.

HOUSE OF LORDS MSS.

1691.

a moiety thereof, subject to taxes. In June following Respondent's agents peaceably took possession, and the tenants of all the estate except the house called Hellens, freely, as did the tenant of Hellens in September after, attorned to Respondent, and paid about 90*l.* of the rents, part of which was paid, by Respondent's order, to the uncle Richard, though the Petitioner falsely affirms that the tenants were constrained to attorn by force in August last. In September following, Petitioner obstructed Respondent in the further receipt of rents, and took forcible possession of the estate, and continued to disturb Respondent in its management; and in June 1691, Respondent's agents having received 40*l.* of a tenant named Rawlins, Petitioner and Noble distrained him and drove away his cattle. The uncle being dead without issue, and the estate thereby being to descend, after the idiot's death, to Noble's wife, the idiot's sister, and Respondent being informed and able to prove that there were agreements made between Noble and Petitioner touching the estate, and that it was not safe for the idiot to be trusted any longer in her keeping, she and Noble then living together, went last August to Hellens to quiet his possession and remove the idiot, and sent a servant before, who finding the doors open, entered and said he came by Respondent's order to take possession. Noble and others, with blunderbusses and other weapons, endeavoured to turn him out, and fired a pistol at Respondent, as he came up, who thereupon removed the force and took possession of the idiot, and having then received above 100*l.* of rents, gave 100*l.* to Petitioner and discharged the tenants of what they had by threats already paid to her. As to her complaint that Respondent has not paid her the 200*l.* a year, she herself obstructed him in the receipt of the rents, out of which the same was intended to be paid, while she had the keeping of the idiot. Prays their Lordships' justice on Petitioner, Mason, and Noble. L. J., XIV. 697. [*See* Notes above.]

(*b.*) 4 Jan. 1691. Affidavits of both parties, viz.* :—

(b^1.) Affidavit of Elizabeth Wynington, of the parish of Much Marcle, in the County of Hereford, Spinster. Deponent was at Hellens House in August last, when the Earl, with an armed company, surprised the house, and broke into the room where Foulk Wallwyn, the idiot child, then was, and placed guards there for about a week. Deponent, who counted a dozen pistols in the room, sat up all the next night with the child and with the mother and nurse and another gentlewoman; and the next morning, the Earl followed her out of doors and kicked her with his jack-boot and threatened to run her through. *Sworn* 12 Dec. 1691 before Abr. Seward. *Signed* by Deponent.

(b^2.) Affidavit of Frances, wife of John Shepheard, Gent. In corn harvest last, Deponent was brought to bed of a child in Hellens House, where her husband then lived; and about two or three days afterwards, hearing a noise on the stairs, she went thither with her sister Noble, and saw four or five persons, with pistols, come up. The foremost of them telling her, in answer to her question, that he was the Earl of Monmouth, Deponent said

* All of these, except Nos. 9, 10, 11, are noticed in Priv. Book of date, as having been read this day, when probably the others also were read. They all form one packet, No. 8 being endorsed by the Clerk.

to him, "'Tis much to your Lordship's honour, if you make my seven children motherless, for I am a dead woman;" and turning into her room, the Earl, with a pistol in his hand, caught hold of her sister and dragged her along in a great passion, bidding her tell him where the idiot was; and on her pointing in a great fright to the door, he kicked at it and entered the room and seized the child. Deponent heard the Earl say that he was resolved to take the house, or else he would have brought his regiment and blown it up, and Deponent saw an axe. But before he left, he spoke kindly to the family and made promises to Deponent, and the Minister of the parish advised her to comply with him, upon the great promises he had made to him, particularly to her husband. *Sworn* at Hereford 22 Dec. 1691, before Abr. Seward. *Signed* by Deponent.

(b^3.) Affidavit of William Clarvo, of Much Marcle, co. Hereford, Joiner. Deponent's mother, Elizabeth Clarvo, widow, was tenant to a small tenement in Much Marcle, the estate of Foulk Wallwyn, the idiot, for which she attorned tenant to the Earl of Monmouth in June last, and covenanted to pay arrears the 1st August then following. She died 11 August last, and after her burial on the 13th, Deponent delivered possession to the Earl's agent, Mr. Richard Hooper. Thereupon Mrs. Wallwyn and Mrs. Frances Shepheard came to the room where Hooper was, and abused him, and Mr. Shepheard and Mr. Noble threatened him and drove him out, and also assaulted one Mr. Robert Aylewey. Mr. John Shepheard's wife and mother, Mrs. Booth, Dorothy Gammon, and Ann Mayo were all in Deponent's house, when Deponent and his sister Mary Turner were forced out; and Mrs. Wallwyn having taken possession, John Noble produced a paper which they forced Deponent to sign, not knowing its contents, under threat of throwing all his goods out into the street. Deponent asked Mr. Wills, the Vicar, who was present during the outrage, to read it to him, but he refused, advising Deponent to sign it, or he would be undone, and telling him that Shepheard and Noble would save him harmless, as they had promised. *Sworn* at Hereford 18 Sept. 2 W. & M. before Abr. Seward. *Signed* by Depondent.

(b^4.) Affidavit of Margaret Tomkins, wife of Thomas Tomkins, of the same parish. Mrs. Wallwyn, after her return from London, about July or August last, sent for Deponent's husband, who being at work, Deponent went to her, and Mrs. Wallwyn told her that her husband was not to pay rent to the Earl, who had no right to it; that all the tenants who had paid him were fools, and that she would save them all harmless who refused payment, in case they should be sued, and would replevin their cattle, if distrained; and bade Deponent tell her husband to refuse rent to any of the Earl's agents and tell them he had no money, adding that Deponent's husband should use the agents as her own son-in-law Mr. Shepheard had done, who had not paid a penny, and never would. *Sworn* 18 Sept. 2 W. & M. before Abr. Seward. *Signed* by Deponent.

(b^5.) Affidavit of John Lewis, of Ayleton, in the County of Hereford, yeoman. After widow Clarvo's funeral, on 13 August last, Deponent, being by her house, heard Mrs. Wallwyn call Mr. Richard Hooper a knave and rascal, asking by what order he had taken possession there, and saying she was come to take possession in behalf of her child, and she bade him leave the

House of Lords MSS.

1691.

house, and said she would send for one that would set him out. Thereupon Mr. John Shepheard, her son-in-law, with a long paddle in his hand, and John Noble with a sword, came and broke open the door of the room where Hooper was, and Shepheard threatened to kill him, but Hooper escaped by a back door, Shepheard following him, and asking which way was the rogue gone. *Sworn* 13 Sept., 2 W. & M., before Abr. Seward. *Signed* by Deponent.

(b^6.) Affidavit of Richard Hodges, of Stoke Edith, in the county of Hereford, yeoman. About May last, Deponent, by order of the Earl of Monmouth, employed one George Worgen and others to fell several acres of coppice wood in Dornington, being part of Foulk Wallwyn's estate. After part of the work had been done, Worgen came to Deponent and told him that Noble and Shepheard had forbidden them to proceed, saying that the Earl had no interest in the woods, and no power to cut them down or sell them, and had also forbidden the tanner, then present, to buy the bark; and he has also threatened Deponent, who is unable to carry out his order. *Sworn* at Hereford, 5 August, 3 W. & M., before Abr. Seward. *Signed* by Deponent.

(b^7.) Affidavit of John Rawlins, the elder, of the parish of Weston Begger, in the county of Hereford, yeoman. About June last, Deponent, hearing that his son John's cattle and sheep were seized by Mr. John Noble and Mr. Shepheard, went to his son's farm, called Dornington Farm, and there found Noble and Shepheard and asked them why they had seized the cattle, and they said it was for rent. Deponent telling them he understood the rent ought to be paid to the Earl of Monmouth, and asking them to forbear until his son had consulted a friend, they replied roughly that the Earl had nothing to do with the idiot, Foulk Wallwyn's estate, and that Mr. Penington, his agent, was a cheating rascal, and that Deponent's son and any other tenants, who paid the Earl, should be severely handled. They then drove the cattle and sheep to Hereford city, and Deponent's son could only get them back by giving a bond to the sheriff. *Sworn* at Exon. Caple, co. Hereford, 26 Dec., 3 W. & M., before Abr. Seward. *Signed* by Deponent, his mark.

(b^8.) Affidavit of John Rawlins, the younger, of the same parish, yeoman, to same effect as proceeding. *Sworn* at Exon Caple 26 Dec., 3 W. & M., before Abr. Seward. *Signed* by Deponent.

(b^9.) Affidavit of John Shepheard, of Hellens House, in the parish of Much Marcle, Gent. In corn harvest last, the Earl of Monmouth, with a company of men armed with swords and pistols, surprised the house by sending a man before them to get into it, and keep the doors open. Deponent and his brother-in-law, Mr. Noble, seeing the man from an out-court with his pistol cocked, went to the door to enter, but the man, whose name Deponent could never learn, threatened to fire on them, whereupon Mr. Noble made in to him and took his pistol from him, and while he and Deponent were thrusting him out, the Earl, with four or five of his men, came up and presenting their pistols, forced them back into the court, and, after keeping them there under guard, had them brought to him indoors, while he searched the house and seized the child, and when Deponent was brought inside, he found his wife, who had been brought to bed but two or three days before, and all the family crying out for fear of their lives. The Earl sate up all the first night in the house, and guards were set there day and night till the child was carried away; but the Earl spoke kindly to the family, before he went away, and promised Deponent, if he would attorn tenant to him, that it would be to his advantage, and Deponent, by the persuasion of the Minister of the parish, who told him that the Earl would give him a commission in his regiment, subscribed to an attornment then produced. Since then, the Earl, by one of his servants, has written to the Minister to require payment of all past rents from Deponent, great part of which, as Deponent is advised, is not due to him, and the Minister, as he says, has answered that the demand is not pursuant to his promises. *Sworn* 22 Dec. 1691, before Abr. Seward, Mag. Cancell. Extraordin. *Signed* by Deponent.

(b^{10}.) Affidavit of Aune Turner, of the same parish, spinster. On Tuesday in August last, the Earl violently surprised the house, and sate up there all the next night, looking after the bolts of the doors, which he said were strong, but that he would open them, and Deponent saw one of his axes. The Earl added that if Mr. Shepheard had not loosed his birding gun, he had done him mischief, and produced a pistol, which he said was charged. Guards were kept in the house till the child was taken away. *Sworn* at Hereford 22 Dec. 1691 before Abr. Seward. *Signed* by Deponent, her mark.

(b^{11}.) Affidavit of John Skyrme of the same parish. Deponent, a servant at Hellen's House, was sent out on 11 August last to harvest work, and on his return found seven or eight strangers, some having pistols, walking about the house, and so they continued all night; and next morning, two of them refusing to let him pass out of the hall door, he went to the back door, where the guard allowed him to go out. *Sworn* at Hereford 22 Dec. 1691 before Abr. Seward. *Signed* by Deponent, his mark.

(*c*.) 11 Jan. 1691–2. Letter from Sir John Somers, Solicitor General, to the Earl of Monmouth, as follows:—"My Lord, I acquainted Mr. Trevor and Sir Thomas Powys with what your Lordship's proposed. viz., 1. That, whereas Mrs. Wallwyn, the mother, was by the order in Chancery to have 200*l*. a year for keeping the idiot, she should have so much paid her, and the idiot paid out of the other part of the estate. 2. That the arrears of the 200*l*. a year should be paid her down presently, though no part of it received out of the estate by your Lordship. 3. That if the mother should live with the child in some convenient place near London, where the idiot might be under her care, and not under the power of the heirs, who are to get by his death, your Lordship would keep the mother and the idiot, and pay her the 200*l*. besides. 4. That because the mother would be destitute of any provision in case of the death of the idiot, your Lordship would agree that, if any copyhold estates fell, they should be granted in trust for the mother, as a subsistence for her. 5. That if there was any surplusage after the 200*l*. paid and the idiot maintained and necessary taxes, and repairs and charges of the estate, your Lordship was resolved that not one farthing of it should be applied to your own use. I hope I did not mistake your Lordship in any of these proposals. Those gentlemen said they would acquaint Mrs. Wallwyn with the proposals; but I have not heard from them since. Indeed, the House of Commons is but just up, where I have been ever since I spoke with Sir Thomas Powys and Mr. Trevor. I am, with all respect, My

Lord, your Lordship's most obedient, humble servant, J. Somers." *Dated* 11 Jan. 1691–2, 5 in the afternoon. *Endorsed:* "Mr. Solicitor General's letter to the E. Monmouth, being Propositions to Mrs. Wallwn." [*See* Notes above.]

(*d.*) 19 Feb. 1691–2. Draft agreement between E. Monmouth and Mary Wallwyn. Whereas by Letters Patent of 11 April, 2 W. & M., the custody of the idiot Foulk Wallwyn's person and estate was committed to the Earl of Monmouth, and by an Order of the Court of Chancery, with the Earl's consent, it was ordered that the person of the said idiot should be in the custody of his mother, who should be paid 200*l.* a year for his maintenance and that of herself and her two daughters; It is agreed that the idiot shall remain henceforth under the care and in the keeping of the Earl, who covenants, for himself and heirs, &c., to pay to Mrs. Wallwyn, her executors, &c. what is due to her for arrears of the 200*l.* a year out of the idiot's estate and also to pay to her, during her life, and so long as the idiot shall continue under the Earl's care, the yearly sum of 200*l.* out of the said estate, by half-yearly payments, beginning next Midsummer. Mrs. Wallwyn, with her servant, at the Earl's charge, may live with her idiot son in such convenient place near London as the Earl shall appoint, and continue to receive the 200*l.* a year, according to the purport of the Order in Chancery. In case any copyhold leases or estates of or in any lands holden of any of the manors, whereto the Earl shall be entitled under the Letters Patent, shall happen to determine during the said idiotcy and the life of Mrs. Wallwyn, the Earl shall grant them to such persons as she shall appoint in trust for her and for a provision to her after the idiot's death, in case she shall survive him. *Endorsed* as dated. [*See* Notes above.]

(*e.*) 19 Feb. 1691–2. Articles of Agreement concluded the (*blank*) day of February, 1691–2, between E. Monmouth and Mary Wallwyn, Widow and Relict of John Wallwyn, late of Hellens, co. Hereford, Esq., deceased. Whereas by an Inquisition taken 7 June, 36 Car. II., by virtue of a Commission in nature of a writ *de Lunatico inquirendo*, Foulk Wallwyn was found an idiot; and whereas by Letters Patent dated April, 2 W. & M., the custody of him and his estate was committed to the Earl of Monmouth; and whereas his person has been in the custody of Mrs. Wallwyn, his mother, for which, and for a provision for his two sisters, the Grant allowed her 200*l.* a year, which is in arrears for 3 years, whereof she received 100*l.* from the Earl last August; it is agreed as follows: The Earl covenants for himself, heirs, &c. to pay Mrs. Wallwyn, her executors, &c. the 500*l.* arrears, and also, during the idiotcy for her and her two daughters, 200*l.* a year in half-yearly payments, beginning next Midsummer, the person of the idiot to remain with Mrs. Wallwyn, so as she shall live with him and keep him under her own care in some place within (*blank*) miles from the City of London, and so as he shall not be under the power of any of his heirs at law. In this case, the Earl will, during the idiotcy of Foulk and his living with her, pay her half-yearly after next Midsummer the further sum of (*blank*) for maintaining him and her. The concluding provision as to copyhold leases is identical with preceding. *Endorsed:* "The Copy of writing agreed to by Mr. Solicitor General, and which was by him sent to my Lord of Monmouth for his Lordship's approbation." [*See* Notes above.]

491. Dec. 18. Fidler *v.* Hanham.—Petition and Appeal of Thomas Fidler, Gent. Respondent, Lady Elizabeth Hanham, sold to one Michael Ayres in 1671 an annuity of 20*l.* a year charged on the manor of Winterborne, Dorset, for the term of 99 years, payable half-yearly, and with clause of distress, in trust for Appellant, which Ayres, pursuant to the trust, assigned to Appellant. The latter received the first half-yearly payment, and in 1 W. & M. sued Respondent at law for arrears, and recovered judgment. Respondent, to prevent execution, brought a Bill in Chancery, suggesting that the annuity was granted on some condition to be performed by Appellant, and subject to a further trust, in case a pretended marriage should take place between Appellant and one other of the Defendants in the Bill, which all the Defendants denied. Although Ayres declared he was a trustee for Appellant, the Court on 16 Nov. 1691 decreed that Appellant should deliver up the deed of 1671 and the assignment to Respondent, to be cancelled, and acknowledge satisfaction of the judgment obtained against her, and continued an injunction, formerly granted, until that was done. Prays that the Decree may be reversed. *Signed* by Appellant; *Countersigned* by Thos. Powys and Robert Dormer. L. J., XIV. 692. [The Appeal was heard on 18 Feb. 1691–2. *Sir Thomas Powys* (for Appellant): 8 Jan. 1671 the Lady Hanham granted an annuity in trust for Fidler. The Decree ought not to be made upon two accounts. There ought to be some stop to these matters. *Mr. Dormer* (for Appellant): The law declares no such resulting trust. The Deed [is] admitted to be absolute. Fidler's Answer in Chancery is read. *Mr. Trevor* (for Respondent): This is a good decree. *Mr. Finch* (for Respondent) is heard. Counsel for Appellant heard in reply. Decree affirmed. (MS. Min., L. J., XV. 83.)]

Annexed:—

(*a.*) 26 Dec. 1691. Answer of Dame Elizabeth Hanham. The pretended deed to Ayres was obtained by evil practices used by Elizabeth Wilson and her sister Dorothy, then servants to Respondent, and without any manner of consideration, nor was ever any trust of the pretended grant declared. Ayres in his answer admitted himself to be a trustee, and though the deed is alleged to be made 23 years since, no payment was ever made pursuant thereto, but the deed was proved to be an imposition on Respondent, who was then very young. Prays that the decree may be confirmed. *Signed* by Respondent; *Countersigned* by Patrick Crawford. *Noted:* Harding of Westminster, Solicitor for Respondent. *Endorsed* as brought in this day.

(*b.*) 15 Jan. 1691–2. Petition of Appellant for an early day for hearing. L. J., XV. 31.

492. Dec. 18. Killigrew *v.* Sawyer (In Error).—Copy Transcript of Record brought in this day, with tenor of Judgment (L. J. XV. 26, *in extenso*) affixed thereto. L. J., XIV. 693. George Sawyer, by his Majesty's consent, agreed with Sir William Killigrew on 27 July, 1682, for his office of Vice-Chamberlain to Katherine, the Queen Consor. Killigrew, by this agreement, was during his life to hold the profits, amounting in all to 516*l.* a year, viz., 200*l.* a year from her Majesty by pension during her life, his new year's gifts of 120*l.* a year, his fees, gifts, and liveries, being 66*l.* a year, and his salary and board-wages from the Cofferer's office of 130*l.* a year. Sawyer was to have no part of these till after Killigrew's death, and he agreed further to lend Killigrew, during his life, the use of his lodging in Somerset House, over

House of Lords MSS. — 1691.

the coach-house. Upon this agreement, Killigrew brought an action of covenant in the Common Pleas for six years arrears of salary, but judgment passed against him both there and on a Writ of Error in the King's Bench, from which he appeals to the House. The pleadings are set out *in extenso* in 4 Modern Rep. 39, where the case below is reported. [The Appeal was heard and dismissed on 12 Jan. 1691-2. *Sir Thomas Powys*, who cited Rolle's Abrid., Croke 202, and *Puncher* v. *Kingston* in Jones 228, 229, appeared with *Mr. Rowe* for Plaintiff; and *Sir Creswell Levinz* and *Mr. Finch* for Defendant. MS. Min., L. J., XV. 26.]

Annexed:—

(*a.*) 22 Dec. 1691. Petition of Plaintiff that Defendant may join issue and that a day may be appointed for hearing. L. J., XIV. 698.

493. Dec. 19. V. Longueville.—Petition of Alexander Davenant, Richard Middlemore and Andrew Card, Sharers and Adventurers in the Playhouse, for removal of the suspension upon them, in which case Petitioners will do their best to prevent the like miscarriage for the future. L. J., XIV. 695. Almost *in extenso*. [On 16 Dec. *L. Longueville* complained to the House of having been assaulted, with his servants, by the Guard at the Playhouse. His witnesses having deposed to the assault, it was *Moved*, That an address be made to his Majesty to suspend the Playhouse from acting. *Moved*, That the Lord Chamberlain be sent to presently to suspend the Players' acting for some time. *Ordered*, That Lieut. Primrose and the Serjeant of the Guard be sent for in custody. Later on, the House being informed that Lieut. Primrose was at the door, he was called in and told that a Peer had received a great affront from his soldiers, who had struck him, and that Primrose was present and told of it. *Lieut. Primrose:* I was below when the thing happened. My Lord took it ill that I asked. I told my Lord he should have satisfaction as soon as the Guard was over. His orders are in writing from the King. He withdrew. *Moved*, That Sir Charles Hero be sent for and bring his orders with him. *Primrose* was then recalled and, after a reprimand, discharged. (L. J., XIV. 688-9; MS. Min.)—On 17 Dec. the *Serjeant of the Guard* was called in, and asked to give an account of the matter. He said that L. Grey and his brother came to the Playhouse, and the sentry stopped him and told him he must take a ticket; and he went down and came back again presently, and threw a guinea to the fellow and went on again. *Mr. Yelverton* (called in): I saw this Serjeant take my Lord by the shoulder and push him. *The Serjeant* says he did not strike his Lordship. *Robert* (*John* in L. J., XIV. 689) *Phinney:* I cannot say it was the Serjeant. The Musketeers struck at me. *The Serjeant:* I was pulled behind. *John Pegue:* I did not know who struck my Lord. They withdraw. Then the two Box-keepers were called in and sworn, the Serjeant being present. *John Browne:* I did not see L. Longueville struck by anyone. His brother fell on the Serjeant and pulled him by the hair. I did not see the Serjeant push him. *William Roberts:* After his Lordship put his hand on his sword, the musketeers got together, and there was clattering of muskets. I never saw the Serjeant take his Lordship by the shoulder. One of the sentinels put his hand between his Lordship and the door. *The Soldier* called in that fired the musket, and was asked why he fired the musket in L. Longueville's face. He says it went off without cocking in the crowd. No word was given to fire, nor did he hear anyone say so. The musket was loaded with powder. *Sir Charles Hero* called in and asked what orders he gave the Guard at the Playhouse. He says he has the King's order. The same, 14 Nov., 1 W. & M., is delivered and *read*. Asked if any orders have been given for punishing the soldiers at the Playhouse who affronted L. Longueville, he says: I found it was before the Lords, and I examined it no further. I was next morning to be at a Court Martial. I received a letter from L. Longueville. The letter and Sir Charles' answer were *read*. The House then ordered the Serjeant and soldier to be sent to the Gatehouse, and an Address that for the future no soldiers should be permitted to guard the Playhouse. (L. J., XIV. 691; MS. Min.) The King answered that he had given orders accordingly. (L. J., XIV. 694.) The suspension on the Players was removed on the above Petition (*ib.* 695), and on 29 Dec. the Serjeant and soldier were, on Petition, released. (L. J., XV. 5; MS. Min.)]

Annexed:—

(*a*.) 29 Dec. Petition of Serjeant John Hutchinson and John Wilson, Sentinel, craving pardon for their offence and praying to be released. L. J., XV. 5.

494. Dec. 21. Cambridge University (Confirmation of Charters) Bill.—Amended* Draft of an Act for confirming the Charters and Liberties of the University of Cambridge and the Colleges and Halls therein. Whereas by an Act of Parliament made in the 13th year of the reign of the late Queen Elizabeth, intituled an Act concerning the several Corporations of the Universities of Oxford and Cambridge, and the confirmation of the charters, liberties, and privileges of either of them, it was amongst other things enacted, that the Letters Patents of the said Queen made and granted unto the Chancellors, Masters and Scholars of the University of Cambridge, bearing date the six and twentieth day of April in the third year of her reign, and also all other Letters Patents by any of the progenitors or predecessors of the said Queen made to the corporate body of the said University of Cambridge, by whatsoever name or names the said Chancellor, Masters and Scholars in any of the said Letters Patents had heretofore been named, should from thenceforth be good, effectual and available in law to all intents, constructions and purposes to the then Chancellor, Masters and Scholars and their successors for evermore, and according to the form, words, sentences, and true meaning of every of the same Letters Patents, as amply, fully, and largely as if the same Letters Patents were recited verbatim in the said Act of Parliament, anything to the contrary in any wise notwithstanding; and that the then Chancellor, Masters and Scholars of the said University and their successors for ever, by the name of Chancellor, Masters and Scholars of the said University of Cambridge, might have, hold, possess and use, to them and to their successors for ever, all manner of manors, lordships, rectories, parsonages, lands, tenements, rents, services, annuities, advowsons of churches, possessions, pensions and hereditaments, and all manner of liberties, franchises, quietances and privileges, view of frank pledge, law days and other things, whatsoever they be, which the said corporate body had held, occupied or enjoyed, or of right ought to have had used, occupied or enjoyed at any time or times before the making of the said Act of Parliament, according to the true intent and meaning as well of the

* The omissions are shown by square brackets, and the additions by italics. These amendments were made in Commitee. (Com. Book, 16 Jan.)

House of Lords MSS.

1691.

said Letters Patents granted by the said Queen to the Chancellor, Masters and Scholars of the said University of Cambridge, as of all other Letters Patents granted by any the progenitors or predecessors of the said Queen, any Statute or other thing or things whatsoever theretofore made or done to the contrary in any wise notwithstanding; and that as well the said letters patents of the said Queen, made and granted to the Chancellor, Masters and Scholars of the said University of Cambridge, as all other letters patents by any of the progenitors or predecessors of her said Highness, and all manner of liberties, franchises, immunities, quietances and privileges, leets, law days and other things whatsoever therein expressed, given or granted to the Chancellor, Masters and Scholars of the University of Cambridge, or to any of their predecessors, by whatsoever name the said Chancellor, Masters and Scholars in any of the said letters patents be named, were, and by virtue of the said Act should be, from thenceforth ratified, stablished and confirmed to the then Chancellor, Masters and Scholars of the said University of Cambridge and their successors for ever, any statute, law, usage, custom, construction or other thing to the contrary notwithstanding. And whereas, since the making of the said Act, the said Queen was pleased to grant to the Chancellor, Masters and Scholars of the said University of Cambridge other letters patents under her Great Seal, for the benefit of the said University bearing date the thirtieth day of August in the one and thirtieth year of her reign; and the late King James the first, by his letters patents under the Great Seal of England, bearing date the twenty-sixth day of August in the third year of his reign, was pleased to grant to the Chancellor, Masters and Scholars of the said University of Cambridge and their successors the perpetual advowson, donation, free deposition and right of patronage of the rectory of Somersham in the county of Huntingdon, together with Colne and Pidley and other chapels and appurtenances thereto belonging, for the better support and maintenance of the Regius Professor or Reader of Divinity in the said University of Cambridge for the time being, and also the perpetual advowson, donation, free disposition, and right of patronage of the rectory of Terrington in the county of Norfolk, with all and singular its appurtenances, for the better support and maintenance of the Lady Margaret's Professor or Reader of Divinity in the said University of Cambridge, for the time being; and whereas, the late King Charles the first, by his Letters Patents, bearing date the sixth day of February in the third year of his reign, did grant and confirm to the Chancellor, Masters and Scholars of the said University of Cambridge, the right and privilege of appointing and having three stationers or printers, and of printing books within the said University of Cambridge. Be it enacted by the King and Queen's most Excellent Majesties, by and with the advice and consent of the Lords spiritual and temporal and the Commons in this present Parliament assembled, and by the authority of the same, that as well the said grants and letters patents, as also all other letters patents and charters by any of the predecessors of their Majesties, kings or queens of this realm, heretofore granted to the corporate body of the said University of Cambridge, by whatsoever name or names the said Chancellor, Masters and Scholars in any of the said letters patents or charters have been heretofore named, shall be from henceforth good, effectual and available in law to all intents, constructions and purposes, to the now Chancellor, Masters and Scholars of the said University of Cambridge and to their successors for evermore, after and according to the form, words, sentences and true meaning of every of the same letters patents and charters, as amply, fully and largely as if the same letters patents and charters were recited verbatim in this present Act; and that all the said letters patents and charters, and all manners of liberties and franchises, immunities, quietances, privileges, powers and authorities, leets, law-days and other things whatsoever in the said Act or in any of the said letters patents or charters expressed, given or granted to the said Chancellor, Masters and Scholars of the said University of Cambridge, or to any of their predecessors, or to any public professor or minister of the said University for the time being, or to the said Chancellor, Masters and Scholars of the said University of Cambridge, or to any other person or persons in trust for the benefit and support of such office or place, by whatsoever name or title the said Chancellor, Masters and Scholars, or the said professors, officers or ministers of the said University of Cambridge, or other persons in any of the said letters patents or charters be named or described, be and by virtue of this present Act shall be from henceforth ratified, stablished, and confirmed unto the said Chancellor, Masters and Scholars, professors, officers, ministers and their successors, according to the true intent and meaning of the said Act, and of all and every the said letters patents and charters, notwithstanding any failure or want of form in law in the said letters patents or charters, or any of them, any statute, law, usage, custom, construction, or other thing to the contrary notwithstanding.

And to the intent the profits and emoluments of the said rectory of Somersham, together with Colne and Pidley, and of the said rectory of Terrington, may be the better appropriated and applied to and for the support and maintenance of the Regius and Margaret Professors of Divinity in the said University of Cambridge, according to the true intent and meaning the said letters patents of King James the first. Be it enacted by the authority aforesaid, that the said rectories of Somersham, with Colne and Pidley and Terrington, with all and singular their appurtenances, shall be and stand appropriated to the Chancellor, Masters and Scholars of the said University of Cambridge and their successors for ever, in trust for better support and maintenance of the Regius and Margaret Professors of Divinity in the said University for the time being respectively, according to the true intent and meaning of the said letters patents of the late King James the first; and the said respective professors for the time being, their executors and administrators, are hereby enabled and empowered, in the name of the Chancellor, Masters and Scholars of the said University of Cambridge, to sue for and recover all tithes, oblations and obventions and other profits arising and renewing within the said respective rectories or either of them, or the titheable places thereof or thereunto belonging, any law or usage to the contrary notwithstanding.

And whereas there is no vicar endowed at Somersham, be it provided and enacted that the Regius Professor of Divinity for the time being, within the said University of Cambridge shall take care of serving the cure there, or shall allow out of the profits of the said rectory [sufficient] *at least* 100*l*. *per annum* for the support and maintenance of curates there, *which curates are hereby obliged to a constant residence upon the said cures on pain of having their licenses withdrawn.* Provided also that no Regius or Margaret Professor of Divinity shall receive the profits of the said rectories, or either of them, for any longer time than he shall hold such his professor's place.

And be it further enacted by the authority aforesaid, that it shall and may be lawful to and for the Vice Chancellor of the said University of Cambridge when, and as often as he cannot attend the keeping of the Court commonly called the Vice Chancellor's Court, within the

House of Lords MSS.

1691.

said University, by reason of his absence from the University, or disability through sickness, or for any other cause, to depute and delegate in his room a sufficient person, at least of the degree of [Master of Arts or Bachelor] *Doctor of Divinity or Doctor* of Law, to keep the said Court in such his absence, who is hereby fully impowered and authorized to keep the same.

And be it further enacted, that all and singular letters patents or charters at any time heretofore made by any of the kings or queens of this realm for the erection, foundation, or corporation or endowment or benefit and advantage of any college or hall within the said University of Cambridge, or for the confirmation of any such charters, letters patents, or grants to them or any of them made, and all instruments, grants, indentures or writings by any other person or persons, bodies politic or corporate, granted or made to or for the endowment, benefit or advantage of any of the governors, masters, provosts, presidents, principal students, fellows and scholars of the said colleges or halls, or any of them respectively, by whatsoever name or names the said governors, masters, provosts, presidents, principal students, fellows and scholars or their predecessors, or any or either of them respectively, in any of the said letters patents, charters, instruments, grants, indentures, or writings, be or are incorporated or named, were and shall be reputed, taken and adjudged to have been good, perfect and effectual in the law for all things contained, according to the true intent and meaning of the same, any thing, matter or cause to the contrary notwithstanding.

And be it enacted, that all and every of the said colleges and halls of the said University shall and may severally have, hold, possess, enjoy and use, to them and their successors for ever, all manner of manors, lordships, rectorics, parsonages, lands, tenements, rents, services, annuities, advowsons of churches, possessions, pensions, portions, and hereditaments, and all manner of liberties, franchises, immunities, quietances and privileges, view of frankpledge, law days and other things, whatsoever they be, the which any of the said respective Corporate bodies of the said colleges or halls had held, occupied or enjoyed, or of right ought to have held, used, occupied and enjoyed at any time or times before the making of this Act, according to the true intent or meaning of any such letters patents, charters, instruments, grants, indentures or writings whatsoever, any law, statute, letters mandatory, or other thing or things whatsoever to the contrary notwithstanding.

And whereas in several of the local statutes, ordinances, and rules of the said colleges and halls, stablished and made in former times, many rites and offices of superstitious devotion had been appointed to be said and observed in the said colleges and halls by the governors, fellows or scholars, or other officers or ministers of such foundation, by saying or singing of masses, dirges, obits, and the like Popish offices and services, contrary to the true profession of the Protestant true Reformed Religion by law established in this realm, Wherefore to remove all occasion of doubt or scruples, which may happen to the minds of weak men concerning such rites and superstitious offices, Be it further enacted, that all such rites and offices of masses, dirges, obits, complines and other Popish offices and services of superstitious devotion, contrary to the profession of the Protestant Reformed Religion, which are mentioned prescribed, stablished or expressed in any such local statutes, rules, or ordinances, shall be, and are hereby for ever abolished to all intents and purposes whatsoever. And no oaths heretofore taken or hereafter to be taken by any manner of person or persons of any such college or hall, for observance of any of the said local statutes, rules, or ordinances, shall be taken or deemed to be or have been meant or intended to relate to any of the said rites or services, or any other such Popish and superstitious offices in any such statutes, rules, or ordinances established or expressed, any such statutes, rules or ordinances, or any other matter or thing to the contrary notwithstanding.

Provided also, and be it enacted, that upon all and every visitation of the said University, or any of the colleges or halls therein, or of the governors, masters, fellows, scholars, members, or officers of the same, by what name or names soever they be known, called or distinguished, all proceedings, sentences and judgments against any offender or offenders therein shall be had or given according to the statutes of this realm or the customs or statutes of the said University, or the several local statutes and ordinances of the respective colleges and halls therein and not otherwise, any law, statute, or usage to the contrary in anywise notwithstanding.

Saving to all and every person and persons, bodies politic and corporate, their heirs and successors, and the heirs and successors of every of them, other *than* the King and Queens Majesties, their heirs and successors, all such rights, titles, interests, leases, entries, conditions, charges, and demands, which they and every of them had, might, and should have had, in or to any of the said manors, lordships, rectories, parsonages, lands, tenements, rents, services, annuities, advowsons of churches, pensions, portions, hereditaments and all other things in the said letters patents, charters, instruments, grants, indentures or writings, or any of them mentioned or comprised, by reason of any right, title, charge, interest or conditions to them or any of them, or to the ancestors or predecessors of them, or any of them, devolved or grown before the several dates of the said letters patents, charters, instruments, grants, indentures, or writings, or by reason of any gift, grant, demise, or other act or acts at any time made or done between the said chancellor, masters and scholars of the said University of Cambridge or any of them and others, or between any governor or masters, students, fellows and scholars, or any of the said colleges or halls respectively, and the corporate bodies of them or any of them and others, by what name or names soever the same were done, in like manner and form, as they and every of them had or might have had the same before the making of this Act, anything therein contained to the contrary notwithstanding.

Provided also and be it enacted, that this Act or anything therein contained shall not extend to the prejudice or hurt of the liberties or privileges of right belonging to the mayor, bailiffs, or burgesses of the town of Cambridge or any of them, before the making of this Act, anything herein to the contrary notwithstanding. [Read 1ª this day. (L. J., XIV. 696.)—In C. W. H., on 13 Jan., the *Bishop of London* in the Chair, the Bill was read through. *Moved*, That the charters mentioned in the Bill may be sent for to be seen. Copies of charters to be produced. Title read and postponed. Preamble read. House resumed. Report made as in L. J., XV., 28, and agreed to. Select Committee appointed accordingly. (MS. Min.)—The Select Committee met on 14 Jan., *E. Bridgewater* in the Chair, but only to adjourn, and again on 16 Jan., *Bishop of London* in the Chair, when, after inspecting the charters, they reported the Bill with the Amendments marked in the text above (Com. Book of dates.) These amendments were agreed to on report, and the Bill was sent to the Commons (L. J., XV. 33, 39), where, on 22 Feb. 1691, it was rejected at the last stage by 119 votes to 69. (C. J., X. 683.)]

HOUSE OF LORDS MSS.

1691.

495. Dec. 22. **Strode and others v. Chichester and another.**—Petition and Appeal of Samuel Strode, Anne, his wife, and Jane, their daughter. The Appellant Samuel, an apothecary in Exeter in good trade and practice under several eminent physicians, was frequently sent for to attend John Chichester, Esq., and Dorothy, his wife (since married to Respondent), at their mansion house at Hall, more than 30 miles off. Dorothy being near related to Appellant, and knowing how his trade suffered from his absence, promised to reward him amply and to provide for his daughter Jane as their own child, and for such considerations as well as for 870*l.*, which she acknowledged to be due to him on an account, made him sole executor of her will and leased to him the moiety of the Baron of Bickleigh, co. Devon, at a yearly rent of 80*l.* for 50 years, determinable on her life, and for years determinable on three lives after her death, with a bond in 1,500*l.* for performance of covenants in the lease, and another in 2,000*l.* for payment of 1,000*l.* to him in trust for her daughter Jane. Respondent, on marrying Dorothy, brought a Bill in Chancery in the name of himself and wife, to avoid the lease and bonds, on the ground that they had been obtained by threats and without payment of the 521*l.* 10*s.* mentioned as consideration. The Lords Commissioners on 7 December last declared the lease and bonds to have been obtained by fraud, and decreed the bond of 2,000*l.* to be delivered up and the lease to be cancelled unless the 521*l.* 10*s.* were paid with interest. Appeal against this decree. *Signed* by Appellants: *Countersigned* by John Rowe and William Spry. L. J. XIV. 698. [The Cause was heard on 26 Jan. 1691–2. *The Solicitor General* (for Appellant) opened the case. *Serjeant Tremayne* (for Respondent): I will prove the threat. He kept possession of the house; this was in June 1685. There was no consideration; it was a fraud. *Mr. Finch:* there is no colour for this, the bond extorted by threats. (Depositions of Christian Greenstead, Wilmot Duck, and Joan Matthews read.) *Mr. Finch:* There was nothing at all due to them. Strode's answer read. Richard Hole, [his answer] to the fourteenth Interrogatory read. *The Solicitor General* (for Appellant) replies as to the fraud and deceit. Mr. Chichester had full notice of this matter. This man is denied to be a relation. We have several letters wherein they call one another cousins. *Mr. Rowe* (for Appellant) heard also. 20 June the lease was dated. A letter read. Counsel withdraw. Decree affirmed. (MS. Min., L. J., XV. 49.)]

Annexed:—

(*a*.) 8 Jan. 1691–2. Answer of Henry Chichester, Esq., and Dorothy, his wife. The Appellant Samuel, an apothecary never of any eminence or great practice, was very liberally paid, far more so than either his attendance and physic deserved. Respondents are not aware of any relationship, though, as John Chichester was related to the ancient family of Strodes in Devonshire and Appellants were of that name, he did sometimes call them cousins, and out of charity maintained Jane for some years, but never promised to give her any portion or make any provision for her. In June 1685, when Dorothy remarried, Samuel treated with her in a threatening manner for the lease in question, offering to pay 521*l.* 10*s.* and 80*l.* rent during her life, and fearing lest she should remarry before sealing the lease, extorted from her a bond to enforce the sealing, which he promised to give back when the lease was sealed. A few weeks before the marriage, he brought her a lease ready drawn up and forced her to seal it, burning at the same time a piece of paper, which he swore was the bond. Afterwards, finding the lease was not so firm as it should be, he brought another, and with it a paper purporting to be an account stated between them, whereby Dorothy was to acknowledge herself to owe him 870*l.*, though she owed him nothing and no items were given. He forced her to sign this account and give a bond for the balance, and also to seal the new lease and acknowledge the receipt of the 521*l.* 10*s.* fine, though not a farthing was paid, he colourably paying her 20 guineas, which he took back as soon as her witnesses had left the room. The Respondent Henry knew nothing of these transactions till after the marriage. Dorothy never entered into any bond to Samuel in trust for his daughter Jane. Respondents having been willing to confirm the pretended lease, if the fine were paid with interest, or to take a surrender of it, if the arrears might be discharged, did for some time receive the 80*l.* rent, and sued Samuel for nonpayment, and it is now in arrear for three quarters. If Appellants have got any will from Dorothy, it was got by ill practices in her widowhood. Nothing was left due at John Chichester's death to Samuel for his attendance. Prays that the Appeal may be dismissed with costs, both in the House and below. *Signed* by Respondents; *Countersigned* by Nic. Hooper. *Endorsed* as brought in this day.

(*b.*) 11 Jan. Petition of Appellants for an early day for hearing. L. J., XV. 23.

496. Dec. 22. Phillipps *v.* Phillipps.—Petition and Appeal of Elizabeth Phillipps. Sir James Phillipps, Bart., having a good personal estate and a real estate of at least 1,000*l.* a year, left by Will, dated 4 Oct. 1688, his personal estate to his wife, the Respondent, subject, however, as well as his real estate, to payment of his debts and legacies, 2,500*l.* of the legacies being made not payable till after the death of his wife, whom he made executrix, with directions to sell so much of the real estate as should pay the debts and legacies, and give the overplus to Appellant, the next heir, to whom was also devised the remainder of his whole real estate, the same being first limited to Respondent so long as she continued his widow, and subject to payment of the interest of his debts at 5 per cent., and to other limitations mentioned in the Will. Respondent being in France, when her husband died, authorised one Peter Cooke to act in her absence, who proved the Will and brought a Bill in Chancery against Appellant to compel her, as heir at law and devisee in remainder, to join with Respondent in the sale of the whole estate without any recompense for so doing. Appellant, by her cross Bill, prayed the personal estate to be applied in the first place to the payment of the debts and legacies, and the real estate to come in aid, and no more thereof to be sold than what sufficed to perform the Will. On 23 June 1691 the Court decreed that Respondent should have the personal estate exempt from all charges, and that the whole real estate should be sold, without any recompense to Appellant, and this Decree was confirmed on a rehearing on 18 Dec. Part of the real estate is sufficient alone to pay all the debts and legacies, and the testator expressly directed that only so much should be sold as was necessary, in order thus to preserve the ancient family seat, which, being above 400*l.* a year, is settled for her jointure on Respondent, though a person but of mean birth and little or no fortune. The reversion ought to come to Appellant and her heirs, whereas by the decree the Respondent will carry away all the personal estate, and also all the real estate during life. Appeals from the decree. *Signed* by Appellant; *Countersigned* by Ambrose Phillipps and Thomas Powys. L. J., XIV. 698. [The Appeal was heard and dismissed on 12 Feb. 1691–2, *Sir Ambrose Phillipps* and *Mr. Finch* being heard for Appellant, and *The Solicitor General* and *Mr. Trevor* for Respondent. (L. J., XV. 72; MS. Min.)]

Annexed:—

(*a.*) 30 Dec. 1691. Petition of Appellant. Prays that, her mother being at Winchester very sick, her friend Robert Napper may enter into Recognisance in her absence. L. J., XV. 6.

(*b.*) 5 Jan. 1691–2. Petition of Appellant. Cooke has had notice, but neglects to answer. Prays for an early day for hearing. L. J., XV. 18. *See* MS. Min., 4 Jan.

(*c.*) 13 Jan. 1691–2. Answer of Dame Marina Phelipps. Respondent's late husband, who died much indebted, left by Will all his personal estate to Respondent, and also his real estate during her widowhood, with full power to sell for payment of his debts and legacies, and the overplus afterwards to her second sister, the Appellant, with a proviso to devise it over to others, if she disturbed the performance of the Will. Cooke waited on Appellant and her mother Lady Elizabeth at Winchester, and desired matters might proceed amicably, and soon after, Napper, came over to Stoke Charity, the mansion seat, and advised Cooke not to remove the papers, promising a friendly proceeding in the performance of the Will; but directly Cooke returned to London, not having stirred a paper except a rental of the estate, Appellant and Napper carried away all the deeds, &c. whereby Respondent is unable to ascertain the value of the real estate, and forced Respondent to proceed against her in Chancery. As to the malicious reflections on Respondent, her father was one Colonel Mitchell and her mother was sister to L. Windsor, and she had between 2,000*l.* and 3,000*l.* a year for her portion. Appellant's late husband had a great regard for Respondent, but little for Appellant, who always behaved vexatiously to him. Prays that the Appeal may be dismissed with costs. *Endorsed* as brought in this day.

(*d.*) 15 Jan. 1691–2. Petition of Appellant for an early day for hearing. L. J., XV. 31.

497. Dec. 22. Herbert and another *v.* Le Brun and others.—Petition and Appeal of Charles Herbert, Gent., and Bartholomew Evans, Yeoman.—John Jones, Esq., about 30 years since was seized in fee of the Lordship of Tregaron and Penarth, co. Cardigan, which, after his death about 17 years since, went to his daughters and co-heirs, Mary Anne and Elianor. In the manor there are two divisions, one called Vaynor Gaeth and the other Penarth, *alias* Ychelder, in each of which Court Leets are held twice a year, and Court Barons every fortnight. The duties, &c. demanded by the Lord of the Manor of every tenant in Vaynor Gaeth, are as follows: (1.) Three quarters of oats of 25 March yearly from every tenant keeping a team; (2.) Upon an alienation, 6*s.* 8*d.*; (3.) At the death of every Freeholder or upon the marriage of every tenant's daughter, 6*s.* 8*d.*; (4.) The delivering and carrying of 4 loads of turf yearly; (5.) One day's ploughing, one day's harrowing, one day's reaping, one day's mowing of hay, yearly; (6.) The carriage of one horse load of lime for liming the Lord's land, which carriage is 20 long miles; (7.) Suit of Mill and to provide and carry thatch at their own charge to thatch the Lords Mill; (8.) Suit of Court and

Chief rents; (9.) To carry and provide stone, timber, and other materails for repairing the Lord's Mill and Millpond, and scouring the same at their own charge. Of the tenants of Penarth, *alias* Ychelder, are demanded in addition to the above, 10*s*. on an alienation, death of a freeholder, or marriage of a tenant's daughter, and three quarters of oats yearly of every tenant keeping a team. Respondents, being the Lords and Ladies of the manor, charged Appellants that they had encroached on the waste of the manor in Vaynor Gaeth, and ought to pay the said duties, &c. in specie. Appellants answered, denying the encroachment, and stating that part of the waste was conveyed to the Appellant, Herbert's father, by John Jones, late Lord, at 1*s*. rent; and that the Appellant Evans was but a tenant in Tregaron at the same rent. They confessed they owed suit of court and suit to the Lord's Mill for the grain raised and consumed in the manor, when there is water in the Lord's Mill, but that no other duties or services had ever been paid for the waste land or the house in Tregaron. The Cause being heard on 30 Nov., 2 Jac. II., it was referred to a trial at law to try what duties, &c. were due in respect of the manor. Appellants' witnesses were not heard, and a verdict was given against them, and a new trial, obtained by paying 32*l*. costs, when their witnesses were examined, had the same result; and the Court of Chancery, on 12 December, 2 W. & M., decreed payment of the said duties, &c., with 217*l*. 10*s*. costs at law and equity, to the ruin of Appellants, who are but two poor tenants, singled out of the whole Lordship. They proved below that the duties, &c. demanded, except the suit of Court and Mill, were only acts of kindness done by some tenants to the Lord, and not obligatory. All the demesne of the manor is but 6*l*. a year and barren ground, and there are above 100 tenants required to do the several duties and services, which is more than the land is capable of, if the pretended duties are allowed, which is a sort of villenage tenure. Pray that the Decree may be set aside, and Respondents ordered to answer. *Signed* by Appellants; *Countersigned* by Thos. Burton and Ro. Price, whose certificate and signatures are copied. L.J., XIV. 698. [The Appeal was heard and dismissed on 29 Jan. 1691–2. (L. J., XV. 55.) The MS. Min. have the following: "Counsel called in. *Mr. Price* (for Appellants): There are 100 tenants to 6*l*. per annum, and they are to carry 100 loads of timber thither, and they keep but two small oxen to a team. *Sir W. Williams* (for Appellants): The Chancery have taken upon them to establish customs by a Decree *Mr. Finch* heard for the Respondent, the Lord of the Manor. *Sir Thomas Powys* (for Respondents): A load of timber may be carried for 2*d*. *Sir W. Williams* (in reply): This Decree they say is to bind all the tenants, and the Bill is brought but against two. Counsel withdrew. Speaker reported. *Holt, C. J.*, heard. House *moved* to reverse the Decree. *Holt, C. J.*, is desired to consider of this case, and give the House an account thereof on Monday next, and the debate adjourned to that day." Nothing further recorded.]

Annexed:—

(*a*.) 21 Jan. 1691–2. Answer of Cornelius Le Brun, Esq., and Anne his wife, Oliver Howells, Gent., and Mary, his wife, and William Corbett and Eleanor, his wife. The matter in dispute coming to be tried at Hereford Assizes, was referred at Appellants' request to two Judges in Westminster Hall, but Appellants refused to proceed in the reference, and so it came to a trial, at which a verdict passed for Respondents, which was confirmed at a new trial. Pray that the Appeal may be dismissed with costs. *Signed* by Respondents. *Endorsed* as brought in this day.

(*b*.) 22 Jan. Petition of Respondents. The Appeal is brought merely for delay. Respondents, who live in Cardiganshire, are obliged to attend in town till it comes to be heard, having no other business here. Pray for an early day for hearing. L. J., XV. 44.

498. Dec. 22. Fountaine's Estate Bill.—Amended Draft* of an Act for divesting the Manors and Lordships of Bushwood and Lapworth and several other lands, tenements and hereditaments in the County of Warwick, out of Andrew Fountaine, Esq., and vesting the same in Trustees for raising and paying a debt due upon a mortgage thereof taken in the name of the said Albert Fountaine. Whereas by a deed of 4 June 1655 between Sir Robert Holt, of Aston, near Birmingham, Bart., and Lady Mary, his wife, of the first part; Stephen Smith, of Covent Garden, London, Esq., and Augustus Walker, of Aston, Gent., of the second part; and James Perrott, of London, Gent., of the third part, and by a fine levied in the same year, Sir Robert Holt, in consideration of 2,500*l*. borrowed of Perrott, mortgaged to him the Manors and Lordships of Bushwood, *alias* Bishopswood, and Lapworth, and all the lands, &c., thereto belonging in Lapworth, Bushwood, Stratford-upon-Avon, Old Stratford, Beudesert, *alias* Belsert, Packwood and Rowington, for 500 years at a pepper-corn rent; And whereas by another deed of 19 August 1658 between Sir Robert Holt and Perrott, the former in consideration of a further loan of 2,500*l*. and for further securing the first loan mortaged to Perrott all his lands, &c. in Birmingham and Witton (except the Great and Lesser Brantleys, the Brantley meadows and the millholms in Witton, and Pemerton's Moors and Bidlees Grounds in Birmingham), as well as the personage, rectory or impropriate tithes, &c. thereto belonging within the manors of Erdington, Witton Castle, Bromwich, Water-Orton, *alias* Water Overton, Saltley, Washwood, Little Bromwich, Wardend, and Duddeston, *alias* Dodston, and elsewhere in the parish of Aston, except the tithes within the manors, &c. of Aston, Rechells, *alias* Assells, and Bordesley, for 500 years from the date of the first deed at a pepper-corn rent, subject to redemption on payment of 5,825*l*. in manner stated in another deed of 20th August, 1658; And whereas Sir Robert Holt on 20 Aug. 1658 acknowledged a recognizance in Chancery to Perrott of 8,000*l*. for performance of the above covenants; And whereas by deed of 31 May, 1664, between Sir Robert Holt and Perrott of the one part, and Andrew Fountaine, of the Inner Temple, Esq., of the other part, Perrott in consideration of 5,000*l*. to be paid by him to Fountaine in satisfaction of the 5,000*l*. principal due to him on the two mortgages, assigned to Fountaine, by direction of Sir Robert, all the lands so mortgaged, subject to redemption by Sir Robert, as stated in a deed of 1 June, 1664; And whereas the said [Sir Robert for further securing of the 5,000*l*. acknowledged a Recognizance in the nature of a Statute Staple for 10,000*l*. to Fountaine and the said] Recognizance was assigned to Fountaine or otherwise kept on foot for his benefit, but subject to a defeazance on his vacating or assigning it on payment of the 5,000*l*. with interest; And whereas the mortgaged lands were not redeemed by Sir Robert at the time limited, and Fountaine having taken possession, Sir Robert in 1671 sued him in Chancery for an account and for recovery of the estate, on payment of what was due, but before the Cause was determined, Elizabeth Cobb,

* The omission is shown by square brackets, and the addition by italics. The other amendments are either consequential or clerical.

widow, Robert Coke, Esq., and William Guavas, Esq., Executors of John Coke, late of Holkham, co. Norfolk, claimed the money due on the mortgage to Fountaine, as part of Coke's personal estate, and Sir Robert could not, therefore, safely pay it without the consent of all parties claiming it, which consent he was unable to obtain; And whereas Coke's said executors in 1672 brought a Bill in Exchequer against Fountaine and Sir Robert for the said money, but the cause remained undetermined for several years, whereby many rents were lost, pending which cause, Sir Robert in 1678, and after his death, his son and heir, Sir Charles Holt, in 1681, offered to pay the same, but Fountaine always refused to reconvey the estate; and though by a Decree of the Court of Exchequer Chamber in 1682, the money is adjudged to be part of John Coke's personal estate, and Fountaine is decreed to transfer the mortgaged estates and deeds to his surviving executors, which Decree has since been affirmed, on appeal, by the House of Lords, yet the Appellant Fountaine still refuses to assign the mortgaged premises and deeds of mortgage and assignment and transfer or vacate the recognizance; And whereas Edward Coke, an infant, the son and heir of the said Robert Coke, by Lady Anne Coke, widow, his mother, and late guardian, claimed the money due on the mortgage, and has obtained a Decree in Exchequer Chamber against John Coke's executors, who have been adjudged to be only executors in trust for Edward Coke, and the money has been decreed for his use and benefit, and he has thereupon claimed the mortgaged estate, so that Sir Charles Holt, though ready to pay what remains due, is like to be deprived of his estate, and has no legal means to get a reconveyance thereof, or sell or dispose of it, and discharge the rest of his lands from the recognizance; The Bill therefore, at the suit of Sir Charles Holt, enacts, That the estate thus mortgaged to Perrott and assigned by him to Fountaine, and all recognizances entered into by Sir Robert Holt as further securities, shall from and after the *twenty-second* day of *October, one thousand, six hundred and ninety-one* be divested out of Fountaine and his assignees and any person claiming them in trust for him or through his default discharged of estates, assignments and incumbrances made or suffered by Fountaine or his assignees; and shall be vested in Fulke, L. Brooke, William, L. Digby, John Grey, Esq., of Enfield, co. Stafford, and Walter Chetwynd, Esq., of Ingestre, co. Stafford, discharged of all estates and incumbrances made or suffered by Fountaine or his assignees or the executors or assigns of John Coke, for the remainder of the term of 500 years, upon trust to raise such money, by lease, mortgage, or sale, as shall satisfy with interest the whole debt due on the mortgage made to Fountaine, discounting all moneys received by Fountaine and paid by Sir Charles Holt into the Court of Exchequer, the interest being at 6 per cent. from the date of the assignment to Fountaine to 1 June 1671, and after that, to the time of raising the money, at 5 per cent., and to pay the money so raised for the use of Edward Coke to Thomas, M. Carmarthen, his present guardian, and the surplus, if any, to Sir Charles Holt; and after payment of the debt and expenses incident to the trust, to assign to Sir Charles Holt, upon his request and at his charge, all the lands, remaining unsold, which until such assignment and after such payment they shall hold in trust for him; and to transfer, vacate, or acknowledge satisfaction of the Recognizances. The Bill concludes with the usual saving clause. [Read 1ª this day. (L. J., XIV. 698.) On 29 Dec. a Petition of Sir Charles Holt (Annex (*a*.) below) was read and referred to a Select Committee then appointed to consider what the House could do in getting their former Judgment obeyed, and whether Petitioner could be relieved in any other way than by Bill. (L. J., XV. 5.) The proceedings of this Select Committee are not recorded, but on 30 Dec. they reported, by E. Rochester, that after hearing the Judges, they were of opinion that no relief could be had except by Bill (*ib.* 6). On 5 Jan. the Bill was accordingly read 2ᵃ and committed, with instructions to the Committee to receive any Propositions and report them to the House (*ib.* 17).—In Committee, on 7 Jan., E. Rochester in the Chair, *Mr. Harrington* (for Mr. Fountaine) offered that Mr. Fountaine should purchase part of the estate by mortgage. We are content that 300*l.* a year may secure our debt, and that the remainder of the estate shall not be subject to the debt. The inheritance of the land will follow the issue of the Cause, and the annual profits will [be] the sequestration, which was obtained pending the Appeal here. *Sir Thomas Powys* (for Sir C. Holt): The Decree was prosecuted to a sequestration before the Appeal. Your Lordships judged the Decree just, so the prosecution is judged to be just and fair. Mr. Fountaine is out of the case. *Mr. Darnell* (for Mr. Coke): Mr. Fountaine is in contempt of the Court. Mr. Coke ought not to be obliged to take 300*l.* a year for his money, when he has a mind to have in his money itself. *Ordered* to acquaint the House with these proposals. (Com. Book.) The House on report, ordered the Committee to proceed on the Bill. (L. J., XV. 19.)—On 11 Jan., in Committee, *Sir Charles Holt* says that the Recognizance mentioned in the Bill is not entered nor to be found; nor does he know plainly whether there is any such, though Mr. Fountaine, in an answer to a Bill of his, has pretended that there is such a one. The Bill was then amended, and ordered to be reported. (Com. Book.) The second reading was negatived in the Commons on 8 Feb. (C. J., X. 657.)]

Annexed:—

(*a.*) 29 Dec. Petition of Sir Charles Holt, Bart. In 1658 Petitioner's father, Sir Robert Holt, mortgaged the manors of Bushwood and Lapworth, co. Warwick, to Mr. James Perrott for 500 years and acknowledged a recognizance of 8,000*l.* to him to secure a loan of 5,000*l.* In 1664, having borrowed 5,000*l.* of William Guavas to pay off this loan, Sir Robert and Perrott, by Guavas' orders, assigned the mortgage and recognizance to Andrew Fountaine (whose name was used, as since appears, only in trust for John Coke, deceased), and Sir Robert acknowledged another recognizance to Fountaine, for 10,000*l.*, as further security. After Coke's death, his executors brought a Bill in Chancery against Fountaine and Sir Robert for the money due on the mortgage, and the Court decreed in 1682 that Fountaine should assign the mortgaged premises to the executors, and deliver up the mortgage deed and assignment. Fountaine refused to obey the decree, and was prosecuted to a sequestration. He then appealed in 1689 to the House to reverse the decree, and their Lordships directed a trial at bar in the Exchequer on two issues, viz., 1. Whether the 5,000*l.* lent to Sir Robert was the money of John Coke, and 2. Whether Coke afterwards gave it to Fountaine. The jury found all the money to be Cokes'. Fountaine did not appear at the trial, and remains in contempt, and is now under a sequestration; and Mr. Coke, the said John Coke's heir, to whom the money due on the securities is decreed, not having the estate in law, and being an infant, cannot recover the estate, and Petitioner, after 20 year's patience, has no hope of having a reconveyance on payment of what is due, unless relieved by their Lordships. Only 6,000*l.* is due on the mortgage, and the estate is worth 14,000*l.* and Petitioner's other estate is encumbered with the two recognizances. He has offered, and is ready to pay what is due on the mortgage, but is forced to remain a debtor against his will, and very likely lose his estate. Prays for relief by Bill or otherwise. *Signed* by Petitioner; *Countersigned* by Thos. Powys and R. West. L. J., XV. 5. [*See* Notes to first paper.]

(*b.*) 11 Jan. 1691–2. Lords' Amendments to the Bill. [Made in Committee and reported this day. Com. Book; L. J., XV. 24.]

499. Dec. 22. D. Leinster's Naturalisation Act.—Draft of an Act for Naturalising of Mainhardt, Duke of Leinster. [Read 1ª this day; Royal Assent, 24 Feb. (L. J., XIV. 698; XV. 93.) 3–4 W. & M. c. 19 in Long Calendar. Com. Book, 11 Jan. The Bill was returned from the Commons with Amendments (C. J., X. 646, *in extenso*), to which the Lords agreed. L. J., XV. 68).]

Annexed:—

(*a.*) 11 Jan. 1691–2. Certificate that his Grace Mainhardt, Duke of Leinster, took the Sacrament in the parish church of St. Martin-in-the-Fields on 20 Dec. 1690. *Signed* by Thos. Tenison, Vicar, and Christopher Cock, Churchwarden. *Attested* by H. Scardeville and Thos. Smyth. [Read in Committee this Day. Com. Book.]

500. Dec. 23. Keble's Estate Act—Amended Draft of an Act to enable John Keble, Gent., to sell certain lands in Stow Market in the county of Suffolk, and to settle other lands of greater value to the said uses. The Lords' Amendments (Com. Book, 23 Jan.) are to insert the names of the Trustees and date of the commencement of the trust, to add the Clause in Annex (*b.*), and to reduce the amount chargeable by John Keble the son on the mortgaged premises from 500*l.* to 400*l.* The Commons' later Amendment is given in C. J., X. 680. [Read 1ª this day; Royal Assent, 24 Feb. (L. J., XIV. 700; XV. 93.) 3–4 W. & M. c. 40. in Long Calendar.]

Annexed:—

(*a.*) 19 Jan. 1691–2. Consent of John Burrell, D.D., and Bridget Keble to the passing of the Bill. *Dated* 8 Dec. 1691. *Attested* by John Chennery and John Turner. [Read in Committee this day. Com. Book.]

(*b.*) 25 Jan. Amended Clause, marked A, vesting certain lands of John Keble called Woodfields in the trustees after 24 March 1691. [Added in Committee 23 Jan. (Com. Book), and reported this day. (L. J., XV. 48.)]

501. Dec. 29. Kynnersley's Estate Bill.—Amended* Draft of an Act to enable Thomas Kynnersley to make a lease or leases for payment of his debts. The Preamble recites that whereas Thomas Kynnersley, Esq., of Loxley, co. Stafford, by a settlement made in 28 Chas. II. on his marriage with Mary, late daughter and only child of John London, Gent., of Islington, deceased, became seized for life (1) of the manors of Great and Little Loxley and the manor-house of Loxley Hall, worth 560*l.* a year, with a limitation of part to her for her jointure, if she survived him, and with power, if she died before him

* The two amendments are purely verbal. Com. Book, 4 Jan. 1691-2.

House of Lords MSS.

1691.

having issue male, to make a jointure to another wife of part of the estate of the yearly value of 60*l.*; and (2) of the reversion, after the death of his mother Mary, a widow, of certain lands in Leeshill, Kingstone, Bromeshall, Caveswall, *alias* Cowershall, Uttoxeter, Horton, Horton Hay, Poshton James and Biddulph, in the County of Stafford, of the yearly value of 700*l.*, remainder to his sons, and remainders to the heirs male and right heirs of his father; And whereas he owes 1,100*l.* to Sir Nathaniel Curzon, Bart., of Kedleston, co. Derby, and 1,200*l.* to Mary London, hereafter named, which debts claim precedence as charges on his estate, as well as other sums to other creditors, as much in all as the profits of his estate in possession will satisfy in 10 years; and the creditors, except Curzon, are willing to accept a lease on certain terms of his estate in possession and reversion for their satisfaction during the 10 years; And whereas his wife is dead, leaving one son only, Thomas, aged 11, and Curzon has agreed to accept, towards satisfaction of his debts, two farms in Great and Little Loxley, formerly possessed or occupied by Edward Pratt and John Burden, and now in the tenure or occupation of William Plant and William Shipley, or their assigns, and other lands in those manors called Kempswood and Kempswood meadow, and the lands in the possession or occupation of Henry Robinson, Richard Hickman, Richard Hamson, and Anne Brough, being of the yearly value of 100*l.*, for the term of 11 years from 21 March 1692, and also a rentcharge of 80*l.* a year out of the said lands in Leeshill, &c. payable half-yearly from the death of Mary Kynnersley till 26 March 1703, unless the debt, with 4 per cent. interest, be satisfied before that date; And whereas Thomas Kynnersley, now aged 38, is desirous to provide for payment of all his creditors, and for that purpose has executed with Mary London an indenture tripartite dated 3 March 1690, and so as the agreement made therein may be performed, to the least possible prejudice of his son, he is willing, not only to relinquish his power of making his second wife a jointure, but that his son (who has a provision of 40*l.* a year already, and after the death of his grandmother, Mary London, will have an estate of 500*l.* a year more in possession) shall also, after the term of years expired, have a third part of his father's estate in possession even in his father's lifetime, as agreed between his father and grandmother, without which agreement he could not in his father's lifetime have any of his father's estate, and the said terms will expire about the time of his coming of age, so that very little or no prejudice will accrue to the infant. The Bill therefore enacts that Sir N. Curzon shall hold the said lands and receive the said rentcharge as aforesaid; and that Francis Cede, of Leighford, co. Stafford, together with Richard Fassett, of London, (named in the said deed,) and Walter Chetwynd, of Millwick, (Thomas Whitby and Richard Sherratt, also named as trustees in the deed, refusing to act in the trust) shall hold all the lands limited to Thomas Kynnersley in possession or reversion, except those appointed for Curzon, for 10 years as aforesaid, on trust to allow Mary London to enjoy the mansion house of Loxley Hall and lands thereto belonging, other than those leased to William Palmer, for 10 *years*, and to pay to her, out of the premises so limited to them, the sum of 50*l.* a year, the rest to go to discharge the debts of such creditors of Kynnersley as shall within six months after notice agree to this provision, Mary London hereby consenting to let their debts have precedence of her own. After the terms of 11 and 10 years are expired, or his father's debts previously satisfied, the infant, although his father be then living, shall have possession of the estate. Provided that no creditor accepting the term of 10 years shall have power to imprison or molest Thomas Kynnersley or his sureties for any of the debts hereby provided for. If any creditor, who shall not accept the said term, shall extend or seize the estate, the other creditors, who have accepted it, may plead any prior mortgage, &c. for their protection. The trustees may have all reasonable charges of the trust out of the estate. The Act shall not prejudice the estate which Mary Kynnersley, the relict, has for life in the lands limited to her by the settlement, nor hinder Curzon from receiving the rentcharge thereout after her death. The Bill concludes with the usual saving clause. [Read 1a this day, L. J., XV. 4. In Committee, E. Warrington in the Chair, the deed mentioned in the preamble was perused. *Mr. Gilby* produced an agreement, under the hands of Mr. Sergeant Birch and Mr. Alexander Stanhope, touching the debt due to him agreable to the Preamble. The Deed relating to Mary London is perused. *Mary London*, the Grandmother, is present and consents to the Bill, which was then ordered to be reported with amendments. (Com. Book, 4 Jan.) The Bill finally dropped in the Commons.]

502. Dec. 29. Howard of Walden Claim of Peerage.—Petition of Elizabeth Felton, by Thomas Felton, Esq., her father, to the King. Thomas Howard, Petitioner's ancestor, was summoned to Parliament by writ of 39 Eliz., as Lord Howard of Walden, and sat and voted as a Peer, and thus his blood was ennobled, and he and his lineal heirs had an inheritance of the said dignity. After the death of the said Thomas, who in 1 Jac. I. was created Earl of Suffolk, the dignity descended to Theophilus, his son and heir; and from Theophilus, to his son and heir James, late E. Suffolk, who died leaving Lady Essex Griffin, his eldest daughter, and Petitioner, his grandchild (only daughter and heir of Lady Elizabeth Felton, his other daughter) his coheirs and also the lineal heirs of the first Lord Walden. The dignity and honour is indivisible, and by the laws and customs of the kingdom his Majesty, as the Sovereign of all honour and dignity, may confer the same on which of the said coheirs his Majesty please. Prays that the dignity may be conferred on Petitioner, as one of the said coheirs and lineal heirs. *Unsigned. Endorsed* with his Majesty's reference to the House, dated Whitehall 22 Dec. 1691 and signed Sydney. L.J., XV. 4. [In Committee for Privileges on 11 Jan., Bishop of Salisbury in the Chair, the Order of Reference and Petition were read and Counsel called in. *The Solicitor-General* (for Petitioner): Instances case of Fiennes, L. Dacre.* An honour is not to be divided. The honour goes so far back to the Crown, that it is in his Majesty power and pleasure to prefer which he pleases. Coke on Lyttleton, fol. 165, and Reports, Part XII., fol. 112, "Mr. Camden, &c." E. Oxford's case, between him and the Lord Willoughby, as to the Office of Great Chamberlain. In the case of Ralph, Lord Cromwell, Sir Humphrey Bourchier was summoned as Lord Cromwell, though he married the younger daughter. *Mr. Holles* (for Petitioner): We say he was called by a general writ. By common law there was no way of creating a Baron but by writ. We only desire your Lordships to report it that the King may give it, if he please. *Sir Thomas Powys* (for Lady Essex Griffin): I agree it is a Barony in fee, and that he did sit in Parliament. The Pedigree is true, but we hope it will be thought necessary this title should come to the Lady Essex Griffin. We say it remains until one of the daughters has male issue to sit in Parliament. Cites Bracton, Book II., Chap. 34; the E. Pembroke's case. He says the Earldom ought to go to the issue of the

* *See* Coke's Inst. 165.

House of Lords MSS.

1691.

eldest daughter. I have 13 [out] of 14 precedents wherein the King has summoned the male of the eldest daughter. Here the eldest daughter has a son, and it would be strange to take it from him and give it to the youngest daughter. Fitzherbert's Abridgment. *Mr. Ward* (for E. Suffolk): If this honour be not in my client, it is in any other person as much as the coheirs. This Barony has always gone with the Earldom, and the Earl has no other Barony but this. Case of Henry de Clifford, E. Cumberland. There were several issues,—Henry, who was son of Francis, was summoned in 1 Jac. 21 (*sic.*). Where there is one as well as two or three. Nevill's case cited. I submit that as this case has gone [it is] with the Earl of Suffolk, and I question not but the King will leave it there. *The Solicitor-General* (in reply): It cannot be a question but an honour will descend to a daughter. This is not like lands descending, it being incorporeal. The question is, whether it is not in the King's power to dispose of it. I cannot say what it is in the power or the King to do. E. Oxford's case, 1625. We hope your Lordships will report that the Barony is so descended and the King may dispose of it. *Mr. Holles* (in reply) recites Acton's case in Coke's Reports. In Bracton's case it is a Barony by tenure. Counsel withdrew. *Ordered* to report that the case, being one of great intricacy, should be heard at the Bar. (Priv Book: L. J., XV. 25.)—On 28 Jan. Counsel were accordingly called in at the Bar. *The Solicitor-General* (for Petitioner): Thomas Howard, second son of Thomas, Lord Howard, was summoned to Parliament by the title of Lord Howard of Walden. Cites several cases. *Mr. Finch* (for Lady Essex Griffin): An heir female is capable to inherit a Barony. The King may declare to which of the sisters it should go. The question is between Lady Essex Griffin and Mrs. Felton. The descendants from the elder sisters have had it all along. Cites many cases, *e.g.*, L. Clifford and L. Audley. It is the best right to have the King's favour. There is a third claim to defeat both the daughters. *Sir Thos. Powys* (for Lady Essex Griffin): Cites cases of L. Grey de Ruthyn* and L. Thanet's claim to the Barony of Clifford.† We hope the E. Suffolk is out of the case. We think it reasonable for his Majesty to suspend this, until there is issue male capable to sit in Parliament. Selden's Titles of Honour, fol. 644, 645. *Mr. Wallop* (for E. Suffolk): These gentlemen would limit this to the heirs female. In E. Suffolk I conceive I am counsel for all the Peers of England in his circumstances, for if the females set up, then all the Baronies in fee will be torn in pieces. If the King's power be limited to the females only, then the Peers are out of all remedy. The Lords in their certificates to the King in E. Oxford's case say they were wholly in the King's power to dispose of. The King is at liberty to grant it to whom he pleases (Car. I., 1625, E. Oxford),‡ and by this we are fairly let in. I conceive we are all here beggars and must leave the King to choose. *Mr. Ward* (for E. Suffolk): We say this is in the King's disposition, as in the case of E. Oxford, upon the Baronies of Bulbeck, Baldermere, &c., Wednesday, 22 March 1625, in which case it was decided that the Baronies were at the King's disposal. Now these Baronies are in E. Oxford. *The Solicitor-General* heard in reply. Mr. Finch: 2 Q. L. Dacre's case the younger brother could not have the honour, their being three coheirs. *Sir Thomas St.*

* L. J., IV. 149.
† L. J., XIV. 568, 574–5, 683; Collins, 306; Cruise, 195.
‡ L. J., III. 537; W. Jones, 96; Collins, 173.

George: I do not find at any time that the heirs female have been summoned to Parliament without the King's pleasure. The sons of the youngest daughters (*sic*). I have not found above one precedent where it has been parted from the earldom. Cites several precedents 1 Rich., Fitzalan, E. Arundel, four daughters and coheirs; Henry, E. Rutland; E. Derby's case declared the three coheirs; L. Cumberland's case. They withdraw. *Ordered* that the Speaker report on 1 Feb. (MS. Min. L. J. XV. 53). On 1 Feb., the Speaker having reported, it was moved to refer the business to the Committee for Privileges to inspect and state the precedents, vizt. L. Grey de Ruthyn, L. Ross, E. Thanet (L. Clifford), E. Oxford. *Note*: E. Derby comes himself from the heirs general and claims not the Barony. *Ordered* accordingly; the Committee to report to a full House. (MS. Min., L.J., XV. 57.) In Committee for Privileges on 19 Feb., E. Stamford in the chair, inquiry being made at the door whether any attend, the Yeoman Usher acquaints the Committee that none attend save Lady Essex Griffin's chaplain, from whom he brings in some papers, but they are not received. *Ordered* that the parties concerned bring to the clerk such precedents as they have in relation to the matter in question, the said precedents to be attested.* The matter adjourned to 22 Feb. (Priv. Book). Nothing further recorded; the Prorogation took place on the 24th. The matter remained unsettled till 1784, when the abeyance was terminated in favour of the nephew of Mrs. Felton's grandchild.]

Annexed:—

(*a*.) 22 Feb. 1691–2. Paper entitled "Baronies by writ allowed to the heir general," as follows: "*Barony of Dacres allowed to the heir general by the King.* William, Lord Dacres was first summoned to Parliament by writ 20 Edw. I., from whom descended Thomas, Lord Dacre, who had issue two sons, Thomas and Humphrey. Thomas, the eldest son, had issue Joan, his daughter, and heir, married to Sir Richard Fenys, [Fienes] knight, who (notwithstanding there was a collateral heir male) was declared Lord Dacres with all preeminences thereto belonging by Patent 37 Hen. VI. and sat in the ancient place of the Lord Dacres accordingly:—*Barony of Dacres again allowed to the heir general by the King and Lords Commissioners for the office of Earl Marshal.* The Barony of Dacres aforesaid, being a barony by writ of 28 Edw. I. and having been adjudged to Fienes who married the heir general temp. Henry VI. continued in the family of Fienes, till 35 Eliz., when by the death of Gregory Fienes, Lord Dacres, it descended to Margaret, his sister and heir, married to Sampson Lennard, Esq., who making claim to the honour, it was declared and adjudged by the Lords Commissioners for exercising the office of Earl Marshal of England, 2 Jac. I., with the privity and assent of the King, that she, the said Margaret, ought to have and enjoy the name, state, degree, style, honour, place, and precedency of the Barons Dacre, to have and to hold to her and the issue of her body, in as full and ample manner, as any of her ancestors did enjoy the same; as also that her children might and should take and enjoy their place and precedence respectively, as the children of her ancestors Barons Dacre formerly had and enjoyed, which title of Lord Dacres was afterwards confirmed to Henry, her son and heir, and is now enjoyed by his descendant the present Earl of

* See Annexes below.

House of Lords MSS.

1691.

Sussex.—*Barony of Dacres of Gillesland refused to be allowed to the heir male collateral by the Commissioners for the office of Earl Marshal, so long as there were coheirs in the right line.* Humphrey Dacres, heir male to the ancient Barons Dacre, some years after the said Barony had been declared to Fienes, who married the heir general, obtained to be summoned as Lord Dacres of Gillesland, anno 22 Edw. IV., by reason he was possessed of the lands and capital seat of the said Barony. From whom descended William, Lord Dacres, who had two sons, Thomas and Leonard. Thomas had issue George, Lord Dacres, who died without issue, 11 Eliz. leaving three sisters and coheirs. Leonard Dacre, their uncle, claimed the Barony; but it was resolved that a Baron by writ, having issue two sons, the eldest having issue three daughters, the Barony shall not descend to the younger son, so long as there are daughters which are heirs general. This resolution is found in Judge Hales' Manuscript in Lincoln's Inn, title "Nobility," in these words: "Baron p̄. B̄r. ad issue deux fils. L'eigné ad issu 3 filles. Le Baronie ne descendr. al puisne filz cy long come sont filles, qui sont Heir "genll. 11 Eliz. Lord Dacres case; resolue p̄. Sp̄.ll Comm^rs. T. 137." This Book is often cited by the lawyers in other cases.—*Barony of Willoughby of Eresby allowed to the heir general by the King.* Robert de Willoughby, (son and heir of William Willoughby, and Alice, his wife, eldest daughter and coheir to John, Lord Bec of Eresby, a Baron by writ,) was summoned to Parliament by writ 7 Edw. II. From whom descended Christopher, Lord Willoughby of Eresby, who had issue two sons, William and Christopher. William had issue Catharine his daughter and heir, married to Richard Bertie, Esq., whose son Peregrine, after the death of his mother was summoned to Parliament 22 Eliz. as Lord Willoughby of Eresby, and was seated according to the seniority of that Barony. Which Barony of Willoughby of Eresby is still in being in that family of Bertie, and Robert, Lord Willoughby, son and heir apparent to the Earl of Lindsey, sits now in the House by that title and in the ancient place. Christopher Willoughby, the second son, had issue William, who was the heir male of the family. But by reason the Barony was descended to the heir general, he was fain to accept of a new creation, by the title of Lord Willoughby of Parham, to him and his heirs male, 1 Edw. VI.—*Barony of Norris allowed to the heir general by the King.* Sir Henry Norris, knight, was summoned to Parliament by writ 14 Eliz. from whom descended Francis, Lord Norris, who was created Earl of Berkshire 18 Jac. I.; which Francis had issue the Lady Elizabeth his sole daughter and heir, married to Edward Wray, Esq.; and the said Elizabeth had likewise one daughter and heir, named Bridget, who became the second wife of Mountague Bertie, Earl of Lindsey, by whom she had issue James Bertie, Esq., her son and heir, who was declared Lord Norris by King Charles II. in 1669, and sat in Parliament accordingly in the place of the first Lord Norris his ancestor, and is now Earl of Abingdon and Lord Norris.—*Barony of Clifton allowed to the heir general in Parliament,* 1674. Sir Gervas Clifton, knight, was summoned to Parliament by the title of Lord Clifton of Leighton Bromswold, by writ, 7 Jac. I., and had issue Catharine his sole daughter and heir, who became the wife of

Esme Stuart, Duke of Lenox, by whom she had issue divers sons, of whom there is no issue remaining, excepting Catharine, the daughter of George, Lord Aubignie, the fourth son, which Catharine making her claim to the title and dignity of the Baroness Clifton, as sole heir to Catharine her grandmother, had that her claim allowed in the Parliament held at Westminster in 1674.—*The title of Viscount Hereford allowed to the heir male 1 W. & M., but the Barony of Lord Ferrers of Chartley allowed to the heir general.* John de Ferrers, of Chartley, was summoned to Parliament by writ 27 Edw. I., from whom descended Sir William Ferrers, knight, son and heir to Edmund, Lord Ferrers of Chartley, which Sir William had issue Anne, his daughter and sole heir, married to Walter Devereux, Esq., who was thereupon summoned to Parliament as Lord Ferrers of Chartley, 1 Edw. IV., from which Walter Devereux, Lord Ferrers, descended Sir Walter Devereux, who in 4 Edw. VI. was created Viscount Hereford, to him and his heirs male; whose heir male was afterwards created Earl of Essex with the like limitation to the heirs male; which honours continued in the male line till 1646, when Robert Devereux, the last Earl of Essex, died without issue, leaving his two sisters his heirs; whereupon the title of Viscount Hereford, by virtue of the entail upon the heirs male, descended to Sir Walter Devereux, Knight and Baronet, and is now enjoyed by Edward Devereux, Viscount Hereford, his grandson and heir, whose title as Viscount Hereford was allowed in Parliament in 1689. But the Barony of Ferrers of Chartley was revived in the issue of one of his sisters and coheirs of the last Earl of Essex above mentioned, by King Charles II. in 1677, and is now enjoyed by Sir Robert Shirley, Baronet, Lord Ferrers.—*Barony of Roos declared to the heir general by the King 14 Jac. I. upon the judgment of the Lords Commissioners for the office of Earl Marshal.* William de Roos, summoned to Parliament by writ 22 Edw. I., from whom descended Edmund, Lord Roos, who died without issue 24 Hen. VII., leaving three sisters his heirs, whereof Eleanor, the eldest, was married to Sir Robert Manners, knight, from whom descended Sir Thomas Manners, who was summoned to Parliament by the title of Lord Roos, 7 Hen. VIII., and was some years after created Earl of Rutland to him and his heirs male. Edward Manners, Earl of Rutland, and Lord Roos, grandson and heir of the said Thomas, the first Earl, died in 1587, 29 Eliz., leaving issue the Lady Elizabeth, his sole daughter and heir, married to William Cecil, Earl of Exeter, whose son, William Cecil, Esq., bearing the title of Lord Roos, 13 Jac. I., the Earl of Rutland, the heir male, disputed it before the Lords Commissioners for the office of Earl Marshal, yet, however, they adjudged that title to Cecil against the Earl of Rutland, and he had the King's Declaration thereupon, dated 22 July, 14 Jac. I.—*Barony of Grey of Ruthyn, adjudged in Parliament to the heir general, against the Earl of Kent the heir male*, 1640. Reginald, Lord Grey of Ruthyn, summoned to Parliament, by writ 23 Edw. I., from whom descended Edmund, Lord Grey of Ruthyn, who was created Earl of Kent 5 Edw. IV. Henry Grey, Earl of Kent and Lord Grey of Ruthyn, the lineal heir male to the said Earl Edmund, died without issue in 1639, leaving Susan his sister, wife of Sir

HOUSE OF LORDS MSS.

1691.

Michael Longvile, knight, his sole heir; whereupon the Earldom of Kent descending to the heir male by virtue of the entail, the Barony of Grey of Ruthyn was claimed by Charles Longvile, Esq., son and heir to the afore-mentioned Susan, as heir general; and, after long dispute in Parliament, in 1640 the said Charles Longvile had it adjudged to him against the Earl of Kent, the heir male, and was thereupon summoned to Parliament by that title by writ dated 6 Feb. 16 Car. I.—*Barony of Fitzwalter heard in Parliament and adjudged to the heir general by the King* 1669. Robert, Lord Fitzwalter summoned to Parliament by writ 23 Edw. I., from whom descended Walter, Lord Fitzwalter, who died 11 Hen. VI., leaving issue, Elizabeth, his daughter and heir, married to Sir John Ratcliff, knight, by whom she had issue Sir John Ratcliff, knight, who was summoned to Parliament by the title of Lord Fitzwalter, 1 Hen. VII., from whom descended Henry Ratcliff, Earl of Sussex and Lord Fitzwalter, who had issue the Lady Frances, married to Sir Thomas Mildmay, knight, by whom she had issue Sir Henry Mildmay, knight, who claimed the Barony of Fitzwalter in Parliament in 1640. But by reason of the troubles there was nothing done therein, till after the Restoration of King Charles II. That Henry Mildmay, Esq., grandson and heir of the said Sir Henry, petitioned the King for the said Barony; which claim being continued by Benjamin Mildmay, his brother and heir, it was at last solemnly adjudged by the King in Council in 1669, whereupon he was summoned to Parliament accordingly and had the ancient place of the Lord Fitzwalter.—These cases are faithfully extracted and reported by me, Gregory King, Lancaster Herald, Register of the College of Arms, 22 Feb. 1691-2."

(*b*.) 22 Feb. 1691-2. Paper entitled "Baronies by Writ descending to Coheirs, revived in the issue of the eldest Coheir," as follows: 1. *Nicholas de Audley* was summoned to Parliament 25 Edw. I., from whom descended Nicholas, Lord Audley, who died without issue 15 Ric. II., leaving his two sisters his heirs, whereof Joan the eldest was married to Thomas Touchet, Esq. John Touchet, his grandson, bore the title of Lord Audley and died 10 Hen. IV., leaving issue James Touchet, his son and heir, who was summoned to Parliament by the title of Lord Audley by writ 8 Hen. V., and had the place of the ancient Lord Audley; which honour has continued in that family ever since, and is now enjoyed by James, Lord Audley and Earl of Castlehaven in Ireland.—2. *John, Lord Maltravers* was first summoned to Parliament by writ of 1 Edw. III., from whom descended John Maltravers, who died in the lifetime of his father, leaving issue two daughters and coheirs Eleanor and Joan, whereof Eleanor the eldest became the wife of John, second son of Richard Fitz-Alan, Earl of Arundel, who was thereupon summoned to Parliament 1 Rich. II. by the title of Lord Maltravers. 3. *Sir Andrew Windsor*, Knt., was first summoned to Parliament by writ 21 Hen. VIII., from whom descended Thomas, Lord Windsor, who died without issue in 1642, leaving two sisters and coheirs, whereof Elizabeth the elder married Dixey Hickman, Esq., and by her had issue Thomas Windsor Hickman, Esq., who was restored to the ancient barony of Windsor by Patent 12 Car. II., and sate in the same place accordingly. He was afterwards created Earl of Plymouth. 4. *John Charlton de Powis* was summoned to Parliament by writ of 7 Edw. II., from whom descended Edward Charlton, Lord Powis, who died 9 Hen. V., leaving issue two daughters and coheirs, whereof Joan the eldest was married to Sir John Grey, Knt., whose posterity was afterwards summoned to Parliament by the title of Lord Powis in 22 Edw. IV. 5. Almarick de St. Amand, Lord St. Amand, first summoned to Parliament by writ 28 Edw. I., from whom descended Almarick, Lord St. Amand, who died 4 Hen. IV., leaving issue two daughters and coheirs, whereof Eleanor the eldest married Gerard Braybroke, Esq., and by her had issue Gerard Braybroke, son and heir, who died 10 Hen. V., leaving three daughters, his heirs, of which Elizabeth the eldest, marrying Sir William Beauchamp, Knt., he was summoned to Parliament by the title of Lord St. Amand, 27 Hen. VI. 6. *Foulk Fitzwarin, Lord Fitzwarin* was summoned to Parliament 22 Edw. I., from whom descended Foulk, Lord Fitzwarin, who died without issue 9 Hen. V., leaving Elizabeth, his sister, married to Sir Richard Hankford, Knt., his sole heir, by whom she had issue three daughters and coheirs, whereof Thomasine, the eldest, marrying to William Bourchier, third son to William, Earl of Ewe, the said William Bourchier was summoned to Parliament as Lord Fitzwarin 27 Hen. VI., and so was his posterity after him. 7. *William de Valence, Earl of Pembroke*, married Joan, one of the cousins and coheirs to Walter Marechal, Earl of Pembroke, by whom he had issue Aymer de Valence, Earl of Pembroke, who died without issue, and three daughters, coheirs to their brother, of which Isabel, the second (Joan the eldest being dead without issue) was married to John, Lord Hastings of Bergavenny; whereupon Laurence de Hastings, grandson and heir of the said Isabel, by reason of his descent from her, was declared Earl of Pembroke by the King, 13 Edw. III.—These are some of the many Precedents of this nature, faithfully extracted from the Records of the College of Arms by Gregory King, Lancaster Herald. Register of the College of Arms. 22 Feb. 1691–2. *Endorsed* "Precedents where the husband or issue of the eldest daughter and coheir has enjoyed a Barony by Writ. Lady Essex Griffin."

(*c*.) Paper stating as follows: "We do not find any Precedents where the daughters and coheirs of a Barony of writ have been at any time settled in their father's Barony; but upon Petition to the King, the son and heir of a coheir has been summoned to Parliament by the titles of his grandfather's Barony, without relation to the son of the eldest or youngest daughter, whereof there are many precedents. We also find divers Precedents that a Barony by Writ, falling into an Earldom, has very seldom been settled in an heir general or severed from such Earldom, as long as the Earldom has continued in an Earl descended from the said Barony. The only Precedent we have observed of a Barony by writ settled in the son of a daughter and heir, when the Earldom has continued in an heir male, descended from the said Barony, is that of the Lady Susan, daughter of Charles Grey, Earl of Kent, whereof the pedigree runs thus viz.:—

HOUSE OF LORDS MSS.

1691.

Charles Grey, Earl of Kent,
Lord Grey of Ruthyn, died 1623.

- Henry Grey, Earl of Kent, who died without issue 1639.
- Susan, sister and heir, was married to Sir Michael Longville, Knt.
  - Charles Longville, Esq.

Upon the death of the said Henry, Earl of Kent, Anthony Grey, son of George Grey, son of Anthony Grey, third son of George Grey, Earl of Kent, Lord Grey of Ruthyn, Charles Longville, Esq., son of Sir Michael Longville as aforesaid, by the Lady Susan Grey, claimed the Barony of Grey of Ruthyn, by Petition to King Charles I., which being by the said King referred to the Lords in Parliament, upon their report, the said King summoned to Parliament the said Charles Longville by the title of Carolus Longville de Grey, Chevalier, which is the first Precedent we have observed of this kind, and he was seated in Parliament in the ancient place of Lord Grey of Ruthyn. By all the other Precedents we have observed it appears to have been other ways, and were as follows :—

Richard Fitz-Alan,
E. of Arundel, L. Fitz-Alan,
Clun and Oswaldestry.

- 1st. Thomas E. Arundel, d. without issue 3 Hen. V.
- 2nd. Richard, 3rd William, both died young.
- 1. Elizabeth, eldest daughter, m. Thos. Mowbray, D. Nottingham.
- 2. Jane, m. W. Beauchamp L. Abergavenny.
- 3. Margaret, m. Sir Rowland Lenthall, Knt.
- 4. Alice, m. John Charlton, L. Powis.

yet, notwithstanding the said Thomas, E. Arundel left his four sisters his coheirs, John Fitz-Alan, son of John Fitz-Alan, Lord Maltravers, grandson of John, Lord Maltravers, next heir male to Thomas, E. Arundel, had and enjoyed the Baronies.

Ferdinand Stanley,
E. Derby, L. Stanley, Strange
of Knocking and of the Isle of
Man, d. 1594.

- Anne, eldest daughter, m. Grey Bruges, L. Chandois.
- Francis, m. Sir John Egerton, after E. Bridgewater.
- Elizabeth, m. Henry, E. Huntingdon.

The Baronies, notwithstanding, were used and enjoyed by William, Earl of Derby, brother and heir male to the said Ferdinand, and being chosen Knight of the Garter (at his installation, according to custom,) the said William's titles and stile were proclaimed in the presence of Queen Elizabeth in 1601, which were William Stanley, Earl of Derby, Lord Stanley, Strange, of Knocking and of the Isle of Man, and were also engraven upon his plate under his arms at the back of his stall, and continue still to be used by the present Earl of Derby, without the least dispute, which we do esteem a good precedent.

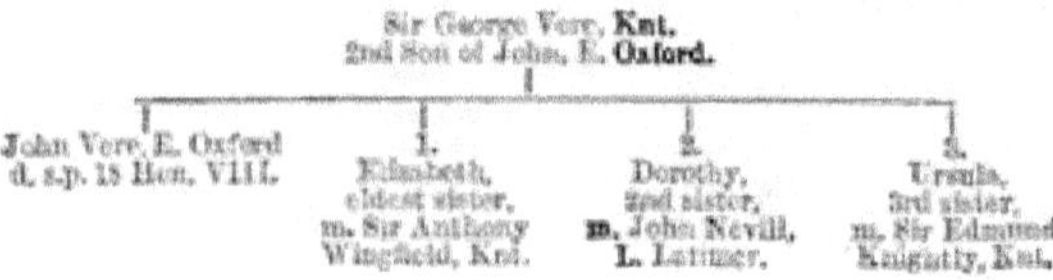

Sir George Vere, Knt.
2nd Son of John, E. Oxford.

- John Vere, E. Oxford, d. s.p. 18 Hen. VIII.
- 1. Elizabeth, eldest sister, m. Sir Anthony Wingfield, Knt.
- 2. Dorothy, 2nd sister, m. John Nevill, L. Latimer.
- 3. Ursula, 3rd sister, m. Sir Edmund Knightly, Knt.

The Baronies, notwithstanding, accompanied the Earldom, and Aubrey de Vere, the present Earl of Oxford, when installed Knight of the Garter, with the title of Earl of Oxford, were also proclaimed his baronies of Bolebec, Sanford and Badelesmer in the presence of the King, and are also engraven upon his plate at the back of his stall at Windsor, which we do esteem also a precedent.

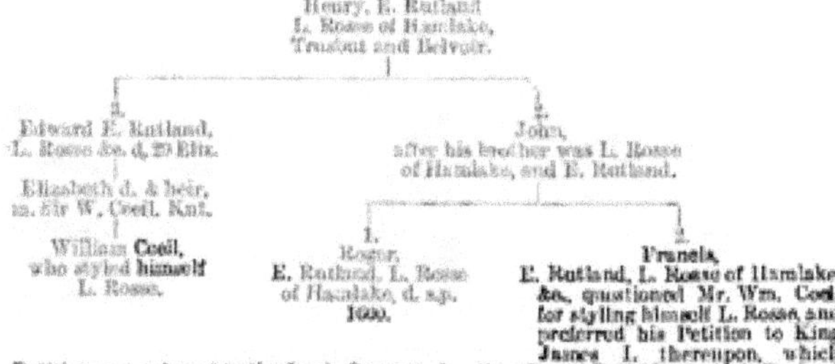

Petition was referred to the Lords Commrs. for the office of Earl Marshal of England to examine and certify to him the state of the case. Their Lordships thereupon ordered the persons interested to attend them with their Counsel, and upon a full hearing of the cause, debated at large by the Counsel of both parties, and the King of Arms, being also called and commanded to show such precedents as might conduce to this matter, after serious consideration thereof, did certify to the King, who thereupon declared his pleasure to be that the Earl of Rutland should retain and continue the said Baronies with the Earldom, as his predecessors had formerly done; and whereas Mr. William Cecil had for many years been styled Lord Rosse and in public employments abroad, the King did also declare his pleasure to be, that the said Mr. William Cecil should be styled and called Lord Rosse, without using the addition of Hamlake or anything else, and this case was determined thus in 1616, and being in the same year elected and installed Knight of the Garter, his style was proclaimed in the King's presence, and engraven also upon his plate, set up at the back of his stall at Windsor, with the Baronies of Rosse of Hamlake, Trushut and Belvoir.

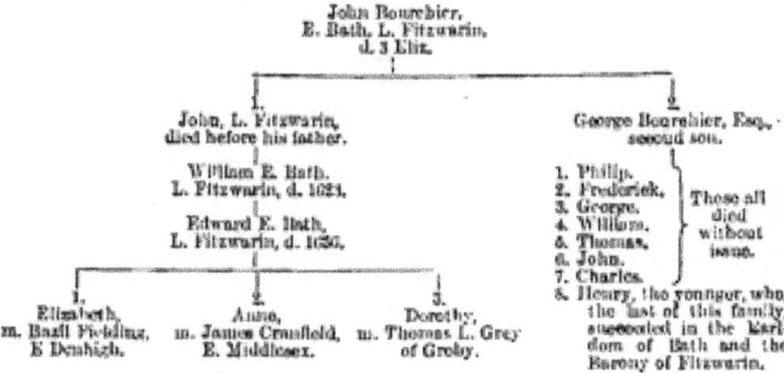

These Pedigrees within mentioned are faithfully transcribed and examined by the originals this 22 Feb. 1691–2 by Peers Mauduit, Windsor. *Endorsed*, E. Suffolk's Paper.

503. Dec. 20. Farrer's Estate Bill.—Draft of an Act for enabling John Farrer, Esq., to pay his debts and raise a portion for his daughter. The Suppliant, John, eldest son of William Farrer, Esq., of Ewood, co. York, deceased, married Elizabeth, only child of James Creswick, of Beale in the same county, with consent of their parents but without any agreement for settlement or portion. His father, by will dated 21 July 1684, left the Manors of Midgley, Sadleworth, and Wortley *alias* Wirkley, in the parish of Leeds, to Suppliant and his sons successively in tail male, and for want of such issue to his three brothers,

House of Lords MSS.

1691.

James, Henry, and Richard successively and their sons in tail male, leaving the reversion in fee to descend to Suppliant, who has power to make leases of any of the lands in Sadleworth for 21 years from the date when existing leases determine, reserving the ancient rents to the person entitled by the will to the freehold. Suppliant, having issue two children, viz. James and Lydia, aged 12 and 14, contracted debts of 1,600*l.* in maintaining his family unassisted, and giving his children a very liberal education; but his father gave him no power to raise money to pay his debts or raise a portion for his daughter, trusting that James Creswick's estate would be available for that purpose after his death, which expectation has become more uncertain, since Suppliant's wife is dead, and her father does not think fit at present to make any settlement. Suppliant is willing, if he can charge his lands to pay his debts and raise the portion, to disburse yearly, as an equivalent, a reasonable sum to educate his son till the age of 21, and maintain him during Suppliant's life. The Bill therefore vests his lands in Sir Thos. Armitage, Bart., of Kirklees, Sir William Lowther, Knt., of Swillington, and Thos. Horton, Esq., of Barkisland, all in co. York, as trustees to raise by mortgage, sale or lease, 1,600*l.* for payment of Suppliant's debts, (*blank*) for a portion for his daughter at the age of 21 or at marriage, and (*blank*) for her maintenance meanwhile, from the date of Suppliant's death; the reversion and equity of redemption of such mortgage, and the reversion expectant on any such lease to belong to the person to whom the lands are limited by the will. The Bill concludes with the usual saving clause. [Read 1a this day; *Question* for rejecting the Bill, negatived. *Ordered* that it shall not be read again until after 12 o'clock. (MS. Min. L. J., XV. 6.) No further proceedings.]

504. Dec. 29. Conyngham *v.* Sir R. Creighton, *alias* Murray.—Petition and Appeal of Henry Conyngham, Esq., son and heir of Sir Albert Conyngham, Knt., lately deceased, on the behalf of himself and others. James Murray, late E. Annandale, in 1653 conveyed his estate in Ireland, co. Donegal, to Sir Robert Maxwell and Robert Browne, in case of failure of his own issue, to the use of Richard Murray, since deceased, and heirs, without any powers of revocation, and died in 1658 without issue. After his death, Sir Robert Creighton, who then took the name of Murray, brought a Bill in Chancery in Ireland to have the conveyance set aside as fraudulent, and have possession under a supposed will of the Earl of 8 Dec. 1658, the day of his death. The Court, on 9 Feb. 1660, directed a trial at law on the issue whether the Earl had conveyed his estate by the deeds in question or not, and the jury on 18 May 1664 found for the deeds, which verdict was confirmed on a new trial by another jury on 5 May 1665, and on 20 Nov. 1665 the Court dismissed the Bill. Richard Murray afterwards obtained possession of the estate on an ejectment in the Court of Exchequer, and in 1667 Sir Albert Conyngham bought from him the lands of Baylagh and other parts of the estate for 4,500*l.*, other parts being sold to other purchasers in 1669. Sir Robert Creighton acquiesced till 1678, by which time Sir Albert had laid out to the value of the estate in improvements, and the witnesses to the deeds were dead, when he began a suit against Richard Murray in Scotland, where the deeds had been perfected, suggesting that they were forged, and by indirect means obtained a Decree cancelling them on the ground of informality. Thereupon a new Bill was brought in Ireland, in the name of Sir Robert Creighton in 1683 against Richard Murray, Sir Albert and the other purchasers, setting forth the Decree in Scotland and praying decree for the will, and

that the deeds might be declared forgeries. The L. Chancellor Boyle in 1685, after several days' hearing, would make no decree, but on 18 June, 1686, the Court admitted the Scotch decree as evidence of forgery, and decreed accordingly, without examining any new witnesses, and left the validity of the will to be tried on an action to recover possession. A Bill of Review being brought, the L. Chancellor Fitton on 7 Nov. 1687 confirmed the said decree, and Sir Robert Creighton afterwards brought actions against Sir Albert and others for possession. Appeals from the two decrees of 1686 and 1687, because (1), the decree and proceedings in Scotland ought not to have been admitted as evidence, (2) The purchasers bought for valuable consideration and were no parties to the decree in Scotland; (3) The title of the deeds and will was purely matter at law, and the two verdicts ought in equity to have been supported; (4) The first decree of 22 Nov. 1665, still standing unreversed, ought not to have been overruled; (5) No proof was ever given that the deeds were forged. Prays that the two decrees may be reversed, the Respondent ordered to answer, and proceedings stayed. *Signed* by Appellant; *Countersigned* by Geo. Treby and John Somers. L.J., XV. 5. [The House, on receiving the Appeal this day, ordered all proceedings in Ireland for altering Petitioner's possession to be stayed. (*Ib.*) On 13 Feb. 1691–2, Counsel were heard on Respondent's Petition of the 11th. (Annex. (a.) below.) *Sir Thomas Powys* (for Petitioner): We are only upon this point, as to the possession. Until the times of trouble, we had possession. We desire our possession may remain as it was. *The Solicitor-General* (for Petitioner) is heard. *Sir Thomas Powys* moved for persons to be sworn, to prove they were in possession. *Sir James Coldwall* (called in and sworn): I have known the estate several years. I suppose the estate was in Sir Albert Conyngham and his tenants. Counsel withdraw. *Ordered* that the order of 29 December last shall stand. (MS. Min., L. J., XV. 75.) The Cause was first heard on 6 Dec. 1692. Counsel being called in, *Counsel* for Appellant consented that the possession should go with the Order of the House. *The Attorney General* (for Appellant) opens the case. By a deed, made in Scotland, he assures the settlement of his Irish estate. In 1658 E. Annandale died in London. It is pretended he made his Will. This Will was made by a little scrivener in Westminster; two apothecaries' boys were witnesses; and under this Will they claim. In December 1658 he died, and then presently they got into possession of some of the estate. Sir Robert Creighton brought a Bill in Ireland to have the deeds set aside. There were two trials, one at the Common Pleas and another at the King's Bench, and both found the deeds were the acts of E. Annandale, and then, upon those verdicts, they had a decree in Ireland. In 1672, when the witnesses were dead, then a suit was set afoot in Scotland. *Sir William Thompson* (for Appellant) is heard, and states the case briefly, and reserves himself for a reply. They read several orders in Ireland. *The Solicitor General* (for Respondent): All along our will was found for us, when the deeds were found for them. *Sir Thomas Powys* (for Respondent) is heard. *Sir William Thompson* (for Appellant) is heard in reply. They offer to read the decree in Scotland for Respondent. Counsel withdrew. *The Speaker* acquainted the House that the matter is as to deeds of lease and release. The Defendant [Respondent] says the deeds are false. There is a decree offered, found in Scotland, whereby the deeds are found false. The question is whether this Scotch decree shall be given in evidence to justify the decree in Ireland. A debate arose, whether this Scotch decree shall be read. House *moved* to ask the Judges what would be

HOUSE OF LORDS MSS.

1691.

done in their Courts. *Ordered* that Counsel and Judges attend on Monday next. (MS. Min., L. J., XV. 135.)—On 13 Dec. *Sir William Thompson* (for Appellant) is heard. The decree in Scotland is a prosecution in a Civil Court, to show that the deeds are forged, and that decree condemns them, and orders the deeds to be torn in pieces. The Court of Chancery in Ireland ought not to be read in Ireland nor here. It concerns a freehold, and ought not to be read. For lands and tenements, it cannot be tried there. *Sir William Williams* states the state of the Court in Scotland. *Sir Thomas Powys:* There is no other Court it can be tried in. States the case how the law stands in Scotland. He may be shot by any persons after this judgment. *Sir William Williams* says by the Information that they are damnified, Counsel withdraw. *Moved* to ask the Judges whether judgments in Scotland may be read in England, as used in evidence here? *Holt, C. J.:* If a sentence be given in Scotland for lands in Ireland, it may be read in Ireland or England, as evidence here. A lease and release; it is surmised these deeds are forged. The cause being heard in the Civil Court, the deeds condemned in Scotland; but he fled. The question is whether this sentence in the Civil Court in Scotland is to be read in Ireland or England. I am of opinion it ought not to be read in England or Ireland. It may be read, if it had been a matter within their jurisdiction. The Case [was] about 12 years since. If this sentence be allowed to be good evidence, it must be conclusive evidence, and takes away his inheritance. The same you may say of France as Scotland. *L. C. Justice of the Common Pleas*, *L. C. Baron Atkyns*, *Powell, B.*, *Nevill, B.*, *Gregory, B.*, *Lechmere, B.*,* *Rokeby, J.*, *Turton, B.*, and *Eyres, J.*,—all of the same opinion. *Holt, C. J.:* As to being under one King, it makes no difference from any other kingdom. If a woman commits adultery in Scotland, the divorce annuls the marriage. The question is, whether she is his wife here. *L. C. Justice:* But that will not affect this case; because they have jurisdiction in it. After debate, the question was put to the Judges, Whether a divorce in Scotland shall bind in England? *Holt, C. J.:* I am not ready. *Treby, C. J.:* I am not ready. *Atkyns, C. B.:* I desire to hear Counsel in the case. *Nevill, B.:* It is new; I desire time. *Rokeby, J.:* I desire time, until it comes before your Lordships. *Eyres, J.:* I think in England she is a femme covert. *Turton, B.:* I desire time. After debate, *Question* put: Whether the Scotch decree shall be given in evidence at the Bar in the cause before the House? Resolved in the *Negative*. Counsel called in again, and the Speaker told Counsel for Respondent that the Lords do not allow the decree to be given in evidence. *The Solicitor General:* Our decree in Ireland was chiefly built upon that decree in Scotland. *Sir Thomas Powys:* The decree in Ireland was upon that decree and other evidence. *Sir William Thompson:* We have no verdicts and [? nor] can they show any evidence at the trials. It is judged in Ireland we are in possession, and we pray the decree and possession. *Sir William Williams:* They decree that the deeds stand suppressed, and that they shall not be given in evidence. Will your Lordships say they are forged, and to be suppressed, and the decree must be affirmed or reversed? The deeds were made in 1653, the Will in 1658. *The Solicitor General* says he will not say there was proof enough for the Chancery to decree, without the Scotch decree. *Counsel* on both sides heard in reply. Counsel withdrew, and the Speaker reported. *Moved* to hear the Judges, whether

* Noted: Different after.

the reversal of this decree will hinder a trial, and a commission for witnesses? *Treby, C. J.:* Notwithstanding this Petition here, the party is at the same liberty, and may exhibit his Bill in Ireland for examining witnesses, and their Counsel will advise them, and you may reverse this decree without prejudice to the proceedings in Ireland for witnesses on trial. *Ordered*, that the decree shall be reversed, and that the Chancery in Ireland [may] shall* issue out a Commission to examine witnesses in Scotland as to the point of forgery. (MS. Min., L. J., XV. 146.)]

Annexed:—

(*a.*) 11 Feb. 1691-2. Petition of Respondent. Has received notice of the Appeal through a friend, while in Scotland. Whatever possession Appellant has of the estate in Ireland must be by force or illegal means. Prays for further time to answer, and for possession of the estate as on 25 Dec. 1688, according to the Act of 1 W. & M. for the Relief of their Majesties' Protestant Subjects in Ireland. L. J., XV. 71.

(*b.*) 11 Feb. 1691-2. Order of the House on preceding Petition. L. J., XV. 71.

(*c.*) 15 Nov. 1692. Petition of Appellant that Respondent may be ordered to answer by a certain day, and that a day may be appointed for hearing, Appellant being detained by the delay from attending their Majesties' service as a Lieut.-Col. in the Army. L. J., XV. 112.

(*d.*) 17 Nov. 1692. Petition of Respondent. Appellant, who leases some lands called Tawine Tallan at about 50*l.* a year, has, under colour of their Lordships' order of 29 Dec. 1691, gained possession, by force or fraud, of all the adjoining lands of Respondent. Prays to be restored to possession thereof. L. J., XV. 114.

(*e.*) 23 Nov. 1692. Petition of Appellant, in answer to preceding Petition. The lands in question belong to Appellant. Most of the tenants voluntarily returned tenants to Appellant's late father and Appellant before the Appeal was brought, there being neither fraud nor force employed, and the few who have not returned continue undisturbed. Prays for a speedy hearing, which Respondent is seeking to delay. *Endorsed* as read this day. (MS. Min. No entry in L. J.)

(*f.*) 24 Nov. 1692. Answer of Respondent. James, late Earl of Annandale, having a particular affection for Respondent, his near kinsman, to whom moreover he owed 5,000*l.* by Scotch bonds, besides loans of 2,200*l.* to other persons, for most of which Respondent stood bound with him, and desiring to provide for payment of his debts, duly made his Will, on 28 Dec. 1658, being then of sound and perfect memory, leaving to Respondent and heirs, according to his previously expressed intentions, all his real and personal estate in England and Ireland and his moveable estate in Scotland, Respondent taking the surname and arms of Murray and paying all his debts and legacies, and died soon afterwards in London. Respondent interred him in Scotland at the expense of at least 1,500*l.*, and duly performed the Will, and in June 1659 went to Ireland and took possession of the estate, which he held till 1661, when Richard Murray,

* This alteration of the judgement was made on 23 Dec., on petition of Respondent. MS. Min., L.J., XV. 164.

HOUSE OF LORDS MSS.

1691.

understanding that the debts were paid or secured, gave out that the estate had been settled on himself by deeds of lease and release, without any provision for such payment. Respondent, being advised that the deeds, if made at all, were not made for valuable consideration, and finding no counterparts thereof, but finding that the Earl had, since the date of the deeds, made two deeds of feoffment in 1665 to one Gregg to secure a jointure to his Countess, which had been witnessed by Appellant's father and one Andrew Lindsay, another of Richard Murray's accomplices, and that the Earl had also leased several parts of his estate since the date of the pretended deeds of lease, and release, and being assured on oath by the Earl of Dumfries that, on showing Richard Murray the Will, the latter had declared that he wished Sir Robert Murray much joy of the estate, and that those who got it might go into mourning for the Earl, and never pretended any deeds of settlement, concluded they were forged, and in August 1661 brought a Bill in Chancery in Ireland to discover them. Respondent appeared to Richard Murray's actions for ejectment in 1663, but could not attend, as Parliament, of which he was a member, was then sitting, but the proceedings went on in Chancery, and by direction of the Court, the issue not only as to the deed but as to the will, which was contested by Richard Murray, was tried at the King's Bench (not at the Common Pleas) Bar on 18 May 1664 (not 1684), but not by a jury settled, as alleged, by consent of Respondent. The Court, being dissatisfied with the verdict, awarded a second trial as to the deeds, when a verdict again passed against Respondent, who was unable to compel witnesses to attend from Scotland to disprove the deeds; and the Court in Nov. 1665 dismissed Respondent's Bill, leaving the reality of the deeds to be tried in a third action by a jury of the county where the lands in question lay. Richard Murray did not obtain judgment and possession upon an ejectment afterwards in Exchequer in the manner suggested, the judgment being merely on a demurrer, not on the general merits. As to the alleged sales of parts of the estate by Richard Murray, Respondent believes that little or nothing was paid him by the purchasers than what Appellant's father and the other confederates, who were to share the estate, if recovered, had expended in maintaining the suits. Respondent never acquiesced, as alleged, but after bringing an ejectment in Common Pleas, was advised that, as the pretended deeds had been executed in Scotland, the question of their forgery should be tried there. The Scotch Judges, before trying the reality of the deeds, apart from the title, desired the Irish Lord Chancellor and Court of King's Bench there, by Letters of Recommendation, to certify whether the matter was *res hactenus judicata* in Ireland, and on the latter reporting on 29 Nov. 1678 that it was not, they decreed, after a full hearing, that the deeds should be cancelled as forgeries. Respondent thereupon having brought an action of ejectment in the Common Pleas in Ireland, Richard Murray and Appellant's father, two of the Defendants, with a view to multiplying defences, brought two Bills in Chancery against Respondent and his Lessee, pretending that the matter was one for equity, and obtained injunctions to stop the suit at law. To save expense and have the benefit of certain depositions &c., Respondent then brought his Bill in Chancery against Sir

Richard Murray and the pretended purchasers, who pleaded the former decree but were overruled, but the Court never refused to allow the parties to enquire into the proceedings in Scotland. The hearing of the Cause before L. Chancellor Boyle and other Judges in 1685 was interrupted by the Lent Assizes, but on its coming on again for hearing before the new L. Chancellor Porter on 18 June, 1686, the Court declared they were fully satisfied the deeds were forged and set up to obviate the Will, and their decree was afterwards confirmed on a Bill of Review. Respondent afterwards obtained a verdict in the Common Pleas in 1686 for two parts of the lands he sued for, at which trial Appellant's father gave in evidence a lease of some lands in Tawine Tallan, made by the late Earl after the making of the pretended deeds, which lands he claimed, as purchaser from those interested under the lessees John, Bishop of Clogher, and his wife. This judgment was affirmed on appeal by the King's Bench, and in 1687 Respondent obtained possession, which he enjoyed till the late troubles in Ireland, when he was disturbed by Appellant, lately made a Lieut.-Col., and his dragoons. As to Appellant's reasons for reversing the decrees complained of: (1) the Scotch decree was properly admitted as evidence in Ireland, the forgery being a matter cognisable, as the Irish Judges reported, in Scotland, where it was contrived; (2) it was proved that Appellant's father and the other pretended purchasers were all along confederates with Richard Murray, and had a common interest in dividing the Earl's estate; (3) the case was one proper for equity, owing to the improper practices of Richard Murray and his confederates; (4) the former decree of dismission amounted to no more than sending Respondent to law for his remedy, and it enabled him to detect the forgery; (5) the verdicts in favour of the deeds were obtained chiefly on the evidence of John Hunand and Thomas McClelland, two notorious persons, who were witnesses to them. As to the allegation that Counsel at the hearing were confined only to speak to the Scotch decree, it is untrue, the parties never having been refused leave to speak on any point they pleased. Prays that the Appeal may be dismissed with costs. *Signed* Ro. Murray. *Endorsed* as brought in this day.

(*g*.) 23 Dec. 1692. Petition of Respondent. Prays that Appellant may not be allowed to continue in possession, and for explanation of their Lordships' judgment directing the Lord Chancellor to issue a Commission into Scotland, *i.e.* as to whether it should be ("may issue") or ("shall issue"). L. J., XV. 164.

505. Dec. 29. Pelham's Estate Act.—Amended draft of an Act for securing out of the manors, lands, tenements and hereditaments of Charles Pelham, of Brockelsby, in the county of Lincoln, Esq., the sum of 5,000*l*. with interest and 1,000*l*. unto Ann Pelham, eldest daughter of the said Charles. [Read 1ª this day; Royal Assent 24 Feb L. J., XV. 5, 93. 3 & 4 W. & M. c. 38, in Long Calendar. Only one amendment, and that a purely clerical, appears in Com. Book (4 Jan.) or on the draft. Comp. L. J., XV. 17.]

506. Dec. 29. Halsted's Act.—Amended draft of an Act to enable Henry Halsted to make a lease for the improvement of his Prebend of Eald Street in the Church of St. Paul's in London. [Read 1ª this day; Royal Assent Feb. 24. L. J., XV. 4, 93. 3 & 4 W. & M. c. 39 in Long Calendar.]

HOUSE OF LORDS MSS.

1691.

Annexed:—

(*a.*) 5 Jan. 1691-2. Minutes of Lords' proceedings in Committee this day.

507. Dec. 30. St. Anne's Church, Westminster, Bill.—Commons' Engrossment of an Act for the making farther Provision for finishing the Parish Church of St. Anne within the Liberties of Westminster, and other buildings directed to be erected and done pursuant to a former Act of Parliament. Whereas by one Act of Parliament made in the first year of the reign of the late King James the Second, intituled An Act to enable the inhabitants of the parish of St. Anne within the Liberty of Westminster to raise money to build a Church to be the Parish Church there, it is enacted that certain Commissioners, thereby constituted supervisors and Commissioners for the said Church, or any seven of them, should make, or cause to be made, an estimate in writing, under the hands of some sufficient person or persons qualified for the same, of the charge of building and finishing the said Church and steeple, and a house for the rector, and a vestry-room, and inclosing the churchyard, and erecting galleries, pulpit, desk, and pews in the said Church, and providing a clock and dial, and one or more bells, for the ordinary usage thereof; And for such sum or sums of money for the said charges as they should judge they should not be able to raise by sale of the pews, to be made and erected therein, they or any nine or more of them might and were thereby empowered equally to assess, or cause the said sum (not exceeding five thousand pounds) to be assessed and levied in four years, by sixteen quarterly payments (over and above the charge of collecting the same upon all and every the inhabitants, owners and occupiers of lands, houses, tenements, and hereditaments, or any personal estate within the said parish, according to an equal pound rate of the yearly value of the lands, tenements, and hereditaments so to be assessed or otherwise, as it might seem meet to the said Commissioners; And the said Commissioners were also thereby enjoined by themselves, or any seven or more of them, to make a yearly account under their hands until the said Church, steeple, house for a rector should be fully finished, to the Lord Bishop of London for the time being, whose allowance thereof under his Seal Episcopal should be to them and every of them a sufficient discharge; But forasmuch as the said sum of five thousand pounds, assessed and levied for the purposes aforesaid, was limited to be done in four years, which are expired, and all the said money expended and accounted for to the said Lord Bishop of London, according to the direction of the said Act, and the house for the rector, and many other of the buildings and things required by the said Act to be performed, could not be effected for want of money to finish the same; And the said Commissioners cannot be discharged of the trust by the said Act in them reposed, until the said Church and steeple, and a house for the rector, vestry room and premises in the said Act appointed to be built shall be finished. Be it enacted by, &c., that the Commissioners by the said recited Act appointed and their successors, or any seven or more of them respectively assembled in the vestry of the said Church, shall, and are hereby authorised equally to assess all such sum or sums as they shall think necessary and needful to build or purchase a convenient house for a rector, and finish and supply all other the buildings and premises in and about the said Church, steeple, vestry room, and other things appointed to be done by the said Act, so as the sum to be assessed and levied exceed not 1,700*l.* over and above the charge of collecting thereof, to be assessed and levied by sixteen quarterly and successive payments in four years upon all and every the inhabitants,

owners, and occupiers of houses, tenements, and hereditaments, which have been or shall be newly erected or finished within the said parish between the expiration of the time limited by the said Act and the end of the time hereby appointed for the assessing, levying, and collecting the same and on any personal estate rateable therein, according to an equal pound rate of the yearly value of the lands, houses, tenements, and hereditaments so to be assessed, or otherwise as it may seem meet to the said Commissioners or any seven or more of them.

Provided always, and be it enacted, that if any assessments made upon any of the inhabitants, owners and occupiers of lands, houses, tenements and hereditaments, or any personal estate in the said parish within the time limited by the said Act have not been collected and are in arrear, It shall and may be lawful for any collectors authorised thereunto, by warrant under the hands and seals of seven or more of the said Commissioners, to levy the same by distress and sale of the goods of such person so in arrear (neglecting or refusing to pay the same upon demand), deducting the sum assessed and reasonable charges of distraining thereof, and then restoring the overplus to the owner of the same.

Provided also that, if any of the said inhabitants, owners and occupiers, as aforesaid, have only paid part of the assessments by the said Act rateable upon them in proportion to other the inhabitants, owners, occupiers of lands, houses, tenements and hereditaments, or any personal estate in the said parish, for and towards the raising the sum in the said Act limited, it shall and may be lawful for the said Commissioners, or any seven or more of them, to re-assess the deficiencies not assessed, or the sums assessed and not paid on all such inhabitants and occupiers so deficient or in arrear to be collected, paid and levied, in such manner as deficiencies by the said Act might be reassessed, or added to any of the quarterly payments thereby appointed.

And be it further enacted, that if the said sum of 1,700*l.* cannot be raised of the persons and by the ways aforesaid within the time hereby limited, it shall and may be lawful for the said Commissioners, or any seven or more of them, within the space of two years after the said time, equally to assess or cause so much as shall not or cannot be so levied and collected within the said time, to be assessed and levied upon all and every the inhabitants, owners and occupiers of lands, houses, tenements and hereditaments of any personal estate within the said parish, according to an equal pound rate or otherwise, as it shall seem meet to the said Commissioners as aforesaid.

And it is hereby further enacted, that the said recited Act, as to the said powers, authorities, rules and directions and all other the clauses therein contained, touching landlords and tenants and other matters relating to the charges, taxes, assessments, disbursements and manner of accounting thereby directed and not otherwise herein limited and appointed, shall be and is hereby revived and in full force and virtue as if they had been herein particularly inserted.

Provided always and be it enacted, that the first quarterly payment of the assessment to be assessed and levied by virtue of this Act shall be made on the 25th day of March, which shall be in the year of Our Lord 1693.

And be it further enacted by the authority aforesaid, that if any action, plaint, suit or information shall be commenced or prosecuted against any person or persons for what he or they shall do in pursuance or execution of this Act, such person or persons so sued may plead the general issue of not guilty, and upon any issue joined give this Act and the special matter in evidence; And if the plaintiffs or prosecutors shall become nonsuit or suffer discontinuance, or if a verdict pass against him, her, or them, the defendants shall recover their treble costs, for which they shall have the like remedy as in any case where costs by the law are given to defendants. *Parchment Collection.* [Brought from the Commons this day; committed 5 Jan. (L. J., XV. 6, 17.) The Committee, E. Bridgewater in the chair, met on Jan. 8 to adjourn to the 13th, when they ordered E. Bolingbroke and all other persons concerned to be heard on the 15th. On Jan. 15 after agreeing to the title and postponing the preamble, they ordered all persons concerned, in the parish and elsewhere, to be heard on the 20th. On 22 Jan. they met, with the Bishop of London in the Chair, but only to adjourn to the 26th, on which day, Bp. of London in the Chair, they ordered to report that they found great difficulties in the Bill, and desired it might be heard at the Bar. (Com. Book of dates.) This Report does not appear to have been made, and the Bill dropped.]

508. Dec. 31. Sutton *v.* Sloughter and another.—In 1677 Paris Sloughter, a Blackwell Hall factor, and others, procured a Commission of Bankrupts against George Hagar, a dyer, and John Catlyn, his partner. After several proceedings thereon, Hagar's estate was assigned to Sloughter, who was no real creditor, except for a sum of 100*l.*, claimed not for moneys lent, but on pretence of breach of an agreement. The Commission for a long time lay dormant, and Hagar having desired Petitioner's assistance to complete an agreement he had come to with his other creditors, Petitioner lent him 800*l.*, and took discharges for Hagar's debts, not knowing that he had been made a bankrupt. Hagar afterwards set up some Paper Mills at Ensham and elsewhere, and drove a considerable trade, and being furnished with money by Petitioner, became indebted to him on his own security only, in upwards of 1,170*l.* Sloughter then procured from the Commissioners of Bankrupts an assignment of the Mills and stock at Ensham to himself, worth above 1,500*l.*, and other estate, goods, and debts of Hagar, amounting to 5,000*l.* at least, part of which he sold for 700*l.* to Edward Highmore, a pretended creditor of Hagar, though a creditor, if at all, since the Commission, like Petitioner. The Commission was afterwards renewed, and Petitioner admitted as a creditor and an assignment made to him of part of Hagar's estate, though he has received no benefit thereby, being obstructed by Sloughter and Highmore, who have got most of the estate into their hands. Petitioner having brought his Bill in Chancery for a discovery and satisfaction of his debt in proportion with other creditors, several Orders were made, and the Master, Sir Robert Legard, reported 1,170*l.* due to Petitioner; and on this report the Court, on 22 July, 2 W. & M., decreed referring it Mr. Meredith, another Master, to examine what was due from Hagar first to Sloughter and then to Highmore for principal, interest, and costs, including, in the case of Sloughter, the charges in contesting the bankruptcy, and that Petitioner should pay what was so found due, and that after such payments, Sloughter should assign to Petitioner all Hagar's estate which was assigned him by the Commissioners, and be paid his own debt out of the surplus of the bankrupt's estate, failing which payment by Petitioner, his Bill to be dismissed with costs. This decree is unjust, as it gives an unfair preference to Sloughter and Highmore, whereas Petitioner lent Hagar money to discharge his real debts incurred before the Commission was taken out, of which moreover Petitioner had no notice at the time of lending the money. Prays that the decree may be reversed, and proceedings stayed. *Signed* by Appellant; *Countersigned* by Thos. Powys and Edm. Bridges, whose signatures appear to be copied. L. J., XV. 9. [The Cause was heard on 8 Feb. 1691–2. *Sir Francis Winnington* (for Appellant) opened the case and stated the proceedings as to the Commission of Bankrupts. *Sir Ambrose Phillipps* (for Respondents) as to the assignee of the Commission. Sutton drew in these shares to be sold and the people to buy, and so secured himself. Mr. Sutton was solicitor in the cause, and he pretends to lose the 11,000*l.* debts, and he may have what bonds he will from Sloughter, they being all one. Hagar gave releases, and yet not one penny paid, and he was to account for the money, Mr. Sutton not actually paying anything. Sutton is a creditor since the bankruptcy. *The Solicitor-General:* We hope this decree is right, and Sutton has no pretence to it. My clients made out their debts before the Master. Sutton could make out none. He gets a Commission executed in Whitefriars. The Court says: they that have made themselves out to be creditors, shall come in. *Sir Francis Winnington:* Reads the order of Chancery, 22 July 1691. Report of the Master read, 17 May, 1690. Sutton pays the creditors, and comes in their places. *Sir Thomas Powys* (for Appellant) is heard. *The Solicitor-General* (for Respondents): His oath will go but little way to make him a creditor. He was a solicitor in the Cause. By the oath of Hagar he is a creditor. We admit that, for that is the roguery of the business. Recites items [of] creditors, and, on the other side, debt to Hagar. He was employed as a solicitor, and with the other creditors' moneys he paid these bonds. Counsel withdrew, and Speaker reported. *Ordered* that the Decree be affirmed, and the Appeal dismissed. (MS. Min., L. J., XV. 60.)]

Annexed:—

(*a.*) 14 Jan. 1691–2. Answer of Paris Sloughter and Edward Highmore. Sloughter employed Hagar and Catlyn, as Dyers, and in April 1677 they owed him by agreement 259*l.*, viz., 208*l.* for 16 tons of woad, 16*l.* by note for more woad, and 35*l.* for woad, out of which were to be deducted the sums of 65*l.* 5*s.* for cloths already dyed by Hagar, 8*l.* and 35*l.* received by Sloughter from Mr. Carey and Mr. Houblond, being due to Hagar but received after he became a bankrupt, and 31*l.* for work done by Hagar and partner after signing the agreement; leaving a balance of 118*l.* 18*s.* Hagar becoming bankrupt in Nov. 1677, a Commission was taken out against him, followed by three or four others against him and his partner, all of which Sloughter had to defend in Chancery, at the expense of above 700*l.*, and the supposed estate of Hagar was duly assigned to him in trust for himself and all the other creditors, but no estate being found to satisfy their debts, the Commission lay dormant till 1684. In 1682 it being pretended and given out that Hagar had invented an improved way of making paper, Appellant, by contrivance with him, was employed to persuade persons to buy shares, and after pressing Sloughter, who refused, he brought in several purchasers to the value of 6,000*l.*, including Highmore, who paid 1,700*l.* for what proved to be a fraud. Highmore afterwards hearing of Hagar's bankruptcy, Appellant, who had known it all along, but kept it secret, was employed by Hagar and those who had bought shares, to compound Hagar's debts and, if possible, get the Commission superseded, and received sums from the shares for that purpose, but failing to account for 30*l.* out of 97*l.* so received, he was entrusted with no more money, but directed merely to agree with Hagar's creditors to take releases for such sums as should be paid them, and Appellant afterwards informed the Sharers that all the creditors were compounded except Sloughter, whose claim was only about 80*l.* and who was tired of prosecuting the Commission, so that the invention might be proceeded with. Hagar having leased a mill at Ensham and built another at Stanwell, in Middlesex, mortgaged the former to Highmore for 550*l.* Sloughter, however, not receiving his debt, procured an assignment from the Commissioners of the mill at Ensham and caused it to be seized, and Highmore was forced to pay him 700*l.* for his interest. Appellant, combining with Hagar to defraud Highmore and other creditors, pretended that Hagar owed him 310*l.* lent on bonds, besides 700*l.* or 800*l.* more, paid by him to compound Hagar's debts, and petitioned to be let in as a creditor, but failed to prove any money lent on the bonds, and was found by the Commissioners to owe the estate 350*l.*, which they assigned over to Sloughter, who is now suing Highmore for it. The Commission abating with the death of Charles II., Appellant in the next reign got it renewed to Commissioners of his own nomination, who sat in Whitefriars and other privileged places, and having, by contrivance, got Hagar to confess himself a debtor for 900*l.*, procured an assignment of his estate and admission as a creditor, and brought his Bill in Chancery, to which Respondents brought a Cross-bill for discovery of his debt. Recites the terms of the Master's report and Decree. Sloughter has been harassed at law and in Chancery more than 13 years, to his cost of at least 1,000*l.* Pray that the Appeal may be dismissed with costs, as vexatious, Appellant having utterly failed to prove his pretended debts. *Signed* by Respondents; *Countersigned* by Thos. Goodinge. *Endorsed* as brought in this day.

509. Dec. 31. King's Speech.—His Majesty's Speech this day, on adjourning Parliament. L. J., XV. 11. *In extenso.*

INDEX.

A.

B.

C.

D.

E.

F.

H.

I.

L.

M.

O.

P.

Q.

R.

S.

T.

U.

V.

W.

X.

Y.

Z.

HISTORICAL MANUSCRIPTS COMMISSION.

Date.	——	Size.	Sessional Paper.	Price.
				s. d.
1870 (Re-printed 1874.)	FIRST REPORT, WITH APPENDIX - Contents :— ENGLAND. House of Lords; Cambridge Colleges; Abingdon, and other Corporations, &c. SCOTLAND. Advocates' Library, Glasgow Corporation, &c. IRELAND. Dublin, Cork, and other Corporations, &c.	f'cap	[C. 55]	1 6
1871	SECOND REPORT, WITH APPENDIX, AND INDEX TO THE FIRST AND SECOND REPORTS - - - - - - Contents :— ENGLAND. House of Lords; Cambridge Colleges; Oxford Colleges; Monastery of Dominican Friars at Woodchester, Duke of Bedford, Earl Spencer, &c. SCOTLAND. Aberdeen and St. Andrew's Universities, &c. IRELAND. Marquis of Ormonde; Dr. Lyons, &c.	"	[C. 441]	3 10
1872	THIRD REPORT, WITH APPENDIX AND INDEX - - - - - - Contents :— ENGLAND. House of Lords; Cambridge Colleges; Stonyhurst College; Bridgewater and other Corporations; Duke of Northumberland, Marquis of Lansdowne, Marquis of Bath, &c. SCOTLAND. University of Glasgow; Duke of Montrose, &c. IRELAND. Marquis of Ormonde; Black Book of Limerick, &c.	"	[C. 673]	[*Out of print.*]
1873	FOURTH REPORT, WITH APPENDIX. PART I. - - - - - - Contents :— ENGLAND. House of Lords; Westminster Abbey; Cambridge and Oxford Colleges; Cinque Ports, Hythe, and other Corporations, Marquis of Bath, Earl of Denbigh, &c. SCOTLAND. Duke of Argyll, &c. IRELAND. Trinity College, Dublin; Marquis of Ormonde.	"	[C. 857]	6 8
1873	DITTO. PART II. INDEX - - - -	"	[C.857i.]	2 6
1876	FIFTH REPORT, WITH APPENDIX. PART I. - Contents :— ENGLAND. House of Lords; Oxford and Cambridge Colleges; Dean and Chapter of Canterbury; Rye, Lydd, and other Corporations, Duke of Sutherland, Marquis of Lansdowne, Reginald Cholmondeley, Esq., &c. SCOTLAND. Earl of Aberdeen, &c.	"	[C.1432]	7 0
"	DITTO. PART II. INDEX - - -	"	[C.1432 i.]	3 6

U 64153.

Date.	—	Size.	Sessional Paper.	Price.
				s. d.
1877	SIXTH REPORT, WITH APPENDIX. PART I. - Contents :— ENGLAND. House of Lords; Oxford and Cambridge Colleges; Lambeth Palace; Black Book of the Archdeacon of Canterbury; Bridport, Wallingford, and other Corporations; Lord Leconfield, Sir Reginald Graham, Sir Henry Ingilby, &c. SCOTLAND. Duke of Argyll, Earl of Moray, &c. IRELAND. Marquis of Ormonde.	f'cap	[C.1745]	8 6
	DITTO. PART II. INDEX - - -	„	[C.2102]	[*Out of print.*]
1879	SEVENTH REPORT, WITH APPENDIX. PART I. - - - - - - Contents :— House of Lords; County of Somerset; Earl of Egmont, Sir Frederick Graham, Sir Harry Verney, &c.	„	[C.2340]	[*Out of print.*]
	DITTO. PART II. APPENDIX AND INDEX - Contents :— Duke of Athole, Marquis of Ormonde, S. F. Livingstone, Esq., &c.	„	[C. 2340 i.]	[*Out of print.*]
1881	EIGHTH REPORT, WITH APPENDIX AND INDEX. PART I. - - - - Contents :— List of collections examined, 1869–1880. ENGLAND. House of Lords; Duke of Marlborough; Magdalen College, Oxford; Royal College of Physicians; Queen Anne's Bounty Office; Corporations of Chester, Leicester, &c. IRELAND. Marquis of Ormonde, Lord Emly, The O'Conor Don, Trinity College, Dublin, &c.	„	[C.3040]	8 6
1881	DITTO. PART II. APPENDIX AND INDEX - Contents :— Duke of Manchester.	„	[C. 3040 i.]	1 9
1881	EIGHTH REPORT. PART III. APPENDIX AND INDEX - - - - - - Contents :— Earl of Ashburnham.	„	[C.3040 ii.]	1 4
1883	NINTH REPORT, WITH APPENDIX AND INDEX. PART I. - - - - Contents :— St. Paul's and Canterbury Cathedrals; Eton College; Carlisle, Yarmouth, Canterbury, and Barnstaple Corporations, &c.	„	[C.3773]	[*Out of print.*]
1884	DITTO. PART II. APPENDIX AND INDEX - Contents :— ENGLAND. House of Lords, Earl of Leicester; C. Pole Gell, Alfred Morrison, Esqs., &c. SCOTLAND. Lord Elphinstone, H. C. Maxwell Stuart, Esq., &c. IRELAND. Duke of Leinster, Marquis of Drogheda, &c.	„	[C.3773 i.]	6 3
1884	DITTO. PART III. APPENDIX AND INDEX - - - - - - Contents :— Mrs. Stopford Sackville.	„	[C.3773 ii.]	1 7

Date.	—	Size.	Sessional Paper.	Price.
				s. d.
1883	CALENDAR OF THE MANUSCRIPTS OF THE MARQUIS OF SALISBURY, K.G. (or CECIL MSS.). PART I. - - - -	8vo.	[C.3777]	[*Out of print.*]
1888	DITTO. PART II. - - -	"	[C.5463]	3 5
1889	DITTO. PART III. - - -	"	[C. 5889 v.]	2 1.
	DITTO. PART IV. - - -	*In the Press.*		
1885	TENTH REPORT - - - - - This is introductory to the following :—	"	[C.4548]	0 8½
1885	(1.) APPENDIX AND INDEX - - - Earl of Eglinton, Sir J. S. Maxwell, Bart., and C. S. H. D. Moray, C. F. Weston Underwood, G. W. Digby, Esqs.	"	[C.4575]	[*Out of print.*]
1885	(2.) APPENDIX AND INDEX - - The Family of Gawdy.	"	[C.4576 iii.]	1 4
1885	(3.) APPENDIX AND INDEX - - Wells Cathedral.	"	[C.4576 ii.]	2 0
1885	(4.) APPENDIX AND INDEX - - Earl of Westmorland ; Capt. Stewart ; Lord Stafford ; Sir N. W. Throckmorton, Stonyhurst College ; Sir P. T. Mainwaring, Misses Boycott, Lord Muncaster, M.P., Capt. J. F. Bagot, Earl of Kilmorey, Earl of Powis, Rev. T. S. Hill and others, the Corporations of Kendal, Wenlock, Bridgnorth, Eye, Plymouth, and the County of Essex.	"	[C.4576]	3 6.
1885	(5.) APPENDIX AND INDEX - - - The Marquis of Ormonde, Earl of Fingall, Corporations of Galway, Waterford, the Sees of Dublin and Ossory, the Jesuits in Ireland.	"	[4576 i.]	[*Out of print.*]
1887	(6.) APPENDIX AND INDEX - - - Marquis of Abergavenny, Lord Braye, G. F. Luttrell, P. P. Bouverie, W. B. Davenport, M.P., R. T. Balfour, Esquires.	"	[C.5242]	1 7
1887	ELEVENTH REPORT - - - - This is introductory to the following :—	"	[C. 5060 vi.]	0 3
1887	(1.) APPENDIX AND INDEX - - - H. D. Skrine, Esq., Salvetti Correspondence.	"	[C.5060]	1 1
1887	(2.) APPENDIX AND INDEX - - - House of Lords. 1678-1688.	"	[C. 5060 i.]	2 0
1887	(3.) APPENDIX AND INDEX - - - Corporations of Southampton and Lynn.	"	[C. 5060 ii.]	1 8
1887	(4.) APPENDIX AND INDEX - - - Marquess Townshend.	"	[C. 5060 iii.]	2 6
1887	(5.) APPENDIX AND INDEX - - - Earl of Dartmouth.	"	[C. 5060 iv.]	2 8

Date.	—	Size.	Sessional Paper.	Price.
				s. d.
1887	(6.) APPENDIX AND INDEX - Duke of Hamilton.	8vo.	[C. 5060 v.]	1 6
1888	(7.) APPENDIX AND INDEX - Duke of Leeds, Marchioness of Waterford, Lord Hothfield, &c.; Bridgwater Trust Office, Reading Corporation, Inner Temple Library.	"	[C.5612]	2 0
1890	TWELFTH REPORT - This is introductory to the following:—	"	[C.5889]	0 3
1888	(1.) APPENDIX Earl Cowper, K.G. (Coke MSS., at Melbourne Hall, Derby) Vol. I.	"	[C.5472]	2 7
1888	(2.) APPENDIX Ditto. Vol. II.	"	[C.5613]	2 5
1889	(3.) APPENDIX AND INDEX - Ditto. Vol. III.	"	[C. 5889 i.]	1 4
1888	(4.) APPENDIX The Duke of Rutland, G.C.B. Vol. I.	"	[C.5614]	3 2
1891	(5.) APPENDIX AND INDEX - Ditto. Vol. II.	"	[C. 5889 ii.]	2 0
1889	(6.) APPENDIX AND INDEX - House of Lords, 1689–1690.	"	[C. 5889 iii.]	2 1½
1890	(7.) APPENDIX AND INDEX - S. H. le Fleming, Esq., of Rydal.	"	[C. 5889 iv.]	1 11
1891	(8.) APPENDIX AND INDEX - The Duke of Athole, K.T., and the Earl of Home.	"	[C.6338]	1 0
1891	(9.) APPENDIX AND INDEX - The Duke of Beaufort, K.G., the Earl of Donoughmore, J. H. Gurney, W. W. B. Hulton, R. W. Ketton, G. A. Aitken, P. V. Smith, Esqs.; Bishop of Ely; Cathedrals of Ely, Gloucester, Lincoln, and Peterborough; Corporations of Gloucester, Higham Ferrers, and Newark; Southwell Minster; Lincoln District Registry.	"	[C. 6338 i.]	2 6
1891	(10.) APPENDIX The First Earl of Charlemont. 1745-1783. Vol. I.	"	[C. 6338 ii.]	1 11
	THIRTEENTH REPORT. This is introductory to the following:—			
1891	(1.) APPENDIX The Duke of Portland. Vol. I.	"	[C.6474]	3 0
	(2.) APPENDIX AND INDEX. Ditto. Vol. II.	*In the Press.*		
1892	(3.) APPENDIX. J. B. Fortescue, Esq. Vol. I.	"	[C.6660]	2 7
	(4.) APPENDIX AND INDEX. Corporations of Rye and Hereford, &c.	*In the Press.*		
	(5.) APPENDIX AND INDEX. House of Lords, 1691 -	*In the Press.*		

www.ingramcontent.com/pod-product-compliance
Lightning Source LLC
Chambersburg PA
CBHW022125020426
42334CB00015B/771
* 9 7 8 3 7 4 2 8 4 4 8 4 2 *